THE BRIEF

AMERICAN PAGEANT

A HISTORY OF THE REPUBLIC

Eighth Edition

VOLUME II

SINCE 1865

David M. Kennedy
Stanford University

Lizabeth Cohen
Harvard University

Mel Piehl
Valparaiso University

WADSWORTH
CENGAGE Learning

Australia • Brazil • Japan • Korea • Mexico • Singapore • Spain • United Kingdom • United States

WADSWORTH
CENGAGE Learning™

**The Brief American Pageant,
Eight Edition**

Kennedy, Cohen, Piehl

Senior Publisher: Suzanne Jeans

Senior Sponsoring Editor: Ann West

Development Editor: Leslie Kauffman

Assistant Editor: Megan Chrisman

Media Editor: Robert St. Laurent

Senior Marketing Manager: Katherine Bates

Marketing Coordinator: Lorreen Pelletier

Marketing Communications Manager:
Caitlin Green

Senior Content Project Manager: Carol
Newman

Senior Art Director: Cate Rickard Barr

Senior Print Buyer: Judy Inouye

Senior Text Rights Acquisition Specialist:
Katie Huha

Senior Image Rights Acquisition Specialist:
Jennifer Meyer Dare

Photo Researcher: Picture Research Consultants

Production Service/Compositor: Integra
Software Services

Text Designer: Lisa Devenish/Devenish Design

Cover Designer: Althea Chen

Cover Image: William J. Glackens, 1870–1938.
Parade, Washington Square, 1912. Oil on
canvas, 21 × 31 in. The Whitney Museum.
Gift of Gertrude Vanderbilt Whitney, 31.215.
Photograph by Geoffrey Clements.

For product information and technology assistance, contact us at
Cengage Learning Customer & Sales Support, 1-800-354-9706

For permission to use material from this text or product,
submit all requests online at **www.cengage.com/permissions.**
Further permissions questions can be emailed to
permissionrequest@cengage.com.

Library of Congress Control Number: 2010939123

Student Edition:
ISBN-13: 978-0-495-91537-9

ISBN-10: 0-495-91537-8

Wadsworth
20 Channel Center Street
Boston, MA 02210
USA

Cengage Learning is a leading provider of customized learning solutions
with office locations around the globe, including Singapore, the United
Kingdom, Australia, Mexico, Brazil and Japan. Locate your local office at
international.cengage.com/region

Cengage Learning products are represented in Canada by Nelson Education, Ltd.

For your course and learning solutions, visit **www.cengage.com.**

Purchase any of our products at your local college store or at our preferred
online store **www.cengagebrain.com.**

Printed in United States of America
1 2 3 4 5 6 7 14 13 12 11 10

CONTENTS

PART FOUR

Forging an Industrial Society

1865–1899

352

PART FIVE

Struggling for Justice at Home and Abroad

1899–1945

460

PART SIX

Making Modern America

1945 to the Present

594

MAPS

CHARTS AND TABLES

PREFACE

This new edition of *The Brief American Pageant,* a concise version of *The American Pageant,* fourteenth edition, includes significant innovations. As always, this Brief Edition presents the core content of *The American Pageant* in an efficient and attractive fashion. In order to further improve the teaching of American history already included within past editions, we have included even more new features designed to enhance core academic skills and foundational knowledge essential to serious academic work in history. This Brief Edition thus aims not only to teach students American history, but also to teach them how to learn history and other subjects more effectively.

The text incorporates these features while preserving the liveliness and readability that have long been *The American Pageant's* hallmark. We are often told that the *Pageant* is the sole American history text that has a distinctive personality—defined by clarity, concreteness, a consistent chronological narrative, strong emphasis on major themes, avoidance of clutter, access to a variety of interpretive perspectives, and a colorful writing style leavened, as appropriate, with wit. That personality, we strongly believe, is what has made the *Pageant* both appealing and useful to countless students for more than four decades. In *The Brief American Pageant,* eighth edition, David Kennedy, Lizabeth Cohen, and Mel Piehl have preserved the parent text's essential character, while making this edition far more useful to students and instructors alike.

New to the Eighth Edition

Like *The American Pageant, The Brief American Pageant* provides students with a firm foundation in American history. And *The Brief American Pageant* has also followed the lead of its parent text in terms of revisions for this most recent edition, including:

- **New Global Emphasis** Within each chapter, the authors have revised the text to help students compare American developments to developments around the world and worldwide trends. Many new box-quotes bring more international voices to the events chronicled in the *Brief Pageant's* historical narrative. In addition, new "Thinking Globally" essays present a different aspect of the American experience contextualized within world history.

- **Redesigned Maps** All of the maps in *The Brief American Pageant, 8e* have been redesigned with topographical detail and clear labels to better communicate the text's analytical points. In addition, a global locator map in a corner of each map provides geographical context for the area under discussion.

- **New Visual Images** New documentary images, graphs, and tables illuminate complex and important historical ideas.

- **New End-of-Chapter Pedagogy** Lists of the chapter "Key Terms" and "People to Know"—created to help students focus on the most significant concepts and people introduced in that chapter—appear at the end of each chapter to help students recall chapter highlights.

- **Expanded Student Website** Now included on the student website are a variety of resources for further study and review, including lists with definitions of "Key Terms" and "People to Know" identified in each text chapter, access to primary sources noted in the chapter margins, self-test quizzes with feedback, annotated links to history sites, flashcards, and other activities. A full, chapter-by-chapter annotated bibliography suitable for deeper research and an extensive visual profile of the United States with charts and graphs illustrating many aspects of the American historical experience may also be found here.

The following revisions have been made to each chapter of this edition.

Part I: Founding the Nation

- **Chapter 1:** Newly rendered maps in this chapter (and others) provide a more complete picture of the principal voyages of discovery, exploration, and trade routes around the globe.

- **Chapter 2:** New maps on early settlements provide better understanding of land disputes and territorial claims.

- **Chapter 3:** More discussion of the settlement of "New Amsterdam" and religious diversity in the New Netherland colony has been added.

- **Chapter 4:** A new "Thinking Globally" feature: The Atlantic Slave Trade, 1500–1860 and further discussion of the causes of English migration to the New World help students analyze colonial origins. Expanded discussion of the transatlantic slave trade with a revised map also assists in this study.

- **Chapter 5:** More coverage of the German and Quaker settlement of the West, additional coverage of the Scots-Irish settlements, and further discussion of the early challenges to Calvinist doctrine make up this revised chapter.

- **Chapter 6:** Revised coverage of the French migration to, and settlement of, the New World with updated images throughout are featured in this chapter.

- **Chapter 7:** More discussion of the buildup to the American Revolution leads students into the final chapters of Part I.

- **Chapter 8:** The American Revolution concludes Part I with more on Thomas Paine's *Common Sense* and its significance, as well as expanded coverage of the impact of the American Revolution on British foreign policy and imperial expansion.

Part II: Building the New Nation

- **Chapter 9:** Expanded discussions of the relations among Britain, France, and America, as well as expanded coverage of the fight for compromise within the government begin Part II.

- **Chapter 10:** A new "Thinking Globally" feature: Two Revolutions, in addition to a greater focus on the global implications of the French Revolution, assist students in gaining an international understanding of America's Revolution.

- **Chapter 11:** Expanded discussion of Jefferson as a "citizen of the world" and more attention given to the slave revolt in Santo Domingo, including its impact on white slave owners in the Americas, draw attention to the international community. Additional coverage of Lewis and Clark and westward exploration highlight America's desire to expand.

- **Chapter 12:** This chapter includes expanded discussion of the causes of the War of 1812 in Europe.

- **Chapter 13:** Expanded discussion of democratic reforms in Europe and added discussion of the impact of market and transportation revolutions on democratic reform are provided.

- **Chapter 14:** This chapter includes a greater focus on the international view of migrations; parallels between immigration to the U.S. and other countries; expanded international context for American industrial revolution; importance of foreign capital; impact of American economic development on societies abroad; discussion of the Colt Revolver as an example of interchangeable parts technology; and added coverage of American participation in the London World's Fair.

- **Chapter 15:** New discussion of English origins of the Shakers concludes Part II.

Part III: Testing the New Nation

- **Chapter 16:** More attention is given to the importance of cotton and slavery in the United States and world economies (with revised maps), while expanded discussion of the abolition of slave trade and later slavery in Britain is also provided. In addition, more coverage of the development of a domestic slave trade as a byproduct of the suppression of international slave trade and expanded discussion of the *Amistad* episode provide students with a detailed understanding of this era in American history.

- **Chapter 17:** Additional coverage of military growth in the aftermath of the Mexican War is included.

- **Chapter 18:** This chapter includes new coverage on other "gold rushes" (Australia), as well as updated images and maps highlighting America's westward expansion.

- **Chapter 19:** Coverage of the influence of slave rebellions on John Brown is included, while paying more attention to the significance of the U.S. Civil War in a global context (the United States as the only nation to fight a war to rid itself of slavery).

- **Chapter 20:** A new "Makers of America" feature: Billy Yank and Johnny Reb are included, as well as new discussion of global cotton production, which was an effect of the Civil War.

- **Chapter 21:** A new "Thinking Globally" feature: The Era of Nationalism is included, as well as new discussion of the comparative context for Civil War casualties.

- **Chapter 22:** New images have been added to show the destruction of the Civil War.

Part IV: Forging an Industrial Society

- **Chapter 23:** This chapter provides added global character to the depression of 1873, more discussion of the role of government in suppressing the railroad strike, more coverage of Chinese immigration, as well as additional attention given to the Chinese Exclusion Act.

- **Chapter 24:** This chapter includes more discussion of railroad building globally (United States vs. elsewhere), added discussion of world cotton production, more emphasis on foreign investment that was crucial to American industrial expansion, and added discussion of the size and integration of the American market as helped by railroad building and mass production methods.

- **Chapter 25:** This chapter includes more discussion of the size of world cities and American urban expansion as a worldwide phenomenon; the Chicago fire cast as part of the dangers of the city; further discussion of the international view of immigrants and parallel immigrations to other countries, particularly South America; new emphasis on the influence of European architecture and planning ideas on the City Beautiful, particularly as expressed in Chicago's World Columbian Exposition; added discussion of the lasting interest in Henry George's ideas shown by the 1903 invention of "Landlord Game"; and added discussion of Horatio Alger and his lesson of the American Dream.

- **Chapter 26:** A new "Thinking Globally" feature: The Great Frontier is included in this chapter, as well as added discussion of buffalo and the impact of its disappearance and more discussion of farmers as part of the world economy.

- **Chapter 27:** A new "Thinking Globally" feature: The Age of Empire, as well as additional information on female missionaries abroad, are included. Discussion concludes with further coverage of the race factor in the Philippines.

Part V: Struggling for Justice at Home and Abroad

- **Chapter 28:** This chapter includes revised discussion of the Progressives, as well as coverage of female activists, while providing more emphasis on European influences on the Progressives.

- **Chapter 29:** A new discussion on how racial views affected American imperialism (in the case of the Philippines) and amended discussion of Wilson and Mexico and sharpened contrast with Taft are highlighted.

- **Chapter 30:** This chapter discusses the women's suffrage movement in the world while integrating recent research on the importance of expanded federal government authority and planning in WWI, not just voluntary mobilization. New discussion of venereal disease in WWI and discussion of the worldwide influenza pandemic from 1918–1919 are also included, as well as more balance provided on Wilson's anti-colonialism vs. imperialism.

- **Chapter 31:** Added discussion of automobiles worldwide per capita has been included. New emphasis on the attraction of American authors to Paris in the 1920s, including to Gertrude Stein's salon, rounds out the chapter revisions.

- **Chapter 32:** This chapter includes updated maps and images to show the changes in American life after WWI.

- **Chapter 33:** The international comparison of unionization rates and discussion of the economic consequences of the Great Depression (in the U.S., UK, and Germany) are addressed.

- **Chapter 34:** Coverage of *Kristallnacht* and the refugee ship *St. Louis* has been incorporated, while adding attention to Stalin's purges and to the Abraham Lincoln Brigades fighting in the Spanish Civil War.

- **Chapter 35:** A new "Thinking Globally" feature: America and the World in Depression and War: A Study of Contrasts (including a table showing the comparative costs of WWII) has been added, as well as updated maps covering American movement in the war.

Part VI: Making Modern America

- **Chapter 36:** A new "Thinking Globally" feature: The Era of Globalization has been added, as well as a new comparison of suburbanization in postwar United States to

urban reconstruction in war-ravaged European cities. Also added is an updated treatment of the early Cold War, particularly consideration of uses of the nuclear bomb.

- **Chapter 37:** Included within this chapter is more on the spread of American mass consumption abroad to Europe, new discussion of rock 'n' roll and its international appeal, and new discussion of McCarthyism and the damage to U.S. reputation in Western Europe. A civil rights discussion has been expanded to include discussion of Cold War pressures to end segregation.

- **Chapter 38:** This chapter provides a new discussion of the moon landing as part of the space race with Russia and watched worldwide; more discussion of America's international involvement, taking focus from Vietnam; more discussion of the international view of 1968; and added material on how gay pride became a worldwide phenomenon.

- **Chapter 39:** This chapter presents environmentalism as a worldwide phenomenon (such as Earth Day 1970); demonstrates the individual aspects of the EPA and OSHA, which had been linked in the chapter but are really different; provides more attention to regulations and business opposition (and has added the Consumer Product Safety Commission); and concludes with the 1973 oil crisis presented as a more international event, including Europe.

- **Chapter 40:** Discussion has been added about American involvement in Kuwait and about Margaret Thatcher in the UK to make the point that the United States was not alone in its conservative turn.

- **Chapter 41:** This chapter has been greatly expanded to cover the Iraq War, including Abu Ghraib; domestic issues such as No Child Left Behind, gay marriage, and Enron; President Bush's second term and the failed effort to privatize social security, as well as conflicts over immigration reform, surveillance in the War on Terror, charges of corruption in the administration, and Hurricane Katrina problems; the election of 2006 and Democratic victory; as well as the 2008 campaign and election of Barack Obama and the beginnings of the Obama administration.

- **Chapter 42:** This concluding chapter provides a revised discussion of social security, addressing Bush proposals for social security reform and their defeat; updated conflicts over immigration policy; and a new section on the "New Media" (focusing on the Internet and online journalism).

New Pedagogical Features

The special pedagogical features of *The Brief American Pageant* are many and varied, and may be used in different ways by students and instructors.

- **"What if...?"** questions at the end of each overview essay prompt students to consider how history might have changed if certain events turned out differently, reinforcing the contingent nature of history.

- **Chapter Outlines** begin each chapter to provide a roadmap for the student.

- **Focus Questions** come at the beginning of each chapter, pointing to the key issues and ideas in the account that follows, and guiding the student's reading and understanding.

- The **Chronology** has been updated to include even more political occurrences and historical events.

- The **Marginal Glossary** highlights and defines key words to expand students' general historical and social science vocabulary.

- **Icons** in the margins direct students to primary sources that are on the companion website.

- All **Key Terms** are listed at the end of the chapter, with page numbers included, for ease of reference.

- The new feature, **People to Know** list, is located at the end of each chapter, providing students with a useful study tool as they learn about some of the most important individuals in American history.

- **Examining the Evidence,** the feature that acquaints students with historical evidence, offers questions to develop historical and critical thinking skills.

- **Map-Reading Skill Builders** early in the book provide questions designed to improve students' map reading ability.

- **Chapter Summaries** provide a handy review that highlights the chapter's main points.

Goals of *The Brief American Pageant*

Like its predecessors, this eighth edition of *The Brief American Pageant* tries to cultivate in its readers the capacity for balanced judgment and informed understanding about American society by holding up to the present, the mirror and measuring rod that is the past. The book's goal is not to teach the art of prophecy but the much subtler and more difficult arts of seeing things in context, of understanding the roots and direction and pace of change, and of distinguishing what is truly new under the sun from what is not. The study of history, it has been rightly said, does not make one smart for the next time, but wise forever.

We hope that *The Brief American Pageant* will help to develop those intellectual assets in its readers, and that those who use the book will take from it both a fresh appreciation of what has gone before and a seasoned perspective on what is to come. And we hope, too, that readers will take as much pleasure in reading *The Brief American Pageant* as we have had in writing it.

Teaching and Learning Aids

These supplements have been created with the diverse needs of today's students and instructors in mind.

Instructor Resources

PowerLecture CD-ROM with ExamView® and JoinIn®
This dual platform, all-in-one multimedia resource includes the Instructor's Resource Manual; Test Bank (with multiple-choice, short answer, and essay questions); Microsoft® PowerPoint® slides of both lecture outlines and images and maps from the text that can be used as offered, or customized by importing personal lecture slides or other material; and *JoinIn®* PowerPoint® slides with clicker content. Also included is ExamView, an easy-to-use assessment and tutorial system that allows instructors to create, deliver, and customize tests in minutes. Instructors can build tests with as many as 250 questions using up to 12 question types, and using ExamView's complete word-processing capabilities, they can enter an unlimited number of new questions or edit existing ones.

HistoryFinder This searchable online database allows instructors to quickly and easily download thousands of assets, including art, photographs, maps, primary sources, and audio/video clips. Each asset downloads directly into a Microsoft® PowerPoint® slide, allowing instructors to easily create exciting PowerPoint presentations for their classrooms.

eInstructor's Resource Manual For each chapter this manual provides chapter themes and summary, lecture suggestions, additional class topics, character sketches, questions for class discussion, and guiding questions and exercises related to the book features. Available on the instructor's companion website—http://login.cengage.com.

WebTutor™ on Blackboard® and WebCT® With WebTutor's text-specific, pre-formatted content and total flexibility, instructors can easily create and manage their own custom course website. WebTutor's course management tool gives instructors the ability to provide virtual office hours, post syllabi, set up threaded discussions, track student progress with the quizzing material, and much more. For students, WebTutor offers real-time access to a full array of study tools, including animations and videos that bring the book's topics to life, plus chapter outlines, summaries, learning objectives, glossary flashcards, practice quizzes, and weblinks.

CourseMate Cengage Learning's History CourseMate brings course concepts to life with interactive learning, study, and exam preparation tools that support the printed textbook. History CourseMate includes an integrated eBook; interactive teaching and learning tools including quizzes, flashcards, videos, and more; and EngagementTracker, a first-of-its-kind tool that monitors student engagement in the course. Learn more at www.cengagebrain.com.

Student Resources

Book Companion Site A website for students is provided that features a wide assortment of resources to help students master the subject matter. The website includes a glossary, flashcards, crossword puzzles, tutorial quizzes, essay questions, critical thinking exercises, weblinks, and suggested readings.

CL eBook This interactive multimedia ebook links out to rich media assets such as video and MP3 chapter summaries. Through this ebook, students can also access self-test quizzes, chapter outlines, focus questions, chronology and matching exercises, and essay questions (for which the answers can be emailed to their instructors), primary source documents with critical thinking questions, and interactive (zoomable) maps. Available at www.cengagebrain.com.

Cengagebrain.com Saves students time and money. *Cengagebrain.com*, Cengage Learning's online store, is a single destination for more than 10,000 new textbooks, eTextbooks, eChapters, study tools, and audio supplements. Students have the freedom to purchase a-la-carte exactly what they need when they need it. Students can save 50% on the electronic textbook, and can pay as little as $1.99 for an individual eChapter.

Wadsworth American History Resource Center Wadsworth's American History Resource Center gives students access to a "virtual reader" with hundreds of primary sources including speeches, letters, legal documents and transcripts, poems, maps, simulations, timelines, and additional images that bring history to life, along with interactive assignable exercises. A map feature including Google Earth™ coordinates and exercises will aid in student comprehension of geography and use of maps. Students can compare the traditional textbook map with an aerial view of the location today.

The History Handbook, 2e Written by Carol Berkin of Baruch College, City University of New York and Betty Anderson of Boston University, this book teaches students both basic and history-specific study skills, such as how to take notes, get the most out of lectures and readings, read primary sources, research historical topics, and correctly cite sources. Substantially less expensive than comparable skill-building texts, *The History Handbook* also offers tips for Internet research and evaluating online sources. Additionally, students can purchase and download the *eAudio* version of *The History Handbook* or any of its eighteen individual units at www.cengagebrain.com to listen to on-the-go.

Reader Program Cengage Learning publishes a number of readers, some containing exclusively primary sources, others a combination of primary and secondary sources, and some designed to guide students through the process of historical inquiry. Visit Cengage.com/history or contact a Cengage Learning sales representative for a complete list of readers appropriate for any course.

Rand McNally Atlas of American History, 2e This comprehensive atlas features more than 80 maps, with new content covering global perspectives, including events in the Middle East from 1945 to 2005, as well as population trends in the U.S. and around the world. Additional maps document voyages of discovery; the settling of the colonies; major U.S. military engagements, including the American Revolution and World Wars I and II; and sources of immigrations, ethnic populations, and patterns of economic change.

Major Problems in American History Series Volumes in this series contain primary source documents (6 to 10 per chapter), secondary sources (2 to 3 per chapter), chapter introductions, separate introductions to documents and essays in every chapter, bibliographies, and full documentation of sources.

Custom Options

Cengage Learning offers custom solutions for any course—whether it's making a small modification to *The Brief American Pageant* to match a syllabus or combining multiple sources to create something truly unique. Instructors can pick and choose chapters, include their own material, and add additional map exercises along with the Rand McNally Atlas to create a text that fits each course. Contact the Cengage Learning representative to explore custom solutions for your course.

Acknowledgments

Many people contributed to the eighth edition of *The Brief American Pageant*. Foremost among them are the countless students and teachers who have written unsolicited letters of comment or inquiry. We also offer thanks to the following colleagues for their particular contributions to improving the text:

Sheryl Ballard-Smith, Houston Community College
Thomas Born, Blinn College
Shearer Bowman, University of Kentucky
Steven Boyd, University of Texas at San Antonio
Tracy Campbell, University of Kentucky
Mike Downs, Tarrant County College Southeast Campus
Jennifer Lawrence, Tarrant County College
Nancy Maurer, University of Central Florida
Bob McConaughy, Austin Community College, Rio Grande Campus
Lindsey McNellis, University of Central Florida
Manuel Medrano, University of Texas at Brownsville
Russell Mitchell, Tarrant County College Southeast Campus
Jaime Olivares, Houston Community College
John Sacher, University of Central Florida
Manfred Silva, El Paso Community College
Sandra Slater, College of Charleston
Gary Topping, Salt Lake Community College
Amanda Wallace-Wittnebel, University of Texas at San Antonio
Chad Wooley, Tarrant County College

D.M.K.
L.C.
M.P.

Sail, sail thy best, ship of Democracy,
Of value is thy freight, 'tis not the Present only,
The Past is also stored in thee,
Thou holdest not the venture of thyself alone, not
    of the Western continent alone,
Earth's résumé entire floats on thy keel, O ship, is
    steadied by thy spars,
With thee Time voyages in trust, the antecedent
    nations sink or swim with thee,
With all their ancient struggles, martyrs, heroes,
    epics, wars, thou bear'st the other continents,
Theirs, theirs as much as thine, the destination-port
    triumphant. . . .

——⚬⚬——

Walt Whitman
Thou Mother with Thy Equal Brood, 1872

22

The Ordeal of Reconstruction

1865–1877

With malice toward none, with charity for all, with firmness in the right as God gives us to see the right, let us strive on to finish the work we are in, to bind up the nation's wounds, to care for him who shall have borne the battle and for his widow and orphan, to do all which may achieve and cherish a just and lasting peace among ourselves and with all nations.

ABRAHAM LINCOLN, SECOND INAUGURAL ADDRESS, MARCH 4, 1865

The battle was done, the buglers silent. Bone-weary and bloodied, the American people, North and South, now faced the staggering challenges of peace. Four questions loomed large. How would the South, physically devastated by war and socially revolutionized by emancipation, be rebuilt? How would the liberated blacks fare as free men and women? How would the Southern states be reintegrated into the Union? And who would direct the process of Reconstruction—the Southern states themselves, the president, or Congress?

FOCUS QUESTIONS

1. What were the major problems facing the South and the nation after the Civil War?

2. How did African Americans and whites, Southerners and Northerners, respond to the end of slavery and conduct race relations under new conditions of freedom?

3. How did Andrew Johnson's blunders enable the Radical Republicans to gain control of Reconstruction policy?

4. What were the actual effects of congressional Reconstruction in the South, and how did militant white opposition and growing northern apathy eventually bring an end to Reconstruction in the Compromise of 1877?

5. What were the primary successes and failures of Reconstruction, and what legacy did it leave for later generations of Americans?

CHRONOLOGY

1863	Lincoln announces "10 percent" Reconstruction plan.		**1867**	Reconstruction Act. Tenure of Office Act. United States purchases Alaska from Russia.
1864	Lincoln vetoes Wade-Davis Bill.		**1868**	Johnson impeached and acquitted. Johnson pardons Confederate leaders.
1865	Lincoln assassinated. Johnson issues Reconstruction proclamation. Congress refuses to seat Southern congressmen. Freedmen's Bureau established. Southern states pass Black Codes.		**1870**	Fifteenth Amendment ratified.
			1870–1871	Force Acts.
			1872	Freedmen's Bureau ended.
1866	Congress passes Civil Rights Bill over Johnson's veto. Congress passes Fourteenth Amendment. Johnson-backed candidates lose congressional election. *Ex parte Milligan* case. Ku Klux Klan founded.		**1877**	Reconstruction ends.

The Problems of Peace

treason *The crime of betrayal of one's country, involving some overt act violating an oath of allegiance or providing illegal aid to a foreign state. In the United States, treason is the only crime specified in the Constitution.*

civil disabilities *Legally imposed restrictions of a person's civil rights or liberties.*

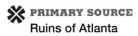
PRIMARY SOURCE
Ruins in Charleston, South Carolina

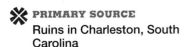
PRIMARY SOURCE
Ruins of the Arsenal at Richmond

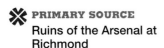
PRIMARY SOURCE
Ruins of Atlanta

PRIMARY SOURCE
Ruins of Petersburg Railroad Bridge

Other questions also clamored for answers. What should be done with the captured Confederate ringleaders? All Confederate officials were subject to charges of treason, and during the war a popular Northern song had been "Hang Jeff Davis to a Sour Apple Tree." Davis was clapped into prison for two years, but no **treason** trials were ever held. President Andrew Johnson pardoned all "rebel" leaders as a sort of Christmas present in 1868. Congress removed their **civil disabilities** thirty years later.

Dismal indeed was the picture presented by the war-wracked South when the rattle of musketry faded. Not only had an age perished, but a civilization had collapsed, in both its economic and its social structure. The moonlight-and-magnolia Old South, largely imaginary in any case, had forever gone with the wind.

Handsome cities of yesteryear, such as Charleston and Richmond, were rubble strewn and weed choked. An Atlantan returned to his once-fair hometown and remarked, "Hell has laid her egg, and right here it hatched." Economic life had creaked to a halt. Banks and businesses had locked their doors, ruined by runaway inflation. Factories were smokeless, silent, dismantled. The transportation system had broken down completely. Efforts to untwist the rails corkscrewed by Sherman's soldiers proved bumpily unsatisfactory.

Agriculture—the economic lifeblood of the South—was almost hopelessly crippled. Once-white cotton fields yielded a lush harvest of nothing but green weeds. The slave-labor system had collapsed, seed was scarce, and livestock had been driven off by plundering Yankees. Pathetic instances were reported of men hitching themselves to plows, while women and children gripped the handles.

The princely planter aristocrats were humbled by the war—at least temporarily. Reduced to proud poverty, they faced charred and gutted mansions, lost investments, and almost worthless land. Their investment of more than $2 billion in slaves, their primary form of wealth, had evaporated with emancipation.

Beaten but unbent, many high-spirited white Southerners remained dangerously defiant. They cursed the "damn yankees" and spoke of "your government" in Washington instead of "our government." Conscious of no crime, these former Confederates continued to believe that their view of secession was correct and that the "lost cause" was still a just war. One popular anti-Union song ran,

> I'm glad I fought agin her, I only wish we'd won,
> And I ain't axed any pardon for anything I've done.

Such attitudes boded ill for the prospects of painlessly binding up the Republic's wounds.

Freedmen Define Freedom

Confusion abounded in the still-smoldering South about the precise meaning of "freedom" for blacks. Emancipation took effect haltingly and unevenly in different parts of the conquered Confederacy. As Union armies marched in and out of various localities, many blacks found themselves emancipated and re-enslaved. A North Carolina slave estimated that he had celebrated freedom about twelve times. In some regions planters stubbornly protested that slavery was legal until state legislatures or the Supreme Court might act. For many slaves the shackles of bondage were not struck off in a single mighty blow; long-suffering blacks often had to pry off their chains link by link.

The variety of responses to emancipation, by whites as well as blacks, illustrated the sometimes startling complexity of the master–slave relationship. Loyalty to the plantation master prompted some slaves to resist the liberating Union armies, while other slaves' pent-up bitterness burst violently forth on the day of liberation. In one instance, a group of Virginia slaves laid twenty lashes on the back of their former master—a painful dose of his own favorite medicine.

Prodded by the bayonets of Yankee armies of occupation, all masters were eventually forced to recognize their slaves' permanent freedom. The once-commanding planter would assemble his former human chattels in front of the porch of the "big house" and announce their liberty. Though some blacks initially responded to news of their emancipation with suspicion and uncertainty, they soon celebrated their newfound freedom. Many took new names in place of the ones given by their masters and demanded that whites formally address them as "Mr." or "Mrs."

Tens of thousands of emancipated blacks took to the roads, some to test their freedom, others to search for long-lost spouses, parents, and children. Emancipation thus strengthened the black family, and many newly freed men and women formalized "slave marriages" for personal and pragmatic reasons, including the desire to make their children legal heirs.

Whole communities sometimes moved together in search of opportunity. From 1878 to 1880, some twenty-five thousand blacks from Louisiana, Texas, and Mississippi surged in a mass exodus to Kansas.

Library of Congress

Charleston, South Carolina, in Ruins, April 1865 Rebel troops evacuating Charleston blew up military supplies to deny them to General William Tecumseh Sherman's forces. The explosions ignited fires that all but destroyed the city.

Houston H. Holloway, age twenty at the time of his emancipation, recalled his feelings upon hearing of his freedom:

"I felt like a bird out of a cage. Amen. Amen. Amen. I could hardly ask to feel any better than I did that day. ... The week passed off in a blaze of glory."

The reunion of long-lost relatives also inspired joy; one Union officer wrote home:

"Men are taking their wives and children, families which had been for a long time broken up are united and oh! such happiness. I am glad I am here."

mutual aid societies *Nonprofit organizations designed to provide their members with financial and social benefits, often including medical aid, life insurance, funeral costs, and disaster relief.*

confiscation *Legal government seizure of private property without compensation.*

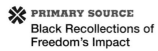 **PRIMARY SOURCE**
Black Recollections of
Freedom's Impact

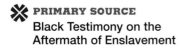 **PRIMARY SOURCE**
Black Testimony on the
Aftermath of Enslavement

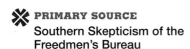 **PRIMARY SOURCE**
Southern Skepticism of the
Freedmen's Bureau

Women from the North enthusiastically embraced the opportunity to go south and teach in Freedmen's Bureau schools for emancipated blacks. One volunteer explained her motives:

"I thought I must do something, not having money at my command, what could I do but give myself to the work. ... I would go to them, and give them my life if necessary."

The church became the focus of black community life in the years following emancipation. As slaves, blacks had worshiped alongside whites, but now they formed their own churches pastored by their own ministers. Black churches grew robustly. The 150,000-member black Baptist Church of 1850 reached 500,000 by 1870, while the African Methodist Episcopal Church quadrupled in size from 100,000 to 400,000 in the first decade after emancipation. These churches formed the bedrock of black community life, and they soon gave rise to other benevolent, fraternal, and **mutual aid societies**. All these organizations helped blacks protect their newly won freedom.

Emancipation also meant education for many blacks. Learning to read and write had been a privilege generally denied to them under slavery. Freedmen wasted no time establishing societies for self-improvement, which undertook to raise funds to purchase land, build schoolhouses, and hire teachers. With qualified black teachers in short supply, they turned for help to Northern white women sent by the American Missionary Association and to the federal government.

The Freedmen's Bureau

Abolitionists had long preached that slavery was a degrading institution. Now the emancipators were faced with the brutal reality that the former slaves were overwhelmingly unskilled, unlettered, without property or money, and with scant knowledge of how to survive as free people. To cope with this problem throughout the conquered South, Congress created the Freedmen's Bureau on March 3, 1865.

On paper at least, the bureau was intended to be a kind of primitive welfare agency. It was to provide food, clothing, and education both to freedmen and to white refugees. The bureau was also authorized to distribute up to forty acres of abandoned or **confiscated** land to black settlers. Headed by General O. O. Howard, who later founded and served as president of Howard University in Washington, D.C., the bureau achieved its greatest successes in education. It taught an estimated 200,000 blacks how to read. Many former slaves had a passion for learning, partly because they wanted to close the gap between themselves and the whites and partly because they longed to read the Word of God.

But in other areas the bureau's accomplishments were meager—or even mischievous. Little confiscated Confederate land actually passed into black hands. Instead local administrators often collaborated with planters in expelling blacks from towns and cajoling them into signing labor contracts to work for their former masters. Still, the white South resented the bureau as a meddlesome federal interloper that threatened to upset white racial dominance. President Andrew Johnson, who shared the white supremacist views of most white Southerners, repeatedly tried to kill it, and the bureau expired in 1872.

Johnson: The Tailor President

Few presidents have ever been faced with a more perplexing sea of troubles than that confronting Andrew Johnson. What manner of man was this dark-eyed, black-haired Tennessean, now chief executive by virtue of the bullet that killed Lincoln?

Tuskegee University Library

Educating Young Freedmen and Women, 1870s Freed slaves in the South regarded schooling as the key to improving their children's lives and the fulfillment of a long-sought right that had been denied blacks in slavery. These well-dressed school children are lined up outside their rural, one-room schoolhouse alongside their teachers, both black and white.

No citizen, not even Lincoln, ever reached the White House from humbler beginnings. Born to impoverished parents in North Carolina and orphaned early, Johnson never attended school but was apprenticed to a tailor at age ten. Ambitious to get ahead, he taught himself to read, and later his wife taught him to write and do simple arithmetic. Like many another self-made man, he was inclined to overpraise his maker.

Johnson early became active in politics in Tennessee, where he had moved when seventeen years old. He shone as an impassioned champion of the poor whites against the planter aristocrats, and as a two-fisted stump speaker before angry and heckling crowds. Elected to Congress, he attracted much favorable attention in the North when he refused to secede with his own state. After Tennessee was partially liberated by Union armies, he was appointed war governor of the state.

Political exigency next thrust Johnson into the vice presidency. Lincoln's Union party in 1864 needed to attract support from the War Democrats and other pro-Southern elements, and Johnson, a Democrat, seemed to be the ideal man.

"Old Andy" Johnson was no doubt a man of parts—unpolished parts. He was intelligent, able, forceful, and steadfastly devoted to duty and to the Constitution. Yet the man who had raised himself from the tailor's bench to the president's chair was a misfit. A Southerner who did not understand the North, a Tennessean who had earned the distrust of the South, a Democrat who had never been accepted by the Republicans, a president who had not been elected to the office, he was not at home in a Republican White House. Hotheaded, contentious, and stubborn, Johnson was the wrong man in the wrong place at the wrong time. A Reconstruction policy devised by the angels might well have failed in his tactless hands.

LETTER FROM A FREEDMAN TO HIS OLD MASTER, 1865

What was it like to experience the transition from slavery to freedom? Four million southern blacks faced this exhilarating and formidable prospect with the end of the war. For historians, recovering the African American perspective on emancipation is challenging. Unlike their white masters, freed blacks left few written records. But one former slave captured in a letter to his "Old Master" (whose surname he bore) the heroic determination of many blacks to build new independent and dignified lives for themselves and their families.

During the war Jordon Anderson escaped slavery in Tennessee with his wife and two daughters. After relocating to the relative safety of Ohio, he received a communication from his former owner asking him to return. In his bold reply, reportedly "dictated by the old servant" himself, Anderson expressed his family's new expectations for life as free people and an uneasiness about his former master's intentions. He made reference to his "comfortable home," his daughters' schooling, the church that he and his wife were free to attend regularly, and the peace of mind that came with knowing that "my girls [would not be] brought to shame by the violence and wickedness of their young masters." To test the white man's sincerity, Anderson and his wife asked for the astronomical figure of $11,680 in back wages from decades as slaves. He closed by reiterating that "the great desire of my life is to give my children an education and have them form virtuous habits." This rare letter demonstrates that many black correspondents may have been illiterate, but they were hardly inarticulate. And they asserted themselves as parents, workers, and citizens not only from the distance of a former free state such as Ohio but also deep within the former slave states of the South.

1. Was the tone of Anderson's letter (and postscript) serious, sarcastic, or tongue-in-cheek? What specific phrases support your answer?

2. How did the eventual accomplishments of Reconstruction correspond with the initial expectations of people like Anderson and his former owner?

3. What does this letter reveal about the complicated relationships between freedmen and their former masters? Is the relationship a "personal" one, or was it entirely dominated by Jordan Anderson's having been held by Colonel P. H. Anderson as "property"?

Letter from a Freedman to his Old Master.

The following is a genuine document. It was *dictated* by the old servant, and contains his ideas and forms of expression. [Cincinnati Commercial.

DAYTON, Ohio, August 7, 1865.
To my Old Master, Col. P. H. ANDERSON, Big Spring, Tennessee.

SIR: I got your letter and was glad to find that you had not forgotten Jordan, and that you wanted me to come back and live with you again, promising to do better for me than anybody else can. I have often felt uneasy about you. I thought the Yankees would have hung you long before this for harboring Rebs they found at your house. I suppose they never heard about your going to Col. Martin's to kill the Union soldier that was left by his company in their stable. Although you shot at me twice before I left you, I did not want to hear of your being hurt, and am glad you are still living. It would do me good to go back to the dear old home again and see Miss Mary and Miss Martha and Allen, Esther, Green and Lee. Give my love to them all, and tell them I hope we will meet in the better world, if not in this. I would have gone back to see you all when I was working in the Nashville Hospital, but one of the neighbors told me Henry intended to shoot me if he ever got a chance.

I want to know particularly what the good chance is you propose to give me. I am doing tolerably well here; I get $25 a month, with victuals and clothing; have a comfortable home for Mandy (the folks here call her Mrs. Anderson), and the children, Milly Jane and Grundy, go to school and are learning well; the teacher says Grundy has a head for a preacher. They go to Sunday-School, and Mandy and me attend church

As to my freedom, which you say I can have, there is nothing to be gained on that score, as I got my free-papers in 1864 from the Provost-Marshal-General of the Department at Nashville. Mandy says she would be afraid to go back without some proof that you are sincerely disposed to treat us justly and kindly—and we have concluded to test your sincerity by asking you to send us our wages for the time we served you. This will make us forget and forgive old sores, and rely on your justice and friendship in the future. I served you faithfully for thirty-two years, and Mandy twenty years, at $25 a month for me, and $2 a week for Mandy. Our earnings would amount to $11,680. Add to this the interest for the time our wages has been kept back and deduct what you paid for our clothing and three doctor's visits to me, and pulling a tooth for Mandy, and the balance will show what we are in justice entitled to. Please send the money by Adams Express, in care of V. Winters, esq., Dayton, Ohio. If you fail to pay us for faithful labors in the past we can have little faith in your promises in the future.

P. S.—Say howdy to George Carter, and thank him for taking the pistol from you when you were shooting at me.

New-York Tribune, August 22, 1865.

Presidential Reconstruction

Even before the shooting war had ended, the political war over Reconstruction had begun. Abraham Lincoln believed that the Southern states had never legally withdrawn from the Union. Their formal restoration to the Union would therefore be relatively simple. Accordingly, Lincoln in 1863 proclaimed his "10 percent" Reconstruction plan. It decreed that a state could be reintegrated into the Union when 10 percent of its voters in the presidential election of 1860 had taken an oath of allegiance to the United States and pledged to abide by emancipation. The next step would be formal erection of a state government. Lincoln would then recognize the purified regime.

Lincoln's proclamation provoked a sharp reaction in Congress, where Republicans feared the restoration of the planter aristocracy to power and the possible re-enslavement of blacks. Republicans therefore rammed through Congress in 1864 the Wade-Davis Bill. The bill required that 50 percent of a state's voters take the oath of allegiance and demanded stronger safeguards for emancipation than Lincoln's as the price of readmission. Republicans were outraged when Lincoln "**pocket-vetoed**" this bill by refusing to sign it after Congress had adjourned.

The controversy surrounding the Wade-Davis Bill had revealed deep differences between the president and Congress. Unlike Lincoln, many in Congress insisted that the seceders had indeed left the Union—had "committed suicide" as republican states—and had therefore forfeited all their rights. They could be readmitted only as "conquered provinces" on such conditions as Congress should decree.

The episode further revealed differences among two emerging Republican factions, moderates and radicals. The majority moderate group tended to agree with Lincoln that the seceded states should be restored to the Union as simply and swiftly as reasonable—though on Congress's terms, not the president's. The minority radical group believed that before the South could be restored, its social structure should be uprooted, the haughty planters punished, and the newly emancipated blacks protected by federal power.

After President Lincoln's assassination in April 1865, some radicals hoped that spiteful Andy Johnson, who shared their hatred for the planter aristocracy, would also share their desire to reconstruct the South with a rod of iron. But Johnson soon disillusioned them. He quickly recognized several of Lincoln's 10 percent governments, and on May 29, 1865, he issued his own Reconstruction proclamation. It disfranchised certain leading Confederates and called for special state conventions, which were required to repeal secession, repudiate all Confederate debts, and ratify the slave-freeing Thirteenth Amendment.

Johnson, savoring his dominance over the high-toned aristocrats who now begged his favor, granted pardons in abundance. Bolstered by the political resurrection of the planter elite, the recently rebellious states moved rapidly in the second half of 1865 to organize governments. But as the pattern of the new governments became clear, Republicans of all stripes grew furious.

pocket veto *The presidential act of blocking a Congressionally passed law not by direct veto but by simply refusing to sign it at the end of a session. (A president can pocket veto a bill within ten days of a session's end or after.)*

The Baleful Black Codes

Among the first acts of the new Southern regimes sanctioned by Johnson was the passage of the iron-toothed Black Codes. These laws were designed to regulate the affairs of the emancipated blacks, much as the slave statutes had done in pre-Civil War days. The Black Codes aimed, first of all, to ensure a stable and subservient labor force. Dire penalties were therefore imposed by the codes on blacks who "jumped" their labor contracts, which usually committed them to work for the same employer for one year, and generally at pittance wages.

The codes also sought to restore as nearly as possible the pre-emancipation system of race relations. Freedom was legally recognized, as were some other privileges, such as the right to marry. But all the codes forbade a black to serve on a jury or vote, and some codes even barred blacks from renting or leasing land.

These oppressive laws mocked the ideal of freedom, so recently purchased by buckets of blood. The Black Codes imposed terrible burdens on the unfettered blacks, struggling against mistreatment and poverty to make their way as free people. Thousands of impoverished former slaves slipped into virtual **peonage** as **sharecropper** farmers, as did many landless whites.

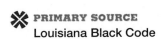 **PRIMARY SOURCE**
Louisiana Black Code

peonage *A system in which debtors are held in servitude, to labor for their creditors.*

sharecropper *An agricultural system in which a tenant receives land, tools, and seed on credit and pledges in return a share of the crop to the creditor.*

The Black Codes made an ugly impression in the North. If the former slaves were being re-enslaved, people asked one another, had not the Boys in Blue spilled their blood in vain? Had the North really won the war?

Congressional Reconstruction

These questions grew more insistent when the congressional delegations from the newly reconstituted Southern states presented themselves in the Capitol in December 1865. To the shock and disgust of the Republicans, many former Confederate leaders were on hand to claim their seats.

The appearance of these ex-rebels was a natural but costly blunder. Voters of the South, seeking able representatives, had turned instinctively to their experienced statesmen. But most of the Southern leaders were tainted by active association with the "lost cause." Among them were four former Confederate generals, five colonels, and various members of the Richmond cabinet and Congress. Worst of all, there was the shrimpy but brainy Alexander Stephens, ex-vice president of the Confederacy, still under indictment for treason.

The presence of these "whitewashed rebels" infuriated the Republicans in Congress. The war had been fought to restore the Union, but not on these kinds of terms. Most Republicans balked at giving up the political advantage they had enjoyed while the South had been "out" from 1861 to 1865. They had passed much legislation that favored the North, such as the Morrill Act, the Pacific Railroad Act, and the Homestead Act. On the first day of the congressional session, December 4, 1865, they banged shut the door in the face of the newly elected Southern delegations.

Looking to the future, the Republicans were alarmed to realize that a restored South would be stronger than ever in national politics. Before the war a black slave had counted as three-fifths of a person in apportioning congressional representation. But now, owing to full counting of free blacks, the eleven rebel states were entitled to twelve more votes in Congress and twelve more presidential electoral votes than they had previously enjoyed. Again, angry voices in the North raised the cry, "Who won the war?"

Republicans had good reason to fear that ultimately they might be elbowed aside. Southerners might join hands with Democrats in the North and win control of Congress or maybe even the White House. If that happened, they could perpetuate the Black Codes, virtually re-enslaving the blacks. They could dismantle the economic program of the Republican party and possibly even repudiate the national debt. President Johnson thus deeply disturbed the congressional Republicans when he announced on December 6, 1865, that the recently rebellious states had satisfied his conditions and that in his view the Union was now restored.

Johnson Clashes with Congress

A clash between president and Congress was now inevitable. It exploded into the open in February 1866, when the president vetoed a bill (later repassed) extending the life of the controversial Freedmen's Bureau.

Aroused, the Republicans swiftly struck back. In March 1866 they passed the Civil Rights Bill, which conferred on blacks the privileges of American citizenship and struck at the Black Codes. President Johnson resolutely vetoed this forward-looking measure, but in April congressmen steamrollered it over his veto—something they repeatedly did henceforth. The hapless president, dubbed "Andy Veto," had his presidential wings clipped short, as Congress increasingly assumed the dominant role in running the government.

The Republicans now undertook to rivet the principles of the Civil Rights Bill into the Constitution as the Fourteenth Amendment. The proposed amendment, as approved by Congress and sent to the states in June 1866 and ratified in 1868, was sweeping. The amendment (1) conferred civil rights, including citizenship but excluding the franchise, on the freedmen; (2) reduced proportionately the representation of a state in Congress and in the Electoral College if it denied blacks the ballot; (3) disqualified from federal and state office former Confederates who as federal officeholders had once sworn to "support the Constitution of the United States"; and (4) guaranteed the federal debt, while repudiating all Confederate debts. (See the text of the Fourteenth Amendment in the Appendix.)

The radical faction was disappointed that the Fourteenth Amendment did not grant the right to vote, but all Republicans agreed that no state should be welcomed back into the Union fold without first ratifying the Fourteenth Amendment. Yet President Johnson advised the Southern states to reject it, and all of the "sinful eleven," except Tennessee, defiantly spurned the amendment.

Swinging 'Round the Circle with Johnson

As 1866 lengthened, the battle grew between Congress and the president. Now the issue was whether Reconstruction was to be carried on with or without the Fourteenth Amendment. The Republicans would settle for nothing less.

The crucial congressional elections of 1866—more crucial than some presidential elections—were fast approaching. Johnson was naturally eager to escape from the clutch of Congress by securing a majority favorable to his soft-on-the-South policy. Invited to dedicate a Chicago monument to Stephen A. Douglas, he undertook to speak at various cities en route in support of his views.

Johnson's famous "swing 'round the circle," beginning in the late summer of 1866, was a seriocomedy of errors. The president delivered a series of "give 'em hell" speeches, in which he accused the radicals in Congress of having planned large-scale antiblack riots and murder in the South. As he spoke, hecklers hurled insults at him. Reverting to his stump-speaking days in Tennessee, he shouted back angry retorts, amid cries of "You be damned!" and "Don't get mad, Andy!" The dignity of his high office sank to a new low.

As a vote-getter, Johnson was highly successful—for the opposition. His inept speech-making heightened the cry to "Stand by Congress" against the "Tailor of the Potomac." When the ballots were counted, the Republicans had rolled up more than a two-thirds majority in both houses of Congress.

Republican Reconstruction

The Republicans now had a veto-proof Congress and virtually unlimited control of Reconstruction policy. But moderates and radicals still disagreed over the best course to pursue in the South.

The radicals were led in the Senate by the courtly and principled idealist Charles Sumner and in the House by crusty and vindictive Pennsylvania Congressman Thaddeus Stevens. Both tirelessly labored not only for black freedom but for racial equality. Still opposed to rapid restoration of the Southern states, the radicals wanted to keep them out as long as possible and apply federal power to bring about a drastic social and economic transformation in the South.

But moderate Republicans, more attuned to time-honored Republican principles of states' rights and self-government, preferred policies that restrained the states from abridging citizens' rights, rather than policies that directly involved the federal government in individual lives. The actual policies adopted by Congress showed the influence of both these schools of thought, though the moderates, as the majority faction, had the upper hand. And one thing both groups had come to agree on by 1867 was the necessity to enfranchise black voters, even if it took federal troops to do it.

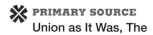
PRIMARY SOURCE
Union as It Was, The

Against a backdrop of vicious and bloody race riots that had erupted in several Southern cities, Congress passed the Reconstruction Act on March 2, 1867. This drastic legislation divided the South into five military districts, each commanded by a Union general and policed by blue-clad soldiers, about twenty thousand all told.

Congress additionally laid down stringent requirements for the readmission of the seceded states. The wayward states were required to ratify the Fourteenth Amendment, giving the former slaves their rights as citizens, and to guarantee in their state constitutions full suffrage for their former adult male slaves. Yet the act, reflecting moderate sentiment, stopped short of giving the freedmen land or education at federal expense. The overriding purpose of the moderates was to create an electorate in Southern states that would vote those states back into the Union on acceptable terms and thus free the federal government

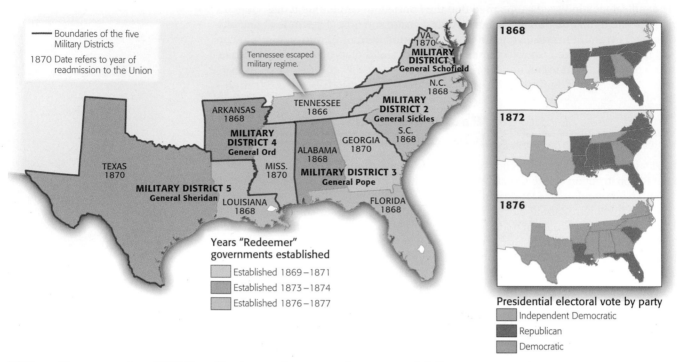

Military Reconstruction, 1867 (five districts and commanding generals) For many white Southerners, military Reconstruction amounted to turning the knife in the wound of defeat. An often-repeated story of later years had a Southerner remark, "I was sixteen years old before I discovered that damnyankee was two words." © Cengage Learning

MAP SKILL-BUILDER Understanding Political Maps

1. This map of military Reconstruction, along with the three sidebar maps on the vote in three presidential elections, provides a wealth of political information about the relationship between the rise and decline of radical Reconstruction in the South. To understand this political information requires examining all *four* maps to look for patterns and correlations. In the election of 1868, which *four* former Confederate states had not yet been readmitted to the Union and therefore cast no electoral votes for president?

2. In 1872—the peak of radical Reconstruction—*two* states that had already been "redeemed" by conservative whites (color-coded yellow on the main Military Reconstruction map) nevertheless *still* voted Republican (Grant) in the election of 1872, suggesting the continuing strength of the radicals. Which states were they?

3. By the election of 1876, radical Reconstruction had declined, and all but four southern states (color-coded green on the Military Reconstruction map) had been "redeemed." Three of those were the only southern states to vote Republican (Hayes) that year, but even one state still under radical rule voted Democratic. Which state was it?

4. Only *one* southern state voted consistently Democratic throughout Reconstruction, even when it was under radical rule, suggesting the weakness of Reconstruction there. Which state was it? Recalling Civil War military events (see pp. 326–328), what might explain the especially deep hostility to Republicans in that state?

from direct responsibility for the protection of black rights. As later events would demonstrate, this approach proved woefully inadequate to the cause of justice for the blacks.

The radical Republicans still worried that once the unrepentant states were readmitted, they would amend their constitutions to withdraw the ballot from the blacks. They therefore sought the ironclad safeguard of incorporating black suffrage in the federal Constitution. This goal was finally achieved by the Fifteenth Amendment, passed by Congress in 1869 and ratified by the required number of states in 1870. (See the Appendix.)

Military Reconstruction of the South not only usurped certain functions of the president as commander in chief but set up a martial regime of dubious legality. The Supreme Court had already ruled, in the case *Ex parte Milligan* (1866), that military tribunals could not try civilians, even during wartime, in areas where the civil courts were open. Peacetime military rule seemed starkly contrary to the spirit of the Constitution, but for the time being the Supreme Court avoided offending the Republican Congress.

Prodded into line by federal bayonets, the Southern states got on with the task of constitution making. By 1870 all of them had reorganized their governments and had been accorded full rights. The hated "bluebellies" remained until the new regimes—usually called "radical" regimes—appeared to be firmly entrenched. Yet when the federal troops finally left a state, its government swiftly passed into the hands of white "Redeemer" regimes, which were inevitably Democratic. Finally, in 1877, the last federal muskets were removed from state politics, and the "solid" Democratic South congealed.

The passage of the three Reconstruction-era Amendments—the Thirteenth, Fourteenth, and Fifteenth—delighted former abolitionists but deeply disappointed advocates of women's rights. Women had played a prominent part in the prewar abolitionist movement, and in the eyes of many women the struggle for black freedom and the crusade for women's rights were one and the same. Now, feminist leaders reeled with shock when the Fourteenth Amendment, which defined equal national citizenship, for the first time inserted the word *male* into the Constitution in referring to a citizen's right to vote. When the Fifteenth Amendment proposed to prohibit denial of the vote on the basis of "race, color, or previous condition of servitude," women's rights leaders Susan B. Anthony and Elizabeth Cady Stanton wanted the word *sex* added to the list. They lost this battle, too. Fifty years would pass before the Constitution granted women the right to vote.

The prominent suffragist and abolitionist Susan B. Anthony (1820–1906) was outraged over the proposed exclusion of women from the Fourteenth Amendment. In a conversation with her former male allies Wendell Phillips and Theodore Tilton, she reportedly held out her arm and declared:

"Look at this, all of you. And hear me swear that I will cut off this right arm of mine before I will ever work for or demand the ballot for the negro and not the woman."

The Realities of Radical Reconstruction in the South

Blacks now had freedom, of a sort. By 1867 Republican hesitation over black voting had given way to a hard determination to enfranchise the former slaves wholesale and immediately, while thousands of white Southerners were being denied the right to vote. By glaring contrast, most of the Northern states, before ratification of the Fifteenth Amendment in 1870, withheld the ballot from their tiny black minorities. White Southerners naturally concluded that the Republicans were hypocritical in insisting that blacks in the South be allowed to vote.

Having gained their right to suffrage, Southern black men seized the initiative and began to organize politically. Their primary vehicle became the Union League, originally a pro-Union organization based in the North. Assisted by Northern blacks, freedmen turned the League into a network of political clubs that educated members in their civic duties and campaigned for Republican candidates. The League's mission soon expanded to include building black churches and schools, representing black grievances before local employers and governments, and recruiting militias to protect black communities from white retaliation.

Though African American women did not obtain the right to vote, they too assumed new political roles. Black women faithfully attended the parades and rallies common in black communities during the early years of Reconstruction and helped assemble mass meetings in the newly constructed black churches. They even showed up at the constitutional conventions held throughout the South in 1867, monitoring the proceedings and participating in informal votes outside the convention halls.

But black men elected as delegates to the state constitutional conventions held the greater political authority. They formed the backbone of the black political community. At the conventions, they sat down with whites to hammer out new state constitutions, which most importantly provided for universal male suffrage.

The sight of former slaves holding office deeply offended their onetime masters, who lashed out with fury at the freedmen's white allies, labeling them "**scalawags**" and "**carpetbaggers**." The so-called scalawags were Southerners, often former Unionists and Whigs, whom former Confederates wildly accused of plundering the treasuries of the Southern radical governments. The carpetbaggers were supposedly sleazy Northerners who had packed all their worldly goods into a carpetbag suitcase at war's end and had come South to seek personal power and profit. In fact, most were former Union soldiers and Northern businessmen and professionals who wanted to play a role in modernizing the "New South."

scalawag *Derogatory term for pro-Union Southerners whom Southern Democrats accused of plundering the resources of the South in collusion with Republican governments after the Civil War.*

carpetbagger *Derogatory term used by Southern whites to describe Northern businessmen and politicians who came to the South after the Civil War to work on Reconstruction projects or invest in Southern infrastructure.*

Freedmen Voting, Richmond, Virginia, 1871 The exercise of democratic rights by former slaves constituted a political and social revolution in the South and was bitterly resented by whites.

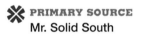

✳ **PRIMARY SOURCE**
Mr. Solid South

The Ku Klux Klan, Tennessee, 1868 This night-riding terrorist has even masked the identity of his horse.

How well did the radical regimes rule? White southerners regularly portrayed the "Black Reconstruction" governments as run by ignorant and corrupt former slaves. Black voters did make up a majority of the electorate in five states, but only in South Carolina did blacks predominate in the lower house of the legislature. Many of the newly elected black legislators were literate and able; more than a few came from the ranks of the prewar free blacks who had acquired considerable education. More than a dozen black congressmen and two black United States senators, Hiram Revels and Blanche K. Bruce, both of Mississippi, did creditable work in the national capital.

In some radical regimes, there was truth to the charges of graft and corruption. This was especially true in South Carolina and Louisiana, where conscienceless promoters and other pocket-padders used politically inexperienced blacks as cat's-paws. The worst "black-and-white" legislatures purchased as "legislative supplies" such "stationery" as hams, perfumes, suspenders, bonnets, corsets, champagne, and a coffin. Yet this sort of corruption was no more outrageous than the scams and felonies being perpetrated in the North at the same time, especially in Boss Tweed's New York.

The radical legislatures also passed much desirable legislation. For the first time in Southern history, steps were taken toward establishing adequate public schools. Tax systems were streamlined; public works were launched; and property rights were guaranteed to women. Many of these reforms were so welcome that they were retained by the all-white "Redeemer" governments that later returned to power.

The Ku Klux Klan

Deeply embittered, some Southern whites resorted to savage measures against "radical" rule. Many whites resented the success and ability of black legislators as much as they resented alleged "corruption." A number of secret organizations mushroomed forth, the most notorious of which was the "Invisible Empire of the South," or Ku Klux Klan, founded in Tennessee in 1866. Hooded nightriders, their horses' hoofs muffled, would pound and hammer on blacks' cabin doors or use other tactics to frighten them. Those stubborn souls who persisted in their "upstart" ways were flogged, mutilated, or even murdered. In one Louisiana parish in 1868, whites in two days killed or wounded two hundred victims; a pile of twenty-five bodies was found half-buried in the woods. Such atrocious **terror** tactics proved partially effective in keeping many blacks from the polls.

Congress, outraged by this night-riding lawlessness, passed the harsh Force Acts of 1870 and 1871. Federal troops were able to stamp out much of the "lash law," but by this time the Invisible Empire had already done its work of intimidation. The Klan remained a refuge for numerous scoundrels and cutthroats who hid under its sheets, often continuing to operate under the guise of "dancing societies," "missionary clubs," and "rifle clubs."

White resistance undermined attempts to empower the blacks politically. The white South for many decades openly flouted the Fourteenth and Fifteenth Amendments. Wholesale disfranchisement of the blacks, starting conspicuously about 1890, was achieved by intimidation, fraud, and trickery. Among various underhanded schemes were the literacy tests, unfairly administered by whites to the advantage of illiterate whites. In the eyes of white Southerners, the goal of white supremacy fully justified these dishonorable devices.

terror (terrorist) *Using violence or the threat of violence in order to create intense fear in the attempt to promote some political policy or objectives.*

Impeachment and Acquittal for Johnson

Radicals meanwhile had been sharpening their hatchets for President Johnson. Not content with curbing his authority, they decided to remove him altogether by constitutional processes.*

As an initial step, Congress in 1867 passed the Tenure of Office Act—as usual over Johnson's veto. Contrary to precedent, the new law required the president to secure the consent of the Senate before he could remove his cabinet members, including the secretary of war, Edwin M. Stanton, a holdover from the Lincoln administration. Although outwardly loyal to Johnson, Stanton was secretly serving as a spy and informer for the radicals.

Johnson provided the radicals with a pretext to begin impeachment proceedings when he abruptly dismissed Stanton early in 1868. The House of Representatives immediately voted 126 to 47 to impeach Andrew Johnson for "high crimes and misdemeanors," as required by the Constitution, charging him with various violations of the Tenure of Office Act. Two additional articles related to Johnson's verbal assaults on the Congress, involving "disgrace, ridicule, hatred, contempt, and reproach."

With evident zeal the radical-led Senate now sat as a court to try Johnson on the dubious impeachment charges. The House conducted the prosecution. The trial aroused intense public interest and, because only one thousand tickets for seats were printed, proved to be the biggest show of 1868. Johnson kept his dignity and maintained a discreet silence. His battery of attorneys argued that the president had fired Stanton merely to put a test case before the Supreme Court. The House prosecutors, including oily-tongued Benjamin F. Butler and embittered Thaddeus Stevens, had a harder time building a compelling case for impeachment.

On May 16, 1868, the day for voting in the Senate, the tension was electric, and heavy breathing could be heard in the galleries. By a margin of only one vote, the radicals failed to muster the two-thirds majority for Johnson's removal. Seven independent-minded Republican senators, courageously putting country above party, voted "not guilty."

Diehard radicals were infuriated. "The Country is going to the Devil!" cried the crippled Stevens as he was carried from the hall. But the nation, though violently aroused, accepted the verdict with a good temper that did credit to its political maturity.

The nation thus narrowly avoided a bad precedent that would have gravely weakened one of the three branches of the federal government. Johnson was clearly guilty of bad speeches, bad judgment, and bad temper, but not of "high crimes and misdemeanors." From the standpoint of the radicals, his greatest crime had been to stand inflexibly in their path.

The Purchase of Alaska

Johnson's administration, though largely reduced to a figurehead, achieved its most enduring success in the field of foreign relations. The Russians by 1867 were in a mood to sell the vast and chilly expanse of land now known as Alaska. The region

The remarkable ex-slave Frederick Douglass (1817?–1895) wrote in 1882:

"Though slavery was abolished, the wrongs of my people were not ended. Though they were not slaves, they were not yet quite free. No man can be truly free whose liberty is dependent upon the thought, feeling, and action of others, and who has himself no means in his own hands for guarding, protecting, defending, and maintaining that liberty. Yet the Negro after his emancipation was precisely in this state of destitution. ... He was free from the individual master, but the slave of society. He had neither money, property, nor friends. He was free from the old plantation, but he had nothing but the dusty road under his feet. He was free from the old quarter that once gave him shelter, but a slave to the rains of summer and the frosts of winter. He was, in a word, literally turned loose, naked, hungry, and destitute, to the open sky."

* For impeachment, see Art. I, Sec. II, para. 5, Art. I, Sec. II, paras. 6, 7, Art. II, Sec. IV, in the Appendix.

Few topics have triggered as much intellectual warfare as the "dark and bloody ground" of Reconstruction. The period provoked questions—sectional, racial, and constitutional—about which people felt deeply and remain deeply divided even today. Scholarly argument goes back conspicuously to a Columbia University historian, William A. Dunning, who wrote about Reconstruction as a kind of national disgrace, foisted on a prostrate region by vindictive and self-seeking radical Republican politicians.

In the 1920s, widespread suspicion that the Civil War itself had been a tragic and unnecessary blunder shifted attention to Northern politicians. Scholars such as Howard Beale argued that the radical Republicans had masked a ruthless desire to exploit Southern resources and expand Republican power in the South behind a false "front" of concern for the freed slaves.

Although ignored by his contemporaries, the scholar and founder of the National Association for the Advancement of Colored People, W. E. B. Du Bois wrote a sympathetic history of Reconstruction in 1935 that became the basis of historians' interpretations ever since. Following World War II, Kenneth Stampp and others, influenced by the modern civil rights movement, built on Du Bois's argument and claimed that Reconstruction had been a noble though ultimately failed attempt to extend American principles of equity and justice. By the early 1970s, this view had become orthodoxy, and it generally holds sway today. Yet some scholars, such as

Michael Benedict and Leon Litwack, disillusioned with the inability to achieve full racial justice in the 1960s and 1970s, claimed to discover that Reconstruction was never really very radical and argued that the Freedmen's Bureau and other agencies had merely allowed white planters to maintain local political and economic control.

More recently, Eric Foner has powerfully reasserted the argument that Reconstruction was a truly radical and noble attempt to establish an interracial democracy. Drawing on the work of Du Bois, Foner has emphasized that Reconstruction allowed blacks to form political organizations and churches and to establish some measure of economic independence. In South Africa, the Caribbean, and other areas once marked by slavery, these opportunities were much harder to come by. Many of the benefits of Reconstruction were erased by white Southerners during the Gilded Age, but in the twentieth century, constitutional principles and organizations developed during Reconstruction provided the foundation for the modern civil rights movement—which some have called the Second Reconstruction.

Steven Hahn's *A Nation Under Our Feet: Black Political Struggles in the Rural South from Slavery to the Great Migration* (2003) is the latest contribution to the literature on Reconstruction. Hahn emphasizes the assertiveness and ingenuity of African Americans in creating new political opportunities for themselves after emancipation.

had been ruthlessly "furred out" and was a growing economic liability to them. The Russians were therefore eager to unload their "frozen asset" on the Americans. They preferred the United States to any other purchaser primarily because they wanted to strengthen further the Republic as a barrier against their ancient enemy, Britain.

In 1867 Secretary of State William Seward, an ardent expansionist, signed a treaty with Russia that transferred Alaska to the United States for the bargain price of $7.2 million. But Seward's enthusiasm for these frigid wastes was not shared by his ignorant or uninformed countrymen, who jeered at "Seward's Folly," "Seward's Icebox," and "Walrussia."

Then why did Congress and the American public sanction the purchase? For one thing Russia, alone among the great powers, had been conspicuously friendly to the North during the recent Civil War. Americans did not feel that they could offend their good friend the tsar by hurling his walrus-covered icebergs back into his face. Besides, the territory was rumored to be still teeming with furs, fish, and gold, and it might yet "pan out" profitably—as it later did with natural resources that included oil and gas.

The Heritage of Reconstruction

Many white Southerners regarded Reconstruction as a more grievous wound than the war itself. It left a festering scar that would take generations to heal. They resented the upending of their social and racial systems, the political empowerment of blacks, and the insult of federal intervention in their local affairs. Yet given the explosiveness of the issues that had caused the war and the bitterness of the fighting, the wonder is that Reconstruction was not far harsher than it was. Northern policymakers groped for the right policies, influenced as much by Southern responses to defeat and emancipation as by any specific plans of their own.

The Republicans acted from a mixture of idealism and political expediency. They wanted both to protect the freed slaves and to promote the fortunes of the Republican party. In the end their efforts backfired badly. Reconstruction conferred only fleeting benefits on the blacks, and it virtually extinguished the Republican party in the South for nearly one hundred years.

Moderate Republicans never fully appreciated the extensive effort necessary to make the freed slaves completely independent citizens, nor the lengths to which Southern whites would go to preserve their system of racial dominance. Had Thaddeus Stevens's radical program of drastic economic reforms and heftier protection of political rights been enacted, things might well have been different. But deep-seated racism, ingrained American resistance to tampering with property rights, and rigid loyalty to the principle of local self-government, combined with spreading indifference in the North to the plight of blacks, formed too formidable an obstacle. Despite good intentions by Republicans, the Old South was in many ways more resurrected than reconstructed.

Chapter Summary

With the Civil War over, the nation faced the difficult problems of rebuilding the South, assisting the freed slaves, reintegrating the Southern states into the Union, and deciding who would direct the Reconstruction process.

The South was economically devastated and socially revolutionized by emancipation. As slave owners reluctantly confronted the end of slave labor, blacks took their first steps in freedom. Black churches and freedmen's schools helped the former slaves begin to shape their own destinies.

The new President Andrew Johnson was politically inept and personally contentious. His attempt to implement a moderate plan of Reconstruction, along the lines originally suggested by Lincoln, fell victim to Southern whites' severe treatment of blacks and his own political blunders.

Republicans imposed harsh military Reconstruction on the South after their gains in the 1866 congressional elections. The Southern states reentered the Union with new radical governments, which rested partly on the newly enfranchised blacks, but also had support from some sectors of Southern society. These governments were sometimes corrupt, but they also implemented important reforms, especially in education. For a time, acting from a mixture of idealism and political expediency, Republicans tried seriously to build a new Republican party in the South to guarantee black rights. But the divisions between moderate and radical Republicans meant that Reconstruction's aims were often limited and confused, despite successful passage of the important Fourteenth and Fifteenth Amendments guaranteeing black civil and voting rights.

Embittered whites hated the radical governments and mobilized reactionary terrorist organizations such as the Ku Klux Klan to restore white supremacy. The radical Republican House of Representatives impeached Johnson, but the Senate failed narrowly to convict him. In the end, the inadequate Reconstruction policy, which never really addressed the deep economic and social legacy of slavery and the Civil War, failed disastrously and created as much or more bitterness than the war itself.

KEY TERMS

treason (338)

civil disabilities (338)

mutual aid societies (340)

confiscation (340)

pocket veto (343)

peonage (343)

sharecropper (343)

scalawag (347)

carpetbagger (347)

terror (terrorist) (349)

PEOPLE TO KNOW

Andrew Johnson

Thaddeus Stevens

Hiram Revels

Edwin M. Stanton

William Seward

Go to the History CourseMate website for primary source links, study tools, and review materials for this chapter. www.cengagebrain.com

PART
FOUR

Forging an Industrial Society

⤬

1865–1899

A nation of farmers fought the Civil War in the 1860s. By the time the Spanish-American War broke out in 1898, America was an industrial nation. For generations Americans had plunged into the wilderness and plowed their fields. Now they settled in cities and toiled in factories. Between the Civil War and the century's end, economic and technological change came so swiftly and massively that it seemed to many Americans that a whole new civilization had emerged.

In some ways it had. The sheer scale of the new industrial civilization was dazzling. Transcontinental railroads knit the country together from sea to sea. New industries such as oil and steel grew to staggering sizes—and made mega-millionaires out of entrepreneurs such as oilman John D. Rockefeller and steel-maker Andrew Carnegie.

Drawn by the allure of industrial employment, Americans moved to the city. In 1860 only about 20 percent of the population were city dwellers. By 1900 that proportion had doubled, as rural Americans and European immigrants alike flocked to mill town and metropolis in search of steady jobs.

These sweeping changes challenged the spirit of individualism that Americans had celebrated since the seventeenth century. Even on the western frontier, that historic bastion of rugged loners, the hand of government was increasingly felt, as large armies were dispatched to subdue the Plains Indians and federal authority was invoked to regulate the use of natural resources. The rise of powerful monopolies called into question the government's traditional hands-off policy toward business, and a growing band of reformers increasingly clamored for government regulation of private enterprise. The mushrooming cities, with their needs for transport systems, schools, hospitals, sanitation, and fire and police protection,

required bigger governments and budgets than an earlier generation could have imagined. As never before, Americans struggled to adapt old ideals of private autonomy to the new realities of industrial civilization.

With economic change came social and political turmoil. Labor violence brought bloodshed to places such as Chicago and Homestead, Pennsylvania. Small farmers, squeezed by debt and foreign competition, rallied behind the People's, or "Populist," party, a radical movement of the 1880s and 1890s that attacked the power of Wall Street, big business, and the banks. Anti-immigrant sentiment swelled. Bitter disputes over tariffs and monetary policy deeply divided the country, setting debtors against lenders, farmers against manufacturers, the West and South against the Northeast. And in this unfamiliar era of big money and expanding government, corruption flourished, from town hall to Congress, fueling loud cries for political reform.

The bloodiest conflict of all pitted Plains Indians against the relentless push of westward expansion. As railroads drove their iron arrows through the heart of the West, the Indians lost their land and life-sustaining buffalo herds. By the 1890s, after three decades of fierce fighting with the U.S. Army, the Indians who had once roamed across the vast rolling prairies were struggling to preserve their shattered cultures within the confinement of reservations.

The South remained the one region largely untouched by the Industrial Revolution sweeping the rest of America. For the most part, the South's rural way of life and its peculiar system of race relations were largely unperturbed by the changes happening elsewhere. On African Americans, the vast majority of whom continued to live in the Old South, the

352

post-emancipation era inflicted new forms of racial injustice. State legislatures systematically deprived black Americans of their political rights, including the right to vote. Segregation of schools, housing, and all kinds of public facilities made a mockery of African Americans' Reconstruction-era hopes for equality before the law.

The new wealth and power of industrial America nurtured a growing sense of national self-confidence. Literature flowered, and a golden age of philanthropy dawned. The reform spirit spread. So did a restless appetite for overseas expansion. In a brief war against Spain in 1898, the United States, born in a revolutionary war of independence and long the champion of colonial peoples yearning to breathe free, seized control of the Philippines and itself became an imperial power. Uncle Sam's venture into empire touched off a bitter national debate about America's role in the world and ushered in a long period of argument over the responsibilities, at home and abroad, of a modern industrial state.

What if ...?

■ What if industrial workers and small farmers in the post-Reconstruction era had joined in a political movement strong enough to challenge the "Captains of Industry" for control of the American economy?

■ How would the course of American economic, social, and political development, and the character of America's foreign policy, have been different?

23

Political Paralysis in the Gilded Age

1869–1896

Grant ... had no right to exist. He should have been extinct for ages. ... That, two thousand years after Alexander the Great and Julius Caesar, a man like Grant should be called—and should actually and truly be— the highest product of the most advanced evolution, made evolution ludicrous. ... The progress of evolution, from President Washington to President Grant, was alone evidence enough to upset Darwin. ... Grant ... should have lived in a cave and worn skins.

HENRY ADAMS, *The Education of Henry Adams*, 1907

The population of the post–Civil War Republic continued to vault upward by vigorous leaps, despite the awful bloodletting in both Union and Confederate ranks. Census takers reported over 39 million people in 1870, a gain of 26.6 percent over the preceding decade, as the immigrant tide surged again. The United States was now the third-largest nation in the Western world, ranking behind Russia and France.

But the civic health of the United States did not keep pace with its physical growth. The Civil War and its aftermath spawned waste, extravagance, speculation, and graft. Disillusionment ran deep among idealistic Americans in the postwar era. They had spilled their blood for the Union, emancipation, and Abraham Lincoln, who had promised "a new birth of freedom." Instead, they got a bitter dose of corruption and political stalemate— beginning with Ulysses S. Grant, a great soldier but an utterly inept politician.

FOCUS QUESTIONS

1. Why was the Gilded Age, by and large, a period of political patronage, corruption, and stalemate between the two major parties? Given these negative factors, why did political participation achieve such high levels?

2. How did the disputed Hayes–Tilden election of 1877 lead to the Compromise of 1877 and the end of Reconstruction?

3. What did the end of Reconstruction mean for blacks, and how did the South's racial system perpetuate an economic and social backwardness that trapped both whites and blacks?

4. What caused the rise of industrial and agricultural conflict in the 1880s–1890s? Why was Grover Cleveland unable to address this discontent?

5. How did the depression of the 1890s stir growing social protest and class conflict and fuel the rise of the radical Populist party?

CHRONOLOGY

1868	Grant defeats Seymour for the presidency.
1869	Fisk and Gould corner gold market.
1871	Tweed scandal in New York.
1872	Crédit Mobilier scandal exposed. Liberal Republicans break with Grant. Grant defeats Greeley for presidency.
1873	Panic of 1873.
1875	Whiskey Ring scandal. Civil Rights Act of 1875. Resumption Act.
1876	Hayes-Tilden election standoff and crisis.
1877	Compromise of 1877. Reconstruction ends. Railroad strikes paralyze nation.
1880	Garfield defeats Hancock for presidency.
1881	Garfield assassinated; Arthur assumes presidency.
1882	Chinese Exclusion Act.
1883	*Civil Rights Cases.* Pendleton Act sets up Civil Service Commission.
1884	Cleveland defeats Blaine for presidency.
1888	Harrison defeats Cleveland for presidency.
1890	"Billion-Dollar" Congress. McKinley Tariff Act. Sherman Silver Purchase Act (repealed 1893).
1892	Homestead steel strike. Coeur d'Alene (Idaho) silver miners' strike. People's party candidate James B. Weaver wins twenty-two electoral votes. Cleveland defeats Harrison and Weaver to regain presidency.
1893	Depression of 1893 begins. Republicans regain House of Representatives.
1895	J. P. Morgan's banking syndicate loans $65 million in gold to federal government.
1896	*Plessy v. Ferguson* legitimizes "separate but equal" doctrine.

The "Bloody Shirt" Elects Grant

Wrangling between Congress and Andrew Johnson had soured the people on professional politicians, and the notion still prevailed that a good general would make a good president. Stubbly bearded General Grant was by far the most popular northern hero to emerge from the war. Grateful citizens of Philadelphia, Washington, and New York showered him with gifts of houses and cash, which the general, silently puffing on his cigar, unapologetically accepted.

Grant was a hapless greenhorn in the political arena. His one presidential vote had been cast for the Democratic ticket in 1856. A better judge of horseflesh than of humans, his cultural background was breathtakingly narrow. He once reportedly remarked that Venice, Italy, would be a fine city if only it were drained.

The Republicans, freed from the Union party **coalition** of war days, enthusiastically nominated Grant for the presidency in 1868. The party's platform sounded a clarion call for continued Reconstruction of the South under the glinting steel of federal bayonets. Yet Grant, always a man of few words, coined a popular campaign slogan when he declared, "Let us have peace."

Expectant Democrats, meeting in their own nominating convention, denounced military Reconstruction but could agree on little else. Wealthy eastern delegates demanded a platform promising that federal war bonds be redeemed in gold, while the poorer midwesterners backed the "Ohio Idea" calling for redemption in greenbacks. Debt-burdened agrarian Democrats thus hoped to keep more money in circulation and to keep interest rates lower. This dispute introduced a bitter contest over monetary policy that continued to convulse the Republic until the century's end.

coalition *A temporary alliance of political factions or parties for some specific purpose.*

Midwestern delegates got the platform but not the candidate. The nominee, former New York governor Horatio Seymour, scuttled the Democrats' faint hope for success by repudiating the Ohio Idea. Republicans whipped up enthusiasm for Grant by energetically "waving the bloody shirt"—that is, reviving gory memories of the Civil War—which became for the first time a prominent feature of a presidential campaign.* "Vote as You Shot" was a powerful Republican slogan aimed at Union army veterans.

Grant won, with 214 electoral votes to 80 for Seymour. But despite his great popularity, the former general scored a majority of only 300,000 in the popular vote (3,013,421 to 2,706,829). Most white voters apparently supported Seymour, and the ballots of three still-unreconstructed southern states (Mississippi, Texas, and Virginia) were not counted at all. An estimated 500,000 former slaves gave Grant his margin of victory. To remain in power, the Republican party somehow had to continue to control the South—and to keep the ballot in the hands of the grateful freedmen. Republicans could not take future victories "for Granted."

The Era of Good Stealings

A few skunks can pollute a large area. Although the great majority of businesspeople and government officials continued to conduct their affairs with decency and honor, the whole postwar atmosphere stunk of corruption. The Man in the Moon, it was said, had to hold his nose when passing over America. Freewheeling railroad promoters sometimes left gullible bond buyers with only "two streaks of rust and a right of way." Unethical stock-market manipulators were a cinder in the public eye. Too many judges and legislators put their power up for hire. Cynics defined an honest politician as one who, when bought, would stay bought.

Notorious in the financial world were two millionaire partners, "Jubilee Jim" Fisk and Jay Gould. The corpulent and unscrupulous Fisk provided the "brass," while the undersized and cunning Gould provided the brains. The crafty pair concocted a plot in 1869 to **corner** the gold market. Their slippery game would work only if the federal Treasury refrained from selling gold. The conspirators worked on President Grant directly, and also through Grant's brother-in-law, who received $25,000 for his complicity. For weeks, Fisk and Gould madly bid the price of gold skyward, so that they could later profit from its heightened value. But on "Black Friday" (September 24, 1869), the bubble burst when the Treasury, contrary to Grant's supposed assurances, was compelled to release gold. The price of gold plunged, and numerous honest businesspeople were driven to the wall. A congressional probe concluded that Grant had done nothing crooked, though he had acted stupidly and indiscreetly.

The infamous Tweed Ring in New York City vividly displayed the ethics (or lack of ethics) typical of the age. Burly "Boss" Tweed—240 pounds of rascality—employed bribery, graft, and fraudulent elections to milk the metropolis of as much as $200 million. Honest citizens were cowed into silence. Protesters found their tax assessments raised.

Tweed's luck finally ran out. The *New York Times* secured damning evidence in 1871 and courageously published it, though offered $5 million not to do so. Gifted cartoonist Thomas Nast pilloried Tweed mercilessly, after spurning a heavy bribe to desist. New York attorney Samuel J. Tilden headed the prosecution, gaining fame that later paved the path to his presidential nomination. Unbailed and unwept, Tweed died behind bars.

More serious than Boss Tweed's peccadilloes were the misdeeds of the federal government. President Grant's cabinet was a rodent's nest of grafters and incompetents. Favor seekers haunted the White House, plying Grant himself with cigars, wine, and horses. Several dozen of Grant's in-laws attached themselves to the public payroll.

corner *To gain exclusive control of a commodity in order to fix its price.*

---

* The expression is said to have derived from a speech by Representative Benjamin F. Butler of Massachusetts, who allegedly waved before the House the bloodstained nightshirt of a Klan-flogged carpetbagger.

The easygoing Grant was first tarred by the Crédit Mobilier scandal, which erupted in 1872. Union Pacific Railway insiders had formed the Crédit Mobilier construction company and then cleverly hired themselves at inflated prices to build the railroad line, earning dividends as high as 348 percent. Fearing that Congress might blow the whistle, the company furtively distributed shares of its valuable stock to key congressmen. A newspaper exposé and congressional investigation of the scandal led to the formal **censure** of two congressmen and the revelation that the vice president of the United States had also accepted payments from Crédit Mobilier.

The breath of scandal in Washington also reeked of alcohol. In 1874–1875 a sprawling Whiskey Ring robbed the Treasury of millions in excise tax revenues. When President Grant's own private secretary turned up among the culprits, the president volunteered a written statement to a jury that helped exonerate the thief. Further rottenness in the Grant administration came to light in 1876, forcing Secretary of War William Belknap to resign after pocketing bribes from suppliers to the Indian reservations. Grant, ever loyal to his crooked cronies, accepted Belknap's resignation "with great regret."

The Liberal Republican Revolt of 1872

By 1872 a powerful wave of disgust with Grantism was beginning to build up throughout the nation, even before some of the worst scandals had been exposed. Reform-minded citizens banded together in the Liberal Republican party. Voicing the slogan "Turn the Rascals Out," they urged purification of the Washington administration as well as an end to military Reconstruction.

The Liberal Republicans muffed their chance when their Cincinnati nominating convention astounded the country by nominating the brilliant but erratic Horace Greeley for the presidency. Although Greeley was a fearless editor of the *New York Tribune*, he was dogmatic, emotional, petulant, and notoriously unsound in his political judgments.

More astonishing still was the action of the office-hungry Democrats, who foolishly proceeded to endorse Greeley's candidacy. In swallowing Greeley the Democrats "ate crow" in large gulps, for the eccentric editor had long blasted them as traitors, slave drivers, saloon keepers, horse thieves, and idiots. Yet Greeley pleased the Democrats, North and South, when he pleaded for clasping hands across "the bloody chasm." The Republicans dutifully renominated Grant. The voters were thus presented with a choice between two candidates who had made their careers in fields other than politics and who were both eminently unqualified, by temperament and lifelong training, for high political office.

In the mud-spattered campaign that followed, regular Republicans denounced Greeley as an atheist, a free-lover, and a vegetarian, while Democrats derided Grant as a drunken swindler. But the regular Republicans, chanting "Grant us another term," pulled the president through. The count in the electoral column was 286 to 66, in the popular column 3,596,745 to 2,843,446.

Liberal Republican agitation frightened the regular Republicans into cleaning their own house before they were thrown out of it. The Republican Congress in 1872

Can the Law Reach Him? 1872 Cartoonist Thomas Nast attacked "Boss" Tweed in a series of cartoons like this one that appeared in *Harper's Weekly* in 1872. Here Nast depicts the corrupt Tweed as a powerful giant, towering over a puny law force.

© Bettmann / Corbis

censure *An official statement of condemnation passed by a legislative body against one of its members or some other official of government. While severe, a censure itself stops short of penalties or* **expulsion***, which is removal from office.*

amnesty *A general pardon for offenses or crimes against a government.*

passed a general **amnesty** act, removing political disabilities from all but some five hundred former Confederate leaders. Congress also moved to reduce high Civil War tariffs and to fumigate the Grant administration with mild civil-service reform. Like many American third parties, the Liberal Republicans left some enduring footprints, even in defeat.

Depression and Demands for Inflation

Grant's woes deepened in the paralyzing economic Panic of 1873. Bursting with startling rapidity, the crash was one of those periodic plummets that roller-coastered the economy in this age of unbridled capitalist expansion. Overreaching promoters had laid more railroad track, sunk more mines, erected more factories, and sowed more grain fields than existing markets could bear. Bankers, in turn, had made too many imprudent loans to finance those enterprises. When profits failed to materialize, loans went unpaid, and the whole credit-based house of cards fluttered down. The United States did not suffer alone. Nations worldwide underwent a similar economic collapse in 1873.

Boom times became gloom times as more than fifteen thousand American businesses went bankrupt. In New York City, an army of unemployed riotously battled police. Black Americans were hard hit. The Freedman's Savings and Trust Company had made

unsecured loans *Money loaned without identification of collateral (existing assets) to be forfeited in case the borrower defaults on the loan.*

unsecured loans to several companies that went under. Black depositers, who had entrusted over $7 million to the bank, lost their savings, and black economic development and black confidence in savings institutions went down with the bank.

Hard times inflicted the worst punishment on debtors, who intensified their clamor for inflationary policies. Proponents of inflation breathed new life into the issue of greenbacks. During the war $450 million of the "folding money" had been issued, but it had depreciated under a cloud of popular mistrust and dubious legality.* By 1868 the Treasury had already withdrawn $100 million of the "battle-born currency" from circulation, and "hard-money" people everywhere looked forward to its complete disappearance. But now afflicted agrarian and debtor groups—"cheap-money" supporters—pressed for a reissuance of the greenbacks. With a crude but essentially accurate grasp of monetary theory, they reasoned that more money meant cheaper money and, hence, rising prices and easier-to-pay debts. Creditors, of course, reasoning from the same premises, advocated precisely the opposite policy.

The "hard-money" advocates took a notable step in 1874 when they persuaded Grant to veto a bill to print more paper money. They scored another victory in the Resumption Act of 1875, which pledged the government to the further withdrawal of greenbacks from circulation and to the redemption of all paper currency in gold at face value, beginning in 1879.

Down but not out, debtors now looked for relief to another precious metal, silver. The "sacred white metal," they claimed, had received a raw deal. In the early 1870s, the Treasury stubbornly and unrealistically maintained that an ounce of silver was worth only one-sixteenth as much as an ounce of gold. Silver miners thus stopped selling their shiny product to the federal mints, and Congress dropped the coinage of silver dollars in 1873. Fate then played a sly joke when new silver discoveries later in the 1870s shot production up and forced silver prices down. Westerners from silver-mining states now joined with debtors in assailing the "Crime of '73," demanding a return to the "Dollar of Our Daddies." Like the demand for more greenbacks, the demand for the coinage of more silver was nothing more nor less than another scheme to promote inflation.

contraction *In finance, reducing the available supply of money, thus tending to raise interest rates and lower prices.*

Hard-money Republicans resisted this scheme and counted on Grant to hold the line against it. He did not disappoint them. The Treasury began to accumulate gold stocks against the appointed day for resumption of metallic-money payments. Coupled with the reduction of greenbacks, this policy was called "**contraction**." It had a noticeable

---

* The Supreme Court in 1870 declared the Civil War Legal Tender Act unconstitutional. With the concurrence of the Senate, Grant thereupon added to the bench two justices who could be counted on to help reverse that decision, which happened in 1871. This is how the Court grew to its current size of nine justices.

deflationary effect—the amount of money per capita in circulation actually decreased between 1870 and 1880, from $19.42 to $19.37. Contraction probably worsened the impact of the depression. But the new policy did restore the government's credit rating, and it brought the embattled greenbacks up to their full face value. When Redemption Day came in 1879, few greenback holders bothered to exchange the lighter and more convenient bills for gold.

Republican hard-money policy had a political backlash. It helped elect a Democratic House of Representatives in 1874, and in 1878 it spawned the Greenback Labor party, which polled over a million votes and elected fourteen members of Congress. The contest over monetary policy was far from over.

Pallid Politics in the Gilded Age

The political seesaw was delicately balanced throughout most of the Gilded Age (a sarcastic name given to the three-decade-long post–Civil War era by Mark Twain in 1873). Even a slight nudge could tip the teeter-totter to the advantage of the opposition party. Every presidential election was a squeaker, and the majority party in the House of Representatives switched six times in the eleven sessions between 1869 and 1891. Wobbling in such shaky equilibrium, politicians tiptoed timidly, producing a political record that was often trivial and petty.

Few significant economic issues separated the major parties. Democrats and Republicans saw very nearly eye-to-eye on questions such as the tariff and civil-service reform, and majorities in both parties substantially agreed even on the much-debated currency question. Yet despite their rough agreement on these national matters, the two parties were ferociously competitive with each other. They were tightly and efficiently organized, and they commanded fierce loyalty from their members. Voter turnouts reached heights unmatched before or since. Nearly 80 percent of eligible voters cast their ballots in presidential elections in the three decades after the Civil War. On election days, droves of the party faithful tramped behind marching bands to the polling places, and "ticket splitting," or failing to vote the straight party line, was as rare as a silver dollar.

How can this apparent paradox of political **consensus** and partisan fervor be explained? The answer lies in the sharp ethnic and cultural differences in the membership of the two parties—in distinctions of style and tone, and especially of religious sentiment. Republican voters tended to adhere to those creeds that traced their lineage to Puritanism. They stressed strict codes of personal morality and believed that government should play a role in regulating both the economic and the moral affairs of society. Democrats, among whom immigrant Lutherans and Roman Catholics figured heavily, were more likely to adhere to faiths that took a less stern view of human weakness. Their religions professed toleration of differences in an imperfect world, and they spurned government efforts to impose a single moral standard on the entire society. These differences in temperament and religious values often produced raucous political contests at the local level, where issues such as prohibition and education loomed large.

Democrats had a solid electoral base in the South and in the northern industrial cities, teeming with immigrants and controlled by well-oiled political machines. Republican strength lay largely in the Midwest and the rural and small-town Northeast. Grateful freedmen in the South continued to vote Republican in significant numbers. Another important bloc of Republican ballots came from the members of the Grand Army of the Republic (GAR)—a politically potent organization of several hundred thousand Union veterans of the Civil War.

The lifeblood of both parties was patronage—disbursing jobs by the bucketful in return for votes, **kickbacks**, and party service. Boisterous infighting over patronage beset the Republican party in the 1870s and 1880s. A "Stalwart" faction, led by the handsome and imperious Senator Roscoe ("Lord Roscoe") Conkling of New York, unblushingly embraced the time-honored system of swapping jobs for votes. Opposed to the Conklingites were the so-called Half-Breeds, who flirted coyly with civil-service reform, but whose real quarrel with the Stalwarts was over who should grasp the ladle that dished out the spoils.

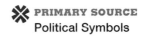

PRIMARY SOURCE
Political Symbols

consensus *Common or unanimous opinion.*

kickback *The return of a portion of the money received in a sale or contract, often secretly or illegally, in exchange for favors.*

The champion of the Half-Breeds was James G. Blaine, a radiantly personable congressman from Maine with a fine physical presence, a thrilling speaking voice, and an elastic conscience. But despite all the color of their personalities, Conkling and Blaine succeeded only in stalemating each other and deadlocking their party.

The Hayes-Tilden Standoff, 1876

Hangers-on around Grant, like fleas urging their ailing dog to live, begged the "Old Man" to try for a third term in 1876. The general, blind to his own ineptitudes, showed a disquieting willingness. But the House, by a lopsided bipartisan vote of 233 to 18, spiked the third-term boom. It passed a resolution that sternly reminded the country—and Grant—of the anti-dictator implications of the two-term tradition.

With Grant out of the running and with the Conklingites and Blaineites neutralizing each other, the Republicans turned to a compromise candidate, Rutherford B. Hayes, who was obscure enough to be dubbed "the Great Unknown." His foremost qualification was having served as three-term governor of the potent "swing" state of Ohio, which was so crucial to the cliffhanging electoral contests of the day that it regularly produced presidential candidates.

Pitted against the humdrum Hayes was the Democratic nominee, Samuel J. Tilden, who had risen to fame as the man who bagged Boss Tweed in New York. Campaigning against Republican scandal, Tilden racked up 184 electoral votes of the needed 185, with 20 votes in four states doubtful because of irregular returns. Oregon eventually fell completely to Hayes, but surely Tilden could pick up at least one of the other three, especially in view of the fact that he had polled 247,448 more popular votes than Hayes, 4,284,020 to 4,036,572.

Both parties scurried to send "visiting statesmen" to the still-contested southern states of Louisiana, South Carolina, and Florida. All three disputed states submitted two sets of returns, one Democratic and one Republican. As the weeks drifted by, the paralysis tightened, generating a dramatic constitutional crisis. The Constitution merely specifies that the electoral returns from the states shall be sent to Congress, and in the presence of the House and Senate they shall be opened by the president of the Senate (see the Twelfth Amendment). But who should count them? On this point the Constitution was silent. If counted by the president of the Senate (a Republican), the Republican returns would be selected. If counted by the Speaker of the House (a Democrat), the Democratic returns would be chosen. How could the impasse be resolved?

The Compromise of 1877 and the End of Reconstruction

Clash or compromise was the stark choice. The danger loomed that there would be no president on inauguration day, March 4, 1877. "Tilden or Blood!" cried Democratic hotheads, and some of their "Minute Men" began to drill with arms. But behind the scenes, frantically laboring statesmen gradually hammered out an agreement in the Henry Clay tradition—the Compromise of 1877.

The election deadlock itself was to be broken by the Electoral Count Act, which passed Congress early in 1877. It set up an electoral commission consisting of fifteen men selected from the Senate, the House, and the Supreme Court.

In February 1877, about a month before Inauguration Day, the Senate and House met together in an electric atmosphere

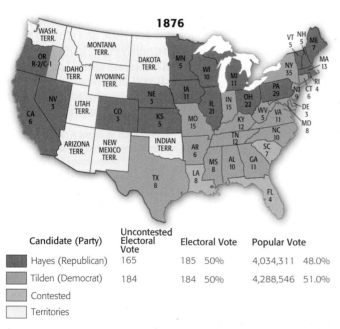

Candidate (Party)	Uncontested Electoral Vote	Electoral Vote		Popular Vote	
Hayes (Republican)	165	185	50%	4,034,311	48.0%
Tilden (Democrat)	184	184	50%	4,288,546	51.0%
Contested					
Territories					

Hayes-Tilden Disputed Election of 1876 (with electoral vote by state) Nineteen of the twenty disputed votes composed the total electoral count of Louisiana, South Carolina, and Florida. The twentieth was one of Oregon's three votes, cast by an elector who turned out to be ineligible because he was a federal officeholder (a postmaster), contrary to the Constitution (see Art. II, Sec. I, para. 2).
© Cengage Learning

to settle the dispute. The roll of the states was tolled off alphabetically. When Florida was reached, the disputed documents were referred to the electoral commission, which sat in a nearby chamber. After prolonged discussion the members agreed, by the partisan vote of eight Republicans to seven Democrats, to accept the Republican returns. Outraged Democrats in Congress, smelling defeat, undertook to launch a filibuster "until hell froze over."

Renewed deadlock was avoided by the rest of the complex Compromise of 1877, already partially concluded behind closed doors. The Democrats reluctantly agreed that Hayes might take office in return for his withdrawing intrusive federal troops from the two states in which they remained, Louisiana and South Carolina. Among various concessions, the Republicans assured the Democrats a place at the presidential patronage trough and support for a bill subsidizing the Texas and Pacific Railroad's construction of a southern transcontinental line. Not all of these promises were kept in later years, including the Texas and Pacific subsidy. But the deal held together long enough to break the dangerous electoral standoff.

The compromise bought peace at a price. Partisan violence was averted by sacrificing the civil rights of southern blacks. With the Hayes-Tilden deal, the Republican party quietly abandoned its commitment to racial equality. That commitment had been weakening in any case. Many Republicans had begun to question the worthiness of Reconstruction and became less willing to send dollars and enlisted sons to bolster southern state governments.

The Civil Rights Act of 1875 was in a sense the last feeble gasp of the congressional radical Republicans. The act supposedly guaranteed equal accommodations in public places and prohibited racial discrimination in jury selection, but the law was born toothless and stayed that way for nearly a century. The Supreme Court pronounced much of the act unconstitutional in the *Civil Rights Cases* (1883), declaring that the Fourteenth Amendment prohibited only *government* violations of civil rights, not the denial of civil rights by *individuals*. When President Hayes withdrew the blue-clad federal troops that were propping up Reconstruction governments, the bayonet-backed Republican regimes collapsed.

✳ PRIMARY SOURCE
The Disputed Election of 1876

═══ The Birth of Jim Crow in the South ═══

Reconstruction was officially ended. Relying shamelessly on fraud and intimidation, white Democrats ("Redeemers") reassumed political power in the South and ruthlessly suppressed the now-friendless blacks. For generations to come, many blacks (as well as poor whites) were forced into sharecropping and tenant farming under conditions scarcely better than slavery. Through the "crop-**lien**" system, storekeepers extended credit to small farmers for food and supplies and in return took a lien on their customers' harvests. Shrewd merchants manipulated the system so that farmers remained perpetually in debt to them.

lien *A legal claim by a lender or another party on a borrower's property as a guarantee of the loan's repayment and a prohibition of any sale of the property.*

With white southerners back in the political saddle, daily discrimination against blacks grew increasingly oppressive. What had started as the informal separation of blacks and whites in the immediate postwar years developed by the 1890s into systematic state-level codes of segregation known as Jim Crow laws. Southern states also enacted literacy requirements, voter-registration laws, and poll taxes—and tolerated violent intimidation of black voters—to ensure full-scale disfranchisement of the South's freedmen. The Supreme Court validated the South's segregationist social order in the case of *Plessy v. Ferguson* (1896). It ruled that "separate but equal" facilities were constitutional under the "equal protection" clause of the Fourteenth Amendment.

But in reality the quality of African American life was grotesquely unequal to that of whites. Segregated in inferior schools and separated from whites in virtually all public facilities, blacks were assaulted daily by reminders of their second-class citizenship. To ensure the stability of this political and economic "new order," southern whites dealt harshly with any black who dared to violate the South's racial code of conduct. A record number of blacks were lynched during the 1890s, most often for the "crime" of asserting themselves as equals. It would take a second Reconstruction, nearly a century later, to redress the racist imbalance of southern society.

deflation (deflationary) *An increase in the value of money in relation to available goods, causing prices to fall.* **Inflation**, *a decrease in the value of money in relation to goods, causes prices to rise.*

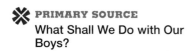

PRIMARY SOURCE
What Shall We Do with Our Boys?

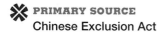

PRIMARY SOURCE
Chinese Exclusion Act

Class Conflicts and Ethnic Clashes

The year 1877 marked more than the end of Reconstruction. As the curtains officially closed on regional warfare, they opened on scenes of class warfare. The explosive atmosphere was largely a by-product of the long years of depression and **deflation** following the panic of 1873. Railroad workers faced particularly hard times, while they watched the railroads continue to rake in huge profits. When the presidents of the nation's four largest railroads collectively decided in 1877 to cut employees' wages by 10 percent, the workers struck back. President Hayes's decision to call in federal troops to quell the unrest brought the striking laborers an outpouring of working-class support. Work stoppages spread like wildfire in cities from Baltimore to St. Louis. When the battling between workers and soldiers ended after several weeks, over one hundred people were dead.

The failure of the great railroad strike exposed the weakness of the labor movement in the face of massive government intervention on the side of the railroads. The federal courts, United States Army, state militias, and local police all lent their muscle to keeping the engines of big business operating at full throttle, and the workers be damned. Meanwhile, racial and ethnic fissures among workers fractured labor unity. Divisions were particularly acute between the Irish and the Chinese in California (see "Makers of America: The Chinese," pp. 364–365). By 1880 the Golden State counted seventy-five thousand Asian newcomers, about 9 percent of its entire population.

Mostly single males from K'uang-t'ung (Guangdong) province in southern China, these newcomers had originally come to labor in the gold fields and on the transcontinental railroads across the West. When those jobs ended, the Chinese who remained worked at the most menial jobs, often as cooks, laundrymen, or domestic servants. Without women or families, they were deprived of the children who in other immigrant communities eased their parent's assimilation through their exposure to the English language and American customs in school.

In San Francisco, Irish-born demagogue Denis Kearney incited his followers, many of them recently arrived European immigrants, to violent abuse of the hapless Chinese. Taking to the streets, gangs of Kearneyites terrorized the Asians by shearing off precious pigtails. Some victims were murdered outright.

Congress finally slammed the door on Chinese immigrant laborers when it passed the Chinese Exclusion Act in 1882, prohibiting nearly all further immigration from China. The door stayed shut until 1943. Some exclusionists even tried to strip native-born Chinese Americans of their citizenship, but the Supreme Court ruled in *U.S. v. Wong Kim Ark* in 1898 that the Fourteenth Amendment guaranteed citizenship to all persons born in the United States. This doctrine of "birthright citizenship" provided important protections to Chinese Americans as well as to other immigrant communities.

Garfield and Arthur

As the presidential campaign of 1880 approached, "Rutherfraud" Hayes was a man without a party, repudiated by the Republican Old Guard. Seeking a new standard-bearer, the Republicans finally settled on a "dark-horse" candidate, Congressman James A. Garfield of Ohio. His vice-presidential running mate was a notorious Stalwart henchman, Chester A. Arthur of New York.

Energetically waving the bloody shirt, Garfield barely squeaked out a victory over the Democratic candidate, Civil War hero Winfield Scott Hancock. Garfield polled only 39,213 more votes than Hancock—4,453,295 to 4,414,082—but his margin in the electoral column was a comfortable 214 to 155.

The new president was an energetic and able man, but he was immediately ensnared in political conflict between his secretary of state, James G. Blaine, and Blaine's Stalwart nemesis, Senator Roscoe Conkling. Then, as the Republican factions dueled, tragedy struck. A disappointed and mentally deranged office seeker, Charles J. Guiteau, shot President Garfield in the back in a Washington railroad station. Garfield died eleven weeks later, on September 19, 1881, and Chester Arthur assumed the presidency.

Garfield's death did have one positive outcome: it shocked politicians into reforming the shameful spoils system. The unlikely instrument of reform was Chester Arthur. Arthur's record of cronyism and fondness for fine wines and elegant clothing (including eighty pairs of trousers) suggested that he was little more than a foppish dandy. But as the new president, Arthur surprised his critics by prosecuting several fraud cases and giving his former Stalwart pals the cold shoulder.

Disgust with Garfield's murder also gave the Republican party itself a previously undetected taste for reform. The medicine finally applied to the long-suffering federal government was the Pendleton Act of 1883—the so-called Magna Carta of civil-service reform. It made compulsory campaign contributions from federal employees illegal, and it established the Civil Service Commission to make appointments to federal jobs on the basis of competitive examinations rather than party pull.

Although at first covering only about 10 percent of federal jobs, **civil service** did rein in the most blatant political abuses. Yet like many well-intentioned reforms, it bred unintended problems of its own. With the "plum" federal posts now beyond their reach, politicians were forced to look elsewhere for money, the "mother's milk of politics." Increasingly, they turned to the bulging coffers of the big corporations. A new breed of boss emerged—less skilled at mobilizing small armies of immigrants and other voters on election day, but more adept at milking dollars from manufacturers and lobbyists.

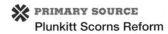

PRIMARY SOURCE
Plunkitt Scorns Reform

civil service *Referring to regular employment by government according to a standardized system of job descriptions, merit qualifications, pay, and promotion, as distinct from* **political appointees** *who receive positions based on affiliation and party loyalty.*

The Blaine-Cleveland Mudslingers of 1884

President Arthur's surprising display of integrity offended too many powerful Republicans, and his ungrateful party refused to nominate him in 1884. Instead they turned to James G. Blaine, whose persistence in pursuit of the presidential nomination finally paid off. The dashing Maine politician, blessed with almost every asset except a reputation for honesty, was enthusiastically nominated by the regulars at the Republican convention in Chicago, though reformers gagged at his candidacy.

Blaine's enemies publicized the Republican nominee's fishy-smelling "Mulligan letters," written by Blaine to a Boston businessman. These damning documents linked Blaine to a corrupt deal involving federal favors to a southern railroad, and one of them ended with the furtive warning "Burn this letter." Some reformers, unable to swallow Blaine, bolted to the Democrats. They were sneeringly dubbed Mugwumps, a word of Indian derivation meaning "sanctimonious" or "holier than thou."

Victory-starved Democrats turned enthusiastically to a noted reformer, Grover Cleveland. A burly bachelor with a soup-straining mustache and a taste for chewing tobacco, Cleveland was a solid but not brilliant lawyer of forty-seven. He had rocketed from the Buffalo mayor's office to the governorship of New York and the presidential nomination in three short years. Known as "Grover the Good," he enjoyed a well-deserved reputation for probity in office.

But Cleveland's admirers soon got a shock. Resolute Republicans, digging for dirt in the past of bachelor Cleveland, unearthed the fact that he had been involved in an amorous affair with a Buffalo widow. Cleveland had provided financial support for her illegitimate son, now eight years old. Demoralized Democratic elders hurried to Cleveland and urged him to lie like a gentleman, but their ruggedly honest candidate insisted, "Tell the truth."

The campaign of 1884 sank to perhaps the lowest level in American experience, as the two parties grunted and shoved for the hog trough of office. Few fundamental differences separated them. Even the bloody shirt had faded to pale pink.* Personalities, not principles, claimed the headlines. Crowds

New York political "boss" Roscoe Conkling (1829–1888) denounced the civil-service reformers in the New York World *(1877):*

"[The reformers'] vocation and ministry is to lament the sins of other people. Their stock in trade is rancid, canting self-righteousness. They are wolves in sheep's clothing. Their real object is office and plunder. When Dr. Johnson defined patriotism as the last refuge of a scoundrel, he was unconscious of the then undeveloped capabilities and uses of the word 'Reform.'"

---

* Neither candidate had served in the Civil War. Cleveland had hired a substitute to go in his stead while he supported his widowed mother and two sisters. Blaine was the only candidate nominated by the Republicans from Grant through McKinley (1868–1900) who had not been a Civil War officer.

The Chinese

Between 1800 and 1925, at least 3 million Chinese left their homeland to labor around the globe. The once great Chinese Empire was disintegrating while its population was exploding, creating severe land shortages and opening up the unstable country to European imperial powers bent on unlocking the riches of a nation closed to outsiders for centuries. Chinese men, faced with economic hardship and political turmoil in their homeland and lured by labor shortages as far afield as Southeast Asia, Australia, and the Americas, migrated by the tens of thousands to work the plantations and dig the mines that fueled a burgeoning global economy. By 1900, more than 300,000 Chinese had entered the United States to contribute their muscle to building the West, wrenching minerals from stubborn rock, and helping to lay the transcontinental railroads that stitched together the American nation.

Until the 1848 discovery of gold in California, there were fewer than fifty Chinese living in the United States. But by 1852, at least twenty-five thousand Chinese had arrived in California, which they dubbed the "golden mountain." At that decade's end, Chinese workers made up nearly a quarter of the state's manual laborers, even though they were only a tenth of the population. Employers nationwide viewed the Chinese as cheap labor, recruiting them to cut sugar cane in the South and break strikes in New England shoe factories.

Although Chinese immigrants included a few merchants and artisans, most were unskilled country folk. In some cases families pooled their money to send out a son, but most travelers, desperately poor, obtained their passage through Chinese middlemen, who advanced them ship fare in return for the emigrants' promise to work off their debts after they landed.

The Chinese America of the late-nineteenth-century West was overwhelmingly a bachelor society. Women of good repute rarely made the passage. Of the very few Chinese women who did venture to California at this time, most became prostitutes. Many of them had been deceived by the false promise of honest jobs.

Although a stream of workers returned to China, many Chinese stayed. "Chinatowns" sprang up wherever economic opportunities presented themselves. Chinese in these settlements spoke their own language, enjoyed the fellowship of their own compatriots, and sought safety from prejudice and violence. Many immigrant clubs and associations were American adaptations of Chinese traditions of loyalty to clan. The poorest and most alienated immigrants also established

of Democrats surged through city streets, chanting—to the rhythm of left, left, left, right, left—"Burn, burn, burn this letter!" Republicans taunted in return, "Ma, ma, where's my pa?" Defiant Democrats shouted back, "Gone to the White House, ha, ha, ha!"

The contest hinged on the state of New York, where Blaine blundered badly in the closing days of the campaign. A witless Republican clergyman damned the Democrats in a speech as the party of "Rum, Romanism, and Rebellion"—insulting with one swift stroke the culture, the faith, and the patriotism of New York's numerous Irish Americans. Blaine was present at the time but lacked the presence of mind to repudiate the statement immediately. The pungent phrase, shortened to "RRR," stung and stuck. Blaine's silence seemed to give assent, and the wavering Irishmen who then deserted his camp helped to account for Cleveland's paper-thin plurality of about a thousand votes in New York State, enough to give him the presidency. Cleveland swept the solid South and squeaked into office with 219 to 182 electoral votes and 4,879,507 to 4,850,293 popular votes.

"Old Grover" Takes Over

Bull-necked Cleveland in 1885 was the first Democrat to take the oath of presidential office since Buchanan, twenty-eight years earlier. Huge question marks hung over his portly frame (5 feet 11 inches, 250 pounds). Could the "party of disunion" be trusted to govern the Union? Would desperate Democrats, ravenously hungry after twenty-four years of exile,

Chinese Butcher Shop, San Francisco, California, c. 1890

tongs—literally, "meeting halls"—secret societies that acquired a sinister reputation among non-Chinese.

Mounting anti-Chinese agitation forced the repudiation of the Burlingame Treaty in 1880, and in 1882 the Chinese Exclusion Act barred nearly all Chinese from the United States for six decades. Many of the bachelors died or returned home. Slowly, however, those men and the few women who remained raised families and reared a new generation of Chinese Americans. They were joined by thousands more immigrants who made the journey illegally or took advantage of the few exceptions permissible under the Exclusion Act. But this second generation still suffered from discrimination, eking out their living in jobs despised by Caucasian laborers or taking daunting risks in small entrepreneurial ventures. Yet many hard-working Chinese did manage to open their own restaurants, laundries, and other small businesses. Such enterprises formed a solid economic foundation for their small community and remain a source of livelihood for many Chinese Americans even today.

trample the frail sprouts of civil-service reform in a stampede to the patronage trough? Could Cleveland restore a measure of respect and power to the maligned and enfeebled presidency?

Cleveland was a man of principles, most of them safely orthodox by the standards of the day. A staunch apostle of the hands-off creed of **laissez-faire**, the new president summed up his political philosophy in 1887 when he vetoed a bill to provide seeds for drought-ravaged Texas farmers. "Though the people support the government," he declared, "the government should not support the people." As tactless as a mirror and as direct as a bulldozer, Cleveland was outspoken, unbending, and profanely hot tempered.

At the outset Cleveland narrowed the North–South chasm by naming to the cabinet two former Confederates. As for the civil service, Cleveland was whipsawed between the demands of the Democratic faithful for jobs and the demands of the Mugwumps, who had helped elect him, for reform. Believing in the merit system, Cleveland at first favored the cause of the reformers, but he eventually caved in to the carpings of Democratic bosses and fired almost two-thirds of the 120,000 federal employees, including 40,000 incumbent (Republican) postmasters, to make room for "deserving Democrats."

Military pensions gave Cleveland some of his most painful political headaches. The politically powerful Grand Army of the Republic (GAR) routinely lobbied hundreds of often questionable private pension bills through a compliant Congress. As a non-veteran, Cleveland was in an awkward position to fight the pension grabbers, but he conscientiously read each bill and ended up vetoing several hundred of them.

laissez-faire *The doctrine of noninterference, especially by the government, in matters of economics or business (literally, "leave alone").*

Puck

"I Want My Pa!"

Cleveland also risked his political neck by prodding the hornet's nest of the tariff issue. Jacked up to new high levels during the Civil War, the tariff duties were producing enormous revenues while comfortably sheltering American industry. By 1881 the Treasury was running an annual surplus amounting to an embarrassing $145 million. Congress could reduce the surplus either by squandering it on pensions or other "**pork-barrel**" bills or by lowering the tariff—something big industrialists vehemently opposed.

With his characteristic bluntness, Cleveland tossed an appeal for lower tariffs like a bombshell into the lap of Congress in late 1887. The response was electric. Democrats were deeply frustrated by the obstinacy of their chief. Republicans rejoiced at his apparent recklessness, bellowing loudly that lower tariffs would mean higher taxes, lower wages, and increased unemployment. The old warrior Blaine gloated, "There's one more president for us in [tariff] protection." For the first time in years, a real issue divided the two parties as the 1888 presidential election loomed.

Dismayed Democrats, seeing no alternative, dejectedly renominated Cleveland at their St. Louis convention, while eager Republicans turned to Benjamin Harrison of Indiana, the grandson of former president William Henry ("Tippecanoe") Harrison. The tariff was the prime issue, and the two parties flooded the country with some 10 million pamphlets on the subject. Republicans raised an unprecedented $3 million war chest, largely by "frying the fat" out of nervous industrialists. The money was widely used to line up corrupt "voting cattle," known as "repeaters" or "floaters," especially in crucial swing states such as Indiana.

On the night before the inauguration of Harrison, a crowd of jubilant Republicans tauntingly serenaded the darkened White House with a popular campaign ditty directed at Grover Cleveland:

Down in the cornfield
Hear that mournful sound;
All the Democrats are weeping—
Grover's in the cold, cold ground!

But Grover was to rise again and serve as president for a second term of four more years.

On election day, Harrison nosed out Cleveland, 233 to 168 electoral votes. A change of about 7,000 ballots in New York would have reversed the outcome. Cleveland actually polled more popular votes, 5,537,857 to 5,447,129, but he nevertheless became the first sitting president to be voted out of his chair since Martin Van Buren in 1840.

Republicans Return under Harrison

After a four-year famine, the Republicans under Harrison licked their lips hungrily for federal offices to lavish upon the party faithful. But in the House of Representatives they had only three votes more than the necessary quorum of 163 members, and the Democrats were preparing to obstruct all House business by refusing to answer roll calls, demanding roll calls to determine the presence of a quorum, and other similar delaying tactics.

Into this tense cockpit stepped the new Republican Speaker of the House, Thomas B. Reed of Maine. A tall, hulking figure, Reed was a master debater who spoke with a harsh nasal drawl and wielded a verbal harpoon of sarcasm. To one congressman who quoted Henry Clay's saying that he would "rather be right than be president," Reed caustically retorted that he "would never be either." Opponents cringed at the crack of his quip.

"Czar" Reed soon bent the intimidated House to his imperious will. Employing clever parliamentary tactics to the full, Reed utterly dominated the "Billion-Dollar" Congress—the first in history to appropriate that sum. Congress showered pensions on Civil War veterans and increased government purchases of silver. To keep the revenues flowing in—and to protect Republican industrialists from foreign competition—the Billion-Dollar Congress also passed the McKinley Tariff Act of 1890, boosting rates to their highest peacetime level ever (an average of 48.4 percent on dutiable goods).

Sponsored in the House of Representatives by rising Republican star William McKinley of Ohio, the new tariff act brought fresh woes to farmers. Debt-burdened farmers had no choice but to buy high-priced manufactured goods from protected American industrialists, but they were compelled to sell their own agricultural products into highly competitive, unprotected world markets. Mounting discontent against Bill McKinley and his McKinley Bill caused many rural voters to rise in wrath. In the congressional elections of 1890, Republicans lost their precarious majority and were reduced to just 88 seats, compared with 235 Democrats. Ominously for conservatives, the new Congress also included nine members of the Farmers' Alliance, a militant organization of southern and western farmers.

The Drumbeat of Discontent

Politics was no longer "as usual" in 1892, when the newly formed People's party, or "Populists," burst upon the scene. Rooted in the Farmers' Alliances in the great agricultural belts of the West and South, the Populists met in Omaha and adopted a scorching platform that denounced the "prolific womb of governmental injustice." They demanded inflation through free and unlimited coinage of silver at the ratio of sixteen ounces of silver to one ounce of gold. They further called for a graduated income tax; government ownership of the railroads, telephone, and telegraph; the direct election of U.S. senators; a one-term limit on the presidency; the adoption of the initiative and referendum to allow citizens to shape legislation more directly; a shorter workday; and immigration restrictions. As their presidential candidate the Populists uproariously nominated the eloquent old Greenbacker, General James B. Weaver.

An epidemic of nationwide strikes in the summer of 1892 raised the prospect that the Populists could weld together a coalition of aggrieved workers and indebted farmers in a revolutionary joint assault on the capitalist order. At Andrew Carnegie's Homestead steel plant near Pittsburgh, company officials called in three hundred armed Pinkerton detectives in July to crush the defiant **Homestead Strike** by steelworkers angry over pay cuts. Defiant strikers, armed with rifles and dynamite, forced their assailants to surrender after a vicious battle that left ten people dead and some sixty wounded. Troops were eventually summoned, and both the strike and the union were broken. That same month, federal troops bloodily smashed a strike among silver miners in Idaho's Coeur d'Alene district.

Homestead Strike *A strike at a Carnegie steel plant in Homestead, Pennsylvania, that ended in an armed battle between the strikers, three hundred armed "Pinkerton" detectives hired by Carnegie, and federal troops, which killed ten people and wounded more than sixty.*

A popular protest song of the 1890s among western farmers was titled "The Hayseed." One stanza ran,

I once was a tool of oppression,
And as green as a sucker could be,
And monopolies banded together
To beat a poor hayseed like me.

The Populists made a remarkable showing in the 1892 presidential election. Singing "Good-bye, Party Bosses," they rolled up 1,029,846 popular votes and 22 electoral votes for General Weaver. They thus became one of the few third parties in U.S. history to break into the electoral column. But they fell far short of an electoral majority. Industrial laborers, especially in the urban East, did not rally to the Populist banner in appreciable numbers. Populist electoral votes came from only six midwestern and western states, four of which (Kansas, Colorado, Idaho, and Nevada) fell completely into the Populist basket.

The South, although a hotbed of agrarian agitation, proved especially unwilling to throw in its lot with the new party. Race was the reason. The more than 1 million southern black farmers, organized in the Colored Farmers' National Alliance, shared a host of complaints with poor white farmers, and for a time their common economic goals promised to overcome their racial differences. Recognizing the crucial edge that black votes could give them in the South, Populist leaders such as Georgia's Tom Watson reached out to the black community. Watson was a wiry redhead who could "talk like the thrust of a Bowie knife." He declared, "There is no reason why the black man should not understand that the law that hurts me, as a farmer, hurts him, as a farmer." Many blacks were disillusioned enough with the Republican party to respond. Alarmed, the conservative white "Bourbon" elite in the South played cynically upon historic racial antagonisms to counter the Populists' appeal for interracial solidarity and woo back poor whites.

Southern blacks were heavy losers. The Populist-inspired reminder of potential black political strength led to the near-total extinction of what little African American suffrage

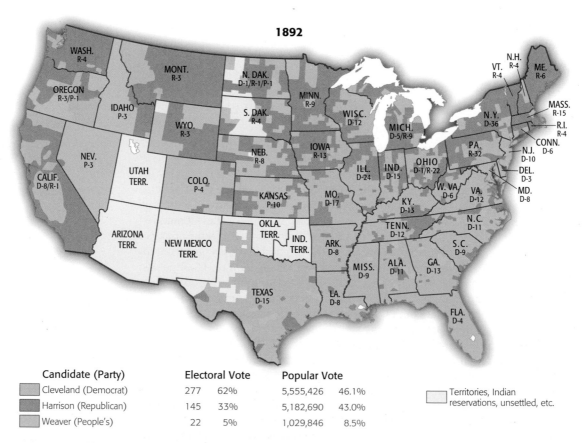

1892

Candidate (Party)	Electoral Vote		Popular Vote	
Cleveland (Democrat)	277	62%	5,555,426	46.1%
Harrison (Republican)	145	33%	5,182,690	43.0%
Weaver (People's)	22	5%	1,029,846	8.5%

Territories, Indian reservations, unsettled, etc.

Presidential Election of 1892 (showing vote by county) Note the concentration of Populist strength in the semiarid farming regions of the western half of the country. © Cengage Learning

Kansas State Historical Society

The Kansas Legislature, 1893 Rifle-bearing Populists seized the Kansas capitol after the election of 1892 to make good their claim that they had won at the polls. Republicans disagreed and eventually prevailed when sergeants at arms, shown here, restored order.

remained in the South. White southerners more aggressively than ever used literacy tests and poll taxes to deny blacks the ballot. The notorious "grandfather clause" exempted from those requirements anyone whose forebear had voted in 1860—when, of course, black slaves had not voted at all. More than half a century would pass before southern blacks could again vote in considerable numbers. Accompanying this disfranchisement were more severe Jim Crow laws designed to enforce racial segregation in public places, including hotels and restaurants, and backed up by atrocious lynchings and other forms of intimidation.

The conservative crusade to eliminate the black vote also had dire consequences for the Populist party itself. Even Tom Watson abandoned his interracial appeals and, in time, became a vociferous racist himself. After 1896 the Populist party lapsed increasingly into vile racism and staunchly advocated black disfranchisement. Such were the bitterly ironic fruits of the Populist campaign in the South.

Grover, Grim Times, and Gold

With the Populists divided and the Republicans discredited, Grover Cleveland took office once again in 1893, the only president ever reelected after defeat. He was the same old bull-necked and bull-headed Cleveland, with a little more weight, polish, conservatism, and self-assertiveness.

But though it was the same old Cleveland, it was not the same old country. Debtors were up in arms, workers were restless, and the advance shadows of panic were falling. Hardly had Cleveland seated himself back in the presidential chair when the devastating depression of 1893 burst about his burly frame. Lasting for about four years, it was the most punishing economic downturn of the nineteenth century. Contributing causes were the splurge of overbuilding and speculation, labor disorders, and the ongoing agricultural depression. Free-silver agitation—the cry to expand the money supply with unlimited coinage of silver— had also damaged American credit abroad, and the pinch on American finances had come when European banking houses began to call in loans from the United States.

Distress ran deep and far. About eight thousand American businesses collapsed in six months. Dozens of railroad lines went into receivership. Soup kitchens fed the unemployed, while gangs of hoboes ("tramps") wandered aimlessly about the country. Local charities did their feeble best, but the federal government, bound by the let-nature-take-its-course philosophy of the times, saw no legitimate way to relieve the suffering masses.

Cleveland, who had earlier been bothered by a surplus, now faced a deepening deficit and a financial crisis. Owners of the paper currency issued under the Sherman Silver Purchase Act of 1890 were presenting the notes for redemption in gold. By law the notes then had to be reissued, and the new holders would then repeat the process, draining away gold in an "endless chain" operation.

Alarmingly, the gold reserve in the Treasury dropped below the $100 million regarded as the safe minimum for supporting about $350 million in outstanding paper currency. Cleveland saw no alternative but to halt the bleeding away of gold by asking Congress to repeal the Sherman Silver Purchase Act of 1890.

The Congressional debate over repeal of the silver act was heated. A silver-tongued young Democratic congressman from Nebraska, thirty-three-year-old William Jennings Bryan, held the galleries spellbound for three hours as he championed the cause of free silver. The friends of silver announced that "hell would freeze over" before Congress passed the repeal measure. But an angered Cleveland used his patronage power to break the filibuster in the Senate and ram the measure through. He thus alienated Democratic silverites such as Bryan and divided his own his party at the very outset of his administration.

Repeal of the Sherman Silver Purchase Act only partially stopped the hemorrhaging of gold from the Treasury. In February 1894 the gold reserve sank to a dismaying $41 million. The United States was now in grave danger of going off the gold standard—a move that would render the nation's currency volatile and unreliable and also mortally cripple America's international trade.

Early in 1895 Cleveland turned in desperation to J. P. Morgan, "the bankers' banker" and the head of a Wall Street syndicate. After tense negotiations at the White House, Morgan and his fellow bankers agreed to lend the government $65 million in gold. They were obviously in business for profit, so they charged a commission amounting to about $7 million. The loan, at least temporarily, helped restore confidence in the nation's finances.

But the gold deal stirred up a storm. In the eyes of the silverites and other debtors, the Wall Street ogre represented all that was wicked and grasping in American politics. President Cleveland's secretive dealings with the mighty "Jupiter" Morgan were savagely condemned as a "sellout" of the national government. But Cleveland was certain that he had done no wrong. Sarcastically denying that he was "Morgan's errand boy," Cleveland asserted, "Without shame and without repentance I confess my share of the guilt."

Cleveland suffered further embarrassment with the passage of the Wilson-Gorman Tariff in 1894. The Democrats had pledged to lower tariffs, but by the time the measure made it through Congress, it had been so loaded with special-interest protection that it made scarcely a dent in the high McKinley Tariff rates. An outraged Cleveland grudgingly allowed the bill, which also contained a 2 percent tax on incomes over $4,000, to become law without his signature. When the Supreme Court struck down the income-tax provision in 1895,[*] the Populists and other disaffected groups found further proof that the courts were only the tools of the plutocrats.

Democratic political fortunes naturally suffered in the face of these setbacks. The tariff dynamite that had blasted the Republicans out of the House in 1890 now dislodged the Democrats, with a strong helping hand from the depression. The revitalized Republicans, singing "Times Are Mighty Hard," won the congressional elections of 1894 in a landslide—244 seats to 105 for the Democrats. Republicans looked forward to the 1896 presidential elections with unconcealed glee.

Despite his gruff integrity and occasional courage, Grover Cleveland failed utterly to cope with the serious economic crisis that befell the country in 1893. He was tied down in office by the same threads that held all the presidents of the day to Lilliputian levels. Grant, Hayes, Garfield, Arthur, Harrison, and Cleveland are often referred to as the "forgettable presidents." Bewhiskered and bland in person, they left mostly blanks—or blots—on the nation's political record, as issues such as the tariff, the money question, and the rights of labor continued to fester. What little political vitality existed in Gilded Age America was to be found in local settings or in Congress, which overshadowed the White House for most of this period. But before the century ended, down-and-out debtors and disgruntled workers would make one last titanic effort to wring reform out of the political system—in the momentous election of 1896.

* PRIMARY SOURCE
The Sacrilegious Candidate

assassination *Politically motivated murder of a public figure.*

---

[*] It violated the "direct tax" clause. See Art. I, Sec. IX, para. 4 in the Appendix. The Sixteenth Amendment of the Constitution, adopted in 1913, permitted an income tax.

Taking their cue from contemporary satirical commentaries such as Mark Twain and Charles Dudley Warner's *The Gilded Age* (1873), the first historians who wrote about the post–Civil War era judged it harshly. They condemned its politicians as petty and corrupt, lamented the emergence of a new plutocratic class, and railed against the arrogance of corporate power. Such a view is conspicuous in Charles and Mary Beard's *The Rise of American Civilization* (4 vols., 1927–1942) and in Vernon Louis Parrington's classic *Main Currents in American Thought* (3 vols., 1927–1930), in which the entire post–Civil War period is contemptuously dismissed as "the great barbecue."

The Beards and Parrington were leaders of the anti-business and pro-reform progressive school of historical writing that flourished in the early years of the twentieth century. Progressive historians identified Populism as virtually the only organized opposition to the social, economic, and political order that took shape in the last decades of the nineteenth century. The Populists thus became heroes to historians such as John D. Hicks, whose work *The Populist Revolt* (1931) is the classic portrayal of the Populists as embattled farmers hurling defiance at Wall Street and the robber barons in defense of their simple, honest way of life. Bowed but unbroken by the defeat of their great champion, William Jennings Bryan, in the election of 1896, the Populists, Hicks claimed, left a reformist legacy that flourished again in the progressive era and the New Deal.

Hicks's point of view was the dominant one until the 1950s, when it was sharply criticized by Richard Hofstadter in *The Age of Reform* (1955). The city-born-and-bred Hofstadter argued that the Populists were best understood not as picturesque protesters, but as "harassed little country businessmen" bristling with provincial prejudices not just against Wall Street, but also irrationally against urbanism, immigrants, the East, and modernity itself. Hofstadter thus exposed a "dark side" of Populism that contained elements of backwoods anti-intellectualism, paranoia, and even anti-Semitism.

In the 1960s several scholars, inspired by the work of C. Vann Woodward, as well as by sympathy with the protest movements of that turbulent decade, began to rehabilitate the Populists as authentic reformers with genuine grievances. Especially notable in this vein was Lawrence Goodwyn's *Democratic Promise: The Populist Movement in America* (1976), which portrayed Populism as the last gasp of popular political revolt against urban industrialism and finance capitalism, a democratic "moment" in American history that expired with the Populists' absorption into the Democratic party.

Two subsequent works, Edward L. Ayers's *Promise of the New South* (1992) and Robert C. McMath's *American Populism* (1993), synthesized many of the older perspectives and presented a balanced view of the Populists as radical in many ways but also limited by their nostalgia for a lost agrarian past.

Chapter Summary

After the soaring ideals and tremendous sacrifices of the Civil War, the post-Civil War era was generally one of political disillusionment and even cynicism. Politicians from the White House to the courthouse were deeply enmeshed in corruption and scandal, while the actual economic, ethnic, and racial problems afflicting industrializing America festered beneath the surface without being seriously addressed.

The popular war hero Grant was a poor politician and his administration was rife with corruption. Despite occasional futile reform efforts by both high-minded "mugwumps" and third-party agrarians, politics in the Gilded Age was monopolized by the two patronage-fattened parties, which competed vigorously for spoils while essentially agreeing on most national policies. Cultural differences, different ethnic and religious constituencies, and deeply felt local issues fueled intense party competition and unprecedented voter participation. Periodic complaints by political reformers and "soft-money" farmers' advocates failed to make much of a dent on politics or the *laissez-faire* business economics of the time.

The deadlocked and bitterly contested 1876 election led to the crass Compromise of 1877, which put an end to Reconstruction at the price of abandoning southern blacks. An oppressive system of tenant farming and racial supremacy and segregation was thereafter fastened on the South, enforced by sometimes lethal violence. Racial prejudice against Chinese immigrants was also linked with labor unrest in the 1870s and 1880s.

Garfield's **assassination** by a disappointed office seeker spurred the beginnings of civil-service reform but made politics more dependent on big business. Cleveland, the first Democratic president since the Civil War, proposed a lower tariff, creating the first real issue in national politics for some time. But the weakness of conventional politics was exposed by a major economic depression that began in 1893. This crisis, the worst of the nineteenth century, deepened the growing outcry from suffering farmers and workers against a government and economic system that seemed biased toward big business and the wealthy.

KEY TERMS

coalition (355)

corner (356)

censure (357)

expulsion (357)

amnesty (358)

unsecured loans (358)

contraction (358)

consensus (359)

kickback (359)

lien (361)

deflation (deflationary) (362)

inflation (inflationary) (362)

civil service (363)

political appointees (363)

laissez-faire (365)

pork-barrel (366)

Homestead Strike (367)

assassination (370)

PEOPLE TO KNOW

Jay Gould

Horace Greeley

Rutherford B. Hayes

James A. Garfield

Chester Arthur

Grover Cleveland

Thomas B. Reed

Tom Watson

William Jennings Bryan

J. P. Morgan

 CourseMate

Go to the History CourseMate
website for primary source links,
study tools, and review materials for this chapter.
www.cengagebrain.com

24

Industry Comes of Age

1865–1900

The wealthy class is becoming more wealthy, but the poorer class is becoming more dependent.
The gulf between the employed and the employer is growing wider; social contrasts
are becoming sharper; as liveried carriages appear, so do barefooted children.

HENRY GEORGE, 1879

⭐ Chapter Outline

As the nineteenth century drew toward a close, observers were asking, "Why are the best men not in politics?" One answer was that they were being lured away from public life by the lusty attractions of the booming private economy. As America's Industrial Revolution slipped into high gear, talented men ached for profits, not the presidency. They dreamed of controlling corporations, not Congress. What the nation lost in civic leadership, it gained in an astounding surge of economic growth. As late as 1870, agriculture was the nation's biggest business. By 1900 its share of the economy was half that. Until the end of the Civil War the United States imported more merchandise than it exported. By 1900 it annually delivered more than $600 million worth of manufactured goods into the world's marketplace. Americans did not achieve this economic transformation all by themselves. Foreign investment, labor, trade, and technology made it possible. Although in many ways still a political dwarf, the United States was about to stand up before the world as an industrial colossus—and the lives of millions of working Americans would be transformed in the process.

FOCUS QUESTIONS

1. How did the transcontinental railroad network promote the post–Civil War transformation of American industry?

2. How did the American economy come to be dominated by monopolistic corporations in industries such as steel and oil, and what was the public and governmental response to these huge combinations?

3. Why was the South generally excluded from industrial development, and what were the economic, social, and racial problems that the region faced as a result?

4. How did industrialization alter American society, particularly the role of the working class and of women?

5. Why did late-nineteenth-century American labor unions generally fail to mobilize American workers?

CHRONOLOGY

1862	Congress authorizes transcontinental railroad.		**1879**	Edison invents electric light.
1866	National Labor Union organized. First working transatlantic telegraph cable.		**1886**	Haymarket Square bombing. *Wabash* case. American Federation of Labor formed.
1869	Transcontinental railroad joined near Ogden, Utah. Knights of Labor organized. Suez Canal completed.		**1887**	Interstate Commerce Act.
			1890	Sherman Anti-Trust Act.
1870	Standard Oil Company organized.		**1901**	United States Steel Corporation formed.
1876	Bell invents telephone.			

The Iron Colt Becomes an Iron Horse

The government-business entanglements that increasingly shaped politics after the Civil War also undergirded the industrial development of the nation. The unparalleled outburst of railroad construction was a crucial case. When Lincoln was shot in 1865, there were only 35,000 miles of steam railways in the United States, mostly east of the Mississippi. By 1900 the figure had spurted up to 192,556 miles, or more than that for all Europe combined, and much of the new trackage ran west of the Mississippi.

Transcontinental railroad building was so costly and risky as to require government subsidies, as it had in many other industrializing nations. Everywhere, the construction of railway systems promised greater national unity and economic growth. Congress began to advance liberal loans to two favored cross-continent companies in 1862 and added enormous donations of acreage paralleling the tracks. All told, Washington rewarded the railroads with 155,504,994 acres, and the western states contributed 49 million more—a total area larger than Texas.

Deadlock in the 1850s over the location of the proposed transcontinental railroad was broken when the South seceded, leaving the field to the North. In 1862, the year after the guns first spoke at Fort Sumter, Congress made provision for starting the long-awaited line. One weighty argument for action was the urgency of bolstering the Union, already disrupted, by binding the Pacific Coast more securely to the rest of the Republic.

The Union Pacific Railroad—note the word *Union*—was thus commissioned by Congress to thrust westward from Omaha, Nebraska. The laying of rails began in earnest after the Civil War ended in 1865, and with juicy loans and land grants available, the "groundhog" promoters made all possible haste.

✳ **PRIMARY SOURCE**
Union Pacific Railway Poster

Sweaty construction gangs, which included many Irish "Paddies" (Patricks), worked at a frantic pace. On one record-breaking day, a sledge-and-shovel army of some five thousand men laid ten miles of track. A favorite song was:

> Then drill, my Paddies, drill;
> Drill, my heroes, drill;
> Drill all day,
> No sugar in your tay [tea]
> Workin' on the U.P. Railway.

When hostile Indians attacked, the laborers would drop their picks and seize their rifles. At rail's end, workers tried to find relaxation and conviviality in tented towns known as "hells on wheels," often teeming with as many as ten thousand men and a sprinkling of painted prostitutes and performers.

Rail laying at the California end was undertaken by the Central Pacific Railroad. This line pushed boldly eastward from boomtown Sacramento, over and through the towering, snow-clogged Sierra Nevada. Four farseeing men—the so-called Big Four—were the chief financial backers of the enterprise. The quartet included the heavyset, enterprising ex-governor Leland Stanford of California, who had useful political connections, and the burly, energetic Collis P. Huntington, an adept lobbyist.

The Central Pacific, which was granted the same princely subsidies as the Union Pacific, had the same incentive to haste. Some ten thousand Chinese laborers sweated from dawn to dusk under their basket hats. Hundreds lost their lives in premature explosions and other mishaps. The towering Sierra Nevada presented a formidable barrier; and the nerves of the Big Four were strained when their workers could chip only a few inches a day through solid rock, while the Union Pacific was sledgehammering westward across the plains.

Federal Land Grants to Railroads The heavy red lines indicate areas within which the railroads might be given specific parcels of land. As shown in the inset, land was reserved in belts of various widths on either side of a railroad's right of way. Until the railroad selected the individual mile-square sections it chose to possess, *all* such sections within the belt were withdrawn from eligibility for settlement. The "time zones" were introduced in 1883 (see p. 377), and their boundaries have since been adjusted. © Cengage Learning

MAP SKILL-BUILDER Understanding Transportation Maps

1. This map reveals the relationship between the expanding transcontinent rail network, the federal government's extensive land grants to railroads, and the railroad-sponsored system of time zones. In which three states did the railroads receive the largest acreage of land grants from the U.S. government?

2. Why were cities such as Chicago, St. Louis, and Kansas especially well positioned to become transportation and economic hubs for the whole nation?

3. Of the four major east-west transcontinental railroad lines that received massive federal land grants, which two had grants extending across only two time zones? (Consider the Union Pacific-Central Pacific route as a single transcontinental rail line.)

PATTERN OF LAND GRANTS

- One square mile held by government or sold
- Right of way: 100 yards wide
- One square mile granted to railroad

Primary federal land grants to railroads

Union Pacific Museum Collection

The Union Pacific and the Central Pacific Link at Promontory Point, Utah, May 10, 1869 Railroad financiers, dignitaries, spectators, and Chinese (Central Pacific) and Irish (Union Pacific) work gangs witnessed the historic joining that created the nation's first transcontinental railroad. After the two locomotives chugged within a few feet of each other, Central Pacific chief and former California governor Leland Stanford tapped a golden spike into a prepared hole on the last tie with a silver-plated maul. The golden spike was whisked away to be preserved for posterity at the Stanford University Museum, but the iron one that replaced it was hardly ordinary. It was wired to a Union Pacific telegraph line, while a copper plate on the maul was connected to a Central Pacific wire. When they touched, they closed a telegraphic circuit that sent the news to cities all over the country.

A "wedding of the rails" was finally consummated near Ogden, Utah, in 1869, as the two locomotives gently kissed cowcatchers. The colorful ceremony included the breaking of champagne bottles and the driving of a last ceremonial (golden) spike, with ex-governor Stanford clumsily wielding a silver sledgehammer.* In all, the Union Pacific built 1,086 miles, the Central Pacific 689 miles.

With the westward trail now blazed, four other transcontinental lines were completed before the century's end. None of them secured monetary loans from the federal government, as had the Union Pacific and the Central Pacific. But all of them except the Great Northern received generous grants of land.

The Northern Pacific Railroad, stretching from Lake Superior to Puget Sound, reached its terminus in 1883. The Atchison, Topeka, and Santa Fe—stretching through the southwestern deserts to California—was completed in 1884. The Southern Pacific ribboned from New Orleans to Los Angeles and was consolidated in the same year.

The last of the five nineteenth-century transcontinental railroads, the Great Northern, ran north of the Northern Pacific from Duluth to Seattle. Its creator was James J. Hill, a far-visioned Canadian–American who perceived that the prosperity of his railroad depended on the prosperity of the area that it served. Hill's sound principles of organization enabled his railroad to ride through later financial storms with flying colors.

---

* The spike was promptly removed and is now exhibited at the Stanford University Museum.

Yet the romance of the rails was not without its sordid side. Pioneer builders were often guilty of gross overoptimism, laying down rails that went "from nowhere to nothing" in order to get the lavish federal land bounties. When prosperity failed to smile, railroad companies went into bankruptcy, carrying down with them the savings of trusting investors. Many of the large railroads in the post–Civil War decades passed through seemingly endless bankruptcies, mergers, or reorganizations.

Revolution by Railways

The metallic fingers of the railroads intimately touched countless phases of American life. For the first time, a sprawling nation became physically bound with ribs of iron and steel. The railroads emerged as the nation's biggest business, employing more people than any other industry and gobbling up nearly 20 percent of investment dollars, from foreign and domestic investors alike.

In 1892 James Baird Weaver (1833–1912), nominee of the Populists, wrote regarding the railroad magnates:

"In their delirium of greed the managers of our transportation systems disregard both private right and the public welfare. Today they will combine and bankrupt their weak rivals, and by the expenditure of a trifling sum possess themselves of properties which cost the outlay of millions. Tomorrow they will capitalize their booty for five times the cost, issue their bonds, and proceed to levy tariffs upon the people to pay dividends upon the fraud."

More than any other single factor, the railroad network spurred the amazing economic growth of the post–Civil War years. By stitching North America together from ocean to ocean, the puffing locomotives opened up the West with its wealth of resources. Trains hauled raw materials to factories and sped them back as finished goods for sale across the continent, making the United States the largest integrated national market in the world. The forging of the rails themselves provided the largest single source of orders for the adolescent steel industry.

The screeching iron horse especially stimulated mining and agriculture, particularly in the West. The railroads took farmers out to their land, carried the fruits of their toil to market, and brought them their manufactured necessities. Clusters of farm settlements paralleled the railroads, just as earlier the settlements had followed the rivers.

Railways were a boon for cities and played a leading role in the great cityward movement of the last decades of the century. The iron monsters could carry food to enormous concentrations of people and at the same time ensure them a livelihood by providing both raw materials and markets.

Railroad companies also stimulated the mighty stream of immigration. Seeking settlers to whom their land grants might be sold at a profit, they advertised seductively in Europe and sometimes offered to transplant the newcomers free to their farms.

The land also felt the impact of the railroad—especially the broad, ecologically fragile midsection of the continent. Settlers following the railroads plowed up the tallgrass prairies of Iowa, Illinois, Kansas, and Nebraska and planted well-drained, rectangular cornfields. On the shortgrass prairies of the high plains in the Dakotas and Montana, range-fed cattle rapidly displaced the buffalo, which were hunted to near extinction. The white pine forests of Michigan, Wisconsin, and Minnesota disappeared into lumber that was rushed by rail to prairie farmers who used it to build houses and fences.

Time itself was bent to the railroads' needs. Until the 1880s every town in the United States had its own "local" time, dictated by the sun's position. When it was noon in Chicago, it was 11:50 A.M. in St. Louis and 12:18 P.M. in Detroit. For railroad operators worried about keeping schedules and avoiding wrecks, this patchwork of local times was a nightmare. Thus, on November 18, 1883, the major rail lines decreed that the continent would henceforth be divided into four "time zones." Most communities quickly adopted railroad "standard" time.

Finally, the railroad, more than any other single factor, was the maker of millionaires. A raw new aristocracy, consisting of "lords of the rail" such as eastern railroad magnate Cornelius Vanderbilt and "palace car" inventor George Pullman, replaced the old southern "lords of the lash." The multi-webbed lines became the playthings of Wall Street, and colossal wealth was amassed by stock speculators and corporate railroad manipulators.

Wrongdoing in Railroading

Corruption lurks nearby when fabulous fortunes can materialize overnight. The fleecings administered by the railroad construction companies, such as the Crédit Mobilier, were but the first of the bunco games that the railroad promoters learned to play. Methods soon became more refined, as fast-fingered financiers executed multimillion-dollar maneuvers beneath the noses of a bedazzled public. Jay Gould was the most adept of these ringmasters of rapacity. For nearly thirty years he boomed and busted the stocks of the Erie, the Kansas Pacific, the Union Pacific, and the Texas and Pacific in an incredible circus of speculative skullduggery.

One of the favorite devices of the moguls of manipulation was "stock watering." The term originally referred to the practice of making cattle thirsty by feeding them salt, which would cause the cattle to bloat themselves with water before they were weighed in for sale. Using a variation of this technique, railroad stock promoters grossly inflated their claims about a given line's assets and profitability and sold stocks and bonds far in excess of the railroad's actual value. "Promoters' profits" were often the tail that wagged the iron horse itself. Railroad managers were forced to charge extortionate rates and wage ruthless competitive battles in order to pay off the exaggerated financial obligations with which they were saddled.

The public interest was frequently trampled underfoot as the railroad titans waged their brutal wars. Crusty old Cornelius Vanderbilt, when told that the law stood in his way, reportedly exclaimed: "Law! What do I care about the law? Hain't I got the power?" His son, William H. Vanderbilt, when asked in 1883 about the discontinuance of a fast mail train, reportedly snorted, "The public be damned!"

While abusing the public, the railroaders blandly bought and sold people in public life. They bribed judges and legislatures, elected their own agents to high office, and showered free passes on journalists and politicians.

Railroad kings were, for a time, virtual industrial monarchs. As manipulators of a huge natural monopoly, they exercised more direct control over the lives of more people than did the president of the United States—and their terms were not limited to four years. They increasingly shunned the crude bloodletting of cutthroat competition and began to cooperate with one another to rule the railroad dominion. Sorely pressed to show at least some returns on their bloated investments, they entered into defensive alliances to protect precious profits.

pool *In business, an agreement to divide a given market in order to avoid competition.*

rebates *A return of a portion of the amount paid for goods or services.*

The earliest form of combination was the "**pool**"—an agreement to divide the business in a given area and share the profits. Other rail barons granted secret **rebates** or kickbacks to powerful shippers in return for steady and assured traffic. Often they slashed their rates on competing lines, but they more than made up the difference on noncompeting ones, where they might actually charge more for a short haul than for a long one. As a result, small farmers usually paid the highest rates, while large customers got the best deals.

Government Bridles the Iron Horse

It was neither healthy nor politically acceptable that so many people should be at the mercy of so few. Impoverished farmers, especially in the Midwest, began to wonder whether the nation had not escaped from the slavery power only to fall into the hands of the money power, as represented by the railroad **plutocracy**.

plutocracy *Government by the wealthy.*

free enterprise *An economic system that permits unrestricted entrepreneurial business activity; capitalism.*

But the American people, usually quick to respond to political injustice, were slow to combat economic injustice. Dedicated to **free enterprise** and to the principle that competition is the soul of trade, they remembered that Jefferson's ideals were hostile to governmental interference with business. Above all, there shimmered the "American dream": the hope that in a catch-as-catch-can economic system, anyone might become a millionaire.

The depression of the 1870s finally goaded the farmers into protesting against being "railroaded" into bankruptcy. Under pressure from organized agrarian groups such as the Grange (see p. 430), many midwestern legislatures tried to regulate the railroad monopoly. The scattered state efforts screeched to a halt in 1886. The Supreme Court, in the *Wabash* case, decreed that individual states had no power to regulate *inter*state commerce. If the mechanical monster were to be corralled, the federal government would have to do the job.

Congress ignored President Cleveland's grumbling indifference to the problem and passed the Interstate Commerce Act in 1887, which prohibited rebates and pools and required the railroads to publish their rates openly. The act also forbade unfair discrimination against shippers and outlawed charging more for a short haul than for a long one over the same line. Most important, the Interstate Commerce Act set up the Interstate Commerce Commission (ICC) to administer and enforce the new legislation.

Despite acclaim, the Interstate Commerce Act emphatically did not represent a popular victory over corporate wealth. One of the leading corporation lawyers of the day, Richard Olney, shrewdly noted that the new commission "can be made of great use to the railroads. It satisfies the popular clamor for a government supervision of railroads, at the same time that such supervision is almost entirely nominal....The part of wisdom is not to destroy the Commission, but to utilize it."

What the new legislation did do was provide an orderly forum where competing business interests could resolve their conflicts in peaceable ways. The country could now avoid ruinous rate wars among the railroads and deflect angry "confiscatory" attacks on the lines by pitchfork-prodded state legislatures. The Interstate Commerce Act tended to stabilize, not revolutionize, the existing business system.

Yet the act still ranks as a red-letter law. It was the first large-scale attempt by Washington to regulate business in the interest of society at large. The act foreshadowed the doom of freewheeling, buccaneering business practices and served full notice that there was a public interest in private enterprise that the government was bound to protect.

PRIMARY SOURCE
The Farmers' Movement in the West

Miracles of Mechanization

Postwar industrial expansion, partly a result of the railroad network, rapidly began to assume mammoth proportions. When Lincoln was elected in 1860, the Republic ranked only fourth among the manufacturing nations of the world. By 1894 it had bounded into first place. Why the sudden upsurge?

Liquid capital, previously scarce, was now becoming abundant. The word *millionaire* had not been coined until the 1840s, and in 1861 only a handful of individuals were eligible for this class. But the Civil War, partly through profiteering, created immense fortunes, and these accumulations could now be combined with borrowings from foreign capitalists. Investors from abroad loaned more money to the United States in the postwar period than any country had previously received. Unlike in other countries, in America they mostly put the money into private hands, not public coffers. Investors primarily from Britain, but from France, Germany, the Netherlands, and Switzerland as well, sometimes owned all or part of an American business. Other times they simply lent their money to the thousands of European companies set up to manage investment in U.S. industry. Either way, Europeans were usually content to let Americans run the business.

Innovations in transport fueled growth, too, by bringing the nation's amazingly abundant natural resources—particularly coal, oil, and iron—to the factory door. A shipping system through the Great Lakes carried the rich iron deposits of the Mesabi range of Minnesota to Chicago and Cleveland for refining. This priceless bonanza, where mountains of red-rusted ore could be scooped up by steam shovels, ultimately became a cornerstone of a vast steel empire. Copper, bauxite, and zinc made similar journeys from mine to manufacture.

The sheer size of the American market encouraged innovators to invent mass production methods. With cheap transportation crisscrossing the nation and an ever larger population able and eager to consume, anyone who could make an appealing new product available for a good price in large quantities—and figure out how to market it—thrived. Industrialists continued to refine the pre–Civil War "American system" of using specialized machinery to make interchangeable parts, culminating in 1913 with Henry Ford's fully developed, moving, assembly line for his Model T (see pp. 167 and 518).

The captains of industry had a major incentive to invent machines. Standardized machines and simplified assembly lines made it possible to replace expensive, skilled craft labor with unskilled workers, now cheap and plentiful thanks to massive immigration. Steel, the keystone industry, built its strength largely on the sweat of low-priced immigrant labor from eastern and southern Europe, working in two, twelve-hour shifts, seven days a week.

✳ **PRIMARY SOURCE**
Carnegie Steel and Black
Diamond Steel Companies
Mills

✳ **PRIMARY SOURCE**
First Recorded Promotional
Message on the Phonograph

Just as industry served as a hothouse of invention, so too could brilliant ideas give rise to whole new lines of business. Between 1860 and 1890, some 440,000 patents were issued. Business operations were facilitated by such machines as the cash register, the stock ticker, and the typewriter ("literary piano"), while the refrigerator car, the electric dynamo, and the electric railway speeded urbanization. One of the most ingenious inventions was the telephone, introduced by Alexander Graham Bell in 1876. America was suddenly turned into a nation of "telephoniacs," as a gigantic communications network was built on Bell's invention. The social impact of the telephone further expanded when it lured "number please" women away from the stove to the switchboard.

The most versatile inventor of all was Thomas Alva Edison (1847–1931), who as a boy had been considered so dull witted that he was taken out of school. Edison was a gifted tinkerer and a tireless worker, not a pure scientist. "Genius," he said, "is one percent inspiration and ninety-nine percent perspiration." Wondrous devices poured out of his "invention factory" in New Jersey—the phonograph, the mimeograph, the dictaphone, and the moving picture. He is probably best known for his perfection in 1879 of the electric light bulb, which turned night into day and transformed ancient human habits as well. People had previously slept an average of nine hours a night; now they slept just a bit more than seven.

The Trust Titan Emerges

Despite pious protests to the contrary, competition was the bugbear of most business leaders of the day. Tycoons such as Andrew Carnegie, the steel king; John D. Rockefeller, the oil baron; and J. Pierpont Morgan, the bankers' banker, exercised their genius in devising ways to circumvent competition. Carnegie pioneered the "vertical integration" of production by directly controlling every phase of his steel-making operation from mining to marketing. His miners dug the ore from Minnesota's Mesabi range; Carnegie ships floated it across the Great Lakes; Carnegie railroads delivered it to blast furnaces at Pittsburgh. When the molten metal finally poured from the glowing crucibles into the waiting ingot molds, no other hands but those in Carnegie's employ had touched the product.

Rockefeller pursued the less economically justifiable technique of "horizontal integration," which simply meant allying with competitors to monopolize a given market. He perfected a device for controlling bothersome rivals—the "**trust**." Stockholders in various smaller oil companies assigned their stock to the board of directors of Rockefeller's Standard Oil Company, formed in 1870, which then consolidated and concerted the operations of the previously competing enterprises. "Let us prey" was said to be Rockefeller's unwritten motto. Ruthlessly wielding vast power, Standard Oil soon cornered virtually the entire world petroleum market. Weaker competitors, left out of the trust agreement, were forced to the wall. Rockefeller's stunning success inspired many imitators, and the word *trust* came to be generally used to describe any large-scale business combination.

The imperial Morgan devised still other schemes for eliminating "wasteful" competition. The depression of the 1890s drove into his welcoming arms many bleeding businesspeople, wounded by cutthroat competition. His prescribed remedy was to consolidate rival enterprises and to ensure future harmony by placing officers of his own banking **syndicate** on their various boards of directors. These came to be known as "interlocking directorates."

trust *A mechanism by which one company grants control over its operations, through ownership of its stock, to another company. The Standard Oil Company became known for this practice in the 1870s as it eliminated its competition by taking control of smaller oil companies.*

syndicate *An association of financiers organized to carry out projects requiring very large amounts of capital.*

The Supremacy of Steel

"Steel is king!" might well have been the exultant war cry of the new industrialized generation. The mighty metal ultimately held together the new civilization, from skyscrapers to coal scuttles, while providing it with food, shelter, and transportation. Steel making, notably rails for railroads, typified the dominance of heavy industry, which concentrated on making "capital goods," as distinct from the production of "consumer goods" such as clothes and shoes.

Now taken for granted, steel was a scarce commodity in the wood-and-brick America of Abraham Lincoln. Yet within an amazing twenty years after 1870, the United States outdistanced all foreign competitors and was pouring out more than one-third of the world's supply of steel. By 1900 the Americans were producing as much as Britain and Germany combined.

What wrought the transformation? Chiefly, the invention in the 1850s of a method of making cheap steel was responsible for the transformation. William Kelly, a Kentucky manufacturer of iron kettles, had earlier discovered that cold air blown on red-hot iron caused the metal to become white-hot by igniting the carbon and thus eliminating impurities. But Kelly was unable to win acceptance for the product. Only after Bessemer, a British inventor, joined forces with Kelly did the Bessemer–Kelly process make possible the new steel civilization.

Kingpin among steelmasters was Andrew Carnegie, an undersized, charming Scotsman. As a towheaded lad of thirteen, he was brought to America by his impoverished parents in 1848 and got a job as a bobbin boy at $1.20 a week. Mounting the ladder of success so fast that he was said to have scorched the rungs, he forged ahead by working hard, doing extra chores, cheerfully assuming responsibility, and smoothly cultivating influential people.

After accumulating some capital, Carnegie entered the steel business in the Pittsburgh area. By 1900 he was producing one-fourth of the nation's Bessemer steel, and the partners in these pre-income tax days were dividing profits of $40 million a year as their take-home pay, with the "Napoleon of the Smokestacks" himself receiving a cool $25 million.

Into the picture now stepped the financial giant of the age, J. Pierpont Morgan. "Jupiter" Morgan had made a legendary reputation for himself and his Wall Street banking house by financing the reorganization of railroads, insurance companies, and banks. An impressive figure of a man, with massive shoulders, shaggy brows, piercing eyes, and a bulbous, acne cursed red nose, he had established an enviable reputation for integrity. Morgan did not believe that "money power" was dangerous, except when in dangerous hands—and he did not regard his own hands as dangerous.

The force of circumstances brought Morgan and Carnegie into collision. By 1900 the canny little Scotsman, weary of turning steel into gold, was eager to sell his holdings. Morgan had meanwhile plunged heavily into the manufacture of steel pipe tubing. Carnegie, cleverly threatening to invade the same business, was ready to ruin his rival if he did not receive his price. The steelmaster's agents haggled with the imperious Morgan for eight agonizing hours, and the financier finally agreed to buy out Carnegie for over $400 million. Fearing that he would die "disgraced" with so much wealth, Carnegie dedicated the remaining years of his life to giving it away for public libraries, pensions for professors, and other such philanthropic purposes—in all disposing of about $350 million.

Morgan moved rapidly to expand his new industrial empire. He took the Carnegie holdings, added others, "watered" the stock liberally, and in 1901 launched the enlarged United States Steel Corporation. Capitalized at $1.4 billion, it was America's first billion-dollar corporation—a larger sum than the total estimated wealth of the nation in 1800. The Industrial Revolution had come into its own.

Rockefeller Grows an American Beauty Rose

Another new industry was born almost overnight when in 1859 the first oil well—"Drake's Folly" in Pennsylvania—poured out its liquid "black gold." Kerosene, derived from petroleum, was the first major product of the infant oil industry. Replacing whale oil as the fuel for America's lamps, kerosene became the country's fourth most valuable export by the 1870s.

But what technology gives, technology takes away. By 1885 Thomas Edison's new electric light bulbs had rendered kerosene largely obsolete. Oil might thus have remained a modest, even a shrinking, industry but for yet another turn of the technological tide—the invention of the automobile. By 1900 the gasoline-burning internal combustion engine had clearly bested its rivals, steam and electricity, and the oil business got a new, long-lasting, and hugely profitable lease on life.

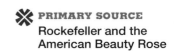

PRIMARY SOURCE
Rockefeller and the
American Beauty Rose

John D. Rockefeller—lanky, shrewd, ambitious, abstemious (he neither drank, smoked, nor swore)—came to dominate the oil industry. Born to a family of precarious income, he became a successful businessman at age nineteen. One upward stride led to another, and in 1870 he organized the Standard Oil Company of Ohio, nucleus of the great trust formed in 1882.

In the jungle world of big business, a kind of primitive savagery prevailed. Rockefeller—"Reckafellow," as Carnegie had once called him—showed little mercy to his competitors. His son later explained that the giant American Beauty rose could be produced "only by sacrificing the early buds that grew up around it." His father pinched off the small buds with complete ruthlessness. By 1877 Rockefeller controlled 95 percent of all the oil refineries in the country. Employing spies and extorting secret rebates from the railroads, he even forced the lines to pay him rebates on the freight bills of his competitors!

Rockefeller thought he was simply obeying a law of nature. "The time was ripe" for aggressive consolidation, he later reflected. "The day of combination is here to stay. Individualism has gone, never to return." On the other side of the ledger, Rockefeller's oil monopoly did turn out a superior product at a relatively cheap price achieved through its large-scale methods of production and distribution. This, in truth, was the tale of the other trusts as well. The efficient use of expensive machinery called for bigness, and consolidation proved more profitable than ruinous price wars.

Other trusts blossomed along with the American Beauty of oil. These included the sugar trust, the tobacco trust, the leather trust, and the harvester trust, which amalgamated some two hundred competitors. The meat industry arose on the backs of bawling western herds, and meat kings such as Gustavus F. Swift and Philip Armour took their places among the new royalty. Wealth was coming to dominate the commonwealth.

These untrustworthy trusts, and the "pirates" who captained them, were disturbingly new. They eclipsed an older American aristocracy of modestly successful merchants and professionals. An arrogant class of "new rich" was now elbowing aside the **patrician** families in the mad scramble for power and prestige. Not surprisingly, the ranks of the antitrust crusaders were frequently spearheaded by the "best men"—genteel old-family do-gooders who were not radicals but conservative defenders of their own vanishing influence.

patrician *Characterized by noble or high social standing.*

The Gospel of Wealth

Monarchs of yore invoked the divine right of kings, and America's industrial plutocrats took a somewhat similar stance. Some candidly credited heavenly help and justified their social position with what came to be known as the "Gospel of Wealth." "Godliness is in league with riches," preached the Episcopal bishop of Massachusetts, and hard fisted John D. Rockefeller piously acknowledged that "the good Lord gave me my money."

But most defenders of wide-open capitalism relied more heavily on the survival-of-the-fittest theories of English philosopher Herbert Spencer and Yale Professor William Graham Sumner. Later mislabeled "**Social Darwinists**," these theorists argued that individuals won their stations in life by competing on the basis of their natural talents. The wealthy and powerful had simply demonstrated greater abilities than the poor. Spencer and Sumner owed less to English evolutionary naturalist Charles Darwin, who stressed the adaptation of organisms, than to British *laissez-faire* economists David Ricardo and Thomas Malthus. In fact, Spencer, not Darwin, coined the phrase "survival of the fittest." "The millionaires are a product of natural selection," Sumner declared. "What do social classes owe each other?" he asked in 1883, then answered his own question: "Nothing." Some Social Darwinists later applied this theory to explain why some nations were more powerful than others or had the right to dominate "lesser peoples," often defined by race.

Self-justification by the wealthy inevitably involved contempt for the poor. Many of the rich, especially the newly rich, had pulled themselves up by their own bootstraps; hence, they concluded that those who stayed poor must be lazy and lacking in enterprise. The Reverend Russell Conwell of Philadelphia became rich by delivering his lecture "Acres of Diamonds" thousands of times. In it he charged, "There is not a poor person in the United States who was not made poor by his own shortcomings." Such attitudes were a formidable roadblock to social reform.

Social Darwinists *Believers in the idea, popular in the late nineteenth century, that people gained wealth by "survival of the fittest." Therefore, the wealthy had simply won a natural competition and owed nothing to the poor, and indeed service to the poor would interfere with this organic process.*

Plutocracy, like the earlier slavocracy, took its stand firmly on the Constitution. The clause that gave Congress sole jurisdiction over interstate commerce was a godsend to the monopolists; their high-priced lawyers used it time and again to thwart controls by the state legislatures. Giant trusts likewise sought refuge behind the Fourteenth Amendment, which had been originally designed to protect the rights of the ex-slaves as persons. The courts ingeniously interpreted a corporation to be a legal "person" and decreed that, as such, it could not be deprived of its property by a state without "due process of law" (see Art. XIV, para. 1 in the Appendix).

Government Tackles the Trust Evil

At long last the masses of the people began to mobilize against monopoly. They first tried to control the trusts through state legislation, as they had earlier attempted to curb the railroads. Failing here, as before, they were forced to appeal to Congress. After prolonged pulling and hauling, the Sherman Anti-Trust Act of 1890 was finally signed into law.

The Sherman Act flatly forbade combinations in restraint of trade, without making any distinction between "good" trusts and "bad" trusts. Bigness, not badness, was the sin. The law proved ineffective, largely because it had only baby teeth or no teeth at all, and because it contained legal loopholes through which clever corporation lawyers could wriggle. But the act was unexpectedly effective in one respect. Contrary to its original intent, the Sherman Act was used to curb labor unions or labor combinations that were deemed to be restraining trade.

Early prosecutions of the trusts by the Justice Department under the Sherman Act of 1890, as it turned out, were neither vigorous nor successful. Not until 1914

Industrial millionaires were condemned in the Populist platform of 1892:

"The fruits of the toil of millions are boldly stolen to build up colossal fortunes for a few…and the possessors of these, in turn despise the Republic and endanger liberty. From the same prolific womb of governmental injustice we breed the two great classes—tramps and millionaires."

The Verdict, January 22, 1900

Washington as Seen by the Trusts, 1900 "What a funny little government," John D. Rockefeller observes in this satirical cartoon. His own wealth and power are presumed to dwarf the resources of the federal government.

were the paper jaws of the Sherman Act fitted with reasonably sharp teeth. Until then, there was some question as to whether the government would control the trusts or the trusts the government.

But the iron grip of monopolistic corporations was being threatened. A revolutionary new principle had been written into the law books by the Sherman Anti-Trust Act of 1890, as well as by the Interstate Commerce Act of 1887. Private greed should henceforth be subordinated to public need.

The South in the Age of Industry

The industrial tidal wave that washed over the North after the Civil War caused only feeble ripples in the backwater of the South. The plantation system had degenerated into a pattern of absentee landownership. White and black sharecroppers now tilled the soil for a share of the crop, or they became tenants, in bondage to landlords who controlled needed credit and supplies.

Southern agriculture received a welcome boost in the 1880s, when machine-made cigarettes replaced the roll-your-own variety and tobacco consumption shot up. James Buchanan Duke took full advantage of the new technology to mass produce the dainty "coffin nails." In 1890, in what was becoming a familiar pattern, he absorbed his main competitors into the American Tobacco Company. The cigarette czar later showed such generosity to Trinity College, near his birthplace in Durham, North Carolina, that the trustees gratefully changed its name to Duke University.

Industrialists tried to coax the agricultural South out of the fields and into the factories, but with only modest success. The region remained overwhelmingly rural. Prominent among the boosters of a "new South" was silver-tongued Henry W. Grady, editor of the *Atlanta Constitution*. He tirelessly exhorted the ex-Confederates to become "Georgia Yankees" and outplay the North at the commercial and industrial game.

Yet formidable obstacles lay in the path of southern industrialization. One was the paper barrier of regional rate-setting systems imposed by the northern-dominated railroad interests. Railroads gave preferential rates to manufactured goods moving southward from the North, but in the opposite direction they discriminated in favor of southern raw materials. The net effect was to keep the South in a kind of "**Third World**" servitude to the Northeast—as a supplier of raw materials to the manufacturing metropolis, unable to develop a substantial industrial base of its own.

A bitter example of this economic discrimination against the South was the "Pittsburgh plus" pricing system in the steel industry. Rich deposits of coal and iron ore near Birmingham, Alabama, worked by low-wage southern labor, should have given steel manufacturers there a competitive edge, especially in southern markets. But the steel lords of Pittsburgh brought pressure to bear on the compliant railroads. As a result, Birmingham steel, no matter where it was delivered, was charged a fictional fee, as if it had been shipped from Pittsburgh. This stunting of the South's natural economic advantages throttled the growth of the Birmingham steel industry.

In manufacturing cotton textiles, the South fared considerably better. Southerners had long resented shipping their fiber to New England, and now their cry was, "Bring the mills to the cotton." Beginning about 1880, northern capital began to erect cotton mills in the South, largely in response to tax benefits and the prospect of cheap and non-unionized labor.

The textile mills proved a mixed blessing to the economically blighted South. Cheap labor was the South's major attraction for potential investors, and keeping labor

Third World *Term developed during the Cold War for nations that were not part of either the Western (First World) or Communist (Second World) blocs; most were Asian, African, or Latin American countries formerly under colonial rule and still economically poor and dependent.*

Henry W. Grady (1851–1889), editor of the Atlanta Constitution, *urged the new South to industrialize. In a Boston speech in 1889, he described the burial in Georgia of a Confederate veteran:*

"The South didn't furnish a thing on earth for that funeral but the corpse and the hole in the ground. ... They buried him in a New York coat and a Boston pair of shoes and a pair of breeches from Chicago and a shirt from Cincinnati, leaving him nothing to carry into the next world with him to remind him of the country in which he lived, and for which he fought for four years, but the chill of blood in his veins and the marrow in his bones."

cheap became almost a religion among southern industrialists. The mills took root in the chronically depressed Piedmont region of southern Appalachia. Blacks were excluded from the mills, so rural southern whites, often derided as "hillbillies" or "lint-heads," worked from dawn to dusk amid the whirring spindles. Paid at half the rate of their northern counterparts, most were perpetually in debt to the company store. But despite their depressed working conditions and poor pay, many southerners saw employment in the mills as a salvation. With many mills anxious to tap the cheap labor of women and children, mill work often offered destitute farm-fugitive families their only chance to remain together.

The Impact of the New Industrial Revolution on America

Economic miracles wrought during the decades after the Civil War enormously increased the wealth of the Republic. The standard of living rose sharply, and well-fed American workers enjoyed more physical comforts than their counterparts in any other industrial nation. Urban centers mushroomed as the insatiable factories demanded more American labor and as immigrants swarmed like honeybees to the new jobs (see "Makers of America: The Poles," pp. 514–515).

Early Jeffersonian ideals were withering before the smudgy blasts from the smokestacks. As agriculture declined in relation to manufacturing, America could no longer aspire to be a nation of small freehold farms. Jefferson's concepts of free enterprise, with neither help nor hindrance by Washington, were being thrown out the factory window.

Older ways of life also wilted in the heat of the factory furnaces. The very concept of time was revolutionized. Rural American migrants and peasant European immigrants, used to living by the languid clock of nature, now had to regiment their lives by the factory whistle. The seemingly arbitrary discipline of industrial labor did not come easily and sometimes had to be forcibly taught by corporate managers.

Probably no single group was more profoundly affected by the new industrial age than women. Propelled into industry by recent inventions, chiefly the typewriter and the telephone switchboard, millions of stenographers and "hello girls" discovered new economic and social opportunities. The "Gibson Girl," a magazine image of an independent and athletic "new woman" created in the 1890s by the artist Charles Dana Gibson, became the romantic ideal of the age. For middle-class women, careers often meant delayed marriages and smaller families. Most women workers, however, toiled neither for independence nor for glamour but out of economic necessity. They faced the same long hours and dangerous working conditions as did their mates and brothers, and they earned less because wages for "women's jobs" were usually set below men's.

The clattering machine age likewise accentuated class division. "Industrial buccaneers" flaunted bloated fortunes, and their rags-to-riches spouses displayed glittering diamonds. Such extravagances evoked bitter criticism. Some of it was envious, but much of the criticism rose from the small and increasingly vocal group of **socialists** and other **radicals**, many of whom were recent European immigrants. The existence of an oligarchy of money was amply demonstrated by the fact that in 1900 about one-tenth of the people owned nine-tenths of the nation's wealth.

Finally, strong pressures for foreign trade developed as the tireless industrial machine threatened to saturate the domestic market. Aided by developments such as the laying of a transatlantic telegraph in 1866 and the opening of the Suez Canal in 1869, international trade became ever faster, cheaper, and easier. American products radiated out all over the world—notably the five-gallon kerosene can of the Standard Oil Company. The flag follows trade, and empire tends to follow the flag—a harsh lesson that America was soon to learn.

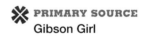
PRIMARY SOURCE
Gibson Girl

socialists (socialism) *Those who hold the political belief in promoting social and economic equality through the ownership and control of the major means of production by the whole community rather than by individuals or corporations.*

radicals *Those who believe in fundamental change in the political, economic, or social system.*

In Unions There Is Strength

The sweat of the laborer lubricated the vast new industrial machine. Yet wage workers did not share proportionately with their employers the benefits of the age of big business.

EXAMINING THE EVIDENCE

THE PHOTOGRAPHY OF LEWIS W. HINE

The pell-mell onrush of industrialization after the Civil War spawned countless human abuses, few more objectionable than the employment of children, often in hazardous jobs. For decades, reformers tried to arouse public outrage against child labor, and they made significant headway at last with the help of photography—especially the photographs of Lewis W. Hine (1874–1940). A native of Wisconsin, Hine in 1908 became the staff photographer for the National Child Labor Committee, an organization committed to ending child labor. This 1909 photo of young "doffers," whose job it was to remove fully wound bobbins from textile spinning machines, is typical of Hine's work. He shows the boys climbing dangerously on the whirling mechanism, and his own caption for the photo names the mill—"Bibb Mill No. 1, Macon, Georgia"—but not the boys, as if to underline the impersonal, dehumanizing nature of their work and the specific responsibilities of their employer. His other subjects included child workers on Colorado beet farms, in Pennsylvania coal mines, and Gulf Coast fish canneries, and in the glass, tobacco, and garment trades. Hine's images contributed heavily to the eventual success of the campaign to end child labor in the New Deal era. Hine is also celebrated as one of the fathers of documentary photography.

✳ **PRIMARY SOURCE**
Child Worker Dies Headline

✳ **PRIMARY SOURCE**
Child Glass Factory Worker

1. Why might Hine's graphic images have succeeded in stirring public opinion more powerfully than factual and statistical demonstrations of the evil of child labor?

2. Given Hine's own reform objectives, can his photographs—or any so-called documentary images—be taken at face value as literal, accurate information about the past?

3. Which details in Lewis Hine's photo especially emphasize the exploitation and dangers experienced by child laborers?

National Archives

The worker, suggestive of the Roman galley slave, was becoming a lever puller in a giant mechanism. Individual originality and creativity were being stifled, and less value than ever before was being placed on manual skills. Before the Civil War, the worker might have toiled in a small plant whose owner hailed the employee in the morning by first name and inquired after the family's health. But now the factory hand was employed by a corporation—depersonalized, bodiless, soulless, and often conscienceless. Employers could take advantage of the vast new railroad network and bring in unemployed workers from the four corners of the country and beyond to beat down high wage levels. During the 1880s and 1890s, several hundred thousand unskilled immigrant workers poured into the country from Europe, creating a labor market more favorable to the boss than the worker.

Individual workers were powerless to battle single handedly against giant industry. The corporation could dispense with the individual worker much more easily than the worker could dispense with the corporation. Employers could retain high-priced lawyers, buy up the local press, import strikebreakers ("scabs"), and employ thugs to beat up labor organizers. In 1886 Jay Gould reputedly boasted, "I can hire one-half of the working class to kill the other half."

Corporations had still other weapons in their arsenals. They could call upon conservative federal judges to issue injunctions against strikers, and if defiance continued, the corporations could then request state or federal authorities to send in troops. Employers could lock the doors of their plants—a procedure called the "**lockout**"—and starve rebellious workers into submission. They could compel them to sign "ironclad oaths" or "**yellow dog contracts**", both solemn agreements not to join a labor union. They could put the names of labor agitators on a "black list" and circulate it among fellow employers. A corporation might even own the "company town," where high-priced grocery stores and "easy" credit often sank workers into perpetual debt—a status that strongly resembled serfdom.

The middle-class public, annoyed by recurrent strikes, grew deaf to the outcry of the worker. Carnegie and Rockefeller had battled their way to the top, and the view was common that the laborer could do likewise. Somehow the strike seemed like a foreign importation—socialistic and hence unpatriotic. Big business might combine into trusts to raise prices, but the worker must not combine into unions to raise wages. Unemployment seemed to be an act of God, who somehow would take care of the laborer.

lockout *The refusal by an employer to allow employees to work unless they agree to his or her terms.*

yellow dog contract *A labor contract in which an employee must agree not to join a union as a condition of holding the job.*

Labor Limps Along

Labor unions, which had been few and disorganized in 1861, were given a strong boost by the Civil War. By 1872, there were several hundred thousand organized workers and thirty-two national unions, representing such crafts as the bricklayers, typesetters, and shoemakers.

The **National Labor Union**, organized in 1866, represented a giant bootstride by workers. One of the earliest national-scale unions to organize in the Americas or Europe, it aimed to unify workers across locales and trades to challenge their ever more powerful bosses. The union lasted six years and attracted the impressive total of some 600,000 members, including the skilled, unskilled, and farmers, though it excluded the Chinese and made only nominal efforts to include women and blacks. Black workers organized their own Colored National Labor Union, but persistent white racism prevented the two national unions from working together. The National Labor Union agitated for the arbitration of industrial disputes and the eight-hour workday, winning the latter for government workers. But the devastating depression of the 1870s dealt it a knockout blow. Wage reductions in 1877 touched off such disruptive strikes on the railroads that nothing short of federal troops could restore order.

A new organization—the Knights of Labor—seized the torch dropped by the defunct National Labor Union. Officially known as the Noble and Holy Order of the Knights of Labor, the organization began inauspiciously in 1869 as a secret society, with a private

National Labor Union *This first national labor organization in U.S. history was founded in 1866 and gained 600,000 members from many parts of the workforce, although it limited the participation of Chinese, women, and blacks. The organization devoted much of its energy to fighting for an eight-hour workday before it dissolved in 1872.*

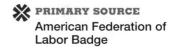
PRIMARY SOURCE
American Federation of
Labor Badge

ritual, passwords, and a secret grip. Secrecy, which continued until 1881, would forestall possible reprisals by employers.

The Knights of Labor, like the National Labor Union, sought to include all workers in "one big union." Their slogan was "An injury to one is the concern of all." A welcome mat was rolled out for the skilled and unskilled, for men and women, for whites and underprivileged blacks, some ninety thousand of whom joined. The Knights barred only liquor dealers, professional gamblers, lawyers, bankers, and stockbrokers.

Setting up broad goals, the embattled Knights campaigned for economic and social reform, including producers' **cooperatives** and codes for safety and health. The ordinary workday was then ten hours or more, and the Knights waged a determined campaign for the eight-hour stint.

Under the eloquent but often erratic leadership of Terence V. Powderly, an Irish American of nimble wit and fluent tongue, the Knights won a number of strikes for the eight-hour day. When the Knights staged a successful strike against Jay Gould's Wabash Railroad in 1885, membership mushroomed to about three-quarters of a million workers.

cooperatives *Organizations for producing, marketing, or consuming goods in which the members share the benefits.*

Unhorsing the Knights of Labor

Despite their outward success, the Knights were riding for a fall. They became involved in a number of May Day strikes in 1886, about half of which failed. A focal point was Chicago, home to about eighty thousand Knights. The city was also honeycombed with a few hundred **anarchists**, many of them foreign-born, who were advocating a violent overthrow of the American government.

Tensions rapidly built up to the bloody Haymarket Square episode. Labor disorders had broken out, and on May 4, 1886, the Chicago police advanced on a meeting called to protest alleged brutalities by the authorities. Suddenly a dynamite bomb was thrown that killed or injured several dozen people including police.

Hysteria swept the Windy City. Eight anarchists were rounded up. Although nobody proved that they had anything to do directly with the bomb, a judge and jury held that because they had preached incendiary doctrines, they could be charged with conspiracy. Five were sentenced to death: one of these men committed suicide, and four were executed. The other three anarchists were given stiff prison terms. They were eventually pardoned in 1892 by Illinois governor John P. Altgeld, a German-born Democrat of strong liberal tendencies.

The Haymarket Square bomb helped blow the props from under the Knights of Labor. They were associated in the public mind, though mistakenly, with the anarchists. The eight-hour movement suffered correspondingly, and subsequent strikes by the Knights met with scant success. By the 1890s the Knights had melted away to 100,000 members, and these members gradually fused with other protest groups of that decade.

anarchists (anarchism) *Those who hold the political belief that all organized, coercive government is wrong in principle and that society should be organized solely on the basis of free cooperation. (Some anarchists practiced violence against the state, while others were nonviolent pacifists.)*

The AF of L to the Fore

The elitist American Federation of Labor, born in 1886, was largely the brainchild of squat, square-jawed Samuel Gompers. This colorful Jewish cigar maker, born in a London tenement and removed from school at age ten, was brought to America when thirteen. Taking his turn at reading informative literature to fellow cigar makers in New York, he was pressed into overtime service because of his strong voice. Rising spectacularly in the labor ranks, he was elected president of the American Federation of Labor every year except one from 1886 to 1924.

Gompers adopted a down-to-earth approach, soft-pedaling attempts to engineer sweeping social reform. A bitter foe of socialism, he shunned politics for economic strategies and goals. Gompers had no quarrel with capitalism, but he demanded a fairer share for labor. All he wanted, he said, was "more." Promoting what he called "pure and simple" unionism, he sought better wages, hours, and working conditions.

The Strike, by Robert Koehler, 1886 Scenes like this were becoming more typical of American life in the late nineteenth century as industrialism advanced spectacularly and sometimes ruthlessly. Here Koehler (1850–1917) shows an entire community of men, women, and children—many of them apparently immigrant newcomers—challenging the power of the "boss." The scene is tense but orderly, though violence seems to be imminent as one striker reaches for a rock.

The AF of L thus established itself on solid but narrow foundations. Although attempting to speak for all workers, it fell far short of being representative of them. Composed of skilled craftsmen, such as the carpenters and bricklayers, it was willing to let unskilled laborers, including women and especially blacks, fend for themselves. The AF of L weathered the panic of 1893 reasonably well, and by 1900 it could boast a membership of 500,000.

Labor disorders continued, peppering the years from 1881 to 1900 with an alarming total of over 23,000 strikes. These disturbances involved 6,610,000 workers, with a total loss to both employers and employees of $450 million. The strikers lost about half their strikes and won or compromised the remainder. Perhaps the gravest weakness of organized labor was that it still embraced only a small minority of all working people—about 3 percent in 1900.

But attitudes toward labor had begun to change perceptibly by 1900. The public was beginning to concede the right of workers to organize, to bargain collectively, and to strike. As a sign of the times, Labor Day was made a legal holiday by act of Congress in 1894. A few enlightened industrialists had come to perceive the wisdom of avoiding costly economic warfare by bargaining with the unions and signing agreements. But the vast majority of employers continued to fight organized labor, which achieved its grudging gains only after recurrent strikes and frequent reverses. Several trouble-fraught decades were to pass before labor was to gain a position of relative equality with capital. If the age of big business had dawned, the age of big labor was still some distance over the horizon.

The capitalists who forged an industrial America in the late nineteenth century were once called captains of industry—a respectful title that bespoke the awe due their wondrous material accomplishments. But these economic innovators have never been universally admired. During the Great Depression of the 1930s, when the entire industrial order they had created seemed to have collapsed utterly, it was fashionable to speak of them as robber barons—a term implying scorn for their high-handed methods. This sneer often issued from the lips and pens of leftist critics such as Matthew Josephson, who sympathized with the working classes allegedly brutalized by the factory system.

Criticism has also come from writers nostalgic for the preindustrial past. These critics believe that industrialization stripped away the traditions, values, and pride of native farmers and immigrant craftspeople. Conceding that economic development elevated the material standard of living for working Americans, this interpretation contends that the Industrial Revolution diminished their spiritual "quality of life." Accordingly, historians such as Herbert Gutman and David Montgomery portray labor's struggle for control of the workplace as the central drama of industrial expansion.

Nevertheless, even these historians concede that class-based protest has never been as powerful a force in the United States as in certain European countries. Many historians believe that this is so because greater social mobility in America dampened class tensions.

In the 1960s, historians led by Stephan Thernstrom began to test this long-standing belief. Looking at such factors as occupation, wealth, and geographic mobility, they tried to gauge the nature and extent of social mobility in the United States. Most of these historians concluded that, although relatively few Americans made rags-to-riches leaps, large numbers experienced small improvements in their economic and social status. Few sons of laborers became corporate tycoons, but many more became line bosses and white-collar clerks.

In recent years such studies have been criticized by historians who point out the difficulties involved in defining "social status." For instance, some white-collar clerical workers received lower wages than manual laborers did. But were they higher or lower on the social scale? Furthermore, James Henretta has pointed out that different groups defined success differently: whereas Jewish immigrants often struggled to give their sons professional educations, the Irish put more emphasis on acquiring land, and Italians on building small family-run businesses.

Meanwhile, leftist historians such as Michael Katz have argued that the degree of social mobility in America has been overrated. These historians argue that industrial capitalism created two classes: a working class that sold its labor and a business class that controlled resources and bought labor. Although most Americans took small steps upward, they generally remained within the class in which they began. Thus, these historians argue, the inequality of a capitalistic class system persisted in America's seemingly fluid society.

Chapter Summary

Aided by government land grant subsidies and loans, the first transcontinental rail line was completed in 1869, soon followed by others. This rail network opened vast new markets and prompted industrial growth. The power and corruption of the railroads led to public demands for regulation. State regulation was declared unconstitutional, but the federal government took a small step with the Interstate Commerce Act (1887).

New technology and types of business organization, sometimes employing harsh competitive practices, led to the growth of huge corporate trusts. Andrew Carnegie and John D. Rockefeller led the way in the steel and oil industries. Initially, the oil industry supplied kerosene for lamps; it eventually expanded by providing gasoline to fuel automobiles. Cheap steel transformed industries from construction to rail building, and the powerful railroads dominated the economy and reshaped American society. Many sectors of the economy came to be dominated by monopolistic trusts that used "interlocking directorates" and other pressure tactics to control competitors. Business-oriented ideologies such as the religious "gospel of wealth" and naturalistic "Social Darwinism"

celebrated the wealthy as "fittest" to survive and denigrated poverty as a sign of moral and natural failure.

While industrialization did raise the general economy and standard of living, its benefits were very unevenly distributed. The South remained in underdeveloped "Third World" dependence, despite "New South" proclamations, while the industrial working class struggled at the bottom of the growing class divisions of American society. Increasingly transformed from independent producers and farmers to dependent wage earners, America's workers became vulnerable to illness, industrial accidents, and unemployment.

Workers' attempts at labor organization were generally ineffective, hindered by corporate and governmental opposition and their own backward-looking ideologies. The National Labor Union enjoyed a brief success before its collapse, and the Knights of Labor also disappeared after the Haymarket bombing. Gompers's AF of L successfully organized skilled craft laborers but ignored most industrial workers, women, and blacks. Middle class public attitudes toward organized labor slowly became more positive after 1900.

KEY TERMS

pool (378)

rebates (378)

plutocracy (378)

free enterprise (378)

trust (380)

syndicate (380)

patrician (382)

Social Darwinists (382)

Third World (384)

socialists (socialism) (385)

radicals (385)

lockout (387)

yellow dog contract (387)

National Labor Union (387)

cooperatives (388)

anarchists (anarchism) (388)

PEOPLE TO KNOW

Cornelius Vanderbilt

Thomas Alva Edison

Andrew Carnegie

John D. Rockfeller

Samuel Gompers

 Go to the History CourseMate website for primary source links, study tools, and review materials for this chapter. www.cengagebrain.com

25

America Moves to the City

1865–1900

What shall we do with our great cities?
What will our great cities do with us...?
[T]he question...does not concern the city alone.
The whole country is affected...
by the condition of its great cities.

LYMAN ABBOT, 1891

Born in the country, America moved to the city in the decades following the Civil War. By the year 1900 the United States' upsurging population nearly doubled from the 40 million people enumerated in the census of 1870. Yet, in the very same period, the population of American cities *tripled*. This cityward drift affected not only the United States but the entire industrializing world. European peasants, pushed off the land in part by competition from cheap American foodstuffs, were pulled into cities—in both Europe and America—by the new lure of industrial jobs. A revolution in American agriculture thus fed the industrial and urban revolutions in Europe, as well as in the United States.

FOCUS QUESTIONS

1. What features characterized the new industrial city, and what was its impact on American society?

2. Why did the massive "New Immigration" from southern and eastern Europe stir opposition from many native-born Americans, and how did political machines, social reformers, and churches adapt to the new urban and immigrant era?

3. What were the major changes in American religious life in the late nineteenth century, and how did the churches respond to the challenges of Darwinism, biblical criticism, and the dramatic growth of Catholicism, Judaism, and other "immigrant" faiths?

4. What were the major changes in American educational and cultural life in the late nineteenth century, and how did the turns toward "realism" and "pragmatism" reflect the new conditions of an urban and scientific civilization?

5. Why were there such fierce debates over morality in the late nineteenth century, especially over issues concerning sex, women, and the family?

CHRONOLOGY

1859	Charles Darwin publishes *On the Origin of Species*.	**1884**	Mark Twain publishes *The Adventures of Huckleberry Finn*.
1862	Morrill Act provides public land for higher education.	**1885**	Louis Sullivan builds the first skyscraper, in Chicago. Linotype invented.
1863	World's first subway system opens in London.	**1886**	Statue of Liberty erected in New York harbor.
1866	American Society for the Prevention of Cruelty to Animals (ASPCA) created.	**1887**	American Protective Association (APA) formed. Hatch Act supplements Morrill Act.
1869	Wyoming Territory grants women the right to vote.	**1888**	Edward Bellamy publishes *Looking Backward*. American all-star baseball team tours world.
1871	*Woodhull and Claflin's Weekly* published.		
1872	Metaphysical Club meets in Cambridge, Massachusetts.	**1889**	Jane Addams founds Hull House in Chicago.
1873	Comstock Law.	**1890**	National American Woman Suffrage Association (NAWSA) formed.
1874	Woman's Christian Temperance Union (WCTU) organized. Chautauqua education movement launched. Impressionist artists debut in Paris.	**1891**	Basketball invented.
		1893	Lillian Wald opens Henry Street Settlement in New York. Anti-Saloon League formed. World's Columbian Exposition held in Chicago. New Zealand grants women right to vote.
1876	Johns Hopkins University graduate school established.		
1879	Henry George publishes *Progress and Poverty*. Dumbbell tenement introduced. Mary Baker Eddy establishes Christian Science. Salvation Army begins work in America.	**1897**	Library of Congress opens.
		1898	Charlotte Perkins Gilman publishes *Women and Economics*.
		1899	Kate Chopin publishes *The Awakening*.
1881	Booker T. Washington becomes head of Tuskegee Institute. American Red Cross founded. Barnum and Bailey first join to stage "Greatest Show on Earth."	**1900**	Theodore Dreiser publishes *Sister Carrie*.
		1907	Henry Adams privately publishes *The Education of Henry Adams*.
1882	First immigration-restriction laws passed.	**1910**	National Association for the Advancement of Colored People (NAACP) founded.
1883	Brooklyn Bridge completed. Metropolitan Opera House built in New York.		

The Urban Frontier

The growth of American metropolises was spectacular. In 1860 no city in the United States could boast a million inhabitants; by 1890 New York, Chicago, and Philadelphia had spurted past the million mark. By 1900 New York, with some 3.5 million people, was the second largest city in the world, outranked only by London. Throughout the world, cities were exploding; not only London, but also Paris, Berlin, Tokyo, Moscow, Mexico City, Calcutta, and Shanghai all doubled or tripled in size between 1850 and 1900. The population of Buenos Aires multiplied by more than ten.

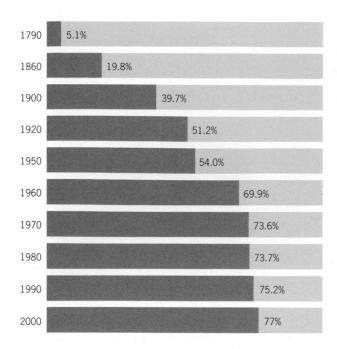

Year	Percentage
1790	5.1%
1860	19.8%
1900	39.7%
1920	51.2%
1950	54.0%
1960	69.9%
1970	73.6%
1980	73.7%
1990	75.2%
2000	77%

The Shift to the City Percentage of total population living in cities of twenty-five hundred or more. Notice the slowing pace of the cityward trend since the 1970s.

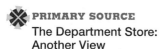

megalopolis *An extensive, heavily populated area, containing several dense urban centers.*

American cities grew both up and out. The cloud-brushing skyscrapers allowed more people and workplaces to be packed onto a parcel of land. Appearing first as a ten-story building in Chicago in 1885, the skyscraper was made usable by the perfecting of the electric elevator. An opinionated Chicago architect, Louis Sullivan (1856–1924), contributed formidably to the further development of the skyscraper with his famous principle that "form follows function."

Cities also spread out, turning many Americans into commuters who traveled daily by mass-transit electric trolleys between urban job and suburban home. The compact and communal "walking city" gave way to the immense and impersonal **megalopolis**, carved into distinctly different districts for business, industry, and residential neighborhoods—which in turn were segregated by race, ethnicity, and social class.

Rural life could not compete with the siren song of the city. Industrial jobs, above all, drew people off farms in America, as well as abroad, and into factory centers. But the urban lifestyle also held powerful attractions. The predawn milking of cows had little appeal when compared with the late-night glitter of city lights, particularly alluring to young adults yearning for independence. Electricity, indoor plumbing, and telephones all made life in the big city more enticing. Engineering marvels such as the skyscraper and New York's awesome Brooklyn Bridge, a harp-like suspension span dedicated in 1883, further added to the seductive glamour of the gleaming cities.

Cavernous department stores such as Macy's in New York and Marshall Field's in Chicago attracted urban middle-class shoppers and provided urban working-class jobs, many of them for women. The bustling emporiums also heralded a dawning era of consumerism and accentuated widening class divisions. When Carrie Meeber, novelist Theodore Dreiser's fictional heroine in *Sister Carrie* (1900), escapes from

PRIMARY SOURCE
The Department Store: Another View

Mulberry Street on New York City's Lower East Side, c. 1900 Population densities in early-twentieth-century American cities were among the highest in the world. Mulberry Street, shown in this photo, was at the heart of New York's "Little Italy" neighborhood.

rural boredom to Chicago, it is the spectacle of the city's dazzling department stores that awakens her fateful yearning for a richer, more elegant way of life.

The move to the city also introduced Americans to new ways of living. Household products sold in bulk at the local store, without wrapping, gave way to city goods that came in throwaway bottles, boxes, bags, and cans. Apartment houses had no adjoining barnyards where residents might toss garbage to the hogs. Waste disposal, in short, was an issue new to the urban age. And the mountains of waste that urbanites generated further testified to a cultural shift away from the virtues of thrift to the convenience of consumerism.

The jagged skyline of America's perpendicular civilization could not fully conceal the canker sores of feverish growth. Criminals flourished like lice in the teeming asphalt jungles. Impure water, uncollected garbage, unwashed bodies, and droppings from draft animals enveloped many cities in a satanic stench.

The cities were monuments of contradiction. They represented "humanity compressed," remarked one observer, "the best and the worst combined, in a strangely composite community." They harbored merchant princes and miserable paupers, stately banks and sooty factories, green-grassed suburbs and stinking **tenements**. The glaring contrasts that assaulted the eye in New York reminded one visitor of "a lady in ball costume, with diamonds in her ears, and her toes out at the boots."

tenement *A multidwelling building, often poor or overcrowded.*

Worst of all were the human pigsties known as slums. They seemed to grow ever more crowded, more filthy, and more rat infested, especially after the perfection in 1879 of the "dumbbell" tenement. So named because of the outline of its floor plan, the dumbbell was usually seven or eight stories high, with shallow, sunless, and ill-smelling air shafts providing minimal ventilation. Several families were sardined onto each floor of the barracks-like structures, and the families shared a malodorous toilet in the hall. Small wonder that slum dwellers strove mightily to escape their wretched surroundings—as many of them did. The slums remained foul places, inhabited by successive waves of newcomers.

Cities were dangerous not only for slum dwellers. In 1871, two-thirds of downtown Chicago burned in a raging fire that left 90,000 people homeless and destroyed more than 15,000 buildings. Closely packed wooden structures fed the insatiable flames, prompting Chicago and other wary cities to require stone and iron buildings downtown. The wealthiest began to leave the risky city behind and head for semirural suburbs. These leafy "bedroom communities" eventually ringed the brick-and-concrete cities with a greenbelt of **affluence**.

affluence *An abundance of wealth.*

The New Immigration

The powerful pull of the American urban magnet was felt even in faraway Europe. A seemingly endless stream of immigrants continued to pour in from the old "mother continent." In each of the three decades from the 1850s through the 1870s, more than 2 million migrants had stepped onto America's shores. By the 1880s the stream had swelled to a rushing torrent, as more than 5 million migrants cascaded into the country.

Until the 1880s most immigrants had come from the British Isles and western Europe, chiefly Germany and Ireland. Also significant were the more than 300,000 Chinese. When these immigrants first arrived, many faced virulent nativism. Most abused were the Irish and the Chinese; the Chinese were legally excluded in 1882 (see pp. 362–365). But by the last decades of the century, the "old" European immigrants had adjusted well to American life by building supportive ethnic organizations and melding into established farm communities or urban craft unions. Although many still lived, worked, and worshipped among their own, they were largely accepted as "American" by the native-born.

But in the 1880s the character of the immigrant stream changed drastically. The so-called New Immigrants—Italians, Croats, Slovaks, Greeks, Poles—came from southern and eastern Europe. Many of them worshiped in Roman Catholic or Eastern Orthodox churches or in Jewish synagogues. Largely illiterate and impoverished, most new immigrants hived together in the "Little Italys" and "Little Polands" of the jam-packed cities. These new peoples totaled only 19 percent of newcomers in the 1880s; but by the first decade of the twentieth century, they constituted an astonishing 66 percent of the total inflow. (See "Makers of America: The Italians," p. 396.)

The Italians

Who were the "New Immigrants"? Who were these southern and eastern European birds of passage that flocked to the United States between 1880 and 1920? Prominent and typical among them were Italians, some 4 million of whom sailed to the United States during the four decades of the New Immigration.

They came from the southern provinces of their native land, the heel and toe of the Italian boot. These areas had lagged behind the prosperous, industrial region of northern Italy. Unification of the nation of Italy had raised hopes of similar progress in the downtrodden south, but it was slow in coming. Southern peasants tilled their fields without fertilizer or machinery, using hand plows and rickety hoes that had been passed down for generations.

From such demeaned conditions, southern Italians set out for the New World. Almost all of them were young men who intended to spend only a few months in America, stuff their pockets with dollars, and return home. Almost half of Italian immigrants did indeed repatriate—as did comparable numbers of the other New Immigrants, with the conspicuous exception of the Jews, who had fled their native lands to escape religious persecution. Almost all Italian immigrants sailed through New York harbor, sighting the Statue of Liberty as they debarked from crowded ships. Many soon moved on to other large cities, but so many remained that, in the early years of the twentieth century, more Italians resided in New York than in Florence, Venice, and Genoa combined.

Although most Italian immigrants huddled in the cities, they did not abandon their rural upbringings entirely. Much to their neighbors' consternation, they often kept chickens and raised vegetables in small garden plots nestled between decaying tenement houses.

Those who bade a permanent farewell to Italy clustered in tightly knit communities that boasted opera clubs, Italian-language newspapers, and courts for playing bocci—a version of lawn bowling imported from the Old Country. Pizza emerged from the hot wood-burning ovens of these Little Italys, its aroma and flavor wafting into the hearts and stomachs of all Americans.

Italians typically earned their daily bread as industrial laborers—most famously as longshoremen and construction workers. They owed their prominence in the building trades to

Most of the struggling new immigrants at first found comfort in tightly bound neighborhoods where their homeland language and religion could be nurtured. There they worshipped in Orthodox or Roman Catholic churches or synagogues and in some cases nourished radical political ideas. There, too, they felt sheltered from Americans who revived old nativist fears that had hounded earlier immigrants in the 1840s and 1850s, fears that these New Immigrants would not—or could not—assimilate to life in their new land. The skeptics—who included some immigrants of the earlier wave—began asking if the nation had become a melting pot or a dumping ground.

Why were these bright-shawled and quaint-jacketed strangers hammering on the gates? In part they left their native countries because Europe seemed to have no room for them. Rapid population growth, American food imports, and European industrialization shook the peasantry loose from its ancient habitats and customary occupations, creating a vast, footloose army of the unemployed. Europeans by the millions drained out of the countryside and into European cities. Most stayed there, but some kept moving and left Europe altogether. About 60 million Europeans abandoned the Old Continent in the nineteenth and early twentieth centuries. More than half of them moved to the United States, while their compatriots spread out across the globe to South America, Canada, Africa, and Australia. Masses of people were already in motion in Europe before they felt the tug of the American magnet. This European diaspora, dominated by immigration to the United States, was, in many ways, simply a by-product of the urbanization of Europe.

Italian Immigrants Arriving at Ellis Island, c. 1910

Brown Brothers

the "padrone system." The *padrone*, or labor boss, met immigrants upon arrival and secured jobs for them in New York, Chicago, or wherever there was an immediate demand for industrial labor.

Lacking education, the Italians, as a group, remained in blue-collar jobs longer than some of their fellow New Immigrants. Many Italians, valuing vocation over schooling, sent their children off to work as early in their young lives as possible. Before World War I, less than 1 percent of Italian children were enrolled in high school. Over the next fifty years, Italian Americans and their offspring gradually prospered, moving out of the cities into the more affluent suburbs. Many served heroically in World War II and availed themselves of the GI Bill to finance the college educations and professional training their immigrant forebears had lacked.

"America fever" proved highly contagious in Europe. The United States was often painted as a land of fabulous opportunity in the "America letters" sent by friends and relatives already transplanted.

The land of the free was also blessed with freedom from military conscription and institutionalized religious persecution. Beginning in the 1880s, savage persecution of minorities in Europe, especially of Jews in Russia, drove tens of thousands of battered refugees to American shores. Virtually unique among the New Immigrants, Jews had experienced city life in Europe, and many of them brought their urban skills of tailoring and shopkeeping to American cities. Destitute and devout, eastern European Jews were frequently given a frosty reception not only by old-stock Americans but also by those German Jews who had arrived decades earlier and prospered in the United States, some of them as garment manufacturers who now condescendingly employed their coreligionists as cheap labor.

The new immigrants struggled heroically to preserve their traditional cultures. Catholics expanded their

✳ **PRIMARY SOURCE**
Because You're a Jew

Mary Antin (1881–1949), who came to America from Russian Poland in 1894 when thirteen years of age, later wrote in The Promised Land *(1912):*

"So at last I was going to America! Really, really going, at last! The boundaries burst. The arch of heaven soared. A million suns shone out for every star. The winds rushed in from outer space, roaring in my ears, 'America! America!'"

parochial *Concerning a religious parish or small district. (By extension, the term is used, often negatively, to refer to narrow or local perspectives as distinct from broad or cosmopolitan outlooks.)*

parochial school system, and Jews established Hebrew schools. Foreign-language newspapers abounded. Yiddish theaters, kosher food stores, Polish parishes, Greek restaurants, and Italian social clubs all attested to the desire to keep old ways alive. Yet time took its toll on these efforts to preserve Old World customs. The children of the immigrants grew up speaking fluent English, sometimes mocking the broken grammar of their parents. They often rejected the Old Country manners of their mothers and fathers in their desire to plunge headlong into the mainstream of American life.

Reactions to the New Immigration

America's government system, nurtured in wide-open spaces, was ill suited to the cement forests of the great cities. Beyond minimal checking to weed out criminals and the insane, the federal government did virtually nothing to ease the assimilation of immigrants into American society. State governments, usually dominated by rural representatives, did even less. City governments, overwhelmed by the sheer scale of rampant urban growth, proved woefully inadequate to the task. By default, the business of ministering to the immigrants' needs fell to the unofficial "governments" of the urban political machines, led by "bosses" such as New York's notorious Boss Tweed.

Taking care of the immigrants was big business, indeed. Trading jobs and services for votes, a powerful boss might claim the loyalty of thousands of followers. In return for their support at the polls, the boss provided jobs on the city's payroll, found housing for new arrivals, tided over the needy with gifts of food and clothing, patched up minor scrapes with the law, and helped get schools, parks, and hospitals built in immigrant neighborhoods. Reformers gagged at this cynical exploitation of the immigrant vote, but the political boss gave valuable assistance that was forthcoming from no other source.

The nation's social conscience gradually awakened to the plight of the cities and their immigrant masses. Prominent in this awakening were some Protestant clergymen such as Walter Rauschenbusch of New York City and Washington Gladden of Columbus, Ohio, who both sought to apply the lessons of Christianity to the slums and factories. Preaching the "social gospel," they insisted that churches tackle the burning social issues of the day.

One middle-class woman who was deeply dedicated to uplifting the urban masses was Jane Addams (1860–1935). Born into a prosperous Illinois family, Addams was one of the first generation of college-educated women and sought suitable outlets for her large talents. Inspired by a visit to England, in 1889 she established Hull House in Chicago as the most prominent American settlement house. Located in a poor immigrant neighborhood of Greeks, Italians, Russians, and Germans, Hull House offered instruction in English, counseling to help newcomers cope with American big-city life, child-care services for working mothers, and cultural activities for neighborhood residents.

Following Jane Addams's lead, women founded settlement houses in other cities as well—notably Lillian Wald's Henry Street Settlement in New York, which opened its doors in 1893. The settlement houses became centers of women's activism and of social reform on behalf of women, children, blacks, and consumers. The women of Hull House, for example, successfully lobbied in 1893 for an Illinois anti-**sweatshop** law that protected women workers and prohibited child labor. They were led by Florence Kelley, a guerrilla warrior in the urban jungle who battled for decades on behalf of the underprivileged at both Hull House and the Henry Street Settlement.

sweatshop *A factory where employees are forced to work long hours under difficult conditions for meager wages.*

The pioneering work of Addams, Wald, and Kelley vividly demonstrated the truth that the city was the frontier of opportunity for women, just as the wilderness had been for men. The urban frontier opened new possibilities for women. More than a million women joined the workforce in the single decade of the 1890s. Strict social codes prescribed which women might work and what jobs they might hold. Because employment for wives and mothers was considered taboo, the vast majority of working women were single. Their jobs depended on their race, ethnicity, and class. Black women had few opportunities beyond domestic service. White-collar jobs as social workers, secretaries, department store clerks, and telephone operators were largely reserved for native-born women. Immigrant women tended to cluster in particular industries, such as food processing or women's garment-making. Although hours were often long, pay low, and advancement limited, a job still bought working women some economic and social independence.

EXAMINING THE EVIDENCE

MANUSCRIPT CENSUS DATA, 1900

Article I of the Constitution requires that a census of the American people be taken every ten years, in order to provide a reliable basis for congressional apportionment. Early censuses gathered little more than basic population numbers, but over the years the census takers have collected information on other matters as well, including occupational categories, educational levels, and citizenship status, yielding copious raw data for historical analysis. The census of 1890 was the first to use punch cards and electric tabulating machines, which greatly expanded the range of data that could be assembled and correlated—though the basic information was still hand recorded by individual canvassers who went door to door to question household members and fill out the census forms. Those handwritten forms, as much as the aggregate numbers printed in the final census tally, can furnish invaluable insights to the historian. Despite its apparent bureaucratic formality, the form shown here richly details the lives of the residents of a tenement house on New York's Lower East Side in 1900. See in particular the entries for the Goldberg family.

1. In what ways does this document reflect the great demographic changes that swept late-nineteenth-century America?

2. What light does the document shed on the character of immigrant "ghettos"?

3. What is the most common occupation of those listed? What is second? What might you conclude about the economic status of these residents of Manhattan?

National Archives

Narrowing the Welcome Mat

Antiforeignism, or "nativism," earlier touched off by the Irish and German arrivals in the 1840s and 1850s, bared its ugly face in the 1880s with fresh ferocity. The New Immigrants had come for much the same reasons as the Old—to escape the poverty and squalor of Europe and to seek new opportunities in America. But "nativists" viewed the eastern and southern Europeans as culturally and religiously exotic hordes and often gave them a rude reception. The newest newcomers aroused widespread alarm. Their high birthrate, common among people with a low standard of living, raised worries that the original Anglo-Saxon stock would soon be outbred and outvoted. Still more horrifying was the prospect that it would be "mongrelized" by a mixture of "inferior" southern European blood and that the fairer Anglo-Saxon types would disappear. One New England writer cried out in anguish:

> O Liberty, white Goddess! is it well
> To leave the gates unguarded?

Native-born Americans voiced additional fears. They blamed the immigrants for the degradation of urban government. Some trade unionists assailed the alien arrivals for their willingness to work for "starvation" wages, which seemed to the immigrants like princely sums, and for importing in their intellectual baggage such seemingly dangerous doctrines as socialism, communism, and anarchism. Many business leaders who had welcomed the flood of cheap manual labor began to fear that they had embraced a Frankenstein's monster.

Antiforeign organizations, reminiscent of the "Know-Nothings" of antebellum days, were now revived in a different guise. Notorious among them was the American Protective Association (APA), which was created in 1887 and soon claimed a million members. In pursuing its nativist goals, the APA urged voting against Roman Catholic candidates for office and sponsored the publication of lustful fantasies about runaway nuns.

Organized labor was quick to throw its growing weight behind the move to choke off the rising tide of foreigners. Frequently used as strikebreakers, the wage-depressing immigrants were hard to unionize because of the language barrier. Labor leaders argued, not illogically, that if American industry was entitled to protection from foreign goods, the American worker was entitled to protection from foreign laborers.

pauper *A poor person, often one who lives on tax-supported charity.*

Congress finally nailed up partial bars against the inpouring immigrants. The first restrictive law, in 1882, banged the gate shut in the faces of **paupers**, criminals, and convicts, all of whom had to be returned at the expense of the greedy or careless shipper. Congress further responded to pained outcries from organized labor when in 1885 it prohibited the importation of foreign workers under contract—usually for substandard wages.

The year 1882, in addition to the first federal restrictions on immigration, brought forth a law to bar completely one ethnic group—the Chinese (see pp. 362–365). Hitherto, America, at least officially, had embraced the oppressed and underprivileged of all races and creeds. Hereafter, the gates would be padlocked against defective undesirables—plus the Chinese.

In later years, other federal laws lengthened the list of undesirables to include the insane, polygamists, prostitutes, alcoholics, anarchists, and people carrying contagious diseases. A proposed literacy test, long a favorite of nativists because it favored the Old Immigrants over the New, met vigorous opposition. The test was not enacted until 1917, after three presidents had vetoed it on the grounds that literacy was more a measure of opportunity than of intelligence.

Looking Backward Older immigrants, trying to keep their own humble arrival in America "in the shadows," sought to close the bridge that had carried them and their ancestors across the Atlantic. Print Collection, Miriam and Ira D. Wallach Division of Art, Prints and Photographs, The New York Public Library, Astor, Lenox and Tilden Foundations

In 1886, four years after the first immigration restrictions were passed, the Statue of Liberty arose in New York harbor, a gift from the people of France. On its base were inscribed the words of Emma Lazarus:

Give me your tired, your poor,
Your huddled masses yearning to breathe free,
The wretched refuse of your teeming shore.

To many nativists, those noble words described only too accurately the "scum" washed up by the New Immigrant tides. Yet the uprooted immigrants, unlike "natives" lucky enough to have had parents who caught an earlier ship, became American citizens the hard way. These new immigrants stepped off the boat ready to put their shoulders to the nation's industrial wheels. The Republic owes much to these latecomers—for their brawn, their brains, their courage, and the yeasty diversity they brought to American society.

═══ Churches Confront the Urban Challenge ═══

The swelling size and changing character of the urban population posed sharp challenges to American churches, which, like other national institutions, had grown up in the country. Protestant churches in particular suffered heavily from the shift to the city, where many of their traditional doctrines and pastoral approaches seemed irrelevant.

As they lost their bearings in the new urban world, some churches were tending to become merely sacred diversions or amusements. Reflecting the wealth of their prosperous parishioners, many of the old-line churches were distressingly slow to raise their voices against social and economic vices. John D. Rockefeller was a pillar of the Baptist Church; J. Pierpont Morgan, of the Episcopal Church. Cynics remarked that the Episcopal Church had become "the Republican party at prayer." The mounting emphasis was on materialism; too many devotees worshiped at the altar of avarice. Money was the accepted measure of achievement, and the new gospel of wealth proclaimed that God caused the righteous to prosper.

Into this spreading moral vacuum stepped a new generation of liberal Protestants. Though earlier embraced by a few dissenters from evangelical orthodoxy, liberal ideas came into the mainstream of American Protestantism between 1875 and 1925. Entrenched in the leadership and seminaries of the dominant denominations, liberal Protestants adapted religious ideas to modern culture, attempting to reconcile Christianity with new scientific and economic doctrines. They rejected biblical literalism, urging Christians to view biblical stories as models for Christian behavior rather than as dogma. They stressed the ethical teachings of the Bible and allied themselves with the reform-oriented "social gospel" movement. Friendly to urban revivalists such as Dwight Moody, a former shoe salesman who captivated audiences with his message of forgiveness, optimistic liberal Protestants sought to mediate between labor and capital, sciences and faith, religious and secular values. Despite frequent and bitter controversies with fundamentalists, liberal leaders' focus on fellowship and personal growth helped many Protestant Americans reconcile their religious faith with modern, cosmopolitan ways of thinking.

Simultaneously, the Roman Catholic and Jewish faiths were gaining enormous strength from the New Immigration. By 1900 Roman Catholics had become the largest single denomination, numbering nearly 9 million communicants. Cardinal James Gibbons (1834–1921) of Baltimore, an urban Catholic leader devoted to American unity, was immensely popular with Roman Catholics and Protestants alike. Acquainted with every president from Andrew Johnson to Warren Harding, he employed his liberal sympathies to assist the American labor movement.

By 1890 the variety-loving Americans could choose from 150 religious denominations, two of them brand new. One was the band-playing Salvation Army, whose soldiers without swords invaded America from England in 1879 and established a beachhead on the street corners. Appealing frankly to the down-and-outers, the boldly named Salvation Army did much practical good, especially with free soup.

The other important new faith was the Church of Christ, Scientist (Christian Science), founded by Mary Baker Eddy in 1879 after she had suffered much ill health.

Chicago History Museum

Morning Service at Moody's Church, 1908 Thousands of Chicagoans found the gospel and a helping hand at evangelist Dwight Lyman Moody's church. Although Moody himself died in 1899, his successors continued to attract throngs of worshipers to his church, which could hold up to ten thousand people.

Preaching that the true practice of Christianity heals sickness, she set forth her views in a book entitled *Science and Health with Key to the Scriptures* (1875), which sold an amazing 400,000 copies before her death. A fertile field for converts was found in America's hurried, nerve-wracked, and urbanized civilization. By the time Eddy died in 1910, she had founded an influential church that embraced several hundred thousand devoted worshipers.

The old-time religion received many blows from modern trends, including a boom sale of books on comparative religion and on historical criticism as applied to the Bible. Most unsettling of all were the writings of the English naturalist Charles Darwin. In the lucid prose of *On the Origin of Species* (1859), Darwin set forth the sensational theory that higher forms of life had slowly evolved from lower forms, through a process of random biological mutation and adaptation.

Darwin's idea of "natural selection" broke new ground. Nature, in his view, blindly selected organisms for survival or death based on random, inheritable variations that they happened to possess. Some traits conferred advantages in the struggle for life and hence better odds of passing them on to offspring. By providing a material explanation for the evolutionary process, Darwin's theory explicitly rejected the "dogma of special creation," which ascribed the design of each fixed species to divine agency.

Darwin's radical ideas evoked the wrath of scientists and laymen alike. Many zoologists, such as Harvard's Louis Agassiz, held fast to the old doctrine of "special creation." By 1875, however, the majority of scientists in America and elsewhere had embraced the theory of organic evolution, though not all endorsed natural selection as its agent.

Clergymen and theologians responded to Darwin's theory in several ways. At first most believers joined scientists in rejecting his ideas outright. After 1875, by which time most natural scientists had embraced evolution, the religious community split into two camps. A conservative minority condemned what they thought was the "bestial hypothesis" of Darwinism. Their rejection of scientific consensus spawned a muscular view of biblical authority that eventually gave rise to **fundamentalism** in the twentieth century.

Most religious thinkers parted company with conservatives and sought ways to reconcile Darwinism with Christianity. These "accommodationists" eventually heralded the

fundamentalism *A Protestant Christian movement emphasizing the literal truth of the Bible and opposing religious modernism, which sought to reconcile religion and science. This movement was especially strong in the Baptist Church and the Church of Christ, first organized in 1906.*

revolutionary theory as a newer and grander revelation of the Almighty. As one commentator observed:

> *Some call it Evolution,*
> *Others call it God.*

While the liberal efforts at compromise did succeed in keeping many Americans in the pews, these compromises also tended to relegate religious teaching to matters of personal faith, private conduct, and family life. As science began to explain more of the external world, commentators on nature and society increasingly refrained from adding religious perspectives to the discussion.

As a student at Harvard Medical School, William James (1842–1910) was influenced by Darwinian science. He reviewed Darwin's theory in his first published article in 1865:

"A doctrine like that of Transmutation of Species ... cannot but be treated with some respect; and when we find that such naturalists, ... many of whom but a few days ago were publicly opposing it, are now coming round, one by one, to espouse it, we may well doubt whether it may not be destined eventually to prevail."

The Lust for Learning

Public education continued its upward climb. The ideal of tax-supported elementary schools was still gathering strength. Beginning about 1870, more and more states were making at least a grade-school education compulsory, and this gain, incidentally, helped check the frightening abuses of child labor.

Spectacular indeed was the spread of the high schools, especially by the 1880s and 1890s. By 1900 some six thousand high schools were educating teenage boys and girls. In addition, the states provided free textbooks in increasing numbers during the last two decades of the century.

Other trends were noteworthy. Teacher-training schools, then called "normal schools," experienced a striking expansion after the Civil War. In 1860 only twelve normal schools were operating; in 1910, there were more than three hundred. Kindergartens, earlier borrowed from Germany, began to gain strong support. The New Immigration in the 1880s and 1890s brought vast new strength to the private Catholic parochial schools, which were fast becoming a major pillar of the nation's educational structure.

Public schools, though showering benefits on children, excluded millions of adults. This deficiency was partially remedied by the Chautauqua movement, launched in 1874 on the shores of Lake Chautauqua in New York. The organizers achieved gratifying success through nationwide public lectures, often held in tents and featuring such well-known speakers as the witty Mark Twain. In addition, Chautauqua offered extensive home-study courses, for which 100,000 people enrolled in 1892 alone.

Crowded cities, despite their cancers, generally provided better educational facilities than the old one-room, one-teacher red schoolhouse. The success of the public schools is confirmed by the falling of the illiteracy rate from 20 percent in 1870 to 10.7 percent in 1900. Americans were developing a profound faith, often misplaced, in formal education as the sovereign remedy for their ills.

Booker T. Washington and Education for Black People

War-torn and impoverished, the South lagged far behind other regions in public education, and African Americans suffered most severely. A staggering 44 percent of nonwhites were illiterate in 1900. Some help came from northern philanthropists, but the foremost champion of black education was an ex-slave, Booker T. Washington, who had slept under a board sidewalk to save pennies for his schooling. Called in 1881 to head the black normal and industrial school at Tuskegee, Alabama, he began with forty students in a tumbledown shanty. Undaunted, he taught black students useful trades so that they could gain self-respect and economic security. But Washington stopped short of advocating *social* equality with whites, acquiescing in segregation in return for the right to develop economic and educational resources of the black community.

❋ **PRIMARY SOURCE**
Booker T. Washington and Others

© Bettmann / Corbis

W. E. B. Du Bois At the end of a long lifetime of struggle for racial justice in the United States, Du Bois renounced his American citizenship in 1961, at the age of 93, and took up residence in the newly independent African state of Ghana.

W. E. B. Du Bois (1868–1963) wrote in his 1903 classic, The Souls of Black Folk:

"It is a peculiar sensation, this double consciousness, this sense of always looking at one's self through the eyes of others, of measuring one's self through the eyes of others. ... One ever feels his two-ness—an American, a Negro; two souls, two thoughts, two unreconciled strivings; two warring ideals in one dark body, whose dogged strength alone keeps it from being torn asunder."

Washington's commitment to training young blacks in agriculture and the trades guided the curriculum at Tuskegee Institute and made it an ideal place for slave-born George Washington Carver to teach and research. After Carver joined the faculty in 1896, he became an internationally famous agricultural chemist who helped the economy of the South by discovering hundreds of new uses for the lowly peanut (shampoo, axle grease), sweet potato (vinegar), and soybean (paints).

Other black leaders, notably Dr. W. E. B. Du Bois, assailed Booker T. Washington as an "Uncle Tom" who was condemning their race to manual labor and perpetual inferiority. Born in Massachusetts, Du Bois was a mixture of African, French, Dutch, and Indian blood ("Thank God, no Anglo-Saxon," he would add). After a determined struggle, he earned a Ph.D. at Harvard, the first of his race to achieve that goal. Du Bois demanded complete equality for blacks, social as well as economic, and helped to found the National Association for the Advancement of Colored People (NAACP) in 1910. Rejecting Washington's gradualism and separatism, he argued that the "talented tenth" of the black community should be given full and immediate access to the mainstream of American life. An exceptionally skilled historian, sociologist, and poet, Du Bois died as a self-exile in Africa in 1963, at the age of ninety-five.

The Hallowed Halls of Ivy

Colleges and universities also shot up like lusty young saplings in the decades after the Civil War. Even women and African Americans were finding new opportunities for higher education. The educational battle for women, only partially won before the war, turned into a rout of the masculine diehards. Women's colleges such as Vassar were gaining ground, and universities open to both genders were blossoming, notably in the Midwest. By 1900 every third college graduate was a woman. By the turn of the century the black institutes and academies planted during Reconstruction had blossomed into a crop of southern black colleges. Howard University in Washington, D.C., Hampton Institute in Virginia, Atlanta University, and numerous others nurtured higher education for blacks until the civil rights movement of the 1960s made widespread attendance at white institutions possible.

The truly phenomenal growth of higher education owed much to the Morrill Act of 1862. This enlightened law provided a generous grant of public lands to the states for support of public higher education. The Hatch Act of 1887 extended the Morrill Act by providing federal funds for the establishment of agricultural experiment stations. Together these two pieces of legislation spawned over a hundred "land-grant colleges" that evolved into state universities, including such institutions as the University of California (1868), Ohio State University (1870), and Texas A&M (1876).

Private philanthropy richly supplemented government grants to higher education. Many of the new industrial millionaires, developing tender social consciences, donated immense fortunes to educational enterprises. In the twenty years from 1878 to 1898 these money barons gave away about $150 million. Among the noteworthy new private universities were Cornell (1865) and Leland Stanford Junior (1891), the latter founded in memory of the deceased fifteen-year-old only child of a builder of the Central Pacific Railroad. The University of Chicago, opened in 1892, speedily forged into a front-rank position, owing largely to the lubricant of John D. Rockefeller's oil millions.

Towering among the new professionalized institutions of higher learning was Johns Hopkins University, opened in 1876, which developed the nation's first high-grade graduate school. Several generations of American scholars, repelled by snobbish English cousins and attracted by painstaking continental methods, had attended German universities. Reputable scholars no longer had to go abroad for a gilt-edged graduate degree; Dr. Woodrow Wilson, among others, received his Ph.D. from Johns Hopkins.

Homegrown influences shaped the modern American university as much as German models. Antebellum colleges had stressed the "unity of truth," or the idea that knowledge and morality existed in a single system united by theology and moral philosophy. After the Darwinian challenge made religion and science seem less compatible, university reformers struggled to preserve the unity of moral and intellectual purpose. When that effort failed, university educators abandoned moral instruction and divorced "facts" from "values."

Other pressures also helped doom the traditional curriculum. Industrialization and science brought insistent demands for "practical" courses, and specialization, not synthesis, became the primary goal of a university education. The turn toward electives and pre-professional training received a powerful boost in the 1870s when Dr. Charles W. Eliot became president of Harvard College. As a sign of the secularizing times, Eliot changed Harvard's motto from *Christo et Ecclesiae* (for Christ and Church) to *Veritas* (Truth).

One of America's most brilliant intellectuals, the slight and sickly William James (1842–1910) served for thirty-five years on the Harvard faculty. Through his numerous writings he made a deep mark on many fields. His *Principles of Psychology* (1890) helped to establish the modern discipline of psychology. In *The Will to Believe* (1897) and *Varieties of Religious Experience* (1902), James explored the philosophy and psychology of religion. In his most famous work, *Pragmatism* (1907), he declared that America's greatest contribution to the history of philosophy was the concept of pragmatism— that truth of an idea was to be tested, above all, by its practical consequences.

✳ **PRIMARY SOURCE**
Morrill Act

The Appeal of the Press

Books continued to be a major source of edification and enjoyment for both juveniles and adults. Public libraries—the poor person's university—made encouraging progress in the late nineteenth century, especially in Boston and New York. The magnificent Library of Congress building, which opened its doors in 1897, provided thirteen acres of floor space in the largest and costliest edifice of its kind in the world. A new era was inaugurated by the generous gifts of Andrew Carnegie, who contributed $60 million for the construction of public libraries all over the country. By 1900 there were about nine thousand free public libraries in America.

Roaring newspaper presses, spurred by the invention of the Linotype in 1885, more than kept pace with the demands of a word-hungry public. But the heavy investment in machinery and plant was accompanied by a growing fear of offending advertisers and subscribers. Bare-knuckle editorials were, to an increasing degree, being supplanted by feature articles and noncontroversial **syndicated** material. The day of slashing, journalistic giants such as Horace Greeley was passing.

Sensationalism, at the same time, was capturing the public taste. The semiliterate immigrants, combined with straphanging urban commuters, created a profitable market for news that was simply and punchily written. Stories of sex, scandal, and other human-interest stories burst into the headlines, as a vulgarization of the press accompanied the growth of circulation. Critics complained in vain about these "presstitutes."

syndicated *In journalism, material that is sold by an organization for publication in several newspapers.*

Educational Levels, 1870–2000

Year	Number Graduating from High School	Number Graduating from College	Median School Years Completed	High School Graduates as a Percentage of 17-Year-Old Population
1870	16,000	9,371		2.0%
1880	24,000	12,896		2.5
1890	44,000	15,539		3.5
1900	95,000	27,410		6.4
1910	156,000	37,199	8.1†	8.8
1920	311,000	48,622	8.2†	16.8
1930	667,000	122,484	8.4†	29.0
1940	1,221,000	186,500	8.6	50.8
1950	1,199,700	432,058	9.3	59.0
1960	1,858,000	392,440	10.5	69.5
1970	2,889,000	792,656	12.2	76.9
1980	3,043,000	929,417	12.5	71.4
1990	2,503,000	1,048,631	12.7	74.2
2001	2,545,000	1,823,036	N.A.	N.A.

*People twenty-five years and over.
†1910–1930 based on retrogressions of 1940 data; 1940 was the first year measured (Folger and Nam, *Education of the American Population,* a 1960 Census Monograph).

Sources: Digest of Education Statistics, 1992, a publication of the National Center for Education Statistics, and *Statistical Abstract of the United States,* relevant years.

tycoon *A wealthy businessperson, especially one who openly displays power and position.*

Two new journalistic **tycoons** emerged. Joseph Pulitzer, Hungarian born and near blind, was a leader in the techniques of sensationalism in St. Louis and in his *New York World.* His use of the colored comic supplements, featuring the "Yellow Kid," gave the name *yellow journalism* to his lurid sheets. A close and ruthless competitor was youthful William Randolph Hearst, who had been expelled from Harvard College for a crude prank. Able to draw on his California father's mining millions, Hearst built up a powerful chain of newspapers, beginning with the *San Francisco Examiner* in 1887. Unfortunately, Pulitzer and Hearst both prostituted the press in their struggle for increased circulation; they "stooped, snooped, and scooped to conquer." Their flair for scandal and sensation was happily somewhat offset by the strengthening of the news-gathering Associated Press, which had been founded in the 1840s.

Apostles of Reform

Magazines partly satisfied the public appetite for good reading, notably old standbys such as *Harper's,* the *Atlantic Monthly,* and *Scribner's Monthly.* Possibly the most influential journal was the liberal and highly intellectual *Nation,* whose modest circulation of ten thousand consisted largely of professors, preachers, and publicists. Launched in 1865 by the Irish-born critic Edwin L. Godkin, the *Nation* crusaded for civil-service reform, honesty in government, and a moderate tariff. Godkin believed that by reaching the nation's leaders his ideas might through the leaders reach millions.

Another journalist-author, Henry George, was an original thinker who left an enduring mark. Poor in formal schooling, he was rich in idealism and in the milk of human kindness. After seeing poverty at its worst in India and land grabbing at its greediest in California, George penned his classic treatise *Progress and Poverty* (1879), which undertook to solve "the great enigma of our times"—"the association of progress with poverty." According to

George, property owners unjustifiably profited from the pressure of growing population on a fixed supply of land. A single 100 percent tax on those windfall profits would eliminate unfair inequalities and stimulate economic growth.

George's controversial single-tax ideas so horrified the propertied classes that his manuscript was rejected by numerous publishers. Finally published in 1879, the book ultimately sold some 3 million copies. George also lectured widely in America, where he influenced thinking about the maldistribution of wealth, and in Britain, where he left an indelible mark on Fabian socialism. George's proposals resounded for decades. As late as 1903 a young female follower took out a patent on her invention of "The Landlord Game," which bore a striking resemblance to the Parker Brothers' later Monopoly, released in 1935, but in which the point was not to amass property but to expose the unfair advantage enjoyed by the landlord and "how the single tax would discourage speculation."

Edward Bellamy, a quiet Massachusetts Yankee, was another journalist-reformer of remarkable power. In 1888 he published a socialistic novel, *Looking Backward,* in which the hero, falling into a hypnotic sleep, awakens in the year 2000. The hero "looks backward" and finds that the social and economic injustices of 1887 have melted away under an idyllic government, which has nationalized big business to serve the public interest. To a nation already alarmed by the trust evil, the book had a magnetic appeal and sold over a million copies. Scores of Bellamy Clubs sprang up to discuss this mild utopian socialism, and they heavily influenced American reform movements near the end of the century.

Postwar Writing

As literacy increased, so did book reading. Post–Civil War Americans devoured millions of "dime novels," usually depicting the wild West. Paint-bedaubed Indians and quick-triggered gunmen such as "Deadwood Dick" shot off vast quantities of gunpowder, and virtue invariably triumphed. These lurid "paperbacks" were frowned on by parents, but goggle-eyed youths read them in haylofts or in schools behind the broad covers of geography books. The king of dime novelists was Harlan F. Halsey, who made a fortune by dashing off about 650 novels, often one in a day.

General Lewis Wallace—lawyer, soldier, and author—was a colorful figure. Having fought with distinction in the Civil War, he sought to combat the prevailing wave of Darwinian skepticism with his novel *Ben Hur: A Tale of the Christ* (1880). A phenomenal success, the book sold an estimated 2 million copies in many languages, including Arabic and Chinese, and later appeared on stage and screen. It was the *Uncle Tom's Cabin* of the anti-Darwinists, who found in it support for the Holy Scriptures.

An even more popular writer was Horatio ("Holy Horatio") Alger, a Puritan-reared New Englander, who in 1866 forsook the pulpit for the pen. He wrote more than a hundred volumes of juvenile fiction that sold over 100 million copies. His stock formula was that a poor boy, through a combination of virtue, honesty, hard work, and bravery, was rewarded with success, wealth, and honor—a kind of survival of the purest, especially nonsmokers, nondrinkers, nonswearers, and nonliars. Although accusations of sexual impropriety haunted Alger throughout his life, he implanted in his readers moral lessons and the conviction that there is always room at the top (especially if one is lucky enough to save the life of the boss's daughter and marry her).

In poetry Walt Whitman was one of the few luminaries of yesteryear who remained active. The assassination of Lincoln inspired him to write two of the most moving poems in American literature, "O Captain! My Captain!" and "When Lilacs Last in the Dooryard Bloom'd."

The curious figure of Emily Dickinson, one of America's most gifted lyric poets, did not emerge until 1886, when she died and her poems were discovered. A Massachusetts recluse, she wrote over a thousand short lyrics on odd scraps of paper. Only two were published during her lifetime, and those without her consent. As she wrote:

> *How dreary to be somebody!*
> *How public, like a frog*
> *To tell your name the livelong day*
> *To an admiring bog!*

Literary Landmarks

In novel writing, the romantic sentimentality of a youthful era was giving way to a rugged realism that reflected more faithfully the materialism of an industrial society. American authors now turned increasingly to the coarse human comedy and tragedy of the world around them to find their subjects.

Two Missouri-born authors with deep connections to the South brought altogether new voices to the late-nineteenth-century literary scene. The daring **feminist** author Kate Chopin (1851–1904) wrote candidly about adultery, suicide, and women's ambitions in *The Awakening* (1899). Largely ignored in her own day, Chopin was rediscovered by later readers who cited her work as suggestive of the feminist yearnings that stirred beneath the surface of "respectability" in the Gilded Age.

feminist (feminism) *One who promotes complete political, social, and economic equality of opportunity for women.*

Mustachioed Mark Twain (1835–1910) leapt to fame with his comic short story "The Celebrated Jumping Frog of Calaveras County" (1867) and *The Innocents Abroad* (1869). He teamed up with Charles Dudley Warner in 1873 to write *The Gilded Age*, an acid satire on post–Civil War politicians and speculators that gave a name to an era. With his scanty formal schooling in frontier Missouri, Twain typified a new breed of American authors in revolt against the elegant refinements of the old New England school of writing. Christened Samuel Langhorne Clemens, he had served for a time as a Mississippi riverboat pilot and later took his pen name, Mark Twain, from the boatman's cry that meant two fathoms. After a brief stint in the armed forces, Twain journeyed to California, a trip he described, with a mixture of truth and tall tales, in *Roughing It* (1872).

Many other books flowed from Twain's busy pen. *The Adventures of Tom Sawyer* (1876) preceded *The Adventures of Huckleberry Finn* (1884), an American masterpiece that defied Twain's own definition of a classic as "a book which people praise and don't read." His later years were soured by bankruptcy growing out of unwise investments, and he was forced to take to the lecture platform and amuse what he called "the damned human race." Twain made his most enduring contribution in recapturing frontier realism and humor in the authentic American dialect.

William Dean Howells (1837–1920), a printer's son from Ohio, could boast of little schoolhouse education, but his busy pen carried him high into the literary circles of the East. In 1871 he became the editor of the prestigious Boston-based *Atlantic Monthly*. Howells wrote about ordinary people and about contemporary and sometimes controversial social themes. *A Modern Instance* (1882) deals with the once-taboo subject of divorce. *The Rise of Silas Lapham* (1885) describes the trials of a newly rich paint manufacturer caught up in the caste system of Brahmin Boston. *A Hazard of New Fortunes* (1890) portrays reformers, strikers, and socialists in Gilded Age New York.

Stephen Crane (1871–1900), the fourteenth son of a Methodist minister, also wrote about the seamy underside of life in urban, industrial America. His *Maggie: A Girl of the Streets* (1893), a brutal tale about a poor prostitute driven to suicide, was too grim to find a publisher. Crane had to have it printed privately. He rose quickly to prominence with *The Red Badge of Courage* (1895), the stirring story of a bloodied young Civil War recruit under fire. Crane himself had never seen a battle and wrote entirely from the printed Civil War records. He died of tuberculosis in 1900, when only twenty-nine.

Not all authors came from humble stock. The gifted Henry Adams (1838–1918)—grandson and great-grandson of American presidents—turned unrivaled family connections into a prolific career as a historian, novelist, and critic. His nine-volume *History of the United States During the Administrations*

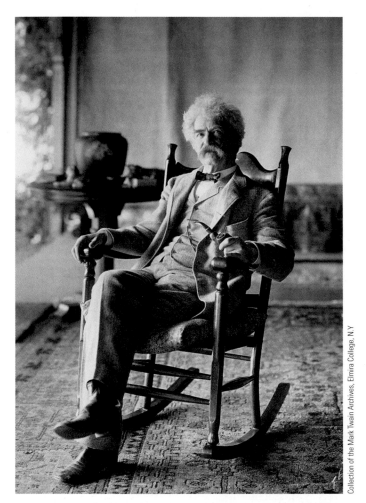

Collection of the Mark Twain Archives, Elmira College, N.Y

Mark Twain (1835–1910) Born Samuel Langhorne Clemens, he was not only America's most popular author but also a renowned platform lecturer. This photograph was taken at his house at Quarry Farm, near Elmira, New York, where he wrote major portions of both *The Adventures of Tom Sawyer* and *The Adventures of Huckleberry Finn*.

of Jefferson and Madison (1889–1891) made his mark as an historian. In *Mont-Saint Michel and Chartres* (1905), Adams penned a paean to the bygone beauty and unity of the High Middle Ages. His well-known autobiography, *The Education of Henry Adams* (1907), similarly reflects his anxieties about modernity and the chaotic forces of twentieth-century life.

Henry James (1843–1916), brother of Harvard philosopher William James, was a New Yorker who took as his dominant literary theme the confrontation of innocent Americans with subtle Europeans. James penned a remarkable number of brilliant novels, including *Daisy Miller* (1879), *The Portrait of a Lady* (1881), and *The Wings of the Dove* (1902). *The Bostonians* (1886) was one of the first novels about the rising feminist movement. James frequently made women his central characters, exploring their inner reactions to complex situations with a deftness that marked him as a master of "psychological realism." Long a resident in England, he became a British subject shortly before his death.

Candid portrayals of contemporary life and social problems were the literary order of the day by the turn of the century. Jack London (1876–1916) turned from his popular nature books such as *The Call of the Wild* (1903) to depicting a possible fascistic revolution in *The Iron Heel* (1907). Frank Norris (1870–1902), like London a Californian, wrote *The Octopus* (1901), an earthy saga of the stranglehold of the railroad and corrupt politicians on California wheat ranchers.

Two black writers, Paul Laurence Dunbar (1872–1906) and Charles W. Chesnutt (1858–1932), brought another kind of realism to late-nineteenth-century literature. In Dunbar's acclaimed book of poetry, *Lyrics of Lowly Life* (1896), he used black dialect and folklore to capture the spontaneity and richness of southern black culture. Chesnutt did the same through his short stories, collected in *Conjure Women* (1899).

Conspicuous among the new "social novelists" rising in the literary firmament was Theodore Dreiser (1871–1945), a homely, gangling writer from Indiana. He burst on the literary scene in 1900 with *Sister Carrie*, a graphically realistic narrative of a poor working girl in Chicago and New York. She becomes one man's mistress, then elopes with another, and finally strikes out on her own to make a career on the stage. The fictional Carrie's disregard for prevailing moral standards so offended Dreiser's publisher that the book was soon withdrawn from circulation, though it later reemerged as an acclaimed American classic.

The New Morality

Victoria Woodhull, who was real flesh and blood, also shook the pillars of conventional morality when she publicly proclaimed her belief in free love in 1871. Woodhull was a beautiful and eloquent divorcée, sometime stockbroker, and tireless feminist propagandist. Together with her sister Tennessee Claflin she published a far-out periodical, *Woodhull and Claflin's Weekly*. The sisters again shocked "respectable" society in 1872 when their journal struck a blow for the new morality by charging that Henry Ward Beecher, the most famous preacher of his day, had for years been carrying on an adulterous affair.

Pure-minded Americans sternly resisted these affronts to their moral principles. Their foremost champion was a portly crusader, Anthony Comstock, who made lifelong war on the "immoral." Armed after 1873 with a federal statute—the notorious Comstock Law—this self-appointed defender of sexual purity boasted that he had confiscated no fewer than 202,679 "obscene pictures and photos"; 4,185 "boxes of pills, powders, etc., used by abortionists"; and 26 "obscene pictures, framed on walls of saloons."

The antics of the Woodhull sisters and Anthony Comstock exposed to daylight the battle going on in late-nineteenth-century America over sexual attitudes and the place of women. Switchboards and typewriters in the booming cities became increasingly the tools of women's independence. Young working women headed to dance halls and nightclubs when the day was done, enjoying a new sense of freedom in the cities. This "new morality" began to be reflected in soaring divorce rates, the spreading practice of birth control, and increasingly frank discussion of sexual topics. By 1913, said one popular magazine, the chimes had struck "sex o'clock in America."

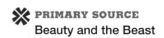

PRIMARY SOURCE
Beauty and the Beast

In 1906 progressive reformer Jane Addams (1860–1935) argued that granting women the vote would improve the social and political condition of American cities:

"City housekeeping has failed partly because women, the traditional housekeepers, have not been consulted as to its multiform activities. The men have been carelessly indifferent to much of the civic housekeeping, as they have been indifferent to the details of the household. ... City government demands the help of minds accustomed to detail and a variety of work, to a sense of obligation to the health and welfare of young children, and to a responsibility for the cleanliness and comfort of other people."

Families and Women in the City

The new urban environment was hard on families. Paradoxically, the crowded cities were emotionally isolating places. Urban families had to go it alone, separated from clan, kin, and village. Many families cracked under the strain of providing the virtually exclusive arena for intimate companionship and emotional satisfaction. The late-nineteenth-century urban era launched the "divorce revolution" that transformed the United States' social landscape in the twentieth century.

Urban life also dictated changes in work habits and even in family size. Not only fathers but mothers and even children as young as ten years old often worked, and usually in widely scattered locations. In the city more children meant more mouths to feed, more crowding in sardine-tin tenements, and more human baggage to carry in the uphill struggle for social mobility. Not surprisingly, birthrates were still dropping, and family size continued to shrink as the nineteenth century lengthened. Marriages were being delayed, and more couples learned the techniques of birth control.

Women were growing more independent in the urban environment, and in 1898 they heard the voice of a major feminist prophet, Charlotte Perkins Gilman. In that year the freethinking and original-minded Gilman published *Women and Economics*. In this classic of feminist literature, Gilman called on women to abandon their dependent status and contribute to the larger life of the community through productive involvement in the economy. Rejecting all claims that biology gave women a fundamentally different character from men, she argued that "our highly specialized motherhood is not so advantageous as believed." She advocated centralized nurseries and cooperative kitchens to facilitate women's participation in the workforce—anticipating by more than half a century the day-care centers and convenience-food services of a later day.

Fiery feminists also continued to insist on the ballot. They had been demanding the vote since before the Civil War, but many high-minded female reformers had temporarily shelved the cause of women to battle for the rights of blacks. In 1890 militant suffragists formed the National American Woman Suffrage Association. Its founders included aging pioneers such as Elizabeth Cady Stanton, who had helped organize the first women's rights convention in 1848, and her long-time comrade Susan B. Anthony, the radical Quaker who had courted jail by trying to cast a ballot in the 1872 presidential election.

By 1900 a new generation of women had taken command of the suffrage battle. Their most effective leader was Carrie Chapman Catt, a pragmatic and businesslike reformer of relentless dedication. Significantly, under Catt the suffragists de-emphasized the argument that women deserved the vote as a matter of right, because they were in all respects the equals of men. Instead Catt stressed the desirability of giving women the vote if they were to continue to discharge their traditional duties as homemakers and mothers in the increasingly public world of the city.

By thus linking the ballot to a traditional definition of women's role, suffragists registered encouraging gains as the new century opened, despite continuing showers of rotten eggs and the jeers of male critics. Women were increasingly permitted to vote in local elections. Wyoming Territory—later called "the Equality State"—granted the first unrestricted suffrage to women in 1869. This important breach in the dike once made, many states followed Wyoming's example. Paralleling these triumphs, most of the states by 1890 had passed laws to permit wives to own or control their property after marriage.

The reborn suffrage movement and other women's organizations excluded black women from their ranks. Fearful that an integrated campaign would handicap its efforts to get the vote, the National American Woman Suffrage Association limited membership to whites. Black women, however, created their own associations. Journalist and teacher

Ida B. Wells inspired black women to mount a nationwide antilynching crusade. She also helped launch the black women's club movement, which culminated in the establishment of the National Association of Colored Women in 1896.

Women also took a lead in the growing crusade against alcohol and the saloon. In 1874 the Women's Christian Temperance Union (WCTU) was organized with the white ribbon as its symbol of purity. The saintly Frances E. Willard—also a champion of planned parenthood—was its leading spirit. Less saintly was the mentally deranged "Kansas Cyclone," Carrie A. Nation, who smashed saloon bottles and bars with her hatchet. Female prohibitionists, singing "The Lips That Touch Liquor Must Never Touch Mine," began sweeping new states into the "dry column"—setting the stage for the great, but temporary, triumph of 1919 when the national prohibition amendment (Eighteenth) was attached to the Constitution.

Artistic Triumphs

John Adams had anticipated that his generation's preoccupation with nation building would allow art to flourish in the future, but the results long proved unspectacular. Portrait painting continued to appeal, as it had since the colonial era, but many of America's finest painters made their livings abroad. James Whistler (1834–1903) did much of his work, including the celebrated portrait of his mother, in England. This eccentric and quarrelsome Massachusetts Yankee had earlier been dropped from West Point after failing chemistry. "Had silicon been a gas," he later jested, "I would have been a major general." Another American painter resident in England, John Singer Sargent (1856–1925), painted highly prized portraits of the British nobility. Mary Cassatt, an American exile in Paris, painted sensitive portrayals of women and children that earned her a place in the pantheon of the French Impressionist painters, whose work revolutionized the European art world after their 1874 debut.

Other brush wielders, no less talented, brightened the artistic horizon. Self-taught George Inness (1825–1894) became America's leading landscapist. Thomas Eakins (1844–1916) attained a high degree of realism in his paintings, a quality not appreciated by portrait sitters who wanted their moles overlooked. Boston-born Winslow Homer (1836–1910), who as a youth had secretly drawn sketches in school, was perhaps the greatest painter of the group. Earthily American and largely resistant to foreign influences, Homer revealed rugged realism and boldness of conception. His canvases of the sea and of fisherfolk were masterly, and probably no American artist has excelled him in portraying the awesome power of the ocean.

Probably the most gifted sculptor yet produced by America was Augustus Saint-Gaudens (1848–1907). Born in Ireland of an Irish mother and a French father, he became an adopted American. Among his most moving works is the Robert Gould Shaw memorial, erected in Boston in 1897. It depicts Colonel Shaw, a young white "Boston Brahmin" officer, leading his black troops into battle in the Civil War.

Music, too, was gaining popularity. America of the 1880s and 1890s was assembling high-quality symphony orchestras, notably in Boston and Chicago. The famed Metropolitan Opera House of New York was erected in 1883. In its fabled "Diamond Horseshoe" the newly rich, often under the pretense of enjoying the imported singers, would flaunt their jewels, gowns, and furs. While symphonies and operas were devoted to bringing European music to elite American audiences, new strains of homegrown American music were sprouting in the South. Black folk traditions such as spirituals and "ragged music" were evolving into the blues, ragtime, and jazz that would transform American popular music in the twentieth century.

A marvelous discovery was the reproduction of music by mechanical means. The phonograph, though a squeakily imperfect instrument when invented by the deaf Edison, had by 1900 reached over 150,000 homes. Americans were rapidly being dosed with "canned music," as the "sitting room" piano increasingly gathered dust.

A new generation of architects and planners looked to Europe to reshape American urban space with the "City Beautiful" movement. They wanted the new American city not just to look beautiful but to convey a confident sense of harmony, order, and monumentality. To achieve these effects they copied European styles of Beaux-Arts classicism and planning ideas from the master builder of Paris, Baron Georges-Eugène Haussmann, who in the 1860s had recast the City of Light with grand boulevards, parks, and public buildings. Aiming to assert America's prominence among the greatest urban cultures of the Western world, architects constructed grandiose urban landmarks such as New York's Grand Central Terminal. City planners such as Daniel Burnham redesigned Chicago and Washington, D.C., in the belief they could make them perfect, progressive cities, inspiring civic virtue in their inhabitants.

Burnham's first major project, one that came to symbolize the City Beautiful movement, was his design for the great World's Columbian Exposition. Held in Chicago in 1893, the exposition, with Burnham's imposing landscape of pavilions and fountains, honored the four-hundredth anniversary of Columbus's first voyage. This so-called dream of loveliness, which was visited by 27 million people, did much to raise American artistic standards and promote city planning, although many fair goers proved more interested in the contortions of a hootchy-kootchy dancer, "Little Egypt."

The Business of Amusement

Fun and frolic were not neglected by the workaday American. The legitimate stage still flourished, as appreciative audiences responded to the lure of the footlights. Vaudeville, with its coarse jokes and graceful acrobats, continued to be immensely popular during the 1880s and 1890s, as were minstrel shows in the South, now performed by black singers and dancers rather than by whites wearing blackface.

The circus—high tented and multiringed—finally emerged full blown. Phineas T. Barnum, the master showman who had early discovered that "the public likes to be humbugged," joined hands with James A. Bailey in 1881 to stage the "Greatest Show on Earth."

Colorful "Wild West" shows, first performed in 1883, were even more distinctively American. Headed by the knightly, goateed, and free-drinking William F. ("Buffalo Bill") Cody, the troupe included war-whooping Indians, live buffalo, and deadeye sharpshooters such as the girlish Annie Oakley. Rifle in hand, at thirty paces she could perforate a tossed-up card half a dozen times before it fluttered to the ground.

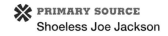
PRIMARY SOURCE
Shoeless Joe Jackson

Baseball, already widely played before the Civil War, was clearly emerging as the national pastime, if not a national mania. A league of professional players was formed in the 1870s, and in 1888 an all-star baseball team toured the world, using the pyramids as a backstop while in Egypt. Basketball was invented in 1891 by James Naismith, a YMCA instructor in Springfield, Massachusetts. Designed as an active, indoor sport that could be played during the winter months, basketball spread rapidly and enjoyed enormous popularity in the next century.

PRIMARY SOURCE
Women Playing Basketball

The trend toward spectator sports was exemplified by football, a rugged game that at first used the dangerous flying-wedge formation. The Yale–Princeton game of 1893 drew fifty thousand cheering fans, while foreigners jeered that the nation was getting "sports on the brain."

Even pugilism, with its long background of bare-knuckle brutality, gained a new gloved respectability in 1892. Agile "Gentleman Jim" Corbett wrested the world championship from the aging and alcoholic John L. Sullivan, the "Boston Strong Boy."

Two crazes swept the country in the closing decades of the century. Croquet became enormously popular, though condemned by moralists of the "naughty nineties" because it exposed feminine ankles and promoted flirtation. Cycling flourished when the low-framed "safety" bicycle replaced the high-seated model. By 1893 a million bicycles were in use, and thousands of young women especially turned to this new "spinning wheel" that offered freedom, not tedium.

The land of the skyscraper was plainly becoming more standardized, owing largely to the new industrialization. Despite their distinct ethnic and racial neighborhoods, Americans increasingly shared a common culture—playing, reading, shopping, and talking alike. As the century drew to a close, the explosion of cities paradoxically made Americans more diverse and more similar at the same time.

Buffalo Bill Historical Center, Cody, Wyoming; Gift of The Coe Foundation, 1.69.74

Buffalo Bill's Wild West Show, c. 1907 By the late 1800s, the "wild" West was already passing into the realm of myth—and popular entertainment. Famed frontiersman William F. ("Buffalo Bill") Cody made his fortune showing off his tame cowboys and Indians to urban audiences.

Chapter Summary

The United States moved from the country to the city in the post–Civil War decades. Mushrooming urban development was attractive and exciting for many who migrated from farms and small towns, but urban development also created severe social problems, including overcrowding and slums.

After the 1880s the cities were also flooded with the "New Immigrants" from southern and eastern Europe. With their culturally different customs and non-Protestant religions, the newcomers often met with nativist hostility and discrimination. Congress began to throw up barriers to immigration, including a complete ban on the Chinese.

Religion had to adjust to social, cultural, and intellectual changes. The immigrant faiths of Roman Catholicism and Judaism gained considerable strength, while conflicts over evolution and biblical interpretation divided American Protestantism into fundamentalist and modernist wings.

American education expanded rapidly, especially at the secondary and collegiate levels; major new research universities were founded, often by wealthy industrialists. Women's opportunities for education advanced in both separate institutions and coeducation. Black leaders Washington and Du Bois divided over the question of manual education versus development of an elite "talented tenth."

Significant conflicts over moral values, especially relating to sexuality and the role of women, began to appear. The new urban environment provided expanded opportunities for women but also created difficulties for the family. Families grew more isolated from society, the divorce rate rose, and average family size shrank.

American literature and art reflected a new social realism, often addressing the social and moral problems of the new urban, industrial age. American culture became more sophisticated and respected. Leisure-time amusements and sports became enormously popular but also more standardized, in keeping with the new industrial nation.

KEY TERMS

megalopolis (394)

tenement (395)

affluence (395)

parochial (398)

sweatshop (398)

pauper (400)

fundamentalism (402)

syndicated (405)

tycoon (406)

feminist (feminism) (408)

PEOPLE TO KNOW

Jane Addams

Charles Darwin

Mark Twain

Booker T. Washington

W. E. B. Du Bois

Joseph Pulitzer

William Randolph Hearst

Carrie Chapman Catt

 CourseMate

Go to the History CourseMate website for primary source links, study tools, and review materials. www.cengagebrain.com

26

The Great West and the Agricultural Revolution

1865–1896

*Up to our own day American history has been in a
large degree the history of the colonization of the
Great West. The existence of an area of free land, its
continuous recession, and the advance of American
settlement westward, explain American development.*

FREDERICK JACKSON TURNER, 1893

*The White Man, who possesses this whole vast country
from sea to sea, ... cannot know the cramp we feel
in this little spot, with the undying remembrance of
the fact ... that every foot of what you proudly call
America, not very long ago belonged to the red man.*

WASHAKIE (SHOSHONE INDIAN), 1878

When the Civil War crashed to a close, the frontier line was still wavering westward. A long fringe of settlement, bulging outward here and there, ran roughly north through central Texas and on to the Canadian border. Between this jagged line and the settled areas on the Pacific slope, there were virtually no white people. The few exceptions were the islands of Mormons in Utah, occasional trading posts and gold camps, and several scattered Mexican settlements throughout the Southwest.

Sprawling in expanse, the Great West was a rough square that measured about a thousand miles on each side. Embracing mountains, plateaus, deserts, and plains, it was the habitat of the Indian, the buffalo, the wild horse, and the coyote. Twenty-five years later—that is, by 1890—the entire domain had been carved into states and the four territories of Utah, Arizona, New Mexico, and "Indian Territory," or Oklahoma. Pioneers flung themselves greedily on this enormous prize, as if to ravish it. Probably never before in human experience had so huge an area been transformed so rapidly.

FOCUS QUESTIONS

1. Why did the western Indians clash with the expanding United States? What were the causes and consequences of their defeat?

2. What were the principal stages of frontier settlement in the West, and how did each affect the region's development?

3. What was the significance of the closing of the frontier in 1890 for American history? Why did the West remain such a distinctive American region?

4. How did the agricultural revolution transform Great Plains farming? What were the consequences for farmers?

5. What were the causes of western and southern farmers' protests? How were their grievances expressed in the Populist Party?

CHRONOLOGY

c. 1700–1800	New Indian peoples move onto Great Plains.
1858	Pike's Peak gold rush.
1859	Nevada Comstock lode discovered.
1862	Homestead Act.
1864	Sand Creek massacre. Nevada admitted to Union.
1867	National Grange organized.
1876	Battle of the Little Bighorn. Colorado admitted to Union.
1877	Nez Percé War.
1881	Helen Hunt Jackson publishes *A Century of Dishonor*.
1884	Federal government outlaws Indian Sun Dance.
1885	Canadian Pacific Railway, first transcontinental rail line, completed across Canada.
1885–1890	Local chapters of Farmers' Alliances formed.
1887	Dawes Severalty Act.
1889	Oklahoma opened to U.S. citizen settlement.
1889–1890	North Dakota, South Dakota, Montana, Washington, Idaho, and Wyoming admitted to Union.
1890	Census Bureau declares frontier line ended. Emergence of People's party (Populists).
1891	Battle of Wounded Knee. Construction of Trans-Siberian Railroad begins.
1892	Populist party candidate James B. Weaver polls more than 1 million votes in presidential election.
1893	Frederick Jackson Turner publishes "The Significance of the Frontier in American History."
1894	"Coxey's Army" marches on Washington. Pullman strike.
1896	McKinley defeats Bryan for presidency. Utah admitted to Union.
1897	Dingley Tariff Act.
1900	Gold Standard Act.
1907	Oklahoma admitted to Union.
1924	Indians granted U.S. citizenship.
1934	Indian Reorganization Act.

The Clash of Cultures in the West

Native Americans numbered about 360,000 in 1860, many of them scattered across the vast grasslands of the trans-Missouri West. But to their misfortune, the Indians stood in the path of the advancing white pioneers. An inevitable clash loomed between an acquisitive, industrializing nation and the Indians' lifeways, highly evolved over centuries to adapt to the demanding environment of the sparsely watered western plains.

Migration and conflict—and sometimes dramatic cultural change—were no strangers to the arid West, even before the whites began to arrive. The Comanches had driven the Apaches off the central plains into the upper Rio Grande valley in the eighteenth century. Harried by the Mandans and Chippewas, the Cheyenne had abandoned their villages along the upper reaches of the Mississippi and Missouri Rivers in the century before the Civil War. The Sioux, displaced from the Great Lakes woodlands in the late eighteenth century, emerged onto the plains to prey upon the Crows, Kiowas, and Pawnees. Mounted on Spanish-introduced horses, peoples such as the Cheyenne and the Sioux transformed themselves into wide-ranging **nomadic** traders and deadly efficient buffalo hunters.

When white soldiers and settlers edged onto the plains just before the Civil War, they accelerated a fateful cycle that exacerbated already fierce enmities among the Indians and ultimately undermined the foundations of Native American culture. White intruders

nomadic (nomad) *A way of life characterized by frequent movement from place to place for economic sustenance.*

unwittingly spread cholera, typhoid, and smallpox among the native peoples of the plains, with devastating results. Equally harmful, whites put further pressure on the shrinking bison population by hunting and by grazing their own livestock on the prairie grasses. As the once-mammoth buffalo herds dwindled, warfare intensified among the Plains tribes for ever-scarcer hunting grounds.

The federal government tried to sign treaties with various "chiefs" at Fort Laramie in 1851. But the white treaty makers misunderstood both Indian government and Indian society. "Tribes" and "chiefs" were often fictions of the white imagination, which could not grasp the fact that many Native Americans, living in scattered bands, recognized only the authority of their immediate families or perhaps a band elder. And the nomadic culture of the Plains Indians was utterly alien to the concept of living out one's life in the confinement of a defined territory.

In the 1860s the federal government tried to herd the Plains Indians into confines such as the "Great Sioux Reservation" in the Dakotas and the Indian Territory of present-day Oklahoma, where dozens of southern Plains tribes were forced to move. Promises from Washington that they would be left alone and provided with food, clothing, and other supplies were often violated by corrupt federal agents who regularly cheated the Indians.

For more than a decade after the Civil War, fierce warfare between Indians and the U.S. Army raged in various parts of the West. Army troops, many of them recent immigrants, met formidable adversaries in the Plains Indians, whose superb horsemanship gave them baffling mobility. Fully one-fifth of all U.S. Army personnel on the frontier were African American—dubbed "Buffalo Soldiers" by the Indians, supposedly because of the resemblance of their hair to the bison's furry coat.

The Buffalo Hunt, by Frederic Remington, 1890 A New Yorker who first went west at the age of nineteen as a cowboy and ranch cook, Remington (1861–1909) became the foremost artist of the vanishing way of life of the old Far West. Once a common sight on the high plains, the kind of buffalo kill that Remington records here was a great rarity by the time he painted this scene in 1890. The once-vast herds of bison had long since been reduced to a pitiful few by the white man's rifles and the increasingly concentrated use of the land by ever more constricted Indians.

immunity *Freedom or exemption from some imposition.*

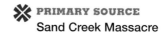
PRIMARY SOURCE
Sand Creek Massacre

reservation *Public lands designated for use by Indians.*

Receding Native Population

The Indian wars in the West were often savage clashes. Aggressive whites sometimes shot peaceful Indians on sight. At Sand Creek, Colorado, in 1864, Colonel J. M. Chivington's militia massacred in cold blood some four hundred Indians who apparently thought they had been promised **immunity**. Women were shot praying for mercy, children had their brains dashed out, and braves were tortured, scalped, and unspeakably mutilated.

Cruelty begot cruelty. In 1866 a Sioux war party ambushed Captain William Fetterman's command of eighty-one soldiers and civilians in Wyoming's Bighorn Mountains, killing every man and mutilating the corpses. As the cycle of ferocious warfare intensified, the federal government in 1868 abandoned its attempt to construct the Bozeman Trail through Montana. The sprawling "Great Sioux **Reservation**" was guaranteed to the Sioux tribes.

One disheartened Indian complained to the white Sioux Commission created by Congress:

"Tell your people that since the Great Father promised that we should never be removed we have been moved five times. ... I think you had better put the Indians on wheels and you can run them about wherever you wish."

But in 1874 a new round of warfare with the Plains Indians began when Colonel George Armstrong Custer, a famed Civil War officer, led a "scientific" expedition into the Black Hills of South Dakota and announced that he had discovered gold there. Hordes of greedy gold-seekers swarmed into the Sioux lands. The aggrieved Sioux, aided by the Cheyenne and Arapaho, took to the warpath, inspirited by the influential and wily Sitting Bull.

Colonel Custer's Seventh Cavalry set out to suppress the Indians and force them onto the reservation. Attacking what turned out to be a superior force of some 2,500 well-armed warriors camped along the Little Bighorn River in present-day Montana, the "White Chief with Yellow Hair" and about 250 officers and men were completely wiped out in 1876 when two supporting columns failed to come to their rescue.* But in a series of battles across the northern plains in the ensuing months, the U.S. Army relentlessly hunted down the Indians who had destroyed Custer's troops.

The Nez Percé Indians of northeastern Oregon were goaded into a daring fight in 1877, when U.S. authorities tried to herd them onto a reservation. Chief Joseph finally

---

* When whites annihilated Indians, the engagement (in white history books) was usually a "battle"; when Indians slaughtered whites, it was a "massacre." "Strategy," when practiced by Indians, was "treachery."

Indian Wars, 1860–1890 Surrendering in 1877, Chief Joseph of the Nez Percés declared: "Our chiefs are killed. … The old men are all dead. … The little children are freezing to death. … I want to have time to look for my children. … Hear me, my chiefs. My heart is sick and sad. From where the sun now stands I will fight no more forever."
© Cengage Learning

surrendered his band after a tortuous, seventeen-hundred-mile, three-month trek across the Continental Divide toward Canada. There Chief Joseph hoped to rendezvous with Sitting Bull, who had taken refuge north of the border after the Battle of Little Bighorn. Betrayed into believing that they would be returned to their ancestral lands in Idaho, the Nez Percés instead were sent to a dusty reservation in Kansas, where 40 percent of them perished from disease. The survivors eventually returned to Idaho.

Fierce Apache tribes of Arizona and New Mexico were the most difficult to subdue. Led by Geronimo, whose eyes blazed hatred of the whites, they were pursued into Mexico by federal troops. Scattered remnants of the warriors were finally persuaded to surrender after the Apache women had been exiled to Florida.

This relentless fire-and-sword policy of the whites at last shattered the spirit of the Indians. The vanquished Native Americans were finally ghettoized on reservations, where they were compelled to eke out an existence as **wards** of the government.

The "taming" of the Indians was engineered by a number of factors. Of cardinal importance was the federal government's willingness to back its land claims with military force. Almost as critical was the railroad, which shot an iron arrow through the heart of the West. The Indians were also ravaged by the white people's diseases, to which they showed little resistance, and by their firewater, which they could resist even less.

Above all, the virtual extermination of the buffalo doomed the Plains Indians' nomadic way of life. When the white Americans ventured onto the Great Plains after the Civil War, some 15 million buffalo, or American bison, still blackened the prairies. In 1868 a Kansas Pacific locomotive had to wait eight hours for a herd to amble across the tracks. These huge, shaggy, lumbering beasts were the staff of life for the Native Americans (see "Makers of America: The Plains Indians," p. 420). Their flesh provided food; their dried dung provided fuel ("buffalo chips"); their hides provided clothing, lariats, and harnesses.

With the building of the railroad, the massacre of the herds began in deadly earnest. The creatures were slain for their hides, for a few choice cuts of meat, or for sheer amusement. The telescope-eyed crack shot William "Buffalo Bill" Cody killed over four thousand buffalo in eighteen months while employed by the Kansas Pacific. "Sportsmen" on lurching railroad trains would lean out the windows and blaze away at the animals to satisfy their lust for slaughter or excitement. Such wholesale butchery left fewer than a thousand buffalo alive by 1885, and the once-numerous beasts were in danger of complete extinction. The whole story is a shocking example of the greed and waste that accompanied the conquest of a continent.

ward *Someone considered incompetent to manage his or her own affairs and therefore placed under the legal guardianship of another person or group.*

The End of the Trail

By the 1880s the national conscience began to stir uneasily over the plight of the Indians. Helen Hunt Jackson, a Massachusetts writer of children's literature, pricked the moral sense of Americans in 1881 when she published *A Century of Dishonor*. The book chronicled the sorry record of governmental ruthlessness and chicanery in dealing with the Indians. Her later novel *Ramona* (1884), a story of injustice to the California Indians, sold some 600,000 copies and further inspired sympathy for the Indians.

Debate seesawed. Humanitarians wanted to treat the Indians kindly and persuade them thereby to "walk the white man's road." Yet hard-liners insisted on the current policy of forced containment and brutal punishment. Neither side showed much respect for Native American culture. Christian reformers, who often administered educational facilities on the reservations, sometimes withheld food to force the Indians to give up their tribal religion and assimilate to white society. In 1884 these zealous white souls joined with military men in successfully persuading the federal government to outlaw the sacred Sun Dance. When the "Ghost Dance" cult later spread to the Dakota Sioux, the army bloodily stamped it out in 1890 at the so-called Battle of Wounded Knee. In the fighting thus provoked, an estimated two hundred Indian men, women, and children were killed, as well as twenty-nine soldiers.

in hand, were replaced by impersonal corporations with their costly machinery and trained engineers.

Yet the mining frontier had played a vital role in conquering the continent. Magnet-like, it attracted population and wealth while advertising the wonders of the Wild West. Women as well as men found opportunity, running boardinghouses or working as prostitutes. They earned a kind of equality on the rough frontier that earned them the vote in Wyoming (1869), Utah (1870), Colorado (1893), and Idaho (1896) long before their sisters in the East could cast a ballot. The amassing of precious metals helped finance the Civil War, facilitated the building of railroads, and injected the silver issue into American politics. Finally, the mining frontier added to American **folklore** and literature, as the writings of Mark Twain so colorfully attest.

Montana Historical Society, Helena

Dance-Hall Girl, Virginia City, Nevada, c. 1890 Women as well as men sought their fortunes in the frontier West—especially in wide-open mining towns such as Virginia City.

folklore *The common traditions and stories of a people.*

Beef Bonanzas and the Long Drive

When the Civil War ended, the grassy plains of Texas supported several million tough, longhorn cattle. These scrawny beasts were killed primarily for their hides. There was no way to get their meat profitably to market.

The problem of marketing was neatly solved when the transcontinental railroads thrust their iron fingers into the West. Cattle could now be shipped alive to the stockyards, and "beef barons" such as the Swifts and Armours turned the highly industrialized meatpacking business into a main pillar of the economy. Drawing on the gigantic stockyards at Kansas City and Chicago, the packers could ship their fresh products to the East Coast in the newly perfected refrigerator cars.

A spectacular feeder of the new slaughterhouses was the "Long Drive." Texas cowboys—black, white, and Mexican—drove herds numbering from one thousand to ten thousand head slowly over the unfenced and unpeopled plains until they reached a railroad terminal. The bawling beasts grazed en route on the free government grass. Favorite terminal points were fly-specked "cow towns" such as Dodge City and Abilene (Kansas), Ogallala (Nebraska), and Cheyenne (Wyoming). From 1866 to 1888, bellowing herds totaling over 4 million steers were driven northward from the beef bowl of Texas.

What the Lord giveth, the Lord also can take away. The railroad made the Long Drive; and the railroad unmade the Long Drive, primarily because the locomotives ran both ways. The same rails that bore the cattle from the open range to the kitchen range brought out the sheepherder and the homesteader. Both of these intruders, sometimes amid flying bullets, built barbed-wire fences that were too numerous to be cut down by the cowboys. Furthermore, the terrible winter of 1886–1887, with blinding blizzards and temperatures reaching 68° below zero, left thousands of dazed cattle starving and freezing. The only escape for the stockman was to make cattle raising a big business and avoid the perils of overproduction. Breeders learned to fence their ranches, lay in winter feed, import blooded bulls, and produce fewer and meatier animals. They also learned to organize. The Wyoming Stock Growers Association, especially in the 1880s, virtually controlled the territory and its legislature.

This was the heyday of the cowboy. The equipment of the lone cowhand—from "shooting irons" and ten-gallon hat to chaps and high-heeled boots—served a useful, not an ornamental, function. A "genuwine" gun-toting cowpuncher, riding where men were men and smelled like horses, could justifiably boast of his toughness.

These bowlegged Knights of the Saddle, with colorful trappings and cattle-lulling songs, became part of American folklore. Many of them, perhaps five thousand, were blacks, who especially enjoyed the newfound freedom of the open range.

Solomon Butcher Collection, Nebraska State Historical Society Photograph Collections

Nebraska Homesteaders in Front of Their Sod House, 1887 These two brothers and their families had escaped to Canada from the slave South during the Civil War. Returning to the United States in the 1880s, they took advantage of the Homestead Act to stake out farms in Custer County, Nebraska.

The Farmers' Frontier

Miners and cattlemen created the romantic legend of the West, but it was the sober sod-buster who wrote the final chapter of frontier history. A fresh day dawned for western farmers with the Homestead Act of 1862. The new law allowed a settler to acquire as much as 160 acres of land (a quarter section) by living on it for five years, improving it, and paying a nominal fee of about $30.

The Homestead Act marked a drastic departure from previous policy. Before the act, public land had been sold primarily for revenue; now it was to be given away to encourage a rapid filling of empty spaces and to provide a stimulus to the family farm—"the backbone of democracy." During the forty years after its passage, about half a million families took advantage of the Homestead Act to carve out new homes in the vast open stretches. Yet five times that many families *purchased* their land from the railroads, land companies, or the states.

The Homestead Act often turned out to be a cruel hoax. The standard 160 acres, quite adequate in the well-watered Mississippi basin, frequently proved pitifully inadequate on the rain-scarce Great Plains. Thousands of homesteaders, perhaps two out of three, were forced to give up the one-sided struggle against drought.

Naked fraud was spawned by the Homestead Act and similar laws. Perhaps ten times more of the public domain wound up in the clutches of land-grabbing promoters than in the hands of bona fide farmers. Unscrupulous corporations would use "dummy" homesteaders—often their employees or immigrants

In making the arduous journey across the western prairies, many women settlers discovered new confidence in their abilities. Early on in her trek, Mary Richardson Walker (1811–1897) confided in her diary that:

"my circumstances are rather trying. So much danger attends me on every hand. A long journey before me, going I know not whither, without mother or sister to attend me, can I expect to survive it all?"

Only a month later, she recorded that:

"in the afternoon we rode thirty-five miles without stopping. Pretty well tired out, all of us. Stood it pretty well myself."

bribed with cash or beer—to grab the best properties, containing timber, minerals, and oil. Settlers would later swear that they had "improved" the property by erecting a "twelve-by-fourteen" dwelling, which turned out to measure twelve by fourteen *inches.*

The railways also played a major role in developing the agricultural West, largely through the profitable marketing of crops. Some railroad companies induced Americans and European immigrants to buy the cheap land earlier granted to the railroads by the government. The Northern Pacific Railroad at one time had nearly a thousand paid agents in Europe distributing roseate leaflets in various languages.

Agriculture expanded once the myth of the Great American Desert was shattered. Pioneer explorers had assumed that the soil must be sterile, simply because it was not heavily watered and did not support immense forests. But once the prairie sod was broken with heavy iron plows pulled by four yokes of oxen, the earth proved astonishingly fruitful.

meridian *In geography, any of the imaginary lines of longitude running north and south on the globe.*

Lured by higher wheat prices resulting from crop failures elsewhere in the world, settlers in the 1870s rashly pushed still farther west, onto the poor, marginal lands beyond the 100th **meridian**. Geologist John Wesley Powell, explorer of the Colorado River's Grand Canyon, warned in 1874 that beyond the 100th meridian so little rain fell that agriculture was impossible without massive **irrigation**. Ignoring Powell's advice, farmers heedlessly chewed up the crusty earth in western Kansas, eastern Colorado, and Montana. They quickly went broke as a six-year drought in the 1880s further desiccated the already dusty region. In the wake of the drought, some pioneers tried the new "dry farming" technique of frequent shallow cultivation. But over time "dry farming" pulverized the surface soil and contributed to the "Dust Bowl" several decades later (see p. 550).

irrigation *Watering land artificially, through canals, pipes, or other means.*

Other adaptations to the western environment were more successful. Tough strains of wheat, resistant to cold and drought, were imported from Russia and blossomed into billowing yellow carpets. Barbed wire, perfected by Joseph F. Glidden in 1874, solved the problem of how to build fences on the treeless prairies. Eventually, federally financed irrigation projects on a colossal scale caused the Great American Desert to bloom. In the long run, hydraulic engineers had more to do with shaping the modern West than all the trappers, miners, cavalrymen, and cowboys ever did.

The Great West experienced a fantastic surge in migration from the 1870s to the 1890s. A parade of new western states proudly joined the Union. Boomtown Colorado, offspring of the Pikes Peak gold rush, was greeted in 1876 as the "Centennial State." In 1889–1890 a Republican Congress, eagerly seeking more Republican electoral and congressional votes, admitted in a wholesale lot six new states: North Dakota, South Dakota, Montana, Washington, Idaho, and Wyoming. The Mormon church—belatedly, in many Americans' eyes—banned polygamy in 1890, but not until 1896 was Utah deemed worthy of admission. Only Oklahoma, New Mexico, and Arizona remained to be lifted into statehood from

contiguous *Joined together by common borders.*

contiguous territory on the mainland of North America.

In a last gaudy fling, the federal government made available to settlers vast stretches of fertile plains formerly occupied by the Indians in Oklahoma ("the Beautiful Land"). Scores of overeager and well-armed "sooners," illegally jumping the gun, entered Oklahoma Territory before the opening date. They had to be evicted repeatedly by federal troops, who on occasion would shoot the intruders' horses. On April 22, 1889, all was in readiness for the legal opening, and some fifty thousand "boomers" were poised expectantly on the boundary line. At high noon the bugle shrilled, and a horde of "eighty-niners" poured in on lathered horses or careening vehicles. That night a lonely spot on the prairie had mushroomed into the tent city of Guthrie, with over ten thousand people. By the end of the year Oklahoma boasted sixty thousand inhabitants, and Congress made it a territory. In 1907 it became the "Sooner State."

The Fading Frontier

PRIMARY SOURCE
Settlement of the Frontier, The

In 1890—a watershed date—the superintendent of the census announced that for the first time in America's experience a frontier line was no longer discernible. All the unsettled areas were now broken into by isolated bodies of American settlement. The "closing" of the frontier inspired one of the most influential essays ever written about American history—Frederick Jackson Turner's "The Significance of the Frontier in American History," in 1893.

EXAMINING THE EVIDENCE

ROBERT LOUIS STEVENSON'S TRANSCONTINENTAL JOURNEY, 1879

The celebrated Scottish writer Robert Louis Stevenson, author of such enduring classics as *Treasure Island, Kidnapped,* and *The Strange Case of Dr. Jekyll and Mr. Hyde,* journeyed from Scotland to California in 1879 to rendezvous with his American fiancée, Frances Osbourne. Between New York and San Francisco, Stevenson traveled on the transcontinental railroad line completed just ten years earlier, and he dutifully recorded his impressions of America, the West in particular, as he made his way toward California. Stevenson's account of his trip provides an unusually gifted writer's vivid portrait of the trans-Mississippi West at the close of the era of the Indian wars. Like all travelogues, Stevenson's colorful tale may reveal as much about the traveler as it does about the things he saw. Yet historians frequently make use of such documents to reconstruct the original appearance and texture of places that were once the exotic destinations of adventurous travelers, before they were transformed by the onrush of modernity.

1. In the passages reproduced here, inspired by the view as Stevenson's train passed through Nebraska and Wyoming, what features of the landscape does the author find most remarkable?

2. What does Stevenson's extended comparison of traveling across the plains to being "at sea" convey about cultured European views of the American West in the late nineteenth century? Why do the buffalo and the few cabins he sees not disrupt his perception of the West's "emptiness"?

3. What is Stevenson's view of the Indians, as well of those who built the railroad (including Chinese laborers)?

THE PLAINS OF NEBRASKA

. . . *We were at sea—there is no other adequate expression—on the plains of Nebraska. . . . It was a world almost without a feature; an empty sky, an empty earth; front and back, the line of railway stretched from horizon to horizon, like a cue across a billiard-board; on either hand, the green plain ran till it touched the skirts of heaven. . . . [G]razing beasts were seen upon the prairie at all degrees of distance and diminution; and now and again we might perceive a few dots beside the railroad which grew more and more distinct as we drew nearer till they turned into wooden cabins, and then dwindled and dwindled in our wake until they melted into their surroundings, and we were once more alone upon the billiard-board. The train toiled over this infinity like a snail; and being the one thing moving, it was wonderful what huge proportions it began to assume in our regard. . . .*

[That] evening we left Laramie [Wyoming]. . . . And yet when day came, it was to shine upon the same broken and unsightly quarter of the world. Mile upon mile, and not a tree, a bird, or a river. Only down the long, sterile cañons, the train shot hooting and awoke the resting echo. That train was the one piece of life in all the deadly land; it was the one actor, the one spectacle fit to be observed in this paralysis of man and nature. And when I think how the railroad has been pushed through this unwatered wilderness and haunt of savage tribes, and now will bear an emigrant for some £12 from the Atlantic to the Golden Gates; how at each stage of the construction, roaring, impromptu cities, full of gold and lust and death, sprang up and then died away again, and are now but wayside stations in the desert; how in these uncouth places pig-tailed Chinese pirates worked side by side with border ruffians and broken men from Europe, talking together in a mixed dialect, mostly oaths, gambling, drinking, quarrelling and murdering like wolves; how the plumed hereditary lord of all America heard, in this last fastness, the scream of the 'bad medicine waggon' charioting his foes; and then when I go on to remember that all this epical turmoil was conducted by gentlemen in frock coats, and with a view to nothing more extraordinary than a fortune and a subsequent visit to Paris, it seems to me, I own, as if this railway were the one typical achievement of the age in which we live, as if it brought together into one plot all the ends of the world and all the degrees of social rank, and offered to some great writer the busiest, the most extended, and the most varied subject for an enduring literary work. . . .

Source: *Across the Plains* by Robert Louis Stevenson (New York: Charles Scribner's Sons, 1897).

As the nineteenth century neared its sunset, the westward-tramping American people were disturbed to find that their fabled free land was going or had gone. The secretary of war had prophesied in 1827 that five hundred years would be needed to fill the West. But as the nation finally recognized that its land was not inexhaustible, seeds were planted to preserve the vanishing resource. The government set aside lands for national parks—first Yellowstone in 1872, followed by Yosemite and Sequoia in 1890.

The frontier was more than a place: It was also a state of mind and a symbol of opportunity. Its passing ended a romantic phase of the nation's internal development and created new economic and psychological problems. Traditionally footloose, Americans have been notorious for their mobility. The nation's farmers, unlike the peasants of Europe, seldom remained rooted to their soil.

Much has been said about the frontier as a "**safety valve**." The theory is that when hard times came, the unemployed who cluttered the city pavements merely moved west, took up farming, and prospered. In truth, relatively few eastern city dwellers migrated to the frontier during depressions. Most of them did not know how to farm; few of them could raise enough money to transport themselves west and then pay for livestock and expensive machinery.

But the safety-valve theory does have some validity. Free acreage did lure to the West a host of immigrant farmers who otherwise might have remained in the eastern cities to clog the job markets and crowd the slums. And the very *possibility* of westward migration may have induced urban employers to maintain wage rates high enough to discourage workers from leaving.

But the real safety valve by the late nineteenth century was in western cities such as Denver, San Francisco, and Seattle, where failed farmers, busted miners, and displaced easterners found the best places to seek their fortunes. Indeed, after about 1880 the area from the Rocky Mountains to the Pacific Coast was the most urbanized region in America, measured by the percentage of people living in cities. U.S. history cannot be properly understood unless it is viewed in light of the westward-moving experience. As Frederick Jackson Turner wrote, "American history has been in a large degree the history of the colonization of the Great West." The story of settling and taming the trans-Mississippi West in the late nineteenth century was but the last chapter in the saga of the colonizing of various American "wests" since Columbus's day.

And yet the trans-Mississippi West formed a distinct chapter in that saga and retains even to this day much of its uniqueness. There the Native American peoples made their last struggle against colonization, and there most Native Americans live today. There "Anglo" culture collided most directly with Hispanic culture, and the Southwest remains the most Hispanicized region in America. There America faced across the Pacific to Asia, and there most Asian Americans dwell today. There the scale and severity of the environment posed their greatest challenges to human ambitions, and there the environment continues to mold social and political life, and the American imagination, as in no other part of the nation.

The westward-moving pioneers and the country they confronted have assumed mythic proportions in the American mind. For better or worse, those pioneers planted the seeds of American civilization in the immense western wilderness. The life we live, they dreamed of; the life they lived, we can only dream.

safety valve *Anything, such as the American frontier, that allegedly serves as a necessary outlet for built-up pressure, energy, and so on.*

The Farm Becomes a Factory

The situation of American farmers, once jacks-and-jills-of-all-trades, was rapidly changing. They had raised their own food, fashioned their own clothing, and bartered for other necessities with neighbors. Now high prices persuaded farmers to concentrate on growing single "cash" crops, such as wheat or corn, and use their profits to buy foodstuffs at the general store and manufactured goods in town or by mail order. The Chicago firm of Aaron Montgomery Ward sent out its first catalogue—a single sheet—in 1872. Farmers were becoming a part of the world economy, as their crops journeyed by rail and ship to distant parts of the globe. Large-scale farmers were now both specialists and businesspeople. As cogs in the vast industrial machine, they were intimately tied to banking, railroading, and manufacturing. They had to buy expensive machinery to plant and to harvest their crops. The speed of harvesting wheat was immensely increased in the 1870s by the twine binder and then in the 1880s by the "combine"—the combined reaper-thresher, which was drawn by twenty to forty horses and both reaped and bagged the grain.

This amazing mechanization of agriculture in the postwar years was almost as striking as the mechanization of industry. Those who remained on the farms achieved miracles of production, making America the world's breadbasket and butcher shop. The farm was attaining the status of a factory—an outdoor grain factory. The enormous bonanza wheat farms of the Minnesota–North Dakota area foreshadowed the gigantic agribusinesses of the next century. By 1890 at least a half-dozen of them were larger than fifteen thousand acres.

Agriculture was a big business from the outset in California's phenomenally productive (and phenomenally irrigated) Central Valley. California farms, carved out of giant Spanish-Mexican land grants and the railroads' huge holdings, were from the outset more than three times larger than the national average. With the advent of the railroad refrigerator car in the 1880s, California fruits and vegetable crops, raised on sprawling tracts by ill-paid migrant Mexican and Chinese farmhands, sold at a handsome profit in the rich urban markets of the East.

Deflation Dooms the Debtor

Once the farmers became chained to a one-crop economy—wheat or corn—they were in the same leaky boat with the southern cotton growers. The grain farmers were no longer the masters of their own destinies. They were engaged in one of the most fiercely competitive of businesses, for the price of their product was determined in a world market by the world output. If the wheat fields of Argentina, Russia, and other foreign countries flourished, the price of the farmers' grain would fall and American sodbusters would face ruin, as they did in the 1880s and 1890s.

Low prices and a deflated currency were the chief worries of the frustrated farmer in all regions. If a family had borrowed $1,000 in 1855, when wheat was worth about a dollar a bushel, they expected to pay back the equivalent of one thousand bushels, plus interest, when the mortgage fell due. But if they let their debt run to 1890, when wheat had fallen to about fifty cents a bushel, they would have to pay back the price of two thousand bushels for the $1,000 they had borrowed, plus interest. This unexpected burden struck them as unjust, though their steely eyed creditors often branded the complaining farmers as slippery and dishonest rascals.

The deflationary pinch on the debtor flowed partly from the static money supply. There were simply not enough dollars to go around, and as a result prices were forced down. In 1870 the currency in circulation for each person was $19.42; in 1890 it was only $22.67. Yet during these twenty years, business and industrial activity, increasing manyfold, had intensified the scramble for available currency.

The forgotten farmers were caught on a treadmill. Despite unremitting toil, they operated year after year at a loss. In a vicious circle, their farm machinery increased their output of grain, lowered the price, and drove them even deeper into debt. Mortgages engulfed homesteads at an alarming rate; by 1890 Nebraska alone reported more than 100,000 farms blanketed with mortgages. The repeated crash of the sheriff-auctioneer's hammer kept announcing to the world that another sturdy American farmer had become landless in a landed nation.

Ruinous rates of interest, running from 8 to 40 percent, were charged on mortgages, largely by agents of eastern loan companies. The windburned sons and daughters of the sod, who felt that they deserved praise for developing the country, cried out in despair against the **loan sharks** and the Wall Street octopus.

Farm tenancy rather than farm ownership was spreading like stinkweed. The trend was especially marked in the sharecropping South, where cotton prices also sank dismayingly. By 1880 one-fourth of all American farms were operated by tenants. The United States was ready to feed the world, but under the new industrial feudalism the farmers were about to sink into a status suggesting Old World **serfdom**.

loan shark *A person who lends money at an exorbitant or illegal rate of interest.*

serfdom *The feudal condition of being permanently bound to land owned by someone else.*

THINKING GLOBALLY

The Great Frontier

The American pioneers who surged westward in the nineteenth century were part of a great global land grab that changed lives and landscapes on several continents. From the Australian outback to the Canadian prairies, from the Argentine pampas to the Russian steppes and the African savannas, millions of mostly white settlers poured into vast new territories and claimed them as their own.

Everywhere, the settlers encountered indigenous people who had lived on those lands since time immemorial. With their superiority in weaponry, transportation, and political organization, everywhere the newcomers prevailed. By the century's close, they had displaced or destroyed countless native peoples and extended their dominion over parts of the planet once considered too remote or rugged to be habitable.

The American frontier soon became the stuff of legend, and even the subject of a scholarly explanation of American uniqueness—Frederick Jackson Turner's fabled "frontier thesis," which hailed the grit and gumption of the pioneers and commended them as the agents of civilization and democracy. Yet far from being unique, those westering Americans had much in common with settlers in sister societies abroad. Argentina had its cowboys (gauchos), and

Australia had its colorful backcountry outlaws, such as Ned Kelly, whose exploits rivaled those of Billy the Kid. The Russians and South Africans had their own versions of "Manifest Destiny," and like the American they often cloaked them in the language of racial superiority.

The world's various frontiers also reflected the particularities of geography and history. Australians soon conceded that much of their continent—the world's driest—was too arid for traditional farming. Most of the Outback proved suitable only for enormous "sheep stations," sometimes measuring tens of thousands of acres. Consequently, small-farm homesteading of the American and Canadian type never took root, nor did cities of any consequence emerge in the parched Australian interior.

Canada's westward movement came later than that in the United States and proceeded more peaceably. Only after the Ottawa government promised in 1871 to build a transcontinental railroad connecting eastern Canada to its western provinces did settlement being in earnest. And unlike in America, where restless pioneers typically struck out on their own and made much mischief among themselves and with the Indians they encountered, in Canada,

Royal Canadian Mounted Police

North-West Mounted Police, c. 1890 Empowered by an act of Parliament in 1873 to establish Canadian authority and order in the Northwest Territories, this force made frontier settlement somewhat more peaceful in Canada than in the United States. In 1920 the North-West Mounted Police absorbed the Dominion Police and became the famed Royal Canadian Mounted Police, or "Mounties."

settlers were generally preceded by government authorities—usually the red-jacketed North-West Mounted Police, or "Mounties"—who established at least a semblance of order before large numbers of pioneers appeared on the scene. As a result, Canada's frontier was markedly less violent than America's. Canada, then and now a more law-abiding society than the United States, never had a "Wild West" like that of its southern neighbor.

In Argentina and Russia, inherited patterns of landholding and politics shaped their nineteenth-century frontiers. When Argentina's General Julio Roca vanquished the native Araucanians in 1879, he flung open the horizonless pampas to white settlement. But he also retained the venerable custom, handed down from Spanish colonial times, of apportioning the land in gigantic estancias (ranches) to a few favored fellow soldiers and friends. These lordly landowners then employed wage workers, mostly Italian immigrants, who turned the fertile Argentine interior into a beef bowl and breadbasket to the world. The immigrants themselves, however, had little hope of ever possessing land of their own.

Russia's frontier lay to the east and long felt the heavy hand of the tsar. For centuries autocratic rulers had strong-armed landowning nobles to move their serfs onto the "virgin lands" beyond the settled edge of European Russia. By the nineteenth century, imperial Russia had pushed its frontier onto the rolling steppes of central Asia, home to Tartars, Kalmyks, Kazahks, and myriad other indigenous peoples. Only military conquest and a strengthened state bureaucracy made possible European settlement in those regions. Between 1867 and 1897, more than a million of the tsar's subjects left for the hinterland. As elsewhere, the railroad proved essential to the growth of the tsarist empire, especially after the government began construction of the Trans-Siberian line in 1891.

The Dutch-descended Afrikaners, or Boers, in southern Africa found their frontier to the north, and unlike their American counterparts, they made scant claim to be spreading democracy. Rather, they sought to escape British rule in the Cape Colony—in particular, to escape from the threat of racial equality for blacks after Britain abolished slavery in the 1830s. The Afrikaners' "Great Trek" took them into the land of the Zulus, who ferociously resisted the oncoming Boers but eventually, like indigenous peoples everywhere, were forced to submit to white rule.

In the Americas, Australia, Asia, and Africa, the great frontier of the nineteenth century was the companion of conquest. The frontier brought opportunity to some and oppression to others. In many places it nurtured democracy; elsewhere it invigorated autocracy. And everywhere it expanded the domains of European civilization—for better or worse.

Unhappy Farmers

Even Mother Nature ceased smiling as her powerful forces conspired against agriculture. Mile-wide clouds of grasshoppers, leaving "nothing but the mortgage," periodically ravaged prairie farms. The terrible cotton boll weevil was also wreaking havoc in the South by the early 1890s.

The good earth was going sour. Floods washed the topsoil off millions of once-lush southern acres. A long succession of droughts seared the trans-Mississippi West, beginning in the summer of 1887. Whole towns were abandoned. "Going home to the wife's folks" and "in God we trusted, in Kansas we busted" were typical laments of many impoverished farmers as they fled their weather-beaten shacks and sunbaked sod houses.

To add to their miseries, the soil-tillers were gouged by their government—local, state, and national. Their land was overassessed, and they paid painful local taxes, whereas wealthy easterners could conceal their stocks and bonds in safe-deposit boxes. High protective tariffs in these years poured profits into the pockets of manufacturers. Farmers, on the other hand, had no choice but to sell their low-priced products in a fiercely competitive, unprotected world market, while buying high-priced manufactured goods in a protected home market.

The farmers were also "farmed" by the corporations. Trusts raised prices on farmers' machinery and supplies to extortionate levels, while operators pushed storage rates to the ceiling at grain warehouses and elevators. The railroad octopus often pushed freight rates so high that the farmers sometimes lost less if they burned their corn for fuel than if they shipped it.

Farmers still made up nearly one-half of the population in 1890, but they were hopelessly disorganized. The manufacturers and the railroad barons knew how to combine to promote their own interests, and so, increasingly, did industrial workers. But the farmers were by nature independent and individualistic—dead set against consolidation or regimentation. They never did organize successfully to restrict production until forced to do so by the federal government nearly half a century later, in Franklin Roosevelt's New Deal days. What they did manage to organize was a monumental political uprising.

The Farmers Take Their Stand

Agrarian unrest had flared forth earlier, in the Greenback movement shortly after the Civil War. Prices sagged in 1868, and a host of farmers unsuccessfully sought relief from low prices and high indebtedness by demanding an inflation of the currency with paper money.

The National Grange of the Patrons of Husbandry—better known as the Grange—was organized in 1867. Its leading spirit was Oliver H. Kelley, a shrewd and energetic Minnesota farmer then working as a clerk in Washington. Kelley's first objective was to enhance the lives of isolated farmers through social, educational, and fraternal activities. The Grange spread like an old-time prairie fire and by 1875 claimed some 800,000 members, chiefly in the Midwest and South.

The Grangers gradually raised their goals from individual self-improvement to improvement of the farmers' collective plight. In a determined effort to escape the clutches of the trusts, they established cooperatively owned stores, grain elevators, and warehouses, and even made a failed attempt to manufacture harvesting machinery.

Embattled Grangers also went into politics, enjoying their most gratifying success in the grain-growing regions of the upper Mississippi Valley. There, through state legislation, they strove to regulate railway rates and the storage fees charged by railroads and grain elevator operators. Many of the state courts, notably in Illinois, were disposed to recognize the principle of public control of private business for the general welfare. A number of the so-called Granger Laws, however, were bitterly fought through the high courts by the well-paid lawyers of the "interests." Following judicial reverses, most severely at the hands of the Supreme Court in the *Wabash* decision of 1886 (see p. 378), the Grangers' influence faded.

Farmers' grievances likewise found a vent in the Greenback Labor party, which combined the inflationary appeal of the earlier Greenbackers with a program for improving

✳ **PRIMARY SOURCE**
Granger at Home, The Granger Abroad

The Granger Collection, New York

The Farmers' Grievances This poster from 1875 expresses one of the agrarian radicals' fundamental premises: that all other walks of life were dependent—or even parasitic—on the indispensable work of farmers. In his famous "Cross of Gold" speech in 1896, Populist presidential candidate William Jennings Bryan put it this way: "Burn down your cities and leave our farms, and your cities will spring up again as if by magic; but destroy our farms and the grass will grow in the streets of every city in the country."

the lot of labor. In 1878, the high-water mark of the movement, the Greenback-Laborites polled over a million votes and elected fourteen members of Congress. In the presidential election of 1880 the Greenbackers ran General James B. Weaver, an old Granger who spoke to perhaps a half-million citizens, but he polled only 3 percent of the popular vote.

Prelude to Populism

A striking manifestation of rural discontent came through the Farmers' Alliance, founded in Texas in the late 1870s (see p. 367). Farmers came together in the Alliance to socialize, but more importantly they hoped to break the strangling grip of the railroads and manufacturers through cooperative buying and selling. Local chapters spread throughout the South and the Great Plains during the 1880s, until by 1890 members numbered more than a million hard-bitten souls.

Unfortunately, the Alliance weakened itself by ignoring the plight of landless tenant farmers, sharecroppers, and farmworkers. Even more debilitating was the Alliance's exclusion of blacks, who counted for nearly half the agricultural population of the South. In the 1880s a separate Colored Farmers' National Alliance emerged to attract black farmers, and by 1890 membership numbered more than 250,000. The long history of racial division in the South, however, made it difficult for white and black farmers to work together in the same organization.

Out of the Farmers' Alliances a new political party emerged in the early 1890s—the People's Party. Better known as the Populists, these frustrated farmers attacked Wall Street and the "money trust." They called for nationalizing the railroads, telephones, and telegraph; instituting a graduated income tax; and building government-owned warehouses where they could store their grain until market prices rose. They also wanted the free and unlimited coinage of silver—yet another of the debtors' demands for inflation that echoed continuously throughout the Gilded Age.

Numerous fiery **prophets** leapt forward to trumpet the Populist cause. William Hope Harvey produced an enormously popular pamphlet called *Coin's Financial School* (1894). Illustrated by clever woodcuts, the booklet showed how "Coin" Harvey overwhelmed the bankers and professors of economics with his brilliant arguments on behalf of free silver. Another notorious spellbinder was red-haired Ignatius Donnelly of Minnesota, three times elected to Congress. The queen of the Populist "calamity howlers" was Mary Elizabeth ("Mary Yellin") Lease, a tall, athletic woman known as the "Kansas Pythoness." She reportedly demanded that Kansans should raise "less corn and more hell." The *New York Evening Post* snarled, "We don't want any more states until we can civilize Kansas." To many easterners, complaint, not corn, was rural America's staple crop.

Yet the Populists, despite their oddities, were not to be laughed away. They were leading a deadly earnest and impassioned campaign to relieve the farmers' many miseries. Smiles faded from Republican and Democratic faces alike as countless thousands of Populists began to sing "Good-bye, My Party, Good-bye."

In 1892 the Populists had jolted the traditional parties by winning several congressional seats and polling more than 1 million votes for their presidential candidate, James B. Weaver. Racial divisions continued to hobble the Populists in the South, but in the West their ranks were swelling. Could the People's Party now reach beyond its regional bases in agrarian America, join hands with urban workers, and mount a successful attack on the northeastern **citadels** of power?

prophet(s) *A person believed to speak with divine power or special gifts, sometimes including predicting the future (hence, any specially talented or eloquent advocate of a cause).*

citadel *A fortress occupying a commanding height.*

Coxey's Army and the Pullman Strike

The panic of 1893 and the severe ensuing depression strengthened the Populists' argument that farmers and laborers alike were being victimized by an oppressive economic and political system. Ragged armies of the unemployed began marching to protest their plight. In the growing hordes of displaced industrial toilers, the Populists saw potential political allies.

After the Pullman strike collapsed, Eugene Debs (1855–1926) said:

"No strike has ever been lost."

In 1897 he declared:

"The issue is Socialism versus Capitalism. I am for Socialism because I am for humanity."

The most famous marcher was "General" Jacob S. Coxey, a wealthy Ohio quarry owner who set out for Washington in 1894 with a small band of supporters. His platform included a demand that the government relieve unemployment by an inflationary $500 million federal public works program. Coxey himself rode in a carriage with his wife and infant son, appropriately named Legal Tender Coxey, while his tiny "army" tramped along behind, singing:

We're coming, Grover Cleveland,
500,000 strong.
We're marching on to Washington
to right the nation's wrong.

The "Commonweal Army" of Coxeyites finally straggled into the nation's capital, but the "invasion" took on the aspects of a comic opera when "General" Coxey and his "lieutenants" were arrested for walking on the grass.

Elsewhere, violent flare-ups accompanied labor protests, notably in Chicago. Most dramatic was the crippling Pullman strike of 1894. Eugene V. Debs, a charismatic labor leader, had helped organize the American Railway Union of about 150,000 members. The Pullman Palace Car Company, which maintained a model town near Chicago for its employees, was hit hard by the depression and cut wages by about one-third, while holding the line on rent for company houses. The workers finally struck—in some places overturning Pullman cars—and paralyzed railway traffic from Chicago to the Pacific Coast.

The turmoil in Chicago was serious but not completely out of hand. At least this was the judgment of Governor John Peter Altgeld of Illinois, a friend of the downtrodden, who had pardoned the Haymarket Square anarchists the year before (see p. 386). But U.S. attorney general Richard Olney, an archconservative and an ex-railroad attorney, urged the dispatch of federal troops on the legal grounds that the strikers were interfering with the U.S. mail. President Cleveland supported Olney with the ringing declaration, "If it takes the entire army and navy to deliver a postal card in Chicago, that card will be delivered."

To the delight of conservatives, federal troops, bayonets fixed, crushed the Pullman strike. Debs was sentenced to six months' imprisonment for contempt of court because he had defied a federal court injunction to cease striking. Ironically, the lean labor agitator spent much of his enforced leisure reading radical literature, which led to his later leadership of the socialist movement in America.

Embittered cries of "government by injunction" now burst from organized labor. This was the first time that such a legal weapon had been used conspicuously by Washington to break a strike, and it was all the more distasteful because defiant workers who were held in contempt could be imprisoned without jury trial. Signs multiplied that employers were striving to smash labor unions by court action. Nonlabor elements of the country, including the Populists and other debtors, were likewise incensed. They saw in the brutal Pullman episode further proof of an unholy alliance between business and the courts.

Golden McKinley and Silver Bryan

The smoldering grievances of the long-suffering farmers and depression-plagued laborers gave ominous significance to the election of 1896. Conservatives of all stripes feared an impending upheaval, while down-and-out husbandmen and discontented workers cast about desperately for political salvation. Increasingly, monetary policy—whether to maintain the gold standard or inflate the currency by monetizing silver—loomed as the issue on which the election would turn.

The leading candidate for the Republican presidential nomination in 1896 was former Congressman William McKinley of Ohio, sponsor of the ill-starred tariff bill of 1890 (see p. 367). He had established a record as a Civil War officer; he hailed from the electorally potent state of Ohio; and he could point to long years of honorable service in Congress.

As a presidential candidate, McKinley was largely the creature of a fellow Ohioan, Marcus Alonzo Hanna, who had made his fortune in the iron business and now coveted the role of president-maker. As a wholehearted Hamiltonian, Hanna believed that a prime function of government was to aid business. He also believed that in some measure prosperity "trickled down" to the laborer, whose dinner pail would be full only when business flourished. Critics assailed this idea as equivalent to feeding the horses in order to feed the sparrows.

The hardheaded Hanna, although something of a novice in politics, organized his preconvention campaign for McKinley with consummate skill and a liberal outpouring of his own money. The convention steamroller, well lubricated with Hanna's dollars, nominated McKinley on the first ballot at St. Louis in June 1896. The Republican platform condemned Democratic incapacity in hard times and declared for the gold standard.

Dissension riddled the Democratic camp. Cleveland no longer led his party. The depression had driven the last nail into his political coffin. Dubbed "the Stuffed Prophet," he was undeniably the most unpopular man in the country. Labor-debtor groups remembered too vividly his intervention in the Pullman strike, the backstairs Morgan bond deal, and especially his stubborn hard-money policies. Ultraconservative in finance, Cleveland now looked more like a Republican than a Democrat on the money issue.

Rudderless, the Democratic convention met in Chicago in July 1896, with the silverites lusting for victory. Shouting insults at the absent Cleveland, the delegates refused to endorse their own administration. They had the enthusiasm and the numbers; all they lacked was a leader.

A new Moses suddenly appeared in the person of William Jennings Bryan of Nebraska. Then only thirty-six years of age and known as "the Boy Orator of the Platte," Bryan stepped confidently onto the platform before fifteen thousand people. His masterful presence was set off by a peninsular jaw and raven-black hair. He radiated honesty, sincerity, and energy.

The convention-hall setting was made to order for a magnificent oratorical effort. A hush fell over the delegates as Bryan stood before them. With an organ-like voice that rolled into the outer corners of the huge hall, he delivered a fervent plea for silver. Rising to supreme heights of eloquence, he thundered, "We will answer their demands for a gold standard by saying to them: 'You shall not press down upon the brow of labor this crown of thorns, you shall not crucify mankind upon a cross of gold'!"

The Cross of Gold speech was a sensation. Swept off its feet in a tumultuous scene, the Democratic convention nominated Bryan the next day on the fifth ballot. The platform demanded inflation through the unlimited coinage of silver at the ratio of sixteen ounces of silver to one of gold, though the market ratio was about thirty-two to one. This meant that the silver in a dollar would be worth about fifty cents.

Democratic "Gold Bugs," unable to swallow Bryan, bolted their party over the silver issue. A conservative senator from New York, when asked if he was a Democrat still, reportedly replied, "Yes, I am a Democrat still—very still." The Democratic minority, including Cleveland, charged that the Populist silverites had stolen both the name and the clothes of their party. Many of them, including Cleveland, not too secretly hoped for a McKinley victory.

The Populists now faced a dilemma because the Democratic majority had appropriated their main plank—"16 to 1," that "heaven-born ratio." The bulk of the Populists, fearing a hard-money McKinley victory, endorsed "fusion" with the Democrats and Bryan for president, sacrificing their identity in the mix. Singing "The Jolly Silver Dollar of the Dads," they became in effect the "Demo-Pop" or "Popocratic" party, though a handful of the original Populists refused to support Bryan and went down with their colors nailed to the mast.

---

* One contemporary sneered that Bryan, like the Platte River, was "six inches deep and six miles wide at the mouth."

The Library of Congress

The Sacrilegious Candidate A hostile cartoonist makes sport of Bryan's flamboyant Cross of Gold speech in 1896.

Class Conflict: Plowholders Versus Bondholders

Mark Hanna smugly assumed that he could make the tariff the focus of the campaign. But Bryan, a dynamo of energy, forced the free-trade issue into a back seat when he took to the stump in behalf of free silver. Sweeping through 27 states and traveling 18,000 miles, Bryan made nearly 600 speeches—36 in one day—and even invaded the East, "the enemy's country." Vachel Lindsay caught the spirit of his oratorical orgy:

> *Prairie avenger, mountain lion,*
> *Bryan, Bryan, Bryan, Bryan,*
> *Gigantic troubadour, speaking like a siege gun,*
> *Smashing Plymouth rock with his boulders from the West.**

Free silver became almost as much a religious as a financial issue. Hordes of fanatical free-silverites, singing "No Crown of Thorns, No Cross of Gold," hailed Bryan as the messiah to lead them out of the wilderness of debt.

Bryan created panic among eastern conservatives with his threat of converting their holdings overnight into fifty-cent dollars. "In God we trust, with Bryan we bust," the Republicans sneered, while one clergyman cried, "That platform was made in Hell." Widespread fear of Bryan and the "silver lunacy" enabled "Dollar Mark" Hanna, now chairman of the Republican National Committee, to shine as a money raiser. He "shook down" the trusts and plutocrats and piled up an enormous "slush fund" for a "campaign of education"—or of propaganda, depending on one's point of view. Republicans appealed to the "belly vote" with their prize slogan, "McKinley and the full dinner pail." The McKinleyites amassed the most formidable political campaign chest thus far in American history—about $16 million, as contrasted with about $1 million for the poorer Democrats (roughly "16 to 1"). With some justification, the Bryanites accused Hanna of "buying" the election and of floating McKinley into the White House on a tidal wave of mud and money.

Bryan's cyclonic campaign began to lose steam as the weeks passed. Fear was probably Hanna's strongest ally, as it was Bryan's worst enemy. Some Republican businesspeople threatened wage reductions or told their workers not to come to work on Wednesday morning if Bryan won. Such were some of the "dirty tricks" of the "Stop Bryan, Save America" crusade.

Hanna's campaign methods paid off. On election day McKinley triumphed decisively. The vote was 271 to 176 in the Electoral College, and 7,102,246 to 6,492,559 in the popular vote. Driven by fear and excitement, an unprecedented outpouring of voters flocked to the polls. McKinley ran strongly in the populous East, where he carried every county of New England, and in the upper Mississippi Valley. Bryan's states, concentrated in the debt-burdened South and the trans-Mississippi West, involved more acreage than McKinley's but less population.

The free-silver election of 1896 was perhaps the most significant political turning point since Lincoln's victories in 1860 and 1864. Despite Bryan's strength in the South and West, the results vividly demonstrated his lack of appeal to the unmortgaged farmer and especially to the eastern urban laborer. Many wage earners in the East, threatened as they were by free silver, voted for their jobs and full dinner pails. Living precariously on a fixed wage, the factory workers had no reason to favor inflation, which was the heart of the Bryanites' program.

The Bryan-McKinley battle heralded the advent of a new era in American politics. The outcome represented a resounding victory for big business, the big cities, middle-class values, and financial conservatism. Bryan's defeat marked the last serious effort to win the White House with mostly agrarian votes. The future of presidential politics lay not on the farms, with their dwindling populations, but in the mushrooming cities, with their growing hordes of freshly arriving immigrants.

The Grand Old Party's smashing victory of 1896 also heralded a Republican grip on the White House for sixteen consecutive years—indeed, for all but eight of the next thirty-six years. McKinley's election thus imparted a new character to the American political system.

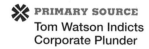

✳ PRIMARY SOURCE
Tom Watson Indicts
Corporate Plunder

---

* Reprinted with permission of Macmillan Publishing Company, Inc., from *Collected Poems*, by Vachel Lindsay. Copyright 1920 by Macmillan Publishing Company, Inc., renewed 1948 by Elizabeth C. Lindsay.

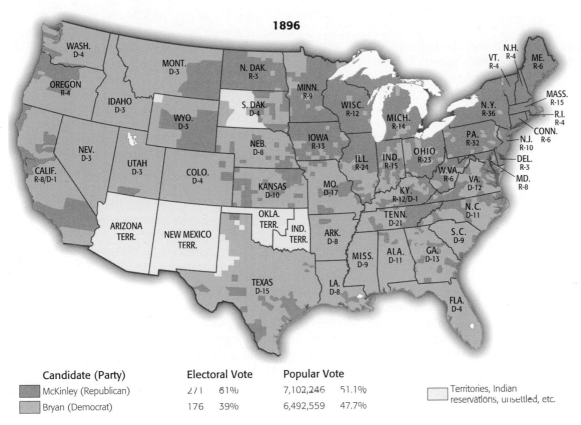

1896

Candidate (Party)	Electoral Vote		Popular Vote	
McKinley (Republican)	271	61%	7,102,246	51.1%
Bryan (Democrat)	176	39%	6,492,559	47.7%

Territories, Indian reservations, unsettled, etc.

Presidential Election of 1896 (with electoral vote by state) This election tolled the death knell of the Gilded Age political party system, with its razor-close elections, strong party loyalties, and high voter turnouts. Bryans' sweep of the southern states and strong showing in the West gave him only 176 electoral votes to McKinley's 271 from the more populous North and East. For years after 1896, Republicans predominated, and citizens showed declining interest in either joining parties or voting.
© Cengage Learning

The long reign of Republican political dominance that it ushered in was accompanied by diminishing voter participation in elections, the weakening of party organizations, and the fading away of issues such as the money question and civil-service reform, which came to be replaced by concern for industrial regulation and the welfare of labor. Scholars have dubbed this new political era the period of the "fourth party system," signaling a break with the previous "third party system," in place since 1860, of remarkably high voter turnouts and close contests between Democrats and Republicans.*

Republican Stand-pattism Enthroned

An eminently "safe" McKinley took the inaugural oath in 1897. Though a man of considerable ability, he was an ear-to-the-ground politician who seldom got far out of line with majority opinion. His cautious, conservative nature caused him to shy away from the flaming banner of reform. Business was given a free rein, and the trusts, which had trusted him in 1896, were allowed to develop more mighty muscles without serious restraints.

---

* The so-called first party system, marked by doubts about the very legitimacy of parties, embraced the Federalist-Republican clashes of the 1790s and early 1800s. The second party system took shape with the emergence of mass-based politics in the Jacksonian era, pitting Democrats against Whigs. The third party system was characterized by the precarious equilibrium between Republicans and Democrats, as well as the high electoral participation, that lasted from the end of the Civil War to McKinley's election. The fourth party system is described above. The fifth party system emerged in Franklin Roosevelt's New Deal, which initiated a long period of Democratic ascendancy. Each "system," except the fifth, lasted about forty years. Debate continues as to whether the nation has entered or is about to enter the era of the sixth party system.

For more than half a century, the Turner thesis dominated historical writing about the West. In his famous essay of 1893, "The Significance of the Frontier in American History," historian Frederick Jackson Turner argued that not only the West but the national character had been uniquely shaped by the westward movement. The struggle to overcome the hazards of the western wilderness had transformed *Europeans* into tough, inventive, and self-reliant *Americans*.

Written just three years after the superintendent of the census declared the frontier closed, Turner's thesis is surely among the most provocative statements ever made about formative influences on the nation's development and character. But as the frontier era recedes ever further into the past, scholars are less persuaded that Turner's thesis adequately explains the character of American society and its differences from Europe.

Modern historians such as David J. Weber challenge Turner's assumptions by suggesting that the line of the frontier did not define the quavering edge of "civilization," but instead marked the boundary between diverse and equally legitimate cultures. The frontier should therefore be understood not as the place where "civilization" triumphed over "savagery," but as the principal site of interaction between those cultures.

Several so-called New Western historians take this argument still further. Scholars such as Patricia Nelson Limerick, Richard White, and Donald Worster suggest that the cultural and ecological damage inflicted by advancing "civilization" must be reckoned with in any final accounting of what these pioneers accomplished. These same scholars insist that the West did not lose its regional identity after 1890. The West, they argue, is still a unique part of the national mosaic, a region whose history, culture, and identity remain every bit as distinctive as those of New England or the Old South.

But where Turner saw the frontier as the principal shaper of the region's character, the New Western historians emphasize the effects of ethnic and racial confrontation, topography, climate, and the roles of government and big business as the factors that have made the modern West. The pioneer "conquests" of Native Americans and Hispanics were less than complete, they contend, and the West therefore remains, uniquely among American regions, an unsettled arena of commingling and competition among these groups. Moreover, in these accounts the West's distinctively challenging climate and geography yielded to human habitation not through the efforts of heroic individual pioneers, but only through massive corporate—and especially federal government—investments in projects like the transcontinental railroads and irrigation systems. Such developments still give western life its special character today.

Almost as soon as McKinley took office, the tariff issue, which had played second fiddle to silver in the "Battle of '96," quickly forced itself to the fore. In due course the Dingley Tariff Bill was jammed through the House in 1897 under the pounding gavel of the rethroned "Czar" Reed. The proposed new rates were high, but not high enough to satisfy the paunchy lobbyists, who once again descended upon the Senate. Over 850 amendments were tacked onto the overburdened bill. The resulting piece of patchwork finally established the average rates at 46.5 percent, substantially higher than the Democratic Wilson-Gorman Act of 1894 and in some categories even higher than the McKinley Act of 1890. (See the chart in the Appendix.)

With the return of prosperity under McKinley in 1897, the money issue that overshadowed politics since the Civil War gradually faded away. The Gold Standard Act of 1900, passed over last-ditch silverite opposition, provided that paper currency was to be freely redeemed in gold. Electrifying discoveries of new gold deposits in Canada's fabled Klondike, as well as in Alaska, South Africa, and Australia, brought huge new quantities of gold onto world markets. Moderate inflation thus took care of the currency needs of an explosively expanding nation, as its circulatory system greatly improved. The tide of "silver heresy" rapidly receded, and the "Popocratic" fish were left gasping high and dry on a golden-sanded beach.

Chapter Summary

At the close of the Civil War, the Great Plains and Mountain West were still controlled by Indians who hunted buffalo on horseback and fiercely resisted white encroachment on their land and way of life. But the whites' railroads, mining, and livestock activities gradually broke up the Indians' territory, while disease and the destruction of the buffalo reduced their numbers and ended their way of life. The federal government eventually forced the Indians onto largely barren reservations where their very existence was threatened.

Attempting to coerce Indians into adopting white ways, the government passed the Dawes Act, which eliminated tribal ownership of land, while often insensitive "humanitarians" created a network of Indian boarding schools that further assaulted traditional culture.

The mining and cattle frontiers created colorful chapters in western history. Farmers carried out the final phase of settlement, lured by free homesteads, railroads, and irrigation. The census declared the end of the frontier in 1890, concluding a formative phase of American history. The frontier was less of a "safety valve" than many believed, but may have had some impact on keeping American wage rates relatively high. The newest western frontier was actually in cities such as Denver, San Francisco, and Seattle, which helped make the West the most urbanized region of the United States by the 1890s.

Beginning in the 1870s, farmers began pushing onto the treeless prairies beyond the 100th meridian, using techniques of dry farming that gradually contributed to soil erosion. Irrigation projects, later financed by the federal government, allowed specialized farming in some areas of the arid West, including California. The "closing" of the frontier in 1890 signified the end of traditional westward expansion, but the Great West remained a unique social and environmental region.

As the farmers opened vast new lands, agriculture was becoming a mechanized business dependent on specialized production and international markets. Once declining prices and other woes doomed the farmers to permanent debt and dependency, they began to protest their lot, first through the Grange and then through the Farmers' Alliances, the prelude to the People's (Populist) Party. The Populists made spectacular gains in the West and the South, but racial divisions undermined southern Populism.

The major depression of the 1890s accelerated farmer protest and labor unrest and strikes, leading to a growing class conflict. In 1896 pro-silverite William Jennings Bryan captured the Democratic Party's nomination, and led a fervent campaign against the "goldbug" Republicans and their candidate William McKinley. McKinley's success in winning urban workers away from Bryan proved a turning point in American politics, signaling the triumph of the city, the middle class, and a new party system. The return of prosperity ended the late-nineteenth-century preoccupation with monetary issues and made Republicans the dominant party for two generations.

KEY TERMS

nomadic (nomad) (416)

immunity (417)

reservation (417)

ward (419)

probationary (421)

folklore (422)

meridian (424)

irrigation (424)

contiguous (424)

safety valve (426)

loan shark (427)

serfdom (427)

prophet(s) (431)

citadel (431)

PEOPLE TO KNOW

Frederick Jackson Turner

Jacob S. Coxey

William McKinley

Marcus Alonzo Hanna

Go to the History CourseMate website for primary source links, study tools, and review materials for this chapter. www.cengagebrain.com

27

Empire and Expansion

1890–1909

*We assert that no nation can long endure half republic and half empire,
and we warn the American people that imperialism abroad will
lead quickly and inevitably to despotism at home.*

DEMOCRATIC NATIONAL PLATFORM, 1900

In the years immediately following the Civil War, Americans remained astonishingly indifferent to the outside world. Enmeshed in struggles over Reconstruction and absorbed in efforts to heal the wounds of civil war, build an industrial economy, make their cities habitable, and settle the sprawling West, most citizens took little interest in international affairs. But the sunset decades of the nineteenth century witnessed a momentous shift in U.S. foreign policy. America's new diplomacy reflected the far-reaching changes that were reshaping agriculture, industry, and the social structure. American statesmen also responded to the intensifying scramble of other nations for international advantage in the dawning "age of empire." By the beginning of the twentieth century, America had acquired its own empire, an astonishing departure from its venerable anticolonial traditions. The world now had to reckon with a new great power, potentially powerful but with diplomatic ambitions and principles that remained to be defined.

FOCUS QUESTIONS

1. Why did the United States abandon its historic isolationism and turn outward to develop imperial great power ambitions at the end of the nineteenth century?

2. What were the causes of the Spanish-American War, and how did the war lead to the acquisition of an American empire in the Philippines and Puerto Rico?

3. Why was there such a vigorous national debate over imperialism, and how did the Filipino rebellion against U.S. rule contribute to doubts about America's overseas role?

4. How did the United States become increasingly involved in China and the rest of East Asia, and what were the Open Door policy toward China and Theodore Roosevelt's diplomacy with Japan intended to achieve?

5. How did Theodore Roosevelt vigorously assert American power in Panama and elsewhere in Latin America, and why did the "Roosevelt Corollary" to the Monroe Doctrine stir controversy?

CHRONOLOGY

1820	New England missionaries arrive in Hawaii.
1889	Samoa crisis with Germany. Pan-American Conference.
1890	Mahan publishes *The Influence of Sea Power upon History*.
1891	New Orleans crisis with Italy.
1892	Valparaiso crisis with Chile.
1893	White planter revolt in Hawaii. Cleveland refuses Hawaii annexation.
1895	Cubans revolt against Spain.
1895–1896	Venezuelan boundary crisis with Britain.
1898	*Maine* explosion in Havana harbor. Spanish-American War. Teller Amendment. Dewey's victory at Manila Bay. Hawaii annexed.
1899	Senate ratifies treaty acquiring Philippines. Aguinaldo launches rebellion against United States in the Philippines. First American Open Door note.
1900	Hawaii receives full territorial status. Foraker Act for Puerto Rico. Boxer Rebellion and U.S. military expedition to China. Second Open Door note. McKinley defeats Bryan for presidency.
1901	Supreme Court *Insular Cases*. Platt Amendment.
	McKinley assassinated; Roosevelt becomes president. Filipino rebellion suppressed. Hay-Pauncefote Treaty with Britain gives United States exclusive right to build Panama Canal.
1902	U.S. troops leave Cuba. Colombian senate rejects U.S. proposal for canal across Panama.
1903	Panamanian revolution against Colombia. Hay–Bunau-Varilla Treaty gives United States control of Canal Zone in newly independent Panama.
1904	Roosevelt Corollary to the Monroe Doctrine.
1904–1914	Construction of the Panama Canal.
1905	United States takes over Dominican Republic customs service. Roosevelt mediates Russo-Japanese peace treaty.
1906	San Francisco Japanese education crisis. Roosevelt arranges Algeciras conference.
1906–1909	U.S. Marines occupy Cuba.
1907	Great White Fleet makes world voyage.
1907–1908	"Gentlemen's Agreement" with Japan.
1908	Root-Takahira agreement.
1917	Puerto Ricans granted U.S. citizenship.

Imperialist Stirrings

Many developments fed the nation's ambition for overseas expansion. Both farmers and factory owners began to look beyond American shores as agricultural and industrial production boomed. Many Americans believed that the United States had to expand or explode. Their country was bursting with a new sense of power generated by the robust growth in population, wealth, and productive capacity—and it was trembling from the hammer blows of labor violence and agrarian unrest. Overseas markets might provide a safety valve to relieve those pressures.

Other forces whetted the popular appetite for overseas involvement. The lurid "yellow press" of Joseph Pulitzer and William Randolph Hearst described foreign exploits as manly adventures, the kind of dashing derring-do that was the stuff of young boys' dreams. Pious missionaries, inspired by books such as the Reverend Josiah Strong's *Our Country: Its Possible Future and Its Present Crisis*, looked overseas for new souls to harvest. Strong trumpeted the superiority of Anglo-Saxon civilization and summoned Americans to spread their religion and their values to "backward" peoples. At the same

The undiplomatic note to Britain by Secretary of State Richard Olney (1835–1917) read:

"Today the United States is practically sovereign on this continent, and its fiat is law upon the subjects to which it confines its interposition. ... Its infinite resources combined with its isolated position render it master of the situation and practically invulnerable as against any or all other powers."

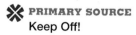
PRIMARY SOURCE
Mahan Defines Security in Terms of Sea Power

indemnity *A payment assessed to compensate for an injury or illegal action.*

arbitration *An arrangement in which a neutral third party conclusively determines the outcome of a dispute between two parties. (In mediation the third party only proposes solutions that the disputing parties may or may not accept.)*

PRIMARY SOURCE
Keep Off!

time, aggressive Americans such as Theodore Roosevelt and Congressman (later Senator) Henry Cabot Lodge were interpreting Darwinism to mean that the earth belonged to the strong and the fit—that is, to Uncle Sam. This view was strengthened as latecomers to the colonial scramble began to scoop up leavings from the banquet table of earlier diners in Africa, China, and elsewhere. If America was to survive in the competition of modern nation-states, perhaps it, too, would have to become an imperial power.

The development of a new steel navy also focused attention overseas. Captain Alfred Thayer Mahan's book of 1890, *The Influence of Sea Power upon History, 1660–1783*, argued that control of the sea was the key to world dominance. Mahan helped stimulate the naval race among the great powers that gained momentum around the turn of the century. Red-blooded Americans joined in the demands for a mightier navy and for an American-built isthmian canal between the Atlantic and the Pacific.

America's new international interest manifested itself in a number of diplomatic crises or near-wars in the late 1880s and early 1890s. The American and German navies nearly came to blows in 1889 over the faraway Samoan Islands in the South Pacific, which were formally divided between the two nations in 1899. (German Samoa eventually became an independent republic; American Samoa remains an American possession.) The lynching of eleven Italians in New Orleans in 1891 brought America and Italy to the brink of war, until the United States agreed to pay compensation. In the ugliest affair, American demands on Chile after the deaths of two American sailors in the port of Valparaiso in 1892 made hostilities between the two countries seem inevitable. The threat of attack by Chile's modern navy spread alarm on the Pacific Coast, until American power finally forced the Chileans to pay an **indemnity**. The willingness of Americans to risk war over such distant and minor disputes demonstrated the aggressive new national mood.

America's new belligerence combined with old-time anti-British feeling to create a serious crisis between the United States and Britain in 1895–1896. The jungle boundary between British Guiana and Venezuela had long been in dispute, but the discovery of gold in the contested area brought the conflict between Britain and Venezuela to a head. President Cleveland and his pugnacious secretary of state, Richard Olney, stepped into the affair with a combative note to Britain invoking the Monroe Doctrine and declaring that the United States was now calling the tune in the Western Hemisphere. Unimpressed British officials shrugged off Olney's salvo as just another twist of the lion's tail and replied that the affair was none of Uncle Sam's business. President Cleveland—"mad clear through," as he put it—sent a bristling special message to Congress that called for a U.S. commission to determine where the line ought to go and threatened war if the British would not accept the boundary it set.

The entire country, irrespective of political party, was swept off its feet in an outburst of hysteria. War seemed inevitable. Fortunately, sober second thoughts prevailed on both sides of the Atlantic. A rising challenge from Kaiser Wilhelm's Germany and a looming war with the Dutch-descended Boers in South Africa left Britain in no mood for war with America. London backed off and consented to **arbitration**.

The chastened British, their eyes fully opened to the European peril, now cultivated Yankee friendship and inaugurated an era of "patting the Eagle's head," which replaced a century or so of America's "twisting the lion's tail." Sometimes called the Great Rapprochement—or reconciliation—between the United States and Britain, the new Anglo-American cordiality became a cornerstone of both nations' foreign policies as the twentieth century opened.

Spurning the Hawaiian Pear

Enchanted Hawaii had early attracted the attention of Americans. In the morning years of the nineteenth century, the breeze-brushed islands were a way station and provisioning point for Yankee shippers, sailors, and whalers. In 1820 the first New England missionaries

United States Expansion, 1857–1917 With the annexation of the Philippines, Hawaii, and Puerto Rico in 1898, the United States became an imperial power. © Cengage Learning

arrived, preaching the twin blessings of Protestant Christianity and protective calico. As American sugar production flourished on the Hawaiian Islands, the U.S. government assumed a greater interest. The State Department, beginning in the 1840s, sternly warned other powers to keep their hands off the islands. America's grip was further tightened in 1887 by a treaty with the native government guaranteeing priceless naval-base rights at spacious Pearl Harbor.

But trouble was brewing in the insular paradise. Old World pathogens had scythed the indigenous Hawaiian population to one-sixth of its size at the time of first European contact, leading the American sugar lords to import large numbers of Asian laborers. By century's end Chinese and Japanese immigrants outnumbered both whites and native Hawaiians, prompting fears that Tokyo might intervene on behalf of its often-abused nationals. Then sugar markets went sour in 1890 when the McKinley Tariff Act raised barriers against the Hawaiian product. White American planters' mounting efforts to secure annexation by the United States were blocked by Queen Liliuokalani, who insisted that native Hawaiians should control the islands. Though only a tiny minority, the white planters staged a successful coup early in 1893. They were openly assisted by American troops, who landed under the unauthorized orders of the expansionist American minister to Honolulu. "The Hawaiian pear is now fully ripe," he wrote exultantly to his superiors in Washington, "and this is the golden hour for the United States to pluck it."

A treaty of annexation was rushed to Washington, but before it could be railroaded through the Senate, Republican president Harrison's term expired and Democratic president Cleveland came in. Suspecting that his powerful nation had gravely wronged the deposed Queen Liliuokalani and her people, "Old Grover" abruptly withdrew the treaty. A subsequent investigation determined that a majority of Hawaiian natives opposed annexation. Although Queen Liliuokalani could not be reinstated, the sugarcoated move for annexation had to be temporarily abandoned. The Hawaiian pear continued to ripen until 1898, when the United States acquired its overseas empire.

War with Spain over Cuba

Cuba's masses, frightfully misgoverned, again rose against their Spanish oppressors in 1895. The roots of their revolt were partly economic. Sugar production—the backbone of the island's prosperity—was crippled when the American tariff of 1894 restored high duties on the toothsome product.

The desperate *insurrectos* sought to drive out their Spanish overlords by adopting a scorched-earth policy, torching canefields and sugar mills and dynamiting passenger trains. American sympathies went out to the Cuban underdogs. Sentiment aside, American business had about $50 million of investment in Cuba and conducted annual trade of about $100 million.

Fuel was added to the Cuban conflagration in 1896 with the coming to power of the Spanish General ("Butcher") Weyler. He undertook to crush the rebellion by herding many civilians into barbed-wire **reconcentration** camps, where they could not give assistance to the armed *insurrectos*. Lacking proper sanitation, these enclosures turned into deadly pestholes; the victims died miserably.

Atrocities in Cuba were red meat for the sensational new "yellow journalism." William R. Hearst and Joseph Pulitzer, then engaged in a titanic duel for circulation, attempted to outdo each other with screeching headlines and hair-raising "scoops." Where **atrocity** stories did not exist, they were invented. Hearst sent the gifted artist Frederic Remington to Cuba to draw sketches, allegedly with the pointed admonition, "You furnish the pictures and I'll furnish the war." Among other outrages, Remington depicted Spanish customs officials brutally disrobing and searching an American woman. Most readers of Hearst's *Journal*, their indignation soaring, had no way of knowing that such tasks were performed by female attendants.

Then early in 1898 Washington sent the battleship *Maine* to Cuba, ostensibly for a "friendly visit" but actually to protect and evacuate Americans if a dangerous flare-up should occur. Tragedy struck on February 15, 1898, when the *Maine* mysteriously blew up in Havana harbor, with a loss of 260 sailors.

Two investigations of the iron coffin ensued, one by U.S. naval officers and the other by Spanish officials. The Spaniards concluded that the explosion had been internal and presumably accidental; the Americans argued that the blast had been caused by a submarine mine. Not until 1976 did U.S. Navy Admiral H. G. Rickover confirm the original Spanish finding with overwhelming evidence that the initial explosion had resulted from spontaneous combustion in one of the coal bunkers adjacent to a powder magazine.

reconcentration *The policy of forcibly removing a population to confined areas in order to deny support to enemy forces.*

atrocity *An act of deliberate and extreme cruelty, often intended to terrorize or destroy its target.*

Chicago History Museum

The Explosion of the *Maine*, February 15, 1898 Encouraged and amplified by the "yellow press," the outcry over the tragedy of the *Maine* helped drive the country into an impulsive war against Spain.

But Americans in 1898, now mad for war, blindly embraced the less likely explanation. Lashed to fury by the yellow press, they leapt to the inaccurate conclusion that the Spanish government had been guilty of intolerable treachery. The battle cry of the hour became:

Remember the Maine!
To hell with Spain!

Nothing would do but to hurl the "dirty" Spanish flag from the hemisphere.

The national war fever burned ever higher, even though American diplomats had already gained Madrid's agreement to Washington's two basic demands: an end to reconcentration and an armistice with the Cuban rebels. The cautious McKinley found himself in a jam. He did not want hostilities, but neither did he want continuing Spanish control or a fully independent Cuba. More impetuous souls denounced the president as "Wobbly Willy" McKinley. Fight-hungry Theodore Roosevelt reportedly snarled that the "white-livered" occupant of the White House did not have "the backbone of a chocolate eclair." McKinley, recognizing the inevitable, eventually yielded and gave the people what they wanted. But public pressure did not fully explain McKinley's course. He did not trust Spanish promises, and he worried that Democrats would win the upcoming presidential election of 1900 if he remained indecisive. On April 11, 1898, McKinley sent his war message to Congress, urging armed intervention to free the oppressed Cubans. The legislators responded uproariously with what was essentially a declaration of war. In a burst of self-righteousness, they likewise adopted the hand-tying Teller Amendment. This **proviso** proclaimed to the world that when the United States had overthrown Spanish misrule, it would give the Cubans their freedom—a declaration that caused imperialistic Europeans to smile skeptically.

PRIMARY SOURCE
Yellow Kid

PRIMARY SOURCE
Maine Explosion

proviso *An article or clause in a statute, treaty, or contract establishing a particular stipulation or condition affecting the whole document.*

Dewey's May Day Victory at Manila

The American people plunged into the war lightheartedly, like schoolchildren off to a picnic. Bands blared incessantly "There'll Be a Hot Time in the Old Town Tonight" and "Hail, Hail, the Gang's All Here," thus leading some foreigners to believe that those were the national anthems.

The war got off to a giddy start for American forces. Even before the declaration of war, on February 25, 1898, while Navy Secretary John D. Long was away from the office, his hot-blooded assistant secretary Theodore Roosevelt took matters into his own hands. Roosevelt cabled Commodore George Dewey, commanding the American Asian squadron, to descend upon Spain's Philippines in the event of war.

Dewey carried out his orders magnificently on May 1, 1898. Sailing boldly with his six warships at night into the fortified harbor of Manila, he trained his guns the next morning on the Spanish fleet. The entire collection of antiquated and overmatched vessels was quickly destroyed.

Taciturn George Dewey became a national hero overnight. An amateur poet blossomed forth with this:

Oh, dewy was the morning
Upon the first of May,
And Dewey was the Admiral
Down in Manila Bay.
And dewy were the Spaniards' eyes,
Them orbs of black and blue;
And dew we feel discouraged?
I dew not think we dew!

Yet Dewey was in a perilous position. He had destroyed the enemy fleet, but he could not storm the forts of Manila with his sailors. His nerves frayed, he was forced to wait in the sweltering bay while troop reinforcements were slowly assembled in America. The appearance of German warships in Manila harbor added to the tension.

Long-awaited American troops, finally arriving in force, captured Manila on August 13, 1898, in collaboration with Filipino insurgents commanded by their well-educated, part-Chinese leader, Emilio Aguinaldo. Dewey, to his later regret, had brought this shrewd and magnetic revolutionary from exile in Asia so that he might weaken Spanish resistance.

These thrilling events in the Philippines had meanwhile focused attention on Hawaii. An impression spread that America needed the archipelago as a coaling and provisioning way station in order to send supplies and reinforcements to Dewey. A joint resolution of annexation was rushed through Congress and approved by McKinley on July 7, 1898. Hawaii received full territorial status in 1900.

The Confused Invasion of Cuba

Shortly after the outbreak of war, the Spanish government ordered a fleet of warships to Cuba. But the decrepit Spanish "armada" was soon forced into bottle-shaped Santiago harbor, where it was blockaded by the much more powerful American fleet. Sound strategy seemed to dictate that an American army be sent in from the rear to drive out the Spanish ships. Leading the ill-equipped American invading force was the grossly overweight General William R. Shafter, a would-be warrior so blubbery that he had to be carried about on a door.

The "Rough Riders," a part of the invading army, now charged onto the stage of history. This colorful regiment of volunteers, short on discipline but long on dash, consisted largely of western cowboys and other hardy characters, with a sprinkling of ex–polo players and ex-convicts. Commanded by Colonel Leonard Wood, the group was organized principally by the glory-hungry Theodore Roosevelt, who had resigned from the Navy Department to serve as lieutenant colonel.

About the middle of June a bewildered American army of seventeen thousand men finally embarked from Tampa, Florida, amid scenes of indescribable confusion. Shafter's landing near Santiago, Cuba, met little opposition. Brisk fighting broke out on July 1 at El Caney and Kettle Hill, up which Colonel Roosevelt and his horseless Rough Riders charged, with strong support from two crack black regiments. They suffered heavy casualties, but the colorful colonel, having the time of his life, shot a Spaniard with his revolver and rejoiced to see his victim double up like a jackrabbit. He later wrote a book on his exploits, which, humorist Finley Peter Dunne's fictional "Mr. Dooley" remarked, ought to have been entitled *Alone in Cubia* [*sic*].

The American army, fast closing in on Santiago, spelled doom for the Spanish fleet. On July 3 the Spanish fleet steamed out of the harbor and into the teeth of the waiting American warships. "Don't cheer, men," Captain Philip of the *Texas* admonished his seamen. "The poor devils are dying." Shortly thereafter Santiago surrendered.

Hasty preparations were then made for a descent on Puerto Rico before the war should end. There the American army met even less resistance. By this time Spain was ready for an armistice, which was signed on August 12, 1898.

If the Spaniards had held out a few months longer in Cuba, the American army might have melted away. Malaria, typhoid fever, dysentery, and yellow fever incapacitated numerous soldiers and sailors. Others suffered from malodorous canned meat known as "embalmed beef." All told, nearly four hundred men lost their lives to bullets; over five thousand succumbed to bacteria and other causes.

America's Course (Curse?) of Empire

Late in 1898 Spanish and American negotiators met in Paris. War-racked Cuba, as expected, was freed from its Spanish overlords. The Americans had little difficulty in securing the remote Pacific island of Guam, which they had captured early in the conflict from astonished Spaniards who had not known that a war was on. Spain also ceded Puerto Rico to the United States. Ironically, the last remnant of Spain's vast New World empire thus became the first territory ever annexed to the United States without the express promise of eventual statehood. In the decades to come, American investment in the island and Puerto Rican immigration to the United States would make this acquisition one of the weightier consequences of this somewhat carefree war (see "Makers of America: The Puerto Ricans," pp. 446–447).

Knottiest of all was the problem of the Philippines, a veritable apple of discord. These lush islands not only embraced an area larger than the British Isles but also contained a completely alien population of some 7 million souls. McKinley was confronted with a devil's dilemma. He did not feel that America could honorably give the islands back to Spanish misrule, especially after it had fought a war to free Cuba. And America would be turning its back on its responsibilities, he believed, if it simply pulled up anchor and sailed away.

McKinley viewed all the choices open to him as trouble-fraught. The Filipinos, if left to govern themselves, might fall into anarchy. One of the major powers, possibly aggressive Germany, might then seize them and suck the United States into a major war. Seemingly the least of the evils was to acquire all the Philippines and then perhaps give the Filipinos their freedom later.

President McKinley, ever sensitive to public opinion, kept a carefully attuned ear to the ground. The rumble that he heard seemed to call for the entire group of islands. Zealous Protestant missionaries were eager to win Filipino converts from Catholicism. (The Philippines had been substantially Christianized by Spanish Catholics before the founding of Jamestown in 1607.) Wall Street had generally opposed the war; but awakened by the booming of Dewey's guns, it was clamoring for profits in the Philippines.

A tormented McKinley later claimed that he went down on his knees seeking divine guidance and heard an inner voice telling him to take all the Philippines and Christianize and civilize them. Accordingly, he decided for outright annexation of the islands. Because Manila had been captured *after* the armistice was signed, the Americans agreed to pay Spain $20 million for the Philippine Islands—the last great Spanish haul from the New World.

The signing of the pact of Paris touched off one of the most impassioned foreign-policy debates in American history. Except for glacial Alaska, coral-reefed Hawaii, and a handful of Pacific atolls, the Republic had hitherto absorbed only contiguous territory on the continent. All previous acquisitions had been thinly peopled and eligible for ultimate statehood. But in the Philippines the nation had on its hands a distant tropical area, thickly populated by Asians of a different culture, tongue, and government institutions.

Opponents of annexation argued that such a step would dishonor and ultimately destroy American's venerable commitments to self-determination and anticolonialism. "Goddamn the United States for its vile conduct in the Philippine Isles!" burst out the usually mild-mannered Professor William James. The Harvard philosopher could not believe that the United States could "puke up its ancient soul in five minutes without a wink of squeamishness." The Anti-Imperialist League sprang into being to fight the McKinley administration's expansionist moves. The organization counted among its members some of the most prominent people in the United States, including the presidents of Stanford and Harvard Universities and the novelist Mark Twain. The anti-imperialist blanket even stretched over such strange bedfellows as the labor leader Samuel Gompers and the steel titan Andrew Carnegie.

Anti-imperialists raised many objections. The Filipinos thirsted for freedom; to annex them would violate the "consent of the governed" philosophy of the Declaration of Independence and the Constitution. Despotism abroad might well beget despotism at home. Imperialism was costly and unlikely ever to turn a profit. Finally, annexation would propel the United States into the political and military cauldron of East Asia.

Yet the expansionists or imperialists could sing a seductive song. They appealed to patriotism, invoked America's "civilizing mission," and played up possible trade profits. Manila, in fact, might become another Hong Kong. Rudyard Kipling, the British poet laureate of imperialism, urged America down the slippery path with a quotable poem:

> Take up the White Man's burden—
> Ye dare not stoop to less—
> Nor call too loud on Freedom
> To cloak your weariness.

In short, the wealthy Americans must help to uplift (and exploit) the underprivileged, underfed, and underclad of the world.

Over heated protests, the Senate approved the treaty with Spain with just one vote to spare on February 6, 1898. America was now officially an empire.

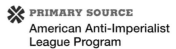

PRIMARY SOURCE
American Anti-Imperialist
League Program

President William McKinley (1843–1901) later described his decision to annex the Philippines:

"When next I realized that the Philippines had dropped into our laps, I confess I did not know what to do with them. ... I went down on my knees and prayed Almighty God for light and guidance. ... And one night late it came to me this way. ... That there was nothing left for us to do but to take them all, and to educate the Filipinos, and uplift and civilize and Christianize them and by God's grace do the very best we could by them, as our fellow men, for whom Christ also died. And then I went to bed and went to sleep, and slept soundly."

The Puerto Ricans

At dawn on July 26, 1898, the U.S. warship *Gloucester* steamed into Puerto Rico's Guanica harbor, fired at the Spanish blockhouse, and landed some thirty-three hundred troops. Within days, the Americans had taken possession of the Caribbean island a thousand miles southeast of Florida. In so doing they set in motion changes on the island that ultimately brought a new wave of immigrants to U.S. shores.

Puerto Rico had been a Spanish possession since Christopher Columbus claimed it for Castile in 1493. The Spaniards enslaved many of the island's forty thousand Taino Indians and set them to work on farms and in mines. Many Tainos died of exhaustion and disease, and in 1511 the Indians rebelled. The Spaniards crushed the uprising, killed thousands of Indians, and began importing African slaves—thus establishing the basis for Puerto Rico's multiracial society.

The first Puerto Rican immigrants to the United States arrived as political exiles in the nineteenth century. From their haven in America, they agitated for the island's independence from Spain. The Puerto Rican political *émigrés* in the United States returned home after the Americans conquered the island in 1898.

But they were soon replaced by poor islanders looking for work. When Congress granted Puerto Ricans U.S. citizenship in 1917, thereby eliminating immigration hurdles, many islanders hurried north to find jobs. During the ensuing decades, Puerto Ricans went to work in Arizona cotton fields, New Jersey soup factories, and Utah mines. The majority, however, clustered in New York City and found work in the city's cigar factories, shipyards, and garment industry. Migration slowed somewhat after the 1920s as the Great Depression shrank the job market on the mainland and as World War II made travel hazardous.

When World War II ended in 1945, the sudden advent of cheap air travel sparked an emigration explosion. As late as the 1930s, the tab for a boat trip to the mainland exceeded the average Puerto Rican's yearly earnings. But with an airplane surplus after World War II, the six-hour flight from Puerto Rico to New York cost under $50. The Puerto Rican population on

Perplexities in Puerto Rico and Cuba

From the outset, the status of Puerto Rico was anomalous—neither a state nor a territory, and with little prospect of eventual independence. The Foraker Act of 1900 accorded the Puerto Ricans a limited degree of popular government, and in 1917 Congress granted Puerto Ricans U.S. citizenship but withheld full self-rule. Although the American regime worked wondrous improvements in education, sanitation, and transportation, many of the inhabitants still aspired to independence. Great numbers of Puerto Ricans ultimately moved to New York City, where they added to the complexity of the melting pot.

The annexation of Puerto Rico (and the Philippines) posed a thorny legal problem: Did the Constitution follow the flag? Did American laws, including tariff laws and the Bill of Rights, apply with full force to the newly acquired possessions? "Who are we?" a group of Puerto Rican petitioners asked Congress in 1900. "Are we citizens or are we subjects?" Beginning in 1901 with the *Insular Cases*, a badly divided Supreme Court decreed, in effect, that the flag did outrun the Constitution, and that the outdistanced document did not necessarily extend with full force to the new windfall. Puerto Ricans (and Filipinos) might be subject to American rule, but they did not enjoy all American rights.

Cuba, scorched and chaotic, presented another headache. An American military government under General Leonard Wood of Rough Rider fame wrought miracles in

The First Puerto Ricans
The Spanish conquistadores treated the native Taino Indian peoples in Puerto Rico with extreme cruelty, and the Indians were virtually extinct by the mid-1500s.

the mainland quadrupled between 1940 and 1950 and tripled again by 1960. In 1970, 1.5 million Puerto Ricans lived in the United States, one-third of the island's total population.

United States citizenship and affordable air travel made it easy for Puerto Ricans to return home. Thus to a far greater degree than most immigrant groups, Puerto Ricans kept one foot in the United States and the other on their native island. By some estimates, 2 million people a year journeyed to and from the island during the postwar period. Puerto Rico's gubernatorial candidates sometimes campaigned in New York for the thousands of voters who were expected to return to the island in time for the election.

Puerto Ricans have fared better economically in the United States than on the island, where, in 1970, 60 percent of all inhabitants lived below the poverty line. In recent years Puerto Ricans have attained more schooling, and many have attended college. Invigorated by the civil rights movement of the 1960s, Puerto Ricans also became more politically active, electing growing numbers of congressmen and state and city officials.

Uncle Sam and People from His Colonies, Postcard, c. 1900 The acquisition of Puerto Rico, the Philippines, Hawaii, and other Pacific islands brought millions of people of color under the American flag and, as depicted here, the paternal watch of "Uncle Sam." Whether they would eventually become citizens or remain colonial subjects was hotly debated in the United States. Many anti-imperialists opposed colonial expansion precisely because they regarded the exotic new peoples as "unassimilable."

government, finance, education, agriculture, and public health. Wood and Colonel William C. Gorgas also launched a frontal attack on yellow fever. Spectacular experiments performed by Dr. Walter Reed and others on American soldiers, who volunteered as human guinea pigs, proved that the stegomyia mosquito was the lethal carrier. Cleaning up breeding places for mosquitoes wiped out yellow fever in Havana.

The United States, honoring its self-denying Teller Amendment of 1898, withdrew from Cuba in 1902. Old World imperialists could scarcely believe their eyes. But the Washington government feared that if Cuba were left on its own a grasping power such as Germany might secure dangerous lodgment near America's soft underbelly. The Cubans were therefore forced to write into their own constitution of 1901 the so-called Platt Amendment.

The Cubans loathed the amendment, which served McKinley's ultimate purpose of bringing Cuba under American control. ("Plattism" survives as a colloquial term of derision even in modern-day Cuba.) The Platt Amendment placed restrictions on Cubans' political and financial autonomy and permitted the United States to intervene with troops to restore order when it saw fit. The Cubans also promised to sell or lease coaling or naval stations to their powerful "benefactor." The United States finally abrogated the amendment in 1934, although Uncle Sam still occupies one remaining base, Guantanamo, under an agreement that can be revoked only by the consent of both parties (see p. 561).

New Horizons in Two Hemispheres

In essence, the Spanish-American War was a kind of colossal coming-out party. Dewey's thundering guns merely advertised the fact that the nation was already a world power. The war itself was short (113 days), spectacular, low in casualties, and theatrically successful—despite the bungling. Secretary of State John Hay called it a "splendid little war." American prestige rose sharply, and the European great powers grudgingly accorded the Republic more respect.

An exhilarating new martial spirit, buoyed along by the newly popular military marching-band music of John Philip Sousa, thrilled America. Most Americans did not start the war with consciously imperialistic motives, but after falling through the cellar door of imperialism in a drunken fit of idealism, they wound up with imperialistic and colonial fruits in their grasp. Captain Mahan's big-navyism seemed vindicated, and popular support grew for more and better battleships. A masterly organizer, Secretary of War Elihu Root, established a general staff and founded the War College in Washington.

One of the most beneficial results of the conflict was the further closing of the "bloody chasm" between North and South. Thousands of patriotic southerners had flocked to the Stars and Stripes, and gray-bearded General Joseph ("Fighting Joe") Wheeler—a Confederate cavalry hero—was given a command in Cuba. He allegedly cried, in the heat of battle, "To hell with the Yankees! Dammit, I mean the Spaniards!"

Even so, the newly imperial nation was not yet prepared to pay the full bill for its new status. By taking on the Philippine Islands, the United States became a full-fledged East Asian power. But the distant islands eventually became a "heel of Achilles"—a kind of indefensible **hostage** given to Japan, as events proved in World War II. Here and elsewhere, the Americans had shortsightedly assumed burdensome commitments that they proved unwilling to defend with appropriate naval and military outlays.

hostage *A person or thing forcibly held in order to obtain certain goals or agreements.*

"Little Brown Brothers" in the Philippines

The liberty-loving Filipinos assumed that they, like the Cubans, would be granted their freedom after the Spanish-American War. They were tragically deceived. Washington excluded them from the peace negotiations with Spain and made clear its intention to stay in the Philippines indefinitely. Bitterness toward the American troops erupted into open insurrection on February 4, 1899, under Emilio Aguinaldo. Having plunged into war with Spain to free Cuba, the United States was now forced to deploy some 126,000 troops ten thousand miles away to rivet shackles onto a people who asked for nothing but freedom—in the American tradition.

The poorly equipped Filipino rebels soon melted into the jungle to wage vicious guerrilla warfare. Just a few months earlier, American soldiers had believed they were rescuing innocent Philippine victims of Spanish tyranny. Now they were fighting the Filipinos, whom they came to see as dangerous enemies of the United States. This shift contributed to a mounting "race war" in which both sides perpetrated sordid atrocities. Uncle Sam's soldiers adopted the "water cure"—forcing water down victims' throats until they yielded information or died. American-built reconcentration camps rivaled those of "Butcher" Weyler in Cuba. Having begun the Spanish war with noble ideals, America now dirtied its hands. One New York newspaper published a reply to Rudyard Kipling's famous poem:

> *We've taken up the white man's burden*
> *Of ebony and brown;*
> *Now will you kindly tell us, Rudyard,*
> *How we may put it down?*

The Americans broke the back of the Filipino insurgency in 1901 when they captured Aguinaldo. But sporadic fighting dragged on for many dreary months, eventually claiming the lives of 4,234 Americans and as many as 600,000 Filipinos.

Future president William H. Taft, an able and amiable Ohioan who weighed some 350 pounds, became civil governor of the Philippines in 1901. Forming a strong attachment to the Filipinos, he called them his "little brown brothers." But McKinley's "benevolent assimilation" of the Philippines proceeded with painful slowness. Millions of American dollars did lead to better roads, improved public sanitation, and an unusually good school system. But all this vast expenditure was ill received. The Filipinos hated compulsory Americanization and pined for liberty. They finally got their freedom on the Fourth of July, 1946. In the meantime, thousands of Filipinos emigrated to the United States (see "Makers of America: The Filipinos," p. 450).

Hinging the Open Door in China

sphere of influence *In international affairs, the territory where a powerful state exercises the dominant control over weaker states or territories.*

Ominous events had meanwhile been brewing in enfeebled China. After its defeat by Japan in 1894–1895, the imperialistic European powers, notably Russia and Germany, moved in. Like sharks attacking a wounded whale, they began to tear away valuable leaseholds and economic **spheres of influence** from the Manchu government.

A growing group of Americans viewed the vivisection of China with alarm. Churches were worried about their missionary strongholds. Merchants feared that Europeans would monopolize Chinese markets. An alarmed American public demanded that Washington do something. Secretary of State John Hay, a witty poet-novelist-diplomat, finally decided upon a dramatic move.

In the summer of 1899, Hay dispatched to all the great powers a communication soon known as the Open Door note. He urged them to announce that in their leaseholds or spheres of influence they would respect certain Chinese rights and the ideal of fair competition. Tellingly, Hay had not bothered to consult the Chinese themselves.

The phrase *Open Door* quickly caught the American public's fancy. But Hay's proposal caused much squirming in the leading world capitals, though all the great powers except Russia eventually agreed to it.

Open Door or not, patriotic Chinese did not care to be used as a doormat by the Europeans. In 1900 a superpatriotic group, known as the "Boxers" for their training in martial arts, broke loose with the cry,

American Missionary Grace Roberts Teaching in China, 1903
A long history of American missionary involvement in China nurtured a sentimental affection for that country among Americans that persisted well into the twentieth century.

By permission of the Houghton Library, Harvard University

The Filipinos

At the beginning of the twentieth century, the United States, its imperial muscles just flexed in the war with Spain, found itself in possession of the Philippines. Uncertain of how to manage this empire, which seethed resentfully against its new masters, the United States promised to build democracy in the Philippines and to ready the islanders for home rule. Almost immediately after annexation, the American governor of the archipelago sent a corps of Filipino students to the United States, hoping to forge future leaders steeped in American ways who would someday govern an independent Philippines.

Most Filipino immigrants to the United States in these years, however, came not to study but to toil. With Chinese immigration banned, Hawaii and the Pacific Coast states turned to the Philippines for cheap agricultural labor. Beginning in 1906, the Hawaiian Sugar Planters Association aggressively recruited Filipino workers. Enlistments grew slowly at first, but by the 1920s thousands of young Filipino men had reached the Hawaiian Islands and been assigned to sugar plantations or pineapple fields.

Those Filipinos venturing as far as the American mainland found work less arduous but also less certain than did their countrymen on Hawaiian plantations. Many mainlanders worked seasonally—in winter as domestic servants, busboys, or bellhops; in summer journeying to the fields to harvest lettuce, strawberries, sugar beets, and potatoes. Eventually Filipinos, along with Mexican immigrants, came to make up the largest share of California's agricultural workforce.

A mobile society, Filipino Americans also were overwhelmingly male; there was only one Filipino woman for every fourteen Filipino men in California in 1930. Thus, the issue of intermarriage became acutely sensitive. California and many other states prohibited the marriage of Asians and Caucasians in demeaning laws that remained on the books until 1948. Undeterred by such overt discrimination and the vigilante violence sometimes directed at them, especially in Washington and California, Filipinos challenged restrictive state laws and the hooligans who found in them an excuse for mayhem. But Filipinos, who did not become eligible for American citizenship until 1946, long lacked political leverage.

After World War II, Filipino immigration accelerated. Between 1950 and 1970, the number of Filipinos in the United States nearly doubled, with women and men stepping aboard the new transpacific airliners in roughly equal numbers. Many of these recent arrivals were solidly middle class and sought in America a better life for their children. Today, the war-torn and perpetually depressed archipelago sends more immigrants to American shores than does any other Asian nation.

Hawaii State Archives

Filipino Workers Arriving in Honolulu, 1940s
Tags around their necks indicated the plantations to which they had been assigned.

"Kill Foreign Devils." In what became known as the Boxer Rebellion, they murdered more than two hundred foreigners and thousands of Chinese Christians and besieged the foreign diplomatic community in the capital, Beijing (Peking).

A multinational rescue force of some eighteen thousand soldiers, including several thousand Americans, arrived in the nick of time to quell the rebellion and prop the Open Door open. The victorious allied invaders acted angrily and vindictively. They assessed prostrate China an excessive indemnity of $333 million, of which America's share was to be $24.5 million. When Washington discovered that this sum was much more than enough to pay damages and expenses, it remitted about $18 million to be used for the education of a selected group of Chinese students in the United States—a not-so-subtle initiative to further the westernization of Asia.

Secretary Hay let fly another paper broadside in 1900, announcing that henceforth the Open Door would embrace the territorial integrity of China. Those principles helped spare China from possible **partition** in these troubled years and were formally incorporated into the Nine-Power Treaty of 1922, only to be callously violated by Japan's takeover of Manchuria a decade later (see p. 539).

partition *In politics, the act of dividing a weaker territory or government among several more powerful states.*

Imperialism or Bryanism in 1900?

President McKinley's renomination by the Republicans in 1900 was a foregone conclusion. He had won a war, acquired rich though burdensome colonial territories for the United States, and brought the promised prosperity of the full dinner pail. An irresistible vice-presidential boom had developed for "Teddy" Roosevelt (TR), the cowboy-hero of the Cuban campaign. Capitalizing on his war-born popularity, he had been elected governor of New York, where the local political bosses had found him headstrong and difficult to manage. They therefore devised a scheme to kick the colorful colonel upstairs into the vice presidency.

This plot to railroad Roosevelt worked beautifully. Gesticulating wildly, Roosevelt sported a cowboy hat that made him stand out like a white crow. To cries of "We Want Teddy!" he was handily nominated. A wary Mark Hanna reportedly moaned that there would now be only one heartbeat between "that damned cowboy" and the presidency of the United States.

William Jennings Bryan was the odds-on choice of the Democrats, meeting at Kansas City. Their platform proclaimed that the paramount issue was Republican overseas imperialism.

McKinley, the soul of dignity, once again campaigned safely from his front porch. Bryan again took to the stump in a cyclonic campaign. Lincoln, he charged, had abolished slavery for 3.5 million Africans; McKinley had reestablished it for 7 million Filipinos. Roosevelt out-Bryaned Bryan, touring the country with revolver-shooting cowboys. Flashing his monumental teeth and pounding his fist into his palm, Roosevelt denounced all the dastards who would haul down Old Glory.

McKinley handily triumphed by a much wider margin than in 1896: 7,218,491 to 6,356,734 popular votes, and 292 to 155 electoral votes. But victory for the Republicans was not a mandate for imperialism. If there was any mandate at all, it was for the two *P*s: prosperity and protectionism. Meanwhile, the New York bosses gleefully looked forward to watching the nettlesome Roosevelt "take the veil" as vice president.

The contest over American imperialism took place on the Senate floor as well as around the globe. In 1900 Senator Albert J. Beveridge (1862–1927), Republican from Indiana, returned from an investigative trip to the Philippines to defend its annexation:

"The Philippines are ours forever. ... And just beyond the Philippines are China's illimitable markets. We will not retreat from either. We will not abandon our opportunity in the Orient. We will not renounce our part in the mission of our race: trustee, under God, of the civilization of the world."

Two years later Senator George F. Hoar (1826–1904), Republican from Massachusetts, broke with his party to denounce American annexation of the Philippines and other territories:

"You cannot maintain despotism in Asia and a republic in America. If you try to deprive even a savage or a barbarian of his just rights you can never do it without becoming a savage or a barbarian yourself."

TR: Brandisher of the Big Stick

Kindly William McKinley had scarcely served another six months when, in September 1901, he was murdered by a deranged anarchist in Buffalo, New York. Roosevelt rode a buckboard out of his campsite in the Adirondack Mountains to take the oath of office, becoming, at age forty-two, the youngest president thus far in American history.

Born into a wealthy and distinguished New York family, Roosevelt, a red-blooded **blue blood**, had fiercely built up his spindly, asthmatic body by a stern and self-imposed routine of exercise. He graduated from Harvard with Phi Beta Kappa honors and published, at the age of twenty-four, the first of some thirty volumes of muscular prose. He worked as a ranch owner and cowboy in the Dakotas before pursuing his political career full time. Barrel-chested, bespectacled, with mulelike molars, squinty eyes, droopy mustache, and piercing voice, he was ever the delight of cartoonists.

The Rough Rider's high-voltage energy was electrifying. Believing that it was better to wear out than to rust out, he would shake the hands of some six thousand people at one stretch or ride long miles on horseback. Incurably boyish and **bellicose**, Roosevelt ceaselessly preached the virile virtues and denounced pacifistic "flubdubs" and "mollycoddles." An ardent champion of military and naval **preparedness**, he adopted as his pet proverb, "Speak softly and carry a big stick, [and] you will go far."

His outsized ego caused it to be said of him that he wanted to be the bride at every wedding and the corpse at every funeral. He loved people and mingled with those of all ranks—from Catholic cardinals to professional prizefighters, one of whom blinded a Rooseveltian eye in a White House bout. "TR" commanded an idolatrous personal following. After visiting him, a journalist wrote, "You go home and wring the personality out of your clothes."

Above all, TR believed that the president should lead boldly. He had no real respect for the delicate checks and balances among the three branches of government. The president, he felt, may take any action in the general interest that is not specifically forbidden by the laws or the Constitution.

blue blood *A person of supposedly "pure blood," presumed to be descended from nobility or aristocracy.*

bellicose *Disposed to fight or go to war.*

preparedness *The accumulation of sufficient armed forces and material to go to war.*

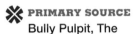

PRIMARY SOURCE
Bully Pulpit, The

Building the Panama Canal

Roosevelt soon applied his bullish energy to foreign affairs. The Spanish-American War had reinvigorated interest in the long-talked-about canal across the Central American isthmus. An isthmian canal would plainly augment the strength of the navy by increasing its mobility. Such a waterway would also make easier the defense of such recent acquisitions as Puerto Rico, Hawaii, and the Philippines.

Big Stick in the Caribbean In 1901 Roosevelt declared: "If a man continually blusters ... a big stick will not save him from trouble; and neither will speaking softly avail, if back of the softness there does not lie strength, power. ... If the boaster is not prepared to back up his words his position becomes absolutely contemptible." © Cengage Learning

Initial obstacles in the path of the canal builders were legal rather than geographical. By the terms of the ancient Clayton-Bulwer Treaty, concluded with Britain in 1850, the United States could not secure exclusive control over an isthmian route. But by 1901 America's British cousins were willing to yield ground. Confronted with an unfriendly Europe and bogged down in the South African Boer War, they consented to the Hay-Pauncefote Treaty in 1901. It not only gave the United States a free hand to build the canal but conceded the right to fortify it as well.

But where exactly should the canal be dug? Many American experts favored a route across Nicaragua, but agents of an old French canal company were eager to salvage something from their costly failure in S-shaped Panama. Represented by a young, energetic, and unscrupulous engineer, Philippe Bunau-Varilla, the New Panama Canal Company suddenly dropped the price of its holdings from $109 million to the fire sale price of $40 million.

Congress in June 1902 finally decided on the Panama route. The scene now shifted to Colombia, of which Panama was a restive part. The Colombian senate rejected an American offer of $10 million and annual payment of $250,000 for a six-mile-wide zone across Panama. Roosevelt railed against "those dagos" who were frustrating his ambitions. Meanwhile, impatient Panamanians were ripe for a revolt. Scheming Bunau-Varilla was no less disturbed by the prospect of losing the company's $40 million. Working hand in glove with the Panama revolutionists, Bunau-Varilla helped incite a rebellion on November 3, 1903. United States naval forces prevented Colombian troops from crossing the isthmus to quell the uprising.

Roosevelt moved rapidly to make steamy Panama a virtual outpost of the United States. Just three days after the insurrection, he hastily extended the right hand of recognition. Fifteen days later, Bunau-Varilla, who was now the Panamanian minister despite his French citizenship, signed the Hay–Bunau-Varilla Treaty in Washington. The price of the canal strip was left the same, but the zone was widened from six to ten miles. The French company gladly pocketed its $40 million from the U.S. Treasury.

Roosevelt, it seems clear, did not actively plot to tear Panama from the side of Colombia. But the conspirators knew of his angrily expressed views, and they counted on his using the big stick to hold Colombia at bay. The Rough Rider became so indiscreetly involved in the Panama affair as to create the impression that he had been a secret party to the intrigue, and the so-called rape of Panama marked an ugly downward lurch in U.S. relations with Latin America.

Theodore Roosevelt and His Big Stick in the Caribbean, 1904
Roosevelt's policies seemed to be turning the Caribbean into a Yankee pond.

Canal construction began in 1904, in the face of daunting difficulties ranging from labor troubles to landslides and lethal tropical diseases. Colonel William C. Gorgas, the quiet and determined exterminator of yellow fever in Havana, ultimately made the Canal Zone "as safe as a health resort." At a cost of some $400 million, an autocratic West Point engineer, Colonel George Washington Goethals, ultimately brought the project to completion in 1914, just as World War I was breaking out.

TR's Perversion of Monroe's Doctrine

Latin American debt defaults prompted further Rooseveltian involvement in affairs south of the border. Nations such as Venezuela and the Dominican Republic were chronically in arrears in their payments to European creditors.

Roosevelt feared that if the Germans or British got their foot in the door as bill collectors, they might remain in Latin America, in flagrant violation of the Monroe Doctrine. He therefore declared a brazen policy of "preventive intervention," better known as the Roosevelt Corollary to the Monroe Doctrine. He announced that in the event of future financial malfeasance by the Latin American nations, the United States itself would intervene, take over the customshouses, pay off the debts, and keep the troublesome Europeans on the other side of the Atlantic. In short, no outsiders could push around the Latin American nations except Uncle Sam, Policeman of the Caribbean. This new brandishing of the big stick in the Caribbean became effective in 1905 when the United States took over management of the Dominican Republic's tariff collections. The big stick was vigorously wielded again in 1906 when revolutionary disorders in Cuba led to the sending of U.S. marines, who policed the country until they were temporarily withdrawn in 1909.

TR's rewriting of the Monroe Doctrine probably did more than any other single step to promote the "Bad Neighbor" policy begun in these years. As time wore on, the new **corollary** was used to justify wholesale interventions and repeated landings of the marines, all of which helped turn the Caribbean into a "Yankee pond." To Latin Americans it seemed as though the revised Monroe Doctrine, far from providing a shield, was a cloak behind which the United States sought to strangle them.

corollary *A secondary inference or deduction from a main proposition that is assumed to be established or proven.*

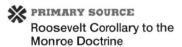
PRIMARY SOURCE
Roosevelt Corollary to the Monroe Doctrine

Roosevelt on the World Stage

Booted and spurred, Roosevelt charged into international affairs far beyond Latin America. The outbreak of war between Russia and Japan in 1904 gave him a chance to perform as a global statesman. The Russians' threatened seizure of China's Manchuria would be a pistol pointed at Japan's strategic heart. The Japanese responded in 1904 with a devastating surprise pounce on the Russian fleet. They proceeded to administer a humiliating series of beatings to the inept Russians. But as the war dragged on, Japan began to run short of men and yen. Tokyo officials therefore approached Roosevelt in the deepest secrecy and asked him to help sponsor peace negotiations.

Roosevelt was happy to oblige, as he wanted to avoid a complete Russian collapse so that the tsar's empire could remain a counterweight to Japan's growing power. At Portsmouth, New Hampshire, in 1905, TR guided the warring parties to a settlement that satisfied neither side. Japan was forced to drop its demands for a cash indemnity and Russian evacuation of Sakhalin Island, though it did gain effective control over Korea, which it formally annexed in 1910.

For achieving this agreement, as well as for helping arrange an international conference at Algeciras, Spain, in 1906 to mediate North African disputes, TR received the Nobel Peace Prize in 1906. But the price of his diplomatic glory was high for U.S. foreign relations. Two historic friendships withered on the windswept plains of Manchuria. America's relations with Russia, once friendly, soured as the Russians implausibly accused Roosevelt of robbing them of military victory. Japan, once America's protégé, felt robbed of its due compensation. Both newly powerful, Japan and America now became rivals in Asia, as fear and jealousy between them grew.

Japanese Laborers in California

America's Pacific Coast soon felt the effects of the Russo-Japanese War. The conflict's dislocations and tax burdens sent a new wave of Japanese immigrants into the spacious valleys of California. Although Japanese residents never amounted to more than 3 percent of the state's population, white Californians ranted about a new "yellow peril" and feared being drowned in an Asian sea.

A showdown on the influx came in 1906 when San Francisco's school board, coping with the aftermath of a frightful earthquake and fire, ordered the segregation of Chinese, Japanese, and Korean students in a special school to free more space for whites. Instantly the incident boiled into an international crisis. The people of Japan, understandably sensitive on questions of race, regarded this discrimination as an insult to them and their beloved children. On both sides of the Pacific, irresponsible war talk sizzled in the yellow press—the real "yellow peril." Roosevelt, the often-bellicose Rough Rider, was in this case unhappy that California might start up a war. He therefore invited the entire San Francisco Board of Education to the White House.

TR finally broke the deadlock, but not until he had brandished his big stick and bared his big teeth. The Californians were induced to repeal the offensive school order and to accept what came to be known as the "Gentlemen's Agreement." By this secret understanding, worked out during 1907–1908, Tokyo agreed to stop the flow of laborers to the American mainland by withholding passports.

Worried that his intercession might be interpreted in Tokyo as prompted by fear, Roosevelt hit upon a dramatic scheme to impress the Japanese with the heft of his big stick. He daringly decided to send the entire U.S. battleship fleet on a highly visible voyage around the world.

Late in 1907, sixteen smoke-belching battleships started from Virginia waters. Their commander pointedly declared that he was ready for "a feast, a frolic, or a fight." The Great White Fleet received tumultuous welcomes in Latin America, Hawaii, New Zealand, and Australia. The high point of the trip was an overwhelming reception in Japan, as tens of

Japanese Workers Building a Road in California, c. 1910

The closing years of the nineteenth century witnessed an unprecedented explosion of imperialism, roughly defined as the forcible imposition of one country's rule on the unwilling inhabitants of another. Between 1870 and the outbreak of World War I in 1914, a handful of European states extended their sway over nearly one-quarter of the earth's surface. Other countries followed suit, notably Japan and eventually the United States.

All the imperial powers had in common a heritage of nationalism and a high degree of industrialization. They commanded the elaborate administrative apparatus of large unified states, along with quantities of wealth, technology, and murderous firepower utterly beyond the capacity of the so-called backward peoples they sought to dominate. As a result, imperialism was, from the start, a lopsided game. As one English wit mordantly noted in 1898:

Whatever happens, we have got
The Maxim gun, and they have not.

Yet ultimately, even with their enormously disproportionate advantages, the imperial states were unable to sustain the age of imperialism for much more than a century.

In many ways, modern imperialism resembled eighteenth-century mercantilism, as economically advanced states backed away from the free-trade doctrines that had energized the early stages of the Industrial Revolution and sought instead to create what one British imperialist called "a great self-sustaining and self-protecting empire." The new imperialism also differed from older colonialism in that the imperial powers sought not merely to exploit but also to transform, modernize, and "westernize" the "backward" societies under their control.

Imperialists often justified their dominion over less-developed societies with high-toned slogans. The British professed to be nobly shouldering "the white man's burden." The French piously invoked their *mission civilisatrice* (civilizing mission). The Germans touted the benefits of spreading their vaunted *Kultur* (culture). The Americans prated about

A Young Ho Chi Minh
Ho Chi Minh (1890–1969) attended the Congress of the Socialist Party in Tours, France, where the French Communist party was created in late December 1920.

the superiority of the Anglo-Saxons, as the Japanese did about their own "Yamato" race.

These protestations may have been sincere, but other motives more powerfully propelled the imperial enterprise. Prominent among them was the quest for new markets, as maturing industrial economies appeared to be exhausting the possibilities for economic growth at home. The need for reliable sources of products such as cotton, sugar, copper, coffee, and tea also figured conspicuously. An even more compelling incentive was the need to protect the huge investments of capital that built the railroads, highways, bridges, ports, mills, foundries, mines, smelters, and telegraphs of the developing world. By the eve of World War I, fully one-quarter of Britain's accumulated wealth was invested overseas.

But perhaps the most important factor driving the imperialist venture was simply the competitive nature of the international system itself. In an unstable, unpredictable world inhabited by ambitious and wary powers, no state thought it could afford to cede an advantage, however ill defined, to any real or imagined rival. Indeed, quite independently of their hard economic value, colonies came to be considered the necessary symbols of great-power status. This perverse logic proved to be a powerful dynamite: Once the imperial race began, it was difficult to stop. As Cecil Rhodes, the fabled British colonizer in southern Africa, once said, "I would annex the planets, if I could. I often think of that."

So when Belgium's King Leopold took an interest in Africa's Congo basin in the 1870s, he touched off a mad imperial scramble that eventually involved Belgium, Britain, Germany, France, Italy, and Portugal. Less than two decades later, with the exceptions of Ethiopia and Liberia, the entire continent, much of it unexplored and of dubious economic value, was under European domination.

In Asia, Germany annexed part of New Guinea in 1884. France completed its annexation of Indochina (present-day Vietnam, Laos, and Cambodia) that same year. Britain acquired Burma (now Myanmar) in 1885 and parts of Borneo and the Malay Peninsula soon after. Japan closed its grip on Okinawa in 1872, Formosa (Taiwan) in 1895, Port Arthur in 1905, and Korea in 1910. All those powers, in addition to Russia, also had designs on China, which despite its venerable history seemed a poor match for the energetic "nations on the make." In the Open Door notes of 1899 and 1900, the United States tried to temper the imperialists' appetites for Chinese territory and concessions, while at the same time America was becoming an imperial power itself with the takeover of the Philippines and Puerto Rico.

The imperialists brought not only their might and their majesty, their capital and their Maxim guns. They also brought their ideas, including concepts of nationalism, self-determination, and democracy. In 1919 a young Vietnamese nationalist named Nguyen Sinh Cung unsuccessfully petitioned the post–World War I peacemakers at Versailles for his country's right to self-determination. A little more than half a century later, under the name Ho Chi Minh, he secured Vietnam's independence by prevailing in a war first against the French and then against the Americans. By that time the United States had long since voluntarily relinquished the Philippines (in 1946, though Puerto Rico remains an American possession), and virtually all of Africa and Asia had been decolonized. With the handover of Hong Kong (1997) and Macao (1999) to the People's Republic of China, the age of empire effectively ended.

VARYING VIEWPOINTS   Why Did America Become a World Power?

American imperialism has long been an embarrassing topic for students of American history, who remember the Republic's own revolutionary origins and anticolonial tradition. Perhaps for that reason, many historians have tried to explain the dramatic overseas expansionism of the 1890s as some kind of aberration—a sudden, singular, and short-lived departure from time-honored American principles and practices. Various explanations have been offered to account for this spasmodic lapse. Scholars such as Julius Pratt pointed to the irresponsible behavior of the yellow press. Richard Hofstadter ascribed America's imperial fling to the "psychic crisis of the 1890s," a crisis brought on, he argued, by the strains of the decade's economic depression and the Populist upheaval. Howard K. Beale emphasized the contagious scramble for imperial possessions by the European powers, as well as Japan, in these years.

In Beale's argument, the United States—and Theodore Roosevelt in particular—succumbed to a kind of international peer pressure: if other countries were expanding their international roles and even establishing colonies around the globe, could the United States safely refrain from doing the same?

Perhaps the most controversial interpretation of American imperialism has come from a so-called New Left school of writers, inspired by William Appleman Williams (and before him by V. I. Lenin's 1916 book *Imperialism:*

The Highest Stage of Capitalism). Historians such as Williams and Walter LaFeber argue that the explanation for political and military expansion abroad is to be found in economic expansion at home. Increasing industrial output, so the argument goes, required ever more raw materials and, especially, overseas markets. That "revisionist" interpretation, in turn, has been sharply criticized by scholars who point out that foreign trade accounted for only a tiny share of American output and that the diplomacy of this period was far too complex to be reduced to "economic need."

Most recently, historians have highlighted the importance of race and gender in the march toward empire. Roosevelt and other imperialists perceived their world in gendered terms. Many feared American society had lost touch with manly virtues and grown soft and "feminine" since the closing of the frontier. Imperialists also saw the nations of the world in a strict racial hierarchy, with "primitive" blacks and Indians at the bottom and "civilized" Anglo-Saxons at the top. In this world view the conquest of "inferior" peoples seemed a natural tonic to restore the nation's masculine virility. Scholars who emphasize these explanations of imperialism are less likely to see the expansionism of the 1890s as an aberration in American history. Instead, they argue, these overseas adventures were part of a long tradition of race-fueled militarism, from the nation's earliest Indian wars to Cold War engagements in Korea and Vietnam.

---

thousands of kimonoed schoolchildren turned out to wave tiny American flags and sing "The Star Spangled Banner."

In the warm diplomatic atmosphere created by the visit of the fleet, the United States signed the Root-Takahira agreement with Japan in 1908. The agreement pledged both powers to respect each other's territorial possessions in the Pacific and to uphold the Open Door in China. For the moment, at least, the two rising rival powers had found a means to maintain the peace.

Chapter Summary

The previously isolated United States dramatically turned attention overseas in the 1890s, leading to a sudden burst of imperialism. Among the stimuli for the new imperialism were the desire for new economic markets, the sensationalistic "yellow press," Protestant missionary fervor, "Social Darwinist" ideology, great-power rivalry, and naval competition.

American intervention in the Venezuelan boundary dispute of 1895–1896 demonstrated an aggressive new assertion of the Monroe Doctrine and led to an American-British rapprochement after a severe war scare. Longtime American involvement in Hawaii climaxed in 1893 with a revolution against native rule by white American planters. The new government sought annexation by the United States, but President Cleveland blocked the effort.

The "splendid little" Spanish-American War began in 1898 over American outrage about Spanish oppression of Cuba. American support for the Cuban rebellion was whipped up into intense popular fervor by the "yellow press." After the mysterious *Maine* explosion in February 1898, this public passion pushed a reluctant President McKinley into war, even though Spain was ready to concede on the major issues.

An astounding first development of the war was Admiral Dewey's naval victory in May 1898 in the rich Spanish islands of the Philippines in the Pacific. American troops, assisted by Filipino rebels, captured the Philippine city of Manila in another dramatic victory. Despite military confusion and many deaths from disease, American forces also easily and quickly overwhelmed the Spanish in Cuba and Puerto Rico.

McKinley's decision to take the Philippines precipitated a long and bitter national debate in Congress and the country over the wisdom and justice of American imperialism. The narrow pro-imperialist victory in the Senate made the Philippines and Puerto Rico American colonial possessions. Despite continuing doubts about the wisdom of imperialism, the United States had asserted itself as a new international power, including in East Asia.

America's decision to take the Philippines aroused violent resistance from the Filipinos, who had expected independence. The brutal war to defeat the Filipino rebels was longer and costlier than the Spanish-American conflict.

Economic interests, missionary efforts, and European imperialistic intrusion led to growing American involvement in China and East Asia. Hay's Open Door policy helped prevent the European great powers from dismembering and colonizing China. The United States joined the international expedition to suppress the Boxer Rebellion.

McKinley readily defeated Bryan's anti-imperialist campaign in 1900 to win reelection. Assuming the presidency after McKinley's death, Theodore Roosevelt brought a new energy and assertiveness to American foreign policy. When his plans to build a canal in Panama were frustrated by the Colombian Senate, he supported a Panamanian revolt that enabled the strategically important canal to be built. He also revised the Monroe Doctrine by adding a "Roosevelt Corollary" that declared an American right to intervene in Latin America, stirring considerable resentment south of the U.S. border.

Roosevelt successfully negotiated an end to the Russo-Japanese War but angered both parties in the process. The United States and Japan were now competitors in the Pacific. Japanese immigration and Pacific Coast fears of a "yellow peril" added to tensions, but Roosevelt's diplomacy enabled the two countries to maintain a fragile peace.

KEY TERMS

indemnity (440)	sphere of influence (449)
arbitration (440)	partition (451)
reconcentration (442)	blue blood (452)
atrocity (442)	bellicose (452)
proviso (443)	preparedness (452)
hostage (448)	corollary (454)

PEOPLE TO KNOW

Josiah Strong	"Butcher" Weyler
Theodore Roosevelt	George Dewey
Alfred Thayer Mahan	Emilio Aguinaldo
Richard Olney	William H. Taft
Liliuokalani	John Hay

Struggling for Justice at Home and Abroad

1899–1945

The new century brought astonishing changes to the United States. Victory in the Spanish-American War made it clear that the United States was a world power. Industrialization ushered in giant corporations, sprawling factories, sweatshop labor, and the ubiquitous automobile. A huge wave of immigration was altering the face of the nation, especially the cities, where a majority of Americans lived by 1920. With bigger cities came bigger fears—of crime, vice, poverty, and disease.

Changes of such magnitude raised vexing questions. What role should the United States play in the world? How could the enormous power of industry be controlled? How would the millions of new immigrants make their way in America? What should the country do about poverty, disease, and the continuing plague of racial inequality? All these issues turned on a fundamental point: should government remain narrowly limited in its powers, or did the times require a more potent government that would actively shape society and secure American interests abroad?

The progressive movement represented the first attempt to answer those questions. Reform-minded men and women from all walks of life and from both major parties shared in the progressive crusade for greater government activism. Buoyed by this outlook, Presidents Theodore Roosevelt, William Howard Taft, and Woodrow Wilson enlarged the capacity of government to fight graft, "bust" business trusts, regulate corporations, and promote fair labor practices, child welfare, conservation, and consumer protection. Progressive

reformers, convinced that women would bring greater morality to politics, bolstered the decades-long struggle for female suffrage. Women finally secured the vote in 1920 with the ratification of the Nineteenth Amendment.

The progressive-era presidents also challenged America's tradition of isolationism in foreign policy. They felt the country had a moral obligation to spread democracy and an economic opportunity to reap profits in foreign markets. Roosevelt and Taft launched diplomatic initiatives in the Caribbean, Central America, and East Asia. Wilson aspired to "make the world safe for democracy" by rallying support for American intervention in the First World War.

The progressive spirit waned, however, as the United States retreated during the 1920s into what President Harding called "normalcy." Isolationist sentiment revived with a vengeance. Blessed with a booming economy, Americans turned their gaze inward to baseball heroes, radio, jazz, movies, and the first mass-produced American automobile, the Model T Ford. Presidents Harding, Coolidge, and Hoover backed off from the economic regulatory zeal of their predecessors.

"Normalcy" also had a brutal side. Thousands of suspected radicals were jailed or deported in the red scare of 1919 and 1920. Anti-immigrant passions flared until immigration quotas in 1924 squeezed the flow of newcomers to a trickle. Race riots scorched several northern cities in the summer of 1919, a sign of how embittered race relations had become in the wake of the "great migration" of southern blacks to wartime jobs in northern industry. A reborn Ku Klux Klan staged a comeback, not just in the South but in the North and West as well.

"Normalcy" itself soon proved short lived, a casualty of the stock market crash of 1929 and the Great Depression that followed. As Americans watched banks fail, businesses collapse, and millions of people lose their jobs, they asked with renewed urgency what role the government should play in rescuing the nation. President Franklin D. Roosevelt's answer was the "New Deal"—an ambitious array of relief programs, public works, and economic regulations that failed to cure the depression but furnished an impressive legacy of social reforms.

Most Americans came to accept an expanded federal governmental role at home under FDR's leadership in the 1930s, but they still clung stubbornly to isolationism. The United States did little in the 1930s to check the rising military aggression of Japan and Germany. By the early 1940s, events forced Americans to reconsider. Once Hitler's Germany had seized control of most of Europe, Roosevelt, who had long opposed the isolationists, found ways to aid a beleaguered Britain.

When Japan attacked the American naval base at Pearl Harbor in December 1941, isolationists at last fell silent. Roosevelt led a stunned but determined nation into the Second World War, and victory in 1945 positioned the United States to assume a commanding position in the postwar world order.

The Great Depression and the Second World War brought to a head a half-century of debate over the role of government and the place of the United States in the world. In the name of a struggle for justice, FDR established a new era of government activism at home and internationalism abroad. The New Deal's legacy set the terms of debate in American political life for the rest of the century.

What If . . . ?

■ **What if the Great Depression had never occurred, or had been swiftly overcome, in America and abroad?**

Would there then have been a New Deal—or a Second World War?

28

Progressivism and the Republican Roosevelt

1901–1912

When I say I believe in a square deal I do not mean . . . to give every man the best hand. If the cards do not come to any man, or if they do come, and he has not got the power to play them, that is his affair. All I mean is that there shall be no crookedness in the dealing.

THEODORE ROOSEVELT, 1905

⭐ Chapter Outline

The Origins of Progressivism

Progressive Political Reforms

Progressive Women at the Forefront

Roosevelt, Labor, and the Trusts

Consumer Protection and Conservation

The Roosevelt Legacy

The Troubled Presidency of William Howard Taft

Roosevelt's Progressive Challenge to Taft

Examining the Evidence: *Muller v. Oregon*, 1908

Makers of America: The Environmentalists

progressive(s) *In politics, one who believes in continuing social advancement, scientific and technological improvement, and morally based reform.*

Nearly 76 million Americans greeted the new century in 1900. Almost one in seven of them was foreign born. In the fourteen years of peace that remained before the Great War of 1914 engulfed the globe, 13 million more migrants would carry their bundles down the gangplanks to the land of promise.

Hardly had the twentieth century dawned on the ethnically and racially mixed American people than they were convulsed by a reform movement, the likes of which the nation had not seen since the 1840s. The new crusaders, who called themselves "**progressives**," waged war on many evils, notably monopoly, corruption, inefficiency, and social injustice. The progressive army was large, diverse, and widely deployed, but it had a single battle cry: "Strengthen the State." The "real heart of the movement," explained one progressive reformer, was to "use the government as an agency of human welfare."

FOCUS QUESTIONS

1. What were the origins and character of the progressive movement?

2. What were the primary achievements of progressivism at the local, state, and national levels, and what role did female reformers play in its success?

3. How did President Theodore Roosevelt apply progressive principles to the American economy and to distinctively progressive causes such as consumer protection and conservation?

4. In what ways did Roosevelt's chosen successor, William Howard Taft, deeply alienate the progressive movement, and why did TR lead a progressive revolt that openly split the Republican party?

CHRONOLOGY

1892	Sierra Club founded.
1899	National Consumers League founded.
1901	Commission system established in Galveston, Texas. Progressive Robert La Follette elected governor of Wisconsin. American Socialist Party formed.
1902	Lincoln Steffens and Ida Tarbell publish muckraking exposés. Anthracite coal strike. Newlands Act.
1903	Department of Commerce and Labor established. Elkins Act. Women's Trade Union League founded.
1904	*Northern Securities* case. Roosevelt defeats Alton B. Parker for presidency.
1905	*Lochner* v. *New York.*
1906	Hepburn Act. Upton Sinclair publishes *The Jungle*. Meat Inspection Act. Pure Food and Drug Act.

1907	"Roosevelt panic."
1908	*Muller* v. *Oregon.* Taft defeats Bryan for presidency.
1909	Payne-Aldrich Tariff.
1910	Ballinger-Pinchot affair. Washington State grants woman suffrage.
1911	Triangle Shirtwaist Company fire. Standard Oil antitrust case. U.S. Steel Corporation antitrust suit. California grants woman suffrage.
1912	Taft wins Republican nomination over Roosevelt. Arizona, Kansas, and Oregon grant woman suffrage. Children's Bureau established in Department of Labor.
1913	Seventeenth Amendment passed (direct election of U.S. senators). Federal Reserve Act.
1920	San Francisco decides to build Hetch Hetchy Reservoir. Women's Bureau established in Department of Labor.

Progressive Roots

The groundswell of the new reformist wave went far back—to the Greenback Labor party of the 1870s and the Populists of the 1890s, to the mounting unrest throughout the land as grasping industrialists concentrated more and more power in fewer and fewer hands. An outworn philosophy of hands-off individualism seemed increasingly out of place in the modern machine age. Progressive theorists were insisting that society could no longer afford the luxury of a limitless "let-alone" (laissez-faire) policy. The people, through government, must substitute mastery for drift.

Well before 1900, perceptive politicians and writers had begun to pinpoint targets for the progressive attack. Bryan, Altgeld, and the Populists loudly branded the "bloated trusts" with the stigma of corruption and wrongdoing. In 1894 Henry Demarest Lloyd charged headlong into the Standard Oil Company with his book entitled *Wealth Against Commonwealth*. Eccentric economist Thorstein Veblen assailed the new rich with his prickly pen in *The Theory of the Leisure Class* (1899), a savage attack on "predatory wealth" and "**conspicuous consumption**."

Other pen-wielding knights likewise entered the fray. The keen-eyed Danish immigrant Jacob A. Riis, a reporter for the *New York Sun,* shocked middle-class Americans in 1890 with *How the Other Half Lives*. His account was a damning indictment of the dirt, disease, vice, and misery of those rat-gnawed human rookeries known as the New York slums. Novelist Theodore Dreiser used his blunt prose to batter promoters and profiteers in *The Financier* (1912) and *The Titan* (1914).

Socialists, many of whom were European immigrants inspired by the strong movements for state socialism in the Old World, began to register appreciable strength at the ballot box. High-minded messengers of the social gospel drew on their religious beliefs to demand

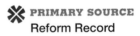
PRIMARY SOURCE
Reform Record

conspicuous consumption *The theory, developed by economist Thorstein Veblen, that much spending by the affluent occurs primarily to display wealth and status to others rather than from enjoyment of the goods or services themselves.*

Library of Congress

George Eastman House

Child Workers Two young girls tend a thread-winding machine. The boy is already a veteran coal miner.

✹ **PRIMARY SOURCE**
Almost Thru the Dark Valley

✹ **PRIMARY SOURCE**
Give Mother the Vote

✹ **PRIMARY SOURCE**
McClure's Magazine

✹ **PRIMARY SOURCE**
Muckrakers

✹ **PRIMARY SOURCE**
Roosevelt Insists on
Regulatory Legislation

better housing and living conditions for the urban poor. University-based economists urged new reforms modeled on European examples, importing policy ideas from Berlin to Baltimore. Feminists in multiplying numbers added social justice to suffrage on their list of needed reforms. With urban pioneers such as Jane Addams blazing the way, women entered the fight to improve the lots of families living and working in the festering cities.

▬▬ Raking Muck with the Muckrakers ▬▬

Beginning about 1902 the exposing of evil became a flourishing industry among American publishers. A group of aggressive popular magazines surged to the front, notably *McClure's, Cosmopolitan, Collier's,* and *Everybody's.* Waging fierce circulation wars, these magazines dug deep for the dirt that the public loved to hate. Enterprising editors financed extensive research and encouraged pugnacious writing by their bright young reporters, whom President Roosevelt branded as "muckrakers" in 1906.

Despite presidential scolding, these muckrakers boomed circulation, and some of their most scandalous exposures were published as best-selling books. In 1902 a brilliant New York reporter, Lincoln Steffens, launched a series of articles in *McClure's* entitled "The Shame of the Cities." He fearlessly unmasked the corrupt alliance between big business and municipal government. Steffens was followed in the same magazine by Ida M. Tarbell, a pioneering woman journalist who published a devastating factual exposé of the Standard Oil Company. (Her father had been ruined by the oil interests.)

Plucky muckrakers fearlessly tilted their pen-lances at varied targets. They assailed the malpractices of life insurance companies and tariff lobbies. They roasted the beef trust, the "money trust," the railroad barons, and the corrupt amassing of American fortunes. David G. Phillips shocked an already startled nation by his series in *Cosmopolitan* entitled "The Treason of the Senate" (1906). He boldly charged that seventy-five of the ninety senators did not represent the people at all but the railroads and trusts.

Some of the most effective fire of the muckrakers was directed at social evils. The ugly list included the immoral "white slave" traffic in women, the rickety slums, and the appalling number of industrial accidents. The sorry subjugation of America's 9 million blacks—of whom 90 percent still lived in the South and one-third were illiterate—was spotlighted in Ray Stannard Baker's *Following the Color Line* (1908). The abuses of child labor were brought luridly to light by John Spargo's *The Bitter Cry of the Children* (1906).

Vendors of potent patent medicines (often heavily spiked with alcohol) likewise came in for bitter criticism. These conscienceless vultures sold incredible quantities of adulterated or habit-forming drugs. Muckraking attacks in *Collier's* were substantiated by Dr. Harvey W. Wiley, chief chemist of the Department of Agriculture, who even performed experiments on himself.

Full of sound and fury, the muckrakers signified much about the nature of the progressive reform movement. They were long on lamentation, but stopped short of revolutionary remedies. To right social wrongs they counted on publicity and an aroused public conscience, not drastic political change. They sought not to overthrow capitalism but to cleanse it. The cure for the ills of American democracy, they earnestly believed, was more democracy.

✳ **PRIMARY SOURCE**
Child Labor in Tenements

✳ **PRIMARY SOURCE**
Patent Medicine Fraud, The

Political Progressivism

The question, "Who were the progressives?" evokes contradictory answers. Progressive reformers included militarists such as Theodore Roosevelt, who thrilled to the strenuous life, as well as pacifists such as Jane Addams, whose loftiest goals included the abolition of war. Female settlement workers hoping to "Americanize" recent immigrants mobilized alongside labor unionists and enlightened businessmen to strengthen the helping hand of government. In diverse ways, and sometimes with divergent aims, the progressives sought to modernize American institutions to achieve two chief goals: to use the state to curb monopoly power and to improve the common person's conditions of life and labor. Progressives emerged in both major parties, in all regions, and at all levels of government. The truth is that progressivism was less a monolithic minority movement and more a broadly dispersed majority mood.

One of the first objectives of progressives was to regain the power that had slipped from the hands of the people into those of the "interests." These ardent reformers pushed for **direct primary** elections so as to undercut power-hungry party bosses. They favored the **"initiative"** so that voters could directly propose legislation themselves, thus bypassing the boss-bought state legislatures. Progressives also agitated for the **"referendum,"** which would give the people the right to reject laws pushed through by free-spending agents of big business. The **"recall"** would enable the voters to remove faithless elected officials who had been bribed by bosses or lobbyists. The secret Australian ballot was likewise introduced in the states to counteract boss rule.

Direct election of U.S. senators became a favorite goal of progressives, especially after muckrakers had exposed the scandalous intimacy between greedy corporations and Congress. Direct election was finally achieved by the Seventeenth Amendment to the Constitution, approved in 1913 (see the Appendix). But the expected improvement in caliber was slow in coming.

Woman suffrage, the goal of female reformers for many decades, likewise received powerful new support from the progressives early in the 1900s. The political reformers believed that women's votes would elevate the political tone, and the foes of the saloon felt that they could count on the support of enfranchised females. Many of the states, especially the more liberal ones in the West such as Washington, California, and Oregon, gradually extended the vote to women. But by 1910 nationwide female suffrage was still a decade away.

direct primary *In politics, the nomination of a party's candidates for office through a special election of that party's voters.*

initiative *A progressive reform measure allowing a defined number of registered voters, through signed petitions, to place a proposed law on the general ballot for approval or rejection by the whole electorate. Like the referendum and recall, it brought democracy directly "to the people" and helped foster a shift toward interest-group politics and away from old political "machines."*

referendum *A progressive reform procedure allowing a defined number of registered voters, through signed petitions, to place on the ballot a law that has already been passed by the legislature, for final approval or rejection by the whole electorate.*

recall *A progressive ballot procedure allowing voters to remove elected officials from office.*

Progressivism in the Cities and States

Progressives scored some of their most impressive gains in the cities. Frustrated by the inefficiency and corruption of machine-oiled city government, many localities followed the pioneering example of Galveston, Texas. In 1901 it had appointed expert-staffed commissions to manage urban

The suffrage campaign of the early twentieth century benefited from a new generation of women who considered themselves "feminists." At a mass meeting in New York in 1914, Marie Jenny Howe (1870–1934), a minister by training as well as a prominent early feminist, proclaimed:

"We intend simply to be ourselves, not just our little female selves, but our whole big human selves."

city manager *An administrator appointed by the city council or other elected body to manage affairs, supposedly in a nonpartisan or professional way.*

red-light district *A section of a city where prostitution is officially or unofficially tolerated.*

franchise *In government, a special privilege or license granted to a company or group to perform a specific function, sometimes for a specified period of time.*

affairs. Other communities adopted the **city manager** system, also designed to take politics out of municipal administration. Some of these "reforms" obviously valued efficiency more highly than democracy, as control of civic affairs was further removed from the people's hands.

Urban reformers likewise attacked "slumlords," juvenile delinquency, and wide-open prostitution (vice-at-a-price), which flourished in **red-light districts** unchallenged by bribed police. Public-spirited Americans looked to British and German cities for lessons on how to clean up their water supplies, light their streets, and run their trolley cars. The vogue of public ownership of utilities swept the nation as local governments tried to halt the corrupt sale of **franchises**.

Progressivism naturally bubbled up to the state level, notably in Wisconsin, which became a yeasty laboratory of reform. Pompadoured Governor Robert M. ("Fighting Bob") La Follette was an undersized but overbearing crusader who emerged as the most militant of the progressive Republican leaders. Elected governor in 1901, he waged a desperate fight to win control of Wisconsin from crooked lumber and railroad interests and return it to the people. He also perfected a scheme for regulating public utilities while laboring in close association with experts on the faculty of the University of Wisconsin at Madison.

Other states marched steadily toward the progressive camp, as they undertook to regulate railroads and trusts, chiefly through public utilities commissions. Oregon was not far behind Wisconsin, and California made giant boot strides under the stocky Hiram W. Johnson. Elected Republican governor in 1910, this dynamic prosecutor of grafters helped break the dominant grip of the Southern Pacific Railroad on California politics and then, like La Follette, set up a political machine of his own.

PRIMARY SOURCE
Election Day!

PRIMARY SOURCE
Factory System's Influence, The

Progressive Women

Women proved themselves an indispensable part of the progressive army. A crucial focus for women's activism was the settlement house movement (see p. 398). At a time when women could neither vote nor hold political office, settlement houses offered a side door to public life. They exposed middle-class women to the numerous problems plaguing American cities and gave them the skill and confidence to tackle those evils. The women's club movement also turned from literary self-improvement to engagement with social issues and current events. "Dante has been dead for several centuries," observed the president of the General Federation of Women's Clubs in 1904. "I think it is time that we dropped the study of his *Inferno* and turned our attention to our own."

Nineteenth-century notions of "separate spheres" dictated that a woman's place was in the home, so most female progressives defended their new activities as an extension—not a rejection—of the traditional roles of wife and mother. Thus they were often drawn to moral and "maternal" issues such as keeping children out of sweatshops or ensuring that only safe food products found their way to the family table. Female activists agitated through organizations such as the National Consumers League (1899) and the Women's Trade Union League (1903) and through two new federal agencies, the Children's Bureau (1912) and the Women's Bureau (1920), both in the Department of Labor.

Campaigns for factory reform and temperance particularly attracted women foot soldiers. Unsafe and unsanitary sweatshops—factories where workers toiled long hours for low wages—were a public scandal in many cities. Florence Kelley, a former resident of Jane Addams's Hull House, became the state of Illinois's first chief factory inspector and one of the leading advocates for improved factory conditions. In 1899 Kelley took control of the newly founded National Consumers League, which mobilized female consumers to pressure for laws safeguarding women and children in the workplace. In the landmark case *Muller* v. *Oregon* (1908), crusading attorney Louis D. Brandeis persuaded the Supreme Court to accept the constitutionality of laws protecting women workers by presenting evidence of the harmful effects of factory labor on women's bodies. Although this argument calling for special protection for women seemed discriminatory by later standards, progressives at the time hailed Brandeis's achievement as a triumph. The American welfare state that emerged from female activism focused more on protecting women and children

Hatwin Collection, Kheel Center, Cornell University

The Wages of Negligence Officials review the charred remains of some of the victims of the catastrophic Triangle Shirtwaist Company fire in 1911. Outrage over this calamity galvanized a generation of reformers to fight for better workplace safety rules.

than on granting benefits to everyone, as was the case in much of western Europe, with its stronger labor overtones.

Crusaders for these humane measures did not always have smooth sailing. One dismaying setback came in 1905, when the Supreme Court in *Lochner* v. *New York* invalidated a New York law establishing a ten-hour day for bakers. Yet the reformist progressive wave finally washed up into the judiciary, and in 1917 the Court upheld a ten-hour law for factory workers.

Laws regulating factories were worthless if not enforced, a truth horribly demonstrated by a lethal fire in 1911 at the Triangle Shirtwaist Company in New York City. Locked doors and other flagrant violations of the fire code turned the factory into a death trap, incinerating 146 workers, most of them young immigrant women. Lashed by the public outcry, the legislature of New York and later other legislatures passed much stronger laws regulating the hours and conditions of sweatshop toil. By 1917 thirty states had put **workers' compensation** laws on their books, providing insurance to workers injured in industrial accidents. Gradually, the concept of the employer's responsibility to society was replacing the old dog-eat-dog philosophy of unregulated free enterprise.

Corner saloons naturally attracted the ire and fire of progressives, especially because the saloons were often intimately connected with prostitution and voter corruption. By 1900 cities such as New York and San Francisco had one saloon for about every two hundred people. Antiliquor campaigners received powerful support from several militant organizations, notably the Woman's Christian Temperance Union (WCTU). Founder Frances E. Willard, who would fall on her knees in prayer on saloon floors, mobilized nearly 1 million women to "make the world homelike" and built the WCTU into the largest organization of women in the world. She found a vigorous ally in the Anti-Saloon League, which was aggressive, well organized, and well financed.

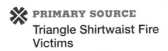 **PRIMARY SOURCE**
Triangle Shirtwaist Fire Victims

workers' (workmen's) compensation *Insurance, provided either by government or employers or both, providing benefits to employees suffering work-related injury or disability.*

Caught up in the crusade, some states and counties passed "dry" laws to control, restrict, or abolish alcohol. The big cities were generally "wet," for they had a large immigrant vote accustomed in the Old Country to the free flow of wine and beer. When World War I erupted in 1914, nearly one-half of the population lived in "dry" territory. Demon Rum was groggy and about to be floored—temporarily—by the Eighteenth Amendment in 1919.

TR's Square Deal for Labor

Theodore Roosevelt, although something of an imperialistic busybody abroad, was touched by the progressive wave at home. Like other reformers, he feared that the "public interest" was being submerged in the drifting seas of indifference. Everybody's interest was nobody's interest. Roosevelt decided to make it his. His sportsman's instincts spurred him into demanding a "square deal" for capital, labor, and the public at large. Broadly speaking, his program embraced three C's: control of the corporations, consumer protection, and conservation of natural resources.

The Square Deal for labor received its acid test in 1902, when a crippling strike broke out in the anthracite coal mines of Pennsylvania. Some 140,000 sooty workers, many of them illiterate immigrants, had long been frightfully exploited and accident plagued. They demanded, among other improvements, a 20 percent increase in pay and a reduction of the working day from ten to nine hours.

Unsympathetic mine owners, confident that a chilled public would react against the miners, refused to arbitrate or even negotiate. One of their spokesmen, multimillionaire George F. Baer, wrote that workers would be cared for "not by the labor agitators, but by the Christian men to whom God in his infinite wisdom has given the control of the property interests of this country."

As coal supplies dwindled, factories and schools were forced to shut down, and even hospitals felt the icy grip of winter. Profoundly annoyed by "extraordinary stupidity and bad temper" of the "wooden-headed" mine owners, Roosevelt threatened to seize the mines and operate them with federal troops. Faced with this first-time-ever threat to use federal bayonets against capital, rather than labor, the owners grudgingly consented to arbitration. A compromise decision ultimately gave the miners a 10 percent pay boost and a working day of nine hours. But their union was not officially recognized as a bargaining agent.

Keenly aware of the mounting antagonisms between capital and labor, Roosevelt urged Congress to create a new Department of Commerce and Labor. This goal was achieved in 1903. (Ten years later the agency was split into two.) An important arm of the new cabinet agency was the Bureau of Corporations, which was authorized to probe businesses engaged in interstate commerce. The bureau was highly useful in helping to break the stranglehold of monopoly and in clearing the road for the era of "trustbusting."

TR Corrals the Corporations

The sprawling railroad octopus sorely needed restraint. The Interstate Commerce Commission, created in 1887 as a feeble sop to the public, had proved woefully inadequate. Railroad barons could simply appeal the commission's decisions on rates to the federal courts—a process that might take ten years.

Spurred by the former-cowboy president, Congress passed effective railroad legislation, beginning with the Elkins Act of 1903. This curb was aimed primarily at the rebate evil. Heavy fines could now be imposed both on the railroads that gave rebates and on the shippers that accepted them.

Still more effective was the Hepburn Act of 1906. Free passes, with their hint of bribery, were severely restricted. The once-infantile Interstate Commerce Commission was expanded, and its reach was extended to include express companies, sleeping-car companies, and pipelines. For the first time, the commission was given real molars when it was authorized to nullify existing shipping rates and stipulate maximum rates.

Railroads also provided Roosevelt with an opportunity to brandish his antitrust bludgeon. *Trusts* had come to be a fighting word in the progressive era. TR was determined to

MULLER V. OREGON, 1908

Court records provide notably fruitful sources for historians. They not only tell often-colorful stories about the lives of ordinary men and women caught up in the legal system; they also by their very nature testify to the norms and values that lawyers employ to make their cases and that judges invoke to explain their decisions. The case of *Muller* v. *Oregon* (see p. 466) is especially instructive on both counts. The official Supreme Court records tell how on September 4, 1905, Joe Haselbock, a supervisor in Curt Muller's Grand Laundry in Portland, Oregon, asked an employee, Mrs. E. Gotcher, to remain after hours to do an extra load of laundry. That request violated Oregon's law prohibiting women from working more than ten hours per day. Mrs. Gotcher later complained to the authorities, and Muller was fined $10.

Muller refused to pay and took his case all the way to the U.S. Supreme Court. In its landmark decision (below), the Court upheld the constitutionality of the Oregon statute, and Muller at last had to cough up his fine.

1. On what grounds did the Court justify its ruling?

2. What does Justice David J. Brewer's argument on behalf of the Court's decision suggest about the cultural identity and social role of women in early-twentieth-century American society?

3. Was Brewer's ruling really a "progressive" one? Why might progressives in the early twentieth century have regarded *Muller* as a great step forward, while Americans of the early twenty-first century might not?

(208 U.S. 412)
CURT MULLER, Plff. in Err.,
v.
STATE OF OREGON.

... That woman's physical structure and the performance of material functions place her at a disadvantage in the struggle for subsistence is obvious. This is especially true when the burdens of motherhood are upon her. ... and as healthy mothers are essential to vigorous offspring, the physical well-being of woman becomes an object of public interest and care in order to preserve the strength and vigor of the race.

Still again, history discloses the fact that woman has always been dependent upon man. He established his control at the outset by superior physical strength, and this control in various forms, with diminishing intensity, has continued to the present. ... It is still true that in the struggle for subsistence she is not an equal competitor with her brother. ... Differentiated by these matters from the other sex, she is properly placed in a class by herself, and legislation designed for her protection may be sustained, even when like legislation is not necessary for men, and could not be sustained. It is impossible to close one's eyes to the fact that she still looks to her brother and depends upon him. ... The two sexes differ in structure of body, in the functions to be performed by each, in the amount of physical strength, in the capacity for long continued labor, particularly when done standing, the influence of vigorous health upon the future well-being of the race, the self-reliance which enables one to assert full rights, and in the capacity to maintain the struggle for subsistence. This difference justifies a difference in legislation, and upholds that which is designed to compensate for some of the burdens which rest upon her.

We have not referred in this discussion to the denial of the elective franchise in the state of Oregon, for while that may disclose a lack of political equality in all things with her brother, that is not of itself decisive. The reason runs deeper, and rests in the inherent difference between the two sexes, and in the different functions in life which they perform. ...

respond to the public outcry against the trusts by curbing but not eliminating them. He believed that there were "good" trusts with public consciences and "bad" trusts greedy for power and that the goal was not to throw out the baby with the bathwater.

Roosevelt, as a trustbuster, first burst into the headlines in 1902 with an attack on the Northern Securities Company, a railroad holding company organized by financial titan J. P. Morgan and empire builder James J. Hill. These Napoleonic moguls of money sought to achieve a virtual monopoly of the railroads in the Northwest. Roosevelt was therefore challenging the most regal potentates of the industrial aristocracy.

The railway promoters appealed to the Supreme Court, which in 1904 upheld Roosevelt's antitrust suit and ordered the Northern Securities Company to be dissolved. The *Northern Securities* decision jolted Wall Street and angered big business but greatly enhanced Roosevelt's reputation as a trust smasher. Roosevelt's big stick crashed down on other giant monopolies, as he initiated over forty legal proceedings against the beef, sugar, fertilizer, harvester, and other monopolies.

Much mythology has inflated Roosevelt's reputation as a trustbuster. The Rough Rider understood the political popularity of monopoly smashing, but he did not consider it sound economic policy. Combination and integration, he felt, were the hallmarks of the age, and to try to stem the tide of economic progress by political means he considered the rankest folly. Bigness was not necessarily badness, so why punish success? Roosevelt's real purpose in assaulting the Goliaths of industry was to prove conclusively that the government, not private business, ruled the country. He believed in regulating, not fragmenting, the big business combines. The threat of dissolution, he felt, might make the sultans of the smokestacks more amenable to federal regulation—and it did.

In truth, Roosevelt never swung his trust-crushing stick with maximum force. His successor, William Howard Taft, actually "busted" more trusts than TR did. In one celebrated instance in 1907, Roosevelt even gave his personal blessing to J. P. Morgan's plan to have United States Steel Corporation absorb the Tennessee Coal and Iron Company, without fear of antitrust reprisals. When Taft then launched a suit against United States Steel in 1911, the political reaction from TR was explosive (see pp. 475–476).

PRIMARY SOURCE
Taft Cartoon

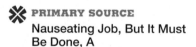

PRIMARY SOURCE
Nauseating Job, But It Must Be Done, A

PRIMARY SOURCE
Attack on the Meatpackers

Caring for the Consumer

Roosevelt backed a noteworthy measure in 1906 that benefited both corporations and consumers. Big meatpackers were being shut out of certain European markets because some American meat had been found to be tainted. Foreign governments were threatening to ban all American meat imports.

At the same time, American consumers hungered for safer products. Their appetite for reform was whetted by Upton Sinclair's sensationalist novel *The Jungle,* published in 1906. Sinclair, a dedicated Socialist, intended his revolting tract to focus attention on the plight of the workers in the big meat-canning factories, but instead he appalled the public with his description of disgustingly unsanitary food products. (As he put it, he aimed for the nation's heart but hit its stomach.) The book described in noxious detail the filth, disease, and putrefaction in Chicago's damp, ill-ventilated slaughterhouses. A cynical jingle of the time ran:

> *Mary had a little lamb,*
> *And when she saw it sicken,*
> *She shipped it off to Packingtown,*
> *And now it's labeled chicken.*

Backed by a nauseated public, Roosevelt induced Congress to pass the Meat Inspection Act of 1906. The act decreed that the preparation of meat shipped over state lines would be subject to federal inspection from corral to can. The largest packers accepted the act as an opportunity to drive their smaller, fly-by-night competitors out of business. At the same time, they could receive the government's seal of approval on their exports. As a companion to the Meat Inspection Act, the Pure Food and Drug Act of 1906 was designed to prevent the adulteration and mislabeling of foods and pharmaceuticals.

Earth Control

Wasteful Americans, assuming that their natural resources were inexhaustible, had looted and polluted their incomparable domain with unparalleled speed and greed. Western ranchers and timber men were especially eager to accelerate the destructive process, for they panted to build up the country, and the environmental consequences be hanged. But even before the end of the nineteenth century, far-visioned leaders saw that such a squandering of the nation's birthright would have to be halted or America would sink from resource richness to despoiled dearth.

A first serious step toward conservation was the Forest Reserve Act of 1891, authorizing the president to set aside public forest land as national forests and other reserves. Under this statute some 46 million acres of magnificent trees were rescued from the lumberman's saw in the 1890s and preserved for posterity.

A new day in the history of conservation dawned with the advent of Roosevelt (see "Makers of America: The Environmentalists," pp. 472–473). Huntsman, naturalist, rancher, lover of the great outdoors, he was appalled by the pillaging of timber and mineral resources. Other dedicated conservationists, notably Gifford Pinchot, head of the federal Division of Forestry, had broken important ground before him. But Roosevelt seized the banner of leadership and charged into the fray with all the weight of his prestige, his energy, his firsthand knowledge, and his slashing invective.

Congress responded to the whip of the Rough Rider by passing the Newlands Act of 1902. This landmark legislation authorized Washington to use funds from the sale of public lands in the sun-baked western states for irrigation projects. Settlers repaid the cost of **reclamation** from their now-productive soil, and the money was put into a revolving fund to finance more such enterprises.

Roosevelt pined to preserve the nation's shrinking forests. By 1900 only about a quarter of the once-vast virgin timberlands remained standing. Lumbermen had already logged off most of the first-growth timber from Maine to Michigan, and the sharp thud of their axes was beginning to split the silence in the great fir forests of the Pacific slope. Roosevelt proceeded to set aside in federal reserves some 125 million acres, or almost three times the acreage thus saved from the saw by his three predecessors. He similarly earmarked millions of acres of coal deposits, as well as water resources useful for irrigation and power.

Conservation may have been Roosevelt's most enduring tangible achievement. He was buoyed in this effort by an upwelling national mood of concern about the disappearance of the frontier. An increasingly citified people worried that too much civilization might not be good for the national soul. City dwellers snapped up Jack London's *Call of the Wild* (1903) and other books about nature, and urban youngsters made the outdoor-oriented Boy Scouts of America the country's largest youth organization. Middle-class clubwomen raised money for nature preserves and organized the Massachusetts—and later National—Audubon Society to save wild native birds by banning the use of plumes to ornament fashionable ladies' hats. The Sierra Club, founded in 1892, dedicated itself to preserving the wildness of the western landscape.

The preservationists lost a major battle in 1913 when the federal government allowed the city of San Francisco to build a dam for its municipal water supply in the spectacular, high-walled Hetch Hetchy Valley in Yosemite National Park. The Hetch Hetchy controversy laid bare a deep division among conservationists that persists to this day.

> *In his annual message to Congress in 1907, Roosevelt declared prophetically:*
>
> **"We are prone to speak of the resources of this country as inexhaustible; this is not so. The mineral wealth of the country, the coal, iron, oil, gas, and the like, does not reproduce itself, and therefore is certain to be exhausted ultimately; and wastefulness in dealing with it today means that our descendants will feel the exhaustion a generation or two before they otherwise would."**

reclamation *The process of bringing or restoring wasteland to productive use.*

Stock Montage

High Point for Conservation Conservationist Roosevelt and famed naturalist-conservationist John Muir visit Glacier Point, on the rim of Yosemite Valley, California. In the distance is Yosemite Falls; a few feet behind Roosevelt is a sheer drop of 3,254 feet (992 meters).

The Environmentalists

Humans have long been awed by nature, but they have also yearned to be its masters. The earliest European colonists saw North America as a "howling wilderness" and toiled mightily with ax and plow to tame it. By the mid-nineteenth century, Americans commanded powerful new technologies that promised unbridled dominion over the natural world. Only then did voices begin to be heard in defense of the wounded earth—the first faint stirrings of what would come to be called "environmentalism."

In a pattern that would often be repeated, nature's earliest defenders tended to be well-off townsfolk and city dwellers such as Henry David Thoreau and Ralph Waldo Emerson. The Americans most likely to appreciate the value of pristine wilderness, it seemed, were those who had ceased to struggle against it. For the loggers, miners, and farmers who continued to sweat their living out of nature's grudging embrace, concern for environmental niceties often seemed like the sanctimonious piety of a privileged elite.

By the dawn of the twentieth century, many genteel, urban Americans had come to romanticize their pioneer forebears. Preservationists such as John Muir waxed lyrical about the mystic allure of unspoiled nature. Seizing the popular mood, Theodore Roosevelt deliberately constructed an image of himself as a manly outdoorsman, and as president he greatly expanded the system of national forests.

But Roosevelt was also a pioneer of another sort—as a prominent promoter of the progressive-era "conservation" movement, composed of a loose coalition of scientists, bureaucrats, and businesspeople dependent on stable access to America's rich endowment of natural resources. Progressive conservationists believed that nature must be neither uncritically reverenced nor wastefully exploited, but must instead be efficiently utilized. Thus the same TR who admired the wonders of Yosemite Valley in the company of John Muir also promoted the "rational use" philosophy that justified the

✱ PRIMARY SOURCE
John Muir on the Dominion of Nature

bureaucracy (bureaucrat) *The management of government or business through organized departments and subdivisions manned by a system of officials (bureaucrats) following defined rules and processes. (The term is often, though not necessarily, disparaging.)*

To the preservationists of the Sierra Club, including famed naturalist John Muir, Hetch Hetchy was a "temple" of nature that should be held inviolable by the civilizing hand of humanity. But other conservationists, including President Roosevelt and his chief forester, Gifford Pinchot, wanted to use the nation's natural endowment intelligently rather than lock it away as wilderness. They sought to combine recreation, sustained-yield logging, watershed protection, and summer stock grazing on the same expanse of federal land.

At first many westerners resisted the federal management of natural resources, but they soon learned how to take advantage of new agencies such as the Forest Service and especially the Bureau of Reclamation. The largest ranches and timber companies in particular figured out how to work hand in glove with federal conservation programs devoted to the rational, large-scale, and long-term use of natural resources. The one-man-and-a-mule logger or the one-man-and-a-dog sheepherder had little clout in the new resources **bureaucracy**. Single-person enterprises were shouldered aside, in the interest of efficiency, by the combined bulk of big business and big government.

The Rough Rider's Second Term

Roosevelt was handily elected president in his own right in 1904 and entered his new term buoyed by his enormous personal popularity. Yet the conservative Republican bosses grew increasingly restive as Roosevelt in his second term called ever more loudly for regulating the corporations, taxing incomes, and protecting workers. Roosevelt, meanwhile, systematic harvesting of millions of trees and the drowning of vast river valleys behind massive dams. This attitude toward nature triumphed in the New Deal era of the 1930s, when the federal government initiated colossal projects that undertook nothing less than reengineering the face of the continent—including the Tennessee Valley Authority, the Soil Conservation Service, and the Shelterbelt tree planting on the Great Plains.

The rise of ecological science in the post–World War II era fundamentally changed the debate about the relation of nature to civilization. Ecologists charged that the apparent "rationality" of the earlier conservationists dangerously neglected the stunningly complex interrelationships that linked together seemingly unrelated organisms—and to the perils of tampering even slightly with the delicate biological fabrics that nature had taken millennia to weave. Rachel Carson helped to popularize this new outlook in her sensational 1962 exposé, *Silent Spring*, about the far-reaching effects of pesticides on birds, plants, and animals—including humans.

The advent of ecological studies coincided with a revival of preservationist sentiment, especially in the suburbs, where Americans increasingly dwelled. Membership in environmental organizations such as the Sierra Club and the Audubon Society soared, as a generation infatuated with nature demanded a clean and green world. The first celebration of Earth Day on April 22, 1970, marked the maturation of modern-day environmentalism, which wedded scientific analysis with respect for nature's majesty. That same year saw the creation of the federal Environmental Protection Agency (EPA), soon to be followed by the Endangered Species Act and other legislation designed to regulate the relationship between humans and nature.

At the outset of the twenty-first century, developments such as global warming served dramatic notice that planet Earth was an ecological system that did not recognize national boundaries. Yet while Americans took pride in the efforts they had made to clean up their own turf, who were they, having long since consumed their timberlands and tamed their free-flowing waters, to tell the Brazilians that they should not cut down their Amazon forest or the Chinese that they should not dam their rivers? For the peoples of the developing world, struggling to match America's standard of living, environmentalists often seemed like spoiled spoilers, preaching the same privileged pieties that had infuriated generations of working Americans.

Gifford Pinchot Going Trout Fishing The father of modern Forest Service, Pinchot championed the concept of "rational use" as the guiding principle of the federal government's natural resource management policies.

had partly defanged himself after his election in 1904 by announcing that under no circumstances would he be a candidate for a third term.

Roosevelt suffered a sharp setback in 1907, when a short but punishing panic descended on Wall Street. The financial flurry featured frightened "runs" on banks, suicides, and criminal indictments against speculators. The financial world hastened to blame Roosevelt for the storm. It cried that this "quack" had unsettled industry with his boat-rocking tactics and branded the current distress the "Roosevelt panic." The hot-tempered president angrily lashed back at his critics when he accused "certain malefactors of great wealth" of having deliberately engineered the crisis to force the government to relax its assaults on trusts.

Still warmly popular in 1908, Roosevelt could easily have won a second presidential nomination and almost certainly the election. But he felt bound by his impulsive post-election promise after his victory in 1904. The departing president thus naturally sought a successor who would carry out "my policies." The man of his choice was amiable and ample-girthed William Howard Taft, secretary of war and a mild progressive.

As heir apparent, Taft had often been called upon in Roosevelt's absence to "sit on the lid"—all 350 pounds of him. At the Republican convention of 1908 in Chicago, Roosevelt used his control of the party machinery—the "steamroller"—to push through Taft's nomination on the first ballot. Three weeks later, in mile-high Denver in the heart of silver country, the Democrats nominated twice-beaten William Jennings Bryan.

The dull campaign of 1908 featured the rotund Taft and the now-balding "Boy Orator" both trying to claim the progressive Roosevelt mantle. The solid Judge Taft read cut-and-dried speeches, while Bryan griped that Roosevelt had stolen his policies from the Bryanite

Sunrise, Yosemite Valley, by Albert Bierstadt, c. 1870 A German-born artist, Bierstadt romanticized the already awesome beauty of the American West. Sunrise, Yosemite Valley, by Albert Beirstadt, 1870, oil on canvas, #1966.1, Amon Carter Museum, Fort Worth, Texas

camp. A majority of voters chose stability with Roosevelt-endorsed Taft, who polled 321 electoral votes to 162 for Bryan. The victor's popular count was 7,675,320 to 6,412,294. The election's only surprise came from the Socialists, who amassed 420,793 votes for Eugene V. Debs, the hero of the Pullman strike of 1894 (see p. 432).

Roosevelt, ever in the limelight, left soon after the election for a lion hunt in Africa. His numerous enemies clinked glasses while toasting "Health to the lions," and a few irreverently prayed that some big cat would "do its duty." But TR survived, still bursting with energy at the age of fifty-one in 1909.

Roosevelt was branded by his adversaries as a wild-eyed radical, but his reputation as an eater of errant industrialists now seems inflated. He fought many a sham battle, and the number of laws that he inspired was certainly not in proportion to the amount of noise he emitted. He was often under attack from the reigning business lords, but the more enlightened of them knew that they had a friend in the White House. Roosevelt should be remembered first and foremost as the cowboy who started to tame the bucking bronco of adolescent capitalism, thus ensuring it a long adult life.

TR's enthusiasm and perpetual youthfulness, like an overgrown Boy Scout's, appealed to the young of all ages. "You must always remember," a British diplomat cautioned his colleagues, "that the president is about six." He served as a political lightning rod to protect capitalists against popular indignation—and against socialism, which Roosevelt regarded as "ominous." He strenuously sought the middle road between unbridled individualism and paternalistic **collectivism**. His conservation crusade, which tried to mediate between the romantic wilderness-preservationists and the rapacious resource-predators, was probably his most typical and his most lasting achievement.

Several other contributions of Roosevelt lasted beyond his presidency. First, he greatly enlarged the power and prestige of the presidential office—and masterfully developed the technique of using the big stick of publicity as a political bludgeon. Second, he helped shape the progressive movement and beyond it the liberal reform campaigns later in the

collectivism *A political or social system in which individuals are subordinated to mass organization and direction.*

Roosevelt, who preached the doctrine of the "strenuous life," practiced it until almost the end. In 1913 he sent a political message on a still-preserved phonograph recording to the Boys' Progressive League:

"Don't flinch, don't foul, and hit the line hard."

century. His Square Deal, in a sense, was the grandfather of the New Deal later launched by his fifth cousin, Franklin D. Roosevelt. Finally, to a greater degree than any of his predecessors, TR opened the eyes of Americans to the fact that they shared the world with other nations. As a great power, they had fallen heir to great responsibilities—and had been seized by great ambitions—from which there was no escaping.

Taft: A Round Peg in a Square Hole

William Howard Taft, with his ruddy complexion and upturned mustache, at first inspired widespread confidence. "Everybody loves a fat man," the saying goes, and the jovial Taft, with "mirthquakes" of laughter bubbling up from his abundant abdomen, was personally popular. He had graduated second in his class at Yale and established an admirable reputation as a lawyer and judge, though he was widely regarded as hostile to labor unions. He had served as a trusted administrator and troubleshooter under Roosevelt—in the Philippines, at home, and in Cuba.

But "good old Will" suffered from lethal political handicaps. Roosevelt had led the conflicting elements of the Republican party by the sheer force of his personality. Taft, in contrast, had none of the arts of a dashing political leader and none of Roosevelt's zest for the fray. Recoiling from the clamor of controversy, he generally adopted an attitude of passivity toward Congress. He was a poor judge of public opinion, and his candor made him a chronic victim of "foot-in-mouth" disease.

"Peaceful Bill" was no doubt a mild progressive, but at heart he was more wedded to the status quo than to change. Significantly, his cabinet did not contain a single representative of the party's "insurgent" wing, which was on fire for reform of current abuses, especially the tariff.

The Dollar Goes Abroad as a Diplomat

Though ordinarily lethargic, Taft bestirred himself to use the lever of American investments to boost American political interests abroad. Washington warmly encouraged Wall Street bankers to sluice their surplus dollars into foreign areas of strategic concern to the United States. New York bankers would thus strengthen American defenses and foreign policies while bringing further prosperity to their homeland—and to themselves. The almighty dollar thereby supplanted the big stick.

China's Manchuria was the object of Taft's most spectacular effort to practice "dollar diplomacy." Newly ambitious Japan and imperialistic Russia, recent foes, controlled the railroads of this strategic province. President Taft saw in the Manchurian railway monopoly a possible slamming of the Open Door in the faces of U.S. merchants. But Secretary of State Philander Knox's attempt in 1909 to persuade U.S. investors to buy the Manchurian railroads and then turn them over to China ran into blunt Japanese and Russian opposition. Taft was showered with ridicule.

Another dangerous new trouble spot was the revolution-riddled Caribbean—now virtually a Yankee lake. Hoping to head off trouble, Washington urged Wall Street bankers to pump dollars into the financial vacuums in Honduras and Haiti. Again necessity was the mother of armed Caribbean intervention. Sporadic disorders in palm-fronded Cuba, Honduras, and the Dominican Republic brought American forces to these countries to restore order and protect American investments. A revolutionary upheaval in Nicaragua, partly fomented by American interests, resulted in the landing of twenty-five hundred marines in 1912. The marines remained in Nicaragua for thirteen years (see the map on p. 484).

Taft the Trustbuster

Taft managed to gain some fame as a smasher of monopolies. The ironic truth is that the colorless Taft brought ninety suits against the trusts during his four years in office, compared with some forty-four for Roosevelt in seven and a half years.

By fateful happenstance the most sensational judicial actions during the Taft regime came in 1911. In that year the Supreme Court ordered dissolution of the mighty Standard Oil Company, which was judged to be a combination in restraint of trade in violation of the Sherman Anti-Trust Act of 1890. At the same time the Court handed down its famous "rule of reason." This doctrine held that only those combinations that "unreasonably" restrained trade were illegal. This fine-point proviso ripped a huge hole in the government's antitrust net.

Even more explosively, in 1911 Taft decided to press an antitrust suit against the U.S. Steel Corporation. This initiative infuriated Roosevelt, who had personally been involved in one of the mergers that prompted the suit. Once Roosevelt's protégé, President Taft was increasingly taking on the role of his antagonist. The stage was being set for a bruising confrontation.

Taft Splits the Republican Party

Lowering the barriers of the formidable protective tariff—the "Mother of Trusts"—was high on the agenda of the progressive members of the Republican party, and they at first thought they had a friend and ally in Taft. When the president called Congress into special session in March 1909, the House passed a moderately reductive bill. But senatorial reactionaries, led by Senator Nelson Aldrich of Rhode Island, tacked on hundreds of upward tariff revisions. Only such items as hides, sea moss, and canary seed were left on the duty-free list.

After much hand-wringing, Taft signed the Payne-Aldrich Bill, thus betraying his campaign promises and outraging the progressive wing of his party, heavily drawn from the Midwest. Taft rubbed salt in the wound by proclaiming it "the best bill that the Republican party ever passed."

Taft revealed a further knack for shooting himself in the foot in his handling of conservation. The portly president was a dedicated conservationist, and his contributions—such as the establishment of the Bureau of Mines to control mineral resources—actually equaled or surpassed those of Roosevelt. But his praiseworthy accomplishments were largely erased in the public mind by the noisy Ballinger-Pinchot quarrel that erupted in 1910.

When Secretary of the Interior Richard Ballinger opened public lands in Wyoming, Montana, and Alaska to corporate development, he was sharply criticized by Gifford Pinchot, chief of the Agriculture Department's Division of Forestry and a stalwart Rooseveltian. When Taft dismissed Pinchot on the narrow grounds of **insubordination**, a storm of protest arose from conservationists and from Roosevelt's friends, who were legion. The whole unsavory episode further widened the growing rift between the president and the former president, onetime bosom political partners.

The reformist wing of the Republican party was now up in arms, as Taft was increasingly drawn into the embrace of the stand-pat Old Guard. By the spring of 1910, the Grand Old Party was split wide open, owing largely to the clumsiness of Taft. A suspicious Roosevelt returned triumphantly to New York in June 1910 and shortly thereafter stirred up a tempest. In a flaming speech at Osawatamie, Kansas, he proclaimed a doctrine—popularly known as the "New Nationalism"—that urged the national government to increase its power to remedy economic and social abuses.

Weakened by these internal divisions, the Republicans lost badly in the congressional elections of 1910. The Democrats emerged from their landslide victory with 228 seats to only 161 for the once-dominant Republicans. In a further symptom of the reforming temper of the times, a Socialist representative, Austrian-born Victor L. Berger, was elected from Milwaukee. (Berger was eventually denied his seat in 1919, during a wave of anti-red hysteria.) The Republicans, by virtue of holdovers, retained the Senate, 51 to 41, but the insurgents in their midst were numerous enough to make that hold precarious.

The Taft-Roosevelt Rupture

The sputtering uprising in Republican ranks had now blossomed into a full-fledged revolt. Early in 1911 the National Progressive Republican League was formed, with the fiery, white-maned Senator Robert La Follette of Wisconsin its leading candidate for the Republican

insubordination *Deliberate disobedience to proper authority.*

Ex-President Theodore Roosevelt Watches President Taft Struggle with the Demands of Government, 1910

presidential nomination. The assumption was that Roosevelt, an anti–third-termer, would not permit himself to be "drafted."

But the restless Rough Rider began to change his views about third terms as he saw Taft, hand in glove with the hated Old Guard, discard "my policies." In February 1912 Roosevelt formally wrote to seven state governors that he was willing to accept the Republican nomination. His reasoning was that the third-term tradition applied to three *consecutive elective* terms. Exuberantly he cried, "My hat is in the ring!" and "The fight is on and I am stripped to the buff!"

Roosevelt forthwith seized the Progressive banner, while La Follette, who had served as a convenient pathbreaker, was protestingly elbowed aside. Girded for battle, the Rough Rider came clattering into the presidential primaries then being held in many states. He shouted through half-clenched teeth that the president had fallen under the thumb of the reactionary bosses and that although Taft "means well, he means well feebly." The once-genial Taft, now in a fighting mood, branded Roosevelt supporters "emotionalists and neurotics."

A Taft-Roosevelt explosion was near in June 1912, when the Republican convention met in Chicago. The Rooseveltites, who were about 100 delegates short of winning the nomination, challenged the right of some 250 Taft delegates to be seated. Most of these contests were arbitrarily settled in favor of Taft, whose supporters held the throttle of the convention steamroller. The Roosevelt adherents, crying "fraud" and "naked theft," in the end refused to vote, and Taft triumphed.

Roosevelt, the supposedly good sportsman, refused to quit the game. Having tasted for the first time the bitter cup of defeat, he was now on fire to lead a third-party crusade.

Chapter Summary

The progressive movement of the early twentieth century became the greatest American reform crusade since abolitionism. Inaugurated by Populists, socialists, social gospelers, female reformers, and muckraking journalists, progressivism became a widely popular effort to strengthen government's power to correct the many social and economic problems associated with industrialization and urbanization.

Progressivism began at the city and state level, where it initially focused "good government" political reforms to corral corrupt bosses. It also turned to correcting a host of social and economic evils that seemed to require national action by the federal government. Women played an especially critical role in galvanizing progressive social concern. Seeing involvement in such issues as reforming child labor, poor tenement housing, and consumer causes as a natural extension of their traditional roles as wives and mothers, female activists brought significant changes in both law and public attitudes in these areas.

At the national level, Roosevelt's Square Deal vigorously deployed the federal government to promote the public interest and mediate conflicts between labor interests on the one hand and the corporate trusts on the other. Rooseveltian progressivism also inspired attention to consumer and environmental concerns. Conservation became an important public crusade under Roosevelt, although sharp disagreements divided wilderness "preservationists" from moderate conservationists such as Roosevelt who favored the "multiple use" of nature.

Roosevelt personally selected his longtime subordinate Taft as his political successor, expecting him to carry out "my policies." But Taft proved to be a poor politician who fell under the thumb of the conservative Republican Old Guard and rapidly lost public support. The progressives' hostility to Taft split the Republican party, and when Roosevelt failed to win the nomination he launched a fiery third-party crusade in the 1912 election.

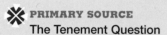 **PRIMARY SOURCE**
The Tenement Question

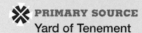 **PRIMARY SOURCE**
Yard of Tenement

KEY TERMS

progressive(s) (462)

conspicuous consumption (463)

direct primary (465)

initiative (465)

referendum (465)

recall (465)

city manager (466)

red-light district (466)

franchise (466)

workers' (workmen's) compensation (467)

reclamation (471)

bureaucracy (bureaucrat) (472)

collectivism (474)

insubordination (476)

PEOPLE TO KNOW

Henry Demarest Lloyd

Thorstein Veblen

Jacob A. Riis

Robert M. ("Fighting Bob") La Follette

Hiram W. Johnson

Florence Kelley

Frances E. Willard

Gifford Pinchot

John Muir

 Go to the History CourseMate website for primary source links, study tools, and review materials www.cengagebrain.com

29

Wilsonian Progressivism at Home and Abroad

1912–1916

American enterprise is not free; the man with only a little capital is finding it harder and harder to get into the field, more and more impossible to compete with the big fellow. Why? Because the laws of this country do not prevent the strong from crushing the weak.

WOODROW WILSON, THE NEW FREEDOM, 1913

⭐ Chapter Outline

The Election of 1912: The New Freedom versus the New Nationalism

Wilsonian Progressivism: Reforming the Tariff, the Banks, and the Trusts

Wilson's Diplomacy in Mexico and Latin America

War in Europe and American Neutrality

The Reelection of Wilson, 1916

Varying Viewpoints: Who Were the Progressives?

Office-hungry Democrats—the "outs" since 1897—were jubilant over the disruptive Republican brawl at Chicago. If they could come up with an outstanding reformist leader, they had an excellent chance to win the White House. Such a leader appeared in Dr. Woodrow Wilson, once a mild conservative but now a militant progressive. Beginning professional life as a brilliant academic scholar of government, Wilson had risen in 1902 to the presidency of Princeton University, where he achieved some sweeping educational reforms.

Wilson entered politics in 1910 when New Jersey bosses, needing a respectable "front" candidate for the governorship, offered him the nomination. They expected to lead the academic novice by the nose, but to their surprise, Wilson waged a passionate reform campaign in which he assailed the "predatory" trusts and promised to return state government to the people. Riding the crest of the progressive wave, the "Schoolmaster in Politics" was swept into office.

Once in the governor's chair, Wilson drove through the legislature a sheaf of forward-looking measures that made reactionary New Jersey one of the more liberal states. Filled with righteous indignation, Wilson revealed irresistible reforming zeal, burning eloquence, superb powers of leadership, and a refreshing habit of appealing over the heads of the scheming bosses to the sovereign people. Now a figure of national eminence, Wilson was being widely mentioned for the presidency.

FOCUS QUESTIONS

1. What made the election of 1912 a debate on fundamental political philosophies rather than a disagreement about particular issues? Was Wilson's victory due primarily to his principles or to the Republican split?

2. How did Wilsonian progressivism overcome the "triple wall of privilege"?

3. What were the features of Wilson's moralistic foreign policy? How did he apply those principles to Latin America and then to Europe in World War I?

4. What was America's response to the outbreak of World War I? Why did Wilson's attempts at neutrality turn into a critical stance toward Germany?

5. What were the basic issues in the election of 1916, and why did Hughes's attempt to straddle isolationist and anti-German sentiment fail?

CHRONOLOGY

1912	Wilson defeats Taft and Roosevelt for presidency.
1913	Underwood Tariff Act.
	Sixteenth Amendment (income tax).
	Federal Reserve Act.
	Huerta takes power in Mexico.
	Seventeenth Amendment (direct election of senators).
1914	Clayton Anti-Trust Act.
	Federal Trade Commission established.
	U.S. occupation of Veracruz, Mexico.
	World War I begins in Europe.
1915	La Follette Seamen's Act.
	Lusitania torpedoed and sunk by German U-boat.

	U.S. Marines sent to Haiti.
	Germany declares submarine war area around British Isles.
1916	*Sussex* ultimatum and pledge.
	U.S. exports to European belligerents skyrocket.
	Workingmen's Compensation Act.
	Federal Farm Loan Act.
	Adamson Act.
	Jones Act.
	Pancho Villa raids New Mexico.
	Brandeis appointed to Supreme Court.
	U.S. Marines sent to Dominican Republic.
	Wilson defeats Hughes for presidency.
1917	United States buys Virgin Islands from Denmark.

The "Bull Moose" Campaign of 1912

When the Democrats met at Baltimore in 1912, Wilson was nominated on the forty-sixth ballot, aided by William Jennings Bryan's switch to his side. The Democrats gave Wilson a strong progressive platform to run on; dubbed the "New Freedom" program, the platform included calls for antitrust legislation, banking reform, and tariff reductions.

Surging events had meanwhile been thrusting Roosevelt to the fore as a candidate for the presidency on a third-party Progressive Republican ticket. The fighting ex-cowboy, angered by his recent rebuff, was eager to lead the charge. A pro-Roosevelt Progressive convention, with about two thousand delegates from forty states, assembled in Chicago in August 1912. Dramatically symbolizing the rising political status of women, as well as Progressive support for the cause of social justice, settlement-house pioneer Jane Addams placed Roosevelt's name in nomination for the presidency. The audience wildly cheered Roosevelt as he fervently cried, "We stand at Armageddon, and we battle for the Lord!" A religious revival atmosphere suffused the convention, as the hoarse delegates sang "Onward Christian Soldiers" and the "Battle Hymn of the Republic."

Fired-up Progressives entered the campaign with righteousness and enthusiasm. Roosevelt boasted that he felt "as strong as a bull moose," so the bull moose took its place with the donkey and the elephant in the American political zoo. As one poet whimsically put it:

I want to be a Bull Moose,
And with the Bull Moose stand
With antlers on my forehead
And a Big Stick in my hand.

Roosevelt and Taft were bound to slit each other's political throats; by dividing the Republican vote they virtually guaranteed a Democratic

GOP Divided by Bull Moose Equals Democratic Victory, 1912

victory. The two antagonists tore into each other as only former friends can. "Death alone can take me out now!" cried the once-jovial Taft, as he branded Roosevelt a "dangerous egotist" and a "demagogue." Roosevelt, fighting mad, assailed Taft as a "fathead" with "the brain of a guinea pig."

Beyond the clashing personalities, the overshadowing question of the 1912 campaign was which of two varieties of progressivism would prevail—Roosevelt's New Nationalism or Wilson's New Freedom. Both men favored a more active government role in economic and social affairs, but they disagreed sharply over specific strategies. Roosevelt preached the theories spun out by the progressive thinker Herbert Croly in his book *The Promise of American Life* (1910). Croly and TR both favored continued consolidation of trusts and labor unions, paralleled by the growth of powerful regulatory agencies in Washington. Roosevelt and his "bull moosers" also campaigned for woman suffrage and a broad program of social welfare, including minimum-wage laws and social insurance. Clearly, the bull moose Progressives looked forward to the kind of activist welfare state that Franklin Roosevelt's New Deal would one day make a reality.

Wilson's New Freedom, by contrast, favored small enterprise, **entrepreneurship**, and the free functioning of unregulated and unmonopolized markets. The Democrats shunned social welfare proposals and pinned their economic faith on competition—on the "man on the make," as Wilson put it. The keynote of Wilson's campaign was not regulation but fragmentation of the big industrial combines, chiefly by means of vigorous enforcement of the antitrust laws. The election of 1912 thus offered the voters a choice not merely of policies but of political and economic philosophies—a rarity in United States history.

The heat of the campaign cooled a bit when, in Milwaukee, Roosevelt was shot in the chest by a fanatic. The Rough Rider suspended active campaigning for more than two weeks after delivering, with bull moose gameness and a bloody shirt, his scheduled speech.

entrepreneurship *The process whereby an individual initiates a business at some risk in order to expand it and thereby earn a profit.*

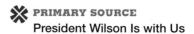

PRIMARY SOURCE
President Wilson Is with Us

═══ Woodrow Wilson: A Minority President ═══

Former professor Wilson won handily, with 435 electoral votes and 6,296,547 popular votes. The "third-party" candidate, Roosevelt, finished second, with 88 electoral votes and 4,118,571 popular votes. Taft won only 8 electoral votes and 3,486,720 popular votes (see the table on p. 482).

The election figures are fascinating. Wilson, with only 41 percent of the popular vote, was clearly a minority president, though his party won a majority in Congress. His popular total was actually smaller than Bryan had amassed in any of his three defeats, despite the increase in population. Taft and Roosevelt together polled over 1.25 million more votes than the Democrats. Progressivism rather than Wilson was the runaway winner. Although the Democratic total obviously included many conservatives in the solid South, the combined progressive vote for Wilson and Roosevelt, totalling 68 percent, far exceeded the tally of the more conservative Taft, who received only 23 percent. To the progressive tally must be added some support for the Socialist candidate, persistent Eugene V. Debs, who rolled up 900,672 votes, 6 percent of the total cast, or more than twice as many as he had netted four years earlier. Starry-eyed Socialists dreamed of being in the White House within eight years.

Roosevelt's lone-wolf course was tragic both for himself and for his former Republican associates. The Progressive party, which was primarily a one-man show, had no future because it had elected few candidates to state and local offices; the Socialists, in contrast, elected more than a thousand. Without patronage plums to hand out to faithful party workers, death by slow starvation was inevitable. Yet the Progressives made a tremendous showing for a hastily organized third party and helped spur the enactment of many of their pet reforms by the Wilsonian Democrats.

As for the Republicans, they were thrust into unaccustomed minority status in Congress for the next six years and were frozen out of the White House for eight years. Taft

The Presidential Vote, 1912

Candidate	Party	Electoral Vote	Popular Vote	Approximate Percentage
Woodrow Wilson	Democratic	435	6,296,547	41%
Theodore Roosevelt	Progressive	88	4,118,571	27
William H. Taft	Republican	8	3,486,720	23
Eugene V. Debs	Socialist	—	900,672	6
E. W. Chafin	Prohibition	—	206,275	1
A. E. Reimer	Socialist-Labor	—	28,750	0.2

himself had a fruitful old age. He taught law for eight pleasant years at Yale University and in 1921 became chief justice of the Supreme Court—a job for which he was far more happily suited than the presidency.

Wilson: The Idealist in Politics

(Thomas) Woodrow Wilson, the second Democratic president since 1861, looked like the ascetic intellectual he was, with clean-cut features, pinched-on eyeglasses, and trim figure. Born in Virginia shortly before the Civil War and reared in Georgia and the Carolinas, the professor-politician was the first man born and raised in one of the seceded southern states to reach the White House since Zachary Taylor, sixty-four years earlier. Wilson's admiration for the Confederacy's attempt to win independence partly inspired his ideal of self-determination for people of other countries. Steeped in the traditions of Jeffersonian democracy, he shared Jefferson's faith in the masses—if they were properly informed.

piety *Devotion to religious duty and practices.*

Son of a Presbyterian minister, Wilson was reared in an atmosphere of fervent **piety**. He later used the presidential pulpit to preach his inspirational political sermons. A moving orator, Wilson could rise on the wings of spiritual power to soaring eloquence. Skillfully using a persuasive voice, he relied not on arm waving but on sincerity and moral appeal. As a lifelong student of finely chiseled words, he turned out to be a "phraseocrat" who coined many noble epigrams. Someone has remarked that he was born halfway between the Bible and the dictionary and never strayed far from either.

Splendid though Wilson's intellectual equipment was, he suffered from serious defects of personality. Though jovial and witty in private, he could be cold and standoffish in public. Incapable of unbending and acting the showman, like "Teddy" Roosevelt, Wilson lacked the common touch. He loved humanity in the mass rather than the individual in person. His academic background caused him to feel most at home with scholars, although he had to work with politicians. An austere and somewhat arrogant intellectual, Wilson looked down his nose through pince-nez glasses upon lesser minds, including journalists. He was especially intolerant of stupid senators, whose "bungalow minds" made him "sick."

Wilson's burning idealism—especially his desire to reform ever-present wickedness—drove him forward faster than lesser spirits were willing to go. His sense of moral righteousness was such that he often found compromise difficult: Black was black, wrong was wrong, and one should never compromise with wrong. Wilson's Scottish Presbyterian ancestors had passed on to him an inflexible stubbornness. When convinced that he was right, Wilson would break before he would bend, unlike the pragmatic Roosevelt.

Wilson Attacks the "Triple Wall of Privilege"

Few presidents have arrived at the White House with a clearer program than Wilson's or one destined to be so completely achieved. The new president called for an all-out assault on what he called the "triple wall of privilege": the tariff, the banks, and the trusts.

He tackled the tariff first. In a precedent-shattering move, he appeared in person before a joint session of Congress in 1913 and presented his appeal with stunning eloquence and effectiveness. Moved by Wilson's aggressive leadership, the House swiftly passed the Underwood Tariff Bill, which provided for a substantial reduction of rates. The bill was also a landmark in tax legislation. Under authority granted by the recently ratified Sixteenth Amendment, Congress enacted a **graduated income tax**, beginning with a modest **levy** on incomes over $3,000 (then considerably higher than the average family's income). By 1917 revenue from the income tax shot ahead of receipts from the tariff, a gap that has since vastly widened.

A second bastion of the "triple wall of privilege" was the antiquated and inadequate banking and currency system, long since outgrown by the Republic's lusty economic expansion. The most serious shortcoming of the country's financial structure, still creaking along under the Civil War National Banking Act, was the **inelasticity** of the currency. Banking reserves were heavily concentrated in New York and a handful of other large cities and could not be mobilized in times of financial stress into areas that were badly pinched.

A House committee chaired by Congressman Arsene Pujo had already stirred public concern about the concentration of financial power by tracing the tentacles of the "money monster" into the hidden vaults of American banking and business. President Wilson's confidant, progressive-minded Massachusetts attorney Louis D. Brandeis, further fanned the flames of reform with his incendiary though scholarly book *Other People's Money and How the Bankers Use It* (1914).

In June 1913, in a second dramatic personal appearance before Congress, the president issued a ringing call for a decentralized bank in government hands, as opposed to mossback Republican Senator Nelson Aldrich's demands for a gigantic private bank—in effect, a third Bank of the United States. Again appealing to the sovereign people, Wilson scored another triumph. In 1913 he signed the Federal Reserve Act, the most important piece of economic legislation between the Civil War and the New Deal.

The new Federal Reserve Board, appointed by the president, oversaw a nationwide system of twelve regional reserve banks. These regional banks were owned by member financial institutions, but the final authority of the Federal Reserve Board guaranteed public control. The board was also empowered to issue paper money—"Federal Reserve notes"—backed by **commercial paper**, such as the **promissory notes** of businesspeople. Thus the amount of money in circulation could be swiftly increased as needed for the legitimate requirements of business. The economy could thus be regulated by effectively raising or lowering interest rates.

The Federal Reserve Act was a red-letter achievement. It carried the nation with flying banners through the financial crises of the First World War of 1914–1918. Without the Federal Reserve Act, the Republic's progress toward the modern economic age would have been seriously retarded.

Without pausing for breath, Wilson pushed toward the last remaining rampart in the "triple wall of privilege"—the trusts. His third personal appearance before Congress in 1914 led to passage of the Federal Trade Commission Act of 1914. The new law empowered a presidentially appointed commission to turn

graduated income tax *A tax on income in which the taxation rates grow progressively higher for those with higher income.*

levy *A forcible tax or other imposition.*

inelasticity *The inability to expand or contract rapidly.*

commercial paper *Any business document having monetary or exchangeable value.*

promissory note *A written pledge to pay a certain person a specified sum of money at a certain time.*

Brown Brothers

Woodrow Wilson (1856–1924) at Princeton Commencement with Andrew Carnegie, 1906 Before his election to the presidency of the United States in 1912, Wilson (left) served as president of Princeton University (1902–1910) and governor of New Jersey (1910–1912). In all three offices he undertook substantial reforms. Fighting desperately later for the League of Nations, at the cost of his health, Wilson said, "I would rather fail in a cause that I know some day will triumph than to win in a cause that I know some day will fail."

a searchlight on industries engaged in interstate commerce, such as the meatpackers. The commissioners were expected to crush monopoly at the source by rooting out unfair trade practices, including unlawful competition, false advertising, mislabeling, adulteration, and bribery.

The knot of monopoly was further cut by the Clayton Anti-Trust Act of 1914. This act lengthened the Sherman Act's list of objectionable business practices to include price discrimination and interlocking directorates (whereby the same individuals served as directors of supposedly competing firms), an end often achieved through holding companies. The Clayton Act also conferred long-overdue benefits on workers by exempting labor organizations from antitrust prosecutions under the Sherman Act and explicitly legalizing strikes and peaceful picketing. Union leader Samuel Gompers hailed the act as the **Magna Carta** of labor because it legally lifted human labor out of the category of "a commodity or article of commerce." But the rejoicing was premature, as conservative judges in later years continued to clip the wings of the union movement.

Magna Carta *The "Great Charter" of England, which feudal nobles of England forced King John to sign in 1215. As the first written guarantee of certain rights, such as trial by a jury of peers, against arbitrary royal power, the Magna Carta served as a model for later claims of Anglo-American liberties.*

Wilsonian Progressivism at High Tide

Energetically scaling the "triple wall of privilege," Woodrow Wilson had treated the nation to a dazzling demonstration of vigorous presidential leadership. He proved nearly irresistible in his first eighteen months in office. For once, a political creed was matched by deed, as the progressive reformers racked up victory after victory.

The United States in the Caribbean, 1898–1941 This map explains why many Latin Americans accused the United States of turning the Caribbean Sea into a "Yankee lake." The map also suggests that Uncle Sam was much less "isolationist" in his own backyard than he was in faraway Europe or Asia. © Cengage Learning

Standing at the peak of his powers at the head of the progressive forces, Wilson pressed ahead with further reforms. The Federal Farm Loan Act of 1916 made credit available to farmers at low rates of interest—as long demanded by the Populists. The La Follette Seamen's Act of 1915 required decent treatment and a living wage for often-abused sailors on American merchant ships.

Wilson further helped workers with the Workingmen's Compensation Act of 1916, granting assistance to federal civil-service employees during periods of disability. In the same year the president approved an act restricting child labor on products flowing into interstate commerce, though the stand-pat Supreme Court soon invalidated the law. The Adamson Act of 1916 established an eight-hour workday for all employees on trains in interstate commerce, with extra pay for overtime.

Wilson earned the enmity of businesspeople and bigots but endeared himself to progressives when in 1916 he nominated for the Supreme Court the prominent reformer Louis D. Brandeis—the first Jew to be called to the high bench. Yet even Wilson's progressivism had its limits, and it clearly stopped short of better treatment for blacks. The southern-bred Wilson actually presided over accelerated segregation in the federal bureaucracy. When a delegation of black leaders personally protested to him, the schoolmasterish president virtually froze them out of his office.

Despite these limitations, Wilson knew that to be reelected in 1916, he needed to identify himself clearly as the candidate of progressivism. Wilson's election in 1912 had been something of a fluke, owing largely to the Taft-Roosevelt split in the Republican ranks. To remain in the White House, the president would have to woo the bull moose voters into the Democratic fold.

New Directions in Foreign Policy

In one important area, Wilson chose not to answer the trumpet call of the bull moosers. In contrast to Roosevelt and even Taft, Wilson recoiled from an aggressive foreign policy. Hating imperialism, he was repelled by TR's big stickism. Suspicious of Wall Street, he detested the so-called dollar diplomacy of Taft.

In office only a week, Wilson declared war on dollar diplomacy. He proclaimed that the government would no longer support American investors in Latin America and China. Shivering from this Wilsonian bucket of cold water, American bankers pulled out of the Taft-engineered six-nation loan to China the next day. Wilson's anti-imperialism also produced the Jones Act of 1916, which granted territorial status to the Philippines and promised independence as soon as a "stable government" could be established. Wilson's racial prejudices, however, made it difficult for him to anticipate anything other than a long political tutelage for the Filipinos. Indeed, not until July 4, 1946—thirty years later—did the United States accept Philippine independence.

Events in the Caribbean soon forced Wilson to eat some of his anti-imperialist words. In response to disorders in Haiti in 1914–1915, the president reluctantly dispatched marines to protect American lives and property. In 1916 he stole a page from the Roosevelt Corollary to the Monroe Doctrine as the United States took over supervision of Haiti's finances and police. In the same year, Wilson sent the leathernecked marines to quell riots in the Dominican Republic, and that debt-cursed land came under the shadow of the American eagle's wings for the next eight years. In 1917 Wilson purchased from Denmark the Virgin Islands in the West Indies. Increasingly, the Caribbean Sea, with its vital approaches to the now-completed Panama Canal, was taking on the earmarks of a Yankee preserve.

Moralistic Diplomacy in Mexico

Rifle bullets whining across the southern border served as a constant reminder that all was not quiet in Mexico. For decades Mexico had been sorely exploited by foreign investors in oil, railroads, and mines. By 1913 American capitalists had sunk about a billion dollars into the underdeveloped but generously endowed country.

But if Mexico was rich, the Mexicans were poor. Fed up with their miserable lot, the Mexicans at last revolted. Their revolution took an ugly turn in early 1913, when a

A Republican congressman voiced complaints against Wilson's Mexican policy in 1916:

"It is characterized by weakness, uncertainty, vacillation, and uncontrollable desire to intermeddle in Mexican affairs. He has not had the courage to go into Mexico nor the courage to stay out. ... I would either go into Mexico and pacify the country or I would keep my hands entirely out of Mexico. If we are too proud to fight, we should be too proud to quarrel. I would not choose between murderers."

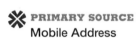

PRIMARY SOURCE
Mobile Address

conscienceless clique (with the support of President Taft's ambassador to Mexico) murdered the popular new revolutionary president and installed General Victoriano Huerta, an Indian, in the president's chair. All this chaos accelerated a massive migration of Mexicans to the United States. More than a million Spanish-speaking newcomers tramped across the southern border in the first three decades of the twentieth century. Settling mostly in Texas, New Mexico, Arizona, and California, they helped to create a unique borderland culture that blended Mexican and American folkways.

The revolutionary bloodshed also menaced American lives and property in Mexico. Cries for intervention burst from the lips of American jingoes such as publisher William Randolph Hearst, himself the owner of a Mexican ranch larger than Rhode Island. Yet once again, President Wilson refused to practice the same old dollar diplomacy of his predecessors, deeming it "perilous" to determine foreign policy "in the terms of material interest."

Wilson strived as best he could to steer a moral course in Mexico. He sent his aggressive ambassador packing, imposed an arms embargo, and refused to recognize officially the murderous government of "that brute" Huerta, even though most foreign powers acknowledged Huerta's bloody-handed regime. "I am going to teach the South American republics to elect good men," the former professor declared. He put his munitions where his mouth was in 1914, when he allowed American arms to flow to Huerta's principal rivals, white-bearded Venustiano Carranza and the firebrand Francisco ("Pancho") Villa.

The Mexican volcano erupted at the Atlantic seaport of Tampico in April 1914, when a small party of American sailors was arrested. The Mexicans promptly released the captives and apologized, but they refused the affronted American admiral's demand for a twenty-one gun salute. Wilson ordered the navy to seize the Mexican port of Veracruz to thwart the arrival of a German steamer carrying Huerta-bound guns and ammunition. Huerta as well as Carranza hotly protested against this high-handed Yankee maneuver.

Just as a full-dress shooting conflict seemed inevitable, Wilson was rescued by an offer of mediation from the ABC powers—Argentina, Brazil, and Chile. Huerta collapsed in July 1914 under pressure from within and without. He was succeeded by his archrival, Venustiano Carranza, still fiercely resentful of Wilson's military meddling. The whole sorry episode did not augur well for the future of United States–Mexican relations.

"Pancho" Villa, a combination of bandit and Robin Hood, had meanwhile emerged as the chief rival of President Carranza, whom Wilson now reluctantly supported. Challenging Carranza's authority while also punishing the gringos, Villa's men ruthlessly killed sixteen American mining engineers in northern Mexico. A month later Villa and his followers, hoping to provoke a war between Wilson and Carranza, blazed across the border into Columbus, New Mexico, and murdered another nineteen Americans.

General John J. ("Black Jack"*) Pershing, a ramrod-erect veteran of the Cuban and Philippine campaigns, was ordered to break up the bandit band. His hastily organized force of several thousand mounted troops penetrated deep into rugged Mexico with surprising speed. They clashed with Carranza's forces and mauled the Villistas but missed capturing Villa himself. As the threat of war with Germany loomed larger, the invading army was withdrawn in January 1917.

A Precarious Neutrality

Europe's powder magazine, long smoldering, blew up in the summer of 1914, when the flaming pistol of a Serb patriot killed the heir to the throne of Austria-Hungary in Sarajevo. An outraged Vienna government, backed by Germany, forthwith presented a stern ultimatum to Serbia.

---

* So called from his earlier service as an officer with the crack black Tenth Cavalry.

An explosive chain reaction followed. Russian mobilization in support of Serbia threatened Germany in the east, even as the tsar's ally, France, confronted Germany in the west. In alarm, the Germans struck suddenly at France through unoffending Belgium. Great Britain in turn was sucked into the conflagration on the side of France.

Almost overnight most of Europe was locked in a fight to the death. On one side were arrayed the Central Powers: Germany and Austria-Hungary, and later Turkey and Bulgaria. On the other side were the Allies, principally France, Britain, and Russia, and later Japan and Italy. Americans thanked God for the ocean moats and self-righteously congratulated themselves on having had ancestors wise enough to have abandoned the hell pits of Europe. Americans felt strong, snug, smug, and secure—but not for long.

President Wilson issued the routine neutrality proclamation and called on Americans to be neutral in thought as well as deed. But such scrupulous evenhandedness proved difficult. Both sides wooed the United States, the great neutral in the West. The British enjoyed the boon of close cultural, linguistic, and economic ties with America and had the added advantage of controlling most of the transatlantic cables. Their **censors** sheared away war stories harmful to the Allies and drenched the United States with tales of German bestiality.

censor *An official who examines publications, mail, literature, and so forth in order to remove or prohibit the distribution of material deemed dangerous or offensive.*

Most Americans were anti-German from the outset, although some German Americans expressed noisy sympathy for the fatherland. With his villainous upturned mustache, Kaiser Wilhelm II seemed the embodiment of arrogant autocracy, an impression strengthened by Germany's ruthless strike at neutral Belgium. The discovery in 1915 of German plans for industrial sabotage in the United States further inflamed opinion against the kaiser and Germany. Yet the great majority of Americans earnestly hoped to stay out of the horrible war.

America Earns Blood Money

When Europe burst into flames in 1914, the United States was bogged down in a worrisome business recession. But British and French war orders soon pulled American industry out of the morass of hard times and onto a peak of war-born prosperity. Part of this boom was financed by American bankers, notably the Wall Street firm of J. P. Morgan and Company, which eventually advanced to the Allies the enormous sum of $2.3 billion during the period of American neutrality. The Central Powers protested bitterly against the immense trade between America and the Allies, but this traffic did not in fact violate international neutrality laws. Germany was technically free to trade with the United States, but the tight British naval blockade prevented it from doing so.

Hard-pressed Germany did not tamely consent to being starved out. In retaliation for the British blockade, in February 1915 Berlin announced a submarine war area around the British Isles. The submarine was a weapon so new that existing international law could not be made to fit it. The old rule that a warship must stop and board merchant ships could hardly apply to submarines, which could easily be rammed or sunk if they surfaced.

torpedo *To launch from a submarine or airplane a self-propelled underwater explosive designed to detonate on impact.*

The cigar-shaped marauders posed a dire threat to the United States—as long as Wilson insisted on maintaining America's neutral rights. Berlin officials declared that they would try not to sink *neutral* shipping, but they warned that mistakes would probably occur. Wilson now determined on a policy of calculated risk. He would continue to claim profitable neutral trading rights while hoping that no high-seas incident would force his hand to grasp the sword of war. He emphatically warned Germany that it would be held to "strict accountability" for any attacks on American vessels or citizens.

The German submarines (known as U-boats, from the German *Unterseeboot,* or "underseas boat") meanwhile began their deadly work. In the first months of 1915, they sank about ninety ships in the war zone. Then the submarine issue became acute when the British passenger liner *Lusitania* was **torpedoed** and sank off the coast of Ireland on May 7, 1915, with the loss of 1,198 lives, including 128 Americans.

The Fatherland, *the chief German-American propaganda newspaper in the United States, cried:*

"We [Americans] prattle about humanity while we manufacture poisoned shrapnel and picric acid for profit. Ten thousand German widows, ten thousand orphans, ten thousand graves bear the legend 'Made in America.'"

Advertisement from the *New York Herald*, May 1, 1915 Six days later the *Lusitania* was sunk. Notice the German warning.

The *Lusitania* was carrying forty-two hundred cases of small-arms ammunition, a fact the Germans used to justify the sinking. But Americans were swept by a wave of shock and anger at this act of "mass murder" and "piracy." The eastern United States, closer to the war, seethed with talk of fighting, but the rest of the country showed a strong distaste for hostilities. The peace-loving Wilson had no stomach for leading a disunited nation into war and relied instead on a series of increasingly strong notes to bring the German warlords sharply to book. "There is such a thing," he said, "as a man being too proud to fight."

Yet Wilson, sticking to his verbal guns, made some diplomatic progress. After another British liner, the *Arabic,* was sunk in August 1915, with the loss of two American lives, Berlin reluctantly agreed not to sink unarmed and unresisting passenger ships *without warning.*

This pledge appeared to be violated in March 1916, when the Germans torpedoed a French passenger steamer, the *Sussex.* The infuriated Wilson informed the Germans that unless they renounced the inhuman practice of sinking merchant ships without warning he would break diplomatic relations—an almost certain prelude to war.

Germany reluctantly knuckled under to President Wilson's *Sussex* ultimatum, agreeing not to sink passenger ships and merchant vessels without giving warning. But the Germans attached a long string to their *Sussex* pledge: The United States would have to persuade the Allies to modify what Berlin regarded as their illegal blockade. This, obviously, was something that Washington could not do. Wilson promptly accepted the German pledge, without accepting the "string." He thus won a temporary but precarious diplomatic victory—precarious because Germany could pull the string whenever it chose, and the president might suddenly find himself tugged over the cliff of war.

Wilson Wins Reelection in 1916

Against this ominous backdrop, the presidential campaign of 1916 gathered speed. Both the bull moose Progressives and the Republicans met in Chicago. The Progressives uproariously renominated Theodore Roosevelt, but the Rough Rider, who loathed Wilson and all his works, had no stomach for splitting the Republicans again and ensuring the reelection of his hated rival. In refusing to run, he sounded the death knell of the Progressive party.

Roosevelt's Republican admirers also clamored for "Teddy," but the Old Guard detested the renegade who had ruptured the party in 1912. Instead, they **drafted** Supreme Court Justice Charles Evans Hughes, the cold, intellectual former governor of New York. The Republican platform condemned the Democratic tariff, assaults on the trusts, and Wilson's wishy-washiness in dealing with Mexico and Germany.

The thick-whiskered Hughes ("an animated feather duster") left the bench for the campaign stump, where he was not at home. In anti-German areas of the country, he assailed Wilson for not standing up to the kaiser, whereas in isolationist areas he took a softer line. This fence-straddling operation led to the jeer, "Charles Evasive Hughes."

Hughes was further plagued by Roosevelt, who was delivering a series of skin-'em-alive speeches against "that damned Presbyterian hypocrite Wilson." Frothing for war, TR privately sneered at Hughes as a "whiskered Wilson." The only difference between the two, he said, was "a shave."

Wilson, nominated by acclamation at the Democratic convention in St. Louis, ignored Hughes on the theory that one should not try to murder a man who is committing suicide. His campaign was built on the slogan "He Kept Us Out of War." Democratic orators warned that by electing Charles Evans Hughes, the nation would be electing a

During the 1916 campaign, J. A. O'Leary, the head of a pro-German and pro-Irish organization, sent a scorching telegram to Wilson condemning him for having been pro-British in approving war loans and ammunition traffic. Wilson shot back an answer:

"Your telegram received. I would feel deeply mortified to have you or anybody like you vote for me. Since you have access to many disloyal Americans and I have not, I will ask you to convey this message to them."

President Wilson's devastating and somewhat insulting response probably won him more votes than it lost.

1916

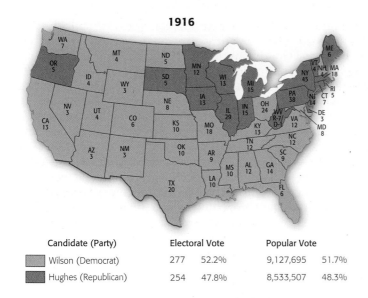

Candidate (Party)	Electoral Vote		Popular Vote	
Wilson (Democrat)	277	52.2%	9,127,695	51.7%
Hughes (Republican)	254	47.8%	8,533,507	48.3%

Presidential Election of 1916 (with electoral vote by state) Wilson was so worried about being a lame-duck president in a time of great international tensions that he drew up a plan whereby Hughes, if victorious, would be appointed secretary of state, Wilson and the vice president would resign, and Hughes would thus succeed immediately to the presidency. © Cengage Learning

fight—with a certain frustrated Rough Rider leading the charge. A Democratic advertisement appealing to American workers read:

> *You are Working;*
> *—Not Fighting!*
> *Alive and Happy;*
> *—Not Cannon Fodder!*
> *Wilson and Peace with Honor?*
> *or*
> *Hughes with Roosevelt and War?*

On election day, Hughes swept the East and looked like a surefire winner. Wilson went to bed that night prepared to accept defeat, while New York newspapers displayed huge portraits of "The President-Elect—Charles Evans Hughes." But the rest of the country turned the tide. Midwesterners and westerners, attracted by Wilson's progressive reforms and antiwar policies, flocked to the polls for the president. The final result, in doubt for several days, hinged on California, which Wilson carried by some 3,800 votes out of about a million cast.

Wilson barely squeaked through, with a final vote of 277 to 254 in the Electoral College and 9,127,695 to 8,533,507 in the popular column. The pro-labor Wilson received strong support from the working class and from renegade bull moosers, whom Republicans failed to lure back into their camp. Wilson had not specifically promised to keep the country out of war, but probably enough voters relied on such implicit assurances to ensure his victory. Their hopeful expectations were soon rudely shattered.

draft *In politics, to choose an individual to run for office without that person's prior solicitation or approval of the nomination. (A military draft, or conscription, legally compels individuals into the armed services.)*

✳ **PRIMARY SOURCE**
My Hat Is Still in the Ring

VARYING VIEWPOINTS   Who Were the Progressives?

Debate about progressivism has revolved mainly around a question that is simple to ask but devilishly difficult to answer: Who were the progressives? It was once taken for granted that progressive reformers were simply the heirs of the Jeffersonian-Jacksonian-Populist reform crusades; they were the oppressed and downtrodden common folk who finally erupted in wrath and demanded their due.

But in his influential *Age of Reform* (1955), Richard Hofstadter astutely challenged that view. Progressive leaders, he argued, were not drawn from the ranks of society's poor and marginalized. Rather, they were middle-class people threatened from above by the emerging power of new corporate elites and from below by a restless working class. It was not economic deprivation, but "status anxiety," Hofstadter insisted, that prompted these people to become reformers. Their psychological motivation, Hofstadter concluded, rendered many of their reform efforts quirky and ineffectual.

By contrast, New Left historians, notably Gabriel Kolko, argue that progressivism was dominated by established business leaders who successfully directed "reform" to their own conservative ends. In this view, government regulation (as embodied in new agencies, such as the Federal Reserve Board and the Federal Tariff Commission, and in legislation, such as the Meat Inspection Act) simply accomplished what two generations of private efforts had failed to accomplish: dampening cutthroat competition, stabilizing markets, and making America safe for monopoly capitalism.

Still other scholars, notably Robert H. Wiebe and Samuel P. Hays, argue that the progressives were neither the psychologically or economically disadvantaged nor the old capitalist elite, but were, rather, members of a rapidly emerging, self-confident social class possessed of the new techniques of scientific management, technological expertise, and organizational know-how. This "organizational school" of historians does not see progressivism as a struggle of the "people" against the "interests," as a confused and nostalgic campaign by status-threatened reformers, or as a conservative coup d'état. The progressive movement, in this view, was by and large an effort to rationalize and modernize many social institutions by introducing the wise and impartial hand of government regulation.

This view has much to recommend it. Yet despite its widespread acceptance among historians, it is an explanation that cannot adequately account for the titanic political struggles of the progressive era over the very reforms that the "organizational school" regards as simple adjustments to modernity. The organizational approach also brushes over the deep philosophical differences that divided progressives themselves—such as the ideological chasm that separated Roosevelt's New Nationalism from Wilson's New Freedom.

Recently, scholars such as Robyn Muncy, Linda Gordon, and Theda Skocpol have stressed the role of women in advocating progressive reforms. Building the American welfare state in the early twentieth century, they argue, was fundamentally a gendered activity inspired by a "female dominion" of social workers and "social feminists." Moreover, in contrast to many European countries where labor movements sought a welfare state to benefit the working class, American female reformers promoted welfare programs specifically to protect women and children.

Chapter Summary

Advocating the "New Freedom," Democrat Woodrow Wilson defeated the Progressive Party candidate Roosevelt and the Republican Taft in the three-way election of 1912. The contest represented an unusual philosophical choice between alternative forms of progressivism. The eloquent, idealistic, but often ideologically self-righteous President Wilson successfully carried out a sweeping program of economic reform of the tariff, money and banking, and the trusts—what Wilson called the "triple wall of privilege." He also achieved substantial social reforms that benefited women and the working classes, but his lack of sympathy for blacks actually furthered segregation.

Wilson's attempt to implement similar progressive moral goals in foreign policy was less successful, as he stumbled into military involvements in the Caribbean and revolutionary Mexico. The outbreak of World War I in Europe brought growing risks of American involvement, especially because of the threat to neutral shipping from German submarine warfare. Led by President Wilson, most Americans earnestly sought to stay clear of the war, though all but a minority sympathized with the Allies more than the Germans.

Wilson temporarily avoided war by extracting the precarious *Sussex* pledge from Germany. His progressive campaign of 1916, appealing to workers and former bull moose supporters, narrowly won him reelection over Charles Evans Hughes and the Republicans, plagued by TR's disaffection and Hughes's deficiencies as a campaigner.

KEY TERMS

entrepreneurship (481)

piety (482)

graduated income tax (483)

levy(483)

inelasticity (483)

commercial paper (483)

promissory note (483)

Magna Carta (484)

censor (487)

torpedo (487)

draft (489)

PEOPLE TO KNOW

Herbert Croly

Louis D. Brandeis

Victoriano Huerta

Venustiano Carranza

Francisco ("Pancho") Villa

John ("Black Jack") Pershing

Charles Evans Hughes

 Go to the History CourseMate website for primary source links, study tools, and review materials for this chapter. www.cengagebrain.com

30

The War to End War

1917–1918

The world must be made safe for democracy. Its peace must be planted upon
the tested foundations of political liberty. We have no selfish ends to serve. We desire
no conquest, no dominion. We seek no indemnities for ourselves, no material
compensation for the sacrifices we shall freely make.

WOODROW WILSON, WAR MESSAGE, APRIL 2, 1917

Destiny dealt cruelly with Woodrow Wilson. The lover of peace, as fate would have it, was forced to lead a hesitant and peace-loving nation into war. As the last days of 1916 slipped through the hourglass, the president made one final, futile attempt to mediate between the embattled belligerents. On January 22, 1917, he delivered one of his most moving addresses, restating America's conviction that only a negotiated "peace without victory" would prove durable.

Germany's warlords responded with a blow of the mailed fist. On January 31, 1917, they announced to an astonished world that they intended to wage *unrestricted* submarine warfare, sinking *all* ships, including America's, in the war zone.

Why this rash act? War with America was the last thing Germany wanted. But after three ghastly years in the trenches, Germany's leaders decided that making distinctions between combatants and noncombatants was a luxury they could no longer afford. Thus they jerked on the string they had attached to their *Sussex* pledge in 1916, desperately hoping to bring Britain to its knees before the United States entered the war. Wilson, his bluff called, broke diplomatic relations with Germany but refused to move closer to war unless the Germans undertook "overt" acts against American lives.

FOCUS QUESTIONS

1. Why did America enter World War I?
2. Why did Woodrow Wilson proclaim America's entry into the war as an ideological crusade for universal democracy and freedom, rather than simply an attempt to curb German military power? How did defining the war that way both inspire patriotic fervor and crush domestic dissent?
3. How did America mobilize for war, and what was the war's impact on labor, women, and African Americans?
4. What were America's economic, military, and diplomatic contributions to the Allied victory, and why was Wilson forced to compromise his idealistic plan for a peace based on the Fourteen Points?
5. Why was the battle over ratifying the Treaty of Versailles so fierce and bitter, and how did Wilson's refusal to compromise with Lodge and others doom the treaty?

CHRONOLOGY

1915	Council of National Defense established.	1918–1919	Armistice ends World War I. Worldwide influenza pandemic.
1917	Germany resumes unrestricted submarine warfare. Zimmermann note. Railroads placed under federal control. United States enters World War I. Espionage Act of 1917. Wilson calls for "peace without victory." Bolshevik Revolution.	1919	Paris Peace Conference and Treaty of Versailles. Wilson's pro-League tour and collapse. Eighteenth Amendment (prohibition of alcohol) passed. First Senate defeat of Versailles Treaty.
1918	Wilson proposes Fourteen Points. Sedition Act of 1918. Battle of Château-Thierry. Second Battle of the Marne. Meuse-Argonne offensive.	1920	Final Senate defeat of Versailles Treaty after reconsideration. Nineteenth Amendment (woman suffrage) passed. Harding defeats Cox for presidency.

War by Act of Germany

To defend American interests short of war, the president asked Congress for authority to arm American merchant ships. When a band of midwestern senators launched a filibuster to block the measure, Wilson denounced them as a "little group of willful men" who were rendering a great nation "helpless and contemptible." But their obstructionism was a powerful reminder of the continuing strength of American **isolationism**.

Meanwhile, the sensational Zimmermann note was intercepted and published on March 1, 1917, infuriating Americans, especially westerners. German foreign secretary Arthur Zimmermann had secretly proposed a German-Mexican alliance, tempting anti-Yankee Mexico with veiled promises of recovering Texas, New Mexico, and Arizona.

On the heels of this provocation came the long-dreaded "overt" acts in the Atlantic, where German U-boats sank four unarmed American merchant vessels in the first two weeks of March. As one Philadelphia newspaper observed, "The difference between war and what we have now is that now we aren't fighting back." Simultaneously came the rousing news that a revolution in Russia had toppled the cruel regime of the tsars. America could now fight foursquare for democracy on the side of the Allies without the black sheep of Russian despotism in the Allied fold.

Subdued and solemn, Wilson at last stood before a hushed joint session of Congress on the evening of April 2, 1917, and asked for a declaration of war. He had lost his gamble that America could pursue the profits of neutral trade without being sucked into the ghastly maelstrom. A myth developed in later years that America was dragged unwittingly into war by munitions makers and Wall Street bankers, desperate to protect their profits and loans. Yet the weapons merchants and financiers were already thriving, unhampered by wartime government restrictions and heavy taxation. The simple truth is that British harassment of American commerce had been galling but endurable; Germany had resorted to the mass killing of civilians. President Wilson had drawn a clear, if risky, line against the depredations of the submarine. The German high command, in a last desperate throw of the dice, chose to cross it. In a figurative sense, America's war declaration of April 6, 1917, bore the unambiguous trademark "Made in Germany."

✳ PRIMARY SOURCE
Zimmermann Telegram

isolationism *In American diplomacy, the traditional belief that the United States should refrain from involvement in overseas politics, alliances, or wars and confine its national security interest to its own borders (sometimes along with the Caribbean and Central America).* ***Internationalism*** *or* ***Wilsonianism*** *is the contrasting belief that America's national security requires continuing involvement in global affairs and diplomatic or military alliances overseas.*

Wilsonian Idealism Enthroned

"It is a fearful thing to lead this great peaceful people into war," Wilson said in his war message. It was fearful indeed, not least of all because of the formidable challenge it posed to Wilson's leadership skills. Ironically, it fell to the scholarly Wilson, deeply respectful of American traditions, to shatter one of the most sacred of those traditions by entangling America in a distant European war.

How could the president arouse the American people to shoulder this unprecedented burden? Isolationism remained strong, and no fewer than six senators and fifty representatives (including the first congresswoman, Jeannette Rankin of Montana) had voted against the war resolution. Wilson could whip up no enthusiasm, especially in the landlocked Midwest, for fighting to make the world safe from the submarine.

To galvanize the country, Wilson would have to proclaim more glorified aims. Radiating the spiritual fervor of his Presbyterian ancestors, he declared the twin goals of "a war to end war" and a crusade "to make the world safe for democracy." Brandishing the sword of righteousness, Wilson virtually hypnotized the nation with his lofty ideals. He contrasted the selfish war aims of the other belligerents, Allied and enemy alike, with America's shining altruism. America, he preached, did not fight for the sake of riches or territorial conquest. The Republic sought only to shape an international order in which democracy could flourish without fear of power-crazed autocrats and militarists.

In Wilsonian idealism the personality of the president and the necessities of history were perfectly matched. The high-minded Wilson genuinely believed in the principles he so eloquently intoned—especially that the modern world could not afford the kind of hyper-destructive war that advanced industrial states were now capable of waging. In this, Wilson's vision was prophetic. In any case, probably no other appeal could have successfully converted the American people from their historic hostility to involvement in European squabbles. Americans, it seemed, could be either isolationists or crusaders, but nothing in between.

Wilson's appeal worked—perhaps too well. Holding aloft the torch of idealism, the president fired up the public mind to a fever pitch. "Force, force to the utmost, force without stint or limit," he cried, while the country responded less elegantly with, "Hang the kaiser!" Lost on the gale was Wilson's earlier plea for "peace without victory."

Wilson's Fourteen Potent Points

Wilson quickly came to be recognized as the moral leader of the Allied cause. He scaled a summit of inspiring oratory on January 8, 1918, when he delivered his famed Fourteen Points Address to an enthusiastic Congress. Wilson's vision inspired all the drooping Allies to make mightier efforts and demoralized the enemy governments by holding out alluring promises to their dissatisfied minorities.

The first five of the Fourteen Points were broad in scope: (1) A proposal to abolish secret treaties pleased liberals of all countries. (2) Freedom of the seas appealed to the Germans, as well as to Americans who distrusted British sea power. (3) A removal of economic barriers among nations had long been the goal of liberal internationalists everywhere. (4) Reduction of armament burdens was gratifying to taxpayers of all countries. (5) An adjustment of colonial claims in the interests of both native peoples and the colonizers was a potentially revolutionary appeal that helped delegitimize old empires and inspire "subject peoples."

Other points among the fourteen proved to be no less seductive. They held out the promise of independence ("self-determination") to oppressed minority groups, such as the Poles, millions of whom lay under the heel of Germany and Austria-Hungary. The capstone point, number fourteen, foreshadowed the League of Nations—an international organization that Wilson dreamed would provide a system of **collective security**. Wilson earnestly prayed that this new scheme would effectively guarantee the political independence and territorial integrity of all countries, whether large or small.

Yet Wilson's appealing points, though raising hopes the world over, were not everywhere applauded. Certain leaders of the Allied nations, with an eye to territorial booty, were less than enthusiastic. Some hard-nosed Republicans at home openly mocked the "fourteen commandments" of "God Almighty Wilson."

collective security *In international affairs, reliance on a group of nations or an international organization as protection against aggressors, rather than on national self-defense alone.*

Creel Manipulates Minds

Mobilizing people's minds for war, both in America and abroad, was an urgent task facing the Washington authorities. The Committee on Public Information, headed by journalist George Creel, was therefore created to sell America on the war and sell the world on Wilsonian war aims. Though outspoken and tactless, Creel was gifted with zeal and imagination. His organization, employing 150,000 workers at home and overseas, proved that words were indeed weapons. It sent out an army of 75,000 "four-minute men"—often longer-winded than that—who delivered countless speeches full of "patriotic pep."

Creel's propaganda took varied forms. Posters were splashed on billboards in the "Battle of the Fences," as artists "rallied to the colors." Millions of leaflets and pamphlets containing the most pungent Wilsonisms were showered like confetti upon the world. Propaganda booklets with red-white-and-blue covers were printed by the millions. Hang-the-kaiser movies, carrying such titles as *The Kaiser, The Beast of Berlin* and *To Hell with the Kaiser,* portrayed the "Hun" at his bloodiest. Arm-waving conductors by the thousands led huge audiences in songs that poured scorn on the enemy and glorified the "boys" in uniform.

The entire nation, catching the frenzied spirit of a religious revival, burst into song. Most memorable of many anthems was George M. Cohan's spine-tingling "Over There":

> *Over there, over there*
> *Send the word, send the word over there,*
> *That the Yanks are coming, the Yanks are coming*
> *The drums rum-tumming everywhere.*

Creel typified American war **mobilization**, which relied more on aroused passion and voluntary compliance than on formal laws. But he oversold the ideals of Wilson and led the world to expect too much. When the president proved to be a mortal and not a god, the resulting disillusionment at home and abroad was disastrous.

Enforcing Loyalty and Stifling Dissent

German Americans numbered over 8 million, counting those with at least one parent foreign-born, out of a total population of 100 million. Most proved to be loyal to the United States. But as emotion mounted, hate hysteria against Germans and things Germanic swept the nation. Orchestras found it unsafe to present German-composed music, such as that of Wagner and Beethoven. German books were removed from library shelves, and German classes were canceled in high schools and colleges. Sauerkraut became "liberty cabbage," hamburger "liberty steak." Even beer became suspect, as patriotic Americans fretted over the loyalty of breweries with names such as Schlitz or Pabst. A few German Americans were tarred, feathered, and beaten; a German Socialist in Illinois was lynched by a drunken mob.

Both the Espionage Act of 1917 and the Sedition Act of 1918 reflected current fears about Germans and antiwar Americans. Especially visible among the nineteen hundred prosecutions undertaken under these laws were antiwar Socialists and members of the radical union Industrial Workers of the World (IWW). Kingpin Socialist Eugene V. Debs was convicted under the Espionage Act in 1918 and sentenced to ten years in a federal penitentiary. IWW leader William D. ("Big Bill") Haywood and ninety-nine associates were similarly convicted. Some leftist journals such as *The Masses* were denied use of the mails.

Virtually any criticism of the government could be censored and punished. Some critics claimed the new laws were bending, if not breaking, the First Amendment. But in *Schenck v.*

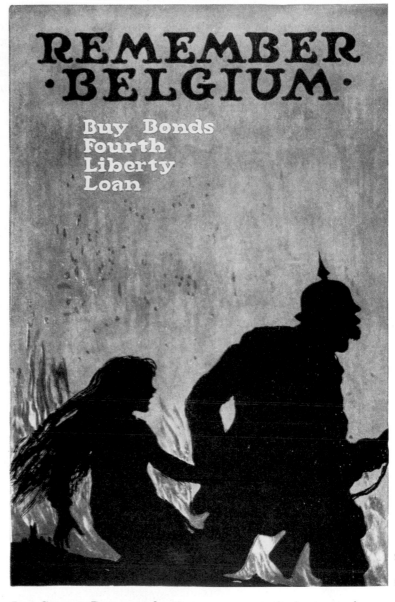

Library of Congress

Anti-German Propaganda The government relied extensively on emotional appeals and hate propaganda to rally support for the First World War, which most Americans regarded as a distant "European" affair. This poster used gendered imagery to evoke the brutal German violation of Belgian neutrality in August 1914.

mobilization *The organization of a nation and its armed forces for war.*

PRIMARY SOURCE
World's Greatest Adventure in Advertising

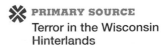

PRIMARY SOURCE
Terror in the Wisconsin Hinterlands

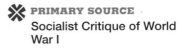

PRIMARY SOURCE
Socialist Critique of World War I

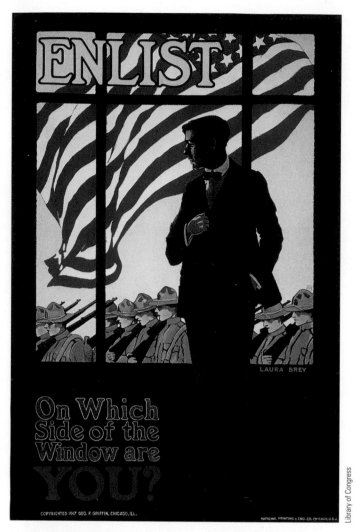

Library of Congress

Patriotic Persuasion Worried about the public's enthusiasm for the war, the government employed all the arts of psychology and propaganda to sustain the martial spirit. The prewar song "I Didn't Raise My Boy to Be a Soldier" was changed to "I Didn't Raise My Boy to Be a Slacker," which in turn inspired the cruel parody "I Didn't Raise My Boy to Be a Sausage."

pardon *The official release of a person from punishment for a crime.*

United States (1919), the Supreme Court affirmed their legality, arguing that freedom of speech could be revoked when such speech posed a "clear and present danger" to the nation.

These prosecutions form an ugly chapter in the history of American civil liberty. With the dawn of peace, presidential **pardons** were rather freely granted, including President Harding's to Eugene Debs in 1921. Yet a few victims lingered behind bars into the 1930s.

Factories and Workers in Wartime

Victory was no foregone conclusion, especially because the Republic was caught flatfootedly unready for its leap into global war. Wilson had only belatedly backed some mild preparedness measures beginning in 1915, including a ship-building program and a civilian Council of National Defense. It would take a herculean effort to mobilize America's daunting but disorganized resources and throw them into the field quickly enough to bolster the Allied war effort.

Towering obstacles confronted economic mobilizers. Sheer ignorance was among the biggest roadblocks. No one knew how much steel or explosive powder the country was capable of producing. Traditional fears of big government hamstrung efforts to orchestrate the economy from Washington.

Late in the war, Wilson finally succeeded in imposing some order on this economic confusion. In March 1918 he appointed Wall Street's Bernard Baruch to head the War Industries Board. Although the War Industries Board had only feeble formal powers, it set a precedent for the federal government to take a central role in economic planning in moments of crisis. It was disbanded within days after the armistice, and Americans returned to their amazingly strong preference for laissez-faire and a weak central government. But in the midst of the Great Depression of the 1930s, policymakers would look back to World War I agencies such as the War Industries Board as models.

Spurred by the slogan "Labor Will Win the War," American workers sweated their way to victory. In 1918 the War Department threatened to draft any unemployed male, but for the most part the government tried to treat labor fairly. The National War Labor Board, chaired by former president Taft, pressed employers to pay higher wages and adopt the eight-hour workday.

Samuel Gompers and his American Federation of Labor (AF of L) loyally supported the war, though some smaller and more radical labor organizations, including the Industrial Workers of the World, known as the "Wobblies," became war resisters. The Wobblies, who were mostly poorly treated workers in the lumber and fruit industries, engineered some damaging industrial sabotage. Mainstream labor's loyalty was rewarded, as union membership doubled to over 3 million, and real wages (adjusting for inflation) had risen 20 percent by war's end.

Yet labor harbored grievances. Recognition of the right to organize still eluded labor's grasp. Some six thousand strikes, several stained by blood, broke out in the war years. In 1919 the greatest strike in American history rocked the steel industry. More than a quarter of a million workers walked off the job in a bid to force their employers to recognize their right to organize and bargain collectively. The steel companies resisted mercilessly. They brought in thirty thousand African American strikebreakers to keep the mills running. After bitter confrontations that left more than a dozen workers dead, the steel strike collapsed, a grievous setback that crippled the union movement for more than a decade.

The black workers who entered the steel mills in 1919 were but a fraction of the tens of thousands of southern blacks drawn to the North by the magnet of war-industry employment. Their sudden appearance in previously all-white areas sometimes sparked interracial violence. An explosive riot in East St. Louis, Illinois, in July 1917 left nine whites and at least forty blacks dead. An equally gruesome riot ripped through Chicago in July 1919, fanned by tensions between white working-class neighborhoods and African Americans who had found jobs as strikebreakers in meatpacking plants. Fifteen whites and twenty-three blacks were killed during nearly two weeks of terror.

Suffering Until Suffrage

Women also heeded the call of patriotism and opportunity. Thousands of female workers flooded into factories and fields, taking up jobs vacated by men who left the assembly line for the front line. But the war split the women's movement deeply. Many progressive feminists were pacifists, inclined to oppose both the participation of America in the war and women in the war effort. This group found a voice in the National Woman's party, led by Quaker activist Alice Paul, which demonstrated against "Kaiser Wilson" with marches and hunger strikes.

But the larger part of the suffrage movement, represented by the National American Woman Suffrage Association, supported Wilson's war. Leaders echoed Wilson's justification for fighting by arguing that women must take part in the war effort to earn a role in shaping the peace. The fight for democracy abroad was women's best chance for winning true democracy at home.

War mobilization gave new momentum to the suffrage fight. Impressed by women's war work, President Wilson endorsed woman suffrage as "a vitally necessary war measure." In 1917 New York voted for suffrage at the state level; Michigan, Oklahoma, and South Dakota followed. The next year, governments in Great Britain, Austria-Hungary, and Germany extended the suffrage to women. Not long after, the United States followed suit. In 1920, more than seventy years after the first calls for suffrage at Seneca Falls, the **Nineteenth Amendment** was ratified, giving all American women the right to vote. (See the Appendix.)

Despite political victory, women's wartime economic gains proved fleeting. When peace arrived, most women workers soon gave up their war jobs. Meanwhile, Congress reaffirmed its support for women in their traditional role as mothers when it passed the Sheppard-Towner Maternity Act of 1921, providing federally financed instruction in maternal and infant health care. But in doing so, Congress also expanded the responsibility of the federal government for family welfare.

Forging a War Economy

Mobilization relied as much on the heated emotions of patriotism as on the cool majesty of the laws. The largely voluntary character of economic war organization testified to ocean-insulated America's safe distance from the fighting—as well as to the still-modest scale of government powers in the progressive-era Republic. But as the war went on, government took greater command of the nation's resources to secure an Allied victory.

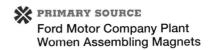

✳ PRIMARY SOURCE
Ford Motor Company Plant
Women Assembling Magnets

In an open address to Congress in 1917, suffragist Carrie Chapman Catt (1859–1947) capitalized on the idealism of the day and invoked the founding principles of American democracy in arguing the case for women's right to vote:

"How can our nation escape the logic it has never failed to follow, when its last unenfranchised class calls for the vote? Behold our Uncle Sam floating the banner with one hand, 'Taxation without representation is tyranny,' and with the other seizing the billions of dollars paid in taxes by women to whom he refuses 'representation.' . . . Is there a single man who can justify such inequality of treatment, such outrageous discrimination? Not one."

As the larder of democracy, America had to feed itself and its allies. By a happy inspiration, the man chosen to head the Food Administration was the Quaker humanitarian Herbert C. Hoover, already a hero for leading a massive drive to feed the starving people of war-racked Belgium.

In common with other American war administrators, Hoover preferred to rely on voluntary compliance rather than on formal edicts. Instead of **rationing** food supplies, he waged a whirlwind propaganda campaign through posters, billboards, newspapers, pulpits, and movies. To save food for export, Hoover proclaimed wheatless Wednesdays and meatless Tuesdays—all on a voluntary basis. Even children, when eating apples, were urged to be "patriotic to the core."

The country soon broke out in a rash of backyard "victory gardens." Congress severely restricted the use of foodstuffs for manufacturing alcoholic beverages. The wartime drive against German-descended brewers aided in the passage of the Eighteenth Amendment in 1919, which prohibited not only beer but all alcoholic drinks.

Thanks to the fervent patriotic wartime spirit, Hoover's voluntary approach worked. Farm production increased by one-fourth, and food exports to the Allies tripled in volume. Hoover's methods were widely imitated in other war agencies. The Fuel Administration exhorted Americans to save fuel with "heatless Mondays" and "gasless Sundays." The Treasury Department sponsored huge parades and invoked slogans such as "Halt the Hun" to promote four great Liberty Loan drives, followed by a Victory Loan campaign in 1919. Together, these efforts netted the then-fantastic sum of about $21 billion, or two-thirds of the current cost of the war to the United States. The remainder was raised by increased taxes.

Despite the Wilson administration's preference for voluntary means of mobilizing the economy, over the course of the war the administration expanded the federal government in size and power. The War Industries Board issued production quotas, allocated raw materials, and set prices for government purchases. Following indescribable traffic snarls in late 1917, Washington took over the railroads. Time itself came under Uncle Sam's control when the entire country was ordered to observe daylight savings time to extend the workday and save on fuel.

rationing *A fixed allowance of food or other scarce commodity.*

Making Plowboys into Doughboys

Most citizens, at the outset, did not dream of sending a mighty force to France. They expected America to ship war materials to the Allies and to supply them with loans. But in April and May of 1917, the Europeans confessed that they were scraping the bottom not only of their money chests but, more ominously, of their manpower barrels. A huge American army would have to be raised, trained, and transported, or the whole western front would collapse.

Conscription was the only answer to the need for raising an immense army with all possible speed. Wilson disliked a draft, but he eventually accepted and eloquently supported conscription as a disagreeable and temporary necessity. After six weeks of criticism and debate, Congress grudgingly passed conscription.

The draft act required the registration of all males between the ages of eighteen and forty-five. The draft machinery, on the whole, worked effectively. No draftee could purchase an exemption or hire a substitute, as in the days of the Civil War. Within a few frantic months the army grew to over 4 million men. For the first time, women were admitted to the armed forces: some 11,000 to the navy and 269 to the marines. African Americans also served in the armed forces, though in strictly segregated units and usually under white officers.

Recruits were supposed to receive six months of training in America and two more months overseas. But so great was the urgency that many "doughboys" were swept swiftly into battle scarcely knowing how to handle a rifle, much less a bayonet.

Ignoring grisly tales of the agonies of trench warfare, many young American men saw an opportunity for adventure and seized it. Author John Dos Passos (1896–1970) recollected how he felt going off to war in 1917:

"We had spent our boyhood in the afterglow of the peaceful nineteenth century. ... What was war like? We wanted to see with our own eyes. We flocked into the volunteer services. I respected the conscientious objectors, and occasionally felt I should take that course myself, but hell, I wanted to see the show."

America Helps Hammer the Hun

Russia's collapse underscored the need for haste. As the communistic **Bolsheviks** withdrew their beaten country from the "capitalistic" war early in 1918, Germany moved its battle-tested forces from the eastern front facing Russia to the western front in France. The Germans hoped to deliver the knockout blow to the Allies in about six months, long before America could get into the struggle.

Berlin's calculations as to American tardiness were surprisingly accurate. No really effective American fighting force reached France until about a year after Congress declared war. Nevertheless, France gradually began to bustle with American doughboys. The first trainees to reach the front were used as replacements in the Allied armies. The newcomers soon made friends with the French girls—or tried to—and one of the most sung-about women in history was the fabled "Mademoiselle from Armentières." One of the printable stanzas ran

> *She was true to me, she was true to you,*
> *She was true to the whole damned army, too.*

Not surprisingly, American soldiers suffered from high rates of venereal disease, which the Army only contributed to by avoiding the subject.

American operations were not confined solely to France; small detachments fought in Belgium, Italy, and notably Russia. The United States, hoping to keep munitions out of German hands, contributed some five thousand troops to an Allied invasion of northern Russia. Wilson likewise sent nearly ten thousand troops to Siberia as part of an Allied expedition. The Bolsheviks long resented these "capitalistic" interventions as high-handed efforts to suffocate their infant communist revolution in its cradle.

The dreaded German drive on the western front exploded in the spring of 1918. Spearheaded by about half a million troops, the enemy rolled forward with terrifying momentum. So dire was the peril that the Allies for the first time united under a supreme commander, the quiet Frenchman Marshal Ferdinand Foch.

At last the ill-trained "Yanks" were coming—and not a moment too soon. Late in May 1918, the forward-rolling Germans, smashing to within forty miles of Paris, threatened to knock out France. Newly arrived American troops, numbering fewer than thirty thousand, were thrown into the breach at Château-Thierry, right in the teeth of the German advance. This was a historic moment—the first significant engagement of American troops in a European war. With their arrival, it was clear that a new American giant had arisen in the West to replace the dying Russian titan in the East.

Bolsheviks *The radical majority faction of the Russian Socialist party that seized power in the October 1917 revolution; they later took the name Communist. (Bolshevik is the Russian word for "majority"; their rivals for power were* **Mensheviks,** *or minority.)*

Over There American troops ("doughboys") man a machine gun in a bomb-blasted forest.

American weight in the scales was now being felt. By July 1918 the awesome German drive had spent its force, and keyed-up American men participated in a Foch counteroffensive in the Second Battle of the Marne. This engagement marked the beginning of a German withdrawal that was never effectively reversed. In September 1918 nine American divisions (about 243,000 men) joined four French divisions to push the Germans from the St. Mihiel **salient**, a German dagger in France's flank.

salient *A portion of a battle line that extends forward into enemy territory.*

The Americans meanwhile demanded and got a separate army. General John J. ("Black Jack") Pershing was finally assigned a front stretching from the Swiss border to the French lines. As part of the last mighty Allied assault, involving several million men, Pershing's army undertook the Meuse-Argonne offensive, from September 26 to November 11, 1918. This battle, the most gargantuan thus far in American history, lasted forty-seven days and engaged 1.2 million American troops. With especially heavy fighting in the rugged Argonne Forest, the killed and wounded mounted to 120,000, or 10 percent of the Americans involved.

Major U.S. Operations in France, 1918 One doughboy recorded in his diary his baptism of fire at St. Mihiel: "Hiked through dark woods. No lights allowed, guided by holding on the pack of the man ahead. Stumbled through underbrush for about half mile into an open field where we waited in soaking rain until about 10:00 P.M. We then started on our hike to the St. Mihiel front, arriving on the crest of a hill at 1:00 A.M. I saw a sight which I shall never forget. It was the zero hour and in one instant the entire front as far as the eye could reach in either direction was a sheet of flame, while the heavy artillery made the earth quake." © Cengage Learning

MAP-READING SKILL BUILDER: Understanding Military Maps

1. In which country did almost all of the major battles of the Western front in 1918 take place? Through which two other countries did smaller portions of the stabilized front of 1914-1917 run between Switzerland and the sea?

2. What critical city on the Seine River was the apparent object of the massive German offensive in spring 1918 that was halted in part by the American troops at Belleau Wood and Chateau-Thierry?

3. The major American battles of St. Mihiel and Meuse-Argonne, fought from September to November 1918, occurred very near the site of which bloody, deadlocked battle of late 1916 between German and French forces?

EXAMINING THE EVIDENCE

"MADEMOISELLE FROM ARMENTIÈRES"

Some familiar songs, such as Julia Ward Howe's stirring Civil War–era melody "Battle Hymn of the Republic," were penned by known composers and have well-established scores and lyrics. But many ballads have no specific author. Songwriters may fit new verses to known tunes, but the songs essentially grow out of the soil of popular culture and take on a life of their own. "Yankee Doodle Dandy," for example, originated during the seventeenth-century English Civil War, was adapted by the American revolutionaries more than a century later, and was parodied by Southerners during the American Civil War:

> Yankee Doodle had a mind
> To whip the Southern "traitors,"
> Because they didn't choose to live
> On codfish and potaters.

"Stagger Lee," or "Stagolee," a blues ballad supposedly based on a murder in Memphis in the 1930s, has been played in countless renditions, with its homicidal subject variously portrayed as a ruthless badman or a civil rights hero.

This process of accretion and adaptation can furnish valuable clues to historians about changing sentiments and sensibilities, just as the ballads themselves give expression to feelings not always evident in the official record. Folklorist Alan Lomax spent a lifetime tracking down American ballads, documenting layers of life and experience not usually excavated by traditional scholars. In the case of the First World War's most notorious song, "Mademoiselle from Armentières" (or "Hinky Dinky, Parley-Voo?"), Lomax compiled from various sources more than six hundred soldier-authored stanzas, some of which are reproduced here (others he delicately described as "not mailable").

> Mademoiselle from Armentières,
> She hadn't been kissed in forty years.
>
> She might have been young for all we knew,
> When Napoleon flopped at Waterloo. . . .
>
> You'll never get your croix de Guerre,
> If you never wash your underwear. . . .
>
> The French, they are a funny race,
> They fight with their feet and save their face.
>
> The cootie [louse] is the national bug of France.
> The cootie's found all over France,
> No matter wear you hang your pants. . . .
>
> Oh, the seventy-seventh went over the top,
> A sous lieutenant, a Jew, and a Wop. . . .
>
> The officers get all the steak,
> And all we get is the belly-ache.
>
> The general got a Croix de Guerre,
> The son-of-a-gun was never there. . . .
>
> There's many and many a married man,
> Wants to go back to France again.
>
> 'Twas a hell of a war as we recall,
> But still 'twas better than none at all.

Source: Excerpt from *American Ballads and Folk Songs*, p. 560. Courtesy of Alan Lomax Archive.

1. What fresh—and irreverent—perspectives do these stanzas reveal about the soldier's-eye view of military life?

2. What view of France and the French people is implied in the lyrics? How do the ordinary American soldiers view their own experience of being in France?

3. What does the implied sexual content of the song and the "Mademoiselle" who supposedly inspired it reveal about this war as a "gendered" activity?

American Ballads and Folk Songs, by John A. Lomax and Alan Lomax. The Macmillan Company, New York, 1934.

Victory was in sight—and fortunately so. The slowly advancing American armies in France were eating up their supplies so rapidly that they were in grave danger of running short. But the battered Germans were staggering under the sledgehammer blows of the Allies and suffering from critical food shortages caused by the British blockade. Propaganda leaflets containing seductive Wilsonian promises rained upon their crumbling lines from balloons, shells, and rockets.

Berlin was now ready to hoist the white flag. The Germans first sought a peace based on the Fourteen Points in October 1918. But Wilson made it clear that the kaiser must be thrown overboard before an armistice could be negotiated. The war-weary Germans then forced the disgraced kaiser to flee to Holland.

The exhausted Germans were through. They laid down their arms at eleven o'clock on the eleventh day of the eleventh month of 1918, and an eerie, numbing silence fell over the western front. War-taut America burst into a delirium of around-the-clock rejoicing, as streets were jammed with laughing, whooping, milling, dancing masses. The war to end wars had ended. But the costs exceeded comprehension: Nearly 9 million soldiers died and more than 20 million suffered grievous wounds. To make matters even worse, some 30 million people perished in a worldwide influenza pandemic that coincided with the war. Over 550,000 Americans—more than ten times the number of combat casualties—died from flu.

The United States' main contribution to the ultimate victory had been foodstuffs, munitions, credits, oil, and manpower—but not battlefield victories. The Yanks fought only two major battles, St. Mihiel and the Meuse-Argonne. It was the *prospect* of endless U.S. troop reserves, rather than America's actual military performance, that eventually demoralized the Germans.

Ironically enough, General Pershing in some ways depended more on the Allies than they depended on him. His army purchased more of its supplies in Europe than it shipped from the United States. The United States was no arsenal of democracy in this war; that role awaited it in the next global conflict, two decades later.

Wilson Steps Down from Olympus

Woodrow Wilson had helped to win the war. What role would he now play in shaping the peace? Expectations ran extravagantly high. As the fighting in Europe crashed to a close, the American president towered at the peak of his popularity and power. No other man had ever occupied so dizzy a pinnacle as moral leader of the world. Wilson also had behind him the prestige of victory and the economic resources of the mightiest nation on earth. But at this fateful moment, his sureness of touch deserted him, and he began to make a series of tragic fumbles.

Under the slogan "Politics is Adjourned," partisan political strife had been kept below the surface during the war crisis. Hoping to strengthen his hand at the Paris peace table, Wilson broke the truce by personally appealing for a Democratic victory in the congressional elections of November 1918. But the maneuver backfired when voters instead returned a narrow Republican majority to Congress. Having staked his reputation on the outcome, Wilson went to Paris as a diminished leader. Unlike all the **parliamentary** statesmen at the table, he did not command a legislative majority at home.

parliamentary *Concerning political systems in which the government is constituted from the controlling party's members in the legislative assembly.*

Grave concern was expressed by General Tasker H. Bliss (1853–1930), one of the five American peace commissioners (December 18, 1918):

"I am disquieted to see how hazy and vague our ideas are. We are going to be up against the wiliest politicians in Europe. There will be nothing hazy or vague about their ideas."

Wilson's decision to go in person to Paris to help make the peace infuriated Republicans, who saw it as flamboyant grandstanding. He further ruffled Republican feathers when he neglected to include a single Republican senator in his official peace delegation. The logical choice was the new chairman of the Senate Committee on Foreign Relations, slender and aristocratically bewhiskered Henry Cabot Lodge of Massachusetts, a Harvard Ph.D. But including Lodge would have been problematic for the president. The senator's mind, quipped one critic, was like the soil of his native New England: "naturally barren but highly cultivated." Wilson loathed him, and the feeling was hotly reciprocated. An accomplished author, Lodge had been known as "the scholar in politics" until Wilson came on the scene. The two men were at daggers drawn, personally and politically.

═══ **Hammering Out the Treaty** ═══

Woodrow Wilson, the great prophet arisen in the West, received tumultuous welcomes from the masses of France, Britain, and Italy late in 1918 and early in 1919. But the realistic statesmen of Italy and France were determined that Wilsonian idealism should not upset their fine-spun imperialistic plans.

The Paris Conference of great and small nations fell into the hands of an inner clique, known as the "Big Four." Wilson, representing the richest and freshest great power, more or less occupied the driver's seat. He was joined by Vittorio Orlando of Italy, David Lloyd George of Britain, and cynical, hard-bitten Georges Clemenceau of France, the seventy-eight-year-old "organizer of victory" known as "the Tiger."

Speed was urgent when the conference opened on January 18, 1919. Europe seemed to be slipping into anarchy; the red tide of communism was licking westward from Bolshevist Russia.

Wilson's ultimate goal was a world parliament to be known as the League of Nations, but he first bent his energies to preventing any cynical parceling out of the former colonies and **protectorates** of the vanquished powers. He forced through a compromise between naked imperialism and Wilsonian idealism, in which the victors received conquered territory only as **trustees** of the League of Nations. But in practice this half-loaf solution was little more than the old prewar colonialism, thinly disguised. In the decades to come, however, anti–colonial-independence movements would effectively wield the Wilsonian ideal of self-determination against their imperial occupiers.

Wilson envisioned a League of Nations containing an assembly with seats for all nations and a council to be controlled by the great powers. He gained a signal victory over the skeptical Old World diplomats in February 1919, when they agreed to make the League Covenant, Wilson's brainchild, an integral part of the final peace treaty.

On a quick trip to America, Wilson discovered that certain Republican senators, led by Senator Lodge, were sharpening their knives. To them the League was either a useless "sewing circle" or an over-potent "superstate." Their hard core was composed of a dozen or so isolationists, led by Senators William Borah of Idaho and Hiram Johnson of California, who were known as "the irreconcilables" or "the battalion of death."

Thirty-nine Republican senators or senators-elect—enough to defeat the treaty—proclaimed that the Senate would not approve the League of Nations in its existing

protectorate *In international affairs, a weaker or smaller country held to be under the guidance or protection of a major power; the arrangement is a weaker form of imperialism or colonialism. (A **colony** is a territory owned outright by a more powerful nation.)*

trustee *A nation that holds the territory of a former colony as the conditional agent of an international body under defined terms.*

Library of Congress

Wilson in Dover, England, 1919 Hailed by many Europeans in early 1919 as the savior of the Western world, Wilson was a fallen idol only a few months later, when his own countrymen repudiated the peace treaty he had helped to craft.

imperfect form. These difficulties delighted Wilson's Allied adversaries in Paris. They were now in a stronger bargaining position because Wilson would have to beg them for changes in the covenant that would safeguard the Monroe Doctrine and other U.S. interests dear to the senators.

As soon as Wilson was back in Paris, hardheaded Premier Clemenceau pressed French demands for the German-inhabited Rhineland and the Saar Valley, a rich coal area. Faced with fierce Wilsonian opposition to this violation of self-determination, France settled for a compromise whereby the Saar basin would remain under the League of Nations for fifteen years, and then a popular vote would determine its fate. (The Saar population voted overwhelmingly to rejoin Germany in 1935.) In exchange for dropping its demands for the Rhineland, France got a security treaty in which both Britain and America pledged to come to its aid in the event of another German invasion. The French later felt betrayed when the pact was quickly pigeonholed by the U.S. Senate, which shied away from all entangling alliances.

Wilson's next battle was with Italy over Fiume, a valuable seaport inhabited by both Italians and Yugoslavs. When Italy demanded Fiume, Wilson insisted that the seaport go to Yugoslavia and appealed over the heads of Italy's leaders to the country's masses. The maneuver fell flat. The Italian delegates went home in a huff, and the Italian masses turned savagely against Wilson.

Another crucial struggle was with Japan over China's Shandong (Shantung) Peninsula and the German islands in the Pacific, which the Japanese had seized during the war. Japan was conceded the strategic Pacific islands under a League of Nations **mandate,*** but Wilson staunchly opposed Japanese control of Shandong as a violation of **self-determination** for its 30 million Chinese residents. But when the Japanese threatened to walk out, Wilson reluctantly accepted a compromise whereby Japan kept Germany's economic holdings in Shandong and merely pledged to return the peninsula to China at a later date. The Chinese were outraged by this imperialistic solution, while Clemenceau jeered that Wilson "talked like Jesus Christ and acted like Lloyd George."

mandate *Under the League of Nations (1919–1939), a specific commission that authorized a trustee to administer a former colonial territory.*

self-determination *The Wilsonian doctrine that each people should have the right to freely choose its own political affiliation and national future, such as independence or incorporation into another nation.*

Wilson's Battle for Ratification

A completed Treaty of Versailles was handed to the Germans in June 1919—almost literally on the point of a bayonet. A careful analysis of the treaty shows that only four of the original Wilsonian points were fully honored. Vengeance, not reconciliation, was the treaty's dominant tone. Loud and bitter cries of betrayal burst from German throats—charges that Adolf Hitler would soon reiterate during his meteoric rise to power in Germany.

Wilson, of course, was guilty of no conscious betrayal. He had been forced to compromise away some of his less-cherished Fourteen Points in order to salvage the more precious League of Nations. He was much more like the mother who had to throw her sickly younger children to the pursuing wolves to save her sturdy firstborn. Greeted a few months earlier with frenzied acclaim in Europe, Wilson was now a fallen idol, condemned alike by disillusioned liberals and frustrated imperialists. He was keenly aware that some injustices had been forced into the treaty. But he was hoping that a potent League of Nations, led by America, would iron out the inequities.

Yet the loudly condemned treaty actually had much to commend it. Not least among its merits was its liberation of many oppressed peoples, such as the Poles, from the yoke of imperial dynasties. Wilson's disappointments and his critics to the contrary, the settlement was almost certainly a fairer one because Wilson had gone to Paris.

Returning to America, Wilson sailed straight into a political typhoon. Isolationists raised a whirlwind of protest against Wilson's commitment to usher the United States into his newfangled League of Nations. Rabid Hun-haters, regarding the pact as not harsh enough, voiced their discontent. Principled liberals, such as the editors of the *Nation* and the *New Republic*, thought it too harsh—and a gross betrayal to boot. German Americans, Italian Americans, Irish Americans, and others whom Wilson termed "hyphenated Americans" were aroused because the peace settlement was not sufficiently favorable to their native lands.

---

* In due time the Japanese illegally fortified these islands—the Marshalls, Marianas, and Carolines—and used them as bases against the United States in World War II.

Despite mounting discontent, a strong majority of the people still seemed favorable to the treaty, with the "Wilson League" firmly riveted as Part I. At this time—early July 1919—Senator Lodge had no real hope of defeating the Treaty of Versailles. His strategy was merely to amend it in such a way as to "Americanize," "Republicanize," or "senatorialize" it.

Lodge effectively used delay to muddle and divide public opinion. He read the entire 264-page treaty aloud in the Senate Foreign Relations Committee and held protracted hearings in which people of various nationalities aired their grievances. With the treaty bogged down in the Senate, Wilson decided to take his case to the country in a spectacular speech-making tour. The strenuous barnstorming campaign was undertaken in the face of protests by physicians and friends. Never robust, Wilson's frail body had begun to sag under the strain of partisan strife, a global war, and a stressful peace conference. But he declared that he was willing to die, like the soldiers he had sent into battle, for the sake of the new world order.

The presidential tour, begun in September 1919, got off to a rather lame start in the Midwest, where German American influence was strong. Trailing after him like bloodhounds came two "irreconcilable" senators, Borah and Johnson, who spoke in the same cities a few days later. Hat-tossing crowds answered their attacks on Wilson, crying, "Impeach him, impeach him!"

But the reception was different in the Rocky Mountain region and the Pacific Coast. These areas, which had elected Wilson in 1916, welcomed him with heartwarming outbursts. The high point—and the breaking point—of the return trip was at Pueblo, Colorado, on September 25, 1919. Wilson, with tears coursing down his cheeks, pleaded for the League of Nations as the only real hope of preventing future wars. That night he collapsed from physical and nervous exhaustion.

Wilson was whisked back in the "funeral train" to Washington, where several days later a stroke paralyzed one side of his body. During the next few weeks he lay in a darkened room in the White House, as much a victim of the war as the unknown soldier buried at Arlington. For seven months he did not meet his cabinet.

Defeat Through Deadlock

Senator Lodge, coldly calculating, was now at the helm. After failing to amend the treaty outright, he came up with fourteen formal **reservations** to protect American sovereignty and guard Congress's constitutional war-declaring power against the League. Wilson, hating Lodge, saw red at the mere suggestion of the Lodge reservations, which he insisted "emasculated" the entire pact.

reservation *A portion of a deed, contract, or treaty that places conditions or restrictions on the general obligations.*

Although too feeble to lead, Wilson was still strong enough to obstruct. When the day finally came for voting in the Senate, he sent word to all true Democrats to vote *against* the treaty with the odious Lodge reservations attached. Loyal Democrats in the Senate, on November 19, 1919, blindly did Wilson's bidding. Combining with the "irreconcilables," mostly Republicans, they rejected the treaty with the Lodge reservations appended, 55 to 39.

The nation was so shocked at this outcome that the Senate was forced to vote a second time in March 1920. There was only one possible path to success. Unless the Senate approved the pact with the Lodge reservations, the entire document would be rejected. But the sickly Wilson signed the treaty's death warrant by again sending word to all loyal Democrats to vote down the treaty with the obnoxious Lodge reservations. On March 19, 1920, the treaty netted a simple majority but failed to get the necessary two-thirds majority by a count of 49 yeas to 35 nays.

Who defeated the treaty? The Lodge-Wilson personal feud, traditionalism, isolationism, disillusionment, and partisanship all contributed to the confused picture. But Wilson himself must bear a substantial share of the responsibility. He asked for all or nothing—and got nothing.

The "Solemn Referendum" of 1920

Wilson's own pet solution for the deadlock was to settle the treaty issue by appealing to the people for a "solemn referendum" in the presidential election of 1920. This was sheer folly, for a true mandate on the League in the noisy arena of politics was clearly an impossibility.

Gathering in Chicago in June 1920, jubilant Republicans devised a masterfully ambiguous platform that could appeal to both pro-League and anti-League sentiment in the party. The nominee would run on a teeter-totter rather than a platform. As the leading presidential contestants jousted with one another, a group of Senate bosses, meeting rather casually in the historic "smoke-filled" Room 404 of the Blackstone Hotel, informally decided on affable, malleable Senator Warren G. Harding of Ohio as the candidate. To run with the "folksy," back-slapping former newspaper editor, the party nominated frugal, grim-faced Governor Calvin ("Silent Cal") Coolidge of Massachusetts.

Meeting in San Francisco, Democrats nominated earnest Governor James M. Cox of Ohio, who strongly supported the League. His running mate was Assistant Navy Secretary Franklin D. Roosevelt, a young, handsome, vibrant New Yorker.

Democratic attempts to make the campaign a referendum on the League were thwarted by Senator Harding, who issued muddled and contradictory statements on the issue from his front porch. Pro-League and anti-League Republicans both claimed that Harding's election would advance their cause, while the candidate suggested that if elected he would work for a vague Association of Nations—*a* league but not *the* League.

With newly enfranchised women swelling the vote totals, Harding was swept into power with a prodigious plurality of over 7 million votes—16,143,407 to 9,130,328 for Cox, the largest victory margin to that date in a presidential election. The electoral count was 404 to 127. Eugene V. Debs, federal prisoner number 9653 in the Atlanta Penitentiary, rolled up the largest vote ever for the left-wing Socialist party—919,799.

Public desire for a change found vent in a resounding repudiation of "high and mighty" Wilsonianism. People were tired of professional high-browism, star-reaching idealism, bothersome do-goodism, moral overstrain, and constant self-sacrifice. Eager to lapse back into "normalcy," they were willing to accept a second-rate president—and they got a third-rate one.

Although the election could not be considered a true referendum, Republican isolationists successfully turned Harding's victory into a death sentence for the League. Politicians increasingly shunned the League as they would a leper. When the legendary Wilson died in 1924, admirers knelt in the snow outside his Washington home. His "great vision" of a league for peace had died long before.

PRIMARY SOURCE
Interrupting the Ceremony

The Betrayal of Great Expectations

America's spurning of the League was tragically shortsighted. The Republic had helped to win a costly war, but it foolishly kicked the fruits of victory under the table. Whether a strong international organization would have averted World War II in 1939 will always be a matter of dispute. But there can be no doubt that the orphaned League of Nations was undercut at the start by the refusal of the mightiest power on the globe to join it. The Allies themselves were largely to blame for the new world conflagration that flared up in 1939, but they found a convenient justification for their own shortcomings by pointing an accusing finger at Uncle Sam.

The ultimate collapse of the Treaty of Versailles must be laid, at least in some degree, at America's doorstep. This complicated pact, tied in with the four other peace treaties through the League Covenant, was a top-heavy structure designed to rest on a four-legged table. The fourth leg, the United States, was never put into place. This rickety structure teetered for over a decade and then crashed in ruins—a debacle that played into the hands of German **demagogue** Adolf Hitler.

demagogue *A politician who arouses fervor by appealing to the lowest emotions, such as fear, hatred, and greed, of a mass audience.*

The United States, as the tragic sequel proved, hurt its own cause when it buried its head in the sand. Granted that the conduct of its Allies had been disillusioning, the United States had its own ends to serve by carrying through the Wilsonian program. It would have been well advised if the United States had forthrightly assumed its war-born responsibilities and resolutely embraced the role of global leader proffered by the hand of destiny. In the interests of its own security, if for no other reason, the United States should have used its enormous strength to shape world-shaking events. Instead it permitted itself blithely to drift toward the abyss of a second and even more bloody international disaster.

As the first president to take the United States into a foreign war, Woodrow Wilson was obliged to make a systematic case to the American people to justify his unprecedented European intervention. His ideas have largely defined the character of American foreign policy ever since—for better or worse.

"Wilsonianism" comprised three closely related principles: (1) the era of American isolation from world affairs had irretrievably ended; (2) the United States must infuse its own founding political and economic ideas—including democracy, the rule of law, free trade, and national self-determination (or anticolonialism)—into the international order; and (3) American influence could eventually steer the world away from rivalry and warfare and toward a cooperative and peaceful international system, maintained by the League of Nations or, later, the United Nations.

Whether that Wilsonian vision constituted hard-nosed realism or starry-eyed idealism has excited scholarly debate for nearly a century. "Realists," such as George F. Kennan and Henry Kissinger, insist that Wilson was anything but a realist. They criticize the president as a naive, impractical dreamer who failed to understand that the international order was, and always will be, an anarchic, unruly arena, outside the rule of law, where only military force can effectively protect the nation's security. In a sharp critique in his 1950 study, *American Diplomacy*, Kennan condemned Wilson's vision as "moralism-legalism." In this view Wilson dangerously threatened to sacrifice American self-interests on the altar of his admirable but ultimately unworkable ideas.

Wilson's defenders, including conspicuously his principal biographer, Arthur S. Link, argue that Wilson's idealism was in fact a kind of higher realism, recognizing as it did that armed conflict on the scale of World War I could never again be tolerated and that some framework of peaceful international relations simply had to be found. The development of nuclear weapons in a later generation gave this argument more force. This "liberal" defense of Wilsonianism derives from the centuries-old liberal faith that, given sufficient intelligence and willpower, the world can be made a better place. Realists reject this notion of moral and political progress as hopelessly innocent, especially as applied to international affairs.

Some leftist scholars, such as William Appleman Williams, have argued that Wilson was in fact a realist of another kind: a subtle and wily imperialist whose stirring rhetoric cloaked a grasping ambition to make the United States the world's dominant economic power. Sometimes called "the imperialism of free trade," this strategy allegedly sought not to decolonialize the world and open up international commerce for the good of peoples elsewhere, but to create a system in which American economic might would irresistibly prevail. This criticism rests on the naive assumption that international relations are a "zero-sum game," in which one nation's gain must necessarily be another nation's loss. By contrast, Wilson's defenders claim that in a Wilsonian world, all parties would be better off; altruism and self-interest need not be mutually exclusive.

Still other scholars, especially John Milton Cooper, Jr., emphasize the absence of economic factors in shaping Wilson's diplomacy. Isolationism, so this argument goes, held such sway over American thinking precisely because the United States had such a puny financial stake abroad—no hard American economic interests were mortally threatened in 1917, nor for a long time thereafter. In these circumstances Wilson—and the Wilsonians who came after him, such as Franklin D. Roosevelt—had no choice but to appeal to abstract ideals and high principles. The "idealistic" Wilsonian strain in American diplomacy, in this view, may have been an unavoidable heritage of America's historically isolated situation. If so, it was Wilson's genius to make practical use of those ideas in his bid for popular support of his diplomacy.

Chapter Summary

Germany's declaration of unlimited submarine warfare, as well as the Zimmermann note proposing a German alliance with Mexico, finally caused the United States to declare war. Wilson aroused the country to patriotic heights by declaring the war an idealistic crusade for democracy and a just peace, based on his ideologically liberal Fourteen Points.

Vigorous wartime propaganda stirred voluntary commitment to the war effort, but at the cost of suppressing dissent. American voluntary mobilization worked wonders in organizing industry, producing food, and financing the war. Labor, including women, made substantial wartime gains. Some progressive women opposed the war, but women's wartime efforts helped spur passage of the Nineteenth (Suffrage) Amendment. The beginnings of black migration to northern cities led to racial tensions and riots.

America's soldiers took nearly a year to arrive in Europe, and they fought in only two major battles at the end of the war. America's main contribution to the Allied victory was to provide new enthusiasm and morale, along with the threat of endless supplies of men and *matériel* to follow. Wilson's immense prestige created high expectations for an idealistic peace based on his Fourteen Points. But his own political blunders and the clever, stubborn opposition of European statesmen forced him to compromise his lofty aims and made the Versailles Treaty considerably harsher than he intended.

Republican opposition to Wilson and the League of Nations grew stronger, particularly in the U.S. Senate. As Lodge stalled the treaty, Wilson tried to rouse the country on behalf of his cherished League. A stroke ended Wilson's pro-League speaking tour, and his stubborn refusal to compromise with Lodge and the Republicans finally killed the treaty and the League. Wilson sought a "solemn referendum" on the League in the election of 1920, but the public delivered a harsh repudiation of Wilsonianism. Republican isolationists turned Harding's victory into a death sentence for the League.

KEY TERMS

isolationism (493)

internationalism (Wilsonianism) (493)

collective security (494)

mobilization (495)

pardon (496)

rationing (498)

Bolsheviks (499)

Mensheviks (499)

salient (500)

parliamentary (502)

protectorate (503)

colony (503)

trustee (503)

mandate (504)

self-determination (504)

reservation (505)

demagogue (506)

PEOPLE TO KNOW

Arthur Zimmerman

George Creel

Eugene V. Debs

William D. ("Big Bill") Haywood

Bernard Baruch

Herbert C. Hoover

Henry Cabot Lodge

David Lloyd George

Go to the History CourseMate website for primary source links, study tools, and review materials for this chapter. www.cengagebrain.com

31

American Life in the Roaring Twenties

1919–1929

America's present need is not heroics but healing; not nostrums but normalcy;

not revolution but restoration; . . . not surgery but serenity.

WARREN G. HARDING, 1920

Bloodied by the war and disillusioned by the peace, Americans turned inward in the 1920s. Shunning diplomatic commitments to foreign countries, they also denounced radical foreign ideas, condemned un-American lifestyles, and clanged shut the immigration gates against foreign peoples. They partly sealed off the domestic economy from the rest of the world and plunged headlong into a dizzying decade of homegrown prosperity.

The boom of the golden twenties showered genuine benefits on Americans, as incomes and living standards rose for many. But there seemed to be something incredible about it all, even as people sang:

> My sister she works in the laundry,
> My father sells bootlegger gin,
> My mother she takes in the washing,
> My God, how the money rolls in!

New technologies, new consumer products, and new forms of leisure and entertainment made the twenties roar. Yet just beneath the surface lurked widespread anxieties about the future and fears that America was losing sight of its traditional ways.

FOCUS QUESTIONS

1. Why was there such a strong movement toward social conservatism in the wake of World War I?

2. What were the major cultural conflicts that occurred over immigration, cultural pluralism, prohibition, and evolution? Why did these issues create such strong polarization among Americans?

3. What were the major features of the new "mass consumer economy," and what effects did it have on the way Americans lived?

4. How did the "new media" of radio, film, and recorded music transform American culture, including the areas of sexuality and the standardization of mass popular taste?

5. How were the new ideas of the times reflected in the American literary renaissance of the 1920s? How was the Harlem Renaissance of black writers similar to and different from artistic movements in the white literary world?

CHRONOLOGY

1903	Wright brothers fly first airplane. First story-sequence motion picture.	**1923**	Equal Rights Amendment (ERA) proposed.
1908	Henry Ford introduces Model T.	**1924**	Immigration Act of 1924.
1917	Bolshevik Revolution in Russia.	**1925**	Scopes trial. Florida real estate boom. Fitzgerald publishes *The Great Gatsby*. Dreiser publishes *An American Tragedy*.
1919	Eighteenth Amendment (prohibition). Volstead Act. Seattle general strike. Anderson publishes *Winesburg, Ohio*.	**1926**	Hughes publishes *The Weary Blues*. Hemingway publishes *The Sun Also Rises*.
1919–1920	"Red scare."	**1927**	Lindbergh flies solo across Atlantic. First talking motion picture, *The Jazz Singer*. Sacco and Vanzetti executed.
1920	Radio broadcasting begins. Fitzgerald publishes *This Side of Paradise*. Lewis publishes *Main Street*.		
1921	Sacco-Vanzetti trial. Emergency Quota Act. Bureau of the Budget created.	**1929**	Faulkner publishes *The Sound and the Fury*. Hemingway publishes *A Farewell to Arms*.
1922	Lewis publishes *Babbitt*. Eliot publishes *The Waste Land*.	**1932**	Al Capone imprisoned.

Seeing Red

Hysterical fears of red Russia continued to color American thinking for several years after Communists came to power in the Bolshevik Revolution of 1917, which spawned a tiny Communist party in America. Tensions were heightened by an epidemic of strikes that convulsed the Republic at war's end, many of them the result of high prices and frustrated union-organizing drives. Upstanding Americans jumped to the conclusion that labor troubles were fomented by bomb-and-whisker Bolsheviks. A general strike in Seattle in 1919, though modest in its demands and orderly in its methods, prompted a call from the mayor for federal troops to head off "the anarchy of Russia." Fire-and-brimstone evangelist Billy Sunday said he would like to "fill the jails so full of [Bolsheviks] that their feet would stick out the window."

The big "red scare" of 1919–1920 resulted in a nationwide crusade against left-wingers whose Americanism was suspect. Attorney General A. Mitchell Palmer earned the title of the "Fighting Quaker" for his excess zeal in rounding up suspects. When a bomb shattered both the nerves and the Washington home of Palmer in June 1919, the "Fighting Quaker" was dubbed the "Quaking Fighter." Late in December 1919, a shipload of 249 alleged alien radicals was deported on the *Buford* ("the Soviet Ark") to the "workers' paradise" of Russia. Hysteria was revived in September 1920 when a still-unexplained bomb blast on Wall Street killed thirty-eight people and wounded several hundred others.

Various states joined the pack in the outcry against radicals. In 1919–1920 a number of legislatures passed criminal **syndicalism** laws that outlawed the mere *advocacy* of violence to secure social change. Critics protested that mere words were not criminal deeds, that there was a great gulf between throwing fits and throwing bombs, and that free screech was for the nasty as well as the nice. Violence was done to traditional American concepts of free speech as IWW members and other radicals were vigorously prosecuted. The hysteria went so far that in 1920 five members of the New York legislature, all lawfully elected, were denied their seats simply because they were Socialists.

The red scare was a godsend to conservative businesspeople, who used it to break the backs of the fledgling unions. Labor's call for the "closed," or all-union, shop was

syndicalism *A theory or movement that advocates bringing all economic and political power into the hands of labor unions by means of strikes.*

denounced as "Sovietism in disguise." Employers, in turn, hailed their own antiunion campaign for the "open" shop as "the American plan."

Anti-redism and antiforeignism were reflected in a notorious case regarded by liberals as a "judicial lynching." Nicola Sacco, a shoe-factory worker, and Bartolomeo Vanzetti, a fish peddler, were convicted in 1921 of the murder of a Massachusetts paymaster and his guard. The jury and judge were prejudiced in some degree against the defendants because they were Italians, atheists, anarchists, and draft dodgers.

Liberals and radicals the world over rallied to the defense of the two aliens doomed to die. The case dragged on for six years until 1927, when the condemned men were electrocuted. Communists and other radicals were thus presented with two martyrs in the "class struggle," while many American liberals hung their heads.

Hooded Hoodlums of the KKK

A new Ku Klux Klan, spawned by the postwar reaction, mushroomed fearsomely in the early 1920s. Despite the familiar sheets and hoods, it more closely resembled the antiforeign nativist movements of the 1850s than the antiblack nightriders of the 1860s. The new KKK was antiforeign, anti-Catholic, antiblack, anti-Jewish, antipacifist, anticommunist, anti-internationalist, anti-evolutionist, anti-adultery, and anti–birth control. It was also pro–Anglo Saxon, pro–native American, and pro-Protestant. In short, the besheeted Klan betokened an extremist, ultraconservative uprising against many of the forces of diversity and modernity that were transforming American culture.

As reconstituted, the Klan spread with astonishing rapidity, especially in the Midwest and the "**Bible Belt**" South where Fundamentalism thrived. At its peak in the mid-1920s, the Klan claimed about 5 million dues-paying members and wielded potent political influence. The "Knights" of the "Invisible Empire" included among their officials Imperial Wizards, Grand Goblins, and King Kleagles. The Klan's most impressive displays were "conclaves" and huge flag-waving parades. The chief warning was the blazing cross. The principal weapon was the bloodied lash, supplemented by tar and feathers.

This reign of hooded horror, so repulsive to the best American ideals, collapsed rather suddenly in the late 1920s. The Klan's bubble burst as decent people at last recoiled from its terrorism, while scandalous embezzling by Klan officials launched a congressional investigation that exposed the movement as a vicious racket. The KKK was an alarming manifestation of the intolerance and prejudice plaguing people anxious about the dizzying pace of social change in the 1920s. Despite the Klan's decline, civil rights activists fought in vain for legislation making lynching a federal crime, as lawmakers feared alienating white southern voters.

Stemming the Foreign Flood

Isolationist America of the 1920s, ingrown and **provincial**, had little use for the immigrants who began to flood into the country again as peace settled soothingly on the war-torn world. Some 800,000 stepped ashore in 1920–1921, about two-thirds of them from southern and eastern Europe. The "one-hundred-percent Americans," shuddering at the sight

Hiram Wesley Evans (1881–1966), imperial wizard of the Ku Klux Klan, in 1926 poignantly described the cultural grievances that fueled the Klan and lay behind much of the Fundamentalist revolt against "Modernism":

"Nordic Americans for the last generation have found themselves increasingly uncomfortable and finally deeply distressed. ... One by one all our traditional moral standards went by the boards, or were so disregarded that they ceased to be binding. The sacredness of our Sabbath, of our homes, of chastity, and finally even of our right to teach our own children in our own schools fundamental facts and truths were torn away from us. Those who maintained the old standards did so only in the face of constant ridicule. ... We found our great cities and the control of much of our industry and commerce taken over by strangers. ... We are a movement of the plain people, very weak in the matter of culture, intellectual support, and trained leadership. ... This is undoubtedly a weakness. It lays us open to the charge of being 'hicks' and 'rubes' and 'drivers of second-hand Fords.' "

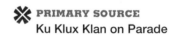

PRIMARY SOURCE
Ku Klux Klan on Parade

Bible Belt *The region of the American South, extending roughly from North Carolina west to Oklahoma and Texas, where Protestant Fundamentalism and belief in literal interpretation of the Bible were traditionally strongest.*

provincial *Narrow and limited; isolated from cosmopolitan influences.*

National Archives

Klanswomen on Parade, 1928 Founded in the Reconstruction Era, the Ku Klux Klan enjoyed a remarkable resurgence in the 1920s. Here, women members, unmasked and unapologetic, march down Pennsylvania Avenue under the very shadow of the Capitol Dome.

A recognized expert on American immigration, Henry P. Fairchild (1880–1956), wrote in 1926:

"The typical immigrant of the present does not really live in America at all, but, from the point of view of nationality, in Italy, Poland, Czecho-Slovakia, or some other foreign country."

of this resumed "New Immigration," once again cried that the famed poem at the base of the Statue of Liberty was all too literally true: they claimed that a sickly Europe was indeed vomiting on America "the wretched refuse of its teeming shore."

Congress temporarily plugged the breach with the Emergency Quota Act of 1921. This stopgap legislation was soon replaced by the Immigration Act of 1924. Quotas for foreigners were drastically cut to 2 percent of persons of each nationality living in the United States in 1890, when comparatively few southern Europeans had arrived.* The purpose was clearly to freeze America's existing ethnic composition, which was largely northern European. A flagrantly discriminatory section of the Immigration Act of 1924 slammed the door absolutely against Japanese immigrants. Only Canadians and Latin Americans were exempt from the quota system.

The quota system effected a pivotal departure in American policy, as the country sacrificed something of its tradition of freedom and opportunity. The Immigration Act of 1924 marked the end of an era—a period of virtually unrestricted immigration that in the previous century had brought some 35 million newcomers to the United States, mostly from

* Five years later the Immigration Act of 1929, using 1920 as the quota base, virtually cut immigration in half by limiting the total to 152,574 a year. In 1965 Congress abolished the national-origins quota system.

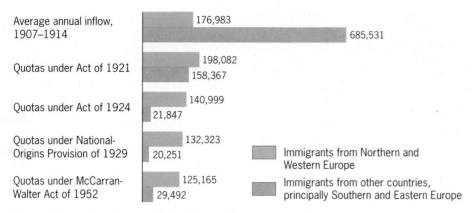

Average annual inflow,
1907–1914

176,983

685,531

Quotas under Act of 1921

198,082

158,367

Quotas under Act of 1924

140,999

21,847

Quotas under National-
Origins Provision of 1929

132,323

20,251

Immigrants from Northern and
Western Europe

Quotas under McCarran-
Walter Act of 1952

125,165

29,492

Immigrants from other countries,
principally Southern and Eastern Europe

Annual Immigration and the Quota Laws

Europe. The immigrant tide now dwindled to a mere trickle, but it left on American shores by the 1920s a patchwork of ethnic communities separated from the larger society and from each other by language, religion, and customs. Many Italians, Jews, Poles, and others lived in isolated enclaves with their own houses of worship, newspapers, and theaters (see "Makers of America: The Poles," pp. 514–515). Efforts to organize labor unions repeatedly foundered on the rocks of ethnic rivalries, which were often played upon by cynical employers. Ethnic variety thus undermined class and political solidarity in America.

Immigration restriction did not appeal to reformers. Particularly opposed was the chorus of "cultural pluralists" who had long criticized the idea than an American "melting pot" would eliminate ethnic differences. Two intellectuals, the philosopher Horace Kallen and critic Randolph Bourne, championed alternative conceptions of the immigrant role in American society. Kallen defended German and Austrian immigrants' right to practice their ancestral customs even during the World War I anti-German hysteria. In Kallen's vision, America's ethnic groups should be like the instruments in a symphony orchestra, each harmonizing with the other while retaining its own identity.

If Kallen stressed the preservation of identity, Bourne advocated greater cross-fertilization among immigrants. Cosmopolitan interchange, Bourne believed, was destined to make America "not a nationalist but a trans-nationality, a weaving back and forth . . . of many threads of all sizes and colors." In this view the United States should serve as the vanguard of a more internationalized and multicultural age.

Other intellectuals, including progressives such as John Dewey, Jane Addams, and Louis Brandeis, joined Kallen and Bourne in their defense of ethnic diversity. Vastly outnumbered in the debate over immigration in the 1920s, these early proponents of "cultural pluralism" planted the seeds for the blooming of "multiculturalism" in the last quarter of the twentieth century.

The Prohibition Experiment

One of the last peculiar spasms of the progressive reform movement was prohibition, loudly supported by crusading churches and by many women. The arid new order was authorized in 1919 by the Eighteenth Amendment (see the Appendix), as implemented by the Volstead Act passed by Congress later that year. Together these laws made the world safe for hypocrisy.

The legal abolition of alcohol was especially popular in the South and the West. Southern whites were eager to keep stimulants out of the hands of blacks, lest they burst out of "their place." In the West, prohibition represented an attack on all the vices associated with the ubiquitous western saloon: public drunkenness, prostitution, and crime. But despite the overwhelming ratification of the "dry" amendment, strong opposition persisted in the larger eastern cities. For many "wet" foreign-born people, sociability was built around beer gardens and corner taverns.

PRIMARY SOURCE
The Genius of Advertising

Makers of America: The Poles

The Poles were among the largest immigrant groups to respond to industrializing America's call for badly needed labor after the Civil War. Between 1870 and World War I, some 2 million Polish-speaking peasants boarded steamships bound for the United States. By the 1920s, when antiforeign feeling led to restrictive legislation that choked the immigrant stream to a trickle, Polish immigrants and their American-born children began to develop new identities as Polish Americans.

The first Poles to arrive in the New World had landed in Jamestown in 1608 and helped to develop that colony's timber industry. Over the ensuing two and a half centuries, scattered religious dissenters and revolutionary nationalists also made their way from Poland to America. During the Revolution about one hundred Poles, including two officers recruited by Benjamin Franklin, served in the Continental Army.

But the Polish hopefuls who poured into the United States in the late nineteenth century came primarily to stave off starvation and to earn money to buy land. Known in their homeland as *za chlebem* ("for bread") emigrants, they belonged to the mass of central and eastern European peasants who had been forced off their farms by growing competition from large-scale, mechanized agriculture. An exceptionally high birthrate among the Catholic Poles compounded this economic pressure, creating an army of the land-poor and landless. With wages in the United States more than eight times higher than in Poland, the American magnet was irresistible.

Many Polish immigrants were also lured by glowing letters from friends and relatives already living in the United States. The first wave of Polish immigrants had established a thriving network of self-help and fraternal associations, organized around Polish Catholic parishes. Often, Polish American entrepreneurs helped their European compatriots make travel arrangements or find jobs in the United States. One of the most successful of these, the energetic Chicago grocer Anton Schermann, is credited with "bringing over" a hundred thousand Poles and causing the Windy City to earn the nickname "the American Warsaw."

Most of the Poles arriving in the United States in the late nineteenth century headed for booming industrial cities such as Buffalo, Pittsburgh, Detroit, Milwaukee, and Chicago. In 1907 four-fifths of the men toiled as unskilled laborers in coal mines, meatpacking factories, textile and steel mills, oil refineries, and garment-making shops. Although married women usually stayed home and contributed to the family's earnings by taking in laundry and boarders, children and single girls often joined their fathers and brothers on the job.

When an independent Poland was created after World War I, few Poles chose to return to their Old World homeland.

Prohibitionists were naive in the extreme. They overlooked the tenacious American tradition of weak control by the central government, especially over private lives. They forgot that the federal authorities had never satisfactorily enforced a law that the majority of the people—or a strong minority—were hostile to. Lawmakers could not legislate away a thirst.

Prohibition simply did not prohibit. The old-time "men-only" corner saloons were replaced by thousands of "speakeasies," each with its tiny grilled window through which the thirsty spoke softly before the barred door was opened. Because of the difficulty of transporting and concealing bottles, hard liquor of high alcoholic content gained in popularity. Illegal rumrunners operating from the West Indies or Canada had their inning. "Home brew" and "bathtub gin" became popular, as law-evading adults engaged in "alky cooking" with toy stills.

Yet the "noble experiment" was not entirely a failure. Bank savings increased, and absenteeism in industry decreased, presumably because of the newly sober ways of formerly soused barflies. On the whole, probably less alcohol was consumed than in the days before prohibition, though strong drink continued to be available. As a legendary tippler remarked, prohibition was "a darn sight better than no liquor at all."

Polish Coal Miners, c. 1905 It was common practice in American mines to segregate mining crews by ethnicity and race.

Instead, like other immigrant groups in the 1920s, they redoubled their efforts to integrate into American society. Polish institutions such as churches and fraternal organizations, which had served to perpetuate a distinctive Polish culture in the New World, now facilitated the transformation of Poles into Polish Americans. When Poland was absorbed into the Communist bloc after World War II, Polish Americans clung still more tightly to their American identity, pushing for landmarks such as Chicago's Pulaski Road to memorialize their culture in the New World.

Prohibition also spawned shocking crimes. The lush profits of illegal alcohol led to bribery of the police. Violent wars broke out in the big cities between rival gangs—often rooted in immigrant neighborhoods—seeking to corner the rich market in booze. Rival triggermen used their sawed-off shotguns and chattering "typewriters" (machine guns) to "erase" bootlegging competitors who were trying to "muscle in" on their "racket." In the gang wars of the 1920s in Chicago, about five hundred mobsters were murdered.

Chicago was by far the most spectacular example of lawlessness. In 1925 "Scarface" Al Capone, a grasping and murderous booze distributor, began six years of gang warfare that netted him millions of blood-spattered dollars. He zoomed through the streets in an armor-plated car with bulletproof windows. Capone could not be convicted of the cold-blooded massacre, on St. Valentine's Day in 1929, of seven rival gang members, but he was finally sent to jail in 1932 for income tax fraud.

Gangsters rapidly moved into other profitable and illicit activities: prostitution, gambling, and narcotics. Honest merchants were forced to pay "protection money" to prevent thugs from destroying their property. **Racketeers** even invaded the ranks of labor unions as organizers and promoters. Organized crime had come to be one of the nation's most gigantic businesses. By 1930 the annual "take" of the **underworld** was estimated to be from $12 billion to $18 billion—several times the income of the Washington government.

racketeers *A person who obtains money illegally by fraud, bootlegging, gambling, or threats of violence. Racketeers invaded the ranks of labor during the 1920s, a decade when gambling and gangsterism were prevalent in American life.*

underworld *Those who live outside society's laws, by vice or crime; organized crime.*

Monkey Business in Tennessee

Education in the 1920s continued to make giant boot-strides. More and more states were requiring young people to remain in school until age sixteen or eighteen, or until graduation from high school. The proportion of seventeen-year-olds who finished high school almost doubled in the 1920s, to more than one in four.

The most revolutionary contribution to educational theory during these yeasty years was made by mild-mannered Professor John Dewey, who served on the faculty of Columbia University from 1904 to 1930. By common consent one of America's few front-rank philosophers, he set forth the principles of "learning by doing" that formed the foundation of so-called progressive education, with its greater "permissiveness." Dewey believed that the workbench was as essential as the blackboard and that "education for life" should be a primary goal of the teacher.

Science also scored wondrous advances in these years. A massive public health program, launched by the Rockefeller Foundation in the South in 1909, had virtually wiped out the ancient affliction of hookworm by the 1920s. Better nutrition and health care helped to increase the life expectancy of a newborn infant from fifty years in 1901 to fifty-nine years in 1929.

Yet both science and progressive education in the 1920s were subjected to unfriendly fire from Fundamentalists. These devoted religionists charged that the teaching of Darwinian evolution was destroying faith in God and the Bible while contributing to the moral breakdown of youth in the jazz age. Numerous attempts were made to secure laws prohibiting the teaching of evolution, "the bestial hypothesis," in the public

The bombastic Fundamentalist evangelist W. A. (Billy) Sunday (1862–1935) declared in 1925:

"If a minister believes and teaches evolution, he is a stinking skunk, a hypocrite, and a liar."

The Battle over Evolution Opponents of Darwin's theories set up shop at the opening of the famed "Scopes Trial" in Dayton, Tennessee, in 1925. The trial was an early battle in an American "culture war" that was still being waged nearly a century later.

schools, and three southern states adopted such shackling measures. The trio of states included Tennessee, in the heart of the so-called Bible Belt South, where evangelical religion was especially robust.

The stage was set for the memorable "Monkey Trial" in the hamlet of Dayton, Tennessee, in 1925. A likable high school biology teacher, John T. Scopes, was indicted for teaching evolution. Batteries of newspaper reporters, armed with notebooks and cameras, descended upon the quiet town to witness the spectacle. Scopes was defended by nationally known attorneys, while former presidential candidate William Jennings Bryan, an ardent Presbyterian Fundamentalist, joined the prosecution. Taking the stand as an expert on the Bible, Bryan was made to appear foolish by the famed criminal lawyer, Clarence Darrow. Five days after the trial was over, Bryan died of a stroke, no doubt brought on by the wilting heat and witness-stand strain.

This historic clash between theology and biology proved inconclusive. Scopes, the forgotten man of the drama, was found guilty and fined $100. But the supreme court of Tennessee, while upholding the law, set aside the fine on a technicality. (The law itself was not formally repealed until 1967.) The Fundamentalists at best won only a hollow victory, for the absurdities of the trial cast ridicule on their cause. Yet even though increasing numbers of Christians were coming to reconcile the revelations of religion with the findings of modern science, Fundamentalism, with its emphasis on literal reading of the Bible, remained a vibrant force in American spiritual life. It was especially strong in the Baptist Church and in the rapidly growing Churches of Christ, organized in 1906.

✳ PRIMARY SOURCE
The Scopes Trial

The Mass-Consumption Economy

Prosperity—real, sustained, and widely shared—put much of the roar into the twenties. The economy kicked off its war harness in 1919, faltered a few steps in the recession of 1920–1921, and then sprinted forward for nearly seven years. Both the recent war and Treasury Secretary Andrew Mellon's tax policies favored the rapid expansion of capital investment. Ingenious machines, powered by cheap energy from newly tapped oil fields, dramatically increased the productivity of the laborer. Assembly-line production was so advanced at Henry Ford's famed Rouge River plant near Detroit that a finished automobile emerged every ten seconds.

Great new industries suddenly sprouted forth. Supplying electrical power for the humming new machines became a giant business in the 1920s. Above all, the automobile, once the horseless chariot of the rich, now became the carriage of the common citizen. By 1930 Americans owned almost 30 million cars. The nation's deepening love affair with the automobile headlined a momentous shift in the character of the economy. American manufacturers seemed to have mastered the problems of production; their worries now focused on consumption. Could they find the mass markets for the goods they had contrived to spew forth in such profusion?

Responding to this need, a new arm of American commerce came into being: advertising. By persuasion and ploy, allure and sexual suggestion, advertisers sought to make Americans chronically discontented with their paltry possessions and want more, more, more. A founder of this new Madison Avenue "profession" was Bruce Barton who published a best seller, *The Man Nobody Knows* (1925), portraying Jesus Christ as the greatest adman of all time. Christ was also an executive who "picked up twelve men from the bottom ranks of business and forged them into an organization that conquered the world."

Sports became big business in the consumer economy of the 1920s. Ballyhooed by the image makers, home-run heroes such as George H. (Babe) Ruth were far better known than most statesmen. In 1921 a Jersey City crowd paid more than a million dollars to watch heavyweight champion Jack Dempsey knock out challenger George Carpentier—the first in a series of million-dollar gates in the golden 1920s.

Buying on **credit** was another innovative feature of the postwar economy. "Possess today and pay tomorrow" was the message directed at buyers. Once-frugal descendants of Puritans went ever deeper into debt to own all kinds of newfangled marvels—refrigerators, vacuum cleaners, and especially cars and radios—*now*. Prosperity thus accumulated an overhanging cloud of debt, and the economy became increasingly vulnerable to disruptions of the credit structure.

credit *In business, the arrangement of purchasing goods or services immediately but making the payment at a later date; a consumer loan.*

Putting America on Rubber Tires

A new industrial revolution slipped into high gear in America in the 1920s. Machinery was the new messiah—and the automobile was its principal prophet. The manufacture of millions of private vehicles heralded an amazing new industrial system based on assembly-line methods and mass-production techniques.

Europeans invented the gasoline engine, but Americans quickly adapted it. By the 1890s a few daring American inventors and promoters, including Henry Ford and Ransom E. Olds (Oldsmobile), were developing the infant automotive industry. By 1910 sixty-nine car companies rolled out a total annual production of 181,000 units. Soon an enormous industry sprang into being, as Detroit became the motorcar capital of America.

It was the lean and silent Ford, the best known of all the industrial wizards, who put America on rubber tires. This ill-educated, multimillionaire mechanic was socially and culturally narrow. "History is bunk," he once testified. But he dedicated himself with one-track devotion to the gospel of standardization and erected an enormous personal empire on the cornerstone of his mechanical genius. After two early failures, he grasped and applied fully the techniques of standardization and assembly-line production—"Fordism." He is supposed to have remarked that the purchaser could have his Model T car in any color he desired just as long as it was black. Before long, Fordism caught fire outside the United States. German engineers were particularly enamored, though their workers resented those "American methods."

The flood of Fords was phenomenal. In 1914 the "Automobile Wizard" turned out his 500,000th Model T. By 1929, when the great bull market collapsed, Ford had produced nearly 20 million vehicles, and a total of 26 million were registered in the United States. This figure, averaging 1 for every 4.9 Americans, represented far more automobiles than existed in all the rest of the world.

PRIMARY SOURCE
Ford Weekly Purchase Plan

The impact of the self-propelled carriage on various aspects of American life was tremendous. A gigantic new industry emerged, employing directly or indirectly about 6 million people by 1930. Thousands of new jobs, moreover, were created in supporting industries such as rubber, glass, and fabrics, to say nothing of thousands of service stations and garages. America's standard of living, responding to this infectious vitality, rose to an enviable level.

Zooming motorcars were agents of social change. At first a luxury, they rapidly became a necessity. Essentially devices for needed transportation, they soon developed into a badge of freedom and equality—a necessary prop for self-respect. Women were further freed from their dependence on men. Buses made possible the consolidation of schools and to some extent of churches. Virtuous home life partially broke down as joyriders of all ages forsook the parlor for the highway. And what might young people get up to in the privacy of a closed-top Model T? An Indiana juvenile judge voiced parents' worst fears when he condemned the automobile as "a house of prostitution on wheels." Yet no sane American would plead for a return of the old horse and buggy, complete with fly-breeding manure. The automobile contributed notably to improved air and environmental quality, despite its later notoriety as a polluter. Life might be cut short on the highways, and smog might poison the air, but the automobile brought more convenience, pleasure, and excitement into more people's lives than almost any other single invention.

Humans Develop Wings

Gasoline engines also provided the power that enabled humans to fulfill the age-old dream of sprouting wings. After near-successful experiments by others with heavier-than-air craft, the Wright brothers, Orville and Wilbur, performed "the miracle at Kitty Hawk," North Carolina. On a historic day—December 17, 1903—Orville Wright took aloft a feebly engined plane that stayed airborne for twelve seconds and 120 feet. Thus the air age was launched by two obscure bicycle repairmen.

Airplanes, once "flying coffins" for stuntmen, were first used with marked success for a serious purpose during the Great War of 1914–1918. Shortly thereafter private companies began to operate passenger lines with airmail contracts, which were in effect a subsidy from Washington. The first transcontinental airmail route was established from New York to San Francisco in 1920.

In 1927 modest and skillful Charles A. Lindbergh electrified the world with the first solo west-to-east conquest of the Atlantic. Seeking a prize of $25,000, the lanky flier courageously piloted his single-engine plane, the *Spirit of St. Louis*, from New York to Paris in a grueling thirty-three hours and thirty-nine minutes.

Lindbergh's exploit swept Americans off their feet. Fed up with the cynicism and debunking of the jazz age, they found in this wholesome and handsome youth a genuine hero. "Lucky Lindy" received an uproarious welcome in the canyons of lower Broadway, as eighteen hundred tons of ticker tape and other confetti showered upon him. Lindbergh's achievement did much to dramatize and popularize flying while giving a strong boost to the infant aviation industry.

The impact of the airplane was tremendous. The floundering railroads received another sharp setback through the loss of passengers and mail. A lethal new weapon was given to the gods of war with the coming of city-busting aerial bombs. The Atlantic Ocean was shriveling to about the size of the Aegean Sea in the days of Socrates, while isolation behind ocean moats was becoming a bygone dream.

The Radio and Film Revolutions

The speed of the airplane was far eclipsed by the speed of radio waves. Guglielmo Marconi, an Italian, invented wireless telegraphy in the 1890s, and his brainchild was used for long-range communication during World War I. Next came the voice-carrying radio, a triumph of many minds. A red-letter day was posted in November 1920, when the Pittsburgh station KDKA broadcast the news of the Harding landslide. Radio knitted the nation together. By the late 1920s, national commercial networks gained control of the new industry and drowned out much local programming. Various regions heard voices with standardized accents, and countless millions tuned in to perennial comedy favorites such as "Amos 'n' Andy." Advertising "commercials" made radio another vehicle for American free enterprise, and brand-named programs such as the "A&P Gypsies" and the "Eveready Hour" helped make radio-touted labels household words and purchases.

The flickering movie, the inventive fruit of Thomas Edison and others, first attracted attention in the naughty peep-show arcades in the 1890s. The first story-sequence movie, a breathless melodrama called *The Great Train Robbery*, was featured in the five-cent theaters, popularly called nickelodeons. Spectacular among the first full-length classics was D. W. Griffith's *The Birth of a Nation* (1915), which glorified the Ku Klux Klan of Reconstruction days and defamed both blacks and northern carpetbaggers. White southerners reputedly fired guns at the screen during the attempted "rape" scene. African Americans were outraged at the film and angrily organized protest marches, petition campaigns, and public hearings.

PRIMARY SOURCE
The Great Train Robbery

A fascinating industry was thus launched. Hollywood, California, quickly became the movie capital of the world, for it enjoyed a maximum of sunshine and other advantages. Early movies featured nudity and heavy-lidded female vampires ("vamps"), and an offended public forced the screen magnates to set up their own rigorous code of censorship. The motion picture really arrived during the World War of 1914–1918, when it was used as an engine of anti-German propaganda.

A new era began in 1927 with the first "talkie"—*The Jazz Singer*, starring white performer Al Jolson in blackface. About the same time, color films began to be produced. Movies eclipsed all other new forms of amusement in the phenomenal growth of their popularity. Movie stars of the first pulchritude commanded much larger salaries than the president of the United States, in some cases as much as $100,000 for a single picture.

Critics bemoaned the vulgarization of popular taste wrought by the technologies of radio and movies. But the effects of the new mass media were not all negative. The insularity of ethnic communities eroded as the immigrants' children, especially, forsook the neighborhood vaudeville theater for the downtown movie palace or turned away from Grandma's Yiddish storytelling to tune in "Amos 'n' Andy." If some of the rich diversity of immigrant cultures was lost, the standardization of tastes and language hastened immigrants' entry into the American mainstream—and set the stage for the emergence of a working-class political coalition that, for a time, would overcome the divisive ethnic differences of the past.

The Dynamic Decade

Far-reaching changes in lifestyles and values paralleled the dramatic upsurge of the economy. The census of 1920 revealed that for the first time most Americans no longer lived in the countryside but in urban areas. Women continued to find new opportunities for employment in the cities, though they tended to cluster in a few low-paying jobs (such as retail clerking and office typing) that quickly became classified as women's work. An organized birth control movement, led by fiery feminist Margaret Sanger, openly championed the use of contraceptives. Alice Paul's National Woman's party began in 1923 to campaign for an Equal Rights Amendment to the Constitution. To some defenders of traditional ways, it seemed that the world had suddenly gone mad.

Even the churches were affected. Fundamentalists lost ground to Modernists, who liked to think that God was a "good guy." To compete with automobiles and golf, some churches turned to providing entertainment of their own, including wholesome moving pictures for young people.

Even before the war, one observer thought the chimes had struck "sex o'clock in America," and the 1920s witnessed what many old-timers thought was a veritable erotic eruption. Advertisers exploited sexual allure to sell everything from soap to car tires. Once-modest maidens now proclaimed their new freedom as "flappers" in bobbed tresses and dresses. Young women appeared with hemlines elevated, stockings rolled, breasts taped flat, cheeks rouged, and lips a crimson gash that held a dangling cigarette. Thus did the "flapper" symbolize a yearned-for and devil-may-care independence (some said wild abandon) in some American women.

Justification for this new sexual frankness could be found in the recently translated writings of Dr. Sigmund Freud. This Viennese physician appeared to argue that sexual **repression** was responsible for a variety of nervous and emotional ills. Thus not pleasure alone but health demanded sexual gratification and liberation.

Many taboos flew out the window as sex-conscious Americans let themselves go. As unknowing Freudians, teenagers pioneered the sexual frontiers. Glued together in rhythmic embrace, they danced to jazz music squeaking from phonographs. The youthful "neckers" and "petters" also poached upon the forbidden territory of each others' bodies in darkened movie houses or in automobiles.

If the flapper was the goddess of the era, jazz was its sacred music. With its virtuoso wanderings and tricky syncopation, jazz moved up from New Orleans along with migrating blacks during World War I. Tunes such as W. C. Handy's "St. Louis Blues" became instant classics, as the wailing saxophone became the trumpet of the new era. Blacks such as Handy, "Jelly Roll" Morton, and Joseph "King" Oliver gave birth to jazz, but

---

✳ PRIMARY SOURCE
Birth Control Clinic Circular

repression *In psychology, the forcing of instincts or ideas painful to the conscious mind into the unconscious, where they continue to exercise influence.*

✳ PRIMARY SOURCE
Impossible Interview: Sigmund Freud vs. Jean Harlow

King Oliver's Creole Jazz Band, Early 1920s Joseph "King" Oliver arrived in Chicago from New Orleans in 1918. His band became the first important black jazz ensemble and made Chicago's Royal Garden Café a magnet for jazz lovers. Left to right: Honoré Dutrey, trombone; Baby Dodds, drums; King Oliver, cornet; Lil Hardin, piano; Bill Johnson, banjo; and Johnny Dodds, clarinet. Kneeling in the foreground is the young Louis Armstrong, playing a trombone.

EXAMINING THE EVIDENCE

THE JAZZ SINGER, 1927

The Jazz Singer was the first feature-length "talkie," a motion picture in which the characters actually speak, and its arrival spelled the end for "silent" films in which the audience read subtitles with live or recorded music as background. Although moviegoers flocked to *The Jazz Singer* to hear recorded sound, when they got there they found a movie concerned with themes of great interest to the urban, first- or second-generation immigrant audiences who were Hollywood's major patrons. *The Jazz Singer* told the story of a poor, assimilating Jewish immigrant torn between following his father's wish that he train as an Orthodox cantor and his own ambition to make a success for himself as a jazz singer, performing in the popular blackface style. The movie's star, Al Jolson, was himself an immigrant Jew who had made his name as a blackface performer. White actors had gradually taken over the southern black minstrel show during the nineteenth century. By the early twentieth century,

Jewish entertainers had entirely monopolized these roles. Jolson, like other Jewish blackface performers, used his ability to impersonate a black person to force his acceptance into mainstream white American society. This use of blackface seems ironic because black Americans in the 1920s were struggling with their own real-life battles against Jim Crow–era segregation, a blatant form of exclusion from American society.

1. Besides the novelty of being a "talkie," what may have made *The Jazz Singer* a box office hit in 1927?

2. How might different types of viewers in the audience have responded to the story?

3. Was the "blackface" tradition of performance by white actors an entirely racist one? Or is there a way in which it acknowledges the great importance of blacks within the wider American culture?

Warner Bros/The Kobal Collection/The Picture Desk

the entertainment industry soon spawned all-white bands—notably Paul Whiteman's. Caucasian impresarios cornered the profits, though not the creative soul, of America's most native music.

A new racial pride also blossomed in the northern black communities that grew so rapidly during and after the war. Harlem in New York City, counting some 100,000 African American residents in the 1920s, was one of the largest black communities in the world. Harlem sustained a vibrant, creative culture that nourished poets such as Langston Hughes, whose first volume of verse, *The Weary Blues*, appeared in 1926.

charismatic *Concerning the personal magnetism or appeal of a leader for his or her followers; literally, "gift of grace."*

Harlem in the 1920s also spawned a **charismatic** leader, Marcus Garvey. The Jamaican-born Garvey founded the United Negro Improvement Association (UNIA) to promote the resettlement of American blacks in Africa. His Black Star Steamship Company and other enterprises failed financially, and Garvey himself was convicted of mail fraud in 1927 and deported by a nervous United States government. But the race pride that Garvey inspired among his 4 million UNIA followers helped these newcomers to northern cities gain self-confidence and self-reliance. And his example proved important to the later founding of the Nation of Islam (Black Muslim) movement.

Literary Liberation

Likewise in literature, an older era seemed to have ground to a halt with the recent war. By the dawn of the 1920s, most of the custodians of an aging genteel culture had died—Henry James in 1916, Henry Adams in 1918, and William Dean Howells ("the Dean of American literature") in 1920. A few novelists who had been popular in the previous decades continued to thrive, notably the well-to-do, cosmopolitan New Yorker Edith Wharton and the Virginia-born Willa Cather, esteemed for her stark but sympathetic portrayals of pioneering on the prairies.

But in the decade after the war, a new generation of writers burst on the scene. Many of them hailed from ethnic and regional backgrounds different from that of the Protestant New Englanders who traditionally had dominated American cultural life. The newcomers exhibited the energy of youth, the ambition of excluded outsiders, and, in many cases the smoldering resentment of ideals betrayed. They bestowed on American literature a new vitality, imaginativeness, and artistic quality.

A patron saint of many young authors was H. L. Mencken, the "Bad Boy of Baltimore." In the pages of his green-covered monthly *American Mercury*, Mencken assailed marriage, patriotism, democracy, prohibition, Rotarians, and the middle-class American "booboisie." The South he contemptuously dismissed as "the Sahara of the Bozart" (a bastardization of *beaux arts*, French for fine arts), and he scathingly attacked do-gooders as Puritans. Puritanism, he jibed, was "the haunting fear that someone, somewhere, might be happy."

The war had jolted many young writers out of their complacency about traditional values and literary standards. With their pens they probed for new codes of morals and understanding, as well as fresh forms of expression. F. Scott Fitzgerald, a handsome, Minnesota-born Princetonian then only twenty-four years old, became an overnight celebrity when he published *This Side of Paradise* in 1920. The book became a kind of bible for the young. It was eagerly devoured by aspiring flappers and their ardent wooers, many of whom affected an air of bewildered abandon toward life. Catching the spirit of the hour (often about 4 a.m.), Fitzgerald found

F. Scott Fitzgerald and His Wife, Zelda They are shown here in the happy, early days of their stormy marriage.

Stock Montage

"all gods dead, all wars fought, all faiths in man shaken." He followed this melancholy success with *The Great Gatsby* (1925), a brilliant commentary on the illusory American ideal of the self-made man. Theodore Dreiser's masterpiece of 1925, *An American Tragedy*, explored the pitfalls of social striving, as it dealt with the murder of a pregnant working girl by her socially ambitious young lover.

Ernest Hemingway, who had seen action on the Italian front in 1917, was among the writers most affected by the war. He responded to pernicious propaganda and the overblown appeal of patriotism by devising his own lean, word-sparing but word-perfect style. In *The Sun Also Rises* (1926) Hemingway told of disillusioned, spiritually numb American expatriates in Europe. In *A Farewell to Arms* (1929) he crafted one of the finest novels in any language about the war experience. A troubled soul, Hemingway finally blew out his brains with a shotgun blast in 1961.

Other writers turned to a caustic probing of American small-town life. Sherwood Anderson dissected various fictional personalities in *Winesburg, Ohio* (1919), finding them all in some way warped by their cramped psychological surroundings. Sinclair Lewis, a hotheaded, heavy-drinking writer from Sauk Centre, Minnesota, sprang into prominence in 1920 with *Main Street*, the story of one woman's unsuccessful war against provincialism. In *Babbitt* (1922) Lewis affectionately pilloried George F. Babbitt, a prosperous, vulgar, slavishly conformist real estate broker. The word "Babbittry" was quickly coined to describe his all-too-familiar lifestyle.

Hemingway, Anderson, and many other writers and painters found shelter and inspiration in the Paris salon of Gertrude Stein, an expatriate American. A literary innovator in her own right, Stein wrote experimental poetry and prose, including *Three Lives* (1909), *Tender Buttons* (1914), and most famously, *The Autobiography of Alice B. Toklas* (1933), named for her lifelong partner.

William Faulkner, a dark-eyed, pensive Mississippian turned his attention to a fictional chronicle of an imaginary, history-rich Deep South county he named "Yoknapatawpha." In powerful books such as *The Sound and the Fury* (1929) and *As I Lay Dying* (1930), Faulkner peeled back layers of time and consciousness from the constricted souls of his ingrown southern characters. His extended meditations on southern themes culminated in what some readers consider his greatest work, *Absalom, Absalom* (1936).

Nowhere was innovation in the 1920s more obvious than in poetry. Ezra Pound, a brilliantly erratic Idahoan who deserted America for Europe, rejected what he called "an old bitch civilization, gone in the teeth," and proclaimed his doctrine: "Make It New." Pound strongly influenced Missouri-born and Harvard-educated T. S. Eliot. After taking up permanent residence in England, Eliot produced *The Waste Land* (1922), one of the most influential poems of the century. Robert Frost, a San Francisco-born poet, wrote hauntingly about his adopted New England.

On the stage, Eugene O'Neill, a New York dramatist and Princeton dropout of globe-trotting background, laid bare Freudian notions of sex in plays such as *Strange Interlude* (1928). A prodigious playwright, he authored more than a dozen productions in the 1920s and won the Nobel Prize in 1936.

O'Neill arose from New York's Greenwich Village, which before and after the war was a seething cauldron of writers, painters, musicians, actors, and other would-be artists. After the war a black cultural renaissance also took root uptown in Harlem, led by such gifted writers as Claude McKay, Langston Hughes, and Zora Neale Hurston, and by jazz artists such as Louis Armstrong and Eubie Blake. In an outpouring of creative expression called the Harlem Renaissance, they proudly exulted in their black culture and argued for a "New Negro" who was a full citizen and a social equal to whites.

Langston Hughes (1902–1967) celebrated Harlem's role in energizing a generation of artists and writers in his poem "Esthete in Harlem" (1930):

"Strange, That in this nigger place I should meet life face to face; When, for years, I had been seeking Life in places gentler-speaking, Until I came to this vile street And found Life stepping on my feet!"*

---

* From *Collected Poems* by Langston Hughes. Copyright © 1994 by the Estate of Langston Hughes. Reprinted by permission of Alfred A. Knopf, Inc.

Architecture also reinvented itself as modern—in diverse ways. At one extreme, Frank Lloyd Wright advanced the theory that buildings should grow from their sites, incorporate indigenous materials, and not slavishly imitate Greek and Roman importations. In a very different kind of paean to modern America, the machine age outdid itself in New York City when it thrust upward the cloud-brushing Empire State Building, 102 stories high.

Wall Street's Big Bull Market

Signals abounded that the economic joyride might end in a crash; even in the best years of the 1920s several hundred banks failed annually. This something-for-nothing craze was well illustrated by real estate speculation, especially the fantastic Florida boom that culminated in 1925. Numerous underwater lots were sold to eager purchasers for preposterous sums. The whole wildcat scheme collapsed when the peninsula was devastated by a hurricane.

The stock exchange provided even greater sensations. Speculation ran wild. An orgy of boom-or-bust trading pushed the bull market to dizzying peaks, as Wall Street gamblers gored one another and fleeced greedy lambs. The stock market became a veritable gambling den.

As the 1920s lurched forward, everybody seemed to be buying stocks "on margin"—that is, with a small down payment. Barbers, stenographers, and elevator boys cashed in on hot tips picked up while on duty. One valet was reported to have parlayed his wages into a quarter of a million dollars. Rags-to-riches Americans eagerly worshiped at the altar of the ticker-tape machine. So powerful was the intoxicant of quick profits that few heeded the voices raised in certain quarters to warn that this kind of tinsel prosperity could not last forever.

Little was done by Washington to curb money mad speculators. In the wartime days of Wilson, the national debt had rocketed from the 1914 figure of $1,188,235,400 to the 1921 peak of $23,976,250,608. Conservative principles of money management pointed to a diversion of surplus funds to reduce this financial burden. But to Secretary of the Treasury Andrew Mellon and his fellow millionaires, the burdensome taxes inherited from the war were especially distasteful. Their theory was that such high levies forced the rich to invest in tax-exempt securities rather than in factories that dispensed prosperous payrolls. The Mellonites also argued, with considerable persuasiveness, that high taxes not only discouraged business but also brought a smaller net return to the Treasury than moderate taxes.

Seeking to succor the "poor" rich people, Mellon helped engineer a series of tax reductions from 1921 to 1926. Congress followed his lead by repealing the excess-profits tax, abolishing the gift tax, and reducing excise taxes, the **surtax**, the income tax, and estate taxes. In 1921 a wealthy person with an income of $1 million had paid $663,000 in income taxes; in 1926 the same person paid about $200,000. Mellon's spare-the-rich policies thus shifted much of the tax burden from the wealthy to middle-income groups.

Mellon, lionized by conservatives as "the greatest Secretary of the Treasury since Hamilton," remains a controversial figure. True, he reduced the national debt by $10 billion—from about $26 billion to $16 billion. But foes of the emaciated multimillionaire charged that he should have bitten an even larger chunk out of the debt, especially while the country was pulsating with prosperity. He was also accused of indirectly encouraging the bull market. If he had absorbed more of the national income in taxes, there would have been less money left for frenzied speculation. His refusal to do so typified the single-mindedly probusiness regime that dominated the political scene throughout the postwar decade.

✳ PRIMARY SOURCE
Aspects of the Financial Merry-Go-Round

surtax *A special tax, usually involving a raised rate on an already existing tax.*

Chapter Summary

After the crusading idealism of World War I, America sharply turned inward, as many citizens became hostile to anything foreign or different. Radicals and immigrants were targeted in the red scare and the Sacco-Vanzetti case, while the resurgent Ku Klux Klan reflected many Protestant Americans' fears of change. New restrictions on immigration reflected prejudice against "non-Anglo-Saxon" groups. Sharp cultural and religious conflicts also occurred over the prohibition experiment and evolution.

A new mass-consumption economy fueled the spectacular prosperity of the 1920s. The automobile industry, led by Henry Ford, transformed the economy and altered American lifestyles.

Charles Lindbergh's flight symbolized the persistence of individual heroism in an age of cynicism and mass standardization.

The pervasive media of radio and film dramatically altered popular culture and values. Jazz music, the Harlem Renaissance, and Marcus Garvey's movement all reflected African Americans' new cultural energy. Birth control and Freudian psychology overturned traditional sexual standards, especially for women. Young literary rebels, many originally from the Midwest, scorned genteel New England and small-town culture and searched for new values, sometimes as expatriates in Europe. The stock-market boom symbolized the free-wheeling spirit of the decade.

KEY TERMS

syndicalism (510)

Bible Belt (511)

provincial (511)

racketeer (515)

underworld (515)

credit (517)

repression (520)

charismatic (522)

surtax (524)

PEOPLE TO KNOW

A. Mitchell Palmer

Nicola Sacco

Bartolomeo Vanzetti

Horace Kallen

Randolph Bourne

Al Capone

John T. Scopes

Henry Ford

Charles A. Lindbergh

Sigmund Freud

Go to the History CourseMate website for primary source links, study tools, and review materials for this chapter. www.cengagebrain.com

32

The Politics of Boom and Bust

1920–1932

We in America today are nearer to the final triumph over poverty than ever before in the history of any land. We have not yet reached the goal—but ... we shall soon, with the help of God, be in sight of the day when poverty will be banished from this nation.

HERBERT HOOVER, 1928

Three Republican presidents—Warren G. Harding, Calvin Coolidge, and Herbert Hoover—steered the nation on the roller-coaster ride of the 1920s, a thrilling ascent from the depths of post–World War I recession to breathtaking heights of prosperity, followed by a terrifying crash into the Great Depression. In a retreat from progressive reform, Republicans sought to serve the public good less by direct government action and more through cooperation with big business. Some corrupt officials served themselves as well, exploiting public resources for personal profit. Meanwhile, the United States retreated from its brief international fling during World War I and resumed with a vengeance its traditional foreign policy of military unpreparedness and political isolationism.

FOCUS QUESTIONS

1. How did the political conservatism and economic prosperity of the 1920s lead to policies advancing the interests of business and attempting to isolate America from the world?

2. What was consistent and what was different in the leadership and policies of the three Republican presidents of the 1920s—Harding, Coolidge, and Hoover?

3. How successfully did the United States address the international economic tangle of loans, war debts, and reparations? Why was there so much resentment of America's actions in Europe?

4. What were the immediate and more fundamental causes of the stock market crash and the Great Depression?

5. In what ways was Hoover's response to the Great Depression a reflection of the older ideology of individualism and *laissez-faire*, and in what ways did his actions reflect a newer view of government responsibility for the nation's collective economic well-being?

CHRONOLOGY

1919	American Legion founded.
1920	Esch-Cummins Transportation Act.
1921	Veterans Bureau created. Capper-Volstead Act.
1922	Five-Power Naval Treaty signed. Four-Power and Nine-Power Treaties on the Far East. Fordney-McCumber Tariff Law.
1923	*Adkins v. Children's Hospital.* Teapot Dome scandal. Harding dies; Coolidge assumes presidency.
1924	Adjusted Compensation Act for veterans. Dawes Plan for international finance. U.S. troops leave Dominican Republic. Coolidge wins three-way presidential election.
1926	U.S. troops occupy Nicaragua.
1928	Kellogg-Briand Pact. Hoover defeats Smith for presidency.
1929	Agricultural Marketing Act sets up Federal Farm Board. Stock-market crash.
1930	Hawley-Smoot Tariff.
1931	Japanese invade Manchuria.
1932	Reconstruction Finance Corporation (RFC) established. Norris–La Guardia Anti-Injunction Act. "Bonus Army" dispersed from Washington, D.C.

The Republican "Old Guard" Returns

Warren G. Harding, inaugurated in 1921, *looked* presidential. With erect figure, broad shoulders, bushy eyebrows, and graying hair, he was one of the best-liked men of his generation. An easygoing, warm-handed backslapper, he exuded graciousness and love of people. Yet the charming, smiling exterior concealed a weak, inept interior. With a mediocre mind, Harding quickly found himself beyond his depth in the presidency. "God! What a job!" was his anguished cry on one occasion.

Harding, like Grant, was unable to detect moral halitosis in his evil associates, and he was soon surrounded by his poker-playing, shirt-sleeved cronies of the "Ohio gang." Harding hated to hurt his friends' feelings by saying no, and designing political leeches capitalized on this weakness. He "was not a bad man," said one Washington observer. "He was just a slob."

Admitting his own scant mental furnishings, Harding appointed to his cabinet some strong and capable Republicans: imperious and brilliant Charles Evans Hughes as secretary of state; lean and elderly Andrew W. Mellon as secretary of the treasury; and chubby-faced Herbert Hoover, famed wartime feeder of the Belgians, as secretary of commerce. But Harding also brought into his cabinet such corrupt characters as Secretary of the Interior Albert B. Fall, a scheming anticonservationist, and Attorney General Harry M. Daugherty, a member of the "Ohio gang" and a big-time crook.

Well intentioned but weak-willed, Harding was a perfect "front" for enterprising industrialists. A McKinley-style old order settled back into place at war's end, crushing the reform seedlings that had sprouted in the progressive era. This new Old Guard hoped to improve on the old business doctrine of laissez-faire. Their plea was not simply for government to keep its hands off business but for government to help guide business along the path to profits. They subtly and effectively achieved their ends by putting the courts and the administrative bureaus into the safekeeping of fellow stand-patters for the duration of the decade.

The Supreme Court was a striking example of this trend. In his short presidency, Harding appointed four justices who were or became deep-dyed reactionaries. In the first years of the 1920s, the Supreme Court axed progressive legislation. It killed a federal child-labor law, stripped away many of labor's hard-won gains, and rigidly restricted governmental intervention in the economy. In the landmark case of *Adkins v. Children's Hospital* (1923), the Court reversed its own reasoning in *Muller v. Oregon* (see p. 469) and

Justice Oliver Wendell Holmes (1841–1935), wryly dissenting in the Adkins *case, said:*

"It would need more than the Nineteenth Amendment to convince me that there are no differences between men and women, or that legislation cannot take those differences into account."

invalidated a minimum-wage law for women. Its strained ruling was that, because females now had the vote (Nineteenth Amendment), they were the legal equals of men and could no longer be protected by special legislation. The contradictory premises of the *Muller* and *Adkins* cases framed a debate over gender differences that would continue for the rest of the century: Were women sufficiently different from men that they merited special legal and social treatment, or were they effectively equal in the eyes of the law and therefore undeserving of special protection and preferences?

Under Harding, corporations could once more relax and expand. Antitrust laws were often ignored, circumvented, or feebly enforced by friendly prosecutors in the attorney general's office. The Interstate Commerce Commission, to single out one agency, came to be dominated by members who were sympathetic to the managers of the railroads.

Big industrialists, striving to lessen competition, now had a free hand to set up trade associations. Cement manufacturers, for example, would use these agencies to agree upon standardization of product, publicity campaigns, and a united front in dealing with the railroads and labor. Although many of these associations ran counter to the spirit of existing antitrust legislation, their formation was encouraged by Secretary of Commerce Herbert Hoover. His sense of engineering efficiency led him to condemn the waste resulting from cutthroat competition and to encourage business self-regulation.

The Aftermath of War

Wartime government controls on the economy were swiftly dismantled. The War Industries Board disappeared with almost indecent haste. With its passing, progressive hopes for more government regulation of big business evaporated.

Washington likewise returned the railroads to private management in 1920. The Esch-Cummins Transportation Act of 1920 encouraged private consolidation of the railroads and obligated the federal Interstate Commerce Commission to guarantee their profitability.

Labor, suddenly deprived of its wartime crutch of friendly government support, limped along badly in the postwar decade. The Railway Labor Board, a successor body to the wartime labor boards, ordered a wage cut of 12 percent in 1922, provoking a two-month strike. It ended when Attorney General Daugherty, who fully shared Harding's big-business bias, clamped on the strikers one of the most sweeping injunctions in American history. Unions wilted in this hostile political environment, and membership dropped by nearly 30 percent between 1920 and 1930.

Needy veterans were among the few nonbusiness groups to reap lasting gains from the war. In 1921 Congress created the Veterans Bureau to operate hospitals and provide vocational rehabilitation for the disabled. The American Legion, founded in Paris in 1919 by Colonel Theodore Roosevelt, Jr., became known for its militant conservative patriotism and aggressive lobbying for veterans' benefits. The Legion demanded "adjusted compensation" to make up for the wages veterans had "lost" while in uniform. Harding vetoed one such bill in 1922, but in 1924 Congress passed the Adjusted Compensation Act over President Calvin Coolidge's veto. This Act gave every former soldier a paid-up insurance policy due in twenty years—adding about $3.5 billion to the total cost of the war.

America Seeks Benefits Without Burdens

Isolation was enthroned in Washington. The Harding administration, with the Senate "irreconcilables" holding a hatchet over its head, continued to regard the League of Nations as a thing unclean.

But disarmament was one international issue on which Harding set isolationism aside and seized the initiative. He was prodded by businesspeople unwilling to dig deeper into their pockets for money to finance the ambitious naval-building program started during the war. A deadly contest was shaping up with Britain and Japan, which watched with alarm as the oceans filled with American vessels. Public agitation in America, fed by worries about British and Japanese cooperation in the Pacific, brought about the headline-making Washington Disarmament Conference in 1921–1922. The double agenda included naval disarmament and the situation in East Asia.

At the outset, Secretary of State Charles Evans Hughes dramatically proposed a ten-year "holiday" on construction of battleships and even the scrapping of some of the huge **dreadnoughts** already built or being built. Hughes proposed that the scaled-down navies of America and Britain should enjoy parity in battleships and aircraft carriers, with Japan on the small end of a 5-5-3 ratio.

dreadnought *A heavily armored battleship with large batteries of twelve-inch guns.*

The conference's Five-Power Naval Treaty of 1922 embodied Hughes's ideas on ship ratios, but only after face-saving compensation for the insecure Japanese. The British and Americans both conceded that they would refrain from fortifying their East Asian possessions, including the Philippines. The Japanese were not subjected to such restraints in their possessions. In addition, a Four-Power Treaty bound Britain, Japan, France, and the United States to preserve the status quo in the Pacific—another concession to the Japanese. Finally, the Washington Conference gave chaotic China—"the sick man of East Asia"—a shot in the arm with the Nine-Power Treaty of 1922, whose signatories agreed to nail wide open the Open Door in China.

The Hardingites boasted of this globe-shaking achievement in disarmament, but their satisfaction was somewhat illusory. No restrictions had been placed on small warships, and the other powers churned ahead with the construction of cruisers, destroyers, and submarines, while penny-pinching Uncle Sam lagged dangerously behind. Ominously, the American people seemed content to rely for their security on words and wishful thinking rather than on weapons and hardheaded realism.

A similar sentimentalism welled up later in the decade, when millions of Americans signed petitions calling for the "outlawry of war." Calvin Coolidge's secretary of state, Frank B. Kellogg, and the French foreign minister, Aristide Briand, signed the Kellogg-Briand Pact forswearing war in 1928, and it was ultimately ratified by sixty-two nations. Lacking both muscles and teeth, this parchment peace was illusory in the extreme. Yet it accurately—and dangerously—reflected the American mind in the 1920s, which was all too ready to be lulled into a false sense of security. This mood took even deeper hold in the ostrich-like neutralism of the 1930s.

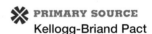

PRIMARY SOURCE
Kellogg-Briand Pact

Hiking the Tariff Higher

A comparable lack of realism afflicted foreign economic policy in the 1920s. Business people, shortsightedly obsessed with the dazzling prospects in the prosperous home market, sought to keep that market to themselves by flinging up insurmountable tariff walls around the United States. Congress passed the Fordney-McCumber Tariff Law of 1922, which boosted schedules from the average of 27 percent under Wilson's Underwood Tariff of 1913 to an average of 38.5 percent.

The high-tariff course thus charted by the Republican regimes set off an ominous chain reaction. European producers felt the squeeze, for the American tariff walls prolonged the postwar chaos. An impoverished Europe needed to sell manufactured goods to the United States, particularly if it hoped to achieve economic recovery and to pay its huge war debt to Washington. America needed to give foreign nations a chance to make a profit from it so that they could buy U.S. manufactured articles and repay debts. International trade, Americans were slow to learn, is a two-way street.

Erecting tariff walls was a game that two could play. The American example spurred European nations, throughout the feverish 1920s, to pile up higher barriers themselves. The whole vicious circle further deepened the international economic distress, providing one more rung on the ladder by which Adolf Hitler scrambled to power.

The Stench of Scandal

The loose morality and get-rich-quickism of the Harding era manifested themselves spectacularly in a series of scandals. Early in 1923 the head of the Veterans Bureau, Colonel Charles R. Forbes, was caught with his hand in the till. An appointee of the gullible Harding, he and his **accomplices** looted the government to the tune of about $200 million, chiefly in connection with the building of veterans' hospitals. Forbes was convicted and sentenced to two years in a federal penitentiary.

Most shocking of all was the Teapot Dome scandal, an affair that involved priceless naval oil reserves at Teapot Dome (Wyoming) and Elk Hills (California). In 1921 the slippery secretary of the interior, Albert B. Fall, induced his careless colleague, the secretary of the navy, to transfer these valuable properties to the Interior Department. Harding indiscreetly signed the secret order. Fall then quietly leased the lands to oilmen Harry F. Sinclair and Edward L. Doheny, but not until they had paid him some $400,000 in bribes ("loans").

Teapot Dome, no tempest in a teapot, finally came to a whistling boil. Details of the crooked transaction leaked out in March 1923. Fall, Sinclair, and Doheny were indicted in 1924. Fall was found guilty of taking a bribe and sentenced to one year in jail. The two bribe givers were acquitted, though Sinclair served time in jail for "shadowing" jurors and for refusing to testify before a Senate committee.

Still more scandals erupted. Persistent reports about the underhanded doings of Attorney General Daugherty brought a Senate investigation in 1924 of the illegal sale of pardons and liquor permits. Forced to resign, the accused official was tried in 1927 but released after a jury twice failed to agree. During the trial, Daugherty hid behind the trousers of the now-dead Harding by implying that persistent probing might uncover crookedness in the White House.

Harding was mercifully spared the full revelation of these iniquities. Just as news of the scandals was beginning to break, he died in San Francisco on August 2, 1923, of pneumonia and thrombosis.

The brutal fact is that Harding simply was not a strong enough man for the presidency—as he himself privately admitted. Such was his weakness that he tolerated people and conditions that subjected the Republic to its worst disgrace since the days of President Grant.

Bargain Day in Washington
If the craze for Government property continues

The Harding Scandals This 1924 cartoon satirizing the misdemeanors of the Harding administration shows the sale of the Capitol, the White House, and even the Washington Monument.

"Silent Cal" Coolidge

News of Harding's death was sped to Vice President Coolidge, then visiting at his father's New England farmhouse. By the light of two kerosene lamps the elder Coolidge, a justice of the peace, used the old family Bible to administer the presidential oath to his son.

This homespun setting was symbolic of Coolidge. Quite unlike Harding, the stern-faced Vermonter, with his thin nose and tightly set lips, embodied the New England virtues of honesty, morality, industry, and frugality. His dour visage prompted the acerbic observation that he had been "weaned on a pickle."

Coolidge seemed to be a crystallization of the commonplace. Painfully shy, he was blessed with only mediocre powers of leadership. He would occasionally display a dry wit in private; but his speeches, delivered in a nasal New England twang, were invariably boring. A staunch apostle of the status quo, he became the "high priest of the great god Business." He believed that "the man who builds a factory builds a temple" and that "the man who works there worships there." The hands-off temperament of "Cautious Cal" perfectly suited the times, and Coolidge "luck" held during his five and a half prosperity-blessed years.

Ever a profile in caution, Coolidge slowly gave the Harding regime a badly needed moral fumigation. Teapot Dome had scalded the Republican party badly, but so transparently honest was the vinegary Vermonter that the scandalous oil did not rub off on him.

Frustrated Farmers

Sun-bronzed farmers were caught squarely in a boom-or-bust cycle in the postwar decade. While the fighting had raged, they had raked in money, hand over gnarled fist. But peace brought an end to high farm prices and to massive purchases by other nations, as foreign production reentered the stream of world commerce.

Machines also threatened to plow the farmer under an avalanche of his own over-abundant crops. The gasoline-engine tractor was working a revolution on American farms. This steel mule was to cultivation and sowing what the McCormick reaper was to harvesting. Blue-denimed farmers could sit on their chugging mechanized chariots and harrow many acres in a single day. But such improved efficiency and expanded agricultural production helped to pile up more price-dampening surpluses. A withering depression swept through agricultural districts in the 1920s, when one farm in four was sold for debt or taxes.

Schemes abounded for bringing relief to the hard-pressed farmers. A bipartisan "farm bloc" from the agricultural states coalesced in Congress in 1921 and succeeded in driving through some helpful laws. Noteworthy was the Capper-Volstead Act, which exempted farmers' marketing cooperatives from antitrust prosecution. The farm bloc's favorite proposal was the McNary-Haugen Bill, pushed energetically from 1924 to 1928. The McNary-Haugen Bill sought to keep agricultural prices high by authorizing the government to buy up surpluses and sell them abroad. Congress twice passed the bill, but frugal Coolidge twice vetoed it. Farm prices stayed low, and the farmers' political temperatures stayed high, reaching fever pitch in the election of 1924.

A Three-Way Race for the White House in 1924

Self-satisfied Republicans, chanting "Keep Cool and Keep Coolidge," nominated "Silent Cal" for the presidency at their convention in Cleveland in the simmering summer of 1924. Squabbling Democrats had more difficulty choosing a candidate when they met in New York's sweltering Madison Square Garden. Reflecting many of the cultural tensions of the decade, the party was hopelessly split between "wets" and "drys," urbanites and farmers, Fundamentalists and Modernists, northern liberals and southern stand-patters, immigrants and old-stock Americans. Deadlocked for an unprecedented 102 ballots, the convention at last turned wearily, sweatily, and unenthusiastically to John W. Davis. A wealthy Wall Street lawyer, the polished nominee was no less conservative than cautious Calvin Coolidge.

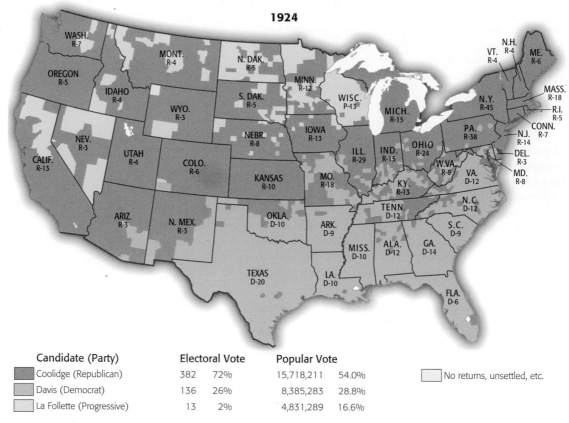

1924

Candidate (Party)	Electoral Vote		Popular Vote	
Coolidge (Republican)	382	72%	15,718,211	54.0%
Davis (Democrat)	136	26%	8,385,283	28.8%
La Follette (Progressive)	13	2%	4,831,289	16.6%

No returns, unsettled, etc.

Presidential Election of 1924 (showing popular vote by county)
Note the concentration of La Follette's votes in the old Populist strongholds of the Midwest and the mountain states. His ticket did especially well in the grain-growing districts battered by the postwar slump in agricultural prices. © Cengage Learning

The field was now wide open for a liberal candidate, and white-pompadoured Senator Robert ("Fighting Bob") La Follette of Wisconsin sprang forward to lead a new Progressive grouping. He gained the support of both the American Federation of Labor and the Socialist party, but his major constituency was the price-pinched farmers. La Follette's new Progressive party, only a shadow of the robust progressive coalition of prewar days, called for government ownership of railroads and relief for farmers, lashed out at monopoly and antilabor injunctions, and urged a constitutional amendment to limit the Supreme Court's power to invalidate laws passed by Congress.

La Follette turned in a respectable showing, polling nearly 5 million votes. But "Cautious Cal" and the oil-smeared Republicans slipped easily back into office, overwhelming Davis, 15,718,211 votes to 8,385,283. The electoral count stood at 382 for Coolidge, 136 for Davis, and 13 for La Follette, all from his home state of Wisconsin.

Foreign-Policy Flounderings

Isolation continued to reign in the Coolidge era. Despite presidential proddings, the Senate proved unwilling to allow America to adhere to the World Court—the judicial arm of the still-suspect League of Nations. Coolidge only halfheartedly—and unsuccessfully—pursued further naval disarmament after the loudly trumpeted agreements worked out at the Washington Conference in 1922.

A glaring exception to the United States' inward-looking indifference to the outside world in the 1920s was the armed interventionism in the Caribbean and Central America. American troops were withdrawn (after an eight-year stay) from the Dominican Republic in 1924, but they remained in Haiti from 1914 to 1934. President Coolidge in 1925 briefly removed American bayonets from troubled Nicaragua, where they had glinted intermittently since 1909, but in 1926 he sent them back, five thousand strong, and they stayed until 1933. When U.S. oil companies clamored for intervention in Mexico in 1926 to protect their interests there, Coolidge kept cool and defused the crisis with some skillful diplomatic negotiating. But his mailed-fist tactics elsewhere bred sore resentments south of the Rio Grande, where angry critics loudly assailed "*yanqui* imperialism."

Overshadowing all other foreign-policy problems in the 1920s was the knotty issue of international debts, a complicated tangle of private loans, Allied war debts, and German **reparations**. The key knot in the debt tangle was the $10 billion that the U.S. Treasury had loaned to the Allies during and immediately after the war. Uncle Sam held their IOUs—and he wanted to be paid. The Allies, in turn, protested that they had held up a wall of flesh and bone against the common foe until America the Unready had finally entered the fray. America, they argued, should write off its loans as war costs, just as the Allies had been tragically forced to write off the lives of millions of young men. And the final straw, protested the Europeans, was that America's postwar tariff walls made it almost impossible for them to sell the goods to earn the dollars to pay their debts.

reparations *Compensation by a defeated nation for damage done to civilians and their property during a war.*

Unraveling the Debt Knot

America's tightfisted insistence on getting its money back helped to harden the hearts of the Allies against conquered Germany. The French and the British demanded that the Germans make enormous reparations payments, totaling some $32 billion, as compensation for war-inflicted damages. The Allies hoped to settle their debts to America with the money received from Germany. The French, seeking to extort lagging reparations payments, sent troops into Germany's industrialized Ruhr Valley in 1923. Berlin responded by permitting its currency to inflate astronomically. At one point in October 1923, a loaf of bread cost 480 million marks, or about $120 million in preinflation money. German society teetered on the brink of mad anarchy, and the whole international house of financial cards threatened to flutter down in colossal chaos.

Sensible statesmen now urged that the war debts and reparations alike be drastically scaled down or canceled outright. But to Americans such proposals smacked of "welshing" on a debt. Scroogelike Calvin Coolidge turned aside suggestions of debt cancellation with a typically terse question: "They hired the money, didn't they?"

Reality finally dawned in the Dawes Plan of 1924. Negotiated largely by Charles Dawes, about to be Coolidge's running mate, it rescheduled German reparations payments and opened the way for further American private loans to Germany. The whole financial cycle now became still more complicated as U.S. bankers loaned money to Germany, Germany paid reparations to France and Britain, and the former Allies paid war debts to the United States. Clearly the source of this monetary merry-go-round was the flowing well of American credit. When that well dried up after the great crash in 1929, the tangled jungle of international finance quickly turned into a desert.

The United States never did get its money, but it harvested a bumper crop of ill will. Throughout Europe Uncle Sam was caricatured as Uncle Shylock, greedily whetting his knife for the last pound of Allied flesh. The bad taste left in American mouths by the whole sorry episode contributed powerfully to the storm-cellar neutrality legislation passed by Congress in the 1930s.

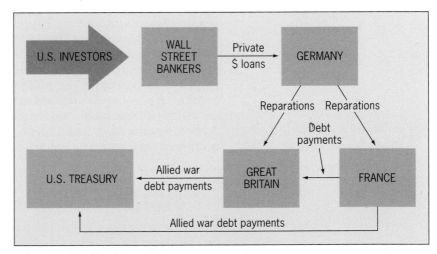

Aspects of the Financial Merry-Go-Round, 1921–1933 Great Britain, with a debt of over $4 billion to the U.S. Treasury, had a huge stake in proposals for inter-Allied debt cancellation, but France's stake was even larger. Less prosperous than Britain in the 1920s, and more battered by the war, which had been fought on its soil, France owed nearly $3.5 billion to the United States and additional billions to Britain.

The Triumph of Herbert Hoover in 1928

Poker-faced Calvin Coolidge, the tight-lipped "Sphinx of the Potomac," bowed out of the 1928 presidential race when he announced, "I do not choose to run." His logical successor was super-Secretary (of Commerce) Herbert Hoover. He was nominated on a platform that clucked contentedly over both prosperity and prohibition.

Still-squabbling Democrats nominated Alfred E. Smith, the wisecracking, glad-handing governor of New York and one of the most colorful personalities in American politics. "Al (cohol)" Smith was soakingly "wet" on prohibition, abrasively urban, and Roman Catholic in an overwhelmingly Protestant—and unfortunately prejudiced—land. Many dry, rural, and Fundamentalist Democrats gagged on his candidacy, and they saddled the wet Smith with a dry running mate and a dry platform.

Radio figured prominently in this campaign for the first time, and it helped Hoover more than Smith. The New Yorker had more personal sparkle, but he could not project it through the radio. Iowa-born Hoover, with his double-breasted dignity, came out of the microphone better than he went in.

Chubby-faced, ruddy-complexioned Herbert Hoover, with his painfully high starched collar, was a living example of the American success story and an intriguing mixture of two centuries. As a poor orphan boy who had worked his way through Stanford University, he had absorbed the nineteenth-century copybook maxims of industry, thrift, and self-reliance. As a fabulously successful mining engineer and businessman, he had honed to a high degree the efficiency doctrines of the progressive era.

A small-town boy from Iowa and Oregon, Hoover had traveled and worked abroad extensively. His experiences there had further strengthened his faith in American individualism, free enterprise, and small government. With his unshaken dignity and Quaker restraint, Hoover was a far cry from the typical backslapping politician. Personally colorless in public, he had been accustomed during much of his life to giving orders to subordinates and did not adapt readily to the necessary give-and-take of political accommodation.

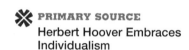

PRIMARY SOURCE
Herbert Hoover Embraces Individualism

As befitted America's newly mechanized civilization, Hoover was the ideal businessperson's candidate. A self-made millionaire, he recoiled from anything suggesting socialism, paternalism, or "planned economy." Yet as secretary of commerce, he had exhibited some progressive instincts. He endorsed labor unions and supported federal regulation of the new radio-broadcasting industry. He even flirted for a time with the idea of government-owned radio, similar to the British Broadcasting Corporation (BBC).

Despite the best efforts of Hoover and Smith, below-the-belt tactics were employed to a disgusting degree by their lower-level campaigners. Religious bigotry raised its hideous head over Smith's Catholicism. An irresponsible whispering campaign claimed that "A vote for Al Smith is a vote for the Pope" and that the White House, under Smith, would become a branch of the Vatican.

Hoover triumphed in a landslide. He bagged 21,391,993 popular votes to 15,016,169 for his embittered opponent, while rolling up an electoral count of 444 to 87. A huge Republican majority was returned to the House of Representatives. Tens of thousands of dry southern Democrats—"Hoovercrats"—rebelled against Al Smith. Hoover carried all the Border States and five states of the former Confederacy, the first Republican candidate in fifty-two years, except for Harding's Tennessee victory, to carry a state that had seceded.

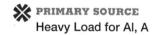

PRIMARY SOURCE
Heavy Load for Al, A

President Hoover's First Moves

Prosperity in the late 1920s smiled broadly as the Hoover years began. Soaring stocks on the bull market continued to defy the laws of financial gravitation. But two immense groups of citizens were not getting their share of the riches flowing from the national cornucopia: the unorganized wage earners and especially the disorganized farmers.

Hoover's administration, in line with its philosophy of promoting self-help, responded to the outcry of the farmers with the Agricultural Marketing Act. Passed by Congress in June 1929, it was designed to help the farmers help themselves, largely through producers' cooperatives. The Agricultural Marketing Act also set up a Federal Farm Board that provided generous loans to farm organizations seeking to buy, sell, and store agricultural surpluses.

Farmers also clutched at the tariff as a possible straw to keep their heads above the water of financial ruin. But the Hawley-Smoot Tariff of 1930, which started out in the House as a fairly reasonable measure designed to assist farmers, acquired more than a thousand amendments in the Senate and turned into the highest protective tariff in the nation's peacetime history. The average duty was raised from 38.5 percent to nearly 60 percent. To angered foreigners, the Hawley-Smoot Tariff seemed like a declaration of economic warfare. It widened the yawning trade gaps and plunged both America and other nations deeper into the terrible depression that had already begun. The Hawley-Smoot Tariff increased international financial chaos and forced the United States further into the bog of economic isolationism, thus directly abetting Adolf Hitler's demagogic rise to power in Germany.

Index of Common Stock Prices (1926 = 100)

The Great Crash Ends the Golden Twenties

When Herbert Hoover confidently took the presidential oath on March 4, 1929, America's productive colossus—stimulated by the automobile, radio, movie, and other new industries—was roaring along at a breathtaking speed that suggested a permanent plateau of prosperity. Prices on the stock exchange continued to spiral upward and create a fool's paradise of paper profits. A few prophets of disaster sounded warnings, but they were drowned out by the mad chatter of the ticker-tape machine.

A catastrophic crash came on "Black Tuesday," October 29, 1929, when 16,410,030 shares of stock were sold in a save-who-may scramble. Wall Street became a wailing wall as gloom and doom replaced boom. Losses, even in blue-chip securities, were unbelievable. By the end of 1929—two months after the initial crash—stockholders had lost $40 billion in paper values, or more than the total cost of World War I to the United States.

The stock-market collapse heralded a business depression, at home and abroad, that was the most prolonged and prostrating in American or world experience. No other industrialized nation suffered so severe a setback. By the end of 1930, more than 4 million workers in the United States were jobless; two years later the figure had about tripled. Hungry and despairing workers pounded pavements in search of nonexistent jobs ("We're firing, not hiring"). Where employees were not discharged, wages and salaries were often slashed. A current jingle ran:

> *Mellon pulled the whistle,*
> *Hoover range the bell*
> *Wall Street gave the signal*
> *And the country went to hell.*

The misery and gloom were incalculable, as forests of dead chimneys stood stark against the sky. Over five thousand banks collapsed in the first three years of the depression, carrying down with them the life savings of tens of thousands of ordinary citizens. Countless thousands of honest, hard-working people lost their homes and farms to the forecloser's hammer.

The Depression spectacle of want in the shadow of surplus moved an observer to write in Current History *(1932):*

"We still pray to be given each day our daily bread. Yet there is too much bread, too much wheat and corn, meat and oil and almost every commodity required by man for his subsistence and material happiness. We are not able to purchase the abundance that modern methods of agriculture, mining and manufacture make available in such bountiful quantities. Why is mankind being asked to go hungry and cold and poverty stricken in the midst of plenty?"

Breadlines formed, soup kitchens dispensed food, and apple sellers stood shivering on street corners trying to peddle their wares for five cents.

Families felt the stress, as jobless fathers nursed their guilt and shame at not being able to provide for their households. Breadless breadwinners often blamed themselves for their plight, despite abundant evidence that the economic system, not individual initiative, had broken down. Mothers meanwhile nursed fewer babies as hard times reached even into the nation's bedrooms, precipitating a decade-long dearth of births. As cash registers gathered cobwebs, the song "My God, How the Money Rolls In" was replaced by "Brother, Can You Spare a Dime?"

The Horn of Plenty Runs Dry

What caused the Great Depression? One basic explanation was overproduction by both farm and factory. Ironically, the depression of the 1930s was one of abundance, not want. It was the "great glut" or the "plague of plenty."

The nation's ability to produce goods had clearly outrun its capacity to consume or pay for them. Too much money was going into the hands of a few wealthy people, who invested it in factories and other agencies of production. Not enough was going into salaries and wages, where revitalizing purchasing power could be more quickly felt. Overexpansion of credit on so-called easy terms also caused many consumers to dive in beyond their depth.

This already bleak picture was further darkened by economic anemia abroad. Britain and the Continent had never fully recovered from the upheaval of World War I. A drying up of international trade, moreover, had been hastened by the shortsighted Hawley-Smoot Tariff of 1930.

By 1930 the depression had become a national calamity. Through no fault of their own, a host of industrious citizens had lost everything. They wanted to work—but there was no work. The insidious effect of all this dazed despair on the spirit was incalculable and long lasting. Hitherto the people had grappled with storms, trees, stones, and other

"Hooverville" in Seattle, 1934 In the early years of the depression, desperate, homeless people constructed shacks with scavenged materials. These shantytowns sprang up in cities across the country.

physical obstacles. But the depression was a baffling wraith they could not grasp. Initiative and self-respect were stifled, as panhandlers begged for food or "charity soup." In extreme cases "ragged individualists" slept under "Hoover blankets" (old newspapers), fought over the contents of garbage cans, or cooked their findings in old oil drums in tin-and-paper shanty-towns cynically named "Hoovervilles." The very foundations of America's social and political structure trembled.

Hoover's exalted reputation as a wonder-worker and effi-ciency engineer crashed about as dismally as the stock market. The perplexed president was impaled on the horns of a cruel dilemma. As a deservedly famed humanitarian, he was pro-foundly distressed by the widespread misery about him. Yet as a "rugged individualist," deeply rooted in an earlier era of free enterprise, he shrank from the heresy of government hand-outs. Convinced that industry, thrift, and self-reliance were the virtues that had made America great, he feared that a govern-ment doling out doles would weaken, or perhaps destroy, the national fiber.

Herbert Hoover (1874–1964) spoke approvingly in a campaign speech in 1928 of "the American system of Rugged Individualism." In 1930 he referred to Cleveland's 1887 veto of a bill to appropriate seed grain for the drought-stricken farmers of Texas:

"I do not believe that the power and duty of the General Government ought to be extended to the relief of individual suffering. ... The lesson should be constantly enforced that though the people support the Government the Government should not support the people."

As the depression nightmare steadily worsened, Hoover was finally forced to turn reluctantly from his doctrine of log-cabin individualism and accept the proposition that the welfare of the people was a direct concern of the national government. The president now worked out a compromise between the old hands-off philosophy and the "soul-destroying" handouts then being used in Britain. He would assist the hard-pressed railroads, banks, and rural credit cor-porations, in the hope that, if financial health were restored at the top of the economic pyramid, unemployment would be relieved at the bottom on a trickle-down basis.

Early in 1932 Congress, responding to Hoover's belated appeal, established the Reconstruction Finance Corporation (RFC). With an initial working capital of half a bil-lion dollars, this agency became a government, lending bank that provided indirect relief to insurance companies, banks, agricultural organizations, railroads, and even struggling

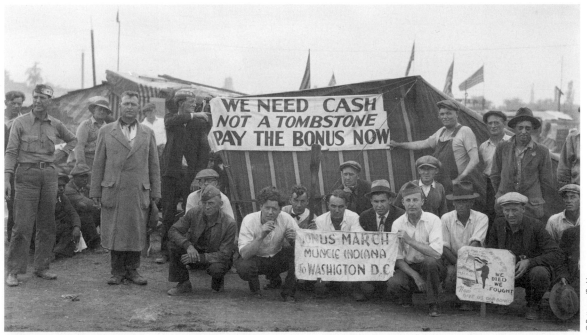

The Bonus Army in Washington, D.C., 1932 World War I veterans from Muncie, Indiana, were among many contingents to set up camp in the capital during the summer of 1932, determined to remain there until they received full payment of their promised bonuses.

EXAMINING THE EVIDENCE

LAMPOONING HOOVER, 1932

The pages of *The American Pageant* are filled with political cartoons that provide pungent commentary on historical events. With one image rather than many words, a cartoonist can convey a point of view much the way an editorial writer does. This cartoon appeared in the *Washington Daily News* on July 25, 1932, three and a half months before Republican president Hoover lost the presidential election to his Democratic challenger, Franklin D. Roosevelt. The cartoonist foretells Hoover's defeat in November and departure from the White House the following March (not January, as at present) and expresses his support for the Home Loan Bank Bill. With this proposal, Hoover sought to come to the aid of home mortgage lenders in order to forestall them from foreclosing on homeowners. The cartoonist jokes that Hoover supported this bill because he identified with homeowners about to lose their homes, but he also cleverly insinuates that Hoover's banking

reform was motivated by electoral opportunism. Surely Hoover sought to win public support in return for his new banking program as he battled for reelection, but the Home Loan Bank Bill also reflected Hoover's growing recognition that the federal government had to take direct action to remedy flaws that had precipitated the crisis of the Great Depression. As Hoover later recorded in his memoirs, "All this seems dull economics, but the poignant American drama revolving around the loss of the old homestead had a million repetitions straight from life, not because of the designing villain but because of a fault in our financial system."

1. How does the cartoonist use caricature to make his point?

2. What accounts for the political cartoon's special power?

3. Are there limitations to this genre? Find another cartoon in this book, and subject it to similar analysis.

The Washington Daily News, July 25, 1932 / The Franklin Delano Roosevelt Library, Hyde Park, New York

538

state and local governments. But to preserve individualism and character, there would be no loans to individuals from this "billion-dollar soup kitchen."

"**Pump-priming**" loans by the RFC were of widespread benefit, but the organization was established many months too late for maximum usefulness. Projects that the RFC supported were largely self-liquidating, and the government as a banker actually profited to the tune of many millions of dollars. Giant corporations so obviously benefited from this assistance that the RFC was dubbed—rather unfairly—"the millionaires' dole."

Hoover's administration also provided some indirect benefits for labor. After stormy debate, Congress passed the Norris–La Guardia Anti-Injunction Act in 1932, and Hoover signed it. The measure outlawed "yellow dog" (antiunion) contracts and forbade the federal courts to issue injunctions to restrain strikes, boycotts, and peaceful picketing.

The truth is that Herbert Hoover, despite criticism of his "heartlessness," did inaugurate a significant new policy. In previous panics the masses had been forced to "sweat it out." Slow though Hoover was to abandon this nineteenth-century bias, by the end of his term he had started down the road toward government assistance for needy citizens—a road that Franklin Roosevelt would travel much further.

Many veterans of World War I were numbered among the hard-hit victims of the depression. A drive developed for the premature payment of the deferred bonus voted by Congress in 1924 and payable in 1945. Thousands of impoverished veterans, both of war and of unemployment, prepared to move on Washington, there to demand of Congress the immediate payment of their *entire* bonuses. The "Bonus Expeditionary Force," which mustered about twenty thousand men, converged on the capital in the summer of 1932. These supplicants promptly set up unsanitary public camps on vacant lots—a gigantic "Hooverville."

Following riots that cost two lives, Hoover ordered the army to evacuate the unwanted guests. The eviction was carried out by General Douglas MacArthur with bayonets and tear gas in the inglorious "Battle of Anacostia Flats." The veterans' shantytown was put to the torch, a few of the former soldiers were injured, and an eleven-month-old "bonus baby" allegedly died from exposure to tear gas.

This brutal episode brought down additional abuse on the once-popular Hoover, who by now was the most loudly booed man in the country. Cynics sneered that the "Great Engineer" had in a few months "ditched, drained, and damned the country." The existing panic was unfairly branded "the Hoover depression." In truth, Hoover had been oversold as a wizard, and the public grumbled when his magician's wand failed to produce rabbits. The time was ripening for the Democratic party—and Franklin D. Roosevelt—to cash in on Hoover's calamities.

Japanese Aggression

The Great Depression, which brewed enough distress at home, added immensely to difficulties abroad. Militaristic Japan stole the East Asian spotlight. In September 1931, Japanese imperialists, noting that the Western world was badly mired down in depression, plunged into Manchuria. Alleging provocation, they rapidly overran the coveted Chinese province and proceeded to bolt shut the Open Door in the conquered area.

Americans were stunned by this act of naked aggression. Many, though by no means a majority, urged strong measures, ranging from boycotts to blockades. Possibly a tight blockade by the League of Nations, backed by the United States, would have brought Japan sharply to book. But the League was handicapped in taking two-fisted action by the non-membership of the United States. Washington flatly rebuffed initial attempts in 1931 to secure American cooperation in applying economic pressure on Japan.

Washington and Secretary of State Henry L. Stimson, in the end, decided to fire only paper bullets at the Japanese aggressors. The so-called Stimson Doctrine, proclaimed in 1932, declared that the United States would not recognize any territorial acquisitions achieved by force. Righteous indignation would substitute for solid initiatives. But there was no real sentiment for stronger measures among a depression-ridden people, who remained strongly isolationist during the 1930s.

pump priming *In economics, the spending or lending of a small amount of funds in order to stimulate a larger flow of economic activity.*

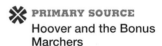 **PRIMARY SOURCE**
Hoover and the Bonus Marchers

Chapter Summary

The Republican governments of the 1920s carried out active, probusiness policies while undermining much of the progressive legacy by neglect or lack of enforcement. The Washington Naval Conference indicated America's strong desire in the 1920s to withdraw from international involvements. Sky-high tariffs protected America's booming industry but caused severe economic troubles elsewhere in the world and deepened the woes of farmers, who did not share in the nation's prosperity.

As the Harding scandals broke, Harding died and the puritanical Calvin Coolidge took office, thus avoiding political repercussions for the Republicans. Bitterly feuding Democrats—divided by region, religion, and culture—and La Follette Progressives fell easy victims to Republican-managed prosperity.

American demands for strict repayment of war debts created international economic difficulties and resentment of the United States. The Dawes Plan provided temporary relief, but the Hawley-Smoot Tariff proved another devastating blow to international trade. Herbert Hoover, a renowned businessman and humanitarian, won a landslide victory over Catholic Al Smith.

The stock-market crash of 1929 brought a sudden end to prosperity and plunged America into a horrible depression. Herbert Hoover's reputation collapsed as he failed to relieve national suffering, although he did make unprecedented but limited efforts to revive the economy through federal assistance.

KEY TERMS

dreadnought (529)

accomplice (530)

reparations (533)

pump priming (539)

PEOPLE TO KNOW

Warren G. Harding

Albert B. Fall

Calvin Coolidge

John W. Davis

Robert M. ("Fighting Bob") La Follette

Alfred E. Smith

Go to the History CourseMate website for primary source links, study tools, and review materials for this chapter. www.cengagebrain.com

33

The Great Depression and the New Deal

1933–1939

The country needs and . . . demands bold, persistent experimentation. It is common sense to take a method and try it. If it fails, admit it frankly and try another. But above all, try something.

FRANKLIN D. ROOSEVELT, CAMPAIGN SPEECH, 1932

✳ PRIMARY SOURCE
Untitled Caricature of FDR and Hoover

Voters were in an ugly mood as the presidential campaign of 1932 neared. Countless factory chimneys remained ominously cold, while more than 11 million unemployed workers and their families sank ever deeper into the pit of poverty.

Hoover, sick at heart, was renominated by the Republican convention in Chicago without great enthusiasm. The rising star in the Democratic firmament was Governor Franklin Delano Roosevelt of New York, a fifth cousin of Theodore Roosevelt. Like the Rough Rider, Franklin Roosevelt had been born to a wealthy New York family, had graduated from Harvard, had been elected as a kid-gloved politician to the New York legislature, had served as governor of the Empire State, had been nominated for the vice presidency (though not elected), and had served capably as assistant secretary of the navy. Although both men were master politicians, adept with the colorful phrase, TR was pugnacious and confrontational, whereas FDR was suave and conciliatory—qualities that appealed strongly to a people traumatized by one of the greatest crises in American history.

FOCUS QUESTIONS

1. What qualities did Franklin Roosevelt bring to the presidency and to his New Deal policies to alleviate the Depression and reform American society?

2. What were the primary New Deal efforts to achieve relief, recovery, and reform?

3. How did the early New Deal affect business, agriculture, and labor? Why did it meet such strong opposition from some quarters, including the Supreme Court?

4. How did Roosevelt politically mobilize the "New Deal coalition" of Southerners, Catholics, Jews, African Americans, and women to achieve his goals and lay the foundations for two generations of Democratic party dominance?

5. What were the New Deal's greatest successes and failures, in both the short term and in the decades after the Great Depression?

CHRONOLOGY

1932	Roosevelt defeats Hoover for presidency.	**1935**	WPA established. Wagner Act. Resettlement Administration. Social Security Act. Public Utility Holding Company Act. *Schechter* "sick chicken" case. CIO organized.
1933	Bank holiday. Emergency Banking Relief Act. Beer and Wine Revenue Act. Hundred Days Congress enacts HOLC, AAA, NRA, PWA, and TVA. Federal Securities Act. Glass-Steagall Banking Reform Act. CWA established. Twentieth Amendment (changed calendar of congressional sessions and date of presidential inauguration). Twenty-first Amendment (prohibition repealed). Nazis legally come to power in Germany with passage of Enabling Act.	**1936**	Soil Conservation and Domestic Allotment Act. Roosevelt defeats Landon for presidency.
		1937	USHA established. Roosevelt announces "court-packing" plan.
		1938	Second AAA. Fair Labor Standards Act.
1934	Gold Reserve Act. Securities and Exchange Commission authorized. Indian Reorganization Act. FHA established. Frazier-Lemke Farm Bankruptcy Act.	**1939**	Hatch Act. Reorganization Act.

FDR: Politician in a Wheelchair

dispossessed *The economically deprived.*

Infantile paralysis, while putting steel braces on Franklin Roosevelt's legs, put additional steel into his soul. Until 1921, when the dread disease struck, young Roosevelt—tall, athletic, and handsome—impressed observers as charming and witty yet at times as a superficial and arrogant "lightweight." But suffering humbled him to the level of common clay. In courageously fighting his way back from complete helplessness to a hobbling mobility, he schooled himself in patience, tolerance, compassion, and strength of will. He once remarked that, after trying for two years to wiggle one big toe, all else seemed easy.

In his successful campaign for the governorship of New York in 1928, Franklin Roosevelt (1882–1945) had played down alleged Democratic "socialism":

"We often hear it said that government operation of anything under the sun is socialistic. If that is so, our postal service is socialistic, so is the parcel post which has largely taken the place of the old express companies; so are the public highways which took the place of the toll roads."

Another of Roosevelt's great personal and political assets was his wife, Eleanor Roosevelt. The niece of Theodore Roosevelt, she was Franklin Roosevelt's distant cousin as well as his spouse. Tall, ungainly, and toothy, she overcame the misery of an unhappy childhood and emerged as a champion of the **dispossessed**—and ultimately as the "conscience of the New Deal." Through her lobbying of her husband, her speeches, and her syndicated newspaper column, Eleanor powerfully influenced the policies of the national government. Always she battled for the impoverished and the oppressed. At one meeting in Birmingham, Alabama, she confounded local authorities and flouted the segregation statutes by deliberately straddling the aisle that separated the black and white seating sections.

Eleanor Roosevelt marched to her own drummer. As a young woman she had worked in a New York settlement house, and later on she joined the Women's Trade Union League and the League of Women Voters. When she and Franklin moved into the White House, she brought an unprecedented number of women activists with her to Washington. This network of reformers helped make her the most active First Lady in history. Sadly, her personal relationship with her husband was often rocky due to his occasional infidelity. Condemned by conservatives and loved by liberals, Eleanor was one of the most controversial—and consequential—public figures of the twentieth century.

Franklin Roosevelt's political appeal was amazing. His commanding presence and his golden speaking voice, despite a sophisticated accent, combined to make him the premier American orator of his generation. He could turn on charm in private conversations as one would turn on a faucet. As a popular depression governor of New York, he had sponsored heavy state spending to relieve human suffering. Though favoring frugality, he believed that money, rather than humanity, was expendable. Roosevelt revealed a deep concern for the plight of the "forgotten man"—a phrase he used in a 1932 speech—although he was assailed by the rich as a "traitor to his class."

Exuberant Democrats met in Chicago in June 1932 and speedily nominated Roosevelt, who flew daringly through stormy weather to Chicago where he smashed precedent to accept the nomination in person. He electrified the delegates and the public with these words: "I pledge you, I pledge myself to a new deal for the American people."

Roosevelt Routs Hoover in 1932

In the campaign that followed, Roosevelt consistently preached a New Deal for the "forgotten man," but he was annoyingly vague and somewhat contradictory. Many of his speeches were ghostwritten by the "Brains Trust" (popularly the "Brain Trust"), a small group of reform-minded intellectuals. They were predominantly youngish college professors who, as a kind of kitchen cabinet, later authored much of the New Deal legislation. Roosevelt rashly promised a balanced budget and berated heavy Hooverian deficits. All of this was to make ironic reading in later months.

The high spirits of the Democrats found expression in the catchy air, "Happy Days Are Here Again." This theme song fit FDR's indestructible smile, his jauntily angled cigarette holder, his breezy optimism, and his promises to do something, even at the risk of bold experimentation. Meanwhile, grim-faced Herbert Hoover predicted on the campaign trail that if the Hawley-Smoot Tariff were repealed, the grass would grow "in the streets of a hundred cities." Such down-at-the-mouth gloom contrasted sharply with Roosevelt's tooth-flashing optimism and sparkling promises.

Hoover had been swept into office on the rising tide of prosperity; he was swept out by the receding tide of depression. The flood of votes totaled 22,809,638 for Roosevelt and 15,758,901 for Hoover; the electoral count stood at 472 to 59. In all, the loser carried only six rock-ribbed Republican states.

One striking feature of the election was a distinct shift of blacks from their traditional home in the Republican party of Lincoln to the Roosevelt camp. Beginning with the election of 1932, they became, notably in the great urban centers of the North, a vital element in the Democratic party.

Eleanor Roosevelt (1884–1962) America's most active First Lady, she commanded enormous popularity and influence during FDR's presidency. Here she emerges, miner's cap in hand, from an Ohio coal mine.

Defeated and repudiated, Hoover continued to be president for four long months, until March 4, 1933. But he was helpless to embark on any long-range policies without the cooperation of Roosevelt. In two meetings with Roosevelt, Hoover tried to bind his successor to an anti-inflationary policy that would have made impossible many of the later New Deal experiments. But Roosevelt refused to assume responsibility without authority and airily remarked to the press, "It's not my baby."

With Washington deadlocked, the vast and vaunted American economic machine clanked to a virtual halt. One worker in four tramped the streets, feet weary and hands idle. Banks were locking their doors all over the nation as people nervously stuffed paper money under their mattresses.

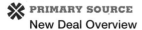

PRIMARY SOURCE
New Deal Overview

FDR and the Three Rs: Relief, Recovery, and Reform

Great crises often call forth gifted leaders, and the hand of destiny tapped Roosevelt on the shoulder. On a dreary inauguration day, March 4, 1933, his vibrant voice provided the American people with inspirational new hope. He denounced the "money changers" who had brought on the calamity, and he declared that the government must wage war on the Great Depression as it would wage war on an armed foe. His clarion note was, "Let me assert my firm belief that the only thing we have to fear is fear itself."

Roosevelt moved decisively. Now that he had full responsibility, he boldly declared a nationwide bank holiday, March 6–10, as a prelude to opening the banks on a sounder basis. He then summoned the overwhelmingly Democratic Congress into special session to cope with the national emergency. For the so-called Hundred Days (March 9–June 16, 1933), members hastily ground out an unprecedented basketful of remedial legislation.

Roosevelt's New Deal program aimed at three R's—relief, recovery, and reform. Short-range goals were relief and immediate recovery, especially in the first two years. Long-range goals were permanent recovery and reform of current abuses, particularly those that had produced the boom-or-bust catastrophe. The three-R objectives often overlapped and got in one another's way. But amid all the topsy-turvy haste, the gigantic New Deal program lurched forward.

Firmly ensconced in the driver's seat, President Roosevelt cracked the whip. A green Congress so fully shared the panicky feeling of the country that it was ready to **rubber-stamp** bills drafted by White House advisers. More than that, Congress gave the president extraordinary **blank-check** powers: some laws it passed expressly delegated legislative authority to the chief executive.

Roosevelt was delighted to exert executive leadership. He was inclined to do things by intuition—off the cuff. He was like the quarterback, as he put it, whose next play depends on the outcome of the previous play. So desperate was the mood of an action-starved public that any movement, even in the wrong direction, seemed better than no movement at all.

The frantic Hundred Days Congress passed many essentials of the New Deal's "three R's," though important long-range measures were added in later sessions. These reforms owed much to the legacy of the pre–World War I progressive movement. Many of them were long overdue, sidetracked by the war in Europe and the Old Guard reaction of the 1920s. In an explosive burst of pent-up energy, New Dealers raided file cabinets full of old pamphlets on German social insurance, English housing and garden cities, Danish agricultural recovery, and American World War I collectivization. In time, the New Dealers embraced progressive ideas such as unemployment insurance, old-age insurance, minimum-wage regulations, conservation and development of natural resources, and restrictions on child labor. They also invented some new schemes, such as the Tennessee Valley Authority (see p. 551). Soon, depression-weary Europeans came to marvel at the exciting din of reform activity underway in the United States.

rubber-stamp *To approve a plan or law quickly or routinely, without examination.*

blank-check *Referring to permission to use an unlimited amount of money or authority.*

The Champ: FDR Chatting with Reporters Roosevelt mastered the press as few presidents before or since have been able to do.

Roosevelt Tackles Money and Banking

Banking chaos cried aloud for immediate action. Congress pulled itself together and in an incredible eight hours had the Emergency Banking Relief Act of 1933 ready for Roosevelt's busy pen. The new law invested the president with power to regulate banking transactions and **foreign exchange** and to reopen solvent banks.

Roosevelt, the master showman, next turned to the radio to deliver the first of thirty famous "fireside chats." As some 35 million people hung on his soothing words, he gave assurances that it was now safer to keep money in a reopened bank than "under the mattress." Confidence returned with a gush, and the banks unlocked their doors.

The Hundred Days Congress also buttressed public reliance on the banking system by enacting the memorable Glass-Steagall Banking Reform Act. This measure provided for the Federal Deposit Insurance Corporation, which insured individual deposits up to $5,000 (later raised).

Roosevelt moved swiftly elsewhere on the financial front, seeking to protect the melting gold reserve and to prevent panicky **hoarding**. He ordered all private holdings of gold to be surrendered to the Treasury in exchange for paper currency and then took the nation off the gold standard.

The goal of Roosevelt's "managed currency" was inflation, which he believed would relieve debtors' burdens and stimulate new production. Roosevelt's principal instrument for achieving inflation was gold buying. He instructed the Treasury Department to purchase gold, ratcheting its price up from $21 an ounce in 1933 to $35 an ounce in 1934, a price that held for nearly four decades. This policy did increase the amount of dollars in circulation, as holders of gold cashed it in at the newly elevated prices, although "sound-money" critics gagged on the "baloney dollar." The gold-buying scheme came

foreign exchange *The transfer of credits or accounts between the citizens or financial institutions of different nations.*

hoarding *Secretly storing up quantities of goods or money.*

**Principal New Deal Acts During Hundred Days Congress, 1933
(items in parentheses indicate secondary purposes)**

Recovery	Relief	Reform
FDR closes banks, March 6, 1933 Emergency Banking Relief Act, March 9, 1933		
(Beer Act)	(Beer Act)	Beer and Wine Revenue Act, March 22, 1933
(CCC)	Unemployment Relief Act, March 31, 1933, creates Civilian Conservation Corps (CCC)	
FDR orders gold surrender, April 5, 1933 FDR abandons gold standard, April 19, 1933		
(FERA)	Federal Emergency Relief Act, May 12, 1933, creates Federal Emergency Relief Administration (FERA)	
(AAA)	Agricultural Adjustment Act (AAA), May 12, 1933	
(TVA)	(TVA)	Tennessee Valley Authority Act (TVA), May 18, 1933 Federal Securities Act, May 27, 1933
Gold-payment clause repealed, June 5, 1933		
(HOLC)	Home Owners' Refinancing Act, June 13, 1933, creates Home Owners' Loan Corporation (HOLC)	
National Industrial Recovery Act, June 16, 1933, creates National Recovery Administration (NRA), Public Works Administration (PWA)	(NRA, PWA)	(NRA)
(Glass-Steagall Act)	(Glass-Steagall Act)	Glass-Steagall Banking Reform Act, June 16, 1933, creates Federal Deposit Insurance Corporation

For later New Deal measures, see p. 556

to an end in February 1934, when FDR returned the nation to a limited gold standard for purposes of international trade only. Thereafter, the United States pledged itself to pay foreign bills, if requested, in gold at the rate of one ounce of gold for every $35 due. But domestic circulation of gold continued to be prohibited, and gold coins became collectors' items.

▪ Creating Jobs for the Jobless ▪

Overwhelming unemployment clamored for prompt remedial action. One out of every four workers was jobless when FDR took his inaugural oath—the highest level of unemployment in the nation's history. Roosevelt had no hesitancy about using federal money to assist the unemployed and at the same time to "prime the pump" of industrial recovery. (A farmer has to pour a little water into a dry pump—that is, "prime it"—to start the flow.)

The Hundred Days Congress responded to Roosevelt's spurs when it created the Civilian Conservation Corps (CCC). This agency provided employment in fresh-air government camps for about 3 million uniformed young men. Their useful work included reforestation, fire fighting, flood control, and swamp drainage. The recruits were required to help their parents by sending home most of their pay. Both human resources and natural resources were thus conserved.

The first major effort of the new Congress to grapple with the millions of adult unemployed was the Federal Emergency Relief Act. Its chief aim was immediate relief rather than long-range recovery. The resulting Federal Emergency Relief Administration (FERA) was handed over to zealous Harry L. Hopkins, a painfully thin, shabbily dressed, chain-smoking New York social worker who had earlier won Roosevelt's friendship and who became one of his most influential advisers. Hopkins's agency finally granted about $3 billion to the states for direct dole payments or preferably for wages on work projects.

Immediate relief was also given to two large and hard pressed special groups by the Hundred Days Congress. One section of the Agricultural Adjustment Act (AAA) made available many millions of dollars to help farmers meet their mortgages. Another law created the Home Owners' Loan Corporation (HOLC). Designed to refinance mortgages on nonfarm homes, it ultimately assisted about a million badly pinched households while simultaneously bailing out mortgage-holding banks.

Harassed by the continuing plague of unemployment, FDR himself established the Civil Works Administration (CWA) under Hopkins's direction late in 1933. Designed to provide temporary jobs during the cruel winter emergency, it employed tens of thousands of jobless people in leaf raking and other make-work tasks. The CWA served a useful purpose, although it was heavily criticized as "**boondoggling**."

Direct relief from Washington to needy families helped pull the nation through the ghastly winter of 1933–1934. But the disheartening persistence of unemployment and suffering demonstrated that emergency relief measures must be not only continued but supplemented.

✳ PRIMARY SOURCE
FDR's First Inaugural Address

boondoggle *To engage in trivial or useless work; any enterprise characterized by such work.*

▪ A Day for Every Demagogue ▪

One danger signal was the appearance of various demagogues, notably a magnetic "microphone messiah," Father Charles Coughlin, a Catholic priest in Michigan who began broadcasting in 1930 with the slogan "Social Justice." His anti–New Deal harangues to some 40 million radio fans finally became so anti-Semitic, fascistic, and demagogic that he was silenced in 1942 by his ecclesiastical superiors.

Also notorious among the new brood of agitators were those who capitalized on popular discontent to make pie-in-the-sky promises. Most conspicuous of these individuals were Dr. Francis E. Townsend, a retired California physician who promised everyone over sixty $200 a month, and Senator Huey P. ("Kingfish") Long of Louisiana, who was said to have more brass than a government mule. Long used his abundant rabble-rousing talents to publicize his "Share Our Wealth" program, which promised to make "Every Man a King." Every family was to receive $5,000, supposedly at the expense of the prosperous. H. L. Mencken called Long's chief lieutenant, former clergyman Gerald L. K. Smith, "the deadliest and damndest orator ever heard on this or any other earth, the champion boob-bumper of all time." Fear of Long's becoming a **fascist** dictator ended when he was shot by an assassin in the Louisiana state capitol in 1935.

Father Coughlin and Huey Long frightened many Americans because they raised troubling questions about the link between fascism and economic crisis. Danger seemed to be lurking ominously in many corners of the world. Authoritarian rule was strengthening in Japan, while Adolf Hitler was acquiring absolute authority in Germany. Some

fascist (fascism) *A political system or philosophy that advocates a mass-based party dictatorship, extreme nationalism, racism, and the glorification of war.*

In 1935 Father Charles Coughlin (1891–1979) single-handedly defeated President Roosevelt's effort to win Senate ratification of a treaty providing for American membership in the World Court, a judicial body of limited authority established by the League of Nations. What FDR saw as a symbolic embrace of international responsibility Coughlin convinced his radio listeners was a conspiracy of international moneyed interests against American sovereignty:

"Our thanks are due to Almighty God in that America retains her sovereignty. Congratulations to the aroused people of the United States who, by more than 200,000 telegrams containing at least 1,000,000 names, demanded that the principles established by Washington and Jefferson shall keep us clear from foreign entanglements and European hatreds."

even worried that Franklin Roosevelt himself would turn into a dictator.

Partly to quiet the groundswell of unrest that might lead to a political explosion, Congress authorized the Works Progress Administration (WPA) in 1935. The objective was employment on useful projects. Launched under the supervision of the ailing but energetic Hopkins, this remarkable agency ultimately spent about $11 billion on thousands of public buildings, bridges, and hard-surfaced roads. The WPA also controlled crickets in Wyoming and built a monkey pen in Oklahoma City. One of the most well-loved WPA programs was the Federal Art Project, which hired artists to create posters and murals—many still adorning post office walls. Critics sneered that WPA meant "We Provide Alms." But the fact is that over a period of eight years, nearly 9 million people were given jobs, not handouts.

Agencies of the WPA also found part-time occupations for needy high school and college students and for such unemployed white-collar workers as actors, musicians, and writers. John Steinbeck, future Nobel Prize novelist, counted dogs in his California county. Cynical taxpayers condemned lessons in tap dancing, as well as the painting of scenes on post office walls. But much precious talent was nourished, self-respect was preserved, and more than a million pieces of art were created, many of them publicly displayed.

New Visibility for Women

Just over a decade after the ratification of the Nineteenth Amendment, American women began to carve a larger space for themselves in the nation's political and intellectual life. First Lady Eleanor Roosevelt may have been the most visible woman in the Roosevelt White House, but she was hardly the only female voice. Secretary of Labor Frances Perkins (1880–1965) became the first woman cabinet member. Mary McLeod Bethune (1875–1955), director of the Office of Minority Affairs in the National Administration, served as the highest ranking African American in the Roosevelt administration.

Women also made important contributions in the social sciences, and especially in the relatively new and open field of anthropology. The landmark book by Ruth Benedict (1887–1948), *Patterns of Culture*, established the study of cultures as collective personalities. One of Benedict's students, Margaret Mead (1901–1978), drew from her own scholarly studies of adolescence among Pacific island peoples to advance bold new ideas about sexuality, gender roles, and intergenerational relationships.

Pearl S. Buck, raised in China by missionary parents, gained fame as a novelist by introducing American readers to Chinese peasant society. Her best-selling novel, *The Good Earth* (1931), earned her the Nobel Prize for literature in 1938.

A Helping Hand for Industry and Labor

A daring attempt to stimulate a nationwide comeback was initiated when the Hundred Days Congress authorized the National Recovery Administration (NRA). This ingenious scheme was by far the most complex and far-reaching effort by the New Dealers to combine immediate relief with long-range recovery and reform. Triple-barreled, the NRA was designed to assist industry, labor, and the unemployed.

Individual industries—over two hundred in all—were to work out codes of "fair competition," under which hours of labor would be reduced so that employment could be spread over more people. A ceiling was placed on the maximum hours of labor; a floor was placed under wages to establish minimum levels.

Labor, under the NRA, was granted additional benefits. Workers were formally guaranteed the right to organize and bargain collectively through representatives *of their own choosing.* The hated "yellow dog," or antiunion, contract was expressly forbidden, and certain safeguarding restrictions were placed on the use of child labor.

Enthusiasm for industrial recovery through the NRA was stirred by patriotic mass meetings and huge parades, which included 200,000 marchers on New York City's Fifth Avenue. A handsome blue eagle was designed as the symbol of the NRA, and Philadelphia's newly formed professional football team was named the Eagles. Such was the enthusiasm for the NRA that for a brief period there was a marked upswing of business activity.

But the high-flying eagle gradually fluttered to earth. The "fair competition" codes required too much self-denial by labor, industry, and the public for such a scheme to work. Critics began to brand the NRA "Nuts Running America," symbolized by what Henry Ford called "that damn Roosevelt buzzard." Complete collapse was imminent when, in 1935, the Supreme Court shot down the dying eagle in the *Schechter* "sick chicken" decision. The learned justices unanimously held that Congress could not "delegate legislative powers" to the executive. They further declared that congressional control of interstate commerce could not properly apply to a local fowl business, such as that of the Schechter brothers in Brooklyn. Roosevelt was incensed by this "horse and buggy" interpretation of the Constitution, but actually the Court helped him out of a bad jam.

The same act of Congress that hatched the NRA eagle also authorized the Public Works Administration (PWA), likewise intended both for industrial recovery and for unemployment relief. The agency was headed by acid-tongued Secretary of the Interior Harold L. Ickes, a free-swinging former bull mooser. Long-range recovery was the primary purpose of the new agency, and in time over $4 billion was spent on some thirty-four thousand projects, which included public buildings, highways, and parkways.

One spectacular PWA achievement was the Grand Coulee Dam on the Columbia River. In the depths of the depression, the towering dam seemed the height of folly. It made possible the irrigation of millions of acres of new farmland—at a time when the government was desperately trying to reduce farm surpluses. It created vast amounts of electrical power—in a region with little industry and virtually no market for additional power. But with the outbreak of World War II and then postwar prosperity, the dam would come to seem a stroke of genius, transforming the entire region with abundant water and power.

Special stimulants aided the recovery of one segment of business—the liquor industry. The Hundred Days Congress, in one of its earliest acts, legalized and taxed "light" wine and beer (3.2 percent alcohol), providing new employment and federal revenue. Prohibition was officially repealed by the Twenty-first Amendment late in 1933 (see Appendix)—and the saloon doors swung open.

Paying Farmers Not to Farm

Ever since the war-boom days of 1918, farmers had suffered from low prices and overproduction, especially of grain. During the depression, conditions became desperate as innumerable mortgages were foreclosed, corn was burned for fuel, and embattled farmers tried to prevent shipment of crops to glutted markets. In Iowa several volatile counties were placed under martial law.

A radical new approach to farm recovery was embraced when the Hundred Days Congress established the Agricultural Adjustment Administration (AAA). Through "artificial scarcity" this agency was to establish "**parity** prices" for basic commodities. "Parity" was the price set for a product that gave it the same real value, in purchasing power, that it had enjoyed during the period from 1909 to 1914. The AAA would eliminate price-depressing surpluses by paying growers to reduce their crop acreage.

Unhappily, the AAA got off to a wobbly start. It was begun after much of the cotton crop for 1933 had been planted, and balky mules, trained otherwise, were forced to plow under countless young plants. Several million squealing pigs were purchased and slaughtered. Much of their meat was distributed to persons on relief, but some of it was used for fertilizer. This "sinful" destruction of food, at a time when thousands of citizens were

parity *Equivalence in monetary value under different conditions; specifically, in the United States, the price for farm products that would give the products the same purchasing power as in the period 1909–1914.*

Novelist John Steinbeck (1902–1968) related in his novel The Grapes of Wrath *(1939) that when the "Okies" and "Arkies" reached California, they found the big growers unwilling to pay more than twenty-five cents an hour for work in the fields. One owner mutters:*

"A Red is any son-of-a-bitch that wants thirty cents an hour when we're paying twenty-five!"

hungry, increased condemnation of the American economic system by many left-leaning voices. The much-criticized AAA was itself plowed under in 1936 by the Supreme Court, which declared its regulatory taxation provisions unconstitutional.

The New Deal recovered from this blow by passing the Soil Conservation and Domestic Allotment Act (1936), which paid subsidies to farmers if they planted soil-conserving crops, such as soybeans, or let their land lie fallow. The Second Agricultural Adjustment Act of 1938 permitted parity payments if farmers observed acreage restrictions on commodities such as cotton and wheat. Other provisions of the new AAA were designed to give farmers not only a fairer price but a more substantial share of the national income. Both goals were partially achieved.

Dust Bowls and Black Blizzards

Nature meanwhile had been providing some unplanned scarcity. Late in 1933 a prolonged drought struck the states of the trans-Mississippi Great Plains. Rainless weeks were followed by furious, whining winds, while the sun was darkened by millions of tons of powdery topsoil torn from homesteads that stretched from eastern Colorado to western Missouri—soon to be dubbed the "Dust Bowl." Despondent citizens sat on front porches with protective masks on their faces, watching their farms swirl by. Overawed victims of the Dust Bowl predicted the end of the world or the second coming of Christ.

Burned and blown out of the Dust Bowl, tens of thousands of refugees fled their ruined acres. In five years about 350,000 Oklahomans and Arkansans—"Okies" and "Arkies"—trekked to southern California in "junkyards on wheels." Undeterred by signs telling them to "KEEP OUT," many found new homes in the San Joaquin Valley, which shared much in common with the southern plains—arid climate, cotton growing, newfound oil deposits, and abundant land. Yet the transition was cruel. Food, shelter, and

clothing were scarce; the winter months, without work and heat, proved nearly unendurable for the migrants. The dismal story of these human tumbleweeds was realistically portrayed in John Steinbeck's best-selling novel *The Grapes of Wrath* (1939), which proved to be the *Uncle Tom's Cabin* of the Dust Bowl.

Zealous New Dealers, sympathetic toward these desperate soil-tillers, made various efforts to relieve their burdens. The Frazier-Lemke Farm Bankruptcy Act, passed in 1934, made possible a suspension of mortgage foreclosures for five years; a revised version was upheld by the Supreme Court. In 1935 the president set up the Resettlement Administration to help farmers move to better land. And more than 200 million young trees were successfully planted on the bare prairies as windbreaks by the young men of the Civilian Conservation Corps.

Native Americans also felt the far-reaching hand of New Deal reform. Commissioner of Indian Affairs John Collier ardently sought to reverse the forced-assimilation policies in place since the Dawes Act of 1887. The Indian Reorganization Act of 1934 (the "Indian New Deal") encouraged tribes to establish local self-government, helped stop the loss of Indian lands, and revived tribes' interest in their identities and cultures. Nearly two hundred tribes established governments under its provisions, though seventy-seven others refused to organize.

Library of Congress

An Okie Family Hits the Road in the 1930s to Escape the Dust Bowl

Reforming Business and Creating Public Power

Reformist New Dealers were determined from the outset to curb the "money changers" who had played fast and loose with gullible investors before the Wall Street crash of 1929. The Hundred Days Congress passed the "Truth in Securities Act" (Federal Securities Act), which required promoters to transmit to the investor sworn information regarding the soundness of their stocks and bonds. In 1934 Congress took further steps to protect the public against fraud, deception, and inside manipulation. It authorized the Securities and Exchange Commission (SEC), which was designed as a watchdog administrative agency. Stock markets henceforth were to operate more as trading marts and less as gambling casinos.

New Dealers likewise directed their fire at public utility holding companies, those super-corporations. When Chicagoan Samuel Insull's multibillion-dollar financial empire crashed in 1932, citizens rebelled against such pyramided layers of big business. The Public Utility Holding Company Act of 1935 delivered a "death sentence" to this type of bloated growth.

Inevitably, the sprawling electric-power industry also attracted the fire of New Deal reformers. Within a few decades it had risen from nothingness to a behemoth with an investment of $13 billion. As a public utility, it reached directly and regularly into the pocketbooks of millions of consumers for vitally needed services. Ardent New Dealers accused the electric-power industry of gouging the public with excessive rates, especially because it owed its success to having secured, often for a song, priceless water-power sites from the public domain.

The tempestuous Tennessee River provided New Dealers with a rare opportunity. With its tributaries, the river drained a badly eroded area about the size of England containing some 2.5 million of the most poverty-stricken people in America. The federal government already owned valuable properties at Muscle Shoals, where it had erected plants for needed nitrates in World War I. By developing the hydroelectric potential of the entire area, Washington could combine the immediate advantage of putting thousands of people to work with a long-term project for reforming the power monopoly.

An act that created the Tennessee Valley Authority (TVA) was passed in 1933 by the Hundred Days Congress. This far-ranging enterprise was largely a result of the steadfast vision and unflagging zeal of Senator George W. Norris of Nebraska, after whom one of the mighty dams was named. From the standpoint of "planned economy," the TVA was by far the most revolutionary of all New Deal schemes.

New Dealers pointed a prideful finger at the amazing achievements of the TVA. The gigantic project brought to the area not only cheap power but full employment, low-cost housing, abundant cheap nitrates, restoration of eroded soil, reforestation, improved navigation, and flood control.

Exulting New Dealers agitated for parallel enterprises in the valleys of the Columbia, Colorado, and Missouri Rivers. Hydroelectric power from federally built dams would drive the growth of the urban West, and the waters the dams diverted would nurture agriculture in the previously bone-dry western deserts. But conservative reaction against the "socialistic" New Deal confined the TVA's brand of federally guided resource management and comprehensive regional development to the Tennessee Valley.

✳ PRIMARY SOURCE
Oct. 29, Dies Irae

Housing Reform and Social Security

The New Deal had meanwhile framed sturdy new policies for housing construction. To speed recovery and improve homes, Roosevelt set up the Federal Housing Administration (FHA) as early as 1934. The building industry was to be stimulated by small loans to householders. So popular did the FHA prove to be that it was one of the few "alphabetical agencies" to outlast the age of Roosevelt.

Congress bolstered the program in 1937 by authorizing the United States Housing Authority (USHA)—an agency designed to lend money to states or communities for low-cost construction. Although units for about 650,000 low-income people were started, new building fell tragically short of needs. New Deal efforts to expand the project collided with brick-wall opposition from real estate promoters, builders, and landlords ("slumlords"), to say nothing of anti–New Dealers who attacked what they considered down-the-rathole spending. Nonetheless, for the first time in a century the slum areas in America ceased growing and even shrank.

Incomparably more important was the success of New Dealers in the field of unemployment insurance and old-age pensions. Their greatest victory was the Social Security Act of 1935—one of the most complicated and far-reaching laws ever to pass Congress. To cushion future depressions, the measure provided for federal-state unemployment insurance. To provide security for old age, specified categories of retired workers were to receive regular payments from Washington, ranging from $10 to $85 a month (later raised), and these pensions were financed by a payroll tax on both employers and employees. Provision was also made for the blind, the physically handicapped, and dependent children.

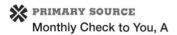

✳ PRIMARY SOURCE
Monthly Check to You, A

Social Security was largely inspired by the example of some of the more highly industrialized nations of Europe. The United States government was now recognizing its responsibility for the economic welfare of its citizens. By 1939 more than 45 million people were eligible for Social Security benefit. In subsequent years further categories of workers were added, belatedly including farm and domestic workers. For decades, millions of poor men and women were excluded from Social Security. In contrast to Europe, where welfare programs generally were universal, American workers had to be employed and in certain kinds of jobs to get coverage.

A New Deal for Unskilled Labor

collective bargaining *Bargaining between an employer and his or her organized work force over hours, wages, and other conditions of employment.*

The NRA blue eagles, with their call for **collective bargaining**, had been a godsend to organized labor. As New Deal expenditures brought some slackening of unemployment, labor began to feel more secure and hence more self-assertive. A rash of walkouts occurred in the summer of 1934, including a paralyzing general strike in San Francisco. When the Supreme Court axed the blue eagle, a Congress sympathetic to labor unions undertook to fill the vacuum. The fruit of its deliberations was the Wagner Act of 1935—known by the name of its congressional sponsor, New York Senator Robert F. Wagner—formally, the National Labor Relations Act. This trailblazing law created a powerful new National Labor Relations Board and reasserted the right of labor to engage in self-organization and to bargain collectively through representatives of its own choice. Considered the Magna Carta of American labor, the Wagner Act proved to be a major milestone for American workers.

Under the encouragement of a highly sympathetic National Labor Relations Board, a host of unskilled workers began to organize themselves into effective unions. The leader of this drive was beetle-browed, domineering, and melodramatic John L. Lewis, boss of the United Mine Workers. In 1935 he succeeded in forming the Committee for Industrial Organization (CIO) within the ranks of the skilled-craft American Federation of Labor. But skilled workers, ever since the days of the ill-fated Knights of Labor in the 1880s, had shown only lukewarm sympathy for the cause of unskilled labor, especially blacks. In 1936, following inevitable friction with the CIO, the older federation suspended the upstart unions associated with the newer organization.

Undaunted, the rebellious CIO moved on a concerted scale into the huge automobile industry. Late in 1936 the workers resorted to a revolutionary technique known as the sit-down strike: they refused to leave the factory buildings of General Motors at Flint, Michigan, and thus prevented the importation of strikebreakers. Conservative respecters of private property were scandalized. The CIO finally won a resounding victory when its union, after heated negotiations, was recognized by General Motors as the sole bargaining agency for its employees.

Roosevelt's "Coddling" of Labor

Unskilled workers now pressed their advantage. The United States Steel Corporation, previously an impossible nut for labor to crack, averted a costly strike when it voluntarily granted rights of unionization to its CIO-organized employees. But the "little steel" companies fought back savagely. Citizens were shocked in 1937 by the Memorial Day massacre at the plant of the Republic Steel Company in South Chicago, where police fire killed or wounded several score picketers.

A better deal for labor continued when Congress, in 1938, passed the memorable Fair Labor Standards Act (Wages and Hours Bill). Industries involved in interstate commerce were to set up minimum-wage and maximum-hour levels. The eventual goals were forty cents an hour (later raised) and a forty-hour week. Labor by children under sixteen (under eighteen if the occupation was dangerous) was forbidden. These reforms were bitterly though futilely opposed by many industrialists, especially by those southern textile manufacturers who had profited from low-wage labor.

In later New Deal days, labor unionization flourished; "Roosevelt wants you to join a union" was the rallying cry of professional organizers. The president received valuable support at ballot-box time from labor leaders and many appreciative working people. One mill worker remarked that Roosevelt was "the only man we ever had in the White House who would know that my boss is an s.o.b."

The CIO surged forward, breaking completely with the AF of L in 1938. On that occasion the *Committee* for Industrial Organization was formally reconstituted as the *Congress* of Industrial Organizations (the new CIO), under the high-handed presidency of John L. Lewis. By 1940 the CIO could claim about 4 million members in its constituent unions, including some 200,000 blacks.

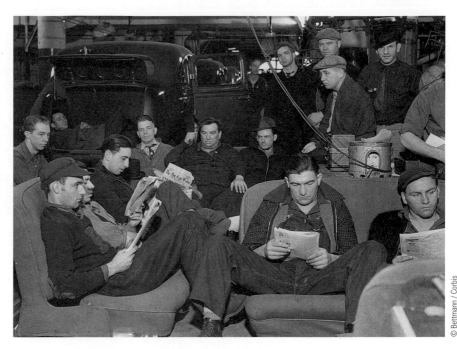

General Motors Sit-Down Strikers, Flint, Michigan, 1937 Strikers like these sometimes kept their spirits up with the song "Sit Down":

When the boss won't talk
Don't take a walk;
Sit down, sit down.

Landon Challenges "the Champ" in 1936

As the presidential campaign of 1936 neared, the New Dealers were on top of the world. They had achieved considerable progress, and millions of "reliefers" were grateful to their bountiful government. The exultant Democrats renominated Roosevelt on a platform squarely endorsing the New Deal.

The Republicans were hard pressed to find someone to feed to "the Champ." They finally settled on the colorless but homespun and honest governor of Kansas, Alfred M. Landon. Landon himself was a moderate who accepted some New Deal reforms, although not the popular Social Security Act. But the Republican platform vigorously condemned the New Deal for its radicalism, experimentation, confusion, and "frightful waste." Backing Landon, ex-president Hoover called for a "holy crusade for liberty," echoing the cry of the American Liberty League, a group of wealthy conservatives organized to fight "socialistic" New Deal schemes.

Roosevelt gave as good as he got. Angry enough to stretch sheet iron, Roosevelt took to the stump and denounced the "economic royalists" who sought to "hide behind the flag and the Constitution." "I welcome their hatred," he proclaimed.

A landslide overwhelmed Landon as the demoralized Republicans carried only two states, Maine and Vermont. The popular vote was 27,752,869 to 16,674,665; the electoral count was 523 to 8—the most lopsided in 116 years. A good-humored newspaper columnist quipped, "If Landon had given one more speech, Roosevelt would have carried Canada, too." Democratic majorities were again returned to Congress. Jubilant Democrats could now claim more than two-thirds of the seats in the House and a like proportion in the Senate.

The battle of 1936, perhaps the most bitter since Bryan's defeat in 1896, partially bore out Republican charges of class warfare. Even more than in 1932, the needy economic groups were lined up against the so-called greedy economic groups. CIO units contributed generously to FDR's campaign chest. Many **left-wingers** turned to Roosevelt, as the

left *(or* **left-wingers***) In politics, groups or parties that traditionally advocate progress, social change, greater economic and social equality, and the welfare of the common person. (The* **right** *or* **right-wing** *is traditionally groups or parties that advocate adherence to tradition, established authorities, and acceptance of a greater degree of economic and social hierarchy.)*

© Bettmann / Corbis

The Rise and Decline of Organized Labor, 1900–2002 The percentage of the total labor force that was organized increased until 1954, and it has declined ever since, except for a brief rise in the 1990s among service and government workers. (Source: Bureau of Labor Statistics, *Statistical Abstract of the United States*, 2003.)

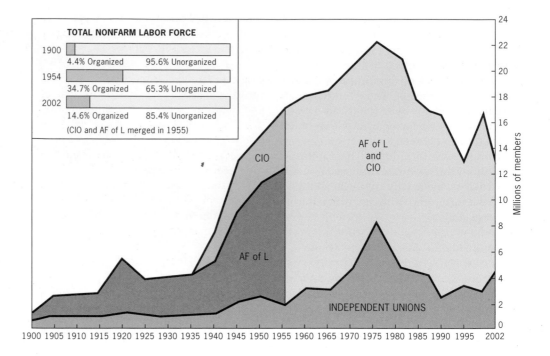

customary third-party protest vote sharply declined. Blacks, several million of whom had also appreciated relief checks, had by now largely shaken off their traditional allegiance to the Republican party. To them, Lincoln was "finally dead."

FDR won primarily because he appealed to the "forgotten man," whom he never forgot. Roosevelt in fact had forged a powerful and enduring coalition of the South, blacks, urbanites, and the poor. He proved especially effective in marshaling the support of the multitudes of "New Immigrants"—mostly Catholics and Jews who had swarmed into the great cities since the turn of the century. These once-scorned newcomers, with their now-numerous sons and daughters, had at last come politically of age. In the 1920s, one out of every twenty-five federal judgeships went to a Catholic; Roosevelt appointed Catholics to one out of every four.

Conflict over the Court

Bowing his head to the sleety blasts, Roosevelt took the presidential oath on January 20, 1937, instead of the traditional March 4. The Twentieth Amendment to the Constitution had been ratified in 1933. (See the Appendix.) It swept away the postelection lame duck session of Congress and shortened by six weeks the awkward period before inauguration.

Flushed with victory, Roosevelt interpreted his reelection as a mandate to continue New Deal reforms. But in his eyes the cloistered old men on the supreme bench, like fossilized stumbling blocks, stood stubbornly in the pathway of progress. In nine major cases involving the New Deal, the Roosevelt administration had been thwarted seven times. The Supreme Court was ultraconservative, and six of the nine oldsters in black were over seventy. As luck would have it, not a single member had been appointed by FDR in his first term.

Roosevelt, his "Dutch up," viewed with mounting impatience what he regarded as the obstructive conservatism of the Court. To overcome such obstructionism, Roosevelt finally hit upon a Court scheme that he regarded as "the answer to a maiden's prayer." In fact, it proved to be one of the most costly political misjudgements of his career. Roosevelt's brainstorm, which caught Congress and the country by complete surprise, was a call for legislation that would permit him to add a new justice to the Supreme Court for every member over seventy who would not retire. The maximum membership could then be fifteen.

✳ PRIMARY SOURCE
Of Course He Can't Want This

Congress and the nation were promptly convulsed over Roosevelt's **"court-packing"** **plan** to expand the Supreme Court. Franklin "Double-crossing" Roosevelt was savagely condemned for attempting to break down the delicate **checks and balances** among the three branches of the government.

The Court had meanwhile seen the ax hanging over its head. Whatever his motives, Justice Owen J. Roberts, formerly regarded as a conservative, began to vote on the side of his liberal colleagues. "A switch in time saves nine" was the classic witticism inspired by this change. By a five-to-four decision, the Court, in March 1937, upheld the principle of a state minimum wage for women, thereby reversing its stand on a different case a year earlier. In succeeding decisions a Court more sympathetic to the New Deal upheld the National Labor Relations Act (Wagner Act) and the Social Security Act.

With these changes under way, Congress refused to endorse the court-packing scheme, and Roosevelt suffered his first major legislative defeat at the hands of his own party. Yet in losing this battle, Roosevelt incidentally won his campaign. The Court, as he had hoped, became markedly more friendly to New Deal reforms. Furthermore, a succession of deaths and resignations enabled him to make nine appointments to the tribunal.

Yet in a sense FDR lost both the Court battle and the war. He so aroused conservatives of both parties in Congress that few New Deal reforms were passed after 1937, the year of the fight to "pack" the Supreme Court. With this catastrophic miscalculation, he squandered much of the political goodwill that had carried him to such a resounding victory in the 1936 election.

court-packing plan *Franklin Roosevelt's politically motivated and ill-fated scheme to add a new justice to the Supreme Court for every member over seventy who would not retire.*

checks and balances *In American politics, the interlocking system of divided and counterweighted authority among the executive, legislative, and judicial branches of government.*

The Twilight of the New Deal

Roosevelt's first term, from 1933 to 1937, did not banish the depression from the land. Unemployment stubbornly persisted in 1936 at about 15 percent, down from the grim 25 percent of 1933 but still miserably high. Despite the inventiveness of New Deal programs and the billions of dollars in "pump priming," recovery had been dishearteningly modest, though the country seemed to be inching its way back to economic health.

Then, in 1937 the economy took another sharp downturn, a surprisingly severe depression-within-the-depression that the president's critics quickly dubbed the "Roosevelt recession." In fact, government policies had caused the nosedive, as new Social Security taxes began to bite into payrolls and as the administration cut back on spending out of continuing reverence for the orthodox economic doctrine of the balanced budget.

Only at this late date did Roosevelt at last frankly and deliberately embrace the recommendations of the British economist John Maynard Keynes. The New Deal had run deficits for several years, but all of them had been rather small and none was intended. Now, in April 1937, FDR announced a bold program to stimulate the economy by planned deficit spending. Although the deficits were still undersized for the Herculean task of conquering the depression, this abrupt policy reversal endorsing "Keynesianism" marked a turning point in the government's relation to the economy. "**Keynesianism**"—the use of government spending and fiscal policy to "prime the pump" of the economy and encourage consumer spending—became the new economic orthodoxy and remained so for decades.

Keynesianism *An economic theory based on the thoughts of British economist John Maynard Keynes, holding that central banks should adjust interest rates and governments should use deficit spending and tax policies to increase purchasing power and hence prosperity.*

Roosevelt had meanwhile been pushing the remaining reform measures of the New Deal. But only a few of his proposals made it through an increasingly conservative Congress. The Reorganization Act gave him limited administrative reforms, including the key new Executive Office in the White House. The Hatch Act of 1939 barred federal officials from political campaigning, soliciting, or using government funds for political purposes. But such clever ways of getting around it were found that the legislation proved disappointing.

By 1938 the New Deal had clearly lost most of its early momentum. Magician Roosevelt could find few dazzling new reform rabbits to pull out of his tall silk hat. In the congressional elections of 1938 the Republicans, for the first time, cut heavily into the New Deal majorities in Congress, though

A basic objective of the New Deal was featured in Roosevelt's second inaugural address (1937):

"I see one-third of a nation ill-housed, ill-clad, ill-nourished. … The test of our progress is not whether we add more to the abundance of those who have much; it is whether we provide enough for those who have too little."

failing to gain control of either house. The international crisis that came to a boil in 1938–1939 shifted public attention away from domestic reform and no doubt helped save the political hide of the Roosevelt "spendocracy." The New Deal, for all practical purposes, had shot its bolt.

New Deal or Raw Deal?

Foes of the New Deal condemned its alleged radicalism, incompetence, confusion, and cross-purposes. New Dealers conceded some weaknesses but defended their record as a necessary and effective response to the depression.

Later Major New Deal Measures, 1933–1939
(items in parentheses indicate secondary purposes)

Recovery	Relief	Reform
(CWA)	FDR establishes Civil Works Administration (CWA), November 9, 1933	
		Securities and Exchange Commission (SEC) authorized by Congress, June 6, 1934 Indian Reorganization Act June 18, 1934
(FHA)	National Housing Act, June 28, 1934, authorizes Federal Housing Administration (FHA)	(FHA)
(Frazier-Lemke Act)	Frazier-Lemke Farm Bankruptcy Act, June 28, 1934	
(Resettlement Administration)	FDR creates Resettlement Administration, April 30, 1935	
(WPA)	FDR creates Works Progress Administration (WPA), May 6, 1935, under act of April 8, 1935	
(Wagner Act)	(Wagner Act)	(Wagner) National Labor Relations Act, July 5, 1935 Social Security Act, August 14, 1935 Public Utility Holding Company Act, August 26, 1935
(Soil Conservation Act)	Soil Conservation and Domestic Allotment Act, February 29, 1936	
(USHA)	(USHA)	United States Housing Authority (USHA) established by Congress, September 1, 1937
(Second AAA)	Second Agricultural Adjustment Act, February 16, 1938	
(Fair Labor Standards)	(Fair Labor Standards)	Fair Labor Standards Act (Wages and Hours Bill), June 25, 1938 Reorganization Act, April 3, 1939 Hatch Act, August 2, 1939

To some conservatives, the New Deal was a radical attempt to make America over in a Bolshevik-Marxist image. They condemned "Rooseveltski" for bringing to Washington "crackpot" college professors, leftist "**pinkos**," and outright Communists. The Hearst newspapers lambasted:

The Red New Deal with a Soviet seal
Endorsed by a Moscow hand,
The strange result of an alien cult
In a liberty-loving land.

pinkos *Disparaging term for someone who is not a "red," or Communist, but is presumed to be sympathetic to communism.*

Roosevelt was further accused by conservatives of tapping too many bright young leftists for his "Jew Deal," or even of being Jewish himself ("Rosenfeld").

More widespread was the charge that the New Deal brought bureaucracy, waste, and a welfare-state mentality that undermined the old American virtues of individualism, thrift, self-reliance, and limited government. The federal government, with its hundreds of thousands of employees, became incomparably the largest single business in the country, as the states faded further into the background. Promises of budget balancing went out the window as the national debt skyrocketed from $19,487,000,000 in 1932 to $40,440,000,000 by 1939. Critics charged that the lavish benefactions of the "handout state" were turning once self-reliant Americans into relief-seeking loafers with wishbones larger than their backbones.

Business was bitter. Accusing the New Deal of fomenting class strife, countless businesspeople, especially Republicans, declared that they could pull themselves out of the depression if they could only get an interventionist big government off their back. Private enterprise, they charged, was being stifled by a "planned economy" and "creeping socialism." Roosevelt's aggressive leadership also came in for denunciation and charges that he was trying to create a "one-man supergovernment."

The most damning indictment of the New Deal was that it failed to cure the depression. Despite some $20 billion poured out in six years of **deficit spending** and lending, many economists came to believe that better results would have been achieved by much greater deficit spending. The New Deal had merely administered aspirin, sedatives, and Band-Aids, with the result that in 1939 millions of dispirited men and women were still

deficit spending *The spending of public funds beyond the amount of income.*

unemployed. Not until World War II increased the national debt from $40 billion in 1939 to $258 billion in 1945 was the unemployment headache solved.

New Dealers staunchly defended their record. Admitting imperfection, they argued that the bureaucratic inefficiency and waste had been trivial in view of the immense sums spent and the obvious need for haste. The New Deal, they insisted, relieved a crisis by demonstrating that the Washington regime was to be used, not feared. The collapse of America's economic system was averted; a fairer distribution of the national income was achieved; and the citizens were enabled to regain and retain their self-respect.

Though hated by business tycoons, FDR should have been their patron saint, so his admirers claimed. He deflected popular resentments against business and may have saved the American system of free enterprise. Roosevelt's quarrel was not with capitalism but with capitalists; he purged American capitalism of some of its worst abuses so that it might be saved from itself. He may even have headed off a more radical swing to the left by a mild dose of what was mistakenly reviled as "socialism." The head of the American Socialist party, when once asked if the New Deal had carried out the Socialist program, reportedly replied that it had indeed—on a stretcher.

Unemployment, 1929–1942 The cold figures can only begin to suggest the widespread human misery caused by mass unemployment. One man wrote to a newspaper in 1932: "I am forty-eight; married twenty-one years; four children, three in school. For the last eight years I was employed as a Pullman conductor. Since September, 1930, they have given me seven months of part-time work. Today I am an object of charity. ... My small, weak, and frail wife and two small children are suffering and I have come to that terrible place where I could easily resort to violence in my desperation."

VARYING VIEWPOINTS   How Radical Was the New Deal?

The Great Depression was both a great calamity and a great opportunity. How effectively Franklin Roosevelt responded to the calamity and what use he made of the opportunity are the two questions that have animated historical debate about the New Deal.

Some historians have denied that there was much of a connection between the depression and the New Deal. Arthur M. Schlesinger, Jr., for example, who believes in "cycles" of reform and reaction in American history, has written that "there would very likely have been some sort of New Deal in the 1930s even without the Depression." But most of the first generation of historians who wrote about the New Deal (in the 1940s, 1950s, and early 1960s) agreed with Carl Degler's judgment that the New Deal was "a revolutionary response to a revolutionary situation." In this view, though Roosevelt never found a means short of war to bring about economic recovery, he shrewdly utilized the stubborn economic crisis as a means to enact sweeping reforms.

Some leftist scholars writing in the 1960s, however, notably Barton J. Bernstein, charged that the New Deal did not reach far enough. This criticism echoed the socialist complaint in the 1930s that the depression represented the total collapse of American capitalism and that the New Deal muffed the chance truly to remake American society. Roosevelt had the chance, these historians argue, to redistribute wealth, improve race relations, and bring the giant corporations to heel. Instead, say these critics, the New Deal simply represented a conservative holding action to shore up a sagging and corrupt capitalist order.

Those charges against the New Deal stimulated another generation of scholars in the 1970s, 1980s, and 1990s to look closely at the concrete institutional, attitudinal, and economic circumstances in which the New Deal unfolded. Historians such as James Patterson, Alan Brinkley, Kenneth Jackson, Harvard Sitkoff, and Lizabeth Cohen—sometimes loosely referred to as the "constraints school"—conclude that the New Deal offered just about as much reform as circumstances allowed and as the majority of Americans wanted. The findings of these historians are impressive: the system of checks and balances limited presidential power; the disproportionate influence of southern Democrats in Congress stalled attempts to move toward racial justice; the federal system, in fact, inhibited all efforts to initiate change from Washington. Most important, a majority of the American people at the time wanted to reform capitalism, not overthrow it.

The best proof of the soundness of that conclusion is probably the durability of the political alliance that Roosevelt assembled. The great "New Deal coalition" that dominated American politics for nearly four decades after Roosevelt's election in 1932 represented a broad consensus in American society about the legitimate limits of government efforts to shape the social and economic order. William Leuchtenburg has offered the most balanced historical assessment in his description of the New Deal as a "half-way revolution," neither radical nor conservative but accurately reflecting the American people's needs and desires in the 1930s—and for a long time thereafter.

Roosevelt, like Jefferson, provided reform without a bloody revolution—at a time in history when some foreign nations were suffering armed uprisings and when many Europeans were predicting either communism or fascism for America. He was upbraided by the left-wing radicals for not going far enough, by the right-wing radicals for going too far. Choosing the middle road, he has been called the greatest American conservative since Hamilton. He was in fact Hamiltonian in his espousal of big government, but Jeffersonian in his concern for the "forgotten man." Demonstrating anew the value of powerful presidential leadership, he exercised that power to relieve the erosion of the nation's greatest physical resource—its people. He helped preserve democracy in America at a time when democracies abroad were disappearing down the sinkhole of dictatorship. And in playing this role, he unwittingly girded the nation for its part in the titanic war that loomed on the horizon—a war in which democracy the world over would be at stake.

Chapter Summary

Franklin Roosevelt, a confident aristocrat with a common touch, swept into office with an urgent mandate to cope with the depression emergency. His bank holiday and frantic Hundred Days legislation lifted America's spirits and created a host of new agencies to provide relief to the unemployed,

economic recovery, and hoped-for permanent reform of a largely unregulated capitalist system.

Roosevelt's early programs put millions of the unemployed back on the job through federal action, but failed to achieve the economic recovery he sought. As popular demagogues such as Huey Long and Father Charles Coughlin gained followings among the suffering population, Roosevelt developed sweeping programs to reform American industry, labor, and agriculture. The Supreme Court declared unconstitutional the most sweeping effort, the National Recovery Administration, and farmers continued to suffer from the Dust Bowl. But the TVA, Social Security, and the Wagner Act brought far-reaching social changes that especially benefited the economically disadvantaged.

Conservatives furiously denounced the New Deal, but Roosevelt formed a powerful coalition of urbanites, labor, "new immigrants," blacks, and the South that swept him to victory in 1936. FDR and especially his vigorously reformist wife Eleanor brought new visibility to women in his administration and the country.

Roosevelt's overreaching court-packing plan failed, but the Supreme Court finally began approving New Deal legislation. The later New Deal encountered mounting conservative opposition and the stubborn persistence of unemployment. Although the New Deal was highly controversial, it steered a middle course between unregulated capitalism and socialism that prevented America from turning toward dictatorship or extreme right-wing or left-wing solutions.

KEY TERMS

dispossessed (542)

rubber-stamp (544)

blank-check (544)

foreign exchange (545)

hoarding (545)

boondoggle (547)

fascist (fascism) (547)

parity (549)

collective bargaining (552)

left (or left-wingers) (553)

court-packing plan (555)

checks and balances (555)

Keynesianism (555)

pinkos (557)

deficit spending (557)

PEOPLE TO KNOW

Franklin Delano Roosevelt

Eleanor Roosevelt

Harry L. Hopkins

Father Charles Coughlin

Francis E. Townsend

Huey P. ("Kingfish") Long

Frances Perkins

Mary McLeod Bethune

 Go to the History CourseMate website for primary source links, study tools, and review materials for this chapter. www.cengagebrain.com

34

Franklin D. Roosevelt and the Shadow of War

1933–1941

The epidemic of world lawlessness is spreading. When an epidemic of physical disease starts to spread, the community approves and joins in a quarantine of the patients in order to protect the health of the community against the spread of the disease. . . . There must be positive endeavors to preserve peace.

FRANKLIN D. ROOSEVELT, CHICAGO QUARANTINE SPEECH, 1937

⭐ Chapter Outline

Roosevelt's Early Foreign Policies

The Rise of Fascism and American Isolationism

War in Europe and the Debate over American Neutrality

Roosevelt's Third-Term Victory and Lend-Lease Aid to Britain

Refugees from Hitler's Holocaust

The Japanese Attack on Pearl Harbor, December 7, 1941

Examining the Evidence: Public Opinion Polling in the 1930s

Americans in the 1930s tried to turn their backs on the world's problems. Their president at first seemed to share these views. The only battle Roosevelt fought was against the Depression. America had its own burdens to shoulder, and the costs of foreign involvement, whether in blood or treasure, simply seemed too great.

But as the clouds of war gathered over Europe, Roosevelt eventually concluded that the United States could no longer remain aloof. Events gradually brought the American people around to his thinking: No nation was safe in an era of international anarchy, and the world could not remain half-enchained and half-free.

FOCUS QUESTIONS

1. What were the motives and effects of Franklin Roosevelt's early foreign policy?

2. How and why did isolationism come to dominate American public opinion and foreign policy in the 1930s?

3. How did the United States gradually awaken to the threat of totalitarian aggression in the late 1930s while still attempting to avoid foreign entanglements?

4. Why did FDR's increasingly bold moves to aid Britain in the fight against Hitler stir such a fierce national debate over the risk of being drawn into war and the best way to preserve America's security?

5. What issues and developments in Japanese-American relations led up to the surprise Japanese attack on Pearl Harbor?

Roosevelt's Early Foreign Policies

The sixty-six nation London Economic Conference in the summer of 1933 revealed how thoroughly Roosevelt's early foreign policy was subordinated to his strategy for domestic economic recovery. The delegates hoped to organize a coordinated international attack on the global depression by stabilizing national currencies. But Roosevelt, unwilling to subordinate his gold-juggling and other inflationary policies to an international agreement

CHRONOLOGY

1933	FDR torpedoes London Economic Conference. United States recognizes Soviet Union. FDR declares Good Neighbor policy toward Latin America. Hitler becomes German chancellor. Germany quits League of Nations.	**1937**	U.S. Neutrality Act of 1937. *Panay* incident. Japan invades China.
1934	Tydings-McDuffie Act provides for Philippine independence on July 4, 1946. Reciprocal Trade Agreements Act. U.S. Marines vacate Haiti.	**1938**	Hitler seizes Austria. Munich Conference. *Kristallnacht* in Germany.
1935	Nuremberg Laws implemented against German Jews. Mussolini invades Ethiopia. U.S. Neutrality Act of 1935. Japan quits League of Nations.	**1939**	Hitler seizes all of Czechoslovakia. Nazi-Soviet pact. World War II begins in Europe with Hitler's invasion of Poland. U.S. Neutrality Act of 1939.
1936	U.S. Neutrality Act of 1936. Mussolini and Hitler form Rome-Berlin Axis. Stalin begins Great Purge. German troops invade Rhineland.	**1940**	Hitler invades Denmark, Norway, Netherlands, and Belgium. Fall of France. United States institutes first peacetime draft. Battle of Britain. Bases-for-destroyers deal with Britain. FDR defeats Willkie for presidency.
1936–1939	Spanish Civil War.	**1941**	Lend-Lease Act. Hitler attacks Soviet Union. Atlantic Charter. Japan attacks Pearl Harbor.

that might tie his hands, torpedoed the conference with a bombshell message that scolded the delegates for even trying to stabilize currencies. Whether the conference could have arrested the worldwide economic slide is debatable, but Roosevelt's every-man-for-himself attitude plunged the planet even deeper into economic crisis. The collapse of the London Conference also strengthened the global trend toward extreme nationalism—a trend that played directly into the hands of power-mad dictators who were determined to shatter the peace of the world.

Roosevelt matched isolationism from Europe with withdrawal from Asia. With the descent into hard times, American taxpayers were eager to throw overboard their expensive tropical liability in the Philippine Islands. Congress passed the Tydings-McGuffie Act in 1934, which provided for the independence of the Philippines in 1946. In truth, the American people were not so much giving freedom to the Philippines as they were freeing themselves *from* the Philippines by imposing economic terms so ungenerous as to threaten the islands with economic prostration. American isolationists rejoiced once again, and Japanese **militarists** calculated that they had little to fear from an inward-looking America.

Closer to home, Roosevelt inaugurated a refreshing new era in relations with Latin America. He proclaimed in his inaugural address, "I would dedicate this nation to the policy of the Good Neighbor." He made it clear from the outset that he was going to renounce armed intervention, particularly the vexatious corollary to the Monroe Doctrine devised by his cousin Theodore Roosevelt.

Accordingly, the United States withdrew the last marines from Haiti in 1934. That same year, after military strongman Fulgencia Batista had come to power, restive Cuba was released from the worst hobbles of the interventionist Platt Amendment, although the United States retained its naval base at Guantanamo (see p. 448). The United States similarly relaxed its grip on Panama in 1936. When the Mexican government seized Yankee oil properties in 1938, Roosevelt successfully resisted business pressure to intervene and eventually thrashed out a settlement in 1941. These earnest acts of friendliness paid rich dividends in goodwill among the peoples to the south, and Roosevelt was cheered with tremendous

militarist *Someone who glorifies military values or institutions and extends them into the political and social spheres.*

enthusiasm when he traveled to an Inter-American Conference at Buenos Aires, Argentina, in 1936. The Colossus of the North now seemed less a vulture and more an eagle.

Taken together, Roosevelt's noninvolvement in Europe and withdrawal from Asia, along with his brotherly embrace of his New World neighbors, suggested that the United States was giving up its ambition to be a world power and would content itself instead with being merely a regional power, its interests and activities confined exclusively to the Western Hemisphere.

Turning Toward Isolationism

totalitarianism *A political system of absolute control, in which all social, moral, and religious values and institutions are put in direct service of the state.*

Post-1918 chaos in Europe, followed by the Great Depression, spawned the ominous spread of **totalitarianism**. The individual was nothing; the state was everything. The Communist USSR led the way, with the crafty and ruthless Joseph Stalin finally emerging as dictator. In 1936, Stalin began to purge his communist state of all suspected dissidents, ultimately executing hundreds of thousands and banishing millions to remote Siberian forced-labor camps. Blustery Benito Mussolini, a swaggering fascist, seized the reins of power in Italy during 1922. And Adolf Hitler, a fanatic with a toothbrush mustache, plotted and harangued his way into control of Germany in 1933 with liberal use of the "big lie."

Hitler was the most dangerous of the dictators because he combined tremendous power with impulsiveness. A frustrated Austrian painter, with hypnotic talents as an orator and leader, Hitler had led the Nazi party to power in Germany by making political capital of the Treaty of Versailles and Germany's depression-spawned unemployment. The desperate German people had fallen in behind the new Pied Piper, for they saw no other hope of escape from the plague of economic chaos and national disgrace. Hitler began clandestinely rearming in 1933, and in 1936 the Nazi Hitler and the Fascist Mussolini allied themselves in the Rome-Berlin Axis.

International gangsterism was likewise spreading in East Asia, where imperial Japan was on the make. Like Germany and Italy, Japan was a so-called have-not power. Like them, Japan resented the ungenerous Treaty of Versailles. Like them, Japan demanded additional space for its teeming millions, cooped up in their crowded island nation. Determined to find a place in the Asian sun, Tokyo terminated the Washington Naval Treaty in 1934 and in the following year accelerated its construction of giant battleships. In 1940 Japan joined arms with Germany and Italy in the Tripartite Pact.

Jut-jawed Mussolini, seeking both glory and empire in Africa, brutally attacked Ethiopia in 1935. The members of the League of Nations could have halted Mussolini's war machine with an oil embargo. But fearing global hostilities they failed to act, and the brave Ethiopians were speedily crushed.

Isolationism, long festering in America, received a strong boost from these alarms abroad. Though disapproving of the dictators, Americans still believed that their encircling seas conferred a kind of mystic immunity. They were continuing to suffer the disillusionment born of their participation in World War I, which they now regarded as a colossal blunder. Americans likewise nursed bitter memories of the ungrateful and defaulting debtors.

Mired down in the Great Depression, Americans had no real appreciation of the revolutionary forces being harnessed by the dictators. Americans were not so much afraid that totalitarian aggression would cause trouble as they were fearful that they might be drawn into it. Strong nationwide sentiment welled up for a constitutional amendment to forbid a declaration of war by Congress—except in case of

#ge792 in the Poster Collection, Hoover Institution Archives

The Wages of Despair Disillusioned and desperate, millions of Germans in the 1930s looked to Adolf Hitler as their savior from the harsh terms of the Treaty of Versailles, which had concluded World War I. This Nazi poster reads, "Our Last Hope: Hitler."

invasion—unless there was a favorable popular referendum. As the gloomy 1930s lengthened, an avalanche of lurid articles and books condemning the munitions manufacturers as war-fomenting "merchants of death" poured forth from American presses. A Senate committee headed by Senator Gerald Nye of North Dakota sensationalized evidence regarding America's entry into World War I, thus shifting the blame away from the German submarines onto the American bankers and arms manufacturers. Because the munitions makers had obviously made money out of the war, many a naive citizen leaped to the illogical conclusion that these soulless scavengers had *caused* the war in order to make money. This kind of reasoning suggested that if the profits could only be removed from the arms traffic—"one hell of a business"—the country could steer clear of any future world conflict.

Responding to overwhelming popular pressure, Congress made haste to legislate the nation out of war. Action was spurred by the danger that Mussolini's Ethiopian assault would plunge the world into a new bloodbath. The Neutrality Acts of 1935, 1936, and 1937, taken together, stipulated that *when the president proclaimed* the existence of a foreign war, certain restrictions would automatically go into effect: No American could legally sail on a belligerent ship, sell or transport munitions to a belligerent, or make loans to a belligerent.

This storm-cellar neutrality proved to be tragically shortsighted. Through its neutrality laws, America served notice that it would make no distinction between brutal aggressors and innocent victims. By striving to hold the scales even, America actually overbalanced the scales in favor of the dictators, who had armed themselves to the teeth. By declining to use its vast industrial strength to aid its democratic friends and defeat its totalitarian foes, America helped goad the aggressors along their blood spattered path of conquest.

The Spanish Civil War of 1936–1939—a proving ground and dress rehearsal in miniature for World War II—was a painful object lesson in the folly of neutrality-by-legislation. Spanish rebels, who rose against the left-leaning republican government in Madrid, were headed by fascistic General Francisco Franco. Generously aided by his fellow conspirators Hitler and Mussolini, he undertook to overthrow the established Loyalist regime, which in turn was assisted on a smaller scale by the Soviet Union. This pipeline from communist Moscow chilled the natural sympathies of many Americans, especially Roman Catholics, for the republican Loyalists. But other Americans burned with passion to defend the struggling republic against Franco's fascist coup. Some three thousand young men and women headed to Spain to fight as volunteers in the Abraham Lincoln Brigade.

Washington continued official relations with the Loyalist government. In accordance with previous American practice, this regime should have been free to purchase desperately needed munitions from the United States. But Congress, with the encouragement of Roosevelt and with only one dissenting vote, amended the existing neutrality legislation so as to apply an arms embargo to both Loyalists and rebels.

Uncle Sam thus sat on the sidelines while Franco, abundantly supplied with arms and men by his fellow dictators, strangled the republican government of Spain. The democracies, including the United States, were so determined to stay out of war that they helped to condemn a fellow democracy to death. In so doing they further encouraged the dictators to take the dangerous road that led over the precipice to World War II.

> *The thirst of Benito Mussolini (1883–1945) for national glory in Ethiopia is indicated by his remark in 1940:*
>
> **"To make a people great it is necessary to send them to battle even if you have to kick them in the pants."**
>
> *(The Italians were notoriously unwarlike.)*
>
> *In 1934 Mussolini proclaimed in a public speech:*
>
> **"We have buried the putrid corpse of liberty."**

Appeasing Japan and Germany

Sulfurous war clouds had meanwhile been gathering in tension-taut East Asia. In 1937 the Japanese militarists, at the Marco Polo Bridge near Beijing (Peking), touched off the explosion that led to an all-out invasion of China. In a sense this attack was the curtain raiser of World War II.

Roosevelt shrewdly declined to invoke the recently passed neutrality legislation by refusing to call the China incident an officially declared war. If he had put the existing restrictions into effect, he would have cut off the tiny trickle of munitions on which the Chinese were desperately dependent. The Japanese, of course, could continue to buy mountains of war supplies in the United States.

In Chicago—unofficial isolationist "capital" of America—President Roosevelt delivered his sensational "Quarantine Speech" in the autumn of 1937. Alarmed by the recent aggression of Italy and Japan, he called for "positive endeavors" to "**quarantine**" the aggressors—presumably by economic embargoes. The speech triggered a cyclone of protest from isolationists and other foes of involvement; They feared that a moral quarantine would lead to a shooting quarantine. Startled by this angry response, Roosevelt retreated and sought less direct means to curb the dictators.

America's isolationist mood intensified in December 1937 when Japanese aviators bombed and sank an American gunboat, the *Panay*, in Chinese waters. Tokyo apologized and paid an indemnity, and Americans breathed a sigh of relief that they need not respond to the outrage.

Adolf Hitler meanwhile grew louder and bolder in Europe. In 1935 he had openly flouted the Treaty of Versailles by introducing compulsory military service in Germany. The next year he boldly marched into the demilitarized German Rhineland, likewise contrary to the detested treaty, while France and Britain looked on in an agony of indecision. Lashing his following into a frenzy, Hitler undertook to persecute and then exterminate the Jewish population in the areas under his control. In the end, he wiped out about 6 million innocent victims, mostly in gas chambers. Calling upon his people to sacrifice butter for guns, he whipped the new German air force and mechanized ground **divisions** into the most devastating military machine the world had yet seen.

Suddenly, in March 1938, Hitler bloodlessly occupied German-speaking Austria, his birthplace. The democratic powers, wringing their hands in despair, prayed that this last grab would satisfy his passion for conquest. But like a drunken reveler calling for madder music and stronger wine, Hitler could not stop. Intoxicated by his recent gains, he began to make bullying demands for the German-inhabited Sudetenland of neighboring Czechoslovakia.

British and French leaders, eager to appease Hitler, frantically arranged a conference with Hitler and Mussolini at Munich, Germany, in September 1938. There they betrayed Czechoslovakia by consenting to the shearing away of the Sudetenland. Europeans and Americans alike hoped that these concessions would bring "peace in our time." Indeed, Hitler publicly promised that the Sudetenland "is the last territorial claim I have to make in Europe."

"Appeasement" of the dictators, symbolized by the ugly word *Munich*, turned out to be merely surrender on the installment plan. It was like giving a cannibal a finger in the hope of saving an arm. In March 1939, scarcely six months later, Hitler suddenly erased the rest of Czechoslovakia from the map, contrary to his solemn vows. The democratic world was again stunned.

Hitler's Belligerency and U.S. Neutrality

Joseph Stalin, the sphinx of the Kremlin, was a key to the peace puzzle. When his efforts to secure a mutual defense treaty with Britain and France fell through in the summer of 1939, the Soviet Union astounded the world by signing, on August 23, 1939, a nonaggression treaty with the German dictator. The notorious Hitler-Stalin pact meant that, contrary to hopes of wishful thinkers in western Europe, the two menaces would not bleed each other to death, but rather join hands to share the spoils.

With the signing of the Nazi-Soviet pact, World War II was only hours away. Hitler now demanded from neighboring Poland a return of the areas wrested from Germany after World War I. Failing to secure satisfaction, he sent his mechanized divisions crashing into Poland at dawn on September 1, 1939. Honoring their commitments, Britain and France promptly declared war. But they were powerless to aid Poland, which was quickly divided between Hitler and his partner in crime, Stalin. Long-dreaded World War II was now fully launched, and the long truce of 1919–1939 had come to an end.

---

quarantine *In politics, isolating a nation by refusing to have economic or diplomatic dealings with it.*

divisions *The major unit of military organization, usually consisting of about 3,000–10,000 soldiers, into which most modern armies are organized.*

President Roosevelt was roused at 3 A.M. on September 1, 1939, by a telephone call from Ambassador William Bullitt (1891–1967) in Paris:

"Mr. President, several German divisions are deep in Polish territory. … There are reports of bombers over the city of Warsaw."

"Well, Bill," FDR replied, "it has come at last. God help us all."

Americans were overwhelmingly anti-Nazi and anti-Hitler, but they were desperately determined to stay out of war; they were not going to be "suckers" again. Neutrality promptly became a heated issue in the United States. Britain and France urgently needed American airplanes and weapons, but the Neutrality Act of 1937 raised a sternly forbidding hand. Roosevelt summoned Congress into special session, and after six weeks of hectic debate it came up with the makeshift Neutrality Act of 1939. This law provided that henceforth the European democracies might buy American war materials, but only on a "cash-and-carry" basis. This meant that they would have to pay for munitions in cash and transport them in their own ships. America would thus avoid loans, war debts, and the torpedoing of American arms-carriers.

Despite its defects, this unneutral neutrality law clearly favored the democracies against the dictators. Because the British and French navies controlled the Atlantic, the European aggressors could not send their ships to buy America's munitions. The United States not only improved its moral position but simultaneously helped its economic position. Overseas demand for war goods brought a sharp upswing from the recession of 1937–1938 and ultimately solved the decade-long unemployment crisis (see the chart on p. 557).

The Fall of France and the Destroyer Deal (1940)

The months following the collapse of Poland, while France and Britain marked time, were known as the "phony war." An ominous silence fell on Europe as Hitler shifted his victorious divisions from Poland for a knockout blow at France. Inaction during this anxious period was relieved by the Soviets, who wantonly attacked neighboring Finland in an effort to secure strategic buffer territory.

An abrupt end to the "phony war" came in April 1940 when Hitler, again without warning, overran his weaker neighbors, Denmark and Norway. Hardly pausing for breath, the next month Hitler attacked the Netherlands and Belgium, followed by a paralyzing blow at France. By late June, France was forced to surrender, but not until Mussolini had pounced on its rear for a jackal's share of the loot. In a pell-mell but successful evacuation from the French port of Dunkirk, the British managed to salvage the bulk of their shattered army. The crisis providentially brought forth an inspired leader in Prime Minister Winston Churchill, the bulldog-jawed orator who nerved the British to fight off the fearful air bombings of their cities.

France's sudden collapse shocked Americans out of their daydreams. Stouthearted Britons, singing "There'll Always Be an England," were all that stood between Hitler and the death of constitutional government in Europe. If Britain went under, Hitler would have at his disposal the workshops, shipyards, and slave labor of western Europe. He might even have the powerful British fleet as well. This frightening possibility, which seemed to pose a dire threat to American security, steeled the American people to a tremendous effort.

Roosevelt moved with electrifying energy and dispatch. He called upon an already debt-burdened nation to build huge air fleets and a two-ocean navy, which could also check Japan. Congress, jarred out of its apathy toward preparedness, within a year appropriated the astounding sum of $37 billion, more than the total cost of fighting World War I. Congress also passed a conscription law on September 6, 1940, America's first peacetime draft.

Refugees from the Holocaust

Aroused by Adolf Hitler, the ancient demon of anti-Semitism brutally bared its fangs. Harsh persecution of Jews began almost immediately when Hitler took power in 1933. More vicious violence appeared with shocking efficiency on the night

Adolf Hitler (1889–1945) promised to win his fellow Germans Lebensraum, *or "living space," and to win it by war if necessary. In his eyes, his nationalist and racist crusade justified every violent means at hand. As he told his commanders:*

"When you start a war, what matters is not who is right, but who wins. Close your hearts to pity. Act with brutality. Eighty million Germans must get what is their due. Their existence must be made secure. The stronger man is in the right."

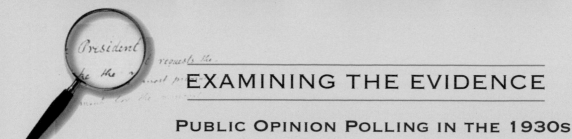

EXAMINING THE EVIDENCE

PUBLIC OPINION POLLING IN THE 1930S

In 1936 the prominent news publication *Literary Digest* made a monumental gaffe when it relied on public-opinion polling data to forecast a victory for the Republican candidate, Alf Landon, over the incumbent, Franklin D. Roosevelt. As it happened, Roosevelt racked up a monstrous majority, winning the electoral votes of all but two states. The *Digest's* error had been to compile its polling lists from records of automobile registration and telephone directories—unwittingly skewing its sample toward relatively well-off voters in an era when fewer than half of American families owned either a car or a telephone. The *Digest's* embarrassing mistake ended an era of informal polling techniques, as new, scientifically sophisticated polling organizations founded by George Gallup and Elmo Roper forged to the fore. From this date forward, polling became a standard tool for marketers and advertisers—as well as for political strategists and historians. Yet controversy has long clouded the relationship between pollsters and politicians, who are often accused of abdicating their roles as leaders and slavishly deferring to public opinion, rather than trying to shape it. Franklin Roosevelt confronted this issue in the 1930s, as polls seemed to confirm the stubborn isolationism of the American people, even as the president grew increasingly convinced that the United States must play a more active international role.

1. What do the poll results suggest about Roosevelt's handling of this issue? What do the results suggest about the reliability of polling data?

2. What are the legitimate political uses of public-opinion polls? How valuable are they to the historian?

3. How might the pollsters' wording of the questions have influenced the results or made them difficult to interpret? Is it possible for polls to avoid terms such as "everything possible" (Question #1) or "becomes necessary" (Question #6) that contain elements of subjective interpretation?

[1.] (U.S. Oct 3 '39) Do you think the United States should do everything possible to help England and France win the war, except go to war ourselves? (AIPO)

Yes 62%   No 38%

[2.] (U.S. Oct 3 '39) If it appears that Germany is defeating England and France, should the United States declare war on Germany and send our army and navy to Europe to fight? (AIPO)

	Yes	No
National total	29%	71%
BY GEOGRAPHICAL SECTION		
New England	33%	67%
Middle Atlantic	27	73
East central	25	75
West central	26	74
South	47	53
West	28	72
(Jan 30 '40) National total	23%	77%

[3.] (U.S. May 29 '40) If the question of the United States going to war against Germany came up for a national vote to go to war (go into the war or stay out of the war)? (AIPO)

Yes 16%   No 84%

(June 11 '40) . . . . Go in 19%   Stay out 81%

[4.] (U.S. Aug 5 '41) Should the United States go to war now against Japan? (AIPO)

	Yes	No		No opinion
	22%	78%	= 100%	11%
(Oct 22 '41)	13	74		13

[5.] (U.S. Sept 17 '41) Should the United States go into the war now and send an army to Europe to fight? (AIPO)

Yes 9%   No 87%   No opinion 4%

[6.] (U.S. Nov 5 '41) If, in trying to defeat Germany, it becomes necessary to send a large American army to Europe, would you favor this step? (AIPO)

Yes 47%   No 46%   No opinion 7%

Source: From Hadley Cantril, ed. *Public Opinion, 1935–1946* (Princeton: Princeton University Press, 1951).

of November 9, 1938. Instigated by a speech by Nazi propagandist Joseph Goebbels, mobs ransacked more than seven thousand Jewish shops and almost all German synagogues. At least ninety-one Jews lost their lives and about thirty thousand were sent to concentration camps in the turbulent wake of *Kristallnacht* ("night of broken glass").

Many Jews attempted to escape from Hitler's racist juggernaut. To take one poignant case, in May 1939, 937 passengers, almost all of them Jewish refugees, boarded the ship *St. Louis* and departed Hamburg for Havana, Cuba. Most, however, were denied entry for lack of valid Cuban visas. The *St. Louis* then sailed for the port of Miami, which proved no more hospitable. President Roosevelt briefly showed some interest in accepting the beleaguered human cargo, but restrictive immigration laws, together with opposition from Southern Democrats and Secretary of State Cordell Hull, nixed his plan. The *St. Louis* eventually deposited its passengers in England, France, Belgium, and the Netherlands, where many of them subsequently perished under the Nazi heel.

By the end of the war, some 6 million Jews had been murdered in the Holocaust. After reports of the genocide began to be verified in 1942, Roosevelt created the War Refugee Board, which saved thousands of Hungarian Jews from deportation to the notorious death camp at Auschwitz. But in the end, only 150,000 Jews—mostly German and Austrian— were to find refuge in the United States before the Holocaust engulfed European Jewry.

Bolstering Britain

Before the fall of France in June 1940, Washington had generally observed a technical neutrality. But now, as Britain alone stood between Hitler and his dream of world domination, the wisdom of neutrality seemed increasingly questionable. Hitler launched air attacks against Britain in August 1940, preparatory to an invasion scheduled for September. For months the Battle of Britain raged in the air over the British Isles. The Royal Air Force's tenacious defense of its native islands eventually led Hitler to postpone his planned invasion indefinitely.

As the Battle of Britain raged in the air over the British Isles, debate intensified in the United States over what foreign policy to embrace. Radio broadcasts from London beamed directly into American homes increased sympathy for Britain, but not yet sufficiently to push the United States into war. Roosevelt faced a historic decision: whether to hunker down in a "Fortress America" posture in the Western Hemisphere, or to bolster beleaguered Britain by all means short of war itself.

Both sides had their advocates. Supporters of aid to Britain formed propaganda groups, the most potent of which was the Committee to Defend America by Aiding the Allies. The isolationists, both numerous and sincere, were by no means silent. Determined to avoid bloodshed at all costs, they organized the America First Committee. Their basic philosophy was "the Yanks are not coming," and their most effective speechmaker was the famed aviator Colonel Charles A. Lindbergh, who, ironically, had narrowed the Atlantic in 1927.

Britain was in critical need of destroyers, for German submarines were again threatening to starve it out with attacks on shipping. Roosevelt moved boldly when, on September 2, 1940, he agreed to transfer to Great Britain fifty old destroyers left over from World War I. In return, the British promised to hand over to the United States eight valuable defensive base sites, stretching from Newfoundland to South America. These strategically located outposts were to remain under the Stars and Stripes for ninety-nine years.

Shifting warships from a neutral United States to a belligerent Britain was, beyond question, a flagrant violation of neutral obligations. But public-opinion polls demonstrated that a majority of Americans were determined to provide the battered British with "all aid short of war."

FDR Shatters the Two-Term Tradition (1940)

In the midst of this crisis came the distracting presidential election of 1940. The two leading Republican candidates were Senator Robert Taft of Ohio, son of the former president, and the energetic boy wonder Thomas E. Dewey of New York. But in one of the miracles of American political history, the Philadelphia convention was swept off its feet by Wendell L. Willkie, a colorful German-descended son of Hoosier Indiana. This dynamic lawyer and public utilities corporation executive—tousle-headed, broad-faced, and large-framed—was a complete novice in politics. With the convention galleries wildly chanting "We Want Willkie," the delegates finally accepted this magnetic political upstart as the only candidate who could possibly beat Roosevelt. The outspoken Willkie was opposed not so much to the New Deal as to its extravagances and inefficiencies. Democratic critics branded him "the simple barefoot Wall Street lawyer."

Roosevelt delayed to the last minute the announcement of his decision to challenge the sacred two-term tradition. Despite what he described as his personal yearning for retirement, he avowed that in so grave a crisis he owed his experienced hand to the service of his country and humanity.

With the country already badly split between interventionists and isolationists, Willkie might have widened the breach dangerously by a violent attack on Roosevelt's aid-to-Britain policies. But the statesmanlike Republican candidate refrained from assailing the president's interventionism and accepted the essential premises of an internationalist foreign policy. Willkie campaigned hard against Rooseveltian "dictatorship" and the third term. Roosevelt, busy at his desk with mounting problems, stayed close to the White House and generally ignored Willkie. But in a speech in Boston he emphatically declared, "Your boys are not going to be sent into any foreign wars"—a pledge that later came back to plague him.

The time-honored argument that one should not change horses in the middle of a stream was strong, especially in an era of war-pumped prosperity. Roosevelt triumphed, although Willkie ran a strong race. The electoral count was 449 to 82. The popular vote was much closer—27,307,819 to 22,321,018. Democratic majorities in Congress remained about the same.

Congress Passes the Landmark Lend-Lease Law

By late 1940 embattled Britain was nearing the end of its financial tether. But Roosevelt, who had bitter memories of the wrangling over the Allied debts of World War I, was determined, as he put it, to eliminate "the silly, foolish, old dollar sign." He finally hit on the scheme of lending or leasing American arms to the reeling democracies. When the shooting was over, to use his comparison, the guns and tanks could be returned, just as one's next-door neighbor would return a garden hose when the threatening fire was put out. But isolationist Senator Robert Taft (who was reputed to have the finest mind in Washington until he made it up) retorted that lending arms was like lending chewing gum: "You don't want it back."

The Lend-Lease Bill, patriotically numbered 1776, was entitled "An Act Further to Promote the Defense of the United States." The underlying concept was "Send guns, not sons" or "Billions, not bodies." America, so President Roosevelt promised, would be the "arsenal of democracy." It would send a limitless supply of arms to the victims of aggression, who in turn would finish the job and keep the war on their side of the Atlantic. Isolationists assailed the lend-lease scheme as "the blank-check bill." Isolationist Senator Burton Wheeler called it "the new triple-A [Agricultural Adjustment Act] bill"—a measure designed to "plow under every fourth American boy." Nevertheless, lend-lease was finally approved in March 1941 by sweeping majorities in both houses of Congress.

Lend-lease was one of the most momentous laws ever to pass Congress; it was a challenge hurled squarely into the teeth of the Axis dictators. America eventually sent about $50 billion worth of arms and equipment to those nations fighting aggressors. By its very nature, the Lend-Lease Bill marked the abandonment of any pretense of neutrality. It was no destroyer deal arranged privately by President Roosevelt. The bill was universally debated over drugstore counters and cracker barrels from California to Maine; and the sovereign citizen at last spoke through convincing majorities in Congress. Lend-lease had the somewhat incidental result of gearing U.S. factories for all-out war production. The enormously increased capacity thus achieved helped to save America's own skin when, at long last, the shooting war burst around its head.

Hitler himself evidently recognized lend-lease as an unofficial declaration of war. Until then, Germany had avoided attacking U.S. ships; memories of America's decisive intervention in 1917–1918 were still fresh in German minds. But after the passing of lend-lease there

✻ PRIMARY SOURCE
Main Flow of Lend-Lease Aid

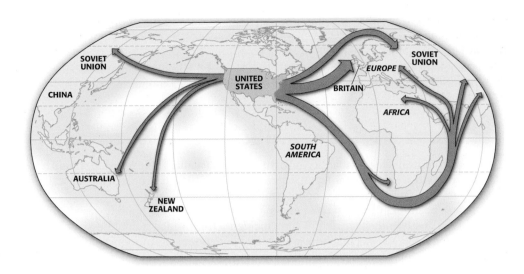

Main Flow of Lend-Lease Aid (width of arrows indicates relative amount) The proud but desperate British prime minister, Winston Churchill, declared in early 1941: "Give us the tools and we will finish the job." Lend-lease eventually provided the British and other Allies with $50 billion worth of "tools." © Cengage Learning

was less point in trying to curry favor with the United States. On May 21, 1941, the *Robin Moor*, an unarmed American merchant ship, was torpedoed and destroyed by a German submarine in the South Atlantic, outside a war zone. The sinking had started, but on a limited scale.

U.S. Destroyers and Hitler's U-Boats Clash

Lend-lease shipments of arms to Britain on British ships were bound to be sunk by German wolf-pack submarines. If the intent was to get the munitions to Britain, not to dump them into the ocean, the freighters would have to be escorted by U.S. warships. Britain simply did not have enough destroyers. Roosevelt made the fateful decision to **convoy** in July 1941, ordering the U.S. Navy to escort lend-lease shipments as far as Iceland. The British would then shepherd them the rest of the way.

Inevitable clashes with submarines ensued on the Iceland run, even though Hitler's orders were to strike American warships only in self-defense. In September 1941, the U.S. destroyer *Greer*, provocatively trailing a German U-boat, was attacked by the undersea craft, without damage to either side. Roosevelt then proclaimed a shoot-on-sight policy. On October 17, 1941, the escorting destroyer *Kearny*, while engaged in a battle with U-boats, lost eleven men when it was crippled but not sent to the bottom. Two weeks later the destroyer *Reuben James* was torpedoed and sunk off southwestern Iceland, with the loss of more than a hundred officers and enlisted men.

Neutrality was still inscribed on the statute books, but not on American hearts. The submarine attacks and Hitler's invasion of the Soviet Union in June 1941 led to closer collaboration between the United States and all of Nazi Germany's foes. With the surrender of the Soviet Union a dread possibility, the United States extended $1 billion of lend-lease aid to help halt the invaders—the first installment on an ultimate total of $11 billion.

Franklin Roosevelt and cherub-faced British Prime Minister Winston Churchill also met on a warship off the foggy coast of Newfoundland in August 1941, where they agreed to the eight-point Atlantic Charter. This covenant, suggestive of Wilson's Fourteen Points, outlined the aspirations of the democracies for a better world at war's end. Arguing for the rights of individuals rather than nations, the Atlantic Charter laid the groundwork for later advocacy on behalf of universal human rights.

Among its key features were self-determination for all peoples, disarmament, and eventually a "permanent system of general security" (a new League of Nations). The

Senator (later president) Harry S Truman (1884–1972) expressed a common reaction to Hitler's invasion of the Soviet Union in 1941:

> "If we see that Germany is winning, we ought to help Russia, and if we see Russia is winning, we ought to help Germany, and that way let them kill as many as possible."

convoy (v.) *To escort militarily, for purposes of protection. The escorting ships or troops are called a* **convoy (n.)**.

Atlantic Charter was cheered by liberals and subject peoples the world over, although roundly condemned by isolationists in the United States.

In November 1941 Congress pulled the teeth from the now-useless Neutrality Act of 1939. Merchant ships could henceforth be legally armed and could enter combat zones. Americans braced themselves for wholesale attacks by Hitler's submarines.

Surprise Assault at Pearl Harbor

The blowup came not in the Atlantic, but in the faraway Pacific. This explosion should have surprised no close observer, for Japan, since September 1940, had been a formal military ally of Nazi Germany—America's shooting foe in the North Atlantic.

Japan's position in East Asia had grown more perilous by the hour. It was still mired down in the costly and exhausting "China incident," from which it could extract neither honor nor victory. Its war machine was fatally dependent on immense shipments of steel, scrap iron, oil, and aviation gasoline from the United States. Such assistance to the Japanese aggressor was highly unpopular in America. But Roosevelt had resolutely held off an embargo, lest he goad the Tokyo **warlords** into a descent upon the oil-rich but defense-poor Dutch East Indies (present-day Indonesia).

Washington, late in 1940, finally imposed the first of its embargoes on Japan-bound supplies. This blow was followed in mid-1941 by a freezing of Japanese assets in the United States and a cessation of all shipments of gasoline and other sinews of war. As the oil gauge dropped, the squeeze on Japan grew steadily more nerve-racking. Japanese leaders were faced with two painful alternatives. They could either knuckle under to the Americans or break out of the embargo ring by a desperate attack on the oil supplies and other riches of Southeast Asia.

Final tense negotiations with Japan took place in Washington during November and early December of 1941. The State Department insisted that the Japanese clear out of China, but to sweeten the pill offered to renew trade relations on a limited basis. Japanese imperialists, after waging a bitter war against the Chinese for more than four years, were unwilling to lose face by withdrawing at the behest of the United States. Faced with capitulation or continued conquest, they chose the sword.

Officials in Washington, having "cracked" the top-secret code of the Japanese, knew that Tokyo's decision was for war. But the United States, as a democracy committed to public debate and action by Congress, could not shoot first. Roosevelt and other officials, misled by Japanese ship movements in the western Pacific, evidently expected the blow to fall on British Malaya or on the Philippines. No one in high authority in Washington evidently believed that the Japanese were either strong enough or foolhardy enough to strike Hawaii.

But the paralyzing blow struck Pearl Harbor, while Tokyo was deliberately prolonging negotiations in Washington. Japanese bombers, winging in from distant aircraft carriers, attacked without warning on the "Black Sunday" morning of December 7, 1941. It was a date, as Roosevelt told Congress, "which will live in infamy." About three thousand casualties were inflicted on American personnel, and many aircraft were destroyed; the battleship fleet was virtually wiped out when all eight of the craft were sunk or otherwise immobilized, and numerous small vessels were damaged or destroyed.

The next day an angered Congress, with only one dissenting vote, officially recognized that war had been "thrust" upon the United States. When Japan's allies, Germany and Italy, also declared war on December 11, 1941, the challenge was accepted by Congress the same day. The unofficial war was now official.

Japan's **hara-kiri** gamble in Hawaii paid off only in the short run. True, the Pacific fleet was largely destroyed or immobilized, but the sneak attack aroused and united America as almost nothing else could have done. To the very day of the blowup, a strong majority of Americans still wanted to keep out of war. But the bombs that pulverized Pearl Harbor blasted the isolationists into silence. The only thing left to do, growled isolationist Senator Wheeler, was "to lick hell out of them."

But Pearl Harbor was not the full answer to the question as to why the United States went to war. This treacherous attack was but the last explosion in a long chain reaction. Following the fall of France, Americans were confronted with a devil's dilemma. They desired above all to stay out of the conflict, yet they did not want Britain to be knocked

warlord(s) *An armed leader or ruler who maintains power by continually waging war, often against other similar petty rulers or local military leaders lacking constitutional or legal legitimacy.*

hara-kiri *Traditional Japanese ritual suicide.*

U.S. Army

The Battleship *West Virginia* The shocking Japanese attack on Pearl Harbor on December 7, 1941, propelled the United States into World War II. One of the first ships to be hit, the USS *West Virginia* quickly sank at its mooring, taking at least seventy sailors down with it. By September 1944 the *West Virginia* had been repaired and was back in service.

out. They also wished to halt Japan, which menaced American security and international peace. To keep Britain from collapsing, the Roosevelt administration felt compelled to extend the unneutral aid that invited attacks from German submarines. To keep Japan from expanding, Washington undertook to cut off vital Japanese supplies with embargoes that invited possible retaliation. Rather than let democracy die and dictatorship rule supreme, most citizens were evidently determined to support a policy that might lead to war. It did.

Chapter Summary

Roosevelt's early foreign policies, such as wrecking the London economic conference and establishing the Good Neighbor policy in Latin America, were governed by his determination to make domestic recovery the national priority and to turn the United States away from commitments elsewhere in the world. America virtually withdrew from all European affairs and promised independence to the Philippines in an attempt to avoid future involvement in East Asia.

Depression-spawned chaos and war in Europe and Asia strengthened the isolationist impulse, as Congress passed a series of Neutrality Acts designed to prevent America from being drawn into foreign wars. The United States adhered to this policy for a time, despite the spreading aggression of Italy, Germany, and Japan. But after the outbreak of World War II in Europe, Roosevelt cautiously began to provide some aid to the Allies.

After the fall of France in June 1940, Roosevelt provided greater assistance to desperate Britain in the destroyers-for-bases deal, and Congress passed the lend-lease program. Still-powerful isolationists protested these measures, but dark-horse Republican nominee Wendell Willkie refrained from attacking Roosevelt's foreign policy in the 1940 campaign.

By the summer of 1941, the United States was fighting an undeclared naval war with Nazi Germany in the North Atlantic. Roosevelt and Winston Churchill issued the Atlantic Charter upholding shared democratic principles and outlining plans for future peace and security. Meanwhile, American pressure against the Japanese invasion of China made Japanese militarists desperate. After negotiations with Japan failed, the surprise attack on Pearl Harbor plunged the United States into World War II.

CHRONOLOGY

1941	United States declares war on Japan.
	Germany declares war on United States.
	Randolph plans black march on
	    Washington.
	Fair Employment Practices Commission
	    (FEPC) established.
	Roosevelt delivers "Four Freedoms" speech.

1942	Japanese Americans sent to internment
	    camps.
	Japan conquers the Philippines.
	Battle of the Coral Sea.
	Battle of Midway.
	United States invades North Africa.
	Congress of Racial Equality (CORE)
	    founded.

1943	Allies hold Casablanca conference. Allies invade Italy. Smith-Connally Anti-Strike Act.

	"Zoot-suit" riots in Los Angeles. Race riot in Detroit. Japanese driven from Guadalcanal. Teheran conference.
1944	*Korematsu v. United States.* D-Day invasion of France. Battle of Marianas. Roosevelt defeats Dewey for presidency.
1944–1945	Battle of the Bulge.

1945	Roosevelt dies; Truman assumes
	    presidency.
	Germany surrenders.
	Battles of Iwo Jima and Okinawa.
	Potsdam conference.
	Atomic bombs dropped on Hiroshima and
	    Nagasaki.
	Japan surrenders.

The get-Germany-first strategy was the solid foundation on which all American military strategy was built. But it encountered much unwarranted criticism from two-fisted Americans who thirsted for revenge against Japan. Aggrieved protests were also registered by shorthanded American commanders in the Pacific and by Chinese and Australian allies. But President Roosevelt, a competent strategist in his own right, wisely resisted these pressures.

Monica Sone (b. 1919), a college-age Japanese American woman in Seattle, recorded the shock she and her brother felt when they learned of Executive Order No. 9066, which authorized the War Department to remove Japanese—aliens and citizens alike—from their homes:

"In anger, Henry and I read and reread the Executive Order. Henry crumbled the newspaper in his hand and threw it against the wall. 'Doesn't my citizenship mean a single blessed thing to anyone? Why doesn't somebody make up my mind for me? First they want me in the army. Now they're going to slap an alien 4-C on me because of my ancestry....' Once more I felt like a despised, pathetic two-headed freak, a Japanese and an American, neither of which seemed to be doing me any good."

The Allies Trade Space for Time

Given time, the Allies seemed bound to triumph. But would they be given time? True, they had on their side the great mass of the world's population, but the wolf is never intimidated by the number of the sheep.

Time, in a sense, was the most needed munition. Expense was no limitation. The overpowering problem confronting America was to retool itself for all-out war production, while praying that the dictators would not meanwhile crush their adversaries who remained in the field—notably Britain and the Soviet Union. Haste was all the more imperative because the highly skilled German scientists might turn up with unbeatable secret weapons, including rocket bombs and perhaps even atomic arms.

America's task was far more complex and backbreaking than during World War I. It had to feed, clothe, and arm itself, as well as transport its forces to regions as far separated as Britain and Burma. More than that, it had to send a vast amount of food and munitions to its hard-pressed allies, who stretched all the way from the USSR to Australia. Could the American people, reputedly "gone soft," measure up to this herculean task? Was democracy "rotten" and "decadent," as the dictators sneeringly proclaimed?

The Shock of War

National unity was no worry, thanks to the electrifying blow by the Japanese at Pearl Harbor. American Communists had denounced the Anglo-French "imperialist" war before Hitler attacked Stalin in 1941, but they now clamored for an unmitigated assault on the Axis powers. A handful of strutting pro-Hitlerites in the United States melted away, while millions of Italian Americans and German Americans loyally supported the nation's war program. In contrast to World War I, when the patriotism of millions of immigrants was hotly questioned, World War II actually speeded the assimilation of many ethnic groups into American society. Immigration had been choked off for almost two decades before 1941, and America's ethnic communities were now composed of well-settled members, whose votes were crucial to Franklin Roosevelt's Democratic party. Consequently, there was virtually no governmental witch-hunting of minority groups, as had happened in World War I.

A painful exception was the plight of some 110,000 Japanese Americans, concentrated on the Pacific Coast (see "Makers of America: The Japanese," pp. 576–577). The Washington top command, fearing that they might act as saboteurs for Japan in case of invasion, forcibly herded them together in concentration camps, though about two-thirds of them were American-born U.S. citizens. This brutal precaution, authorized under Executive Order No. 9066, was both unnecessary and unfair, as the loyalty and combat record of Japanese Americans proved to be admirable. But a wave of post–Pearl Harbor hysteria, backed by the long historical swell of anti-Japanese prejudice on the West Coast, temporarily robbed many Americans of their good sense—and their sense of justice. The internment camps deprived these uprooted Americans of dignity and basic rights; the internees also lost hundreds of millions of dollars in property and forgone earnings. The wartime Supreme Court in 1944 upheld the constitutionality of the Japanese relocation in *Korematsu v. United States.* But more than four decades later in 1988, the U.S. government officially apologized for its actions and approved the payment of reparations of $20,000 to each camp survivor.

The war prompted other changes in the American mood. Many programs of the once-popular New Deal were wiped out by the conservative Congress elected in 1942, and even President Roosevelt declared in 1943 that "Dr. New Deal" was going into retirement to be replaced by "Dr. Win-the-War." The era of New Deal reform was over.

World War II was no idealistic crusade as World War I had been. The Washington government emphasized action rather than propaganda. According to opinion polls during the war, a majority or near-majority of citizens confessed to having "no clear idea what the war is about." All Americans knew was that they had a dirty job on their hands and that the only way out was forward. They went about their bloody task with astonishing efficiency.

Building the War Machine

The war crisis made the drooping American economy snap to attention. Massive military orders—over $100 billion in 1942 alone—almost instantly soaked up the idle industrial capacity of the still-lingering Great Depression. Orchestrated by the War Production Board, American factories poured forth an avalanche of weaponry: 40 billion bullets, 300,000 aircraft, 76,000 ships, 86,000 tanks, and 2.6 million machine guns. Farmers, too, rolled up their sleeves and increased their output. The armed forces drained the farms of workers, but heavy new investment in agricultural machinery and improved fertilizers more than made up the difference. In 1944 and 1945, blue-jeaned farmers hauled in record-breaking billion-bushel wheat harvests.

These wonders of production also brought economic strains. Full employment and scarce consumer goods fueled a sharp inflationary surge in 1942. The Office of Price Administration eventually brought ascending prices under control with extensive regulations. Rationing held down the consumption of critical goods, such as meat and butter, though some "black marketeers" and "meatleggers" cheated the system. The National War Labor Board (WLB) imposed ceilings on wage increases.

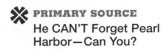

PRIMARY SOURCE
He CAN'T Forget Pearl Harbor—Can You?

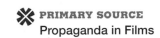

PRIMARY SOURCE
Propaganda in Films

Freedom of Speech   *Freedom of Worship*

Freedom from Want   *Freedom from Fear*

National Archives, Norman Rockwell Family Agency

The Four Freedoms, by Norman Rockwell In his January 6, 1941, speech to Congress requesting lend-lease aid to the Allies, President Roosevelt spoke eloquently of the "four freedoms" then threatened by Nazi and Japanese aggression. Those freedoms are here given pictorial representation by Norman Rockwell, probably the most popular and best-loved American artist of the time.

The Japanese

In 1853 the American commodore Matthew Perry sailed four gunboats into Japan's Uraga Bay and demanded that the nation open itself to diplomatic and commercial exchange with the United States. Within two decades of Perry's arrival, Japan's new "Meiji" government had launched the nation on an ambitious program of industrialization and militarization designed to make it the economic and political equal of the Western powers.

As Japan rapidly modernized, its citizens increasingly took ship for America. A steep land tax drove more than 300,000 Japanese farmers off their land. In 1884 the Meiji government permitted Hawaiian planters to recruit contract laborers from among this displaced population. By the 1890s many Japanese were sailing beyond Hawaii to the ports of Long Beach, San Francisco, and Seattle.

Between 1885 and 1924, roughly 200,000 Japanese migrated to Hawaii, and around 180,000 more ventured to the U.S. mainland. They were a select group: because the Meiji government saw overseas Japanese as representatives of their homeland, it strictly regulated emigration. Thus Japanese immigrants to America arrived with more money and better education than their European counterparts.

Women as well as men migrated. The Japanese government, wanting to avoid the problems of an itinerant bachelor society that it observed among the Chinese in the United States, actively promoted women's migration. Although most Japanese immigrants were young men in their twenties and thirties, thousands of women also ventured to Hawaii and the mainland as contract laborers or "picture brides," so called because their courtships had consisted exclusively of exchanges of photographs with their prospective husbands.

In Hawaii most Japanese labored on the vast sugar cane plantations. On the mainland they initially found migratory work on the railroads or in fish, fruit, or vegetable canneries. A separate Japanese economy of restaurants, stores, and boardinghouses soon sprang up in cities to serve the immigrants' needs.

From such humble beginnings, many Japanese—particularly those on the Pacific Coast—quickly moved into farming. In the late nineteenth century, the spread of irrigation shifted California agriculture from grain to fruits and vegetables, and the invention of the refrigerated railcar opened hungry new markets in the East. The Japanese, with centuries of experience in intensive farming, arrived just in time to take advantage of these developments. By 1940 Japanese farmers produced most of the state's strawberries, beans, and tomatoes.

But the very success of the Japanese proved a lightning rod for trouble. On the West Coast, Japanese immigrants had long endured racist barbs and social segregation. Increasingly, white workers and farmers, jealous of Japanese success, pushed for immigration restrictions. Bowing to this pressure, President Theodore Roosevelt in 1908 negotiated the

Labor unions, whose memberships grew from about 10 million to more than 13 million workers during the war, fiercely resented the government-dictated wage ceilings. Despite the no-strike pledges of most major unions, a rash of labor walkouts plagued the war effort. Threats of lost production through strikes became so worrisome that Congress, in June 1943, passed the Smith-Connally Anti-Strike Act, which authorized the federal government to seize and operate tied-up industries. Under the act, Washington took over the coal mines and, for a brief period, the railroads. Yet work stoppages accounted for less than 1 percent of the total working hours of the United States' wartime laboring force.

Manpower and Womanpower

The armed services enlisted nearly 15 million men in World War II, and some 216,000 women, who were employed for noncombat duties. Best known of these "women in arms" were the WAACS (army), WAVES (navy), and SPARS (Coast Guard).

"Gentlemen's Agreement," under which the Japanese government voluntarily agreed to limit emigration. In 1913 the California legislature denied Japanese immigrants already living in the United States the right to own land.

✳ **PRIMARY SOURCE**
Window Sign After
Relocation

✳ **PRIMARY SOURCE**
Japanese Americans Arrive
at Assembly Center

Legally barred from becoming citizens, Japanese immigrants (the "Issei," from the Japanese word for *first*) became more determined than ever that their American-born children (the "Nissei," from the Japanese word for *second*) would reap the full benefits of their birthright. Japanese parents encouraged their children to learn English, to excel in school, and to get a college education. Many Nissei grew up in two worlds, a fact they often recognized by Americanizing their Japanese names. Although education and acculturation did not protect the Nissei from the hysteria of World War II, those assets did give them a springboard to success in the postwar era.

Japanese American Evacuees, 1942 After the U.S. Army's Western Defense Command ordered the forced evacuation of all Japanese and Japanese Americans living on the Pacific Coast, families had no choice but to pack up whatever they could carry and move to the "relocation centers" hastily erected farther inland.

Despite exemptions for key categories of industrial and agricultural workers, the draft left the nation's farms and factories so short of personnel that new workers had to be found. An agreement with Mexico in 1942 brought thousands of Mexican agricultural workers, called **braceros**, across the border to harvest the fruit and grain crops of the West. The *bracero* program outlived the war by some twenty years, becoming a fixed feature of the agricultural economy in many western states.

Even more dramatic was the march of women onto the factory floor. More than 6 million women took up jobs outside the home; over half of them had never before worked for wages. Many of them were mothers, and the government was obliged to set up some three thousand day-care centers to care for "Rosie the Riveter's" children while Rosie drilled the fuselage of a heavy bomber or joined the links of a tank track. When the war ended, Rosie and many of her sisters wanted to keep on working and often did. The war thus foreshadowed an eventual revolution in the roles of women in American society.

Yet the war's immediate impact on women's lives has frequently been exaggerated. The great majority of women—especially those with husbands present in the home or

bracero *A Mexican farm laborer temporarily brought into the United States.*

✳ **PRIMARY SOURCE**
Women Welders at the
Landers, Frary, and Clark
Plant

577

with small children to care for—did not work for wages in the wartime economy but continued in their traditional roles. In both Britain and the Soviet Union, a far greater percentage of women, including mothers, were pressed into industrial employment as the gods of war laid a much heavier hand on those societies than they did on the United States.

At war's end, two-thirds of women war workers left the labor force. Many of them were forced out of their jobs by employers or unions, but half of them quit their jobs voluntarily because of family obligations. The immediate postwar period witnessed not a permanent widening of women's employment opportunities but a widespread rush into suburban domesticity and the mothering of the "baby boomers," who were born by the tens of millions in the decade and a half after 1945. America was destined to experience a revolution in women's status later in the postwar period, but that epochal change was only beginning to gather momentum in the war years.

The war also proved to be a demographic cauldron, churning and shifting the American population. Many of the 15 million men and women in uniform, having seen new sights and glimpsed new horizons, chose not to go home again at war's end. War industries sucked people into boomtowns such as Los Angeles, Detroit, Seattle, and Baton Rouge. California's population grew by nearly 2 million. The South experienced especially dramatic changes. The states of the old Confederacy received a disproportionate share of defense contracts, including nearly $6 billion of federally financed industrial facilities. Here were the seeds of the postwar blossoming of the "Sunbelt."

Despite this economic stimulus in the South, some 1.6 million blacks left the land of their past enslavement to seek jobs in the war plants of the West and North. Forever after, race relations constituted a national, not a regional, issue. Explosive tensions developed over employment, housing, and segregated facilities. Black leader A. Philip Randolph, head of the Brotherhood of Sleeping Car Porters, threatened a massive "Negro March on Washington" in 1941 to demand equal opportunities for blacks in war jobs and in the armed forces. Roosevelt's response was to issue an executive order forbidding discrimination in defense industries and to establish the Fair Employment Practices Commission (FEPC) to monitor compliance with his edict.

Blacks were also drafted into the armed forces, though they were generally assigned to service branches rather than combat units. But in general the war helped to embolden blacks in their long struggle for equality. Membership in the National Association for the Advancement of Colored People (NAACP) shot up almost to the half-million mark, and a new militant organization committed to nonviolent "direct action," the Congress of Racial Equality (CORE), was founded in 1942.

The northward migration of African Americans accelerated after the war, thanks to the advent of the mechanical cotton picker—an invention whose impact rivaled that of Eli Whitney's cotton gin. Overnight, the Cotton South's historic need for cheap labor disappeared. Their muscle no longer required in Dixie, some 5 million black tenant farmers and sharecroppers headed north in the three decades after the war. Within a single generation, a near-majority of African Americans gave up their historic homeland and their rural way of life. By 1970 half of all blacks lived outside the South, and *urban* had become almost a synonym for *black*.

The war also prompted an exodus of Native Americans from the reservations. Thousands of Indian men and women found war work in the major cities, and thousands more answered Uncle Sam's call to arms. More than 90 percent of Indians resided on reservations in 1940; six decades later almost half lived in cities.

The sudden rubbing against one another of unfamiliar peoples produced some distressingly violent friction. In 1943 young "zoot-suit"-clad Mexicans and Mexican Americans in Los Angeles were viciously attacked by Anglo sailors who cruised the streets in taxicabs, searching for victims. At almost the same time, an even more brutal race riot that killed twenty-five blacks and nine whites erupted in Detroit.

An African American soldier angrily complained about segregation in the armed forces during World War II:

"Why is it we Negro soldiers who are as much a part of Uncle Sam's great military machine as any cannot be treated with equality and the respect due us? The same respect which white soldiers expect and demand from us? ... There is great need for drastic change in this man's Army! How can we be trained to protect America, which is called a *free* nation, when all around us rears the ugly head of segregation?"

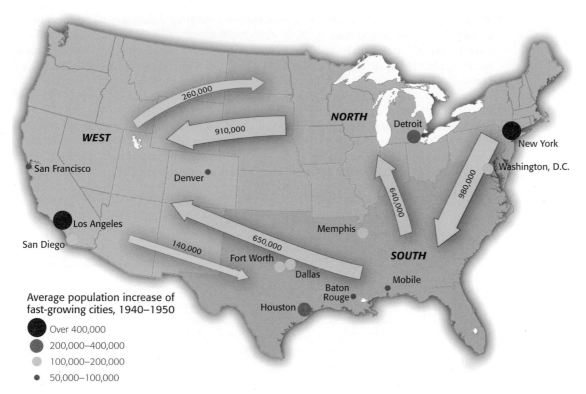

Average population increase of fast-growing cities, 1940–1950

- ● Over 400,000
- ● 200,000–400,000
- ● 100,000–200,000
- ● 50,000–100,000

Internal Migration in the United States during World War II Few events in American history have moved the American people about so massively as World War II. The West and the South boomed, and several war-industry cities grew explosively. A majority of migrants from the South were blacks; 1.6 million African Americans left the region in the 1940s. (Source: United States Department of Labor, Bureau of Labor Statistics.) © Cengage Learning

MAP SKILL-BUILDER: Understanding Demographic-Political Maps

1. With its combination of demographic and political information, this map conveys both a broad impression of the wartime migration (through the graphic arrows) and specific *quantitative* data that can be further analyzed if the reader chooses. During World War II, what was the approximate *net* migration of civilian population from the East to the West? (Net migration is the number of westward migrants minus the number of those who moved east.)
2. Of the nine fastest-growing cities during the 1940s, how many were located in the West and South? (Consider Washington, D.C., as a southern city.) Which were the two fastest-growing cities in the North?

Holding the Home Front

Despite these ugly episodes, Americans on the home front suffered little from the war compared with the peoples of the other fighting nations. By war's end much of the planet was a smoking ruin. But in America the war invigorated the economy and lifted the country out of a decade-long depression. The gross national product vaulted from less than $100 billion in 1940 to more than $200 billion in 1945. Corporate profits approximately doubled during the war. Despite wage ceilings, overtime pay fattened pay envelopes. On December 7, 1944, the third anniversary of Pearl Harbor, Macy's department store rang up the biggest sales day in its history. Americans had never had it so good—and they wanted it a lot better.

The hand of government touched more American lives more intimately during the war than ever before. The war, perhaps even more than the New Deal, pointed the way to the post-1945 era of big-government interventionism. Millions of men and women worked for Uncle Sam in the armed forces or defense industries, and their personal needs were cared for by government-sponsored housing projects, day-care facilities, and health plans. The Office of Scientific Research and Development channeled hundreds of millions of dollars into university-based scientific research, establishing the partnership between the government and universities that underwrote America's technological and economic leadership in the postwar era.

The flood of war dollars—not the relatively modest rivulet of New Deal spending—at last swept the plague of unemployment from the land. War, not enlightened social policy, cured the depression. As the postwar economy continued to depend dangerously on military spending for its health, many observers looked back to the years 1941–1945 and saw the origins of a "warfare-welfare state."

The conflict was phenomenally expensive. The wartime bill amounted to more than $330 billion—ten times the direct cost of World War I and twice as much as *all* previous federal spending since 1776. Despite an expanded income tax and higher tax rates, only about two-fifths of the war costs were paid from current revenues. The remainder was borrowed. The national debt skyrocketed from $49 billion in 1941 to $259 billion in 1945.

The Rising Sun in the Pacific

bastion *A fortified stronghold, often including earthworks or stoneworks, that guards against enemy attack.*

Early successes of the efficient Japanese militarists were breathtaking: they realized that they would have to win quickly or lose slowly. Simultaneously with the assault on Pearl Harbor, the Japanese launched widespread and uniformly successful attacks on various **bastions** in the Pacific and East Asia. These included the American outposts of Guam, Wake, and the Philippines, as well as Hong Kong and British Malaya, with its critically important supplies of rubber and tin.

Nor did the Japanese tide stop there. The soldiers of the emperor, plunging into the snake-infested jungles of Burma, cut the famed Burma road. This was the route over which the United States had been trucking a trickle of munitions to the armies of Chinese generalissimo Jiang Jieshi (Chiang Kai-shek), who was still resisting the Japanese invader in China. Thereafter, intrepid American aviators were forced to fly a handful of war supplies to Jiang "over the hump" of the towering Himalaya Mountains from the India-Burma theater. Meanwhile, the Japanese had lunged southward against the oil-rich Dutch East Indies, which speedily fell to the assailants.

In the Philippines General Douglas MacArthur, the eloquent and egotistical American commander, slowed the invading Japanese army's advance for five months. Twenty thousand American troops and a larger force of Filipinos withdrew to a strong defensive position at Bataan, near Manila, where they held off violent Japanese attacks until April 9, 1942. Before the inevitable American surrender, MacArthur was ordered to depart secretly for Australia, but he proclaimed as he departed, "I shall return." The battered remnants of his army were treated with vicious cruelty in the infamous eighty-mile Bataan death march to prisoner-of-war camps. The island fortress of Corregidor, in Manila harbor, held out until May 6, 1942, when it surrendered and left Japanese forces in complete control of the Philippine archipelago.

Japan's High Tide at Midway

The aggressive warriors from Japan, making hay while the Rising Sun shone, pushed relentlessly southward. They invaded the turtle-shaped island of New Guinea, north of Australia, and landed on the Solomon Islands, from which they threatened Australia itself. Their onrush was finally checked by a crucial naval battle in the Coral Sea, in May 1942. An American carrier task force, with Australian support, inflicted heavy losses on the victory-flushed Japanese. For the first time in history, the fighting was all done by carrier-based aircraft.

Japan next undertook to seize Midway Island, more than a thousand miles northwest of Honolulu. From this strategic base, it could launch devastating assaults on Pearl Harbor and perhaps force the weakened American Pacific fleet into destructive combat. An epochal naval battle was fought near Midway on June 3–6, 1942. Admiral Chester W. Nimitz, a high-grade naval strategist, directed a smaller but skillfully maneuvered carrier force

United States Thrusts in the Pacific, 1942–1945 American strategists had to choose among four proposed plans for waging the war against Japan:

1. Defeating the Japanese in China by funneling supplies over the Himalayan "hump" from India.
2. Carrying the war into Southeast Asia (a proposal much favored by the British, who could thus regain Singapore).
3. Heavy bombing of Japan from Chinese air bases.
4. "Island-hopping" from the South Pacific to within striking distance of the Japanese home islands. The fourth strategy, favored by General Douglas MacArthur, was the one finally emphasized.

against the powerful invading fleet. The fighting was all done by aircraft, and the Japanese broke off action after losing four vitally important carriers.

The Battle of Midway was a pivotal victory. Combined with the Battle of Coral Sea, the U.S. success at Midway halted Japan's juggernaut. But the thrust of the Japanese into the eastern Pacific did net them America's fog-girt islands of Kiska and Attu in the Aleutian archipelago, off Alaska. This easy conquest aroused fear of an invasion of the United States from the northwest. Much American strength was consequently diverted to the defense of Alaska.

Yet the Japanese imperialists, overextended in 1942, suffered from "victory disease." Their appetites were bigger than their stomachs. If they had only dug in and consolidated their gains, they would have been much more difficult to dislodge once the tide turned.

American Leapfrogging Toward Tokyo

Following the heartening victory at Midway, the United States for the first time was able to seize the initiative in the Pacific. In August 1942 American ground forces gained a toehold on Guadalcanal Island, in the Solomons, in an effort to protect the lifeline from America to Australia through the Southwest Pacific. After several desperate sea battles for naval control of the area, the Japanese troops evacuated Guadalcanal in February 1943.

American and Australian forces, under General MacArthur, meanwhile had been hanging on courageously to the southeastern tip of New Guinea, the last buffer protecting Australia. Aided by American naval forces, MacArthur eventually fought his way westward through the tropical jungle hells and completed the conquest of New Guinea by August 1944.

The U.S. Navy, with marines and army divisions doing the meat-grinder fighting, had meanwhile been "leapfrogging" the Japanese-held islands in the Pacific. Old-fashioned strategy dictated that the American forces, as they drove toward Tokyo, should reduce the fortified Japanese outposts on their flank. The new American strategy of island-hopping called for bypassing some of the most heavily fortified Japanese posts, capturing nearby islands, setting up airfields on them, and then neutralizing the enemy bases through heavy bombing. Deprived of essential supplies from the homeland, Japan's outposts would slowly wither on the vine—as they did.

With Admiral Nimitz skillfully coordinating the efforts of naval, air, and ground units, the American attacks achieved brilliant success. In May and August 1943, Attu and Kiska in the Aleutians were easily retaken. In November 1943 "bloody Tarawa" and Makin in the Gilbert Islands fell after suicidal resistance, and key outposts in the Marshall Islands succumbed after savage fighting in January and February 1944. The conquest of Guam and other islands in the Marianas in July and August 1944 provided airfields for America's new B-29 super-bombers to carry out round-trip bombing raids on Japan's home islands. With these unsinkable aircraft carriers now available, virtual around-the-clock bombing of Japan began in November 1944.

The Allied Halting of Hitler

Early setbacks for America in the Pacific were paralleled in the Atlantic. Hitler had entered the war with a formidable fleet of ultramodern submarines, which ultimately operated in "wolf packs" with frightful effect. During ten months of 1942 more than five hundred merchant ships were lost. Not until the spring of 1943 did the Allies clearly gain the upper hand against the **U-boat**.

The turning point of the land-air war against Hitler came late in 1942. The British, who had launched a thousand-plane raid on Cologne in May, were joined by the American air force in cascading bombs on German cities. The Germans under Marshal Erwin Rommel—the "Desert Fox"—had driven eastward across the hot sands of North Africa into Egypt, perilously close to the Suez Canal. A breakthrough would have spelled disaster for the Allies. But late in October 1942, British general Bernard Montgomery delivered a withering attack at El Alamein, west of Cairo. With the aid of several hundred hastily shipped American Sherman tanks, he speedily drove the enemy back to Tunisia, more than a thousand miles away.

On the Soviet front, the unexpected successes of the Red army gave a new lift to the Allied cause. In September 1942 the Russians halted the German steamroller at rubble-strewn Stalingrad, graveyard of Hitler's hopes. In November 1942 the resilient Russians unleashed a crushing counteroffensive, which was never seriously reversed. A year later, Stalin had regained about two-thirds of the blood-soaked Soviet motherland wrested from him by the German invader.

U-boat *A German submarine, named for the German* Unterseeboot, *or "undersea boat," which proved deadly for Allied ships in the war zone. U-boat attacks played an important role in drawing the United States into the war.*

A Second Front from North Africa to Rome

Soviet losses were already staggering in 1942; millions of soldiers and civilians lay dead, and Hitler's armies had laid waste a vast territory equivalent in the United States to the area from Chicago to the Atlantic seaboard. Small wonder that Kremlin leaders clamored for a second front to divert the German strength westward.

Many Americans, including FDR, were eager to begin an invasion of France in 1942 or 1943. They feared that the Soviets might make a separate peace with Germany, as they had in 1918, and leave the Western Allies to face Hitler's fury alone. But British military

World War II in Europe and North Africa, 1939–1945 © Cengage Learning

planners, remembering their appalling losses in France in 1914–1918, preferred to attack Hitler's Fortress Europe through the "soft underbelly" of the Mediterranean. Faced with British boot-dragging, the Americans reluctantly agreed to postpone a massive invasion of Europe.

An assault on French-held North Africa was a compromise second front. The highly secret attack, launched in November 1942, was headed by a gifted and easy-smiling American general, Dwight D. ("Ike") Eisenhower, a master of organization and conciliation. The joint Allied operation, ultimately involving some 400,000 men and about 850 ships, was highly successful. After savage fighting, the remnants of the German-Italian army were finally trapped in Tunisia and surrendered in May 1943.

At Casablanca, in newly occupied French Morocco, President Roosevelt met with Winston Churchill in January 1943 to plan new blows. The Big Two agreed to step up the Pacific war, invade Sicily, increase pressure on Italy, and insist on "unconditional surrender" by the enemy. Designed to hearten the ultra suspicious Soviets, who professed to fear separate Allied peace negotiations, "unconditional surrender" proved to be one of the most controversial moves of the war. The main criticism was that it steeled the enemy to fight to a last-bunker resistance, while discouraging antiwar groups in Germany from revolting. Although there was some truth in these charges, no one can prove that "unconditional surrender" either shortened or lengthened the war. But this is known: by helping to destroy the German government utterly, the harsh policy forced a thorough postwar reconstruction.

depose *Forcibly remove from office or position.*

beachhead *The first position on a beach secured by an invading force and used to land further troops and supplies.*

Allied forces, victorious in Africa, now turned against the not-so-soft underbelly of Europe. Sicily fell in August 1943 after sporadic but sometimes bitter resistance. Shortly before the conquest of the island, Mussolini was **deposed**, and Italy surrendered unconditionally soon thereafter, in September 1943.

But if Italy dropped out of the war, the Germans did not drop out of Italy. Hitler's well-trained troops stubbornly resisted the Allied invaders now pouring into the toe of the Italian boot. "Sunny Italy" proceeded to belie its name, for in the snow-covered and mud-caked mountains of its elongated peninsula occurred some of the filthiest, bloodiest, and most frustrating fighting of the war. After a touch-and-go assault on the Anzio **beachhead**, Rome was finally taken on June 4, 1944. But painful fighting continued in northern Italy, and not until May 2, 1945, did several hundred thousand Axis troops in Italy lay down their arms. While the Italian second front opened the Mediterranean and diverted some German divisions from the blazing Soviet and French battle lines, it also may have delayed the main Allied invasion of France by many months—allowing more time for the Soviet army to advance into Eastern Europe.

D-Day: June 6, 1944

The Soviets never ceased their clamor for an all-out second front. Plans for a major Allied invasion were finally settled at a conference of Stalin, Churchill, and Roosevelt in Teheran, Iran, held from November 28 to December 1, 1943. The Soviets agreed to launch attacks on Germany from the east simultaneously with the prospective Allied assault from the west.

Preparations for the cross-channel invasion of France were gigantic. Britain's fast-anchored isle virtually groaned with munitions, supplies, and troops, as nearly 3 million fighting men were readied. Because the United States was to provide most of the Allied warriors, the overall command was entrusted to an American, General Eisenhower.

French Normandy, less heavily defended than other parts of the European coast, was pinpointed for the invasion assault. On D-Day, June 6, 1944, the enormous operation, which involved some forty-six hundred vessels, unwound. Stiff resistance was encountered from the Germans, who had been misled by a feint into expecting the blow to fall farther north.

The Allied beachhead, at first clung to with fingertips, was gradually enlarged, consolidated, and reinforced. After desperate fighting, the invaders finally broke out of the German iron ring that enclosed the Normandy landing zone. Most spectacular were the lunges across France by American armored divisions, brilliantly commanded by blustery and profane General George S. ("Blood 'n' Guts") Patton. The retreat of the German defenders was hastened when an American-French force landed in August 1944 on the southern coast of France and swept northward. With the assistance of the French "**underground**," Paris was liberated in August 1944.

Allied forces rolled irresistibly toward Germany. The first important German city (Aachen) fell to the Americans in October 1944, and the days of Hitler's "thousand-year Reich" were numbered.

underground *A secret or illegal movement organized in a country to resist or overthrow the government.*

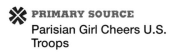
PRIMARY SOURCE
Parisian Girl Cheers U.S. Troops

FDR: The Fourth Term of 1944

The presidential campaign of 1944 came awkwardly as the awful conflict roared to its climax. Meeting in Chicago, victory-starved Republicans nominated short, mustachioed, and dapper Thomas Dewey, the popular governor of New York. A former prosecutor, Dewey was only forty-two years of age, causing one veteran New Dealer to sneer that the candidate had cast his diaper into the ring. To offset Dewey's mild internationalism, the convention nominated for the vice presidency a strong isolationist, Senator John W. Bricker of Ohio.

FDR, aging under the strain but still the "indispensable man," was nominated by **acclamation** for a fourth term. The scramble for the vice-presidential plum turned into a free-for-all. Roosevelt's third-term vice president, former agriculture secretary Henry

acclamation *A general and unanimous action of approval or nomination by a large public body, without a vote.*

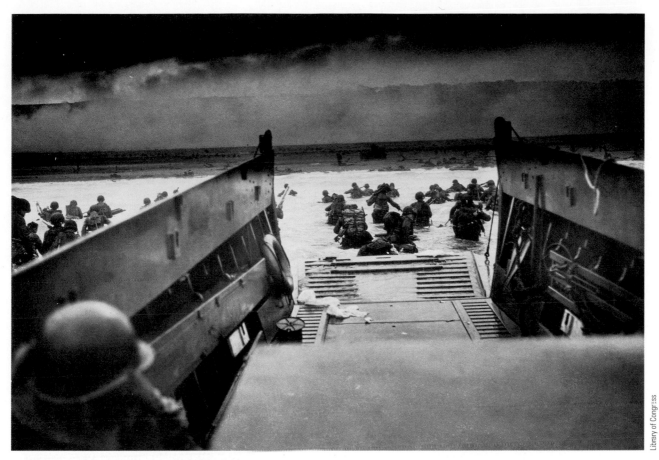

Library of Congress

Allies Landing in Normandy, June 6, 1944 Nine-foot ocean swells on invasion day made loading the assault landing craft, such as the one pictured here, treacherous business. Many men were injured or tossed into the sea as the bathtub-like amphibious vessels bobbed wildly up and down alongside the troop transports. As the vulnerable boats churned toward the beach, some officers led their tense, grim-faced troops in prayer. One major, recalling the remarkable Battle of Agincourt in 1415, quoted from Shakespeare's *Henry V*: "He that outlives this day, and comes safe home/Will stand a tip-toe when this day is named."

A. Wallace, was a committed liberal who desired renomination. Conservative Democrats concocted a "ditch Wallace" movement that developed tremendous momentum and finally won Roosevelt's blessing. The vice presidential nomination then went to smiling and self-assured Senator Harry S Truman of Missouri, who had recently attained national visibility as the efficient chairman of a Senate committee investigating wasteful war expenditures.

A dynamic Dewey took the offensive in the campaign, proclaiming in his beautiful baritone voice that it was "time for a change" after "twelve long years" of New Dealism. In the closing weeks of the campaign, Roosevelt left his desk for the stump. He was eager to show himself, even in chilling rains, to spike well-founded rumors of failing health.

Democrats relied heavily on the new political action committee of the CIO, which provided union funds and campaign workers. Roosevelt, as customary, won a sweeping victory: 432 to 99 in the Electoral College, 25,606,585 to 22,014,745 in the popular totals. Elated, Roosevelt quipped that, "the first twelve years are the hardest."

The Last Days of Hitler

By mid-December 1944, the month after Roosevelt's fourth-term victory, Germany seemed to be wobbling on its last legs. The Soviet surge had penetrated eastern Germany. Allied aerial "blockbuster" bombs, making the "rubble bounce" with around-the-clock attacks, were falling like giant explosive hailstones on cities, factories, and transportation arteries.

EXAMINING THE EVIDENCE

FRANKLIN ROOSEVELT AT TEHERAN, 1943

In late 1943 the "Big Three" wartime leaders—British prime minister Winston Churchill, American president Franklin Roosevelt, and Soviet leader Marshal Joseph Stalin—gathered together for the first time. They met amid growing Soviet frustration with the British and the Americans for their failure thus far to open a "second front" against Germany in Western Europe, while the Soviets continued to suffer horrendous losses in the savage fighting in Eastern Europe. American military planners were eager to open a second front as soon as possible, but the British, who would necessarily have to supply most of the troops until America was fully mobilized, balked. Tension among the three leaders over the second-front plan—code-named OVERLORD, the operation that resulted in the Anglo-American invasion of Normandy on "D-Day," June 6, 1944—is evident in this report of their discussions in the Iranian city of Teheran on November 28, 1943. The excerpts printed here are actually taken from two separate accounts: one composed by the American diplomat and Roosevelt's official translator Charles Bohlen, the other written by a military officer on behalf of the United States Joint Chiefs of Staff. Both versions were published in *Foreign Relations of the United States*, a compilation of American diplomatic records since 1861. The Soviets and the British also kept their own records of the Teheran meetings, giving historians remarkably rich sources with which to reconstruct the crucial negotiations and decisions that shaped wartime diplomacy.

1. Why might the history of diplomacy be so lavishly documented?

2. At this meeting, what were the principal objectives that each leader pursued? How did each man address his task?

3. In what ways was the future of the war—and the postwar world—here foreshadowed?

FIRST PLENARY MEETING, NOVEMBER 28, 1943, 4 P. M., CONFERENCE ROOM, SOVIET EMBASSY

Bohlen Minutes

SECRET

THE PRESIDENT said as the youngest of the three present he ventured to welcome his elders. He said he wished to welcome the new members to the family circle and tell them that meetings of this character were conducted as between friends with complete frankness on all sides with nothing that was said to be made public. . . .

Chief of Staff Minutes

MARSHAL STALIN asked who will be the commander in this Operation Overlord. (THE PRESIDENT and PRIME MINISTER interpolated this was not yet decided.) MARSHAL STALIN continued, "Then nothing will come out of these operations." . . .

THE PRESIDENT said we again come back to the problem of the timing for OVERLORD. It was believed that it would be good for OVERLORD to take place about 1 May, or certainly not later than 15 May or 20 May, if possible.

THE PRIME MINISTER said that he could not agree to that. . . .

. . . He said he (the Prime Minister) was going to do everything in the power of His Majesty's Government to begin OVERLORD at the earliest possible moment. However, he did not think that the many great possibilities in the Mediterranean should be ruthlessly cast aside as valueless merely on the question of a month's delay in OVERLORD.

MARSHAL STALIN said all the Mediterranean operations are diversions, . . .

THE PRESIDENT said he found that his staff places emphasis on OVERLORD. While on the other hand the Prime Minister and his staff also emphasize OVERLORD, nevertheless the United States does not feel that OVERLORD should be put off.

THE PRESIDENT questioned whether it would not be possible for the *ad hoc* committee to go ahead with their deliberations without any further directive and to produce an answer by tomorrow morning.

MARSHAL STALIN questioned, "What can such a committee do?" He said, "We Chiefs of State have more power and more authority than a committee. General Brooke cannot force our opinions and there are many questions which can be decided only by us." He said he would like to ask if the British are thinking seriously of OVERLORD only in order to satisfy the U.S.S.R.

THE PRIME MINISTER replied that if the conditions specified at Moscow regarding OVERLORD should exist, he firmly believed it would be England's duty to hurl every ounce of strength she had across the Channel at the Germans.

THE PRESIDENT observed that in an hour a very good dinner would be awaiting all and people would be very hungry. He suggested that the staffs should meet tomorrow morning and discuss the matter. . . .

The German western front seemed about to buckle under the sledgehammer blows of the United States and its Allies.

Hitler then staked everything on one last throw of his reserves. Secretly concentrating a powerful force, he hurled it, on December 16, 1944, against the thinly held American lines in the heavily befogged and snow-shrouded Ardennes Forest. Caught off guard, the outmanned Americans were driven back, creating a deep "bulge" in the Allied line. The ten-day penetration was finally halted after the 101st Airborne Division had stood firm at the vital bastion of Bastogne. The commander, Brigadier General A. C. McAuliffe, defiantly answered the German demand for surrender with one word: "Nuts." Reinforcements were rushed up, and the last-gasp Hitlerian offensive was at length bloodily stemmed in the Battle of the Bulge.

In March 1945, forward-driving American troops reached Germany's Rhine River, where, by incredibly good luck, they found one strategic bridge not demolished. Pressing their advantage, General Eisenhower's troops reached the Elbe River in April 1945. There, a short distance south of Berlin, American and Soviet advance guards dramatically clasped hands.

The conquering Americans were horrified to find blood-bespattered **concentration camps**, where the German Nazis had engaged in scientific mass murder of "undesirables," including an estimated 6 million Jews. The Washington government had long been informed about Hitler's campaign of **genocide** against the Jews and had been reprehensibly slow to take steps against it—such as bombing rail lines that carried the victims to the camps. But until the war's end, the full dimensions of the "Holocaust" were not known. When the details were revealed, the whole world was aghast.

The vengeful Soviets, clawing their way forward from the east, reached Berlin in April 1945. After desperate house-to-house fighting, followed by an orgy of pillage and rape, they captured the bomb-shattered city. Adolf Hitler, after a hasty marriage to his mistress, committed suicide in an underground bunker on April 30, 1945.

Tragedy had meanwhile struck the United States. President Roosevelt, while relaxing at Warm Springs, Georgia, suddenly died from a massive cerebral hemorrhage on April 12, 1945. Knots of confused, leaderless citizens gathered to discuss the future anxiously, as bewildered, unbriefed Vice President Truman took the helm.

On May 7, 1945, what was left of the German government surrendered unconditionally. May 8 was officially proclaimed V-E (Victory in Europe) Day and was greeted with frenzied rejoicing in the Allied countries.

concentration camp *A place of confinement for prisoners or others a government considers dangerous or undesirable.*

genocide *The systematic extermination or killing of an entire people.*

Japan Dies Hard

Japan's rickety bamboo empire meanwhile was tottering to its fall. American submarines— "the silent service"—were sending the Japanese merchant marine to the bottom so fast they were running out of prey. All told, these undersea craft destroyed 1,042 ships, or about 50 percent of Japan's entire life-sustaining merchant fleet.

Giant bomber attacks were more spectacular. Launched from Saipan and other captured Mariana islands, they were reducing the enemy's fragile cities to cinders. The massive fire-bomb raid on Tokyo, March 9–10, 1945, was annihilating. It destroyed over 250,000 buildings, gutted a quarter of the city, and killed an estimated 83,000 people—a loss comparable to that later inflicted by the atomic bombs.

General MacArthur was also on the move. Completing the conquest of jungle-draped New Guinea, he headed northwest for the Philippines, en route to Japan, with six hundred ships and 250,000 men. In a scene well staged for the photographers, he splashed ashore at Leyte Island, on October 20, 1944, with the summons, "People of the Philippines, I have returned...Rally to me." The ravaged city of Manila on the main island of Luzon fell in March 1945, but the Philippines were not finally conquered until July, after bitter fighting against holed-in Japanese, who took a toll of over sixty thousand American casualties.

America's steel vise was tightening mercilessly around Japan. The tiny island of Iwo Jima was captured in March 1945, after a desperate assault that cost over four thousand American dead. The island of Okinawa, well defended by Japanese soldiers who fought with incredible courage from their caves, was finally taken in June 1945, at the cost of fifty thousand American casualties and far heavier Japanese losses. The U.S. Navy, which

The scientific director of the Manhattan Project, J. Robert Oppenheimer (1904–1967), recalled his reaction as he witnessed the detonation of the first atomic bomb at the Trinity test site in Alamogordo, New Mexico, in July 1945. He was not only awed by the extraordinary force of this new weapon. He also feared the power to do harm that it gave to humans:

"I remembered the line from the Hindu scripture, the *Bhagavad-Gita:* 'Now I am become Death, the destroyer of Worlds.' "

covered the invasion of Okinawa, sustained severe damage. Japanese suicide pilots ("kamikazes"), in an exhibition of mass hara-kiri for their emperor, smashed their bomb-laden planes onto the decks of the invading fleet, sinking over thirty ships and damaging scores more.

The Atomic Bombs

Strategists in Washington were meanwhile planning an all-out invasion of the main islands of Japan—an invasion that presumably would cost hundreds of thousands of American (and even more Japanese) casualties. Tokyo, recognizing imminent defeat, had secretly sent peace feelers to Moscow, which had not yet entered the East Asian war. But bomb-scorched Japan still showed no outward willingness to surrender *unconditionally* to the Allies.

The Potsdam conference, held near Berlin in July 1945, sounded the death knell of the Japanese. There President Truman, still new on his job, met in a seventeen-day parley with Joseph Stalin and the British leaders. The conferees issued a stern ultimatum to Japan: surrender or be destroyed. But no encouraging response was forthcoming.

America had a fantastic ace up its sleeve. Early in 1940, after Hitler's wanton assault on Poland, Roosevelt was persuaded by American and exiled scientists, notably German-born Albert Einstein, to push ahead with preparations for unlocking the secret of an atomic bomb. Congress, at Roosevelt's blank-check request, blindly made available nearly $2 billion.

What was called the Manhattan Project pushed feverishly forward, as American know-how and industrial power were combined with the most advanced scientific knowledge. Much technical skill was provided by refugee scientists who had fled the torture chambers of the dictators. Finally, in the desert near Alamogordo, New Mexico, on July 16, 1945, the experts detonated the first awesome and devastating atomic device.

With Japan still refusing to surrender, the Potsdam threat was fulfilled. On August 6, 1945, a lone American bomber dropped one atomic bomb on the city of Hiroshima, Japan. In a blinding flash of death, followed by a funnel-shaped cloud, about 180,000 people were left killed, wounded, or missing. Some 70,000 of them died instantaneously. Sixty thousand more soon perished from burns and radiation disease.

Two days later, on August 8, Stalin entered the war against Japan, exactly on the deadline date previously agreed upon with his allies. Soviet armies speedily overran the depleted Japanese defenses in Manchuria and Korea in a six-day "victory parade" that involved several thousand Russian casualties. Stalin was evidently determined to be in on the kill, lest he lose a voice in the final division of Japan's holdings.

On August 9, American aviators dropped a second atomic bomb on the city of Nagasaki. The explosion took a horrible toll of about eighty thousand people killed or missing (see "Varying Viewpoints," p. 592). The Japanese nation could endure no more. On August 10, 1945, Tokyo sued for peace on one condition: that Hirohito, the bespectacled Son of Heaven, be allowed to remain on his ancestral throne as nominal emperor. Despite their "unconditional surrender" policy, the Allies accepted this condition on August 14, 1945. The official surrender ceremonies took place on the battleship *Missouri* on September 2, 1945. At the same time, Americans at home celebrated V-J (Victory in Japan) Day, after the most horrible war in history had ended in mushrooming atomic clouds.

PRIMARY SOURCE
Announcing the Use of the
A-Bomb at Hiroshima

PRIMARY SOURCE
Unconditional Surrender of
Japan

The Allies Triumphant

World War II proved to be terribly costly. American forces suffered some 1 million casualties, about one-third of which were deaths. Compared with other wars, the proportion killed by wounds and disease was sharply reduced, owing in part to the use of blood plasma and "miracle" drugs, notably penicillin.

America was fortunate in emerging with its mainland virtually unscathed. Much of the rest of the world was utterly destroyed and destitute. America alone was untouched and healthy—oiled and muscled like a prize bull, standing astride the world's ruined landscape.

This complex conflict was the best-fought war in America's history. Though unprepared for it at the outset, the nation was better prepared than for the others, partly because America had begun to buckle on its armor about a year and a half before the war officially began. In the end the United States showed itself to be resourceful, tough, adaptable—able to accommodate itself to the tactics of an enemy who was relentless and ruthless.

American military leadership proved to be of the highest order. A new crop of war heroes emerged in brilliant generals such as Eisenhower, MacArthur, and George Marshall (chief of staff) and in imaginative admirals such as Nimitz. President Roosevelt and Prime Minister Churchill, as kindred spirits, collaborated closely in planning strategy. "It is fun to be in the same decade with you," FDR once cabled Churchill.

Industrial leaders were no less skilled, for marvels of production were performed almost daily. Assembly lines proved as important as battle lines, and victory went again to the side with the most smokestacks. The enemy was almost literally smothered by bayonets, bullets, **bazookas**, and bombs. Hitler and his Axis coconspirators had chosen to make war with machines, and the ingenious Yankees could ask for nothing better. They demonstrated again, as they had in World War I, that the American way of war was simply more—more men, more weapons, more machines, more technology, and more money than any enemy could hope to match. From 1940 to 1945, the output of American factories was simply phenomenal.

Hermann Goering, a Nazi leader, had sneered, "The Americans can't build planes—only electric iceboxes and razor blades." Democracy had given its answer, as the dictators, despite long preparation, were overthrown and discredited. It is true that an unusual amount of direct control was exercised over the individual by the Washington authorities during the war emergency. But the American people preserved their precious liberties without serious impairment.

bazooka *A metal-tubed weapon from which armor-piercing rockets are electronically fired.*

36

The Cold War Begins

1945–1952

America stands at this moment at the summit of the world.

WINSTON CHURCHILL, 1945

The American people, 140 million strong, cheered their nation's victories in Europe and Asia at the conclusion of World War II. But before the shouting had even faded, many Americans began to worry about their futures. Four fiery years of global war had not entirely driven from their minds the painful memories of twelve desperate years of the Great Depression. Still more ominously, victory celebrations had barely ended before America's crumbling relations with its wartime ally, the Soviet Union, threatened a new and even more terrible international conflict.

FOCUS QUESTIONS

1. What were the causes and consequences of the post–World War II economic boom?

2. What were the principal short-term and long-term changes in American society caused by the postwar "baby boom"?

3. What were the sources of the emerging Cold War between the United States and the Soviet Union, and what key events in Germany and Eastern Europe brought the two sides to the brink of confrontation?

4. How did the United States attempt to "contain" the Soviet Union, and later Communist China, and what were the effects of this policy in Europe and East Asia (including Korea)?

5. How did the Cold War affect domestic American society, and what were the results of the widespread fear of both Soviet spying and domestic Communist subversion?

Postwar Economic Anxieties

The decade of the 1930s had left deep scars. Joblessness and insecurity had dampened the marriage rate. Babies went unborn as pinched budgets and sagging self-esteem wrought a sexual depression in American bedrooms. The war had banished the blight of depression, but grim-faced observers warned that peace would bring the return of hard times.

CHRONOLOGY

1944	Servicemen's Readjustment Act (GI Bill). Bretton Woods economic conference.
1945	Spock publishes *The Common Sense Book of Baby and Child Care.* Yalta conference. United States ends lend-lease to USSR. United Nations established.
1945–1946	Nuremberg war crimes trials in Germany.
1946	Employment Act creates Council of Economic Advisers.
1946–1948	Iran crisis.
1947	Truman Doctrine. Marshall Plan. Taft-Hartley Act. National Security Act creates Department of Defense, National Security Council (NSC), and Central Intelligence Agency (CIA).
1948	Israel founded; United States recognizes it. Alger Hiss case begins. Truman defeats Dewey for presidency.
1948–1949	Berlin blockade.
1949	NATO established. Communists defeat Nationalists in China. Soviets explode their first atomic bomb.
1950	American economy begins postwar growth. McCarthy Red hunt begins. McCarran Internal Security Act passed by Congress over Truman's veto.
1950–1953	Korean War.
1951	Truman fires MacArthur. Rosenbergs convicted of treason.
1952	United States explodes first hydrogen bomb.
1957	Postwar peak of U.S. birthrate.
1973	U.S. birthrate falls below replacement level.

The faltering economy in the initial postwar years threatened to confirm the worst predictions of the doomsayers who foresaw another Great Depression. Real **gross national product** (GNP) slumped sickeningly in 1946 and 1947 from its wartime peak. With the removal of wartime price controls, prices giddily levitated by 33 percent in 1946–1947. An epidemic of strikes swept the country. During 1946 alone some 4.6 million laborers laid down their tools, fearful that soon they would barely be able to afford the autos and other goods they themselves were manufacturing.

gross national product *The total value of a nation's annual output of goods and services.*

The growing muscle of organized labor deeply annoyed many conservatives. They had their revenge against labor's New Deal gains in 1947, when a Republican-controlled Congress (the first in fourteen years) passed the Taft-Hartley Act over President Truman's vigorous veto. Labor leaders condemned the Taft-Hartley Act as a "slave-labor law." It outlawed the "closed" (all-union) shop, made unions liable for damages resulting from jurisdictional disputes, and required union leaders to take a noncommunist oath.

The Democratic administration meanwhile took steps of its own to forestall an economic downturn. It sold war factories and other government installations to private businesses at fire-sale prices. It secured passage of the Employment Act of 1946, which created a three-member Council of Economic Advisers to advise the president on government policy to "promote maximum employment, production, and purchasing power."

Most dramatic was the passage of the Servicemen's Readjustment Act of 1944—better known as the GI Bill of Rights, or the GI Bill. Enacted partly out of fear that the employment markets would never be able to absorb 15 million returning veterans at war's end, the GI Bill made generous provisions for sending the former soldiers to school. In the postwar decade, some 8 million veterans advanced their educations at Uncle Sam's expense. The majority attended technical and vocational schools, but colleges and universities were crowded to the blackboards as more than 2 million ex-GIs stormed the halls of higher learning. The total eventually spent for education was some $14.5 billion in taxpayer dollars. The act also enabled the Veterans Administration (VA) to guarantee about $16 billion in loans

The GI Bill Financed by the federal government, thousands of World War II veterans crowded into college classrooms in the 1940s. Here a fresh crop of ex-soldier students lays in supplies for the new term.

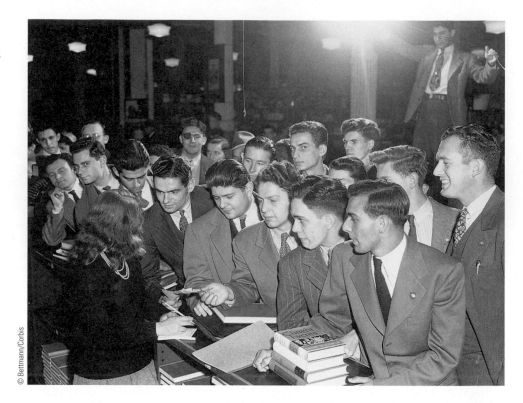

© Bettmann/Corbis

for veterans to buy homes, farms, and small businesses. By raising educational levels and stimulating the construction industry, the GI Bill powerfully nurtured the robust and long-lived economic expansion that eventually took hold in the late 1940s and that profoundly shaped the entire history of the postwar era.

The Long Economic Boom, 1950–1970

Gross national product began to climb haltingly in 1948. Then, beginning about 1950, the American economy surged onto a dazzling plateau of sustained growth that was to last virtually uninterrupted for two decades. America's economic performance became the envy of the world. National income nearly doubled in the 1950s and almost doubled again in the 1960s, shooting through the trillion-dollar mark in 1973. Americans, some 6 percent of the world's people, were enjoying about 40 percent of the planet's wealth. Nothing loomed larger in the history of the post–World War II era than this fantastic eruption of affluence. It did not enrich all Americans, and it did not touch all people evenly, but it transformed the lives of a majority of citizens and molded the agenda of politics and society for at least two generations. Prosperity underwrote social mobility, funded vast new welfare programs such as Medicare, and gave Americans the confidence to exercise unprecedented international leadership in the Cold War era.

As the gusher of prosperity poured forth its riches, Americans drank deeply from the gilded goblet. Millions of depression-pinched souls sought to make up for the sufferings of the 1930s. They determined to "get theirs" while the getting was good. A people who had once considered a chicken in every pot the standard of comfort and security now hungered for two cars in every garage, swimming pools in their backyards, vacation homes, and gas-guzzling recreational vehicles. The size of the "middle class," defined as households earning between $3,000 and $10,000 a year, doubled from pre–Great Depression days and included 60 percent of the American people by the mid-1950s. By the end of that decade, the vast majority of American families owned their own cars and washing machines, and nearly 90 percent owned a television set. In another revolution of sweeping consequences, almost 60 percent of American families owned their own homes by 1960, compared with less than 40 percent in the 1920s.

Of all the beneficiaries of postwar prosperity, none reaped greater rewards than women. More than ever, urban offices and shops provided them with a bonanza of employment, as the service sector of the economy dramatically outgrew the old industrial and manufacturing sectors. Women accounted for a quarter of the American work force at the end of World War II and for nearly half the labor pool five decades later. Yet even as women continued their march into the workplace in the 1940s and 1950s, popular culture glorified the traditional feminine roles of homemaker and mother. The clash between the demands of suburban housewifery and the realities of employment eventually sparked a feminist revolt in the 1960s.

What propelled this unprecedented economic explosion? The Second World War itself provided a powerful stimulus. While other countries had been ravaged by years of fighting, the United States had used the war crisis to fire up its smokeless factories and rebuild its depression-plagued economy. Invigorated by battle, America had almost effortlessly come to dominate the ruined global landscape of the postwar period.

Ominously, much of the glittering prosperity of the 1950s and 1960s rested on the underpinnings of colossal military budgets, leading some critics to speak of a "permanent war economy." The economic upturn of 1950 was fueled by massive appropriations for the Korean War, and defense spending accounted for some 10 percent of the GNP throughout the ensuing decade. Pentagon dollars primed the pumps of high-technology industries such as aerospace, plastics, and electronics and also financed much of the scientific research and development ("R and D") that spurred the economy.

Cheap energy also fed the economic boom. American and European companies controlled the flow of abundant petroleum from the Middle East, and they kept their prices low. Americans doubled their consumption of inexpensive and seemingly inexhaustible oil in the quarter century after the war. Anticipating a limitless future of low-cost fuels, they flung out endless ribbons of highways, installed air conditioning in their homes, and engineered a sixfold increase in the country's electricity-generating capacity between 1945 and 1970.

With the forces of nature increasingly harnessed in their hands, workers chalked up spectacular gains in productivity—the amount of output per hour of work. In the two decades after the outbreak of the Korean War in 1950, productivity increased at an average rate of more than 3 percent per year. Gains in productivity were also enhanced by the rising educational level of the workforce. By 1970 nearly 90 percent of the school-age population were enrolled in educational institutions—a dramatic contrast with the opening years of the century, when only half of this age group had attended school. Better educated and better equipped, American workers in 1970 could produce nearly twice as much in an hour's labor as they had done in 1950. Productivity was the key to prosperity. Rising productivity in the 1950s and 1960s virtually doubled the average American's standard of living in the postwar quarter century.

The Smiling Sunbelt

The convulsive economic changes of the post-1945 period shook and shifted the American people, amplifying the population redistribution set in motion by World War II. As immigrants and westward-trekking pioneers, Americans had always been a people on the move, but they were astonishingly footloose in the postwar years. For some three decades after 1945, an average of 30 million persons changed residences every year. Families especially felt the strain, as distance divided parents from children, and brothers and sisters from one another. One sign of this sort of stress was the phenomenal popularity of advice books on child rearing, especially Dr. Benjamin Spock's *The Common Sense Book of Baby and Child Care*. First published in 1945, the book instructed millions of parents during the ensuing decades in the kind of homely wisdom that was once transmitted naturally from grandparent to parent, and from parent to child.

Especially striking was the growth of the "Sunbelt"—a fifteen-state area stretching in a smiling crescent from Virginia through Florida and Texas to Arizona and California. This region increased its population at a rate nearly double that of the old industrial zones of the Northeast (the "Frostbelt"). In the 1950s California alone accounted for one-fifth of the entire nation's population growth and by 1963 had outdistanced New York as the most populous state—a position it still holds in the early years of the twenty-first century, with more than 36 million people, or more than one out of every eight Americans.

Sunbelt Prosperity The old and new West are evident in this view of booming Dallas.

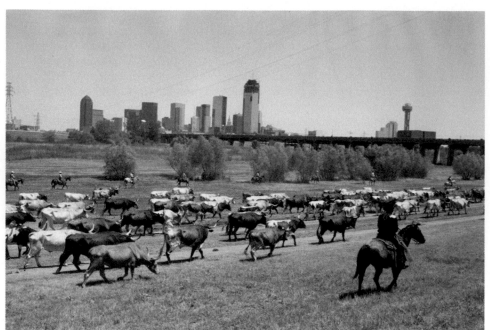

© Bettmann/CORBIS

A Niagara of federal dollars accounted for much of the Sunbelt's prosperity, though, ironically, southern and western politicians led the cry against government spending. By the early twenty-first century, states in the South and West were annually receiving some $444 billion more in federal funds than those in the Northeast and Midwest. Northeasterners and their allies from the hard-hit region of the Ohio Valley tried to rally political support with the sarcastic slogan "The North shall rise again."

These dramatic shifts of population and wealth further broke the historic grip of the North on the nation's political life. Every occupant of the White House from 1964 has hailed from the Sunbelt, and the region's congressional representation rose as its population grew. With their frontier ethic of unbridled individualism and their devotion to unregulated economic growth, the Sunbelters were redrawing the Republic's political map.

★ PRIMARY SOURCE
Population Increases in the Sunbelt States

The Rush to the Suburbs

In all regions, America's modern migrants—if they were white—fled from the cities to the burgeoning new suburbs (see "Makers of America: The Suburbanites," pp. 602–603). While other industrial countries struggled to rebuild their war-ravaged cities, government policies in the United States encouraged movement away from urban centers. Federal Housing Authority (FHA) and Veterans Administration (VA) home-loan guarantees made it more economically attractive to own a home in the suburbs than to rent an apartment in the city. Tax deductions for interest payments on home mortgages provided additional financial incentive. And government-built highways that sped commuters from suburban homes to city jobs further facilitated this mass migration. By 1960 one in every four Americans dwelt in suburbia, and a half century later, more than half the nation's population did.

The construction industry boomed in the 1950s and 1960s to satisfy this demand. Pioneered by innovators such as the Levitt brothers, whose first "Levittown" sprouted on New York's Long Island in the 1940s, builders developed efficient new techniques of mass-produced housing construction. Snooty critics wailed about the aesthetic monotony of the suburban "tract" developments, but eager homebuyers nevertheless moved into them by the millions.

★ PRIMARY SOURCE
Levittown

"White flight" to the leafy green suburbs left the inner cities—especially in the Northeast and Midwest—black, brown, and broke. Migrating blacks from the South filled up the urban neighborhoods abandoned by the departing white middle class (see "Makers

ADVERTISING PROSPERITY, 1956

This Ford advertisement in a popular magazine encouraged readers to buy a second car. By the mid-1950s, once manufacturers had met the demand for cars, homes, appliances, and other consumer goods that a decade and a half of depression and world war had pent up, they worried about how to keep expanding their markets. "Planned obsolescence"—changing design frequently enough to necessitate replacement purchasing—was one strategy. Altering expectations about what consumers needed was another. This advertisement suggests that the up-to-date family, living in its modern-style suburban home, had no choice but to own two cars, one for the male breadwinner's business, the other for the wife's "ferrying the family."

1. What gender-role prescriptions are reinforced in this advertisement?

2. What assumptions has Ford made about prospective buyers of its cars?

3. How much can mass advertising tell us about the actual values of Americans living at a particular time?

of America: The Great African American Migration," pp. 626–627). Taxpaying businesses fled with their affluent customers from downtown shops to suburban shopping malls.

Government policies sometimes aggravated this spreading pattern of residential segregation. FHA administrators often refused home mortgage loans to blacks and "other unharmonious racial or nationality groups," thus limiting black mobility out of the inner cities. Even public housing programs frequently built housing for blacks in neighborhoods that were already predominantly black—thus solidifying racial separation.

The Suburbanites

Few images evoke more vividly the prosperity of the postwar era than aerial photographs of sprawling suburbs. Neat rows of look-alike tract houses, each with driveway and lawn and here and there a backyard swimming pool, came to symbolize the capacity of the economy to deliver the "American dream" to millions of families.

Suburbanization was hardly new. Well-off city dwellers had beaten paths to leafy outlying neighborhoods since the nineteenth century. But after 1945 the steady flow became a stampede. The baby boom, new highways, government guarantees for mortgage lending, and favorable tax policies all made suburbia blossom.

Who were the Americans racing to the new postwar suburbs? War veterans led the way in the immediate postwar years, aided by low-interest Veterans Administration mortgages. People of all kinds followed, heading for neighborhoods that varied from the posh to the plain. Yet the overwhelming majority of suburbanites were white and middle class. In 1967 sociologist Herbert Gans published *The Levittowners*, based on his own move to a Levitt-built community outside Philadelphia. He described suburban families in tract developments as predominantly third- or fourth-generation Americans with some college education and at least two children. Men tended to work in either white-collar jobs or upper-level blue-collar positions. Women usually worked in the home, so much so that suburbia came to symbolize domestic confinement for feminists of the 1960s and 1970s.

The house itself became more important than ever as postwar suburbanites built their leisure lives around television, home improvement projects, and barbecues on the patio. The center of family life shifted to the fenced-in backyard, and institutions that had thrived as social centers in the city—churches, women's clubs, fraternal organizations, taverns—had a tougher time attracting patrons in the privatized world of postwar surburbia.

Life in the suburbs was a boon to the automobile, as parents jumped behind the wheel to shuttle children, groceries, and golf clubs to and fro. Drive-thru restaurants and drive-in movies sprang up, and roadside shopping centers edged out downtowns as places to shop. Meanwhile, the new interstate highway system enabled breadwinners to live far from their jobs and still commute to work daily.

Wherever they worked, suburbanites turned their backs on the city and its problems. They fought to maintain their independent municipalities as secluded retreats, with their own taxes, schools, and zoning restrictions designed to keep out public housing and the poor. Even the naming of towns such as Elmwood Park and Maple Grove Village reflected the pastoral ideal. With a majority of Americans living in suburbs by the 1980s, cities lost their political clout. Bereft of state and federal aid, cities festered with worsening social problems: poverty, drug addiction, and crime.

Middle-class African Americans began to move to the suburbs in substantial numbers by the 1980s, but even that

✳ **PRIMARY SOURCE**
Emergence of the
Suburbanite

The Postwar Baby Boom

Of all the upheavals in postwar America, none was more dramatic than the "baby boom"—the huge leap in the birthrate in the decade and a half after 1945. Confident young men and women tied the nuptial knot in record numbers at war's end, and they began immediately to fill the nation's empty cradles. They thus touched off a demographic explosion that added more than 50 million bawling babies to the nation's population by the end of the 1950s. The soaring birthrate finally crested in 1957 and was followed by a deepening birth dearth. By 1973 fertility rates had dropped below the point necessary to maintain existing population figures without further immigration.

population curve *The varying size and age structure of a given nation or other group, measured over time.*

This boom-or-bust cycle of births begat a bulging wave along the American **population curve**. As the oversize postwar generation grew to maturity, it was migration failed to alter dramatically the racial divide of metropolitan America. Black suburbanites settled in black middle-class suburbs within white-majority counties. By the end of the twentieth century, suburbia as a whole was more racially diverse than at midcentury. But old patterns of urban "white flight" and residential segregation endured.

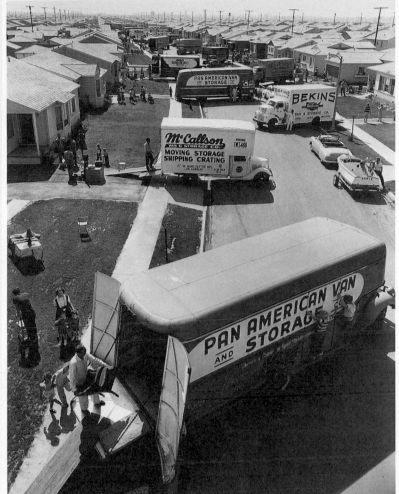

Moving to the Suburbs After World War II, Americans by the millions moved to suburban housing developments like this one. Although criticized for their architectural monotony and cultural barrenness, the suburbs provided inexpensive and spacious housing for growing families seeking to escape the crowded confines of the cities.

destined—like the fabled pig passing through the python—to strain and distort many aspects of American life. Elementary-school enrollments, for example, swelled to nearly 34 million pupils in 1970. Then began a steady decline, as the onward-marching age group left in its wake closed schools and unemployed teachers.

The maturing babies of postwar boom sent economic shock waves undulating through the decades. The baby boomers created lucrative markets for toys and baby food in the 1940s and 1950s and for clothes and recorded rock music in the 1960s. In the 1980s the hordes of baby boomers bumped and jostled one another in the job market, struggling to get a foothold on the crowded ladder of social mobility. As the boomers entered middle age, a "secondary boom" of children peaked in the early 1990s—a faint demographic echo of the postwar population explosion. The impact of the huge postwar generation will continue to ripple through American society well into the twenty-first century, when its members pass eventually into retirement, placing enormous strains on the Social Security system.

Truman: The "Gutty" Man from Missouri

precinct *The smallest subdivision of a city, as it is organized for purposes of police administration, politics, voting, and so on.*

protégé *Someone under the patronage, protection, or tutelage of another person or group.*

Presiding over the opening of the postwar period was the "accidental president"—Harry S Truman. "The moon, the stars, and all the planets" had fallen on him, he remarked when he was called upon to shoulder Roosevelt's awesome burdens of leadership. Trim and owlishly bespectacled, with graying hair and a friendly, toothy grin, Truman was called "the average man's average man." The first president in many years without a college education, he had farmed, served as an artillery officer in France during World War I, and failed as a haberdasher. He then tried his hand at **precinct**-level Missouri politics, through which he rose from a judgeship to the U.S. Senate. Though a **protégé** of a notorious political machine in Kansas City, Truman had managed to keep his own hands clean.

The problems of the postwar period were staggering, and the suddenly burdened new president at first approached his tasks with humility. But he gradually evolved from a shrinking pipsqueak into a scrappy little cuss, gaining confidence to the point of cockiness. A smallish man thrust suddenly into a giant job, Truman permitted designing old associates of the "Missouri gang" to gather around him and, like Grant, was stubbornly loyal to them when they were caught with cream on their whiskers. On occasion he would send critics hot-tempered and profane "s.o.b." letters. Most troubling, in trying to demonstrate to a skeptical public his decisiveness and power of command, he was inclined to go off half cocked or stick mulishly to some wrongheaded notion.

But if Truman was sometimes small in the small things, he was often big in the big things. He had down-home authenticity, few pretensions, rock-solid probity, and a lot of that old-fashioned character trait called moxie. Not one to dodge responsibility, he placed a sign on his White House desk that read, "The buck stops here." Among his favorite sayings was, "If you can't stand the heat, get out of the kitchen."

Yalta: Bargain or Betrayal?

Vast and silent, the Soviet Union continued to be the great enigma. The conference in Teheran in 1943, where Roosevelt had first met Joseph Stalin man to man, had done something to clear the air, but much had remained unresolved—especially questions about the postwar fates of Germany, Eastern Europe, and Asia.

A final fateful conference of the Big Three had taken place in February 1945 at Yalta. At this former tsarist resort on the relatively warm shores of the Black Sea, Stalin, Churchill, and the fast-failing Roosevelt reached momentous agreements. Stalin agreed that Poland, with revised boundaries, should have a representative government based on free elections—a pledge he soon broke. Bulgaria and Romania were likewise to have free elections—a promise also flouted. The Big Three further announced plans for fashioning a new international peace-keeping organization—the United Nations.

The most controversial decision at Yalta concerned Moscow's entry into the war against Japan. Uncertain of the untested atomic bomb, and expecting frightful American casualties in the projected assault on Japan, Roosevelt was willing to offer inducements to the Soviets to enter the Asian war and pin down Japanese troops in Manchuria and Korea. Horse trader Stalin was in a position at Yalta to exact a high price. He agreed to attack Japan within three months after the collapse of Germany, but only if the Soviets were promised the southern half of Sakhalin Island, Japan's Kurile Islands, and control of key industrial centers in China's Manchuria. The Americans agreed, and Stalin later redeemed his pledge in full.

As it turned out, Moscow's muscle was not necessary to knock out Japan. Critics charged that Roosevelt had sold Jiang Jieshi (Chiang Kai-shek) down the river and contributed to his overthrow by the Chinese communists four years later. Roosevelt's defenders countered that Stalin's mighty Red army could have secured much more of China if he had wished and that the Yalta conference really set limits to his ambitions. Apologists for Roosevelt also noted that Soviet troops had already occupied much of Eastern Europe, and a war to throw them out was unthinkable.

The Communist Menace First appearing in the *New York Daily News* on January 6, 1946, this map reflected the rising anxiety in post–World War II America that the Soviet Union was an aggressively expansionist power, relentlessly gobbling up territory and imposing its will across both Europe and Asia.

The fact is that the Big Three at Yalta were not drafting a comprehensive peace settlement; at most they were sketching general intentions and testing one another's reactions. In the case of Poland, Roosevelt admitted that the Yalta agreement was "so elastic that the Russians can stretch it all the way from Yalta to Washington without ever technically breaking it." More specific understandings among the wartime allies—especially the two emerging **superpowers**, the United States and the Soviet Union— awaited the arrival of peace.

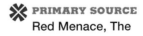 **PRIMARY SOURCE**
Red Menace, The

superpower *One of the two overwhelmingly dominant international powers after World War II—the United States and the Soviet Union.*

The United States and
the Soviet Union

History provided little hope that the United States and the Soviet Union would reach cordial understandings about the shape of the postwar world. Mutual suspicions were ancient, abundant, and deep. Communism and capitalism were historically hostile social philosophies. The United States had refused officially to recognize the Bolshevik revolutionary government in Moscow until 1933. Soviet skepticism was also aroused by American delays in opening a second front against Germany, by the abrupt termination of vital lend-lease aid in 1945, and by the refusal of Moscow's plea for a $6 billion reconstruction loan—while approving a similar loan of $3.75 billion to Britain in 1946.

Different visions of the postwar world also separated the two superpowers. Stalin aimed above all to guarantee the security of the Soviet Union by establishing friendly governments along its western border, especially in Poland. By maintaining an extensive Soviet sphere of influence in Eastern and central Europe, the USSR could protect itself and consolidate its revolutionary base as the world's leading communist country.

To many Americans, that "sphere of influence" looked like an ill-gained "empire." Doubting that Soviet goals were purely defensive, they remembered the earlier Bolshevik call for world revolution. Stalin's emphasis on "spheres" also clashed with Franklin Roosevelt's Wilsonian dream of an "open world," decolonized, demilitarized, and democratized, with a strong international organization to oversee the global peace.

Even the ways in which the United States and the Soviet Union resembled each other were troublesome. Both countries had been largely isolated from world affairs before World War II. Both nations also had a history of conducting a kind of "missionary" diplomacy—of trying to export to all the world the political doctrines precipitated out of their respective revolutionary origins.

Unaccustomed to their great-power roles, America and the USSR suddenly found themselves staring eyeball-to-eyeball over the prostrate body of battered Europe—a Europe that had been the traditional center of international affairs. The wartime "Grand Alliance" of the United States, the Soviet Union, and Britain had been a child of necessity. When the hated Hitler fell, suspicion and rivalry between communistic, despotic Russia and capitalistic, democratic America were all but inevitable. In a fateful progression of events, marked often by misperceptions as well as by genuine conflicts of interest, the two powers provoked each other into a tense standoff known as the Cold War. Enduring four and a half decades, the Cold War not only shaped Soviet–American relations; it overshadowed the entire postwar international order in every corner of the globe.

Shaping the Postwar World

Bretton Woods Conference (1944) *Meeting of Western allies to establish a postwar international economic order to avoid crises like the one that spawned World War II.*

underdeveloped *Economically and industrially deficient.*

Despite these obstacles, the United States did manage at war's end to erect some of the structures that would support Roosevelt's vision of an open world. At the **Bretton Woods Conference** in Bretton Woods, New Hampshire, in 1944, the Western Allies established the International Monetary Fund (IMF) to encourage world trade and the International Bank for Reconstruction and Development (World Bank) to promote economic growth in war-ravaged and **underdeveloped** areas. In contrast to its behavior after World War I, the United States took the lead in creating these important international bodies.

Meeting in San Francisco in April 1945, representatives from fifty nations fashioned the United Nations Charter. The United Nations (UN) was a successor to the old League of Nations, but it differed from its predecessor in significant ways. The League had adopted rules denying veto power to any party in a dispute. The UN, by contrast, more realistically provided that no member of the Security Council, dominated by the Big Five powers (the United States, Britain, the USSR, France, and China), could have action taken against it without its consent. The League, in short, presumed great-power conflict; the UN presumed great-power cooperation. The UN also featured an Assembly, which could be controlled by smaller countries. In contrast to the U.S. rejection of the League in 1919, the Senate overwhelmingly approved the UN Charter on July 28, 1945, by a vote of 89 to 2.

The United Nations had some gratifying initial successes. It helped preserve peace in Iran, Kashmir, and other trouble spots. It played a large role in creating the new Jewish state of Israel. The UN Trusteeship Council guided former colonies to independence. Through such arms as UNESCO (United Nations Educational, Scientific, and Cultural Organization), FAO (Food and Agricultural Organization), and WHO (World Health Organization), the UN brought benefits to peoples the world over.

But it proved far less successful in controlling the fearsome new technology of the atom. The Soviets rejected an American proposal in 1946 for a UN agency to prevent the manufacture of nuclear weapons. The atomic clock ticked ominously on for the next forty-five years, shadowing all relations between the Soviet Union and the United States and threatening the very future of the human race.

The Era of Globalization

Woodrow Wilson had envisioned a world order organized around the principles of self-determination and free trade—a world "made safe for democracy." But Wilson's dream perished in the turbulent aftermath of World War I. The United States retreated into a selfish and shortsighted isolationism: hiking tariffs to record levels, refusing to join the new League of Nations, and stoutly asserting its neutrality, even as the Great Depression plunged the planet into economic chaos and World War II eventually wreathed the globe in fire and destruction.

Franklin Roosevelt had served Wilson as assistant secretary of the navy. He had shared his chief's idealistic goals, as well as Wilson's bitter disappointment when they failed to be achieved. FDR also believed that many of the ills that beset the world in the post–World War I era could have been avoided if only the United States had played an international role commensurate with its power and its own highest ideals. He resolved not to squander another opportunity for American international leadership.

So on August 9, 1941, as much of Europe writhed under the Nazi jackboot, President Roosevelt rendezvoused with British prime minister Winston Churchill aboard two warships anchored off the coast of Newfoundland. After three days of talks, they publicly announced their vision of the postwar world. What came to be called the "Atlantic Charter" proclaimed for all nations the rights to self-determination and free access to trade. It also foresaw the creation of a new international organization to replace the defunct League of Nations. And it declared that a postwar peace must ensure "freedom from fear and want" for all individuals, everywhere—the first time global economic prosperity was formally declared to be an objective of any country's foreign policy. Roosevelt and Churchill had drafted the charter for a new era in American diplomacy and for a new phase of world history as well.

After World War II, the United States, victorious and robust at the end of a conflict that had laid waste all the traditional great powers, was uniquely positioned to shape the world order. To a remarkable degree, it followed the Wilsonian principles embodied in the Atlantic Charter. The United States gave birth to an array of multilateral institutions to promote trade and international investment, support the rule of law, and nurture democracy. The new institutions included the World Bank, to fund postwar reconstruction; the International Monetary Fund (IMF), to stabilize world currencies; and the General Agreement on Tariffs and Trade (GATT), to lower barriers to international commerce. In the ensuing decades, 102 nations, accounting for 80 percent of world trade, signed GATT (succeeded by the World Trade Organization, or WTO, in the 1990s). The United States also took the lead in founding and funding the United Nations (UN), which worked to arbitrate international disputes, improve standards of living worldwide, and encourage decolonization, particularly in Asia and Africa.

United Nations, 1947 by Henry Rowland Eveleigh

Great Hope for World Peace with the United Nations, 1947 The achievements of the new international regime were dramatic. International trade doubled in the 1950s and again in the 1960s. By century's end, the volume of global commerce was ten times larger than in 1950. Increased trade fueled postwar recovery in Europe and Japan and set several underdeveloped countries—notably Taiwan, Singapore, South Korea, India, and China—on the path to modernization and prosperity.

As Roosevelt and Churchill anticipated, the benefits of trade extended far beyond rising incomes. As goods flowed across borders, so too did advances in medicine and nutrition. Since 1950 the average life expectancy worldwide has increased by twenty years, with the biggest gains in the developing world.

Rising prosperity and improved standards of living also strengthened the middle classes in developing countries, with democracy often following in the footsteps of globalization. The number of electoral democracies increased from 44 in 1950 to 120 in 2000. Recent studies confirm that states with open trade policies are three times more likely to protect civil liberties than those without such policies.

For some four decades, the full effects of this liberalized world order were muffled by the Cold War. Eastern Europe and the Soviet Union in particular were conspicuous nonparticipants in the emerging global economy, and the United States often supported repressive, undemocratic regimes simply to keep them out of the Soviet camp. But the end of the Cold War and the dissolution of the Soviet bloc in the early 1990s unleashed the full force of globalization. International trade, investment, and migration exploded. More than fifty new electoral democracies, notably in Eastern Europe, Asia, and Latin America, emerged in the last decade of the twentieth century. Global trade, already at record levels, doubled between 1990 and 2003.

Despite these gains, problems persist. Critics decry the job insecurity, exploitative labor practices, inflationary pressures, widening income disparities both within and between nations, and environmental degradation that have accompanied worldwide industrial growth. Many African nations have proved chronically unable to overcome political instability, systemic poverty, and devastating epidemics. The persistent inability of most nations in Africa and the Middle East to establish working democracies and develop sustained economic prosperity for their people proves that the American-sponsored ideals and institutions have not attained universal success. Yet the liberalized world order that the United States took the lead in building after World War II left an impressive legacy of international stability, burgeoning prosperity, and freedom from fear and want for millions of human beings—a lasting testament to Wilson's vision and to Roosevelt's leadership.

Former prime minister Winston Churchill (1874–1965), in a highly controversial speech at Fulton, Missouri (March 1946), warned of Soviet expansionism:

"From Stettin in the Baltic to Trieste in the Adriatic an iron curtain has descended across the Continent."

Nuremberg Trials *Highly publicized proceedings against former Nazi leaders for war crimes and crimes against humanity as part of the Allies' denazification program in postwar Germany.*

military occupation *The holding and control of a territory and its citizenry by the conquering forces of another nation.*

The Problem of Germany

Hitler's ruined Reich posed especially thorny problems for all the wartime Allies. They agreed only that the cancer of Nazism had to be cut out of the German body politic, which involved punishing Nazi leaders for war crimes. The Allies joined in trying twenty-two top culprits at the **Nuremberg Trials** at Nuremberg, Germany, during 1945–1946. Accusations included committing crimes against the laws of war and humanity and plotting aggressions contrary to solemn treaty pledges. Justice, Nuremberg-style, was harsh. Twelve of the accused Nazis swung from the gallows, and seven were sentenced to long jail terms.

Beyond punishing the top Nazis, the Allies could agree on little about postwar Germany. Some American Hitler-haters wanted to deindustrialize Germany, while the Soviets sought to extract enormous reparations from the Germans. Both these desires clashed headlong with the reality that an industrial, healthy German economy was indispensable to the recovery of Europe. The Americans soon came to appreciate that fact, but the fearful Soviets resisted all efforts to revitalize Germany.

Along with Austria, Germany had been divided at war's end into four **military occupation** zones, each assigned to one of the Big Four powers (France, Britain, America, and the USSR). Before long, it was apparent that Germany would remain indefinitely divided. West Germany eventually became an independent country, wedded to the West. East Germany and the other Soviet-dominated Eastern European countries became nominally independent "satellite" states, bound to the Soviet Union. Eastern Europe virtually disappeared from Western sight behind the "iron curtain" of secrecy and isolation that Stalin clanged down across Europe from the Baltic to the Adriatic. The division of Europe would endure for more than four decades.

With Germany now split in two, there remained the problem of the rubble heap known as Berlin. Lying deep within the Soviet zone (see the map on p. 610), this beleaguered isle in a red sea had been broken, like Germany as a whole, into sectors occupied by troops of each of the four victorious powers. In 1948 the Soviets abruptly choked off all rail and highway access to Berlin, evidently reasoning that the Allies would be starved out.

Berlin became a hugely symbolic issue as well as a test of wills for both sides. The Americans organized the gigantic Berlin Airlift in the midst of hair-trigger tension. For nearly a year American pilots ferried thousands of tons of supplies to the grateful Berliners, their former enemies. The Soviets, their bluff dramatically called, finally lifted their blockade in May 1949. In the same year the governments of the two Germanies, East and West, were formally established. The Cold War had icily congealed.

Crystallizing the Cold War

A crafty Stalin also probed the West's resolve at other sensitive points, including oil-rich Iran. In 1946 he broke an agreement to remove his troops from Iran's northernmost province, which the USSR had occupied, with British and American approval, during World War II. Truman sent off a stinging protest, and the Soviet dictator backed down.

Moscow's hard-line policies in Germany, Eastern Europe, and the Middle East wrought a psychological Pearl Harbor. Any remaining goodwill from the period of comradeship-in-arms evaporated in a cloud of dark distrust. "I'm tired of babying the Soviets," Truman remarked privately in 1946, as attitudes on both sides began to harden frostily.

Truman's piecemeal responses to various Soviet challenges took on intellectual coherence in 1947 with the formulation of the "**containment** doctrine." Crafted by a brilliant young diplomat and Soviet specialist, George F. Kennan, this concept held that Russia, whether tsarist or communist, was relentlessly expansionary. But the Kremlin was also cautious, Kennan argued, and the flow of Soviet power into "every nook and cranny available to it" could be stemmed by "firm and vigilant containment."

Truman embraced Kennan's advice when he formally and publicly adopted a "get-tough-with-Russia" policy in 1947. His first dramatic move was triggered by word that heavily burdened Britain could no longer bear the financial and military load of defending Greece against communist pressures. If Greece fell, Turkey would presumably collapse, and the strategic eastern Mediterranean would pass into the Soviet orbit.

In a surprise appearance before Congress on March 12, 1947, the president announced what came to be called the Truman Doctrine. He requested $400 million to bolster Greece and Turkey, which Congress quickly granted. More generally, he declared that "it must be the policy of the United States to support free peoples who are resisting attempted subjugation by armed minorities or outside pressures"—a sweeping and open-ended commitment of vast and worrisome proportions.

Critics then and later charged that the Truman Doctrine committed the United States to backing any tinhorn despot who claimed to be resisting "Communist aggression," needlessly polarized the world into pro-Soviet and pro-American camps, and unwisely construed the Soviet threat as primarily military in nature. Apologists for Truman have explained that it was Truman's fear of a revived isolationism that led him to exaggerate the Soviet threat and to pitch his message in the charged language of a holy global war against godless communism—a description of the Cold War that straitjacketed future policymakers who would seek to tone down Soviet–American competition and animosity.

Truman found support for casting the Cold War as a battle between good and evil from theologians such as the influential liberal Protestant clergyman Reinhold Niebuhr (1892–1971). In the 1940s and 1950s, Niebuhr raised a Christian voice against fascism, pacifism, and communism. Niebuhr divided the world into the "children of light" and the "children of darkness." He argued that Christian justice, including force if necessary, required a "realist" response to "children of darkness" such as Hitler and Stalin.

A threat of a different sort loomed in Western Europe—especially France, Italy, and Germany. Still suffering from the hunger and economic chaos spawned by the war, these key nations were in grave danger of being taken over from the inside by Communist parties that could exploit these hardships. President Truman responded with a bold policy. On June 5, 1947, Secretary of State George C. Marshall invited the Europeans to work out a *joint* plan for their economic recovery. If they did so, then the United States would provide substantial financial assistance. The democratic nations of Europe enthusiastically accepted the life-giving Marshall Plan at a Paris conference in July 1947. Marshall offered the same aid to the Soviet Union and its allies, but nobody was surprised when the Soviets denounced the "Martial Plan" as one more capitalist trick.

Congress at first balked at the Marshall Plan's proposal for spending the mammoth sum of $12.5 billion over four years in sixteen countries. But a Soviet-sponsored communist coup in Czechoslovakia finally awakened the legislators to reality, and they voted the initial appropriations in April 1948. Truman's Marshall Plan was a spectacular success. American dollars pumped reviving blood into the economic veins of the anemic Western European nations. Within a few years, an "economic miracle" drenched Europe in prosperity. The Communist parties in Italy and France lost ground, and these two keystone countries were saved from the westward thrust of communism.

containment *In international affairs, the blocking of another nation's expansion through the application of military and political pressure short of war.*

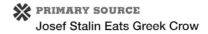 **PRIMARY SOURCE**
Josef Stalin Eats Greek Crow

Postwar Partition of Germany Germany lost much of its territory in the east to Poland and the Soviet Union. The military occupation zones were the bases for the formation of two separate countries in 1949, when the British, French, and American zones became West Germany, and the Soviet zone became East Germany. (The two Germanies were reunited in 1990.) Berlin remained under joint four-power occupation from 1945 to 1990 and became a focus and symbol of Cold War tensions. © Cengage Learning

A resolute Truman made another fateful decision in 1948. Access to Middle Eastern oil was crucial to the European recovery program and, increasingly, to the health of the U.S. economy, given finite American oil reserves. Yet the Arab oil countries adamantly opposed the creation of the Jewish state of Israel in the British mandate territory of Palestine. Defying Arab wrath and his own State and Defense Departments, Truman officially recognized the state of Israel on the day of its birth, May 14, 1948. Humanitarian sympathy for the Jewish survivors of the Holocaust ranked high among his reasons, as did his wishes to preempt Soviet influence in the Jewish state and to retain the support of American Jewish voters. Truman's policy of strong support for Israel would vastly complicate U.S. relations with the Arab world in the decades ahead.

America Begins to Rearm

The Cold War, the struggle to contain Soviet communism, was not war, yet it was not peace. The standoff with the Kremlin banished the dreams of tax-fatigued Americans that tanks could be beaten into automobiles.

The Soviet menace spurred the unification of the armed services as well as the creation of a huge new national security apparatus. Congress in 1947 passed the National Security Act, creating the Department of Defense. The uniformed heads of each service were brought together as the Joint Chiefs of Staff. The National Security Act also established the National Security Council (NSC) to advise the president on security matters and the Central Intelligence Agency (CIA) to coordinate the government's foreign fact gathering. In the same year, Congress resurrected the military draft, providing for the conscription of selected young men from nineteen to twenty-five years of age. The forbidding presence of the Selective Service System shaped millions of young people's educational, marital, and career plans in the following quarter century. One shoe at a time, a war-weary America was reluctantly returning to a war footing.

The Soviet threat was also forcing the democracies of Western Europe into an unforeseen degree of unity under the leadership of the United States. On April 4, 1949, twelve nations signed the North Atlantic Treaty, which pledged the signatories to regard an attack on one as an attack on all and to respond with "armed force," if necessary. Despite last-ditch howls from immovable isolationists, the U.S. Senate approved the treaty on July 21, 1949, by a vote of 82 to 13.

The NATO pact was epochal. The formation of the North Atlantic Treaty Organization (NATO) marked a dramatic departure from the traditional American avoidance of entangling alliances, especially in peacetime, and a significant step in the militarization of the Cold War. NATO became the cornerstone of all Cold War American policy toward Europe. With good reason, pundits summed up NATO's threefold purpose: "to keep the Russians out, the Germans down, and the Americans in."

Reconstruction and Revolution in Asia

Reconstruction in Japan was simpler than in Germany, primarily because it was largely a one-man show. The occupying American army, led by General Douglas MacArthur as a kind of Yankee *mikado*, implemented his program for the democratization of Japan with stunning success. The Japanese cooperated to an astonishing degree. They saw that good behavior and the adoption of democracy would speed the end of occupation—and it did. A MacArthur-dictated constitution, adopted in 1946, paved the way for a phenomenal economic recovery that within a few decades made Japan one of the world's mightiest industrial powers.

If Japan was a success story for American policymakers, the opposite was true in China, where a bitter civil war had raged for years between Nationalists and communists. Washington had halfheartedly supported the Nationalist government of Generalissimo Jiang Jieshi in his struggle with the communists under Mao Zedong (Mao Tse-tung). But ineptitude and corruption within the generalissimo's regime eroded his people's confidence and enabled the communist armies to sweep to victory late in 1949. Jiang was forced to flee with the remnants of his force to the island of Taiwan.

The collapse of Nationalist China was a depressing defeat for America and its allies in the Cold War. At one fell swoop nearly one-fourth of the world's population—some 500 million people—was swept into the communist camp. Seeking scapegoats, the Republicans charged that President Truman and his British-appearing secretary of state, Dean Acheson, had "lost China." Democrats heatedly replied that, when a regime has forfeited the support of its people, no amount of outside help will save it. Truman, the argument ran, did not "lose" China because he never had China to lose.

More bad news came in September 1949 when President Truman shocked the nation by announcing that the Soviets had exploded an atomic bomb—approximately three years earlier than many experts had thought possible. To outpace the Soviets in nuclear weaponry, Truman ordered the development of the "H-bomb" (hydrogen bomb)—a city-smashing thermonuclear weapon that was a thousand times more powerful than the atomic bomb. Physicist Albert Einstein and J. Robert Oppenheimer, former scientific director of the Manhattan Project and current chair of the Atomic Energy Commission, led a group of scientists in opposition to the crash program to design thermonuclear weapons.

But Einstein and Oppenheimer, the nation's two most famous scientists, could not persuade Truman, anxious over communist threats in East Asia. The United States exploded its first hydrogen device on a South Pacific atoll in 1952. Not to be outdone, the Soviets exploded their first H-bomb in 1953, and the nuclear arms race entered a perilously competitive cycle. Nuclear "superiority" became a dangerous and elusive dream, as each side tried to outdo the other in the scramble to build more destructive weapons. If the Cold War should ever blaze into a hot war, there might be no world left for the communists to communize or the democracies to democratize—a chilling thought that constrained both camps. Peace through mutual terror brought a shaky stability to the superpower standoff.

PRIMARY SOURCE
USSR's First Atomic Bomb

In August 1949 Secretary of State Dean Acheson (1893–1971) explained publicly why America had "dumped" Jiang Jieshi:

"The unfortunate but inescapable fact is that the ominous result of the civil war in China was beyond the control of the government of the United States. Nothing that this country did or could have done within the reasonable limits of its capabilities could have changed that result; nothing that was left undone by this country has contributed to it. It was the product of internal Chinese forces, forces which this country tried to influence but could not."

Ferreting Out Alleged Communists

One of the most active Cold War fronts was at home, where a new anti-Red chase was in full cry. Many nervous citizens feared that communists were undermining the government and treacherously misdirecting foreign policy. In 1947 Truman launched a massive "loyalty" program. A Loyalty Review Board investigated more than 3 million federal employees, some three thousand of whom either resigned or were dismissed, none under formal indictment.

Individual states likewise became intensely security conscious. Loyalty oaths in increasing numbers were demanded of employees, especially teachers. The gnawing question for many earnest Americans was: Could the nation continue to enjoy traditional freedoms in a Cold War climate?

In 1949 eleven communists were convicted of advocating the overthrow of the American government under the Smith Act of 1940 and sent to prison. In 1948 Congressman Richard M. Nixon, a member of the House Un-American Activities Committee (HUAC) and an ambitious Red-catcher, led the chase after Alger Hiss, a prominent ex–New Dealer and a distinguished member of the "eastern establishment." Accused of being a communist agent in the 1930s, Hiss dramatically confronted his chief accuser before the committee and denied everything. But Hiss was caught in embarrassing falsehoods, convicted of perjury in 1950, and sentenced to five years in prison.

Was America really riddled with Soviet spies? Soviet agents did infiltrate certain government agencies, and espionage may have helped the Soviets develop an atomic bomb somewhat sooner than they would have otherwise. But for many ordinary Americans, the hunt for communists was not just about fending off the military threat of the Soviet Union. Unsettling dangers lurked closer to home. While men such as Nixon and Senator Joseph McCarthy led the search for communists in Washington, conservative politicians at the state and local levels discovered that all manner of real or perceived social changes—including declining religious sentiment, increased sexual freedom, and agitation for civil rights—could be tarred with a Red brush. Anticommunist crusaders ransacked school libraries for "subversive" books and drove debtors, drinkers, and homosexuals, all alleged to be security risks, from their jobs.

Richard Nixon, Red-Hunter Congressman Nixon examines the microfilm that figured as important evidence in Alger Hiss's conviction for perjury in 1950.

Some Americans, including President Truman, realized that the Red hunt was turning into a witch hunt. In 1950 Truman vetoed the McCarran Internal Security Bill, which authorized the president to arrest and detain suspicious persons during an "internal security emergency." But the congressional guardians of the Republic's liberties enacted the bill over Truman's veto.

The stunning success of Soviet scientists in developing an atomic bomb was attributed by many to the cleverness of communist spies in stealing American secrets. In 1951 two American citizens, Julius and Ethel Rosenberg, were convicted of "leaking" atomic data to Moscow. Their sensational trial and eventual electrocution in 1953 began to sour some sober citizens on the excesses of the Red-hunters.

Democratic Divisions in 1948

Attacking high prices and "High-Tax Harry" Truman, the Republicans had won control of Congress in the congressional elections of 1946. Their prospects had seldom looked rosier as they gathered in Philadelphia to choose their 1948 presidential candidate. They noisily renominated New York governor Thomas E. Dewey, still as debonair as if he had stepped out of a bandbox.

Also gathering in Philadelphia, Democratic politicos looked without enthusiasm on their hand-me-down president and sang "I'm Just Mild About Harry." But their "dump Truman" movement collapsed when war hero Dwight D. Eisenhower refused to be drafted. The peppery president, unwanted but undaunted, was then chosen in the face of vehement opposition by southern delegates. They were alienated by his strong stand in favor of civil rights for blacks—especially his decision in 1948 to desegregate the military.

Truman's nomination split the party wide open. Embittered southern Democrats from thirteen states, like their "fire-eating" forebears of 1860, met in their own convention in Birmingham, Alabama, with Confederate flags brashly in evidence. Amid scenes of heated defiance, these "Dixiecrats" nominated Governor J. Strom Thurmond of South Carolina on a States' Rights party ticket.

To add to the confusion within Democratic ranks, former vice president Henry A. Wallace threw his hat into the ring. Having parted company with the administration over its get-tough-with-Russia policy, he was nominated at Philadelphia by the new Progressive party—a bizarre collection of disgruntled former New Dealers, starry-eyed pacifists, well-meaning liberals, and **communist-fronters**.

Wallace, a vigorous if misguided liberal, assailed Uncle Sam's "dollar imperialism" from the stump. This so-called Pied Piper of the **Politburo** took an apparently pro-Soviet line that earned him drenchings with rotten eggs in hostile cities. But to many Americans, Wallace raised the only hopeful voice in the deepening gloom of the Cold War.

With the Democrats deeply split three ways and the Republican congressional victory of 1946 just past, Dewey's victory seemed assured. Succumbing to overconfidence engendered by his massive lead in public-opinion polls, the cold, smug Dewey confined himself to dispensing soothing-syrup trivialities such as "Our future lies before us."

The seemingly doomed Truman, with little money and few active supporters, had to rely on his "gut-fighter" instincts and folksy personality. Traveling the country by train to deliver some three hundred "give 'em hell" speeches, he lashed out at the Taft-Hartley "slave labor" law and the "do-nothing" Republican Congress while whipping up support for his program of civil rights, improved labor benefits, and health insurance. "Pour it on 'em, Harry!" cried increasingly large and enthusiastic crowds as the pugnacious president rained a barrage of verbal uppercuts on his opponent.

On election night the *Chicago Tribune* ran off an early edition with the headline "DEWEY DEFEATS TRUMAN." But in the morning it turned out that "President" Dewey had

communist-fronter(s) *One who belongs to an ostensibly independent political, economic, or social organization that is secretly controlled by the Communist party.*

Politburo *The small ruling executive body that controlled the Central Committee of the Soviet Communist party and hence dictated the political policies of the Soviet, Chinese, and other Communist parties (from "Political Bureau").*

In his inaugural address, January 1949, President Harry S Truman (1884–1972) said:

"Communism is based on the belief that man is so weak and inadequate that he is unable to govern himself, and therefore requires the rule of strong masters. ... Democracy is based on the conviction that man has the moral and intellectual capacity, as well as the inalienable right, to govern himself with reason and justice."

embarrassingly snatched defeat from the jaws of victory. Truman had swept to a stunning triumph, to the complete bewilderment of politicians, pollsters, prophets, and pundits. Even though Thurmond took away 39 electoral votes in the South, Truman won 303 electoral votes, primarily from the South, Midwest, and West. Dewey's 189 electoral votes came principally from the East. The popular vote was 24,179,345 for Truman, 21,991,291 for Dewey, 1,176,125 for Thurmond, and 1,157,326 for Wallace. To make the victory sweeter, the Democrats regained control of Congress as well.

Truman's victory rested on farmers, workers, and blacks, all of whom were Republican wary. Republican overconfidence and Truman's lone-wolf, never-say-die campaign also won him the support of many Americans who admired his "guts." No one wanted him, someone remarked, except the people.

✱ PRIMARY SOURCE
Tipping the Scales (1948)

Smiling and self-assured Truman sounded a clarion note in his inaugural address, when he called for a "bold new program," known thereafter as "Point Four," to lend U.S. money and technical aid to underdeveloped lands to help them help themselves. Truman wanted to spend millions to keep underprivileged peoples from becoming communists rather than to spend billions to shoot them after they had become communists. This far-seeing program was officially launched in 1950, and it brought badly needed assistance to impoverished countries, notably in Latin America, Africa, the Middle East, and East Asia.

At home Truman outlined a sweeping "Fair Deal" program in his 1949 message to Congress. The program called for improved housing, full employment, a higher minimum wage, better farm price supports, new TVAs, and an extension of Social Security. But most of the Fair Deal fell victim to congressional opposition from Republicans and southern Democrats. The only major successes came in raising the minimum wage, providing for public housing in the Housing Act of 1949, and extending old-age insurance to many more beneficiaries in the Social Security Act of 1950.

The Korean Volcano Erupts (1950)

✱ PRIMARY SOURCE
Korea—The War That Could Have Set Off World War III

That Ain't the Way I Heard It! Truman wins.

Korea, the Land of the Morning Calm, heralded a new and more ominous phase of the Cold War—a shooting phase—in June 1950. When Japan collapsed in 1945, Soviet troops had accepted the Japanese surrender north of the thirty-eighth parallel on the Korean peninsula, and American troops had done likewise south of that line. Both superpowers professed to want the reunification and independence of Korea, a Japanese colony since

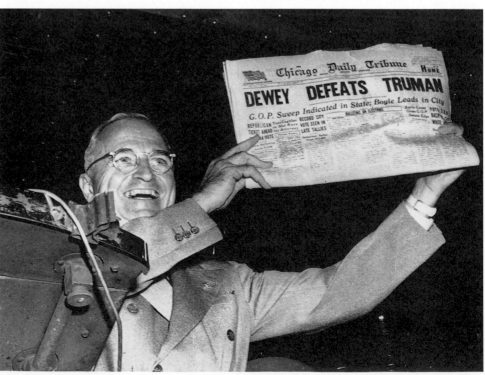

1910. But, as in Germany, each helped to set up rival regimes above and below the parallel. When the Soviets and Americans withdrew in 1949, the entire peninsula was a bristling armed camp.

Secretary of State Acheson seemed to wash his hands of the dispute early in 1950, when he declared that Korea was outside the essential United States defense **perimeter** in the Pacific. But when North Korean army columns rumbled across the thirty-eighth parallel on June 25, 1950, shoving the South Koreans southward into a tiny defensive area around Pusan, President Truman sprang quickly into the breach. The invasion seemed to provide devastating proof of a fundamental premise in the "containment doctrine" that shaped Washington's foreign policy: that even a slight relaxation of America's guard was an invitation to communist aggression somewhere.

The Korean invasion prompted a massive expansion of the American military. A few months before, Truman's National Security Council had issued its famous **National Security Council Memorandum Number 68 (NSC-68)**, recommending that the United States quadruple its defense spending. Ignored at first because it seemed politically impossible to implement, NSC-68 got a new lease on life from the Korean crisis. "Korea saved us," Secretary of State Acheson later commented. Truman now ordered a massive military buildup, well beyond what was necessary for Korea. Soon the United States had 3.5 million men under arms and was spending $50 billion per year on the defense budget—some 13 percent of the GNP.

NSC-68 was a key document of the Cold War period, not only because it marked a major step in the militarization of American foreign policy, but also because it vividly reflected the sense of almost limitless possibility that pervaded postwar American society. NSC-68 rested on the assumption that the enormous American economy could bear without strain the huge costs of a gigantic rearmament program.

Truman took full advantage of a temporary Soviet absence from the United Nations Security Council to obtain a unanimous condemnation of North Korea as an aggressor. The Council also called upon all UN members, including the United States, to "render every assistance" to restore peace. Two days later, without consulting Congress, Truman ordered American armed forces under General Douglas MacArthur to support South Korea. So began the ill-fated **Korean War**. Officially, the United States was simply participating in a United Nations "police action," but in fact the United States made up the overwhelming bulk of the UN contingents.

The Military Seesaw in Korea

Rather than fight his way out of the southern Pusan perimeter, MacArthur launched a daring amphibious landing behind the enemy's lines at Inchon. This bold gamble, on September 15, 1950, succeeded brilliantly; within two weeks the North Koreans had scrambled back behind the "sanctuary" of the thirty-eighth parallel. Truman's avowed intention was to restore South Korea to its former borders, but there seemed little point in permitting the North Koreans to regroup north of the parallel and come again. The UN General Assembly tacitly authorized a crossing by MacArthur, whom President Truman ordered northward, provided that there was no intervention in force by the Chinese or Soviets.

The Americans thus raised the stakes in Korea, and in so doing they quickened the fears of another potential player in

perimeter *The outer boundary of a defined territory.*

National Security Council Memorandum Number 68 (NSC-68) *National Security Council recommendation to quadruple defense spending and rapidly expand peace-time armed forces to address Cold War tensions.*

Korean War *First "hot war" of the Cold war. The Korean War began in 1950 when the Soviet-backed North Koreans invaded South Korea before meeting a counteroffensive by UN forces, dominated by the United States. The war ended in stalemate in 1953.*

The Shifting Front in Korea © Cengage Learning

37

The Eisenhower Era

1952–1960

Every warship launched, every rocket fired signified . . .
a theft from those who hunger and are not fed,
those who are cold and are not clothed.

DWIGHT D. EISENHOWER, APRIL 16, 1953

In President Dwight D. Eisenhower, the man and the hour met. Americans yearned for a period of calm in which they could pursue without distraction their new visions of consumerist affluence. The nation sorely needed a respite from twenty years of depression and war. Yet the American people unexpectedly found themselves in the early 1950s dug into the frontlines of the Cold War abroad and dangerously divided at home over the explosive issues of communist subversion and civil rights. They longed for reassuring leadership. "Ike" seemed ready both to reassure and to lead.

FOCUS QUESTIONS

1. What changes occurred in the American consumer economy of the 1950s, and how did those changes fuel the rise of mass "popular culture"?

2. What caused the sudden rise and equally sudden fall of Senator Joseph McCarthy and "McCarthyism"?

3. What were the origins of the modern American civil rights movement, and what successes and challenges did it face against the generally conservative political and social environment of the 1950s?

4. What were the fundamental principles of Dwight Eisenhower's Cold War foreign policies, in relation to the Soviet Union as well as Vietnam, Cuba, and the Middle East?

5. What were the central issues in the tight Kennedy-Nixon presidential campaign of 1960? In what ways did the candidates differ, and in what ways did they reflect the general American consensus of the time?

═══ Changing Economic Patterns ═══

The continuing post–World War II economic boom wrought wondrous changes in American society in the 1950s. Prosperity triggered a fabulous surge in home construction: One of every four homes standing in America in 1960 had been built in the 1950s, and 83 percent of those new homes were in the suburbs.

CHRONOLOGY

1952	Eisenhower defeats Stevenson for presidency. Ellison publishes *Invisible Man*.
1953	CIA-engineered coup installs shah of Iran. Joseph Stalin dies.
1954	French defeated at Dienbienphu in Vietnam. Army-McCarthy hearings. *Brown v. Board of Education*. Southeast Asia Treaty Organization (SEATO) formed. CIA-sponsored coup in Guatemala.
1955	Montgomery bus boycott by blacks begins; emergence of Martin Luther King, Jr. Geneva summit meeting on Vietnam. Soviet Union withdraws troops from Austria. Warsaw Pact signed. AF of L merges with CIO. Tennessee Williams's *Cat on a Hot Tin Roof* first performed.
1956	Soviets crush Hungarian revolt. Suez crisis. Eisenhower defeats Stevenson for presidency.
1957	Little Rock school desegregation crisis. Civil Rights Act passed. Southern Christian Leadership Conference (SCLC) formed. Eisenhower Doctrine. Soviet Union launches *Sputnik* satellites.
1958	U.S. troops sent to Lebanon. NDEA authorizes loans and grants for science and language education. Galbraith publishes *The Affluent Society*.
1958–1959	Berlin crisis.
1959	Castro seizes power in Cuba. Landrum-Griffin Act. Alaska and Hawaii attain statehood.
1960	Sit-in movement for civil rights begins. U-2 incident sabotages Paris summit. OPEC formed. Kennedy defeats Nixon for presidency.

More than ever, science and technology drove economic growth. The invention of the transistor in 1948 sparked a revolution in electronics, and especially in computers. The first electronic computers in the 1940s were massive machines, but transistors and, later, printed circuits on silicon wafers made possible dramatic miniaturization and phenomenal computational speed. Eventually personal computers contained more computing power than room-size earlier models.

Aerospace industries also grew fantastically in the 1950s, thanks both to Eisenhower's aggressive buildup of the Strategic Air Command and to a robustly expanding passenger airline business. Connections between military and civilian aircraft production were evident when Seattle-based Boeing Company brought out the first large passenger jet, the "707," in 1957. Its design owed much to the previous development of SAC's long-range strategic bomber.

The nature of the workforce was also changing. A quiet revolution was marked in 1956 when "white-collar" workers for the first time outnumbered "blue-collar" workers, signaling the passage from an industrial to a postindustrial or service-based economy. Keeping pace with that fundamental transformation, organized labor withered as a percentage of the labor force, after peaking at about 35 percent in 1954.

The surge in white-collar employment opened special opportunities for women. Postwar popular culture developed a "cult of domesticity" celebrating the conventional female roles of wife and mother. Popular television programs such as "Ozzie and Harriet" and "Leave It to Beaver" depicted idyllic suburban homes with a working husband, two children, and a wife who did not work outside the home. But they did so without irony; much of middle-class America really did live that way.

But as the 1950s progressed, another quiet revolution was gaining momentum that was destined to transform women's roles and even the character of the American family. Of some 40 million new jobs created in the three decades after 1950, more than 30 million were in clerical and service work. Women filled the huge majority of these new positions.

Exploding employment opportunities for women unleashed a groundswell of social and psychological change that mounted to tidal-wave proportions in the decades that followed. In the new urban age, women's dual role as *both* workers and homemakers raised urgent questions about family life and about traditional definitions of gender differences.

Feminist Betty Friedan gave focus and fuel to women's feelings in 1963 when she published *The Feminine Mystique*, a runaway best-seller and a classic of the modern women's movement. Friedan spoke in rousing accents to millions of able, educated women who were already working for wages but also struggling against the guilt and frustration of trying to live up to the feminine "ideal" as defined by the postwar "cult of domesticity."

Consumer Culture in the Fifties

The 1950s witnessed a huge expansion of the middle class and the blossoming of a consumer culture. Diner's Club introduced the plastic credit card in 1949, just one year after the first fast-food style McDonald's hamburger stand opened in San Bernardino, California. In 1955 Disneyland opened its doors in Anaheim, California. Easy credit, high-volume "fast-food" production, and new forms of leisure marked an emerging affluent lifestyle that soon moved beyond America's borders. Manufacturers, retailers, and advertisers spread American-style consumer capitalism throughout much of the non-communist world.

Crucial to the development of that lifestyle was the rapid rise of the new technology of television. Only six TV stations were broadcasting in 1946; a decade later 442 stations were operating. TV sets were rich people's novelties in the 1940s, but 7 million sets were sold in 1951. By 1960 virtually every American home had one, in a stunning display of the speed with which new technologies can pervade and transform modern societies. By the mid-1950s advertisers annually spent $10 billion to hawk their wares on television, while critics fumed that the wildly popular new mass medium was degrading the public's aesthetic, moral, political, and educational standards.

Even religion capitalized on the powerful new electronic pulpit. "Televangelists" such as the Baptist Billy Graham, the **Pentecostal** and Holiness preacher Oral Roberts, and the Roman Catholic Fulton J. Sheen took to the airwaves to spread the Christian gospel. Television also catalyzed the commercialization of professional sports, as viewing audiences that once numbered in the stadium-capacity thousands could now be counted in the couch-potato millions.

Sports also reflected the shift in population toward the West and South. In 1958 baseball's New York Giants moved to San Francisco, and the Brooklyn Dodgers abandoned Flatbush for Los Angeles. Those moves touched off a new westward and southward movement of sports franchises. Shifting population and spreading affluence led eventually to substantial expansion of the major baseball leagues and the principal football and basketball leagues as well.

Popular music was also dramatically transformed in the 1950s. The chief revolutionary was Elvis Presley, a white singer born in 1935 in Tupelo, Mississippi. Fusing black rhythm and blues with white bluegrass and country styles, Elvis created a new musical idiom known forever after as rock and roll. Rock was "crossover" music, carrying its heavy beat and driving rhythms across the cultural divide that separated black and white musical traditions. Listening and dancing to rock n' roll became a rite of passage for millions of young people around the world, from Japan to working-class Liverpool, England, where Elvis's music inspired teenagers John Lennon and Paul McCartney to form a band that would become the Beatles.

Traditionalists were repelled by Presley, and they found much more to upset them in the affluent decade. Movie star Marilyn Monroe, with her ingenuous smile and mandolin-curved hips, helped to popularize—and commercialize—new standards of sensuous sexuality. So did *Playboy* magazine, whose first issue Monroe graced in 1953. As the decade closed, Americans were well on their way to becoming free-spending consumers of mass-produced, standardized products advertised on the electronic medium of television and often sold for their alleged sexual allure.

Pentecostal *A family of Protestant Christian churches that emphasize a "second baptism" of the holy spirit, speaking in tongues, faith healing, and intense emotionalism in worship.*

PRIMARY SOURCE
Report on the Baby Boom

The King Rock star Elvis Presley revolutionized popular music in the 1950s.

© Bettmann/Corbis

Many critics lamented the implications of this new consumerist lifestyle. Harvard sociologist David Riesman criticized the postwar generation as a pack of conformists in *The Lonely Crowd* (1950), as did William H. Whyte, Jr., in *The Organization Man*. Harvard economist John Kenneth Galbraith highlighted the troublesome connection between private opulence and public squalor in a series of books beginning with *The Affluent Society* (1958). Americans had televisions in their homes but garbage in their streets. They ate rich food but breathed foul air. But Galbraith's call for social spending to match private purchasing fell on mostly deaf ears in the giddily affluent 1950s.

The Advent of Eisenhower

Democratic prospects in the presidential election of 1952 were blighted by the military deadlock in Korea, Truman's clash with MacArthur, war-bred inflation, and whiffs of scandal from the White House. Dispirited Democrats nominated a reluctant Adlai E. Stevenson, the witty, eloquent, and idealistic governor of Illinois. Republicans enthusiastically chose war hero General Dwight D. Eisenhower. As Ike's running mate the convention selected California senator Richard M. Nixon, who had gained notoriety as a relentless Red-hunter.

Eisenhower was already the most popular American of his time, as "I Like Ike" buttons everywhere testified. Striking a grandfatherly, nonpartisan pose, Eisenhower left the rough campaigning to Nixon, who relished bare-knuckle political combat. The vice-presidential candidate lambasted his opponents with charges that they had cultivated corruption, caved in on Korea, and coddled communists. He particularly blasted the cerebral Stevenson as "Adlai the appeaser," with a "Ph.D. from [Secretary of State] Dean Acheson's College of Cowardly Communist Containment."

Nixon himself faltered late in the campaign amid accusations that he had accepted illegal donations. Responding with a self-pitying live address on television, Nixon denied the charges and solemnly declared that the only campaign gift he had ever received was the family cocker spaniel, Checkers. The shameless and mawkish **"Checkers Speech"** saved Nixon's spot on the ticket and spotlighted a fundamental change in American politics.

Soon even Eisenhower was reluctantly appearing in the short televised "spots" that amounted, one critic observed, to "selling the President like toothpaste." Television

Checkers Speech *Nationally televised address by vice-presidential candidate Richard Nixon. Using the new mass medium of television shortly before the 1952 election, the vice-presidential candidate saved his place on the ticket by defending himself against accusations of corruption.*

allowed politicians to bypass the traditional political party organizations and speak directly to the voters. But its origins in entertainment and advertising meant that political messages would be increasingly tuned to the standards of show business and commercialism.

The outcome of the presidential election of 1952 was never really in doubt. Given an extra prod by Eisenhower's last-minute pledge to go personally to Korea to end the war, the voters overwhelmingly declared for Ike. He garnered 33,963,234 votes to Stevenson's 27,314,992. He cracked the solid South wide open, ringing up 442 electoral votes to 89 for his opponent. He garnered 33,936,234 votes to Stevenson's 27,314,992, ringing up 442 electoral votes to 89 for his opponent. Ike also managed to pull enough Republican legislators into office on his military coattails to gain GOP control of the new Congress by a hair's breadth.

True to his campaign pledge, president-elect Eisenhower undertook a flying three-day visit to Korea in December 1952. But it took seven more months of hard negotiations before an armistice was finally signed. The brutal and futile fighting had lasted three years. About fifty-four thousand Americans lay dead, joined by perhaps more than a million Chinese, North Koreans, and South Koreans. Tens of billions of American dollars had been poured down the Asian sinkhole. Yet this terrible toll in blood and treasure bought only a return to the conditions of 1950; Korea remained divided at the thirty-eighth parallel, Communist in the North, Western-looking in the South. Americans took what little comfort they could from the fact that communism had been "contained" and that the bloodletting had been "limited" to something less than full-scale global war. The shooting had ended, but the Cold War remained frigidly frozen.

As a military commander, Eisenhower had cultivated a leadership style that self-consciously projected an image of sincerity, fairness, and optimism. Ike thus seemed ideally suited to soothe the anxieties of troubled Americans, much as a distinguished and well-loved grandfather brings stability to his family. He played this role well as he presided over a decade of shaky peace and shining prosperity. Yet critics charged that he unwisely hoarded the "asset" of his immense popularity, rather than spend it for a good cause (especially civil rights), and that he cared much more for social harmony than for social justice.

The Rise and Fall of Joseph McCarthy

One of the first problems Eisenhower faced was the swelling popularity and swaggering power of an obstreperous anticommunist crusader, Wisconsin Republican Senator Joseph R. McCarthy. Elected to the Senate on the basis of a trumped-up war record, McCarthy had crashed into the limelight in February 1950 when he accused Secretary of State Dean Acheson of knowingly employing 205 Communist party members. Pressed to reveal the names, McCarthy later conceded that there were only 57 genuine communists and in the end failed to root out even one. McCarthy's Republican colleagues nevertheless realized the usefulness of this kind of attack on the Democratic administration. Ohio's Senator John Bricker reportedly said, "Joe, you're a dirty s.o.b., but there are times when you've got to have an s.o.b. around, and this is one of them."

McCarthy's rhetoric grew bolder and his accusations spread more wildly after the Republican victory in 1952. McCarthy saw the Red hand of Moscow everywhere. Incredibly, he even denounced General George Marshall, former army chief of staff and ex–secretary of state, as "part of a conspiracy so immense and an infamy so black as to dwarf any previous venture in the history of man."

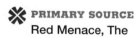
PRIMARY SOURCE
Red Menace, The

McCarthy—and what became known as McCarthyism—flourished in the seething Cold War atmosphere of suspicion and fear. The Senator was neither the first nor the most effective Red-hunter, but he was surely the most ruthless, and he did the most damage to American traditions of fair play and free speech. The careers of countless officials, writers, and actors were ruined after "Low-Blow Joe" had "named" them, often unfairly, as communists or communist sympathizers. Politicians trembled in the face of such onslaughts, especially when opinion polls showed that a majority of the American people approved of McCarthy's crusade.

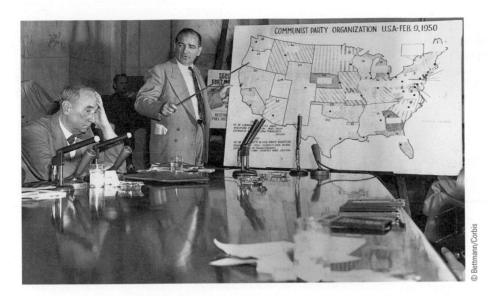

Exposing "Reds" Senator McCarthy makes a point at the Army-McCarthy hearings in 1954 while army counsel Joseph Welch ponders a reply. McCarthy declared in a speech in 1951: "Let me assure you that regardless of how high-pitched becomes the squealing and screaming of those leftwing, bleeding-heart, phony liberals, this battle is going to go on."

Eisenhower privately loathed McCarthy but publicly tried to stay out of his way. Trying to appease the brash demagogue from Wisconsin, Eisenhower allowed him, in effect, to control personnel policy at the State Department. One baleful result was severe damage to the morale and effectiveness of the professional foreign service. In particular, McCarthyite purges deprived the government of a number of Asian specialists who might have counseled a wiser course in Vietnam in the fateful decade that followed. McCarthy's extreme antics also damaged America's international reputation for fair and open democracy at a moment when it was important to keep Western European allies on the U.S. side in an intensifying Cold War.

McCarthy finally bent the bow too far when he attacked the U.S. Army. The embattled military men fought back in thirty-five days of televised hearings in the spring of 1954. The political power of the new broadcast medium was again demonstrated as up to 20 million Americans watched the Army-McCarthy hearings in fascination, where a boorish, surly McCarthy cut his own throat by parading his essential meanness and irresponsibility. A few months later the Senate condemned him for "conduct unbecoming a member." Three years later McCarthy died unwept and unsung. But "**McCarthyism**" passed into the English language as a label for the dangerous forces of unfairness and fear that a democratic society can unleash only at its peril.

McCarthyism *The practice of making sweeping, unfounded charges against innocent people, with consequent loss of reputation, job, and so on.*

Desegregating the South

America counted some 15 million black citizens in 1950, two-thirds of whom still made their homes in the South. There they lived bound by the iron folkways of a segregated society. A rigid set of antiquated rules known as "Jim Crow" laws governed all aspects of their existence, from the schoolroom to the restroom. Blacks everywhere in the South not only attended segregated schools but were compelled to use separate public toilets, drinking fountains, restaurants, and waiting rooms. Trains and buses had "whites only" and "colored only" seating. Only about 20 percent of eligible southern blacks were registered to vote, and fewer than 5 percent in some Deep South states such as Mississippi and Alabama.

Where the law proved insufficient to enforce this regime, vigilante violence did the job. Six black war veterans,

In a moment of high drama during the Army-McCarthy hearings, attorney Joseph Welch (1890–1960) reproached McCarthy in front of a huge national television audience for threatening to slander a young lawyer on Welch's staff:

"Until this moment, Senator, I think I never really gauged your cruelty or your recklessness. Little did I dream you could be so cruel as to do an injury to that lad.... If it were in my power to forgive you for your reckless cruelty, I would do so. I like to think that I am a gentleman, but your forgiveness will have to come from someone other than me. ... Have you no decency, sir, at long last? Have you left no sense of decency?"

A black woman described the day-in, day-out humiliations of life in a Jim Crow South:

"You could not go to a white restaurant; you sat in a special place at the movie house; and Lord knows, you sat in the back of the bus. It didn't make any difference if you were rich or poor, if you were black you were nothing. You might have a hundred dollars in your pocket, but if you went to the store you would wait at the side until all the clerks got through with all the white folks, no matter if they didn't have change for a dollar. Then the clerk would finally look at you and say, 'Oh, did you want something? I didn't see you there.'"

PRIMARY SOURCE
Rosa Parks Sits in Front Again

New York Times Company/Hulton Archive/Getty Images

The Face of Segregation These women in the segregated South of the 1950s were compelled to enter the movie theater through the "Colored Entrance." Once inside, they were restricted to a separate seating section, usually in the rear of the theater.

claiming the rights for which they had fought overseas, were murdered in the summer of 1946. In 1955 a fourteen-year-old black boy, Emmett Till, was lynched in Mississippi for allegedly leering at a white woman. It is small wonder that a black clergyman declared that "everywhere I go in the South the Negro is forced to choose between his hide and his soul."

Segregation also tarnished America's international image, much as McCarthyism did. After the war, African American entertainers such as Paul Robeson and Josephine Baker toured widely in Europe and Latin America, informing audiences about the horrors of Jim Crow and raising doubts about America's place as the beacon of freedom against Soviet communism. In response, the State Department confiscated Robeson's passport but had to find other ways to silence Baker, who had assumed French citizenship. Intellectuals as well poured on criticism. Swedish scholar Gunnar Myrdal published his landmark book, *An American Dilemma*, exposing the scandalous contradiction between "The American Creed"—allegiance to the values of "progress, liberty, equality, and humanitarianism"—and the nation's shameful treatment of black citizens.

International pressure combined with grassroots and legal activism to propel some racial progress in the North after World War II. In a growing number of northern cities and states, African Americans battled for—and won—equal access to public accommodations such as restaurants, hotels, theaters, and beaches. Jackie Robinson cracked baseball's color barrier when the Brooklyn Dodgers signed him in 1946. The national conscience was slowly awakening from its centuries-long slumber, but black suffering still continued, especially in the South.

Increasingly, however, African Americans refused to suffer in silence. The war had generated a new militancy and restlessness among many members of the black community (see "Makers of America: The Great African American Migration," pp. 626–627). The National Association for the Advancement of Colored People (NAACP) had for years pushed doggedly to dismantle the legal underpinnings of segregation and now enjoyed some success. In 1950 NAACP chief legal counsel Thurgood Marshall (himself later a Supreme Court justice), in the case of *Sweatt v. Painter*, wrung from the High Court a ruling that separate professional schools for blacks failed to meet the test of equality.

On a chilly day in December 1955, Rosa Parks, a college-educated black seamstress, made history in Montgomery, Alabama. She boarded a bus, took a seat in the "whites only" section, and refused to give it up to a white person, as the law required. Her arrest for violating the city's Jim Crow statutes sparked a yearlong black boycott of the city buses and served notice throughout the South that blacks would no longer submit meekly to the absurdities and indignities of segregation.

The Montgomery bus boycott also catapulted to prominence a young pastor at Montgomery's Dexter Avenue Baptist Church, the Reverend Martin Luther King, Jr. Barely twenty-seven years old, King became a champion of the downtrodden and disfranchised. His oratorical skill, his passionate devotion to biblical and constitutional conceptions of justice, and his devotion to the nonviolent principles

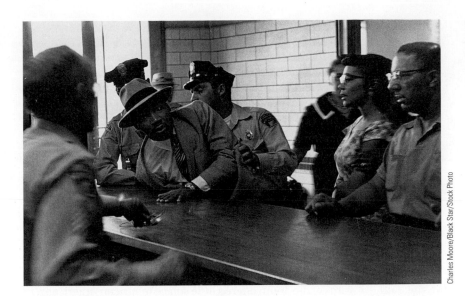

Martin Luther King, Jr., and His Wife, Coretta, Arrested King and his wife were arrested for the first time in Montgomery, Alabama, in 1955 while organizing a bus boycott.

of India's Mohandas Gandhi thrust him to the forefront of the black revolution that soon pulsed across the South and the rest of the nation.

Seeds of the Civil Rights Revolution

In 1946 President Harry Truman commissioned a report on blacks entitled "To Secure These Rights." Following the report's recommendations, Truman in 1948 ended segregation in federal civil service and ordered "equality of treatment and opportunity" in the armed forces. Yet Congress stubbornly resisted passing civil rights legislation, and Truman's successor, Dwight Eisenhower, showed no real interest in the racial issue.

It was the Supreme Court that assumed civil rights leadership. Chief Justice Earl Warren, former governor of California, shocked traditionalists with his active judicial intervention in previously **taboo** social issues. Publicly snubbed and privately criticized by President Dwight Eisenhower, Warren courageously led the Court to address urgent issues that Congress and the president preferred to avoid.

The unanimous decision of the Warren Court in *Brown v. Board of Education of Topeka, Kansas* in May 1954 was epochal. In a forceful opinion, the learned justices ruled that segregation in the public schools was "inherently unequal" and thus unconstitutional. The uncompromising sweep of the decision startled conservatives like an exploding time bomb, for it reversed the Court's earlier declaration of 1896 in *Plessy v. Ferguson* (see p. 361) that "separate but equal" facilities were allowable under the Constitution. That doctrine was now dead. Desegregation, the justices insisted, must go ahead with "all deliberate speed."

The Border States generally made reasonable efforts to comply with this ruling, but in the Deep South diehards organized "massive resistance" against the Court's annulment of the principle of "separate but equal." More than a hundred southern congressmen and senators pledged their unyielding resistance to desegregation, and several states diverted funds to hastily created "private" schools. Throughout the South, white citizens' councils, sometimes with fire and hemp, thwarted attempts to make integration a reality. Ten years after the Court's momentous ruling, fewer than 2 percent of the eligible blacks in the Deep South were sitting in classrooms with whites.

President Eisenhower remained reluctant to promote integration. He shied away from employing his vast popularity and the prestige of his office to educate white Americans about the need for racial justice. He complained that the Supreme Court's decision in *Brown v. Board of Education* had upset "the customs and convictions of at least two generations of Americans," and he steadfastly refused to issue a public statement endorsing

taboo *A social prohibition or rule that results from strict tradition or convention.*

The Great African American Migration

Among the groups most affected by the great social upheavals of World War II were African Americans. Predominantly a rural, southern people before 1940, African Americans were propelled by the war into the cities of the North and West, and by 1970 a majority lived outside the states of the Old Confederacy. The results of that massive demographic shift were momentous, for African Americans and for all of American society.

So many black southerners took to the roads during World War II that local officials lost track of the numbers. Black workers on the move crowded into boardinghouses, camped out in cars, and clustered in the juke joints of roadside America en route to their new lives.

Southern cotton fields and tobacco plantations had yielded but slender sustenance to African American farmers, most of whom struggled to make ends meet as tenants and sharecroppers. The Great Depression dealt yet another blow for when New Deal farm programs paid growers to leave their land fallow, many landlords simply pocketed the money and evicted their tenants—white as well as black. As the Depression deepened, dispossessed former sharecroppers toiled as seasonal farmworkers or languished without jobs.

The spanking new munitions plants and bustling shipyards of the South offered little solace to African Americans. In 1940 and 1941 the labor-hungry war machine soaked up unemployed white workers but commonly denied jobs to blacks. Fed up with such injustices, many African Americans headed for shipyards, factories, and foundries on the Pacific Coast or north of the Mason-Dixon line, where their willing hands found work awaiting them.

Angered by continuing racism, black leaders cajoled President Roosevelt into issuing Executive Order 8802 in June 1941 declaring that "there shall be no discrimination in the employment of workers in defense industries or government because of race, creed, color, or national origin." Roosevelt's action was a tenuous, hesitant step, yet it was the first time since Reconstruction that the federal government had committed itself to ensuring justice for African Americans.

the Court's conclusions. "I do not believe," he explained, "that prejudices, even palpably unjustifiable prejudices, will succumb to compulsion."

But in September 1957 Ike was forced to act. Arkansas Governor Orval Faubus mobilized the National Guard to prevent nine black students from enrolling in Little Rock's Central High School. Confronted with a direct challenge to federal authority, Eisenhower sent troops to escort the children to their classes. In the same year Congress passed the first civil rights bill since Reconstruction, setting up a Civil Rights commission to investigate violations of civil rights. Eisenhower characteristically reassured a southern senator that the legislation represented "the mildest civil rights bill possible."

Blacks meanwhile continued to take the civil rights movement into their own hands. Martin Luther King, Jr., formed the Southern Christian Leadership Conference (SCLC) in 1957. The churches were the largest and best-organized black institutions that had been allowed to flourish in a segregated society, and the SCLC aimed to mobilize their vast power on behalf of black rights.

More spontaneous was the "sit-in" movement launched on February 1, 1960, by four black college freshmen in Greensboro, North Carolina. Without a detailed plan or institutional support, they demanded service at a whites-only Woolworth's lunch counter. The following day, eighty-five students joined in; by the end of the week, a thousand. The sit-in movement rolled swiftly across the South, swelling into a wave of wade-ins, lie-ins, and

By war's end the great wartime exodus had scattered hundreds of thousands of African Americans to new regions and ways of life. In western and northern cities, blacks now competed for housing and jobs, and they also voted—many of them for the first time in their lives.

As early as 1945, NAACP leader Walter White concluded that the war "immeasurably magnified the Negro's awareness of the disparity between the American profession and practice of democracy." The wartime migration thus set the stage for the success of the civil rights movement. With their new political base outside the Old South, and with new support from the Democratic party, African Americans eventually forced an end to the hated segregationist practices that kept them from enjoying their full rights as citizens.

Detroit Race Riot, 1943 A woman passenger climbs from the rear of a streetcar in Detroit, Michigan, June 21, 1943, after a mob blocked the car in an effort to seize black passengers during the Detroit race riots.

pray-ins to compel equal treatment in restaurants, transportation, employment, housing, and voter registration. In April 1960 southern black students formed the Student Non-Violent Coordinating Committee (SNCC, pronounced "snick") to give more focus and force to these efforts. Young and impassioned, SNCC members would eventually lose patience with the more stately tactics of the SCLC and the even more deliberate legalisms of the NAACP.

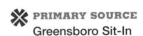

PRIMARY SOURCE
Greensboro Sit-In

Eisenhower Republicanism at Home

The balding, sixty-two-year-old General Eisenhower had entered the White House in 1953 pledging his administration to a philosophy of "dynamic conservatism." Above all, he strove to balance the federal budget and guard the Republic from what he called "creeping socialism." True to his small-government philosophy, Eisenhower supported the transfer of control over offshore oil fields from the federal government to the states. Ike also tried to curb the TVA by encouraging a private power company to build a generating plant to compete with the massive public utility spawned by the New Deal. Eisenhower's secretary of health, education, and welfare condemned free distribution of Salk antipolio vaccine as "socialized medicine."

Highway Act of 1956 *Eisenhower-sponsored program to develop a massive system of limited-access interstate highways across the United States, officially in order to enhance national defense.*

Eisenhower responded to the Mexican government's worry that illegal Mexican immigration to the United States would undercut the *bracero* program of legally imported farmworkers inaugurated during World War II (see p. 577). In a massive roundup of illegal aliens, as many as 1 million Mexicans were apprehended and returned to Mexico in 1954.

In yet another of the rude and arbitrary reversals that have long afflicted the government's relations with Native Americans, Eisenhower sought to cancel the tribal preservation policies of the "Indian New Deal," in place since 1934 (see p. 550). He proposed to "terminate" the tribes as legal entities and to return to the assimilationist goals of the Dawes Severalty Act of 1887 (see p. 421). Most Indians resisted termination, and the policy was abandoned in 1961.

Eisenhower obviously could not unscramble all the eggs that had been fried by New Dealers and Fair Dealers for twenty long years. He pragmatically accepted and thereby legitimated many New Dealish programs. In some ways Eisenhower even did the New Deal one better. In a public works project that dwarfed anything the New Dealers had ever dreamed of, Ike backed the Federal **Highway Act of 1956**, a $27 billion plan to build forty-two thousand miles of sleek, fast motorways. The former general believed that such roads were essential to national defense, allowing U.S. troops to mobilize anywhere in the country in the event of a Soviet invasion. Beyond being a defense strategy, the construction of these modern, multilane roads created countless construction jobs, speeded the suburbanization of America, and exacerbated problems of air quality and energy consumption.

Ike's Foreign Policies

The 1952 Republican platform condemned the mere "containment" of communism as "negative, futile, and immoral." Incoming secretary of state John Foster Dulles promised not just to stem the Red tide but to "roll back" its gains and "liberate captive peoples." At the same time, the new administration promised to balance the budget by cutting military spending.

How were these two contradictory goals to be reached? Dulles answered with a "policy of boldness" in early 1954. Eisenhower would relegate the army and navy to the back seat and build up an air fleet of superbombers (called the Strategic Air Command, or SAC) with city-flattening nuclear bombs. These fearsome weapons would inflict "massive retaliation" on the Soviets or the Chinese if they got out of hand, with a much cheaper price tag than conventional forces—"more bang for the buck." At the same time, Eisenhower sought a thaw in the Cold War through negotiations with the new Soviet leaders who came to power after dictator Joseph Stalin's death in 1953.

In the end, the touted "new look" proved illusory. The burly new Soviet premier, Nikita Khrushchev, rudely rejected Ike's call in 1955 for "open skies" over both the Soviet Union and the United States. In 1956 the Hungarians rose up against their Soviet masters and felt badly betrayed when the United States refused their desperate appeals for aid. The brutally crushed Hungarian uprising revealed the sober truth that America's mighty nuclear sledgehammer was too heavy a weapon to be used in such a relatively minor crisis.

Western Europe, thanks to the Marshall Plan and NATO, seemed reasonably secure by the early 1950s, but Southeast Asia was a different can of worms. In Vietnam and elsewhere, nationalist movements had fought for years to throw off the yoke of French colonialism. The legendary Vietnamese leader, goateed Ho Chi Minh, had tried to appeal personally to Woodrow Wilson as early as 1919 to support self-determination for the people of Southeast Asia.

But Cold War events dampened the dreams of anticolonial Asian peoples. Their leaders—including Ho Chi Minh—became increasingly communist while the United States became increasingly anticommunist. By 1954 American taxpayers were financing nearly 80 percent of the costs of a bottomless French colonial war in Vietnam. The United States' share amounted to about $1 billion a year.

Despite this massive aid, French forces continued to crumble under pressure from Ho Chi Minh's nationalist guerilla forces, called the Viet Minh. In March 1954 a key French garrison was trapped hopelessly in the fortress of Dienbienphu. The new "policy of boldness" was now put to the test. Secretary Dulles, Vice President Nixon, and the chairman of the Joint Chiefs of Staff favored intervention with American bombers to help bail out the beleaguered French. But Eisenhower, wary about another war in Asia soon after Korea, held back.

The **Battle of Dienbienphu** proved a victory for the nationalists, and a multination conference at Geneva roughly halved Vietnam at the seventeenth parallel (see map). The victorious Ho Chi Minh in the north consented to this arrangement on the assurance that Vietnam-wide elections would be held within two years. In the south a pro-Western government under Ngo Dinh Diem was soon entrenched in Saigon. The Vietnamese never held the promised elections, primarily because the communists seemed certain to win, and Vietnam remained a dangerously divided country.

American aid continued as communist guerrillas heated up their campaign against Diem. The Americans had evidently backed a losing horse but could see no easy way to call off their bet.

East and Southeast Asia, 1955–1956 © Cengage Learning

Battle of Dienbienphu *The decisive 1954 battle in which Ho Chi Minh's Vietnamese Communists defeated French forces, leading to the Geneva Conference that ended French colonialism in Vietnam.*

Cold War Crises in Europe and the Middle East

The United States had initially backed the French in Vietnam in part to win French approval of a plan to rearm West Germany. Despite French fears, the Germans were finally welcomed into the NATO fold in 1955. In the same year, the Eastern European countries and the Soviets signed the Warsaw Pact, creating a Red military counterweight to the newly bolstered NATO forces in the West.

Despite these hardening military lines, the Cold War seemed to be thawing a bit in 1955. In May the Soviets rather surprisingly agreed to end their occupation of Austria. A summit conference in Geneva, Switzerland, in July produced little progress on the burning issues, but it bred a conciliatory "spirit of Geneva" that caused a modest blush of optimism to pass over the face of the Western world.

Violent events late in 1956 ended the post-Geneva lull. When the liberty-loving Hungarians struck for their freedom, they were ruthlessly overpowered by Soviet tanks while the Western world looked on in horror.

Fears of Soviet penetration in the oil-rich Middle East also heightened Cold War tensions. The government of Iran, supposedly influenced by the Kremlin, began to resist the power of the gigantic Western companies that controlled Iranian petroleum. In response, the American Central Intelligence Agency (CIA) engineered a coup in 1953 that installed the youthful shah of Iran, Mohammad Reza Pahlavi, as a kind of dictator. Though successful in the short run in securing Iranian oil for the West, the American intervention left a bitter legacy of resentment among many Iranians. More than two decades later, they took their revenge on the shah and his American allies (see p. 672).

The Suez crisis proved far messier than the swift strike in Iran. President Gamal Abdel Nasser of Egypt, an ardent Arab nationalist, had tentatively obtained American and British aid to build an immense dam on the Nile. But when Nasser began to flirt openly with the communist camp, Secretary of State Dulles dramatically withdrew the dam offer. Nasser promptly regained face by nationalizing the Suez Canal, owned chiefly by British and French stockholders.

Nasser's action placed a razor's edge at the jugular vein of Western Europe's oil supply. America's jittery British and French allies, deliberately keeping Washington in the dark, joined with Israel in an attack on Egypt late in October 1956. The French and British had calculated that the oil-rich United States would supply them while their Middle Eastern supplies were disrupted. But a furious President Eisenhower resolved to let them "boil in their own oil" and refused to release emergency supplies. The oilless French and British resentfully withdrew their troops.

The Suez crisis marked the last time in history that the United States could brandish its "oil weapon." As recently as 1940, the United States had produced two-thirds of the world's oil, but by 1948 America had become a net oil importer. Its days as an "oil power" clearly were numbered as the economic and strategic importance of the Middle East oil region grew dramatically.

The U.S. president and Congress proclaimed the Eisenhower Doctrine in 1957, pledging U.S. military and economic aid to Middle Eastern nations threatened by communist aggression. The real threat to U.S. interests in the Middle East, however, was not communism but nationalism. The poor Arab countries increasingly resolved to reap for themselves the lion's share of the enormous oil wealth that Western companies pumped out of the scorching Middle Eastern deserts. In a portentous move, Saudi Arabia, Kuwait, Iraq, and Iran joined with Venezuela in 1960 to form the Organization of Petroleum Exporting Countries (OPEC). In the next two decades, OPEC's stranglehold on the Western economies would tighten.

Round Two for Ike

The election of 1956 was a replay of the 1952 contest, with President Eisenhower pitted once more against Adlai Stevenson. The Democrats were hard pressed to find issues with which to attack the genial general in a time of prosperity and peace, and the voters made it clear that they still liked Ike. Eisenhower piled up an enormous majority of 35,590,472 popular votes to Stevenson's 26,022,752; in the Electoral College the vote was even more unbalanced at 457 to 73. But the general's coattails this time were not so stiff or broad. He failed to win for his party either house of Congress.

Eisenhower began his second term in fragile health, and critics charged that he had his hands on his golf clubs, fly rod, and shotgun more often than on the levers of power. But in his last years in office Ike rallied himself to do less golfing and more governing.

A key area in which the president bestirred himself was labor legislation. Congressional investigations produced scandalous revelations of gangsterism and brass-knuckle tactics in many American unions, especially the Teamsters Union. The AF of L–CIO, born of a merger of the two giants in 1955, expelled the Teamsters in 1957 for choosing leaders such as two-fisted James R. "Jimmy" Hoffa. Convicted of **jury tampering**, Hoffa served part of his sentence before disappearing without a trace—evidently the victim of gangsters he had crossed. To counter such corruption, Eisenhower persuaded Congress to pass the Landrum-Griffin Act in 1959. The act was designed to bring labor leaders to book for financial shenanigans and bullying tactics, but it also expanded some of the anti-labor strictures of the earlier Taft-Hartley Act.

Soviet scientists astounded the world on October 4, 1957, by lofting into orbit around the globe a beep-beeping "baby moon" (*Sputnik I*), weighing 184 pounds. A month later they sent aloft an even larger satellite (*Sputnik II*), weighing 1,120 pounds and carrying a dog. This amazing scientific breakthrough rattled American self-confidence. It cast doubts on America's vaunted scientific superiority and raised sobering military questions. If the Soviets could fire heavy objects into outer space, they certainly could reach America with intercontinental ballistic missiles (ICBMs).

"Rocket fever" swept the nation. Eisenhower established the National Aeronautics and Space Administration (NASA) and directed billions of dollars to missile development. After humiliating and well-advertised failures—notably the Vanguard missile, which blew up on national television just a few feet above the ground in 1957—in February 1958 the United States managed to put into orbit a grapefruit-sized satellite weighing 2.5 pounds. By the end of the decade, several satellites had been launched, and the United States had successfully tested its own ICBMs.

The *Sputnik* success led to a critical comparison of the American educational system, which was already under fire as too easygoing, with that of the Soviet Union. A strong move now developed in the United States to replace "frills" with solid subjects—to substitute square roots for square dancing. Congress rejected demands for federal scholarships, but late in 1958 the National Defense and Education Act (NDEA) authorized $887 million for college student loans and grants for the improvement of teaching the sciences and languages.

jury tampering *The felony of bribing, threatening, or otherwise interfering with the autonomous deliberations and decisions of a jury.*

The Continuing Cold War

The fantastic race toward nuclear annihilation continued unabated. Humanity-minded scientists urged that nuclear tests be stopped before the atmosphere became so polluted as to produce generations of deformed mutants. The Soviets, after completing an intensive series of exceptionally "dirty" tests, proclaimed a suspension in March 1958 and urged the Western world to follow. Beginning in October 1958, Washington did halt both underground and atmospheric testing. But attempts to regularize such suspensions by proper inspection sank on the reef of mutual mistrust.

Thermonuclear suicide seemed nearer in July 1958, when both Egyptian and communist plotting threatened to engulf Western-oriented Lebanon. After Lebanon's president had called for aid under the Eisenhower Doctrine, the United States boldly landed several thousand troops and helped restore order.

The burly Khrushchev, seeking new propaganda laurels, was eager to meet with Eisenhower and pave the way for a "summit conference" with Western leaders. Despite grave misgivings as to any tangible results, the president invited him to America in 1959. Khrushchev appeared before the UN General Assembly in New York and then went to Camp David, the presidential retreat in Maryland, to meet with Eisenhower. Khrushchev emerged saying that his ultimatum for the evacuation of Berlin would be extended indefinitely. The relieved world gave prayerful but premature thanks for the "spirit of Camp David."

The Camp David spirit quickly evaporated when the follow-up Paris "summit conference," scheduled for May 1960, turned out to be an incredible fiasco. Both Moscow and Washington had publicly taken a firm stand on the burning Berlin issue, and neither could risk a public back down. Then, on the eve of the conference, an American U-2 spy plane was shot down deep in the heart of Russia. After bungling bureaucratic denials in Washington, "honest Ike" took the unprecedented step of assuming personal responsibility. Khrushchev stormed into Paris filling the air with invective, and the conference collapsed before it could get off the ground. The concord of Camp David was replaced with the grapes of wrath.

thermonuclear *Concerning the heat released in nuclear fission; specifically, the use of that heat in hydrogen bombs.*

✳ **PRIMARY SOURCE**
Duck Test

confiscation *The seizure of property by a public authority, often as a penalty.*

What's So Funny? 1960 Premier Khrushchev gloats over Ike's spying discomfiture.

Cuba's Castroism Spells Communism

Latin Americans bitterly resented Uncle Sam's lavishing of billions of dollars on Europe while doling out only millions to the poor relations to the south. They also chafed at Washington's habit of intervening in Latin American affairs—as in a CIA-directed coup that ousted a leftist government in Guatemala in 1954. On the other hand Washington continued to support bloody dictators who claimed to be combating communists.

Most ominous of all was the communist beachhead in Cuba. Ironfisted Cuban dictator Fulgencio Batista, in power since the 1930s, had encouraged huge investments of American capital, and Washington in turn had given him some support. But early in 1959 black-bearded Fidel Castro engineered a revolution that ousted Batista. Castro then denounced the Yankee imperialists and began to expropriate valuable American properties in pursuing a land-distribution program. Washington, finally losing patience, released Cuba from "imperialistic slavery" by cutting off the heavy U.S. imports of Cuban sugar. Castro retaliated with further wholesale **confiscations** of Yankee property and in effect made his leftwing dictatorship an economic and military satellite of Moscow. An exodus of anti-Castro Cubans headed for the United States, especially Florida. Nearly 1 million arrived between 1960 and 2000. Washington broke diplomatic relations with Castro's government early in 1961 and imposed a strict embargo on trade with Cuba. Strengthened by the Helms-Burton Act in 1996, the embargo has remained in place, even after Castro's departure from power in 2008. Americans talked seriously of invoking the Monroe Doctrine before the Soviets set up a communist base only ninety miles from their shores. Khrushchev angrily proclaimed that the Monroe Doctrine was dead and indicated that he would shower missiles on the United States if it attacked his new friend Castro.

Kennedy Challenges Nixon for the Presidency

Republicans approached the 1960 presidential campaign with Vice President Richard Nixon as their heir apparent. The "old" Nixon had been a no-holds-barred campaigner, especially in assailing Democrats and left-wingers. The "new" Nixon was represented as a mature, seasoned statesman who had gained stature with his global travels. Nixon handily won the Republican nomination; his running mate was the patrician Henry Cabot Lodge, Jr., of Massachusetts (grandson of Woodrow Wilson's arch-foe).

By contrast, the Democratic race for the presidential nomination started as a free-for-all. John F. Kennedy—a tall, youthful, dark-haired millionaire senator from Massachusetts—won impressive victories in the primaries. He then scored a first-ballot triumph in Los Angeles over his closest rival, Senator Lyndon B. Johnson, the Senate majority leader from Texas. A disappointed South was not completely appeased when Johnson accepted second place on the ticket.

Bigotry inevitably showed its snarling face. Senator Kennedy was a Roman Catholic, the first to be nominated since Al Smith's ill-starred campaign in 1928. Smear artists revived the ancient charges about the Pope's controlling the White House. Kennedy pointed to his fourteen years of service in Congress, denied that he would be swayed by Rome, and asked if some 40 million Catholic Americans were to be condemned to second-class citizenship from birth.

Kennedy's Catholicism aroused misgivings in the Protestant Bible Belt South, which was ordinarily Democratic. "I fear Catholicism more than I fear communism," declaimed one Baptist minister in North Carolina. But the religious issue largely canceled itself out. If many southern Democrats stayed away from the polls because of Kennedy's Catholicism, northern Democrats in unusually large numbers supported Kennedy because of the bitter attacks on their Catholic faith.

Kennedy charged that the Soviets, with their nuclear bombs and circling *Sputniks*, had gained on America in prestige and power. Nixon retorted that the nation's prestige had not slipped, although Kennedy was causing it to do so by his unpatriotic talk. A series of television debates between the contestants may have tipped the scales. Nobody "won" the debates, but Kennedy held his own with the more experienced Nixon. The debates once again demonstrated the importance of image over substance in a television age. Many viewers found Kennedy's glamour and vitality far more appealing than Nixon's tired and pallid appearance.

Kennedy squeezed through by the rather comfortable margin of 303 electoral votes to 219,* but with a breathtakingly close popular margin of only 118,574 votes out of over 68 million cast. He was the first Roman Catholic and the youngest person to

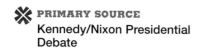

PRIMARY SOURCE
Kennedy/Nixon Presidential Debate

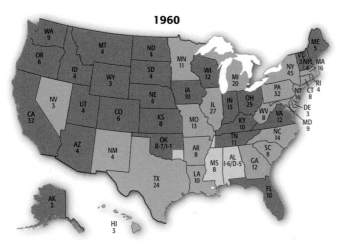

1960

Candidate (Party)	Electoral Vote		Popular Vote	
Kennedy (Democrat)	303	56.50%	34,266,731	49.7%
Nixon (Republican)	219	40.75%	34,108,157	49.5%
Byrd (Independent)	15	2.75%	501,643	0.7%

Presidential Election of 1960 (with electoral vote by state) Kennedy owed his hairbreadth triumph to his victories in twenty-six of the forty largest cities—and to Lyndon Johnson's strenuous campaigning in the South, where Kennedy's Catholic religion may have been a hotter issue than his stand on civil rights. © Cengage Learning

---

*Six Democratic electors in Alabama, all eight unpledged Democratic electors in Mississippi, and one Republican elector in Oklahoma voted for Virginia Senator Harry F. Byrd, who ran as an independent.

date to be elected president. Like Franklin Roosevelt, Kennedy ran well in the large industrial centers, where he had strong support from workers, Catholics, and African Americans. (He had solicitously telephoned the pregnant Coretta King, whose husband, Martin Luther King, Jr., was then imprisoned in Georgia for participating in a sit-in.) Although losing a few seats, the Democrats swept both houses of Congress by wide margins.

An Old General Fades Away

President Eisenhower continued to enjoy extraordinary popularity to the final curtain. Despite Democratic gibes about "eight years of golfing and goofing," Eisenhower was universally admired and respected for his dignity, decency, sincerity, goodwill, and moderation.

Pessimists had predicted that Eisenhower would be a seriously crippled lame duck during his second term, owing to the barrier against reelection erected by the Twenty-second Amendment, ratified in 1951 (see the Appendix). In truth, he displayed more vigor, more political know-how, and more aggressive leadership during his last two years as president than ever before.

America was fabulously prosperous in the Eisenhower years, despite pockets of poverty and unemployment, recurrent recessions, and perennial farm problems. To the north the vast St. Lawrence waterway project, constructed jointly with Canada and completed in 1959, had turned the cities of the Great Lakes into bustling ocean seaports.

"Old Glory" could now proudly display fifty stars. Alaska and Hawaii both attained statehood in 1959. Alaska, though gigantic, was thinly populated and noncontiguous, but these objections were overcome in a Democratic Congress that expected Alaska to vote Democratic. Hawaii had ample population (largely of Asian descent), advanced democratic institutions, and more acreage than Rhode Island, Delaware, or Connecticut. As the first noncontiguous states to join the Union, Alaska and Hawaii helped turn America's face toward the Pacific and East Asia.

Though a crusading general, Eisenhower as president mounted no moral crusade for civil rights. This was perhaps his greatest failing. Yet he was no bigot, and he had done far more than grin away problems. As a Republican president, he had further woven the reforms of the Democratic New Deal and Fair Deal into the fabric of national life. As a former general, he had exercised wise restraint in his use of military power and had soberly guided foreign policy away from countless threats to peace. He had ended one war and avoided all others. As the decades lengthened, appreciation of him grew.

Candidate John F. Kennedy (1917–1963), in a speech to a Houston group of Protestant ministers (September 12, 1960), declared:

"I believe in an America where the separation of church and state is absolute—where no Catholic prelate would tell the President, should he be a Catholic, how to act, and no Protestant minister would tell his parishioners for whom to vote … and where no man is denied public office because his religion differs from the President who might appoint him or the people who might elect him."

The Life of the Mind in Postwar America

America's affluence in the heady post–World War II decades was matched by a mother lode of literary gems. In fiction writing some of the prewar realists continued to ply their trade, notably Ernest Hemingway in *The Old Man and the Sea* (1952). A Nobel laureate in 1954, Hemingway was dead by his own duck gun in 1961. John Steinbeck, another prewar writer who persisted in graphic portrayals of American society, such as *East of Eden* (1952) and *Travels with Charley* (1962), received the Nobel Prize for literature in 1962, the seventh American to be so honored.

Curiously, World War II did not inspire the same kind of literary outpouring that World War I had. Searing realism, the trademark style of war writers in the 1920s, characterized the earliest novels that portrayed soldierly life in World War II, such as Norman Mailer's *The Naked and the Dead* (1948) and James Jones's *From Here to Eternity* (1951). But as time passed, realistic writing fell from favor. Authors tended increasingly to write about the war in fantastic and even psychedelic prose. Joseph Heller's *Catch-22* (1961) dealt with

EXAMINING THE EVIDENCE

THE SHOPPING MALL AS NEW TOWN SQUARE, 1960

In this photograph Democratic presidential candidate John F. Kennedy is campaigning at the Bergen Mall in Paramus, New Jersey. Just one presidential contest earlier, a regional shopping center would have been a rare campaign stop. The Bergen Mall opened in 1957, a time when similar shopping centers were popping up in suburbanizing metropolitan areas all over the United States. Real estate developers watched Americans flee cities for suburbs, and they followed the money, locating shopping centers strategically at new highway intersections or along the busiest thoroughfares. As suburbanites increasingly found branches of their favorite department and chain stores closer to home during the 1950s and 1960s, they found it less and less necessary to go downtown. Shopping centers for their part went out of their way to sell themselves as modern-style downtowns worthy of being the public core of new suburban communities, even though legally they were privately owned space. They provided the full range of shops and services once found in city centers, including restaurants, post offices, Laundromats, banks, and even

chapels. Shopping centers offered entertainment, from movie theaters and skating rinks to free open-air concerts, carnivals, and exhibitions. They made auditoriums available for community meetings. And they attracted public events such as Kennedy on the stump.

1. Look closely at this photograph. What kind of audience greeted candidate Kennedy at the Bergen Mall in 1960? How different might the crowd have looked in a more socially diverse urban center such as Manhattan or in nearby Newark, the largest city in New Jersey at the time?

2. What did it mean for sites of consumption, such as privately owned shopping centers, to take on the roles and responsibilities previously associated with urban streets, squares, and parks?

3. How might current struggles of downtown merchants against "big-box" chain stores such as Walmart be compared to this history of continuing changes in American public and consumer spaces?

Courtesy of the Newark Public Library

the improbable antics and anguish of American airmen in the wartime Mediterranean. A savage satire, it made readers hurt when they laughed. The supercharged imagination of Kurt Vonnegut, Jr., produced works of sometimes impenetrably inventive prose, including the dark comedy war tale *Slaughterhouse Five* (1969).

The dilemmas created by the new mobility and affluence of American life were explored by Pennsylvania-born John Updike in books such as *Rabbit, Run* (1960) and *Couples* (1968) and by Massachusetts-bred John Cheever in *The Wapshot Chronicle* (1957) and *The Wapshot Scandal* (1964). These writers represented the rear guard of an older WASP (White Anglo-Saxon Protestant) elite that had long dominated American writing.

Younger poets were also coming to the fore during the postwar period. Pacific north-westerner Theodore Roethke wrote lyrically about the land until his premature death in a Seattle suburb in 1963. Robert Lowell, descended from a long line of patrician New Englanders, sought to apply the wisdom of the Puritan past to the perplexing present in allegorical poems such as *For the Union Dead* (1964). Troubled Sylvia Plath crafted the moving verses of *Ariel* (published posthumously in 1966) and a disturbing novel, *The Bell Jar* (1963), but her career was cut short when she took her own life in 1963. Anne Sexton produced brooding autobiographical poems until her death by apparent suicide in 1974. Another brilliant poet of the period, John Berryman, ended it all in 1972 by leaping from a Minneapolis bridge onto the frozen bank of the Mississippi River. Writing poetry seemed to be a dangerous pursuit in modern America. The life of the poet, it was said, began in sadness and ended in madness.

Playwrights were also active. Tennessee Williams wrote a series of searing dramas about psychological misfits struggling to hold themselves together amid the disintegrating forces of modern life. Noteworthy were *A Streetcar Named Desire* (1947) and *Cat on a Hot Tin Roof* (1955). Arthur Miller brought to the stage searching probes of American values, notably *Death of a Salesman* (1949) and *The Crucible* (1953), which treated the Salem witch trials as a dark parable warning against the dangers of McCarthyism. Lorraine Hansberry offered an affecting portrait of African American life in *A Raisin in the Sun* (1959). In the 1960s Edward Albee exposed the rapacious underside of middle-class life in *Who's Afraid of Virginia Woolf?* (1962).

Books by black authors also made the best-seller lists, beginning with Richard Wright's chilling portrait of a black Chicago killer in *Native Son* (1940). Ralph Ellison depicted the black individual's quest for personal identity in *Invisible Man* (1952), a haunting novel narrated by a nameless black person who finds that none of his supposed supporters— white philanthropists, black nationalists, and Communist party members—can see him as a real man. James Baldwin won plaudits as a novelist and essayist, particularly for his sensitive reflections on the racial question in *The Fire Next Time* (1963). Black nationalist LeRoi Jones, who changed his name to Imamu Amiri Baraka, crafted powerful plays such as *Dutchman* (1964).

After Nobel Prize recipient William Faulkner died in 1962, his fellow Mississippians Walker Percy and Eudora Welty grasped the torch of southern letters. Tennesseean Robert Penn Warren immortalized Louisiana politico Huey Long in *All the King's Men* (1946). Flannery O'Connor wrote perceptively of her native Georgia, and Virginian William Styron confronted the harsh history of his home state in a controversial fictional representation of an 1831 slave rebellion, *The Confessions of Nat Turner* (1967).

Especially bountiful was the harvest of books by Jewish novelists. Some critics quipped that a knowledge of Yiddish was becoming necessary to understanding much of the dialogue presented in modern American novels. J. D. Salinger painted an unforgettable portrait of a sensitive, upper-class, Anglo-Saxon adolescent in *Catcher in the Rye* (1951), but other Jewish writers found their favorite subject matter in the experience of lower- and middle-class Jewish immigrants. Bernard Malamud rendered a touching portrait of a family of New York Jewish storekeepers in *The Assistant* (1957). Philip Roth penned an uproarious account of a sexually obsessed middle-aged New Yorker in *Portnoy's Complaint* (1969). Chicagoan Saul Bellow contributed masterful sketches of Jewish urban and literary life in *The Adventures of Augie March* (1953) and *Herzog* (1962). Bellow became the eighth American Nobel laureate for literature in 1976.

Chapter Summary

Using the new medium of television to enhance his already great popularity, grandfatherly "Ike" was ideally suited to soothe an America badly shaken by the Cold War and Korea. Eisenhower was slow to go after Joseph McCarthy, but the demagogue's bubble finally burst when he attacked the U.S. Army. Eisenhower also reacted cautiously to the beginnings of the civil rights movement but sent troops to Little Rock to enforce court orders for desegregation. Eisenhower's domestic policies were moderately conservative; they left most of the New Deal in place.

Despite John Foster Dulles's tough talk, Eisenhower's foreign policies were also generally cautious. He avoided military involvement in Vietnam, although aiding Diem, and pressured Britain, France, and Israel to resolve the Suez crisis.

He also refused to intervene in the Hungarian revolt and sought negotiations to thaw the frigid Cold War. Dealing with Nikita Khrushchev proved difficult, as *Sputnik,* the Berlin Crisis, the U-2 incident, and Fidel Castro's Cuban revolution all kept Cold War tensions high. In a tight election, Senator John Kennedy defeated Eisenhower's vice president, Richard Nixon, by calling for the country to "get moving again" by more vigorously countering the Soviets.

American society grew ever more prosperous in the Eisenhower era, as science, technology, and the Cold War fueled burgeoning new industries such as electronics and aviation. Women joined the movement into the increasingly white-collar workforce and chafed at widespread restrictions they faced.

A new consumer culture, centered around television, fostered a new ethic of leisure and enjoyment, including more open expressions of sexuality in popular entertainment. Intellectuals and artists criticized the focus on private affluence rather than the public good. Jewish, African American, and southern writers had a striking new impact on American thought and writing.

KEY TERMS

Pentecostal (620)

Checkers Speech (621)

McCarthyism (623)

taboo (625)

Highway Act of 1956 (628)

Battle of Dien Bien Phu (629)

jury tampering (630)

thermonuclear (631)

confiscation (631)

PEOPLE TO KNOW

Dwight D. ("Ike")
 Eisenhower

Richard M. Nixon

Betty Friedan

Elvis Presley

Joseph McCarthy

Rosa Parks

Martin Luther King, Jr.

Earl Warren

John Foster Dulles

Nikita Khrushchev

Ho Chi Minh

Gamal Abdel Nasser

Fidel Castro

John F. Kennedy

Lyndon B. Johnson

Go to the History CourseMate website for primary source links, study tools, and review materials for this chapter.
www.cengagebrain.com

38

The Stormy Sixties

1960–1968

*Let the word go forth from this time and place,
to friend and foe alike, that the torch has been
passed to a new generation of Americans.*

JOHN F. KENNEDY, INAUGURAL, 1961

Complacent and comfortable as the 1950s closed, Americans elected in 1960 a young, vigorous president who pledged "to get the country moving again." Neither the nation nor the new president had any inkling, as the new decade opened, of just how action-packed it would be, both at home and abroad. The 1960s would bring a sexual revolution, a civil rights revolution, the emergence of a "youth culture," a devastating war in Vietnam, and the beginnings, at least, of a feminist revolution. By the end of the stormy sixties, many Americans would yearn nostalgically for the comparative calm of the fifties.

FOCUS QUESTIONS

1. Why did John F. Kennedy's "New Frontier" raise such high expectations, and to what extent were those expectations met?

2. How was Lyndon Johnson able to pass the flood of legislation intended to achieve his "Great Society"?

3. How was the idealistic and nonviolent spirit of the civil rights movement overcome in the mid-1960s by white racial "backlash," black power, and urban rioting?

4. How did Lyndon Johnson and his advisers lead the United States deeper into the Vietnam quagmire, and why did that war create such deep divisions in American politics and society?

5. What were the roots of the cultural rebellion of the 1960s, and what were its short-term and long-term consequences?

CHRONOLOGY

1957	European Economic Community (EEC, Common Market) created by Treaty of Rome.
1961	Berlin Wall built. Bay of Pigs invasion. Alliance for Progress. Kennedy sends "military advisers" to South Vietnam.
1962	Pressure from Kennedy results in rollback of steel prices. Trade Expansion Act. Laos neutralized. Cuban missile crisis.
1963	France vetoes British membership in EEC. Anti-Diem coup in South Vietnam. Civil rights march in Washington, D.C. Kennedy assassinated; Johnson assumes presidency.
1964	Twenty-fourth Amendment (abolishing poll tax in federal elections) ratified. "Freedom Summer" voter registration in the South. Gulf of Tonkin Resolution. Johnson defeats Goldwater for presidency. War on Poverty begins. Civil Rights Act.
1965	Great Society legislation. Voting Rights Act. U.S. troops occupy Dominican Republic.
1965–1968	Race riots in U.S. cities.
1966	France withdraws from NATO.
1967	Six-Day War between Israel and Egypt.
1968	North Vietnamese army launches Tet offensive in South Vietnam. Worldwide protests. Martin Luther King, Jr., and Robert Kennedy assassinated. Prague Spring crushed by Soviet army. Nixon defeats Humphrey and Wallace for presidency.
1969	Astronauts land on moon. Stonewall Inn riot in New York City.

Kennedy's New Frontier

Hatless and topcoatless in the twenty-two-degree chill, John F. Kennedy delivered a stirring inaugural address on January 20, 1961. Tall, elegantly handsome, speaking crisply and with staccato finger jabs at the air, Kennedy personified the glamour and vitality of the new administration. The youngest president ever elected, he assembled one of the youngest cabinets, including his thirty-five-year-old brother, Robert, as attorney general. "Bobby," the president quipped, would find "some legal experience" useful when he began to practice law.

From the outset Kennedy inspired high expectations, especially among the young. His challenge of a "New Frontier" quickened patriotic pulses. He brought a warm heart to the Cold War when he proposed the Peace Corps, an army of idealistic and mostly youthful volunteers to bring American skills to underdeveloped countries. He summoned citizens to service with his clarion call to "ask not what your country can do for you but what you can do for your country." The president's personal grace and wit won him the deep affection of many of his fellow citizens.

Kennedy came into office with fragile Democratic majorities in Congress. Southern Democrats threatened to team up with Republicans and ax New Frontier proposals such as medical assistance for the aged and increased federal aid to education. Kennedy forced an expansion of the conservative-dominated House Rules Committee, but despite this victory his key medical and education bills remained stalled in Congress.

Richard Goodwin (b. 1931), a young Peace Corps staffer, eloquently summed up the buoyantly optimistic mood of the early 1960s:

"For a moment, it seemed as if the entire country, the whole spinning globe, rested, malleable and receptive, in our beneficent hands."

Another vexing problem was the economy. Kennedy had campaigned on the theme of revitalizing the economy after the recessions of the Eisenhower years. Kennedy's administration helped negotiate a noninflationary wage agreement in the steel industry in early 1962. The assumption was that the companies, for their part, would keep the lid on prices. But almost immediately, steel management announced significant price increases, thereby seemingly demonstrating bad faith. The president erupted in wrath. "My father always told me that all businessmen were sons of bitches," he said, "but I never believed him till now." He called the "big steel" men onto the Oval Office carpet and unleashed his Irish temper. Overawed, the steel operators backed down.

The steel episode provoked fiery attacks by big business on the New Frontier, but Kennedy soon appealed to believers in free enterprise when he announced his support of a general tax-cut bill. He chose to stimulate the economy by slashing taxes and putting more money directly into private hands. When he announced his policy before a big-business group, one observer called it "the most Republican speech since McKinley."

Kennedy's New Frontier vision also extended to the "final frontier." Early in his term, the president promoted a multibillion-dollar project dedicated, as he put it, to "landing a man on the Moon and returning him safely to earth." When skeptics objected that the money could be better spent elsewhere, Kennedy summoned stirring rhetoric of rising to challenges and expanding human possibilities. In reality, the moon shot was a calculated plan to restore America's prestige in the space race, severely damaged by the Soviet *Sputnik* successes (see p. 630). Twenty-four billion dollars later, in July 1969, two NASA astronauts triumphantly planted their footprints—and the American flag—on the moon's dusty surface. As people around the globe huddled around televisions to watch the **Apollo** mission live, the world had never seemed so small and interconnected, nor the United States so dominant.

Apollo *The American space program, launched by President John Kennedy, that aimed to land a man on the moon by the end of the 1960s.*

free world *During the Cold War, the noncommunist democracies of the Western world, as opposed to the communist states.*

Rumblings in Europe

A few months after settling into the White House, the new president met Soviet Premier Nikita Khrushchev at Vienna in June 1961. The tough-talking Soviet leader adopted a belligerent attitude, threatening to cut off Western access to Berlin. Though visibly shaken, the president refused to be bullied. The Soviets backed off from their most bellicose threats but suddenly began to construct the Berlin Wall in August 1961. A barbed-wire-and-concrete barrier, the "Wall of Shame" looked to the **free world** like a gigantic enclosure around a concentration camp. The Wall stood for almost three decades as an ugly scar symbolizing the post–World War II division of Europe into two hostile camps.

Kennedy meanwhile turned his attention to Western Europe, now miraculously prospering after the Marshall Plan and the growth of the **European Economic Community (EEC)**, the free-trade area that later evolved into the European Union. Kennedy finally secured passage of the Trade Expansion Act in 1962, authorizing tariff cuts of up to 50 percent to promote trade with the EEC countries. This act led to the so-called Kennedy Round of tariff negotiations, concluded in 1967, and to a significant expansion of European-American trade. These liberalized trade policies inaugurated a new era of such robustly invigorated international commerce that a new word was coined to describe it: "globalization."

But not all of Kennedy's ambitious designs for Europe were realized. American policymakers were dedicated to an economically and militarily united "Atlantic Community," with the United States the dominant partner. But they found their way blocked by towering, stiff-backed Charles de Gaulle, president of France. De Gaulle vetoed British membership in the Common Market with a haughty *"non,"* and sought to preserve French freedom of action by developing his own small atomic force. Despite the perils of **nuclear proliferation** or Soviet domination, de Gaulle demanded an independent Europe, free of Yankee influence.

European Economic Community (EEC) *Free trade zone in Western Europe created by Treaty of Rome in 1957. The body eventually expanded to become the European Union, which by 2010 included twenty-seven member states.*

nuclear proliferation *The spreading of nuclear weapons to nations that have not previously had them.*

Foreign Flare-Ups and "Flexible Response"

Special problems for U.S. foreign policy emerged from the worldwide decolonization of European overseas possessions after World War II. Sparsely populated Laos, freed of its French colonial overlords in 1954, was teetering dangerously under pressure from an aggressive communist movement by the time Kennedy came into office. A Red Laos, many observers feared, would be a river on which the influence of communist China would flood into all of Southeast Asia.

As the Laotian civil war raged, Kennedy's military advisers seriously considered sending in American troops. But the president sought a diplomatic escape hatch in the fourteen-power Geneva conference, which imposed a shaky peace in Laos in 1962.

These "brushfire wars" intensified the pressure for a shift away from Secretary Dulles's dubious doctrine of "massive retaliation." Kennedy felt hamstrung by the knowledge that in a crisis he had the Devil's choice between humiliation and nuclear incineration. With Defense Secretary Robert S. McNamara, Kennedy pushed the strategy of "flexible response"—that is, developing an array of military "options" that could be precisely matched to gravity of the crisis at hand. To this end, Kennedy increased spending on conventional military forces and bolstered the Special Forces (Green Berets). They were an elite anti-guerrilla outfit trained to survive on snake meat and to kill with scientific finesse.

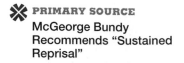

PRIMARY SOURCE
McGeorge Bundy
Recommends "Sustained
Reprisal"

Stepping into the Vietnam Quagmire

The doctrine of "flexible response" seemed sane enough, but it contained lethal logic. It potentially lowered the level at which diplomacy would give way to shooting. "Flexible response" also provided a mechanism for a progressive, and possibly endless, stepping-up of the use of force. Vietnam soon presented a grisly proof of these pitfalls.

The corrupt, right-wing Ngo Dinh Diem government in Saigon, despite a deluge of American dollars, had ruled shakily since the partition of Vietnam in 1954 (see pp. 628–629). Anti-Diem agitators noisily threatened to topple the pro-American government from power. In a fateful decision late in 1961, Kennedy ordered a sharp increase in the number of "military advisers" (U.S. troops) in South Vietnam.

American forces allegedly entered Vietnam to foster political stability—to help protect Diem from the communists long enough to allow him to enact basic social reforms favored by the Americans. But the Kennedy administration eventually despaired of the reactionary Diem and encouraged a successful coup against him in November 1963. Ironically, the United States thus contributed to a long process of political disintegration that its original policy had meant to prevent. Kennedy still told the South Vietnamese that it was "their war," but he had made dangerously deep political commitments. By the time of his death, Kennedy had ordered more than fifteen thousand American men into the far-off Asian slaughter pen. A graceful pullout was becoming increasingly difficult.

Backbone The United States supports South Vietnam.

Cuban Confrontations

Although the United States regarded Latin America as its backyard, its southern neighbors feared and resented the powerful Colossus of the North. In 1961 Kennedy extended the hand of friendship with the Alliance for Progress (*Alianza para el Progreso*), hailed as a Marshall Plan for Latin America. But results were disappointing; there was little alliance and even less progress. American handouts had little positive impact on Latin America's immense social problems.

President Kennedy also struck below the border with the mailed fist. He had inherited from the Eisenhower administration a CIA-backed scheme to topple Fidel Castro from power by invading Cuba with anticommunist **exiles**. On April 17, 1961, some twelve hundred exiles landed at Cuba's Bay of Pigs. When the ill-starred invasion quickly bogged down, Kennedy stood fast in his decision to keep hands off, and the bullet-riddled band of anti-Castroites surrendered. President Kennedy assumed full responsibility for the failure, remarking that "victory has a hundred fathers, and defeat is an orphan."

The Bay of Pigs blunder, along with continuing American covert efforts to assassinate Castro and overthrow his government, naturally pushed the Cuban leader even further into the Soviet embrace. Wily Chairman Khrushchev lost little time taking full advantage of his Cuban comrade's position just ninety miles off Florida's coast. In October 1962 the aerial photographs of American spy planes revealed that the Soviets were secretly and speedily installing nuclear-tipped missiles in Cuba.

Kennedy and Khrushchev now began a nerve-racking game of "nuclear chicken." The president, on October 22, 1962, ordered a naval "quarantine" of Cuba and demanded immediate removal of the threatening weaponry. He also served notice on Khrushchev that any attack on the United States from Cuba would be regarded as coming from the Soviet Union and would trigger nuclear retaliation against the Russian heartland. For an anxious week, Americans waited while Soviet ships approached the patrol line established by the U.S. Navy off Cuba. The world teetered breathlessly on the brink of global atomization.

In this tense eyeball-to-eyeball confrontation, Khrushchev finally flinched. On October 28 he agreed to a partially face-saving compromise, by which he would pull the missiles out of Cuba. The United States in return indicated that it would not invade the island and would quietly remove some of its own missiles from Turkey.

Fallout from the Cuban missile crisis was considerable. A disgraced Khrushchev was ultimately hounded out of the Kremlin and became an "unperson." Kennedy, apparently sobered by the appalling risks he had just run, pushed harder for a nuclear test-ban treaty with the Soviet Union. After prolonged negotiations in Moscow, a pact prohibiting trial nuclear explosions in the atmosphere was signed in late 1963.

Most significant was Kennedy's speech at American University, Washington, D.C., in June 1963. The president urged Americans to abandon a view of the Soviet Union as a Devil-ridden land filled with fanatics and instead to deal with the world "as it is, not as it might have been had the history of the last eighteen years been different." Kennedy thus tried to lay the foundations for a realistic policy of **peaceful coexistence** with the Soviet Union. Here were the modest origins of the policy that later came to be known as *détente* (French for "relaxation of tension").

exile(s) *A person who has been banished or driven from her or his country by the authorities.*

peaceful coexistence *The principle or policy that communists and noncommunists—specifically, the United States and the Soviet Union—ought to live together without trying to dominate or destroy each other.*

détente *In international affairs, a period of relaxation of tension and agreement in areas of mutual interest between rival powers—but something short of alliance or friendship.*

The Struggle for Civil Rights

Kennedy had campaigned with a strong appeal to black voters, but he proceeded gingerly to redeem his promises. Although he had pledged to eliminate racial discrimination in housing "with a stroke of the pen," it took him nearly two years to find the right pen. Civil rights groups meanwhile sent thousands of pens to the White House in an "Ink for Jack" protest against the president's slowness.

Political concerns stayed the president's hand on civil rights. Elected by a wafer-thin margin and with shaky control over Congress, Kennedy needed the support of southern legislators to pass his economic and social legislation, especially his medical and educational bills.

But events soon scrambled these careful calculations. After the wave of **sit-ins** that surged across the South in 1960, groups of Freedom Riders fanned out to end segregation in facilities serving interstate bus passengers. A white mob torched a Freedom Ride bus near Anniston, Alabama, in May 1961, and Attorney General Robert Kennedy's personal representative was beaten unconscious in another anti–Freedom Ride riot in Montgomery. When southern officials proved unwilling or unable to stem the violence, Washington dispatched federal marshals to protect the Freedom Riders.

Reluctantly but fatefully, the Kennedy administration had now joined hands with the civil rights movement. For the most part, the relationship between Martin Luther King, Jr., and the Kennedys was a fruitful one. Encouraged by Robert Kennedy, SNCC and other

sit-in *A demonstration in which people occupy a facility for a sustained period to achieve political or economic goals.*

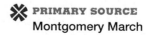 **PRIMARY SOURCE**
Montgomery March

Freedom Ride, 1961
Rampaging whites near Anniston, Alabama, burned this bus carrying an interracial group of Freedom Riders on May 14, 1961.

© Bettmann/Corbis

civil rights groups inaugurated a Voter Education Project to register the South's historically disfranchised blacks.

Integrating southern universities threatened to provoke wholesale slaughter. Some desegregated painlessly, but the University of Mississippi ("Ole Miss") became a volcano. A twenty-nine-year-old air force veteran, James Meredith, encountered violent opposition when he attempted to register in October 1962. In the end, President Kennedy was forced to send in four hundred federal marshals and three thousand troops to enroll Meredith in his first class—in colonial American history.

In the spring of 1963, Martin Luther King, Jr., launched a campaign against discrimination in Birmingham, Alabama, the most segregated big city in America. Although they constituted nearly half the city's population, blacks made up fewer than 15 percent of the city's voters. Knowing that cross burnings and bomb attacks on civil rights activists were common, King told his organizers that "some of the people sitting here will not come back alive from this campaign." Events soon confirmed this grim prediction. Watching developments on television screens, a horrified world saw peaceful civil rights marchers repeatedly repelled by police with attack dogs and electric cattle prods. Most fearsome were the high-pressure fire hoses that delivered water with enough force to knock bricks loose from buildings or strip bark from trees at a distance of one hundred feet. Water from the hoses bowled little children down the street like tumbleweed.

Jolted by these vicious confrontations, President Kennedy delivered a memorable televised speech to the nation on June 11, 1963. Pleading for new civil rights legislation, he called the situation a "moral crisis" and declared that the principle at stake "is as old as the Scriptures and as clear as the American Constitution." In August Martin Luther King, Jr., led 200,000 black and white demonstrators in a peaceful "March on Washington" in support of the proposed legislation. Still the violence continued. On the very night of Kennedy's stirring television address a white gunman shot down Medgar Evers, a black Mississippi civil rights worker. In September 1963 an explosion blasted a Baptist church in Birmingham, killing four black girls who had just finished their Sunday school lesson called "The Love That Forgives."

In his civil rights address of June 11, 1963, President John F. Kennedy (1917–1963) said:

"If an American, because his skin is dark, cannot eat lunch in a restaurant open to the public; if he cannot send his children to the best public school available; if he cannot vote for the public officials who represent him; if, in short, he cannot enjoy the full and free life which all of us want, then who among us would be content to have the color of his skin changed and stand in his place?"

The Killing of Kennedy

Violence haunted America in the mid-1960s, and it stalked onto center stage on November 22, 1963. While riding in an open limousine in downtown Dallas, Texas, President Kennedy was shot in the brain by a concealed rifleman and died within seconds. As a stunned nation grieved, the tragedy grew still more unbelievable. The alleged assassin, a furtive figure named Lee Harvey Oswald, was himself shot to death in front of the television cameras by a self-appointed avenger, Jack Ruby. So bizarre were the events surrounding the two murders that even an elaborate official investigation conducted by Chief Justice Warren could not quiet all doubts and theories about what had really happened. Vice President Johnson, sworn in as president on an airplane in Dallas, managed a dignified and efficient transition and pledged continuity with his slain predecessor's policies.

For several days, the nation was steeped in sorrow. Not until then did many Americans realize how fully their young, vibrant president and his captivating wife had cast a spell over them. Chopped down in his prime after only slightly more than a thousand days in the White House, Kennedy was acclaimed more for the ideals he had enunciated and the spirit he had kindled than for his concrete achievements. Kennedy had laid one myth to rest forever—that a Catholic could not be trusted with the presidency of the United States.

In later years revelations about Kennedy's womanizing and allegations about his involvement with organized crime figures tarnished his reputation. But despite those accusations, his vigor, charisma, and idealism made him an inspirational figure for the generation of Americans who came of age in the 1960s—including Bill Clinton, who as a boy had briefly met President Kennedy and would himself be elected president in 1992.

The LBJ Brand on the Presidency

The torch passed to craggy-faced Lyndon Baines Johnson, a Texan who towered six feet three inches. The new president hailed from the populist hill country west of Austin, Texas, and had supported New Deal measures as a young Congressman. But Johnson had trimmed his sails to the right in order to win statewide elections in Texas, and as Senate Majority Leader he developed into a master wheeler-dealer. He could move political mountains or checkmate opponents as the occasion demanded, using what came to be known as the "Johnson treatment"—a flashing display of backslapping, flesh-pressing, and arm-twisting that overbore friend and foe alike. His ego and vanity were legendary.

As president, Johnson quickly shed the conservative coloration of his Senate years to reveal the latent liberal underneath. With Johnson's vigorous prodding, and after a lengthy conservative filibuster, Congress at last passed the landmark **Civil Rights Act of 1964**. The act banned racial discrimination in most private facilities open to the public, including theaters, hospitals, and restaurants. It strengthened the federal government's power to end segregation in schools and other public places. Title VII of the Act barred employers from discriminating based on race or national origin in hiring, and empowered the Equal Employment Opportunity Commission (EEOC) (a body John F. Kennedy had created in 1961) to enforce the law.

When conservatives tried to derail the legislation by adding a prohibition on sexual, as well as racial, discrimination, the tactic backfired. The bill's opponents cynically calculated that liberals would not be able to support a bill that threatened to wipe out laws that singled out women for special protection because of their sex. But the act's Title VII passed with the sexual clause intact. It soon proved to be a powerful instrument of federally enforced gender equality, as well as racial equality. Johnson struck another blow for women and minorities in 1965 when he issued an executive order requiring all federal contractors to take "**affirmative action**" against discrimination.

Johnson dubbed his popular domestic program the "Great Society"—a sweeping set of New Dealish economic and welfare measures aimed at transforming the American way of life. Public support for LBJ's antipoverty war was aroused by Michael Harrington's *The Other America* (1962), which revealed that in affluent America 20 percent of the population—and more than 40 percent of the black population—suffered in poverty.

Civil Rights Act of 1964 *Federal law that banned racial discrimination in public facilities and strengthened the federal government's power to fight segregation in schools.*

affirmative action *Program designed to redress historic racial and gender imbalances in jobs and education.*

EXAMINING THE EVIDENCE

CONFLICTING PRESS ACCOUNTS OF THE MARCH ON WASHINGTON, 1963

The day after the March on Washington of August 28, 1963 (see p. 642), newspapers all over the country carried reports of this historic assembly of more than 200,000 people to demand civil rights and equal job opportunities for African Americans. Although the basic outlines of the story were the same in most papers, ancillary articles, photographs, and editorials revealed deep-seated biases in coverage. Shown here are continuations from the front-page stories in the *New York Times*, a bastion of northeastern liberalism (below), and the *Atlanta Constitution*, a major southern newspaper (right). While the *Times* called the march "orderly" in its headline, the *Constitution*'s story in its columns highlighted the potential for violence and the precautions taken by police. The article read: "There was such a force of uniformed officers on hand to cope with any possible trouble that one senator was prompted to comment: 'It almost looks like we had a military coup d'état during the night.'" In addition to stressing the march's potential for disruption, the *Constitution* ran an advertisement right below the March on Washington story for a National Ku Klux Klan Rally two days hence, featuring prominent speakers and a cross burning. This comparison of newspaper coverage of a controversial event serves as a reminder that press reporting must always be scrutinized for biases when it is used as historical evidence.

1. What other differences in coverage separated these two newspapers?

2. What factors contribute to press biases?

3. How are both President Kennedy and the marchers and their leaders portrayed in the two stories? Which portrays the marchers as taking more initiative, and why?

March a Big Boost for Bill, Kennedy Tells 10 Leaders

Atlanta Journal-Constitution, Thursday, August 29, 1963

(PAID ADVERTISEMENT)

NATIONAL KU KLUX KLAN RALLY

Prominent Speakers
Cross Burning

STONE MOUNTAIN, GA.
AUGUST 31, 1963
7:30 P.M.

Largest Ever Held in the Country
Delegations from 46 States
Press Representatives from 5 Foreign Countries

PUBLIC INVITED

Klansmen and families urged to attend

FREE PARKING

200,000 Join Orderly March in Capital for Civil Rights; Kennedy Sees Negro Gain

LEADERS OF RALLY URGE ACTION 'NOW'

Ask Laws Against Inequity
—Picnic Air Prevails as Crowds Clap and Sing

President Meets March Chiefs; Urges Bipartisan Aid on Rights

LEADERS MEET WITH KENNEDY: From left Whitney M. Young Jr., of National Urban League; the Rev. Dr. Martin Luther King Jr., Southern Christian Leadership Conference; John Lewis, partly hidden, Student Nonviolent Coordinating Committee; Rabbi Joachim Prinz, American Jewish Congress; the Rev. Dr. Eugene Carson Blake, United Presbyterian Church in U.S.A.; A. Philip Randolph, Negro American Labor Council; the President; Walter P. Reuther, the United Automobile Workers; Vice President Johnson, almost hidden, and Roy Wilkins, N.A.A.C.P. Mr. Kennedy and Mr. Johnson met with leaders of the civil rights march at the White House after the ceremonies at the Lincoln Memorial.

The New York Times, August 29, 1963, page 16/The New York Times Agency

Johnson's nomination by the Democrats in 1964 was a foregone conclusion, and he was chosen by acclamation at the party's convention in Atlantic City. The Republicans, convening in San Francisco, nominated box-jawed Senator Barry Goldwater of Arizona, a bronzed and bespectacled champion of rock-ribbed conservatism. The American stage was thus set for a historic clash of political principles.

Goldwater's forces had galloped out of the Southwest to ride roughshod over the moderate Republican "eastern **establishment**." Goldwater attacked the federal income tax, the Social Security system, the Tennessee Valley Authority, civil rights legislation, the nuclear test-ban treaty, and, most loudly, the Great Society. His fiercely dedicated followers proclaimed, "In Your Heart You Know He's Right," which prompted the Democratic response, "In Your Guts You Know He's Nuts." Goldwater warmed right-wing hearts when he proclaimed that "extremism in the defense of liberty is no vice. And ... moderation in the pursuit of justice is no virtue."

establishment *The ruling inner circle of a nation and its principal institutions.*

Johnson cultivated the contrasting image of a resolute statesman by seizing upon the Tonkin Gulf episode early in August 1964. Unbeknownst to the American public or Congress, U.S. Navy ships had been cooperating with South Vietnamese gunboats in provocative raids along the coast of North Vietnam. Two of these American destroyers were allegedly fired upon by the North Vietnamese on August 2 and 4, although exactly what happened remains unclear. Later investigations strongly suggested that the North Vietnamese fired in self-defense on August 2 and that the "attack" of August 4 never happened. Johnson later wisecracked, "For all I know, the Navy was shooting at whales out there."

Johnson nevertheless promptly called the attacks "unprovoked" and moved swiftly to make political hay out of this episode. He ordered a "limited" retaliatory air raid against the North Vietnamese bases, loudly proclaiming that he sought "no wider war"—thus implying that the truculent Goldwater did. Johnson also used the incident to spur congressional passage of the all-purpose Tonkin Gulf Resolution. With only two dissenting votes in both houses, the lawmakers virtually abdicated their war-declaring powers and handed the president a blank check to use further force in Southeast Asia.

The towering Texan rode to a spectacular victory in November 1964. The voters were herded into Johnson's column by fondness for the Kennedy legacy, faith in Great Society promises, and fear of Goldwater. A stampede of 43,129,566 Johnson votes trampled the Republican ticket, with its 27,178,188 supporters. The tally in the Electoral College was 486 to 52. Goldwater carried only his native Arizona and five other states—all of them, significantly, in the racially restless South. Johnson's record-breaking 61 percent of the popular vote swept lopsided Democratic majorities into both houses of Congress.

The Great Society Congress

Johnson's huge victory temporarily smashed the conservative congressional coalition of southern Democrats and northern Republicans. A wide-open legislative road stretched before the Great Society programs, as the president skillfully ringmastered his two-to-one Democratic majorities. Congress poured out a flood of legislation, comparable only to the output of the New Dealers in the Hundred Days Congress of 1933, as Johnson fully delivered on long-delayed Democratic promises of social reform.

Besides a greatly expanded War on Poverty, a tireless Johnson also prodded the Congress into creating two new cabinet offices: the Department of Transportation and the Department of Housing and Urban Development (HUD). He named noted economist Robert C. Weaver to be secretary of HUD and the nation's first black cabinet member. Other noteworthy laws established the National Endowment for the Arts and the National Endowment for the Humanities, designed to lift the level of American cultural life.

Even more impressive were the Big Four legislative achievements that crowned LBJ's Great Society: aid to education, medical care for the elderly and indigent, immigration reform, and a new voting rights bill.

Johnson's federal program for education neatly avoided the thorny question of church and state by channeling educational aid to students, thus allowing funds to flow to hard-pressed parochial institutions. With a keen eye for the dramatic, LBJ signed the education bill in the humble one-room Texas schoolhouse he had attended as a boy.

Medicare for the elderly, accompanied by Medicaid for the poor, became a reality in 1965. Like the New Deal's Social Security program, Medicare and Medicaid created "entitlements." That is, they conferred rights on certain categories of Americans virtually in perpetuity. These programs materially improved the lives of millions of Americans—but also eventually undermined the federal government's financial health.

Immigration reform was the third of Johnson's Big Four feats. The Immigration and Nationality Act of 1965 abolished at last the "national-origins" quota that had been in place since 1921 (see p. 512), doubled to 290,000 the number of immigrants allowed to enter annually, and provided for the admission of close relatives of U.S. citizens without limits. The "family unification" provision swelled immigration, and to the surprise of the act's sponsors, the sources of immigration shifted heavily from Europe to Latin America and Asia.

Great Society programs came in for rancorous political attack in later years. Conservatives charged the billions spent for "social engineering" had simply been flushed down the waste pipe. Yet the poverty rate declined measurably in the ensuing decade. Medicare dramatically reduced poverty among America's elderly, and antipoverty programs such as Project Head Start sharply improved the educational performance of underprivileged youth. Lyndon Johnson was not fully victorious in the war against poverty, but he did win several noteworthy battles.

Battling for Black Rights

With the last of his Big Four reforms, the Voting Rights Act of 1965, Johnson made heartening headway against one of the most persistent American evils, racial discrimination. The Civil Rights Act of 1964 had prohibited racial discrimination in public accommodations and employment and strengthened school desegregation. But the problem of voting rights remained. In Mississippi and throughout the South, only about 5 percent of eligible blacks were registered to vote. Ballot-denying devices such as the poll tax, **literacy tests**, and bare-faced intimidation still barred black people from the political process.

Beginning in 1964, opening up the polling booths became the chief goal of the black movement in the South. The Twenty-fourth Amendment, ratified in January 1964, abolished the poll tax in federal elections. (See the Appendix.) Singing "We Shall Overcome," blacks joined hands with white civil rights workers—many of them student volunteers from the North—in a massive voter-registration drive in Mississippi during the "Freedom Summer" of 1964.

But events soon blighted bright hopes. In late June 1964, one black and two white civil rights workers disappeared in Mississippi. Their badly beaten bodies were later found buried beneath an earthen dam. In August an integrated "Mississippi Freedom Democratic Party" delegation was denied its seat at the national Democratic convention.

Early in 1965 Martin Luther King, Jr., resumed the voter-registration campaign in Selma, Alabama. State troopers with tear gas and whips assaulted King's peaceful demonstrators. A Boston Unitarian minister was killed, and a few days later a white Detroit woman was shotgunned to death by Klansmen on the highway near Selma.

As the nation recoiled in horror before these violent scenes, President Johnson, speaking in soft southern accents, delivered a compelling address on television. What happened in Selma, he insisted, concerned all Americans, "who must overcome the crippling legacy of bigotry and injustice." Then, in a stirring adaptation of the anthem of the civil rights movement, the president concluded: "And we shall overcome." Following words with deeds, Johnson speedily shepherded through Congress the landmark Voting Rights Act of 1965, signed into law on August 6. It outlawed literacy tests and sent federal voter registrars into several southern states.

The passage of the Voting Rights Act, exactly one hundred years after the conclusion of the Civil War, climaxed a century of awful abuse and robust resurgence for African Americans in the South. The act did not end discrimination and oppression overnight, but it placed an awesome lever for change in blacks' hands. Black southerners now had power and began to wield it without fear of reprisals. In the following decade, for the first time since emancipation, African Americans began to migrate *into* the South.

literacy test *A literacy examination that a person must pass before being allowed to vote.*

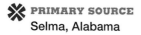
PRIMARY SOURCE
Selma, Alabama

Black Power

The Voting Rights Act of 1965 marked the end of an era in the history of the civil rights movement—the era of nonviolent demonstrations, focused on the South, led by peaceful moderates such as Martin Luther King, Jr., and aimed at integrating blacks into American society. As if to symbolize the turn of events, just five days after President Johnson signed the landmark voting law, a bloody riot erupted in Watts, a black **ghetto** in Los Angeles. The week-long violence left thirty-one blacks and three whites dead, more than a thousand people injured, and hundreds of buildings charred and gutted. The Watts explosion heralded a new phase of the black struggle—increasingly marked by militant confrontation, focusing on northern and western cities, led by radical and sometimes violent spokespersons, and often aiming not at interracial cooperation but at black separatism.

The pious Christian moderation of Martin Luther King, Jr., came under heavy fire from this second generation of younger black leaders. Deepening division among black leaders was highlighted by the career of Malcolm X. Born Malcolm Little, he was at first inspired by the **militant** black nationalist Nation of Islam founded by Elijah Muhammad. A brilliant and charismatic preacher, Malcolm X trumpeted **black separatism** and inveighed against the "blue-eyed white devils." Eventually, Malcolm distanced himself from Elijah Muhammad's separatist preachings and moved toward mainstream Islam. In early 1965 he was cut down by Nation of Islam gunmen while speaking to a large crowd in New York City.

The Black Panther party meanwhile openly brandished weapons in the streets of Oakland, California. Then in 1966 Trinidad-born Stokely Carmichael, a leader of the Student Non-Violent Coordinating Committee (SNCC), began to preach the doctrine of "Black Power," which, he said, "will smash everything Western civilization has created." Some advocates of Black Power insisted that they simply intended the slogan to describe a broad-front effort to exercise the political and economic rights gained by the civil rights movement. But other African Americans, recollecting previous black nationalist movements such as that of Marcus Garvey earlier in the century (see p. 522), breathed a vibrant separatist meaning into the concept of Black Power. Advocates of Black Power emphasized African American distinctiveness, shed their "white" names for new African identities, and demanded black studies programs in colleges and universities.

Ironically, just as the civil rights movement had achieved its greatest legal and political triumphs, city-shaking riots erupted in the black ghettoes of several American cities. A bloody outburst in Newark, New Jersey, in the summer of 1967, took twenty-five lives. Federal troops restored order in Detroit, Michigan, after forty-three people died in the streets. As in Los Angeles, black rioters torched their own neighborhoods, attacking police officers, and even firefighters, who had to battle both flames and mobs chanting, "Burn, baby, burn." These outbursts angered many white Americans, who threatened to retaliate with their own "backlash" against ghetto arsonists and killers. Inner-city anarchy baffled many northerners, who had considered racial problems a purely "southern" question. But black concerns had moved north—as had nearly half the nation's black people. In the North the Black Power movement now focused less on civil rights and more on economic demands. Black unemployment, for example, was nearly double that for whites. These oppressive problems seemed even less likely to be solved peaceably than the struggle for voting rights in the South.

Despair deepened when the magnetic and moderate voice of Martin Luther King, Jr., was forever silenced by a sniper's bullet in Memphis, Tennessee, on April 4, 1968. A martyr for justice, King had bled and died against the peculiarly American thorn of race. The killing of King cruelly robbed the American people of one of the most inspirational leaders in their history—at a time when they could least afford to lose him. This outrage triggered a nationwide orgy of ghetto-gutting and violence that cost more than forty lives.

Dr. Martin Luther King, Jr. (1929–1968) and Malcolm X (1925–1965) not only differed in the goals they held out to their fellow African Americans—King urging racial integration and Malcolm X black separatism—but also in the means they advocated to achieve them. In his famous "I Have a Dream" speech during the interracial March on Washington on August 28, 1963, King proclaimed to a quarter of a million people assembled at the Lincoln Memorial:

"In the process of gaining our rightful place we must not be guilty of wrongful deeds. Let us not seek to satisfy our thirst for freedom by drinking from the cup of bitterness and hatred. ... We must not allow our creative protest to degenerate into physical violence. Again and again we must rise to the majestic heights of meeting physical force with soul force."

ghetto *The district of a city where members of a religious or racial minority are forced to live, either by legal restriction or by informal social pressure. (Originally, ghettoes were enclosed Jewish districts in Europe.)*

militant *In politics, someone who pursues political goals in a belligerent way, often using paramilitary means.*

black separatism *The doctrine that blacks in the United States ought to separate themselves from whites, either in separate institutions or in a separate political territory.*

Rioters noisily made news, but thousands of other blacks quietly made history. Their voter registration had shot upward, and by the late 1960s several hundred blacks held elected office in the Old South. Cleveland, Ohio, and Gary, Indiana, elected black mayors. By 1972 nearly half of southern black children sat in integrated classrooms. Actually, more schools in the South were integrated than in the North. About a third of black families had risen economically into the ranks of the middle class—though an equal proportion remained below the "poverty line." King left a shining legacy of racial progress, but he was cut down when the job was far from completed.

Combating Communism in Two Hemispheres

PRIMARY SOURCE
President Lyndon Johnson's
Defense of the American ...

Violence at home eclipsed Johnson's legislative triumphs, while foreign flare-ups threatened his political life. Discontented Dominicans rose in revolt against their military government in April 1965. Johnson speedily announced that the Dominican Republic was the target of a Castro-like coup by "Communist conspirators," and he dispatched some twenty-five thousand American troops to restore order. But the evidence of a communist takeover was fragmentary at best. Johnson was widely condemned, at home and in Latin America, for his temporary reversion to "gunboat diplomacy."

At about the same time, Johnson was sinking deeper into the monsoon mud of Vietnam. Guerillas loyal to the North Vietnamese communists, called Viet Cong, attacked an American air base at Pleiku, South Vietnam, in February 1965. The president immediately ordered retaliatory bombing raids against military installations in North Vietnam and for the first time ordered U.S. troops to land. By the middle of March 1965, the Americans had "Operation Rolling Thunder" in full swing—regular full-scale bombing attacks against North Vietnam. Before 1965 ended, some 184,000 American troops were slogging through the jungles and rice paddies of South Vietnam searching for guerrillas.

Johnson had now taken the first fateful steps down a slippery path. He and his advisers believed that a fine-tuned, step-by-step escalation in American force would drive the enemy to defeat with a minimum loss of life. But the enemy matched every increase in American firepower with more men and more wiliness in the art of guerrilla warfare.

The South Vietnamese themselves were meanwhile becoming spectators in their own war, as the fighting became increasingly Americanized. Corrupt and collapsible governments succeeded each other in Saigon with bewildering rapidity. Yet American officials continued to talk of defending a faithful democratic ally. Washington spokespeople also defended the action as a test of Uncle Sam's "commitment" and of the reliability of his numerous treaty pledges to resist communist encroachment. Persuaded by such panicky thinking, Johnson steadily raised the military stakes in Vietnam. By 1968 he had poured more than half a million troops into Southeast Asia, and the annual bill for the war was exceeding $30 billion. Yet the end was nowhere in sight.

Vietnam Vexations

America could not defeat the enemy in Vietnam, but it seemed to be defeating itself. World opinion grew increasingly hostile; the blasting of an underdeveloped country by a mighty superpower struck many critics as obscene. Several nations expelled American Peace Corps volunteers. Ever-censorious Charles de Gaulle withdrew France from NATO in 1966 and ordered all American troops out of the country.

Overcommitment in Southeast Asia also tied America's hands elsewhere. Attacked by Soviet-backed Egypt, Jordan, and Syria, a beleaguered Israel stunned the world with a military triumph in June 1967. When the smoke cleared after the **Six-Day War**, Israel expanded to control new territories in the Sinai Peninsula, the Golan Heights, the Gaza Strip, and the West Bank of the Jordan River, including Jerusalem. The Israelis eventually withdrew from the Sinai after signing a peace treaty with Egypt, but they refused to relinquish the other areas without a treaty and began moving Jewish settlers into the heavily Arab district of the West Bank. The Six-Day War markedly intensified the problems of the already volatile Middle East, leading to an intractable standoff between the Israelis and Palestinians, now

Six-Day War (1967) *Military conflict between Israel and its Arab neighbors, including Syria, Egypt, and Jordan. The war ended with an Israeli victory and territorial expansion into the Sinai Peninsula, the Golan Heights, the Gaza Strip, and the West Bank.*

Vietnam and Southeast Asia, 1954–1975 Le Ly Hayslip (1949–) was born in a peasant village in South Vietnam, just south of Danang. In her memoir, *When Heaven and Earth Changed Places*, she describes the trauma endured by ordinary Vietnamese from America's fight against the Viet Cong. "[I]n 1963—the year the Viet Cong came to my village—American warplanes bombed Man Quang. It was at noon, just when the children were getting out of school. My aunt Thu and her pregnant daughter-in-law were making lunch for her husband and four grandchildren when the air-raid signal blared. They all jumped under the wooden table and sheltered the pregnant woman with their bodies—even the little kids. A bomb fell in Aunt Thu's front yard. ... Hot shrapnel tore through everyone except the pregnant woman. Aunt Thu and one of her grandchildren were killed. The passing fragment left only a weeping hole where her generous heart had been." © Cengage Learning led by Yasir Arafat (1929–2004), head of the Palestine Liberation Organization (PLO). The Middle East became an ever more dangerously packed powder keg that the war-plagued United States proved powerless to defuse.

Domestic discontent festered as the Vietnamese entanglement dragged on. Antiwar demonstrations had begun on a small scale with campus "teach-ins" in 1965, and gradually these protests mounted to tidal-wave proportions. As the long arm of the military draft dragged more and more young men off to the Southeast Asian slaughterpen, resistance stiffened. Thousands of draft registrants fled to Canada; others publicly burned their draft cards. Hundreds of thousands of chanting marchers filled the streets of New York, San Francisco, and other cities. Many Americans felt pangs of conscience at the ghastly spectacle of their countrymen burning peasant huts and blistering civilians with ghastly napalm.

Opposition in Congress to the Vietnam involvement centered in the influential Senate Committee on Foreign Relations, headed by Senator J. William Fulbright of Arkansas. A constant thorn in the side of the president, he staged a series of widely viewed televised hearings in 1966 and 1967, during which prominent personages aired their views, largely antiwar. Gradually the public came to feel that it had been lied to about both the causes and the "winnability" of the war. A yawning "credibility gap" opened between the government and the people. New flocks of antiwar "**doves**" were hatching daily.

By early 1968 the brutal and futile struggle had become the longest and most unpopular foreign war in the nation's history. The government had failed utterly to explain to the people what was supposed to be at stake in Vietnam. Casualties, killed and wounded, already exceeded 100,000. More bombs had been dropped on Vietnam than on all enemy territory in World War II.

The war was ripping apart the fabric of American society and even threatening to shred the Constitution. In 1967 President Johnson ordered the CIA, in clear violation of its charter as a *foreign* intelligence agency, to spy on domestic antiwar activities. He also encouraged the FBI to turn its counterintelligence program against the peace movement, subverting leading "doves" with false accusations that they were communist sympathizers. These clandestine tactics made the FBI look like a totalitarian state police rather than a guardian of American democracy.

As the war dragged on, evidence mounted that America had been entrapped in an Asian civil war, fighting against highly motivated rebels who were striving to overthrow an oppressive regime. Yet Johnson clung to his basic strategy of ratcheting up the pressure bit by bit. He stubbornly assured doubting Americans that he could see "the light at the end of the tunnel." But to growing numbers of Americans, it seemed that Johnson was bent on "saving" Vietnam by destroying it.

✳ PRIMARY SOURCE
Child from Vietnam War on TV Screen

dove(s) *During the Vietnam War, someone who opposed the war and favored de-escalation or withdrawal by the United States.*

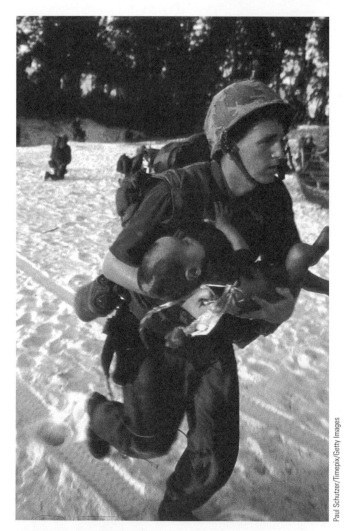

Paul Schutzer/Timepix/Getty Images

The Agony of War, 1965 A U.S. marine carries a South Vietnamese baby to safety. The child was wounded by American jets during the opening stages of a military operation at Cape Batangan, Vietnam.

Vietnam Topples Johnson

Hawkish illusions that the struggle was about to be won were shattered by a blistering communist offensive launched in late January 1968, during Tet, the Vietnamese New Year. At a time when the Viet Cong were supposedly licking their wounds, they suddenly and simultaneously mounted savage attacks on twenty-seven key South Vietnamese cities, including the capital, Saigon. Although eventually beaten off with heavy losses, they demonstrated anew that victory could not be gained by Johnson's strategy of gradual escalation. With an increasingly insistent voice, American public opinion demanded a speedy end to the war. But American military leaders responded to the Tet attacks with a request for 200,000 more troops. The size of the request staggered many policymakers.

Meanwhile, Senator Eugene J. McCarthy of Minnesota was sharply challenging the president from within his own party for the 1968 Democratic presidential nomination. McCarthy, a sometime poet and devout Catholic, gathered a small army of antiwar college students as campaign workers. Going "clean for Gene," with shaven faces and shortened locks, they helped him gain an impressive 41.4 percent of the Democratic vote in the New Hampshire primary on March 12, 1968. Although still second to Johnson's 49.6 percent, McCarthy's showing was devastating for the president. Johnson's star fell further four days later when Senator Robert F. Kennedy, now a senator from New York and an outspoken dove on the war, threw his hat into the ring. The charismatic and handsome Kennedy, heir to his murdered brother's mantle of leadership, stirred a passionate response among workers, African Americans, Latinos, and young people.

These startling events abroad and at home were not lost on LBJ. In a bombshell address on March 31, 1968, he announced that he would freeze American troop levels and scale down the bombing. Johnson startled his vast audience by firmly declaring that he would not be a candidate for the presidency in 1968.

Johnson's "abdication" had the effect of preserving the military status quo. The United States could maintain the maximum *acceptable* level of military activity in Vietnam with one hand, while trying to negotiate a settlement with the other. North Vietnam shortly agreed to negotiations in Paris, but progress was glacially slow, as prolonged bickering developed over the very shape of the conference table.

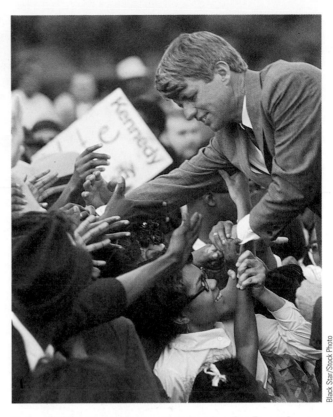

Black Star/Stock Photo

Robert F. Kennedy Campaigning for the Presidency, 1968 Wrapped in the Kennedy family mystique and exuding his own boyish charm, Kennedy excited partisan crowds to wildly adulatory outpourings.

The Presidential Sweepstakes of 1968

The summer of 1968 was one of the hottest political seasons in the nation's history. Johnson's heir apparent for the Democratic nomination was his loyal vice president, Hubert Humphrey. Senators McCarthy and Kennedy meanwhile dueled in several state primaries, with Kennedy's bandwagon gathering ever-increasing speed. But on June 5, 1968, on the night of an exciting victory in the California primary, Kennedy was shot to death by a young Arab immigrant.

Angry antiwar forces, deprived by an assassin's bullet of their leading candidate, streamed menacingly into Chicago for the Democratic convention in August 1968. Mayor Richard Daley responded by arranging for barbed-wire barricades around the convention hall, as well as thousands of police and National Guard reinforcements. Some militant demonstrators baited the officers in blue by calling them "pigs," shouting obscenities, and hurling bags of excrement at police lines. As people the world over watched on television, the exasperated "peace officers" broke into a "police riot," clubbing and manhandling innocent and guilty alike. Acrid tear gas fumes hung over the city even as Humphrey steamrollered to a first-ballot nomination. The Humphrey forces blocked the dovish McCarthyites' attempt to secure an antiwar platform plank and rammed through their own declaration that armed force would be relentlessly applied until the enemy showed more willingness to negotiate.

Scenting victory over the badly divided Democrats, the Republicans convened in plush Miami Beach, Florida, where former vice president Richard Nixon rose from his political grave to win the nomination. As a "**hawk**" on Vietnam and a right-leaning middle-of-the-roader on domestic policy, Nixon pleased the Goldwater conservatives and was acceptable to party moderates. He appealed to white southern voters and to the "law and order" element when he tapped as his running mate Maryland governor Spiro T. Agnew, noted for his tough stands against **dissidents** and black militants. The Republican platform called for victory in Vietnam and a strong anticrime policy.

Adding color and confusion to the campaign was the third-party candidacy of the segregationist former Alabama governor George C. Wallace. Wallace jabbed repeatedly at "pointy-headed bureaucrats" and taunted hecklers as "bums" who needed a bath. He also called for prodding blacks back into their place. He and his running mate, former air force general Curtis LeMay, also proposed smashing the North Vietnamese to smithereens by "bombing them back to the Stone Age."

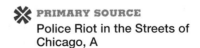 **PRIMARY SOURCE**
Police Riot in the Streets of Chicago, A

hawk *During the Vietnam War, someone who favored vigorous prosecution or escalation of the conflict.*

dissident(s) *Someone who dissents, especially from an established or normative institution or position.*

1968

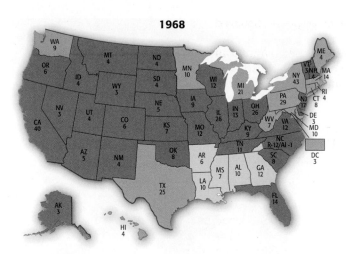

Candidate (Party)	Electoral Vote		Popular Vote	
Nixon (Republican)	301	56.1%	31,785,480	43.4%
Humphrey (Democrat)	191	35.5%	31,275,166	42.7%
Wallace (American Independent)	46	8.4%	9,906,473	13.5%

Presidential Election of 1968 (with electoral vote by state) George Wallace won in five states and denied a clear majority to either of the two major-party candidates in twenty-five other states. A shift of some fifty thousand votes might have thrown the election into the House of Representatives, giving Wallace the strategic bargaining position that he sought. © Cengage Learning

Between the positions of the Republicans and the Democrats on Vietnam, there was little choice. Both candidates were committed to keeping on the war until the enemy would settle for an "honorable peace," which seemed to mean an "American victory." The millions of "doves" had no place to roost, and many refused to vote at all. Humphrey, scorched by the LBJ brand, went down to defeat as a loyal prisoner of his chief's policies.

Nixon, who had lost a cliffhanger to Kennedy in 1960, won one in 1968. He garnered 301 electoral votes with 43.4 percent of the popular tally (31,785,480), compared with 191 electoral votes and 42.7 percent of the popular votes (31,275,166) for Humphrey. Unlike most new presidents, Nixon faced congressional majorities by the opposing party in both houses. Wallace won an impressive 9,906,473 popular votes and 46 electoral votes, all from five states of the Deep South, four of which the Republican Goldwater had carried in 1964. Wallace remained a formidable force, for he had amassed the largest third-party popular vote in American history to that point and was the last third-party candidate to win any electoral votes. (Ross Perot in 1992 enjoyed a greater popular vote margin but won no states; see p. 694). Wallace had also resoundingly demonstrated the continuing power of "populist" politics, which appealed to voters' fears and resentments rather than to the better angels of their nature. His candidacy foreshadowed a coarsening of American political life that would take deep root in the ensuing decades.

The Obituary of Lyndon Johnson

Talented but tragedy-struck Lyndon Johnson returned to his Texas ranch in January 1969 and died there four years later. His party was defeated, and his "me-too" Hubert Humphrey was repudiated. Yet Johnson's legislative leadership for a time had been remarkable. No president since Lincoln worked harder or did more for civil rights. None showed more compassion for the poor, blacks, and the ill educated.

But by 1966 Johnson was already sinking into the Vietnam quicksand. Great Society programs began to wither on the vine as soaring war costs sucked tax dollars into the military machine. Johnson promised guns and butter but could not deliver both. The War on Poverty met resistance as stubborn as the Viet Cong and eventually went down to defeat. Great want persisted alongside great wealth.

The Southeast Asian quagmire engulfed Johnson's noblest intentions. He was evidently persuaded by his brightest advisers, both civilian and military, that massive aerial bombing and limited troop commitments would make a "cheap" victory possible. His decision not to escalate the fighting further offended the "hawks," and his refusal to back off altogether antagonized the "doves." Like the Calvinists of colonial days, luckless Lyndon Johnson was damned if he did and damned if he did not.

The Cultural Upheaval of the 1960s

The struggles of the 1960s against racism, poverty, and the war in Vietnam had momentous cultural consequences. The decade came to be seen as a watershed dividing two distinct eras in terms of values, morals, and behavior.

Everywhere in 1960s America, a newly negative attitude toward all kinds of authority began to take hold. Disillusioned by the discovery that American society was not free of racism, sexism, imperialism, and oppression, many young people lost their traditional moral rudders. Neither families, nor churches, nor schools seemed to be able to define values and shape behavior with the certainty of shared purpose that many people believed had once existed.

The nation's mainstream Protestant denominations, which had dominated American religious life for centuries, lost their grip and many of their churchgoing parishioners. The liberal Protestant churches suffered the most. They increasingly ceded religious authority to conservative evangelicals while surrendering cultural authority to secular professionals and academic social scientists. A new cultural divide began to take shape, as educated Americans became increasingly secular and the less educated became more religious. Religious upheaval even churned the tradition-bound Roman Catholic Church, among the world's oldest and most conservative institutions. Clerics abandoned their Roman collars and the Latin Mass; folk songs replaced Gregorian chants; and meatless Fridays became ancient history. No matter what the topic, conventional wisdom and inherited ideas came under fire. "Trust no one over thirty" was a popular sneer of rebellious youth.

Skepticism about authority had deep historical roots in American culture, and it had even bloomed in the supposedly complacent and conformist 1950s. "Beat" poets such as Allen Ginsberg and iconoclastic novelists such as Jack Kerouac had voiced dark disillusion with the materialistic pursuits of "establishment" culture in the Eisenhower era. In movies such as *Rebel Without a Cause* (1955), the attractive young actor James Dean expressed the restless frustration of many young people.

The disaffection of the young reached crisis proportions in the tumultuous 1960s. One of the first organized protests against established authority broke out at the University of California at Berkeley in 1964, in the aptly named Free Speech Movement. Students objected to an administrative ban on the use of campus space for political debate, and accused the Cold War "megaversity" of promoting corporate interests rather than humane values.

But in only a few years, the clean-cut Berkeley activists and their sober-minded sit-ins would seem downright quaint. Fired by outrage against the war in Vietnam, some sons and daughters of the middle class became radical political rebels. Others turned to mind-bending drugs, tuned in to "acid rock," and dropped out of "straight" society. Others "did their own thing" in communes or "alternative" institutions. Patriotism became a dirty word. Beflowered women in trousers and long-haired men with earrings heralded the rise of a self-conscious "counterculture" vehemently opposed to traditional American ways.

Social upheaval in the 1960s was far from an American-only phenomenon. As people born in the wake of World War II came of age across the world, they questioned established authority. Waves of protests and calls for individual rights and political freedom spread like wildfire. The year 1968 was so stormy that it became synonymous with unrest in many languages. In May of that year, leftist French students organized city-crippling strikes against their country's antiquated university system. Joined by millions of workers,

The Free Speech Movement, Berkeley, California, 1964 Student leader Mario Savio addresses a crowd at the University of California at Berkeley. The Free Speech Movement marked the first of the large-scale student mobilizations that would rock campuses across the country throughout the rest of the 1960s.

© Bettmann/Corbis

and Japanese people had meanwhile scratched their way out of the ruins of war and built wholly new factories with the most up-to-date technology and management techniques. By the 1970s their efforts paid handsome rewards, as they came to dominate industries such as steel, automobiles, and consumer electronics—fields in which the United States had once been unchallengeable.

The poor economic performance of the 1970s hung over the decade like a pall. It frustrated both policymakers and citizens who keenly remembered the growth and optimism of the quarter-century since World War II. Now a stalemated, unpopular war and a stagnant, unresponsive economy heralded the end of the self-confident postwar era. With it ended the liberal dream, vivid since New Deal days, that an affluent society could spend its way to social justice.

moratorium *A period in which economic or social activity is suspended, often to achieve certain defined goals.*

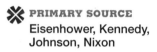
PRIMARY SOURCE
Eisenhower, Kennedy, Johnson, Nixon

PRIMARY SOURCE
Letters Home from Vietnam

My Lai Massacre (1968) *Military assault in a small Vietnamese village on March 16, 1968, in which American soldiers under the command of 2nd Lieutenant William Calley murdered hundreds of unarmed Vietnamese civilians, mostly women and children.*

Nixon "Vietnamizes" the War

Inaugurated on January 20, 1969, Richard Nixon urged the American people, torn with dissension over Vietnam and race relations, to "stop shouting at one another." Yet the new president seemed an unlikely conciliator of the clashing forces that appeared to be ripping apart American society. Solitary and suspicious by nature, Nixon could be brittle and testy in the face of opposition. He also harbored bitter resentments against the "liberal establishment." Yet Nixon brought one hugely valuable asset with him to the White House—his broad knowledge and thoughtful expertise in foreign affairs.

The first burning need of American foreign policy was to quiet the public uproar over Vietnam. President Nixon's announced policy, called "Vietnamization," was to withdraw the 540,000 U.S. troops in South Vietnam over an extended period. The South Vietnamese—with American money, weapons, training, and advice—could then gradually take over the burden of fighting their own war. The so-called Nixon Doctrine furthermore proclaimed that in the future, Asians and others would have to fight their own wars without the support of large bodies of American ground troops.

Nixon sought not to end the war but to win it without the further spilling of American blood. But even this much involvement was distasteful to the American "doves," and many of them demanded a withdrawal that was prompt, complete, unconditional, and irreversible. Antiwar protesters staged a massive national Vietnam **moratorium** in October 1969, as nearly 100,000 people jammed Boston Common and some 50,000 filed by the White House carrying lighted candles.

Undaunted, Nixon launched a counteroffensive by appealing to the "silent majority" who presumably supported the war. Though ostensibly conciliatory, Nixon's approach was in fact deeply divisive. His intentions became clear when he unleashed tough-talking Vice President Agnew to attack the "nattering nabobs of negativism" who demanded quick withdrawal from Vietnam. Nixon himself in 1970 sneered at the student antiwar demonstrators as "bums."

By January 1970 the Vietnam conflict had become the longest in American history and, with some 40,000 killed and more than 250,000 wounded, the third most costly foreign war in the nation's experience. Especially in the war's early stages, African Americans were disproportionately represented in the army and accounted for a disproportionately high share of combat casualties. Black and white soldiers alike floundered through booby-trapped swamps and steaming jungles, often unable to distinguish friend from foe among the Vietnamese peasants. Morale plummeted, as drug abuse, mutiny, and sabotage dulled the army's fighting edge.

Domestic disgust with the war was further deepened in 1970 by revelations of the **My Lai Massacre**, that in 1968 American troops had murdered innocent women and children in the village of My Lai. Increasingly desperate for a quick end to the demoralizing conflict, Nixon widened the war in 1970 by ordering an attack on Vietnam's neighbor, Cambodia.

A Marine Corps officer expressed the disillusion that beset many American troops in Vietnam:

"For years we disposed of the enemy dead like so much garbage. We stuck cigarettes in the mouths of corpses, put *Playboy* magazines in their hands, cut off their ears to wear around our necks. We incinerated them with napalm, atomized them with B-52 strikes, shoved them out the doors of helicopters above the South China Sea. . . . All we did was count, count bodies. Count dead human beings. . . . That was our fundamental military strategy. Body count. And the count kept going up."

"Cambodianizing" the Vietnam War

Suddenly, on April 29, 1970, without consulting Congress, Nixon ordered American troops to invade officially neutral Cambodia, which the North Vietnamese and Viet Cong had long used as a springboard for troops, weapons, and supplies. Angry students nationwide responded to the Cambodian invasion with rock throwing, window smashing, and arson. At Kent State University in Ohio, jumpy members of the National Guard fired into a noisy crowd, killing four and wounding many more; at historically black Jackson State College in Mississippi, the highway patrol killed two students.

Nixon withdrew the American troops from Cambodia after only two months. But in America the Cambodian invasion deepened the bitterness between "hawks" and "doves," as right-wing groups physically assaulted leftists. Disillusionment with "whitey's war" increased ominously among African Americans in the armed forces. The Senate (though not the House) overwhelmingly repealed the Gulf of Tonkin blank check that Congress had given Johnson in 1964 and sought ways to restrain Nixon. The youth of America were only slightly mollified when the government reduced draft calls, introduced a draft lottery, and lowered the voting age to eighteen through approval of the Twenty-sixth Amendment in 1971 (see Appendix).

New combustibles fueled the fires of antiwar discontent in June 1971, when a former Pentagon official leaked to the *New York Times* the "Pentagon Papers," a top-secret Pentagon study that documented the blunders and deceptions of the Kennedy and Johnson administrations, especially the provoking of the 1964 North Vietnamese attack in the Gulf of Tonkin.

John Filo/Premium Archive/Getty Images

The War at Home, Spring 1970 President Nixon's order to invade Cambodia sparked angry protests on American campuses. At Kent State University in Ohio, the nation watched in horror as four student demonstrators were shot by jittery National Guardsmen.

Nixon's Détente with Beijing and Moscow

As the antiwar firestorm flared ever higher, Nixon concluded that the road out of Vietnam ran through Beijing and Moscow. He perceived that tensions between the Chinese and the Soviets afforded the United States an opportunity to play off one antagonist against the other and to enlist the aid of both in pressuring North Vietnam into peace. Nixon's thinking was reinforced by his bespectacled and German-accented national security adviser, Dr. Henry A. Kissinger, who in 1969 began negotiating secretly with North Vietnamese officials in Paris while preparing the president's path to Beijing and Moscow.

Nixon, heretofore an uncompromising anticommunist, startled the nation by making an historic journey to China in February 1972. He capped the visit with the Shanghai Communiqué, in which the two nations agreed to "normalize" their relationship. Nixon next traveled to Moscow in May 1972 to play his "China card" in a game of high-stakes diplomacy in the **Kremlin**. The Soviets, hungry for American foodstuffs and alarmed over the possibility of intensified rivalry with an American-backed China, were ready to deal.

Nixon's visits ushered in an era of *détente*, or relaxed tension, with the two communist powers and produced several significant agreements in 1972, including the sale of $750 million worth of wheat, corn, and other grain to the Soviet Union. More important, the United States and the USSR agreed to an **antiballistic missile** (ABM) treaty, which limited each nation to two clusters of defensive missiles, and to a series of arms-reduction agreements known as SALT (Strategic Arms Limitations Talks) aimed at freezing the numbers of long-range nuclear missiles for five years.

These accords constituted long-overdue first steps toward slowing the arms race. Yet even though the ABM treaty forbade elaborate defensive systems, the United States forged ahead with the development of "MIRVs" (multiple independently targeted reentry vehicles), designed to overcome any defense by "saturating" it with large numbers of warheads, several to a rocket. Predictably, the Soviets proceeded to "MIRV" their own

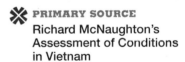

PRIMARY SOURCE
Richard McNaughton's Assessment of Conditions in Vietnam

Kremlin *The extensive palace complex in Moscow that houses the Soviet (Russian) government; hence, a shorthand term for the Soviet or Russian government.*

antiballistic missile *A defensive missile designed to intercept and destroy an offensive missile in flight.*

missiles, and the arms race ratcheted up to a still more perilous plateau, with more than sixteen thousand nuclear warheads deployed by both sides by the end of the 1980s.

Nixon's détente diplomacy did, to some extent, de-ice the Cold War. Yet Nixon remained staunchly anticommunist when the occasion seemed to demand it. He strongly opposed the election of the outspoken Marxist Salvador Allende as president of Chile in 1970. His administration and the Central Intelligence Agency worked covertly to undermine the legitimately elected leftist president. When the Chilean army overthrew and killed Allende in 1973, many observers smelled a Yankee rat. Even so, by checkmating and co-opting the two great communist powers, the president had cleverly set the stage for America's exit from Vietnam, although the concluding act in that wrenching tragedy still remained to be played.

Nixon on the Home Front

Nixon had lashed out during the campaign at the "permissiveness" and "judicial activism" of the Supreme Court, presided over by Chief Justice Earl Warren. The Warren Court's controversial decisions on sexual freedom, civil rights, criminal law, the practice of religion, and the structure of political representation had reflected its deep concern for the individual, no matter how lowly.

Miranda Warning *A statement of an arrested person's constitutional rights, which police officers must read during an arrest.*

In *Griswold v. Connecticut* (1965), the Court struck down a state law that prohibited the use of contraceptives, even among married couples. The Court proclaimed (critics said "invented") a "right of privacy" that soon provided the basis for decisions protecting women's abortion rights. Controversial decisions in the cases of *Escobedo* (1964) and *Miranda* (1966) gave accused criminals the right to remain silent. The latter case gave rise to the "**Miranda Warning**" that arresting officers must read to suspects. These several court rulings sought to prevent abusive police tactics, but they appeared to conservatives to coddle criminals and subvert law and order.

Conservatives also objected to the Court's views on religion. In two stunning decisions, *Engel v. Vitale* (1962) and *School District of Abington Township v. Schempp* (1963), the justices argued that the First Amendment's separation of church and state meant that public schools could not require prayers or Bible readings. Social conservatives raised anew the battle cry "Impeach Earl Warren."

From 1954 on, the Court came under relentless criticism, the bitterest since New Deal days. Fulfilling campaign promises, President Nixon undertook to change the Court's philosophical complexion. He sought appointees who would strictly interpret the Constitution, cease "meddling" in social and political questions, and not coddle radicals or criminals. The Senate in 1969 speedily confirmed his nomination of white-maned Warren E. Burger of Minnesota to succeed the retiring Earl Warren as chief justice. Before the end of 1971 the Court counted four conservative Nixon appointments out of nine members.

Yet Nixon was to learn the ironic lesson that many presidents have learned about their Supreme Court appointees: Once seated on the high bench, the justices are fully free to think and decide according to their own beliefs, not according to the president's expectations. The Burger Court that Nixon shaped proved reluctant to dismantle the "liberal" rulings of the Warren Court; it even produced the most controversial judicial opinion of modern times, the momentous *Roe v. Wade* decision in 1973, which legalized abortion (see p. 667).

Surprisingly Nixon presided over significant expansion of the welfare programs that conservative Republicans routinely denounced. He approved increased funds for entitlements such as Food Stamps, Medicaid, and Aid to Families with Dependent Children (AFDC), and he added a generous new program, Supplemental Security Income (SSI), to aid the indigent, blind, and disabled. Nixon also signed legislation in 1972 guaranteeing automatic Social Security cost-of-living increases to protect the elderly against the ravages of inflation. Ironically, this "indexing" actually helped to fuel the inflationary fires.

Amid much controversy, Nixon in 1969 implemented his so-called Philadelphia Plan requiring construction unions to establish "goals and timetables" for the hiring of black apprentices. Soon extended to all federal contracts, the Philadelphia Plan required employers to meet hiring quotas or to establish "set-asides" for minority contractors. Nixon's policy had far-reaching implications, because it went beyond earlier definitions of "affirmative action" designed to aid *individuals,* and instead conferred privileges on certain *groups.* While opening broad employment and educational opportunities for minorities and women, this approach opened a Pandora's box of protest from critics who assailed this "reverse discrimination" created by executive orders and unelected courts, not by democratically elected representatives.

Among Nixon's legacies was the creation in 1970 of the **Environmental Protection Agency (EPA),** which climaxed two decades of mounting concern for the environment. Scientist and author Rachel Carson gave the environmental movement a huge boost in 1962 when she published *Silent Spring,* an enormously effective piece of latter-day muckraking that exposed the poisonous effects of pesticides. On April 22, 1970, millions of environmentalists around the world celebrated the first "Earth Day" to raise awareness and to encourage their leaders to act. In the wake of what became a yearly event, the U.S. Congress passed the Clean Air Act of 1970 and the Endangered Species Act of 1973. The EPA now stood on the frontline of the battle for ecological sanity and made notable progress in reducing automobile emissions and cleaning up befouled waterways and toxic waste sites.

The federal government also expanded its regulatory reach on behalf of workers and consumers. Late in 1970, Nixon signed the Occupational Safety and Health Administration (OSHA) into law, creating an agency dedicated to improving working conditions, preventing work-related accidents and deaths, and issuing safety standards. The Consumer Product Safety Commission (CPSC) followed two years later, holding companies to account for selling dangerous products.

Elected as a minority president, with only 43 percent of the vote in 1968, Nixon devised a clever but cynical plan—called the "southern strategy"—to achieve a solid majority in 1972. Appointing conservative Supreme Court justices, soft-pedaling civil rights, and opposing school busing to achieve racial balance were all parts of the strategy.

Environmental Protection Agency (EPA) *A governmental organization signed into law by Richard Nixon in 1970 designed to regulate pollution, emissions, and other factors that negatively influence the natural environment.*

The Nixon Landslide of 1972

But the southern strategy became superfluous as foreign policy dominated the presidential campaign of 1972. Vietnam continued to be the burning issue. Nearly four years had passed since Nixon had promised, as a presidential candidate, to end the war and "win" the peace. Yet in the spring of 1972 the fighting escalated anew to alarming levels when the North Vietnamese, heavily equipped with foreign tanks, burst through the demilitarized zone separating the two Vietnams. Nixon reacted promptly by launching massive bombing attacks on strategic centers in North Vietnam, including Hanoi, the capital. Gambling heavily on Moscow's and Beijing's forbearance, Nixon also ordered the dropping of contact mines to blockade the principal harbors of North Vietnam.

The continuing Vietnam conflict spurred the rise of South Dakota senator George McGovern to the 1972 Democratic nomination. McGovern's promise to pull the remaining American troops out of Vietnam in ninety days earned him the backing of the large antiwar element in the party. But his appeal to racial minorities, feminists, leftists, and youth alienated the traditional working-class backbone of his party. Moreover, the discovery shortly after the convention that McGovern's running mate, Missouri senator Thomas Eagleton, had undergone psychiatric care—including electroshock therapy—forced Eagleton's ouster from the ticket and virtually doomed the Democrat's hope of recapturing the White House.

Nixon's campaign emphasized that he had wound down the "Democratic war" in Vietnam from some 540,000 troops to about 30,000. His candidacy received an added boost just twelve days before the election when the high-flying Dr. Kissinger announced that "peace is at hand" in Vietnam and that an agreement would be settled in a few days.

Nixon won the election in a landslide. His lopsided victory encompassed every state except Massachusetts and the nonstate District of Columbia (which was granted electoral votes by the Twenty-third Amendment in 1961 (see Appendix). He piled up 520 electoral votes to 17 and a popular majority of 47,169,911 votes to 29,170,383. McGovern had counted on a large vote from young people, but less than half the 18–21 group even bothered to vote.

The dove of peace, "at hand" in Vietnam just before the balloting, took flight after the election. Fighting on both sides escalated again, and Nixon launched a furious two-week bombing of North Vietnam. This merciless pounding drove the North Vietnamese negotiators to agree to cease-fire arrangements on January 23, 1973, nearly three months after peace was prematurely proclaimed.

Nixon hailed the face-saving cease-fire agreement as "peace with honor," but the boast rang hollow. The United States was to withdraw its remaining 27,000 or so troops and could reclaim some 560 American prisoners of war. The North Vietnamese were allowed to keep some 145,000 troops in South Vietnam, where they still occupied about 30 percent of the country. This shaky "peace" was in reality little more than a thinly disguised American retreat.

The Secret Bombing of Cambodia and the War Powers Act

The constitutionality of Nixon's continued aerial battering of Cambodia had meanwhile been coming under increasing fire. In July 1973 America was shocked to learn that the U.S. Air Force had already secretly conducted some thirty-five hundred bombing raids against North Vietnamese positions in Cambodia, beginning in March 1969 and continued for some fourteen months prior to the open American incursion in May 1970. The most disturbing feature of these sky **forays** was that, while they were going on, American officials, including the president, had sworn that Cambodian neutrality was being respected. Countless Americans began to wonder what kind of representative government they had if they were fighting a war they knew nothing about.

foray *A single, defined movement or attack by a military unit.*

Defiance followed secretiveness. After the Vietnam cease-fire in January 1973, Nixon brazenly continued large-scale bombing of communist forces in order to help the rightist Cambodian government, and he repeatedly vetoed congressional efforts to stop him. The years of bombing inflicted grisly wounds on Cambodia, blasting its people and revolutionizing its politics. The long-suffering Cambodians soon groaned under the sadistic heel of Pol Pot, a murderous tyrant who dispatched as many as 2 million of his people to their graves.

Congressional opposition to the expansion of presidential war-making powers by Johnson and Nixon led to the War Powers Act in November 1973. Passed over Nixon's veto, it required the president to report to Congress within forty-eight hours after committing troops to a foreign conflict. Such a limited authorization would have to end within sixty days unless Congress extended it for thirty more days.

The War Powers Act was but one manifestation of what came to be called the "New Isolationism," a mood of caution and restraint in the conduct of the nation's foreign affairs after the bloody and futile misadventure in Vietnam. Meanwhile, the draft ended in January 1973, although it was retained on a standby basis. The armed forces were to be all volunteers.

The Washington Post *(July 19, 1973) carried this news item:*

"American B-52 bombers dropped about 104,000 tons of explosives on Communist sanctuaries in neutralist Cambodia during a series of raids in 1969 and 1970.... The secret bombing was acknowledged by the Pentagon the Monday after a former Air Force major... described how he falsified reports on Cambodian air operations and destroyed records on the bombing missions actually flown."

The Arab Oil Embargo and the Energy Crisis

The long-rumbling Middle East erupted anew in October 1973, when the rearmed Syrians and Egyptians unleashed surprise attacks on Israel. Kissinger, who had become secretary of state in September, hastily flew to Moscow in an effort to restrain the Soviets, who were arming the attackers. Believing that the Kremlin was poised to fly combat troops to the Suez area, Nixon placed America's nuclear forces on alert and ordered a gigantic airlift of nearly $2 billion in war materials to the Israelis. This assistance helped save the day, as the Israelis aggressively turned the tide and threatened Cairo until American diplomacy brought about an uneasy cease-fire.

America's policy of backing Israel against its oil-rich neighbors exacted a heavy penalty. Late in October 1973, the OPEC nations announced an embargo on oil shipments to the United States and several European allies supporting Israel, especially the Netherlands. What was more, the oil-rich Arab states cut their oil production, further ratcheting pressure on the entire West, whose citizens suffered a long winter of lowered thermostats and speedometers. Lines at gas stations grew longer as tempers grew shorter. The shortage triggered a major economic **recession** not just in America, but also in France and Britain, whose non-support for Israel had exempted them from the embargo. But in an increasingly globalized, interconnected world, all nations soon felt the crunch.

recession *A moderate and short-term economic downturn, less severe than a depression. (Economists define a recession as two consecutive quarters, i.e., six months, of declining gross domestic product.)*

The "energy crisis" suddenly energized a number of long-deferred projects. Congress approved a costly Alaska pipeline and a national speed limit of fifty-five miles per hour to conserve fuel. Agitation mounted for heavier use of coal and nuclear power, despite the environmental threat they posed.

The five months of the Arab "blackmail" embargo in 1974 clearly signaled the end of an era—a period of cheap and abundant energy. American oil production peaked in 1970 and then began an irreversible decline. Blissfully unaware of their dependence on foreign suppliers, Americans, like revelers on a binge, had more than tripled their oil consumption since the end of World War II. The number of automobiles increased 350 percent between 1949 and 1972, and Detroit's engineers gave nary a thought to building more fuel-efficient engines.

By 1974 America was oil-addicted and extremely vulnerable to any interruption in supplies. That stark fact would deeply color the diplomatic and economic history of the next three decades and beyond, as the Middle East loomed ever larger on the map of America's strategic interests. OPEC approximately quadrupled its price for crude oil after lifting the embargo in 1974.

Watergate Woes

Nixon's electoral triumph in 1972 was almost immediately sullied—and eventually undone—by the Watergate scandal. On June 17, 1972, five men were arrested inside the Watergate office complex in Washington after attempting to plant electronic "bugs" in the Democratic party's headquarters. They were soon revealed to be working for the Republican Committee to Re-Elect the President—popularly known as CREEP. The Watergate break-in turned out to be just one in a series of Nixon administration "dirty tricks" that included forging documents to discredit Democrats, using the Internal Revenue Service to harass innocent citizens named on a White House "enemies list," burglarizing the office of the psychiatrist who had treated the leaker of the Pentagon Papers, and perverting the FBI and CIA to cover the tricksters' track.

Meanwhile, the moral stench hanging over the White House worsened when Vice President Spiro Agnew was forced to resign in October 1973 for taking bribes from Maryland contractors. In the first use of the Twenty-fifth Amendment (see Appendix), Nixon nominated and Congress confirmed Agnew's successor, a twelve-term congressman from Michigan, Gerald ("Jerry") Ford.

Amid a mood of growing national outrage, a select Senate committee conducted widely televised hearings about the Watergate affair in 1973–1974. Nixon indignantly denied any prior knowledge of the break-in and any involvement in the legal proceedings against the burglars. But John Dean III, a former White House lawyer with a remarkable memory, accused top White House officials, including the president, of obstructing justice by trying

Nixon, the Law-and-Order-Man

attorney general *The presidentially appointed head of the Department of Justice and chief legal officer of the federal government.*

executive privilege *In American government, the claim that certain information known to the president or the executive branch of government should be unavailable to Congress or the courts because of the principle of separation of powers.*

"smoking gun" tape *The White House tape recordings, released in July 1974, that proved that President Nixon had corruptly used the CIA to block the FBI's investigation of the Watergate burglary. The tape forced Nixon to resign the presidency.*

PRIMARY SOURCE
Nixon Incriminates Himself

PRIMARY SOURCE
House Judiciary Committee's
Conclusion on Impeachment

to cover up the Watergate break-in and silence its perpetrators. Then another former White House aide revealed that a secret taping system had recorded most of Nixon's Oval Office conversations. Now, Dean's sensational testimony could be checked against the White House tapes, and the Senate committee could better determine who was telling the truth. But Nixon, stubbornly citing his "executive privilege," refused to hand over the tapes. Then, on October 20, 1973, he ordered the "Saturday Night Massacre," firing the special prosecutor who demanded the evidence, as well as his **attorney general** and deputy attorney general who had refused orders to dismiss the prosecutor.

Nixon finally acceded in the spring of 1974 to the House Judiciary Committee's demand for the Watergate tapes, though with many sections missing (including Nixon's frequent obscenities, which were excised with the phrase "expletive deleted"). But on July 24, 1974, the president suffered a disastrous setback when the Supreme Court unanimously ruled that **"executive privilege"** gave him no right to withhold from the special prosecutor portions of tapes relevant to criminal activity. Skating on thin ice over hot water, Nixon reluctantly complied.

Nixon now made public three subpoenaed tapes of conversations with his chief aide on June 23, 1972. Fatally for his own case, one of them—the notorious **"smoking gun" tape** (see p. 665) revealed the president giving orders, six days after the Watergate break-in, to use the CIA to hold back an inquiry by the FBI. Nixon's own tape-recorded words convicted him of having been an active party to the attempted cover-up. The House Judiciary Committee proceeded to draw up articles of impeachment, based on obstruction of justice, abuse of the powers of the presidential office, and contempt of Congress.

The public's wrath proved to be overwhelming. Republican leaders in Congress concluded that the guilty and unpredictable Nixon was a loose cannon on the deck of the ship of state. They frankly informed the president that his impeachment by the full House and removal by the Senate were foregone conclusions and that he would do best to resign.

Left with no better choice, Nixon choked back his tears and announced his resignation in a dramatic television appearance on August 8, 1974. Few presidents had flown so high, and none had sunk so low. In his Farewell Address, Nixon admitted having made some "judgments" that "were wrong" but insisted that he had always acted "in what I believed at the time to be the best interests of the nation." Unconvinced, countless Americans would change the song "Hail to the Chief" to "Jail to the Chief."

The nation had survived a wrenching constitutional crisis, which proved that the impeachment machinery forged by the Founding Fathers could work when public opinion overwhelmingly demanded that it be implemented. The principles that no person is above the law and that presidents must be held to strict accountability for their acts were strengthened. The United States of America, on the eve of its two-hundredth birthday as a republic, had eventually cleaned its own sullied house, giving an impressive demonstration of self-discipline and self-government to the rest of the world.

The First Unelected President

Gerald Rudolph Ford, the first man to be made president solely by a vote of Congress, entered the besmirched White House in August 1974 with serious handicaps. He was widely—and unfairly—suspected of being little more than a dim-witted former college football player. President Johnson had sneered that "Jerry" was so lacking in brainpower that he could not walk and chew gum at the same time. Worse, Ford had been selected, not elected, vice president, following Spiro Agnew's resignation in disgrace. The sour odor of illegitimacy hung about this president without precedent.

Then, out of a clear sky, Ford granted a complete pardon to Nixon for any crimes he may have committed as president, discovered or undiscovered. Democrats were outraged, and lingering suspicions about the pardon cast a dark shadow over Ford's prospects of being elected president in his own right in 1976.

Ford at first sought to enhance the so-called détente with the Soviet Union that Nixon had crafted. In July 1975 President Ford joined leaders from thirty-four other nations in Helsinki, Finland, to sign several sets of historic accords. One group of agreements officially wrote an end to World War II by finally legitimizing the Soviet-dictated boundaries of

EXAMINING THE EVIDENCE

THE "SMOKING GUN" TAPE, JUNE 23, 1972, 10:04–11:39 A.M.

The technological capability to record Oval Office conversations combined with Richard Nixon's obsession with documenting his presidency to give the public—and the Senate committee investigating his role in the break-in of the Democratic National Committee headquarters in the Watergate Office Tower—rare access to personal conversations between the president and his closest advisers. This tape, which undeniably exposed Nixon's central role in constructing a "cover-up" of the Watergate break-in, was made on Nixon's first day back in Washington after the botched burglary of June 17, 1972. In this conversation with White House Chief of Staff H. R. Haldeman, Nixon devised a plan to block a widening FBI investigation by instructing the director of the CIA to deflect any further FBI snooping on the grounds that it would endanger sensitive CIA operations. Nixon refused to turn over this and other tapes to Senate investigators until so ordered by the Supreme Court on July 24, 1974. Within four days of its release on August 5, Nixon was forced to resign. After eighteen months of protesting his innocence of the crime and his ignorance of any effort to obstruct justice, Nixon was finally undone by the evidence in this incriminating "smoking gun" tape. While tapes documented two straight years of Nixon's Oval Office conversations, other presidents, such as Franklin Roosevelt, John F. Kennedy, and Lyndon Baines Johnson, recorded important meetings and crisis deliberations. Since Watergate, however, it is unlikely that any president has permitted extensive tape recording, depriving historians of a unique insight into the inner workings of the White House.

1. Should taped White House discussions be part of the public record of a presidency? If so, who should have access to the records?

2. What else might historians learn about the president and the administration from a tape such as this one, besides the specific details of the Watergate cover-up?

3. Why did this conversation especially lead to near-unanimous calls for Nixon's impeachment or resignation from Republicans and Democrats alike?

Haldeman: . . . yesterday, they concluded it was not the White House, but are now convinced it is a CIA thing, so the CIA turn off would . . .

President: Well, not sure of their analysis, I'm not going to get that involved. I'm (unintelligible).

Haldeman: No, sir. We don't want you to.

President: You call them in.

President: Good. Good deal! Play it tough. That's the way they play it and that's the way we are going to play it.

Haldeman: O.K. We'll do it.

President: Yeah, when I saw that news summary item, I of course knew it was a bunch of crap, but I thought ah, well it's good to have them off on this wild hair [sic] thing because when they start bugging us, which they have, we'll know our little boys will not know how to handle it. I hope they will though. You never know. Maybe, you think about it. Good!

President: When you get in these people when you . . . get these people in, say: "Look, the problem is that this will open the whole, the whole Bay of Pigs thing, and the President just feels that" ah, without going into the details . . . don't, don't lie to them to the extent to say there is no involvement, but just say this is sort of a comedy of errors, bizarre, without getting into it, "the President believes that it is going to open the whole Bay of Pigs thing up again. And, ah because these people are plugging for, for keeps and that they should call the FBI in and say that we wish for the country, don't go any further into this case," period!

The "Smoking Gun" Tape, June 23, 1972, 10:04–11:39 A.M.

Source: Nixon Presidential Materials Project, National Archives and Records Administration

---

Poland and other Eastern European countries. In return, the Soviets signed a "third basket" of agreements, guaranteeing more liberal exchanges of people and information between East and West and protecting certain basic human rights. The Helsinki accords kindled small dissident movements in Eastern Europe and even in the USSR itself, but the Soviets soon poured ice water on these sputtering flames of freedom.

Western Europeans cheered the Helsinki conference as a milestone of détente. But in the United States critics increasingly charged that détente was proving to be a one-way street. American grain and technology flowed to the USSR, and little of comparable importance flowed back. Moscow also continued its human rights violations, including restrictions on Jewish emigration. Despite these difficulties, Ford at first clung stubbornly to détente. But the American public's fury over Moscow's double-dealing steadily mounted. The thaw in the Cold War was threatening to prove chillingly brief.

Passing the Buck A satirical view of where responsibility for the Vietnam debacle should be laid.

Defeat in Vietnam

Early in 1975 the North Vietnamese gave full throttle to their long-expected drive southward. President Ford urged Congress to vote still more weapons for Vietnam. But his plea was in vain, and without the crutch of massive American aid, the South Vietnamese quickly and ingloriously collapsed.

The dam burst so rapidly that the remaining Americans had to be frantically evacuated by helicopter, the last of them on April 29, 1975. Also rescued were about 140,000 South Vietnamese, most of them so dangerously identified with the Americans that they feared a bloodbath by the victorious communists. Ford compassionately admitted these people to the United States, adding further seasoning to the melting pot. Eventually some 500,000 arrived (see "Makers of America: The Vietnamese," pp. 668–669).

America's longest, most frustrating war thus ended not with a bang but a whimper. In a technical sense the Americans had not lost the war; their client nation had. The United States had fought the North Vietnamese to a standstill and had then withdrawn its troops in 1973, leaving the South Vietnamese to fight their own war, with generous shipments of costly American weaponry. The estimated cost to America was $118 billion in current outlays, together with some 56,000 dead and 300,000 wounded. The people of the United States had in fact provided just about everything, except the will to win—and that could not be injected by outsiders.

Technicalities aside, America had lost more than a war. It had lost face in the eyes of foreigners, lost its own self-esteem, lost confidence in its military prowess—and lost much of the economic muscle that had made possible its global leadership since World War II. Americans reluctantly came to realize that their power as well as their pride had been deeply wounded in Vietnam and that recovery would be slow and painful.

Feminist Victories and Defeats

As the army limped home from Vietnam, most of the protest movements of the 1960s, including the antiwar movement, had long since splintered and stalled. One major exception to this pattern stood out: the American feminist movement. Although they had their differences, feminists showed vitality and momentum by winning legislative and judicial victories and provoking an intense rethinking of gender roles. (On the roots of this movement, see "Makers of America: The Feminists," pp. 670–671).

Thousands of women marched in the Women's Stride for Equality on the fiftieth anniversary of woman suffrage in 1970. In 1972 Congress passed Title IX of the Education Amendments, prohibiting sex discrimination in any federally assisted educational program. This act created opportunities for girls' and women's athletics at schools and colleges, giving birth to a new "Title IX generation" that would reach maturity in the 1980s and 1990s and help professionalize women's sports as well. The Equal Rights Amendment (ERA) to the Constitution won congressional approval in 1972. It declared, "Equality of rights under the law shall not be denied or abridged by the United States or by any State on account of sex." Twenty-eight states quickly ratified the amendment, first proposed by suffragists in 1923. Hopes rose that the ERA would soon be the law of the land.

Even the Supreme Court seemed to be on the movement's side. In *Reed v. Reed* and *Frontiero v. Richardson* (1973), the Court challenged sex discrimination in legislation and employment. And in the landmark case of *Roe v. Wade* (1973), the Court struck down laws prohibiting abortion, arguing that a woman's decision to terminate a pregnancy was protected by the constitutional right of privacy.

But the feminist movement soon faced a formidable backlash. In 1972 President Nixon vetoed a proposal to set up nationwide public day care, saying it would weaken the American family. The Catholic Church and the religious right organized a powerful grassroots movement to oppose the legalization of abortion. For many feminists, the most bitter defeat was the death of the ERA. Anti-feminists, led by conservative activist Phyllis Schlafly, argued that the ERA would in fact remove traditional protections women enjoyed by forcing the law to see them as men's equals. They further believed the amendment would threaten the basic family structure of American society. Schlafly charged that the ERA's advocates were just "bitter women seeking a constitutional cure for their personal problems." In 1979 Congress extended the deadline for ratification, as the ERA was still short of the thirty-eight states needed, but opponents dug in their heels. The amendment died in 1982, three states short of success.

PRIMARY SOURCE
Women's Liberation March

The Seventies in Black and White

Although the civil rights movement had fractured, race remained an explosive issue in the 1970s. The Supreme Court in *Milliken v. Bradley* blind-sided school integrationists when it ruled that desegregation plans could not require students to move across school-district lines. The decision effectively exempted suburban districts from shouldering any part of the burden of desegregating inner-city schools, thereby reinforcing "white flight" to the suburbs and forcing all the problems of desegregation into the least prosperous districts. Conflicts over desegregation often pitted the poorest, most disadvantaged elements of the white and black communities against one another.

Affirmative action programs also remained highly controversial. White workers who were denied advancement and white students who were refused college admission cried "reverse discrimination," charging that race or ethnic background was now outweighing ability in employment or admissions. In 1978 the Supreme Court, by a narrow five-to-four margin, upheld the claim of one white Californian, Allan Bakke, that he had been denied admission to medical school because of a program that favored minority applicants. In a tortured decision, the Court ordered the University of California at Davis medical school to admit Bakke, and declared that preference in admissions could not be based on ethnic or racial identity alone. Yet at the same time, the Court said that racial factors might be taken into account in a school's overall admissions policy for purposes of assembling a diverse student body. In an impassioned dissent, the Court's only black justice, Thurgood Marshall, warned that denial of racial preferences might sweep away years of civil rights progress. But many conservatives cheered the decision as affirming the principle that justice is colorblind.

Inspired by the civil rights movement, Native Americans in the 1970s gained remarkable power through using the courts and well-planned acts of civil disobedience. But while blacks had fought against segregation, Indians used the tactics of the civil rights movement to assert their status as separate semisovereign peoples. Indian activists captured the nation's attention by seizing the island of Alcatraz in 1970 and the village of Wounded Knee, South Dakota, in 1972. In the case of *United States v. Wheeler* (1978), the Supreme Court declared that Indian tribes possessed a "unique and limited" sovereignty, subject to the will of Congress but not to individual states.

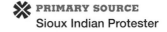

PRIMARY SOURCE
Sioux Indian Protester

The Vietnamese

At first glance, the towns of Westminster and Fountain Valley, California, seem to resemble other California communities nearby. Tract homes line residential streets; shopping centers flank the busy thoroughfares. But these are no ordinary American suburbs. Instead, they make up "Little Saigons," vibrant outposts of Vietnamese culture in the contemporary United States.

Before South Vietnam fell in 1975, few Vietnamese ventured across the Pacific. Only in 1966 did U.S. immigration authorities even designate "Vietnamese" as a separate category of newcomers, and most early immigrants were the wives and children of U.S. servicemen. But as the communists closed in on Saigon, many Vietnamese, particularly those who had worked closely with American or South Vietnamese authorities, feared for their future. Gathering together as many of their extended-family members as they could assemble, thousands of Vietnamese fled for their lives. In a few hectic days in 1975, some 140,000 escaped before the approaching gunfire, a few dramatically clinging to the bottoms of departing helicopters. Another 60,000 less fortunate refugees escaped at the same time over land and sea to Hong Kong and Thailand, where they waited nervously for permission to move on.

To accommodate the refugees, the U.S. government set up camps across the nation. Arrivals were crowded into army barracks affording little room and less privacy. These were boot camps not for military service but for assimilation into American society. A rigorous program trained the Vietnamese in English, forbade children from speaking their native language in the classroom, and even immersed them in American slang. Many resented this attempt to mold them and strip them of their culture.

Vietnamese discontent boiled over when authorities prepared to release the refugees from camps and board them with families around the nation. The resettlement officials had decided to find a sponsor for each Vietnamese family—an American family that would provide food, shelter, and assistance for the refugees until they could fend for themselves. But the Vietnamese people cherish their traditional extended families—grandparents, uncles, aunts, and cousins living communally with parents and children. As soon as refugees could, they relocated from the rural districts where they had

The Bicentennial Campaign and the Carter Victory

America's two-hundredth birthday, in 1976, fell during a presidential election year—a fitting coincidence for a proud democracy. President Gerald Ford energetically sought the Republican nomination in his own right and defeated challenger Ronald Reagan, former actor and governor of California, who ran as a more conservative candidate.

The Democratic standard-bearer was fifty-one-year-old James Earl Carter, Jr., a dark-horse candidate who galloped out of obscurity during the long primary-election season. A former Georgia governor who insisted on humble "Jimmy" as his first name, this **born-again** Baptist touched many people with his down-home sincerity. Untainted by ties with a corrupt and cynical Washington, Carter ran against the memory of Nixon and Watergate as much as he ran against Ford. His most effective campaign pitch was his promise that "I'll never lie to you."

Carter squeezed out a narrow victory on election day, with 51 percent of the popular vote. The electoral count stood at 297 to 240. The winner swept every state except Virginia in his native South. Especially important were the votes of African Americans, 97 percent of whom cast their ballots for Carter.

born-again *The evangelical Christian belief in a spiritual renewal or rebirth, involving a personal experience of conversion and a commitment to moral transformation.*

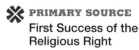 **PRIMARY SOURCE**
First Success of the Religious Right

Preserving the Past A Vietnamese American boy learns classical calligraphy from his grandfather.

been scattered to established Vietnamese enclaves around San Francisco, Los Angeles, and Dallas.

Soon a second throng of Vietnamese immigrants pushed into these Little Saigons. Fleeing from the ravages of poverty and from the oppressive communist government, these stragglers had crammed themselves and their few possessions into little boats, hoping to reach Hong Kong or get picked up by friendly ships. Eventually, many of these "boat people" reached the United States. Usually less educated than the first arrivals and receiving far less resettlement aid from the U.S. government, they were, however, more willing to start at the bottom. Today these two groups total more than half a million people. Differing in experience and expectations, the Vietnamese share a new home in a strange land. Their uprooting is an immense, unreckoned consequence of America's longest war.

Carter enjoyed hefty Democratic majorities in both houses of Congress. Hopes ran high that the stalemate of the Nixon-Ford years between a Republican White House and a Democratic Capitol Hill would now be ended. At first Carter enjoyed notable political success, as Congress granted his requests to create a new cabinet-level Department of Energy and to cut taxes. But Carter's honeymoon did not last long. An inexperienced outsider, he had campaigned against the Washington "establishment" and never quite made the transition to being an insider himself. Carter repeatedly rubbed congressional fur the wrong way, and critics charged that he isolated himself in a shallow pool of fellow Georgians whose ignorance of the ways of Washington compounded the problems of their greenhorn chief.

Carter's Humanitarian Diplomacy

As a committed Christian, President Carter displayed from the outset an overriding concern for human rights as the guiding principle of his foreign policy. In the African nations of Rhodesia (later Zimbabwe) and South Africa, Carter and his eloquent United Nations ambassador, Andrew Young, championed the oppressed black majority.

The Feminists

A well-to-do housewife and mother of seven, Elizabeth Cady Stanton (1815–1902) was an unlikely revolutionary. Yet this founding mother of American feminism devoted seven decades of her life to the fight for women's rights.

Young Elizabeth Cady drew her inspiration from the fight against slavery. When she and her new husband, abolitionist Henry Stanton, attended the World Anti-Slavery Convention in London, she was insulted that women were forced to sit in a screened-off balcony above the convention floor. Stanton went on to organize the Seneca Falls Convention in 1848. There she presented her Declaration of Sentiments, which proclaimed that "all men *and women* are created equal" and demanded women's rights to own property, enter the professions, and vote.

Early feminists encountered a mountain of hostility to their cause. Stanton failed to have women included in the Fourteenth Amendment to the Constitution, which granted equal citizenship to African Americans, and she died nearly twenty years before her dream of woman suffrage was realized in the Nineteenth Amendment (1920). Yet by imagining women's emancipation as an expansion of America's founding principles of citizenship, Stanton charted a path that other feminists would follow a century later.

Historians use the terms "first wave" and "second wave" to distinguish the women's movement of the nineteenth century from that of the late twentieth century. The woman most often credited with launching the "second wave" is Betty Friedan (1921–2006). Friedan, who had seen her mother sacrifice her own career in journalism to raise a family, wrote the best seller *The Feminine Mystique* to expose the quiet desperation of millions of housewives trapped in the "comfortable concentration camp" of the suburban home. In 1966 Friedan cofounded the National Organization for Women (NOW), the chief political arm of second-wave feminism.

Just as first-wave feminism grew out of abolitionism, the second wave drew ideas, leaders, and tactics from the civil rights movement of the 1960s. Civil rights workers and feminists alike focused on equal rights. NOW campaigned vigorously for an Equal Rights Amendment, which in 1982 fell just three states short of ratification.

Second-wave feminism also had an avowedly radical wing, supported by younger women eager to challenge almost every traditional male and female gender role and to take the feminist cause to the streets. Among these women was Robin Morgan, a civil rights activist in organizations such as the Congress of Racial Equality (CORE) and SNCC (Student Non-Violent Coordinating Committee). Women in the movement who protested against gender discrimination met ridicule, as in SNCC leader Stokely Carmichael's retort that "the only position for women in SNCC is prone." Morgan went on to found WITCH (Women's International Terrorist Conspiracy from Hell), made famous by its protest at the 1968 Miss America pageant in Atlantic City, New Jersey. There demonstrators threw symbols of women's oppression—bras, girdles, dishcloths—into trash cans. (Contrary to news stories, they did not burn the bras.)

As the contrast between WITCH and NOW suggests, second-wave feminism was a remarkably diverse movement.

The president's most spectacular foreign-policy achievement came in September 1978 when he invited President Anwar Sadat of Egypt and Prime Minister Menachem Begin of Israel to the woodsy presidential retreat at Camp David, Maryland, in an attempt to prevent another blowup in the misery-drenched Middle East. Skillfully serving as go-between, Carter persuaded the two visitors to sign an accord (September 17, 1978) under whose terms Israel agreed to withdraw from territory conquered in the 1967 war and Egypt promised to respect Israel's borders. Both parties pledged themselves to sign a formal peace treaty within three months.

Carter achieved further diplomatic success by resuming full diplomatic relations with China in 1979. He also concluded two treaties turning over ownership of the Panama Canal to the Panamanians. The United States gave up complete control on December 31, 1999.

Despite these dramatic accomplishments, trouble stalked Carter's foreign policy. Overshadowing all international issues was the ominous reheating of the Cold War with the Soviet Union. Détente fell into disrepute as thousands of Cuban troops, assisted by

Marching for Women's Rights, 1977 A multiethnic and multiracial group of women, accompanied by noted "second-wave" feminists Bella Abzug (in hat) and Betty Friedan (far right), helped to carry a torch from Seneca Falls, New York, birthplace of the feminist movement, to Houston, Texas, site of the National Women's Conference.

Feminists in the late twentieth century disagreed over many issues—from pornography and marriage to how much to expect from government, capitalism, and men. Some feminists placed a priority on gender equality, whereas others defended a feminism of gender difference.

Still, beyond these differences feminists had much in common. Most advocated a woman's right to choose abortion and regarded the law as a key weapon against gender discrimination. By century's end radical and moderate feminists alike could take pride in a host of achievements that had changed the landscape of gender relations. Yet, like Elizabeth Cady Stanton, second-wave feminists also shared the burden of understanding that the goals of genuine equality would take more than a lifetime to achieve.

Soviet advisers, appeared in Angola, Ethiopia, and elsewhere in Africa to support revolutionary factions. Arms-control negotiations with Moscow stalled in the face of this Soviet military meddling.

Economic and Energy Woes

Adding to Carter's mushrooming troubles was the failing health of the economy. A stinging recession during Ford's presidency brought the inflation rate down slightly to just under 6 percent, but from the moment Carter took over, prices resumed their dizzying ascent, driving the inflation rate well above 13 percent by 1980. The soaring bill for imported oil plunged America's **balance of payments** deeply into the red (an unprecedented $40 billion in 1978).

balance of payments *The net ratio, expressed as a positive or negative sum, of a nation's exports in relation to its imports. (It may be calculated in relation to one particular foreign nation or to all foreign states collectively.)*

President Jimmy Carter (b. 1924) delivered what became known as his "malaise" speech (although he never used the word) on television in 1979. In time cultural conservatives would take up his theme to support their call for a return to "traditional values":

"In a nation that was proud of hard work, strong families, close-knit communities, and our faith in God, too many of us now tend to worship self-indulgence and consumption. Human identity is no longer defined by what one does, but by what one owns. But we've discovered that owning things and consuming things does not satisfy our longing for meaning. We've learned that piling up material goods cannot fill the emptiness of lives which have no confidence or purpose. ... The symptoms of this crisis of the American spirit are all around us."

The "oil shocks" of the 1970s taught Americans a painful but necessary lesson: they could never again seriously consider a policy of economic isolation, as they had tried to do between the two world wars. For most of American history, foreign trade had accounted for no more than 10 percent of gross national product (GNP). But huge foreign-oil bills drove that figure upward in the 1970s so that, by century's end, some 27 percent of GNP depended on foreign trade. Unable to dominate international trade and finance as they once had, Americans would have to master foreign languages and study foreign cultures if they wanted to prosper in the rapidly globalizing economy.

Yawning deficits in the federal budget, reaching nearly $60 billion in 1980, further aggravated the U.S. economy's inflationary ailments. The elderly and other Americans living on fixed incomes suffered from the shrinking dollar. People with money to lend pushed interest rates ever higher. The "prime rate" (the rate of interest that banks charged their very best customers) vaulted to an unheard-of 20 percent in early 1980. The high cost of borrowing money shoved small businesses to the wall and strangled the construction industry.

Carter diagnosed America's economic disease as stemming primarily from the nation's costly dependence on foreign oil. Unfortunately, his legislative proposals in April 1977 for energy conservation ignited a blaze of indifference among the American people, who had already forgotten the long gasoline lines of 1973.

Events in Iran jolted Americans out of their complacency about energy supplies in 1979. The imperious Mohammed Reza Pahlevi, installed as shah of Iran with help from America's CIA in 1953, had long ruled his oil-rich land with a will of steel. His repressive regime was finally overthrown in January 1979 in a violent revolution spearheaded by Muslim fundamentalists. The revolutionary upheavals soon crippled Iran's oil fields. As Iranian oil supplies stopped flowing, Americans once more found themselves waiting impatiently in long lines at gas stations or buying high-priced gasoline only on specified days.

As the oil crisis deepened, President Carter sensed the rising temperature of popular discontent. In July 1979 he retreated to the mountain hideaway of Camp David, where he remained largely out of public view for ten days. Like a royal potentate of old summoning the wise men of the realm for their counsel in a time of crisis, Carter called in more than one hundred leaders from all walks of life to give him their views. Meanwhile, the nation anxiously awaited the results of these extraordinary deliberations.

When Carter finally came down from the mountaintop on July 15, 1979, he stunned a perplexed nation with his "malaise speech," chiding his fellow citizens for falling into a "moral and spiritual crisis" and for being too concerned with "material goods." A few days later, the president fired four of his cabinet secretaries and circled the wagons of his Georgia advisers more tightly about the White House. Critics began to wonder aloud whether Carter, the professed man of the people, was losing touch with the popular mood of the country.

Foreign Affairs and the Iranian Imbroglio

Hopes for a less dangerous world rose slightly in June 1979, when President Carter met with Soviet leader Leonid Brezhnev in Vienna to sign the long-stalled SALT II agreements, limiting the levels of lethal strategic weapons in the Soviet and American arsenals. But conservative critics of the president's defense policies, still regarding the Soviet Union as the Wicked Witch of the East, unsheathed their long knives to carve up the SALT treaty when it came to the Senate for debate in the summer of 1979.

Political earthquakes in the petroleum-rich Persian Gulf region finally buried all hopes of ratifying the **SALT II** arms limitation treaty between the Soviets and the United States. On November 4, 1979, a howling mob of rabidly anti-American Muslim militants stormed the United States embassy in Teheran, Iran, and took all of its occupants hostage. The captors demanded that American authorities ship the exiled shah from the United States back to Iran. Americans agonized over both the fate of the hostages and the stability of the entire Persian Gulf region, so dangerously close to the Soviet Union. The Soviet army then aroused the West's worst fears on December 27, 1979, when it blitzed into the mountainous nation of Afghanistan, next door to Iran, and appeared to be poised for a thrust at the oil jugular of the gulf.

President Carter reacted vigorously to these alarming events. He slapped an embargo on the export of grain and high-technology machinery to the USSR, called for a boycott of the upcoming Olympic Games in Moscow, and requested that young people (including women) be made to register for a possible military draft. Proclaiming that the United States would "use any means necessary, including force," to protect the Persian Gulf against Soviet incursions, Carter grimly conceded that he had misjudged the Soviets. The SALT treaty became a dead letter in the Senate. Meanwhile, the Soviet army met unexpectedly stiff resistance in Afghanistan and became bogged down in a nasty, decade-long guerrilla war that came to be called "Russia's Vietnam."

The Iranian hostage crisis was Carter's—and America's—bed of nails. The captured Americans languished in cruel captivity, while the nightly news broadcasts showed humiliating scenes of Iranian mobs burning the American flag and spitting on effigies of Uncle Sam.

Carter at first tried to apply economic sanctions and the pressure of world opinion against the Iranians. But the president's frustration grew as the political turmoil in Iran rumbled on endlessly. Carter at last ordered a daring rescue mission. A highly trained **commando** team penetrated deep into Iran's sandy interior, but when equipment failures prevented some members of the team from reaching their destination, the mission had to be scrapped. As the commandos withdrew in the dark desert night, two of their aircraft collided, killing eight of the would-be rescuers.

The disastrous failure of the rescue raid proved anguishing for Americans. The episode seemed to underscore the nation's helplessness and even incompetence in the face of a mortifying insult to the national honor. The stalemate with Iran dragged on throughout the rest of Carter's term, providing an embarrassing backdrop to the embattled president's struggle for reelection.

SALT II *Strategic Arms Limitation Treaty agreement between Soviet leader Leonid Brezhnev and American president Jimmy Carter. Despite an accord to limit weapons between the two leaders, the agreement was ultimately scuttled in the U.S. Senate following the Soviet invasion of Afghanistan in 1979.*

commando *Member of a small, elite military force trained to carry out difficult missions, often within territory controlled by the enemy.*

Chapter Summary

Nixon's "Vietnamization" policy reduced American ground participation in the war, but his Cambodia invasion sparked massive protest. Nixon's journeys to Communist Moscow and Beijing (Peking) established a new rapprochement with these powers. In domestic policy, Nixon and the Supreme Court promoted affirmative action and environmental protection.

Nixon's landslide 1972 election victory was negated as the widespread Watergate scandal erupted. A cease-fire provided cover for withdrawal of the last American troops from Vietnam, but Congressional protest over the secret bombing of Cambodia led to the War Powers Act. The Middle East War of 1973 and the Arab oil embargo created an energy and economic crisis that lasted through the decade and ended the long era of postwar prosperity. Americans gradually awoke to their costly and dangerous dependence on Middle Eastern oil, and began to take tentative steps toward conservation and alternative energy sources.

Nonelected Gerald Ford took over after Watergate forced Nixon to resign. The Communist Vietnamese finally overran the South Vietnamese government in 1975. The defeat in Vietnam added to a general sense of disillusionment with government and society and a new sense of the limits of American power. The major social movement to survive the sixties was feminism, which achieved widespread social breakthroughs though failing to pass the Equal Rights Amendment. Race remained an explosive issue, as divisive issues of busing and affirmative action eroded the good will created by the civil rights movement.

Campaigning against Watergate and a corrupt Washington, outsider Jimmy Carter won a slender victory over Ford in 1976, but proved unable to work with Congress or improve the economy once he took office. His Camp David agreement brought peace between Egypt and Israel, but the Iranian revolution led to a new energy crisis that compounded already severe inflation and recession. The Soviet invasion of Afghanistan and the holding of American hostages in Iran added to Carter's woes and a general American sense of frustration and helplessness.

KEY TERMS

moratorium (658)

My Lai Massacre (1968) (658)

Kremlin (659)

antiballistic missile (659)

Miranda Warning (660)

Environmental Protection Agency (EPA) (661)

foray (662)

recession (663)

attorney general (664)

executive privilege (664)

"smoking gun" tape (664)

born-again (668)

balance of payments (671)

SALT II (673)

commando (673)

PEOPLE TO KNOW

Henry A. Kissinger

Warren E. Burger

George McGovern

Gerald ("Jerry") Ford

John Dean III

James Earl ("Jimmy") Carter, Jr.

Leonid Brezhnev

Go to the History CourseMate website for primary source links, study tools, and review materials for this chapter. www.cengagebrain.com

40

The Resurgence of Conservatism

1980–1992

It will be my intention to curb the size and influence of the federal establishment and to demand recognition of the distinction between the powers granted to the federal government and those reserved to the states or to the people.

RONALD REAGAN, INAUGURAL ADDRESS, 1981

⭐ Chapter Outline

Ronald Reagan and the New Right

"Reaganomics" and Its Consequences

Reagan Renews the Cold War

The Iran-Contra Scandal

Reagan's Economic Legacy

The Religious Right and Conflict over Abortion

George H. W. Bush

The End of the Cold War

The Persian Gulf War, 1991

Bush's Battles at Home

Varying Viewpoints: Where Did Modern Conservatism Come From?

"It's morning in America" was the slogan of Republican candidate Ronald Reagan in his 1984 presidential campaign. Certainly the 1980s were a new day for America's conservative right. Census figures confirmed that the average American was older than in the stormy sixties and much more likely to live in the South or West, the traditional bastions of the "Old Right," where many residents harbored suspicions of federal power. The conservative cause drew added strength from the emergence of a "New Right" movement, partly in response to the countercultural protests of the 1960s. Spearheading the New Right were evangelical Christian groups such as the Moral Majority, dedicated believers who enjoyed startling success as political fund-raisers and organizers.

Many New Right activists were far less agitated about economic questions than about cultural concerns—the so-called social issues. New Right activists denounced abortion, pornography, homosexuality, feminism, and especially affirmative action. Activists championed prayer in the schools and tougher penalties for criminals. Together, the Old and New Right added up to a powerful political combination, devoted to changing the very character of American society.

FOCUS QUESTIONS

1. What social and cultural developments led to the dramatic rise of Ronald Reagan and the "new right" in the early 1980s?

2. What were the essential elements of the "Reagan revolution" in economic and social policy, and what were Reaganism's short-term and long-term consequences?

3. How did the renewed Cold War of the early 1980s eventually lead to the Reagan-Gorbachev agreements of the late 1980s and the end of the Cold War? What caused the collapse of communism and the Soviet Union in 1989–1991?

4. How did the religious right transform American politics, and how did issues such as abortion and affirmative action create disagreement in the Supreme Court and the country?

5. How did the United States become more involved in the Middle East, leading up to the military intervention of the Persian Gulf War?

CHRONOLOGY

1980	Reagan defeats Carter for presidency.	**1987**	U.S. naval escorts begin in Persian Gulf. Stock market plunges 508 points. Senate rejects Supreme Court nomination of Robert Bork. Third Reagan-Gorbachev summit meeting in Washington, D.C.; INF treaty signed.
1981	Iran releases American hostages. "Reaganomics" spending and tax cuts passed. Solidarity movement in Poland. O'Connor appointed to Supreme Court (first woman justice).	**1988**	Fourth Reagan-Gorbachev summit meeting in Moscow. Bush defeats Dukakis for presidency.
1981–1991	United States aids anti-leftist forces in Central America.	**1989**	Chinese government suppresses prodemocracy demonstrators in Tiananmen Square. *Webster v. Reproductive Health Services.* Eastern European countries oust communist governments. Berlin Wall torn down.
1982	Recession hits U.S. economy. Israel invades Lebanon.		
1983	Reagan announces SDI plan (Star Wars). U.S. marines killed in Beirut, Lebanon. U.S. invasion of Grenada.	**1990**	Iraq invades Kuwait. East and West Germany unite. Americans with Disabilities Act (ADA).
1984	Reagan defeats Mondale for presidency. Soviet Union boycotts Summer Olympics in Los Angeles.	**1991**	Persian Gulf War. Thomas appointed to Supreme Court. Gorbachev survives coup attempt and resigns as Soviet president. Soviet Union dissolves; republics form Commonwealth of Independent States.
1985	Gorbachev comes to power in Soviet Union, announces *glasnost* and *perestroika.* First Reagan-Gorbachev summit meeting in Geneva.		
1986	Reagan administration backs Aquino in Philippines. Iran-Contra affair revealed. Second Reagan-Gorbachev summit meeting in Reykjavik, Iceland.	**1992**	Twenty-seventh Amendment (prohibiting congressional pay raises from taking effect until an election seats a new session of Congress) ratified. *Planned Parenthood v. Casey*

✳ **PRIMARY SOURCE**
Reagan for President

The Election of Ronald Reagan, 1980

Ronald Reagan was well suited to lead the gathering conservative crusade. Reared in a generation whose values were formed well before the upheavals of the 1960s, he naturally sided with the New Right on social issues. In economic and social matters alike, he denounced the activist government and failed "social engineering" of the 1960s. Just as his early political hero, Franklin Roosevelt, had championed the "forgotten man" against big business, Reagan championed the "common man" against big government. He aimed especially to win over from the Democratic column working-class and lower-middle-class white voters by implying that the Democratic party had become the exclusive tool of its minority constituents.

Though Reagan was no intellectual, he drew on the ideas of a small but influential group of thinkers known as "**neoconservatives.**" Their ranks included Norman Podhoretz, editor of *Commentary* magazine, and Irving Kristol, editor of *The Public Interest.* Reacting against what they saw as the excesses of 1960s liberalism, the neoconservatives championed free-market capitalism liberated from government restraints, and they took tough, harshly anti-Soviet positions in foreign policy. They also questioned liberal welfare programs and affirmative-action policies and called for reassertion of traditional values of individualism and the centrality of the family.

neoconservatives (neoconservatism)
Political activists and thinkers, mostly former liberals, who turned to a defense of traditional social and moral values and a strongly anticommunist foreign policy in the 1970s and 1980s.

An actor-turned-politician, Reagan enjoyed enormous popularity with his crooked grin and aw-shucks manner. The son of an impoverished Irish-American father from a small Illinois town, Reagan got his start in the depressed 1930s as a radio sports announcer. He became a B-grade Hollywood star in the 1940s and helped purge communists from the Screen Actors Guild as the organization's president in the 1950s. In 1954 he became a spokesman for General Electric and began preaching a conservative, antigovernment line. Reagan's growing skill at promoting the conservative cause inspired a group of wealthy California businessmen to help him launch his political career as governor of California from 1966 to 1974.

By 1980 the Republican party was ready to challenge the Democrats' hold on the White House. Bedeviled abroad and becalmed at home, Jimmy Carter's administration struck many Americans as bungling and befuddled. Carter's inability to control double-digit inflation was especially damaging. Disaffection with Carter's apparent ineptitude ran deep even in his own Democratic party, in which an "ABC" (Anybody But Carter) movement gathered steam. The liberal wing of the party found their champion in Senator Edward Kennedy of Massachusetts, the last survivor of the assassin-plagued Kennedy brothers. He and Carter slugged it out in a series of bruising primary elections, while delighted Republicans decorously proceeded to name Reagan their presidential nominee. In the end Kennedy's candidacy fell victim to the country's conservative mood and to lingering suspicions about a 1969 automobile accident on Chappaquiddick Island, Massachusetts, in which a young woman assistant was drowned when Kennedy's car plunged off a bridge. A badly battered Carter, his party divided and in disarray, was left to do battle with Reagan.

The Republican candidate proved to be a formidable campaigner. Using his professional acting skills to great advantage, Reagan attacked the incumbent's fumbling performance in foreign policy and blasted the Democratic party's "big-government philosophy." Galloping inflation, sky-high interest rates, and a faltering economy also put the incumbent president on the defensive. Carter countered ineffectively with charges that Reagan was a trigger-happy cold warrior who might push the country into nuclear war.

Carter's spotty record in office was no defense against Reagan's popular appeal. On election day Reagan rang up a spectacular victory, bagging more than 51 percent of the popular vote while 41 percent went to Carter. Reflecting a small but vocal protest against both candidates, nearly 7 percent of the electorate voted for liberal Republican congressman John Anderson, who ran as an independent. The electoral count stood at 489 for Reagan and 49 for Carter, making Carter the first elected president to be unseated by voters since Herbert Hoover in 1932. Equally startling, the Republicans gained control of the Senate for the first time in twenty-six years. Leading Democratic liberals, including George McGovern, had been targeted for defeat by well-heeled New Right groups. They went down like dead timber in the conservative windstorm that swept the country.

Carter showed dignity in defeat. An unusually intelligent, articulate, and well-meaning president, he had been hampered by his lack of managerial talent and badly buffeted by events beyond his control, such as the soaring price of oil, runaway inflation, and the galling insult of the hostages still held in Iran. Though unsuccessful in the White House, Carter earned much admiration in later years for his humanitarian and human rights activities. He received the Nobel Peace Prize in 2002.

In a speech to the National Association of Evangelicals on March 8, 1983, President Ronald Reagan (1911-2004) defined his stand on school prayer:

"The Declaration of Independence mentions the Supreme Being no less than four times. 'In God We Trust' is engraved on our coinage. The Supreme Court opens its proceedings with a religious invocation. And the Members of Congress open their sessions with a prayer. I just happen to believe the schoolchildren of the United States are entitled to the same privileges as Supreme Court Justices and Congressmen."

✳ PRIMARY SOURCE
Re-elect Carter-Mondale

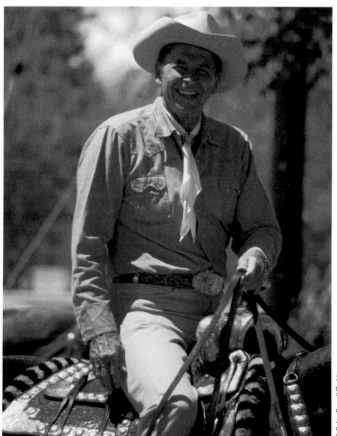

© Galen Rowell/Corbis

President Ronald Reagan The oldest man ever elected to the presidency, Reagan displayed youthful vigor both on the campaign trail and in office.

The Reagan Revolution

Reagan's arrival in Washington was triumphal. The Iranians contributed to the festive mood by releasing the hostages on Reagan's Inauguration Day, January 20, 1981, after 444 days of captivity. The new president, a hale and hearty sixty-nine-year-old, was devoted to fiscal fitness and a leaner federal government. He sought nothing less than the dismantling of the welfare state and the reversal of the political evolution of the preceding half century. Years of New Deal–style tax-and-spend programs, Reagan jested, had created a federal government that reminded him of the definition of a baby as a creature who was all appetite at one end, with no sense of responsibility at the other.

On his conservative crusade for smaller government, less bureaucracy, and freer markets, Reagan found common cause with the new leader of America's oldest ally, Great Britain. Conservative Margaret Thatcher became Britain's first female Prime Minister in 1979. With a mandate to improve her nation's economy—suffering through the 1970s as the United States had—she embarked on a mission to reduce the power of labor unions and government involvement in business, two of Reagan's chief goals. The philosophic kinship between "Ronnie and Maggie," as the press dubbed the two heads of state, went beyond economics. Emboldened by each other, they strengthened the Anglo-American alliance through muscular foreign policy against a number of foes, especially the Soviet bloc. Their common refrain was that free markets made free peoples, and that shrinking government meant keeping their nations safer from communism.

By the early 1980s, this antigovernment message found a receptive audience in the United States. In the two decades since 1960, federal spending had risen from about 18 percent of gross national product to nearly 23 percent. After four decades of advancing New Deal and Great Society programs, a strong countercurrent took hold. Californians staged a "tax revolt" in 1978 (known by its official ballot title of "Proposition 13") that slashed property taxes and forced painful cuts in government services. The California "tax quake" jolted other state capitals and rocked even Washington, D.C. Ronald Reagan had ridden this political shock wave to presidential victory in 1980 and proceeded to rattle the "**welfare state**" to its very foundations

Reagan pursued his smaller-government policies with near-religious zeal and remarkable effectiveness. He proposed a new federal budget that necessitated cuts of some $35 billion, mostly in social programs such as food stamps and federally funded job-training centers. Reagan worked naturally in harness with the Republican majority in the Senate, while in the Democratic House he enterprisingly wooed a group of mostly southern conservative Democrats (dubbed "boll weevils"), who abandoned their own party's leadership to follow the president. The new president seemed strong and motivated, all the more so after a failed assassination attempt in March 1981 brought an outpouring of sympathy and support.

The Battle of the Budget

Swept along on a tide of presidential popularity, Congress swallowed Reagan's budget proposals. The new president's triumph amazed political observers, especially defeated Democrats. He had descended on Washington like an avenging angel of conservatism, kicking up a blinding whirlwind of political change. His impressive performance demonstrated the power of the presidency with a skill not seen since Lyndon Johnson's day.

Reagan hardly rested to savor the sweetness of his victory. The second part of his economic program called for substantial reductions in marginal tax rates over a period of three years. Many Democrats, the president quipped, had "never met a tax they didn't hike." Thanks largely to Reagan's skill as a television performer and the continued defection of the "boll weevils" from the Democratic camp, the president again had his way. In late 1981 Congress approved a set of far-reaching tax reforms that lowered individual tax rates, reduced federal estate taxes, and created new tax-free savings plans for small investors. Reagan's "**supply-side**" economic advisers assured him that the combination of budgetary discipline and tax reduction would stimulate new

welfare state *The political system, typical of modern industrial societies, in which government assumes responsibility for the economic well-being of its citizens by providing social benefits.*

supply-side *In economics, the theory that investment incentives such as lowered federal spending and tax cuts will stimulate economic growth and increased employment.*

investment, boost productivity, foster dramatic economic growth, and eventually even reduce the deficit.

But at first, supply-side economics seemed to be a beautiful theory mugged by a gang of brutal facts, as the economy slid into its deepest recession since the 1930s. Unemployment reached nearly 11 percent in 1982, businesses folded, and several bank failures jolted the nation's entire financial system. The automobile industry, once the brightest jewel in America's industrial crown, reported losses in the hundreds of millions of dollars.

Ignoring the yawping pack of Democratic critics, President Reagan and his economic advisers serenely waited for their supply-side economic policies ("Reaganomics") to produce the promised results. The supply-siders seemed to be vindicated when a healthy economic recovery finally got under way in 1983. Yet the economy of the 1980s was not uniformly sound. For the first time in the twentieth century, income gaps widened between the richest and the poorest Americans. The poor got poorer and the very rich grew fabulously richer, while middle-class incomes largely stagnated. Symbolic of the new income stratification was the emergence of "yuppies," or young urban professionals. Sporting Rolex watches and BMW sports cars, they made a near-religion out of conspicuous consumption. Though numbering only about 1.5 million people, yuppies showcased the values of materialism and the pursuit of wealth that came to symbolize the high-rolling 1980s.

Some economists located the sources of the economic upturn neither in the president's budget cuts and tax reforms nor in the go-get-'em avarice of the yuppies. Rather, they pointed to his massive expenditures for the military. Reagan cascaded nearly 2 trillion dollars onto the Pentagon in the 1980s, asserting the need to close the "window of vulnerability" in the armaments race with the Soviet Union. Ironically, this conservative president thereby plunged the government into a red-ink bath of deficit spending that made the New Deal look downright stingy. Federal budget deficits topped $100 billion in 1982, and the government's books were nearly $200 billion out of balance in every subsequent year of the 1980s. Massive government borrowing to cover these deficits kept interest rates high. The soaring dollar caused by high interest rates dealt crippling blows to American exporters, as the American international trade deficit reached a record $152 billion in 1987. The masters of international commerce and finance for a generation after World War II, Americans suddenly became the world's heaviest borrowers in the global economy of the 1980s.

✳ **PRIMARY SOURCE**
Federal Budget, The

Reagan Renews the Cold War

Hard as nails toward the Soviet Union in his campaign speeches, Reagan saw no reason to soften up after he checked in at the White House. He claimed that the Soviets were "prepared to commit any crime, to lie, to cheat" in pursuit of their goals of world conquest. He denounced the Soviet empire as "the focus of evil in the modern world."

Reagan believed in negotiating with the Soviets—but only from a position of overwhelming strength. Accordingly, his strategy for dealing with Moscow was simple: by enormously expanding U.S. military capabilities, he could threaten the Soviet leaders with a fantastically expensive new round of the arms race. Desperate to avoid economic ruin, Kremlin leaders would come to the bargaining table and sing Reagan's tune.

This strategy resembled a riverboat gambler's ploy. It wagered the enormous sum of Reagan's defense budgets on the hope that the other side would not call Washington's bluff and initiate a new cycle of arms competition. Reagan played his trump card in this risky game in March 1983 when he announced his intention to pursue a high-technology missile defense system called the Strategic Defense Initiative (SDI), popularly known as "Star Wars." The plan called for orbiting battle stations in space that could fire laser beams or other forms of concentrated energy to vaporize intercontinental missiles on liftoff. Most scientists considered this an impossible goal, but the deeper logic of SDI lay in its fit with Reagan's overall Soviet strategy. By pitching the arms contest onto a stratospherically high plane of technology and astronomical expense, it would further force the Kremlin's hand.

Shrinking the federal government and reducing taxes had been the main objectives of Reagan's first term; foreign-policy issues dominated his second term. The president soon found himself contending for the world's attention with a charismatic new Soviet leader, Mikhail Gorbachev, installed as chairman of the Soviet Communist party in March 1985. Gorbachev was personable, energetic, imaginative, and committed to radical reforms in the Soviet Union. He announced two policies with remarkable, even revolutionary, implications. *Glasnost,* or "openness," aimed to ventilate the secretive, repressive stuffiness of Soviet society by introducing free speech and a measure of political liberty. *Perestroika,* or "restructuring," was intended to revive the moribund Soviet economy by adopting many of the free-market practices of the capitalist West.

Both *glasnost* and *perestroika* required that the Soviet Union shrink the size of its enormous military machine and redirect its energies to the civilian economy. That requirement, in turn, necessitated an end to the Cold War. Gorbachev accordingly made warm overtures to the West, including an announcement in April 1985 that the Soviet Union would cease to deploy intermediate-range nuclear forces (INF) targeted on Western Europe, pending an agreement on their complete elimination. He pushed this goal when he met with Ronald Reagan at their first of four summit meetings, in Geneva in November 1985. A second summit meeting, in Reykjavik, Iceland, in October 1986, broke down when a furious Reagan stormed out, convinced that Gorbachev had come to end plans for the beloved SDI. But at a third summit, in Washington, D.C., in December 1987, the two leaders at last signed the Intermediate-Range Nuclear Forces (INF) Treaty, banning all of these missiles from Europe. Reagan and Gorbachev capped their new friendship in May 1988 at a final summit in Moscow. There President Reagan, who had entered office condemning the "evil empire" of Soviet communism, warmly praised Gorbachev. Reagan, the consummate cold warrior, had been flexible and savvy enough to seize a historic opportunity to join with the Soviet chief to bring the Cold War to a kind of conclusion. For this, history would give both leaders high marks.

Central America and the Caribbean This region, so important to the United States throughout its history, remained a hotbed of unrest through the last years of the Cold War and beyond. © Cengage Learning

The Iran-Contra Imbroglio

Two foreign-policy problems seemed insoluble to Reagan: the continuing captivity of a number of American hostages seized by Muslim extremist groups in bleeding, battered Lebanon; and the continuing grip on power of the left-wing Sandinista government in Nicaragua. The president repeatedly requested that Congress provide military aid to the contra rebels fighting against the Sandinista regime. Congress repeatedly refused, and the administration grew increasingly frustrated, even obsessed, in its search for a means to help the contras.

Unknown to the American public, some Washington officials saw a possible linkage between the two thorny problems of the Middle Eastern hostages and the Central American Sandinistas. In 1985 American diplomats secretly arranged arms sales to Iran, which was mired in a devastating territorial war with neighboring Iraq. In return, the Iranians helped obtain the release of at least one American hostage held by Middle Eastern terrorists. Meanwhile, the money Iran paid for the American weapons was diverted to the contras in Nicaragua. These actions brazenly violated a congressional ban on military aid to the Nicaraguan rebels—not to mention Reagan's repeated vow that he would never negotiate with terrorists. Washington also continued to support Iraqi dictator Saddam Hussein, to whom it sold weapons he then used against Iran.

News of these secret dealings broke in November 1986 and ignited a firestorm of controversy. President Reagan claimed he was innocent of wrongdoing and ignorant of his subordinates' activities. Although Reagan was never found to have lied outright, a congressional committee condemned the "secrecy, deception, and disdain for the law" displayed by administration officials and concluded that "if the president did not know what his national security advisers were doing, he should have."

The Iran-Contra affair cast a dark shadow over Reagan's record in foreign policy, tending to obscure the president's achievement in establishing a new relationship with the Soviets. Although the several Iran-Contra investigations presented damaging revelations of Reagan's weaknesses and laziness as a chief executive, he remained among the most popular and beloved presidents in modern American history.

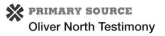

Contra Rebel Troops Head for Battle These rebels were long-seasoned and battle-scarred veterans of Nicaragua's civil war by the time this photograph was taken in 1987.

✳ PRIMARY SOURCE
Oliver North Testimony

Reagan's Economic Legacy

Ronald Reagan had taken office vowing to invigorate the American economy by rolling back government regulations, lowering taxes, and balancing the budget. He did ease many regulatory rules, and he pushed major tax-reform bills through Congress in 1981 and 1986. But a balanced budget remained grotesquely out of reach. The combination of tax reduction and huge increases in military spending opened a vast "revenue hole" of $200 billion in annual deficits. In his eight years in office, President Reagan added nearly $2 trillion to the national debt—more than all his predecessors combined.

The staggering deficits of the Reagan years assuredly constituted a great economic failure. And because foreign lenders, especially the Japanese, financed so much of the Reagan-era debt, the deficits virtually guaranteed that future generations of Americans would have to either work harder than their parents, lower their standard of living, or both to pay their foreign creditors.

On March 4, 1987, President Ronald Reagan somewhat confusingly tried to explain his role (or lack of role) in the arms-for-hostages deal with Iran:

"A few months ago I told the American people I did not trade arms for hostages. My heart and my best intentions still tell me that is true, but the facts and the evidence tell me it is not."

Hollywood director Oliver Stone's (b. 1946) film Wall Street *both romanticized and vilified the business culture of the 1980s. The character of Gordon Gekko, inspired by real-life corporate raider Ivan Boesky, captured the spirit of the times:*

"Ladies and gentlemen, greed is good. Greed works, greed is right. ... Greed for life, money, love, knowledge, has marked the upward surge of mankind— and greed, mark my words, will save the malfunctioning corporation called the U.S.A."

✳ **PRIMARY SOURCE**
Teenagers Against Abortion

But if the deficits represented an economic failure, they also constituted, strangely enough, a kind of political triumph. By making new social spending both practically and politically impossible, the deficits achieved one of Reagan's paramount goals: slowing the growth of government and blocking or even repealing the social programs launched in the era of Lyndon Johnson's Great Society. The deficits achieved, in short, Reagan's highest political objective: the containment of the welfare state. Ronald Reagan thus ensured the long-term perpetuation of his values to a degree that few presidents have managed to achieve. For better or worse, the consequences of "Reaganomics" would be large and durable.

The Religious Right

Religion pervaded American politics in the 1980s. Especially conspicuous was a coalition of conservative evangelical Christians known as the religious right. In 1979 the Reverend Jerry Falwell, an evangelical minister from Lynchburg, Virginia, founded a political organization called the Moral Majority. Falwell preached with great success against sexual permissiveness, abortion, feminism, and the spread of gay rights. In its first two years, the Moral Majority registered between 2 million and 3 million voters. Using radio, direct-mail marketing, and cable TV, "televangelists" reached huge audiences in the 1980s, collected millions of dollars, and became aggressive political advocates of conservative causes.

Members of the religious right were sometimes called "movement conservatives," a term that recalls the left-wing protest movements of the 1960s. In many ways the religious right of the 1980s was a reflection of, or an answer to, sixties radicalism. Feminists in the 1960s declared that "the personal was political." The religious right did the same. What had in the past been personal matters—gender roles, homosexuality, and prayer—became the organizing ground for a powerful political movement. Like advocates of multiculturalism and affirmative action, the religious right practiced a form of "identity politics." But rather than defining themselves as Latino voters or gay voters, they declared themselves Christian or pro-life voters. The New Right also mimicked the New Left in some of its tactics. If the left had consciousness-raising sessions, the right had prayer meetings. If protesters in the 1960s blocked entrances to draft offices, protesters in the 1980s blocked entrances to abortion clinics.

Several leaders of the religious right fell from grace by engaging in financial or sexual misconduct in the latter part of the decade. But such scandals would not shake the faith of America's conservative Christians or diminish the new political clout of activist, evangelical religionists.

Conservatism in the Courts

If the budget was Reagan's chief weapon in the war against the welfare state, the courts became his principal instrument in the "cultural wars" demanded by the religious right. By the time he left office, Reagan had appointed a near-majority of all sitting federal judges. Equally important, Reagan had named three conservative-minded justices to the U.S. Supreme Court. They included Sandra Day O'Connor, a brilliant, public-spirited Arizona judge. When she was sworn in on September 25, 1981, she became the first woman to ascend to the high bench in the Court's nearly two-hundred-year history.

Reaganism repudiated two great icons of the liberal political culture: affirmative action and abortion. The Court showed its newly conservative colors in 1984, when it decreed, in a case involving Memphis fire fighters, that union rules about job seniority could outweigh affirmative-action concerns in guiding promotion policies in the city's fire department. In two cases in 1989 (*Ward's Cove Packing v. Antonia* and *Martin* v. *Wilks*), the Court made it more difficult to prove that an employer practiced racial discrimination in hiring and made it easier for white males to argue that they were the victims of reverse discrimination. Congress passed legislation in 1991 that partially limited the effects of these decisions.

The contentious issue of abortion also reached the Court in 1989. In the case of *Roe v. Wade* in 1973, the Supreme Court had prohibited states from making laws that interfered with a woman's right to an abortion during the early months of pregnancy. For nearly two decades, that decision had been the bedrock principle on which "pro-choice" advocates built their case for abortion rights. *Roe v. Wade* also provoked bitter criticism from Roman Catholics and various "right-to-life" groups, who wanted a virtually absolute ban on all abortions. In *Webster v. Reproductive Health Services*, the Court in July 1989 did not entirely overturn *Roe*, but it seriously compromised *Roe*'s protection of abortion rights. By approving a Missouri law that imposed certain restrictions on abortion, the Court signaled that it was inviting the states to legislate in an area in which *Roe* had previously forbidden them to legislate.

Right-to-life advocates were at first delighted by the *Webster* decision. But the Court's ruling also galvanized pro-choice organizations into a new militancy. Bruising, divisive battles loomed as state legislatures across the land confronted abortion. This painful cultural conflict over the unborn was also part of the Reagan era's bequest to the future.

Referendum on Reaganism in 1988

Republicans lost control of the Senate in the off-year elections of November 1986. Hopes rose among Democrats that the "Reagan revolution" might be showing signs of political vulnerability at last. The newly Democratic majority in the Senate flexed its political muscle in 1987 when it rejected an ultraconservative nominee for the Supreme Court.

Disquieting signs of economic trouble also seemed to open political opportunities for Democrats. The double mountain of deficits—the federal budget deficit and international trade deficit—continued to mount ominously. Falling real estate prices caused hundreds of savings and loan (S&L) institutions to fail, especially in the Southwest. A massive federal rescue operation for the S&Ls cost well over $500 billion. A wave of mergers, acquisitions, and **leveraged buyouts** washed over Wall Street, leaving many brokers and traders mega rich and many companies saddled with mega debt. A cold spasm of fear struck the money markets on "Black Monday," October 19, 1987, when the leading stock-market index plunged 508 points—the largest one-day decline in history to that point. This crash, said *Newsweek* magazine, heralded "the final collapse of the money culture . . . , the death knell of the 1980s." But as Mark Twain famously commented about his own obituary, this announcement proved premature.

leveraged buyouts *The purchase of one company by another using money borrowed on the expectation of selling a portion of assets after the acquisition.*

Hoping to cash in on these ethical and economic anxieties, a pack of Democrats—dubbed the "Seven Dwarfs" by derisive Republicans—chased after their party's 1988 presidential nomination. The handsome and charismatic Democratic front runner, former Colorado senator Gary Hart, was forced to drop out of the race after charges of sexual misconduct. African American candidate Jesse Jackson, a rousing speechmaker who hoped to forge a "rainbow coalition" of minorities and the disadvantaged, campaigned energetically. But the Democratic nomination in the end went to the coolly cerebral governor of Massachusetts, Michael Dukakis. Republicans nominated Reagan's vice president, George Bush, who ran largely on the Reagan record of tax cuts, strong defense policies, toughness on crime, opposition to abortion, and a long-running if hardly robust economic expansion. Dukakis made little headway exploiting the ethical and economic sore spots and came across to television viewers as almost supernaturally devoid of emotion. On election day the voters gave him just 41,016,429 votes to 47,946,422 for Bush. The Electoral College count was 111 to 426.

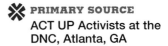
PRIMARY SOURCE
ACT UP Activists at the
DNC, Atlanta, GA

George Bush and the End of the Cold War

George Herbert Walker Bush was born with a silver ladle in his mouth. His father had served as a U.S. senator from Connecticut, and young George enjoyed a first-rate education at Yale. After service in World War II and success in the Texas oil business, he turned to public service. Bush served briefly as a congressman from Texas and then held various posts in several Republican administrations, including emissary to China, ambassador to the United Nations, director of the Central Intelligence Agency, and vice president. He

In his state of the union address on January 31, 1990, President George H. W. Bush (b. 1924) declared:

"The events of the year just ended, the revolution of '89, have been a chain reaction, changes so striking that it marks the beginning of a new era in the world's affairs."

Just six months later, speaking at Stanford University, Soviet president Mikhail Gorbachev (b. 1931) said:

"The Cold War is now behind us. Let us not wrangle over who won it. It is in the common interest of our two countries and nations not to fight this trend toward cooperation, but rather to promote it."

autocratic (autocracy) *Relating to authoritarian or repressive government or institutional practices.*

✳ **PRIMARY SOURCE**
Reagan in Front of Berlin Wall

capped this long political career when he was inaugurated as president of the United States in January 1989, promising to work for "a kinder, gentler America."

In the first months of the Bush administration, the communist world commanded the planet's fascinated attention. Everywhere in the communist bloc it seemed, astoundingly, that the season of democracy had arrived.

In China hundreds of thousands of prodemocracy demonstrators thronged Beijing's Tiananmen Square in the spring of 1989. But in June of that year, China's aging and **autocratic** rulers brutally crushed the prodemocracy movement. Tanks rolled over the crowds, and machine-gunners killed hundreds of protesters. World opinion roundly condemned the bloody suppression of the prodemocracy demonstrators. President Bush joined in the criticism. Yet despite angry demands in Congress for punitive restrictions on trade with China, the president insisted on maintaining normal relations with Beijing.

Stunning changes also shook Eastern Europe. Long oppressed by puppet regimes propped up by Soviet guns, the region was revolutionized in just a few startling months in 1989. The Solidarity movement in Poland led the way when it toppled Poland's communist government in August. With dizzying speed, communist regimes collapsed in Hungary, Czechoslovakia, East Germany, and even hyperrepressive Romania. In December 1989, jubilant Germans danced atop the hated Berlin Wall, symbol of the division of Germany and all of Europe into two armed and hostile camps. The Wall itself soon came down, heralding the imminent end of the forty-five-year-long Cold War. With the approval of the victorious Allied powers of World War II, the two Germanies, divided since 1945, were at last reunited in October 1990.

AP Photo/Jeff Widener

Tiananmen Square, Beijing, China, June 1989 The Chinese communist state mobilized all its forces against students demonstrating for a more democratic China.

Most startling of all were the changes that rolled over the heartland of world communism, the Soviet Union itself. Mikhail Gorbachev's policies of *glasnost* and *perestroika* had set in motion a groundswell that surged out of his control. Old-guard hard-liners, in a last-gasp effort to preserve the tottering communist system, attempted to dislodge Gorbachev with a military coup in August 1991. With the support of Boris Yeltsin, president of the Russian Republic (one of several republics that composed the Union of Soviet Socialist Republics), Gorbachev foiled the plotters. But his days were numbered. In December 1991 Gorbachev resigned as president, and the Soviet Union dissolved into fifteen sovereign republics, with Russia the most powerful state and Yeltsin the dominant leader.

The demise of the Soviet Union wrote a definitive finish to the Cold War era. More than four decades of nail-biting tension between the two nuclear superpowers, the Soviet Union and the United States, evaporated when the USSR dismantled itself. With the Soviet Union swept into the dustbin of history and communism all but extinct, Bush spoke hopefully of a "new world order," where democracy would reign and diplomacy would supersede weaponry. Some observers even saw in these developments the "end of history," in the sense that democracy, victorious in its two-century-long struggle against foes on the left and right, had no ideological battles left to fight.

But the disintegration of the Soviet Union posed serious new questions. Who would honor arms-control agreements with the United States? Which of the successor states of the former Soviet Union would take command of the formidable Soviet nuclear arsenal?

Throughout the former Soviet empire, waves of nationalistic fervor and long-suppressed ethnic and racial hatred rolled across the vast land as communism's roots were wrenched out. A particularly nasty conflict erupted in 1991, when the Chechnyan minority tried to declare their independence from Russia, prompting President Yeltsin to send in Russian troops. Ethnic warfare flared in other former communist countries as well, notably in misery-drenched former Yugoslavia, racked by vicious "ethnic cleansing" against minorities. The cruel and paradoxical truth stood revealed that the calcified communist regimes of Eastern Europe, whatever their sins, had at least bottled up the ancient ethnic antagonisms that were the region's peculiar curse and that now erupted in all their historical fury.

Refugees from the strife-torn regions flooded into Western Europe. The sturdy German economy, the foundation of European prosperity, wobbled under the awesome burden of absorbing technologically backward, physically decrepit East Germany. The Western democracies, which for more than four decades had feared the military *strength* of the Eastern bloc, now saw their well-being threatened by the social and economic *weakness* of the former communist lands.

The end of the Cold War also proved a mixed blessing for the United States. The nearly half century of the Cold War had been the only lengthy period in American history when the United States had consistently pursued an internationalist foreign policy. With the Soviet threat canceled, would the United States revert to its traditional isolationism? The Soviet-American rivalry, with its demands for high levels of military preparedness, had also sustained huge sectors of the American economy such as aerospace. When the Pentagon in 1991 closed thirty-four military bases and canceled numerous weapons orders, unemployment soared in southern California and other areas that had once been deluged with Pentagon dollars. The problems of weaning the U.S. economy from its decades of dependence on defense spending tempered the euphoria of Americans as they welcomed the Cold War's long-awaited finale.

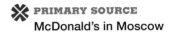

✳ PRIMARY SOURCE
McDonald's in Moscow

The Persian Gulf War

Sadly, the end of the Cold War did not mean the end of all wars. President Bush flexed the United States' still-intimidating military muscle in tiny Panama in December 1989, when he sent airborne troops to capture dictator Manuel Noriega.

Still more ominous events in the summer of 1990 severely tested Bush's dream of a democratic and peaceful new world order. On August 2 Saddam Hussein, the brutal and

Communist regimes overthrown since 1989
Soviet Union, dissolved in 1991
Yugoslavia, dissolved in civil war, 1991–1992

ATLANTIC OCEAN

North Sea

SWEDEN
NORWAY
FINLAND
Arctic Circle

IRELAND
UNITED KINGDOM
DENMARK

Elections, 1989

ESTONIA
LATVIA
LITHUANIA
RUSSIA

NETH.
BELG.
LUX.
GERMANY
Berlin

Largest and most influential of the former Soviet republics after 1991

Berlin Wall opened, Nov. 1989
German reunification, 1990

POLAND
BELARUS

R U S S I A
Moscow

Gorbachev in power, 1985–1991
Moscow coup fails; Boris Yeltsin declared president of Russia, 1990

FRANCE
SWITZ.
CZECH REP.
AUSTRIA SLOVAKIA
HUNGARY
ITALY

Czechoslovakia broke into Czech Republic and Slovakia in 1993

UKRAINE
MOLDOVA

KAZAKHSTAN

Aral Sea

PORTUGAL
SPAIN

ROMANIA

Chechnya declares independence 1991; Russia attacks, 1994

Mediterranean Sea

ALBANIA BULGARIA

Black Sea

GEORGIA CHECHNYA

Caspian Sea

UZBEKISTAN

KYRGYZSTAN

ALGERIA
TUNISIA
MALTA
GREECE

TURKEY
ARMENIA
AZERBAIJAN

TURKMENISTAN

CHINA
TAJIKISTAN

CYPRUS
LEBANON
ISRAEL
SYRIA
IRAQ
JORDAN

I R A N

AFGHANISTAN

PAKISTAN

SLOVENIA
CROATIA
BOSNIA-HERZEGOVINA
SERBIA
MONTENEGRO
KOSOVO
F.Y.R. MACEDONIA

NATO airwar against Serbia to protect Kosovo, 1994

U.S. troops join NATO peacekeeping forces, Dec. 1995

Adriatic Sea

EGYPT
SAUDI ARABIA
KUWAIT
Red Sea
Persian Gulf

0 250 500 Km.
0 250 500 Mi.

The End of the Cold War Changes the Map of Europe © Cengage Learning

---

ambitious ruler of Iraq, sent his armies to overrun Kuwait, a tiny, oil-rich desert sheikdom on Iraq's southern frontier. Oil fueled Saddam's aggression. With his hand on the world's jugular vein, he would be able to dictate the terms of oil supplies to the industrial nations, and perhaps totally extinguish the Arabs' enemy, Israel.

The speed and audacity of the Iraqi invasion of Kuwait were stunning. But the world responded just as swiftly. The United Nations Security Council unanimously condemned the invasion on August 3, 1990, and demanded the immediate and unconditional withdrawal of Iraq's troops. In November the Security Council delivered an ultimatum: Saddam must leave Kuwait by January 15, 1991, or UN forces would "use all necessary means" to expel his troops. For perhaps the first time in the post–World War II era, the UN seemed to be fulfilling its founders' dreams that it could preserve international order by putting guns where its mouth was. In a **logistical** operation of astonishing complexity, the United States spearheaded a massive international military deployment on the sandy Arabian peninsula. As the January 15 deadline approached, some 539,000 U.S. soldiers, sailors, and pilots—many of them women and all of them members of the new, post-Vietnam, all-volunteer American military—swarmed into the Persian Gulf region. They were joined by nearly 270,000 troops from twenty-eight other countries in the coalition opposed to Iraq. When all diplomatic efforts to resolve the crisis failed, the U.S. Congress voted on January 12, 1991, to approve the use of force.

The United States and its UN allies first unleashed a thirty-seven-day air attack that pummeled targets in occupied Kuwait and in Iraq itself. Iraq responded to this pounding by launching several dozen "Scud" short-range ballistic missiles against military and civilian targets in Saudi Arabia and Israel. These missile attacks claimed several lives but did no significant military damage.

The allied commander, the beefy and blunt American general Norman ("Stormin' Norman") Schwarzkopf, could take nothing for granted as he prepared for the ground phase of the war. Saddam, who had threatened to wage "the mother of all battles," had

logistical *Relating to the organization and movement of substantial quantities of people and material in connection with some defined objective.*

the capacity to inflict awful damage through the use of chemical or biological weapons. His tactics also included releasing a gigantic oil slick into the Persian Gulf to forestall amphibious assault, and igniting hundreds of oil-well fires whose smoky plumes shrouded the ground from aerial view. Faced with these horrifying tactics, Schwarzkopf's strategy was starkly simple: soften the Iraqis with relentless bombing, then suffocate them on the ground with a tidal-wave rush of troops and armor.

On February 23, 1991, the dreaded and long-awaited land war began. Dubbed "Operation Desert Storm," it lasted only four days—the "hundred-hour war." With light-ning speed the UN forces penetrated deep into Iraq, outflanking the occupying army in Kuwait and blocking the enemy's ability either to retreat or to reinforce. Allied casual-ties were amazingly light, whereas much of Iraq's remaining fighting force was quickly destroyed or captured. On February 27 Saddam accepted a cease-fire, and Kuwait was liberated.

Most Americans cheered the war's rapid and enormously successful conclusion. Many people echoed President Bush's sentiments when he declared, "By God, we've kicked the Vietnam Syndrome once and for all!" But when the smoke cleared, Saddam Hussein had survived to menace the world another day. America and its allies had agreed to the liberation of Kuwait, but Bush, fearing that a full assault on Baghdad would cost many lives and much public support, stopped well short of overthrowing the tyrant Saddam. The perpetually troubled Middle East knew scarcely less trouble after Desert Storm had ceased to thunder, and the United States, for better or worse, found itself more deeply ensnared in the region's web of mortal hatreds and intractable conflicts.

Bush on the Home Front

George Bush partly redeemed his promise to work for a "kinder, gentler America" when he signed the Americans with Disabilities Act (ADA) in 1990, a landmark law pro-hibiting discrimination against the 43 million U.S. citizens with physical or mental disabilities. The president also signed a major water projects bill in 1992 that put the interests of the environment ahead of agriculture, especially in California's heavily irri-gated Central Valley.

The new president continued to aggravate the explosive "social issues" that had so divided Americans throughout the 1980s, especially the nettlesome questions of affirmative action and abortion. Bush challenged the legality of college scholarships targeted for racial minorities, and he only grudgingly accepted a watered-down civil rights bill in 1991 that made it easier for employees to prove discrimination in hiring and promotion.

Most provocatively, in 1991 Bush nominated for the Supreme Court the conserva-tive African American jurist Clarence Thomas, a stern critic of affirmative-action policies. Thomas's nomination was loudly opposed by labor, civil rights, and women's organiza-tions. Reflecting irreconcilable divisions over affirmative action and abortion, the Senate Judiciary Committee concluded its hearings with a divided 7-to-7 vote and forwarded the matter to the Senate without a recommendation.

Then, just days before the Senate was scheduled to vote in early October 1991, a press leak revealed that Anita Hill, a University of Oklahoma law professor, had accused Thomas of sexual harassment. The Senate Judiciary Committee was forced to reopen its hearings. For days, a prurient American public sat glued to their television sets as Hill graphically detailed her charges of sexual improprieties and Thomas angrily responded. In the end, by a 52-to-48 vote, the Senate narrowly confirmed Thomas as the second African American ever to sit on the supreme bench (Thurgood Marshall was the first). While many Americans hailed Hill as a heroine for focusing the nation's attention on issues of sexual harassment, Thomas maintained that Hill's widely publicized, unproved allegations amounted to "a high-tech lynching for uppity blacks who in any way deign to think for themselves, to do for themselves."

The furor over Clarence Thomas's confirmation suggested that the social issues that had helped produce three Republican presidential victories in the 1980s were losing some of their electoral appeal. Many women, enraged by the all-male judiciary com-mittee's behavior in the Thomas hearings, grew increasingly critical of the president's

Ronald Reagan's elections surprised many historians. Reflecting a liberal political outlook that is common among academic scholars, they were long accustomed to understanding American history as an inexorable, almost evolutionary, unfolding of liberal principles, including the quests for economic equality, social justice, and active government. Progressive historians of the early twentieth century such as Charles and Mary Beard portrayed conservatives as rich, privileged elites bent on preserving their wealth and power (see "Varying Viewpoints: The Populists: Radicals or Reactionaries?" on p. 356).

Even the "New Left" revisionists of the 1960s, while critical of the celebratory tone of their progressive forebears, were convinced that the deep currents of American history flowed leftward. But whether they were liberal or revisionist, most scholars writing in the first three post–World War II decades dismissed conservatism as an obsolete political creed. Conservatives were seen as fringe wackos—paranoid McCarthyites or racist demagogues who, in the words of liberal critic Lionel Trilling, trafficked only in "irritable mental gestures which seem to resemble ideas." Such an outlook is conspicuous in books such as Daniel Bell, ed., *The Radical Right* (1963), and Richard Hofstadter, *The Paranoid Style in American Politics* (1965).

Yet what flowed out of the turbulent decade of the 1960s was not a strengthened liberalism but a revived conservatism. Ronald Reagan's huge political success compelled a thorough reexamination of the tradition of American conservatism and the sources of its modern resurgence.

Historians such as Leo Ribuffo and Alan Brinkley have argued that characters once dismissed as irrational crackpots or colorful irrelevancies—including religious fundamentalists and depression-era figures such as Huey Long and Father Charles Coughlin—articulated values deeply rooted and widely shared in American culture. These conservative spokespersons, whatever their peculiarities, offered a vision of free individuals, minimal government, and autonomous local communities that harkened back to the "civic republicanism" in the era of young nationhood.

But modern conservatism, however deep its roots, is also a product of the recent historical past. As scholars such as Thomas Sugrue and Thomas Edsall have shown, the economic stagnation that set in after 1970 made many Americans insecure about their futures and receptive to new political doctrines. At the same time, as commentator Kevin Phillips has stressed, "social issues" with little or no apparent economic content, became increasingly prominent as movements for sexual liberation, abortion on demand, women's rights, and race relations sharply challenged traditional beliefs. Finally, the failure of government policies in Vietnam, runaway inflation in the 1970s, as well as the disillusioning Watergate episode, cast doubt on the legitimacy and even the morality of "big government."

Many modern conservatives, including the pundit George Will, stress the deep historical roots of American conservatism. In their view, as Will once put it, it took sixteen years to count the ballots from the 1964 (Goldwater versus Johnson) election, and Goldwater won after all. But that argument is surely overstated. Goldwater ran against the legacy of the New Deal and was overwhelmingly defeated. Reagan ran against the consequences of the Great Society and won decisively. Many conservatives, in short, apparently acknowledge the legitimacy of the New Deal and the stake that many middle-class Americans feel they have in its programs of Social Security, home mortgage subsidies, farm price supports, and similar policies. But conservatives reject the philosophy of the Great Society with its more focused attack on urban poverty and its vigorous support of affirmative action. Modern conservatism springs less from a repudiation of government per se and more from a disapproval of the particular priorities and strategies of the Great Society. The different historical fates of the New Deal and the Great Society suggest the key to the rise of modern conservatism.

uncompromising stand on abortion. A "gender gap" opened between the two political parties, as pro-choice women grew increasingly cool toward the strong anti-abortion stand of the Republicans.

Still more damaging to President Bush's political health, the economy sputtered and stalled almost at the outset of his administration. By 1992 the unemployment rate exceeded 7 percent, while the federal budget deficit continued to mushroom, topping $250 billion in each year of Bush's presidency. In a desperate attempt to stop the hemorrhage of **red ink**, Bush agreed in 1990 to a budget that included $133 billion in new taxes.

Bush's 1990 tax and budget package added up to a political catastrophe. In his 1988 presidential campaign, Bush had belligerently declared, "Read my lips—no new taxes." Now he had flagrantly broken that campaign promise.

red ink *A deficit in a financial account, with expenditures or debts larger than income or assets; from the early accounting practice of marking such deficits in red.*

Chapter Summary

Reagan led Republicans to sweeping victories in 1980 and 1984 over divided and demoralized Democrats. Riding a conservative national tide, Reagan pushed both his "supply-side" economic program of lower taxes and the "new-right" social policies, especially opposition to affirmative action, abortion, and drugs. These policies brought economic recovery and lower inflation, as well as record budget deficits that severely restricted "big government." The Supreme Court under Reagan and his successor, George Bush, became increasingly conservative, while the confirmation hearings of Justice Clarence Thomas highlighted issues of sexual harassment. Religious conservatives assumed growing influence on American politics, borrowing many tactics from the sixties New Left.

Reagan revived the Cold War confrontation with the Soviet Union, and engaged the United States in assertive military support for anti-leftist forces in Latin America and elsewhere. The ratcheting up of military spending, along with the attempted reforms led by Mikhail Gorbachev, contributed to the unraveling of Communism in Eastern Europe and the Soviet Union in 1989–1991. With America as the only remaining superpower, George Bush led an international coalition to victory in the Persian Gulf War, but the Middle East remained a dangerous tinderbox despite new efforts to resolve the Israel-Arab conflict. Bush supported the Americans with Disabilities Act, but also pushed conservative social issues and nominated the controversial Clarence Thomas to the Supreme Court. Economic recession and a growing "gender gap" raised Democrats' hopes as the election of 1992 approached.

KEY TERMS

neoconservatives
   (neoconservatism) (676)

welfare state (678)

supply-side (678)

oligarchs (680)

leveraged buyouts (685)

autocratic (autocracy) (686)

logistical (688)

red ink (690)

PEOPLE TO KNOW

Ronald Reagan

Mikhail Gorbachev

Saddam Hussein

Jerry Falwell

Sandra Day O'Connor

George H. W. Bush

Boris Yeltsin

Manuel Noriega

Norman ("Stormin'
   Norman") Schwarzkopf

Clarence Thomas

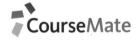

Go to the History CourseMate website for primary source links, study tools, and review materials for this chapter. www.cengagebrain.com

41

America Confronts the Post–Cold War Era

1992–2010

There is nothing wrong with America that cannot be cured with what is right in America.

WILLIAM J. CLINTON, INAUGURAL, 1993

★ Chapter Outline

The collapse of the Soviet Union and the democratization of its client regimes in Eastern Europe ended the four-decade-old Cold War and left the United States the world's sole remaining superpower. The culture wars that had started in the 1960s fed ferociously partisan political squabbles that weakened the Clinton presidency and distracted the nation from its urgent task of clearly defining its role in the dawning age of globalization. In 2000, George W. Bush won a bitterly contested presidential election that deepened national divisions, until a spectacular terrorist attack on September 11, 2001, called forth a resurgence of national unity that proved temporary. Bush responded to the 9/11 attacks by invading the terrorist haven of Afghanistan and then, more controversially, invading Iraq as well. The Iraq War proved a prolonged and excruciating conflict that inflicted rising casualties and divided the country. Weary of war and shocked by a major economic collapse in 2008, voters made history by electing Illinois Senator Barack Obama the first African American president of the United States. Taking office as the United States experienced the worst economic collapse since the Great Depression, Obama promoted strong government reforms in the economy and health care. His vigorous pro-government stance, along with the economy's continuing struggles, fueled a revived conservative Republican opposition.

FOCUS QUESTIONS

1. How did Bill Clinton attempt to navigate between traditional liberal Democratic values and his claim to be a centrist "new Democrat"?

2. What caused the growing partisanship and polarization between the conservative Republican movement and the Clinton administration, and how did these conflicts play out in Clinton's impeachment?

3. What was the impact of the September 11, 2001, attacks on American society and on U.S. national security policies in the Middle East and elsewhere?

4. What were the major foreign and domestic policies of the George W. Bush administration, and why did they meet growing opposition in Bush's second term?

5. Why did Senator Barack Obama win such a convincing victory in the election of 2008, and how did his early administration address the major economic crisis that the United States faced?

CHRONOLOGY

1992	Clinton defeats Bush and Perot for presidency.
1993	NAFTA signed.
1994	Republicans win majorities in both houses of Congress.
1996	Welfare Reform Bill becomes law. Clinton defeats Dole for presidency.
1998	Clinton-Lewinsky scandal. United States and Britain launch military strikes against Iraq. House of Representatives impeaches Clinton.
1999	Senate acquits Clinton on impeachment charges. Kosovo crisis; NATO warfare with Serbia. Protest in Seattle against World Trade Organization.
2000	"Million Mom March" against guns in Washington, D.C. United States normalizes trade relations with China. George W. Bush wins presidency in Electoral College; Albert Gore takes popular vote.
2001	Terrorists attack New York City and Washington, D.C., on September 11. United States invades Afghanistan. Congress passes USA Patriot Act. Energy trader Enron collapses amid accounting scandals.
2002	Congress passes "No Child Left Behind" Act. Bush labels Iraq, Iran, and North Korea an "axis of evil." Telecommunications giant WorldCom declares bankruptcy. Congress authorizes use of force against Iraq. U.N. Security Council demands that Iraq comply with weapons inspections. Republicans regain Senate.
2003	North Korea withdraws from Nuclear Non-Proliferation Treaty. United States invades Iraq. Bush signs drug prescription bill for seniors. Saddam Hussein captured in Iraq. Supreme Court narrowly approves affirmative action.
2004	Gay marriage controversy erupts. Iraqi interim government is installed. Bush defeats Kerry for presidency.
2005	Iraq elects permanent government but quickly descends into sectarian conflict.
2006	Saddam Hussein executed.
2007	U.S. troop surge in Iraq.
2008	Barack Obama elected 44th president of the United States. U.S. financial markets crash; beginning of "Great Recession"
2010	Deepwater Horizon oil spill in Gulf of Mexico

Bill Clinton: The First Baby-Boomer President

As the last decade of the twentieth century opened, the slumbering economy, the widening gender gap, and the rising anti-incumbent spirit spelled opportunity for Democrats, frozen out of the White House for all but four years since 1968. In a bruising round of primary elections, Governor William Jefferson Clinton of Arkansas weathered blistering accusations of womanizing and draft evasion to emerge as his party's standard-bearer, with another southern moderate, Tennessee Senator Albert Gore, as his vice presidential running mate.

Clinton claimed to be a "new" Democrat, chastened by his party's long exile in the political wilderness. Clinton and other centrist Democrats attempted to point their party away from its traditional antibusiness, dovish, champion-of-the-underdog orientation and toward pro-growth, strong defense, and anticrime policies. The youthful and phenomenally articulate Clinton campaigned vigorously on promises to stimulate the economy, reform the welfare system, and overhaul the nation's scandalously expensive and inefficient health care apparatus.

Trying to wring one more win out of the social issues that had underwritten two Reagan and one Bush presidential victories, the Republican convention in Houston emphasized "family values" as it renominated George Bush and Vice President J. Danforth Quayle for a

PRIMARY SOURCE
Arsenio Hall and Bill Clinton

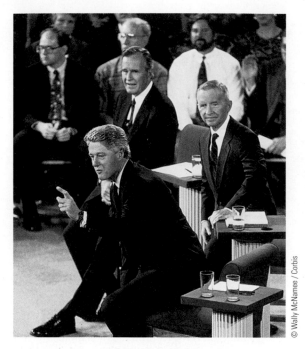

Presidential Campaign Debate, 1992
George Bush, Ross Perot, and Bill Clinton squared off at the University of Richmond (Virginia) on October 16, 1992. The telegenic Clinton handily dominated the television debates, especially in the "talk-show" format used on this occasion.

second term. But Bush's listless campaign could not keep pace with that of his youthful rival, the super-energetic and phenomenally articulate Clinton. Bush claimed credit for ending the Cold War and trumpeted his leadership in the Persian Gulf War. But pocketbook problems as the economy dipped into recession swayed more voters than pride in past foreign policy. The purchasing power of the average worker's paycheck had actually declined during Bush's presidency. At Clinton's campaign headquarters, a simple sign reminded staffers of his principal campaign theme: "It's the economy, stupid."

Reflecting pervasive economic unease and the virulence of the throw-the-bums-out national mood, nearly 20 percent of voters cast their ballots for independent presidential candidate H. Ross Perot, a bantam-weight, jug-eared Texas billionaire who harped incessantly on federal deficit problems and boasted of the fact that he had never held any public office. With a record turnout of voters on election day, the final tallies gave Clinton 43,728,275 popular votes and 370 in the Electoral College. Bush polled 38,167,416 popular and 168 electoral votes. Perot won no electoral votes but did gather 19,237,247 in the popular count—the strongest showing for an independent or third-party candidate since Theodore Roosevelt ran on the Bull Moose ticket in 1912. Democrats also racked up clear majorities in both houses of Congress. The new Congress included thirty-nine African Americans and record numbers of Hispanics, Asian Americans, Indians, and women as well.

Women and minorities figured prominently in President Clinton's cabinet, as he fulfilled his pledge to shape a government that "looks like America." Janet Reno became the first female attorney general, and former University of Wisconsin president Donna Shalala was appointed secretary of health and human services. Carol Moseley-Braun of Illinois became the first African American woman elected to the U.S. Senate, where she joined five other women in the largest female contingent in the upper chamber to that point. Clinton also seized the opportunity in 1993 to nominate Ruth Bader Ginsburg to the Supreme Court, where she joined Sandra Day O'Connor to make a pair of women justices.

A False Start for Reform

Badly overestimating his electoral mandate for liberal reform, the young president made a series of costly blunders upon entering the White House. Clinton stirred a hornet's nest of controversy by advocating an end to the ban on gays and lesbians in the armed forces. Confronted with fierce opposition, the president finally settled for a "don't ask, don't tell" policy that quietly accepted gay and lesbian soldiers and sailors without officially acknowledging their presence in the military.

Even more damaging to Clinton's political standing was the fiasco of his attempt to reform the nation's health care system. In a dramatic but risky move, the president appointed his wife, Hillary Rodham Clinton, as director of a task force charged with redesigning the medical-service industry. Their stupefyingly complicated plan was dead on arrival when it was presented to Congress in October 1993. The First Lady was doused with a torrent of abuse, although she eventually rehabilitated herself and won election as U.S. senator from New York in 2000—the first First Lady ever to hold elective office—and later became President Obama's Secretary of State..

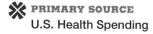

PRIMARY SOURCE
U.S. Health Spending

Clinton had better luck with a deficit-reduction bill in 1993, which combined with an increasingly buoyant economy by 1996 to shrink the federal deficit to its lowest level in more than a decade. By 1998 Clinton's policies seemed to have caged the ravenous deficit monster, as Congress argued over the unfamiliar question of how to spend projected federal budget *surpluses*.

The new president also induced Congress in 1993 to pass a gun-control law, the "Brady Bill," named for presidential aide James Brady, who had been wounded and disabled by gunfire in the assassination attempt on President Ronald Reagan in 1981. In July 1994, Clinton made further progress against the national plague of firearms when he persuaded

Bombing of Federal Building in Oklahoma City, 1995 A truck bomb killed 168 people in this federal office building in the worst act of terrorism in the United States until September 11, 2001. Convicted on eleven counts for the attack, antigovernment militant Timothy McVeigh became the first person executed by the federal government in nearly forty years in 2001.

Congress to pass a $30 billion anticrime bill, which contained a ban on several types of assault weapons until the law sunsetted in 2004.

These measures aimed to hold the line against an epidemic of violence that rocked American society in the 1990s. A huge explosion destroyed a federal office building in Oklahoma City in 1995, taking 168 lives, presumably in retribution for a 1993 standoff in Waco, Texas, between federal agents and the fundamentalist Branch Davidians. That showdown ended in the destruction of the sect's compound and the deaths of many Branch Davidians, including women and children. Events such as the Oklahoma City bombing brought to light a secretive underground of **paramilitary** private "militias," armed to the teeth and ultrasuspicious of all government.

paramilitary *Unauthorized or voluntary groups that employ military organization, methods, and equipment outside the official military system of command and organization.*

Even many law-abiding citizens shared to some degree in the antigovernment attitudes that drove the militia members to murderous extremes. Thanks largely to the disillusioning agony of Vietnam and the naked cynicism of Richard Nixon in the Watergate scandal, the confidence in government that came naturally to the generation that licked the Great Depression and won the Second World War was in short supply by century's end. Reflecting the pervasive disenchantment with politics and politicians, several states passed term-limit laws for elected officials, although the Supreme Court ruled in 1995 that the restrictions did not apply to federal officeholders.

The Politics of Distrust

Clinton's failed initiatives and widespread antigovernment sentiment offered conservative Republicans a golden opportunity in 1994, and they seized it aggressively. Led by outspoken Georgia representative Newt Gingrich, Republicans offered voters a "Contract with America" that promised an all-out assault on budget deficits and radical reductions in welfare programs. Their campaign succeeded fabulously, as a right-wing tornado roared across the land in the 1994 congressional elections. Republicans picked up eleven governorships, eight Senate seats, and fifty-three seats in the House (where Gingrich became Speaker), giving them control of both chambers of Congress for the first time in forty years.

But if President Clinton had overplayed his mandate for liberal reform in 1993, the congressional Republicans now proceeded to overplay their mandate for conservative retrenchment. The new Republican majority did achieve one long-standing conservative goal by restricting "unfunded mandates"—federal laws that imposed new obligations on state and local governments without providing new revenues. And in 1996 the new Congress achieved a major conservative victory when Clinton signed, over the howls of old-line liberal Democrats, a Welfare Reform Bill that severely slashed welfare grants and required able-bodied welfare recipients to find employment. Many Americans gradually came to feel that the Gingrich Republicans were bending the bow too far, especially when Speaker Gingrich advocated provocative ideas such as sending the children of welfare families to orphanages. In a tense confrontation between the Democratic president and the Republican Congress, the federal government actually had to shut down for several days at the end of 1995, until a budget package was agreed upon. These outlandishly partisan antics bred a backlash that helped President Clinton rebound from his political near-death experience.

As the 1996 election approached, the Republicans chose Kansas Senator Robert Dole as their presidential candidate. A decorated World War II veteran, Dole ran a torpid campaign. Clinton, buoyed by a healthy economy and his artful trimming to the conservative wind, breezed to an easy victory, with 47,401,898 popular votes to Dole's 39,198,482. The Reform party's egomaniacal leader, Ross Perot, ran a sorry third, picking up less than half the votes he had garnered in 1992. Clinton won 379 electoral votes, Dole only 159. But Republicans retained control of Congress.

Clinton Again

As Clinton began his second term—the first Democratic president since Franklin Delano Roosevelt to be reelected—the heady promises of far-reaching reform with which he had entered the White House four years earlier were no longer heard. Still facing Republican majorities in both houses of Congress, Clinton proposed only modest legislative goals, even though soaring tax revenues generated by the prosperous economy produced in 1998 a balanced federal budget for the first time in three decades.

Clinton cleverly managed to put Republicans on the defensive by claiming the political middle ground on contentious welfare and affirmative-action issues. He now warmly embraced the landmark Welfare Reform Bill of 1996 that he had initially been slow to endorse. Juggling the political hot potato of affirmative action, Clinton pledged to "mend it, not end it." When voters in California in 1996 approved Proposition 209, prohibiting affirmative-action preferences in government and higher education, the number of minority students in the state's public universities temporarily plummeted. A federal appeals court decision, *Hopwood v. Texas*, had similar effects in Texas, Mississippi, and Louisiana (the three states in the federal court's jurisdiction). Clinton criticized these broad assaults on affirmative action but stopped short of trying to reverse them, aware that public support for affirmative action, especially among white Americans, had diminished since the 1970s.

Clinton's major political advantage continued to be the roaring economy, which by 2000 had sustained the longest period of growth in American history, driven by low-interest, easy-money policies at the Federal Reserve Board, and by new Internet ("dot. com") businesses and other high-tech and media companies. While unemployment crept down below 4 percent and businesses scrambled madly for workers, inflationary pressure remained remarkably low.

Prosperity did not make Clinton immune to controversy over trade policy. During his first term, he had displayed political courage by supporting the North American Free Trade Agreement (NAFTA), creating in 1993 a free-trade zone encompassing Mexico, Canada, and the United States. Clinton took another step in 1994 toward a global free-trade system when he vigorously promoted the creation of the World Trade Organization (WTO). But simmering discontent over the human and environmental costs of "globalization" spurred protests in the United States and elsewhere and hampered Clinton's push for further expansion of free trade.

Problems Abroad

The end of the Cold War dismantled the framework within which the United States had conducted foreign policy for nearly half a century. Clinton groped for a new formula to replace anticommunism as the basic premise of American diplomacy.

Absorbed by domestic issues, President Clinton at first seemed uncertain and even amateurish in his conduct of foreign policy. He followed his predecessor's lead in dispatching American peacekeeping troops to Somalia, but quietly withdrew them after Somali rebels killed more than a dozen Americans in late 1993. Burned in Somalia, Washington stood on the sidelines in 1994 when catastrophic ethnic violence in the central African country of Rwanda killed half a million people.

Clinton also struggled to define a policy with respect to China, which was rapidly emerging as an economic and political powerhouse. Clinton soft-pedaled his earlier criticism of the Beijing regime on human rights issues and instead began seeking improved trade relations with that robustly industrializing country and potential market bonanza. By 2000 Clinton was crusading for a controversial China trade bill. Congress passed it in May 2000, making the Asian giant a full-fledged trading partner of the United States.

Clinton's approach to the tormented Balkans in southeastern Europe showed a similar initial hesitation, followed eventually by firm leadership. In the former Yugoslavia, as vicious ethnic conflict raged through Bosnia, the Washington government dithered until finally deciding to commit American troops to a NATO peacekeeping contingent in late 1995. When Serbian president Slobodan Milosević in 1999 unleashed a new round of "ethnic cleansing" in the region, this time against ethnic Albanians in the province of Kosovo, U.S.-led NATO forces launched an air war against Serbia. The bombing campaign initially failed to stop ethnic terror, as refugees flooded into neighboring countries, but it eventually forced Milosević to accept a NATO peacekeeping force in Kosovo. Milosevic was arrested in 2001 and put on trial before the International Criminal Court in The Hague, where he died in 2006 before the trial was completed.

The Middle East remained a major focus of American diplomacy right up to the end of Clinton's tenure. At a historic White House meeting in 1993, Clinton persuaded Israeli prime minister Yitzhak Rabin and Palestinian Liberation Organization leader Yasir Arafat to agree in principle on self-rule for the Palestinians within Israel. But hopes flickered low two years later when Rabin fell to an assassin's bullet. Clinton and his second-term secretary of state, Madeleine Albright, spent the rest of the 1990s struggling in vain to broker the permanent settlement that continued to elude Israelis and Palestinians.

Seeking a legacy as a peacemaker, Clinton stepped up his personal efforts to resolve festering international conflicts in Northern Ireland, the Korean peninsula, and southern Asia. But the guiding principles of American foreign policy in the post–Cold War era remained ill-defined and elusive.

Scandal and Impeachment

Scandal had dogged Bill Clinton from the beginning of his presidency. Critics brought charges of everything from philandering to illegal financial transactions. Allegations of corruption stemming from a real estate deal called the **Whitewater** Land Corporation while he was governor of Arkansas triggered an investigation by a special prosecutor, but no indictment ever materialized.

All the previous scandals were overshadowed by the revelation in January 1998 that Clinton had engaged in a sexual affair with a young White House intern, Monica Lewinsky, and then blatantly lied about it when he testified under oath in another woman's civil suit accusing him of sexual harassment. Caught in his bold lie, the president made a humiliating confession, but his political opponents smelled blood in the water. In September 1998, the special prosecutor investigating Whitewater, who had broad powers to investigate *any* evidence of presidential malfeasance, presented a stinging report, including lurid sexual details, to the Republican-controlled House of Representatives. That report charged Clinton with eleven possible grounds for impeachment, all related to lying about the Lewinsky affair.

Whitewater *A series of scandals during the Clinton administration that stemmed from a failed real-estate investment from which the Clintons were alleged to have illicitly profited. The accusations prompted the appointment of a special federal prosecutor, though no indictments.*

The House quickly cranked up the rusty machinery of impeachment. As an acrid partisan atmosphere enveloped the capital, House Republicans in December 1998 eventually passed two articles of impeachment against the president: perjury before a grand jury and obstruction of justice. Crying foul, the Democratic minority charged that, however deplorable Clinton's personal misconduct, sexual transgressions did not rise to the level of "high crimes and misdemeanors" prescribed as grounds for impeachment in the Constitution (see Art. II, Sec. IV in the Appendix). The House Republican managers (prosecutors) of impeachment replied that perjury and obstruction were grave public issues and that nothing less than "the rule of law" was at stake.

As cries of "honor the Constitution" and "sexual McCarthyism" filled the air, the nation debated whether the president's peccadilloes amounted to high crimes or low follies. Most Americans apparently leaned toward the latter conclusion. In the 1998 midterm elections, voters reduced the House Republicans' majority, causing fiery House Speaker Newt Gingrich to resign his post. Although Americans held a low opinion of Clinton's slipshod personal morals, most liked the president's political and economic policies and wanted him to stay in office.

In early 1999, for the first time in 130 years the nation witnessed an impeachment proceeding in the U.S. Senate. Dusting off ancient precedents from Andrew Johnson's trial, the one hundred senators solemnly heard arguments and evidence in the case, with Chief Justice William Rehnquist presiding. With the facts widely known and the two parties' political positions firmly locked in, the trial's outcome was a foregone conclusion. On the key obstruction of justice charge, five northeastern Republicans joined all forty-five Democratic senators in voting not guilty. The fifty Republican votes for conviction fell far short of the constitutionally required two-thirds majority. The vote on the perjury charge was forty-five guilty, fifty-five not guilty.

Clinton's Legacy and the 2000 Election

Beyond the obvious stain of impeachment, Clinton's legacy was a mixed one for his country and his party. His sound economic policies encouraged growth and trade in a rapidly globalizing, post–Cold War world. Yet as a "New Democrat" and avowed centrist, Clinton did more to consolidate than to reverse the Reagan-Bush revolution against New Deal liberalism that had for half a century provided the compass for the Democratic party and the nation. Further, by setting such a low standard in his personal conduct, he replenished the sad reservoir of public cynicism about politics that Vietnam and Watergate had created a generation before.

Nonetheless, as the end of the Clinton term and the beginning of the new millennium approached, the Democrats stayed on their political course and nominated loyal vice president Albert Gore for president. Gore faced the tricky challenge of linking himself to Clinton-era peace and prosperity while at the same time distancing himself from his boss's personal foibles. He chose as his running mate Connecticut Senator Joseph Lieberman, an outspoken Clinton critic and the first Jew nominated to a major national ticket. Their Republican challenger, George W. Bush, won the nomination on the strength of his father's name and his years as governor of Texas. Bush surrounded himself with Washington insiders and, in a clear jab at Clinton, promised to "restore dignity to the White House."

Rosy estimates that the federal budget would produce a surplus of some $2 trillion in the coming decade set the stage for the presidential contest. Echoing the Republican creed of smaller government, Bush argued for returning the budget surplus to "the people" through massive tax cuts and for promoting private-sector programs, such as school **vouchers** and a reliance on "faith-based" institutions to help the poor. Gore proposed smaller tax cuts, targeted at middle- and lower-class people, and strengthening Social Security. In an era of peace, foreign policy figured hardly at all in the campaigns, although Bush struck a moderate note when he urged that America act like "a humble nation."

Pollsters predicted a close election, but none foresaw the epochal cliffhanger that Election 2000 became. On election day, the country split nearly evenly between the two candidates, and it was soon clear that Florida's electoral votes would determine the winner. Television news programs announced that Bush had won the Sunshine State, and Al Gore called the Texas governor to concede defeat. Yet just an hour later Gore's camp decided

vouchers *Officially granted certificates for benefits of a particular kind, redeemable by a designated agency or service provider.*

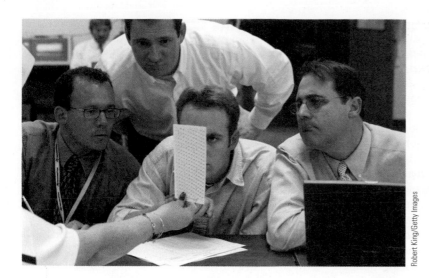

Counting Chads With Bush and Gore neck-and-neck in Florida's presidential vote count, election officials in Broward County examined by eye paper ballots disqualified by machine because the punched chads had not fully separated from the ballots. They hoped that close scrutiny would reveal the voters' intentions.

that Florida was too close to call and the vice president—in perhaps the most awkward phone call in modern politics—retracted his concession.

What ensued was a five-week political stand-off over how to count the votes in Florida. Democrats argued that some ballots were confusing or misread by machines, and asked for recounts in several counties. Republicans claimed that such a recount would amount to "changing the rules in the middle of the game" and would thwart the rule of law. After weeks of legal bickering, with the presidency in the balance, the Supreme Court finally intervened. By a 5–4 vote along partisan lines, the Court reasoned that, because neither Florida's legislature nor its courts had established a uniform standard for evaluating disputed ballots, the hand counts amounted to an unconstitutional breach of the Fourteenth Amendment's equal protection clause.

That ruling gave Bush the White House but cast a dark shadow of illegitimacy over his presidency. Bush officially won Florida by 537 votes out of 6 million cast, and he squeaked by in the Electoral College, 271 to 266 (see Maps 41.3 and 41.4). The national popular vote, on the other hand, went decisively to Gore, 50,999,897 to 50,456,002. For the first time since 1888, a candidate had won the White House getting fewer votes than his opponent. Calls to abolish the Electoral College, however, were few and muted (see Art. V of the Constitution).

PRIMARY SOURCE
Clothespin Vote

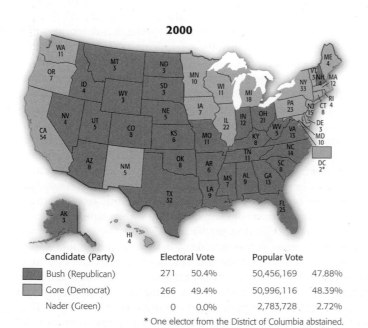

Presidential Election of 2000 (with electoral vote by state) Although Democrat Albert Gore won the popular election for president by half a million votes, George W. Bush's contested 537-vote advantage in Florida gave him a slight lead in the Electoral College. The 2.7 million popular votes won by Green party candidate and consumer activist Ralph Nader almost surely deprived Gore of victory, casting Nader in the role of spoiler. Bush's failure to win the popular vote inspired critics to protest at his inauguration with placards reading "Hail to the Thief." © Cengage Learning

Candidate (Party)	Electoral Vote		Popular Vote	
Bush (Republican)	271	50.4%	50,456,169	47.88%
Gore (Democrat)	266	49.4%	50,996,116	48.39%
Nader (Green)	0	0.0%	2,783,728	2.72%

* One elector from the District of Columbia abstained.

Bush Begins

As the son of the forty-first president, George W. Bush became the first presidential offspring since John Quincy Adams to reach the White House. Affecting the chummy manner of a self-made good ol' boy—though he held degrees from Yale and Harvard—Bush promised to bring to Washington the conciliatory skills he had honed as the Republican governor of Texas.

But as president, Bush soon proved to be more of a divider than a uniter, less a "compassionate conservative" than a crusading ideologue. Religious traditionalists cheered but liberals jeered when he withdrew American support from international health programs that sanctioned abortion. Bush pleased corporate chieftains but angered environmentalists by challenging scientific findings on global warming and repudiating the Kyoto Treaty limiting greenhouse gas emissions (negotiated by the Clinton administration but never ratified by the Senate). Bush pressed ahead with a whopping $1.3 trillion tax cut that, together with a softening economy, turned the federal budget surpluses of the late 1990s into yawning deficits that reached nearly $500 billion by 2006.

These polarizing policies both reflected and deepened the cultural chasm that increasingly divided "red-state" (conservative, Republican) from "blue-state" (liberal, Democratic) America. The new president's initiatives proved so divisive that a member of his own party, Vermont senator James Jeffords, left the Republican party in May 2001, thereby briefly returning control of the Senate to the Democrats—though Republicans regained control following the 2002 elections.

Terrorism Comes to America

On September 11, 2001, the long era of America's impregnable national security violently ended. On a balmy late-summer morning, suicidal terrorists slammed two hijacked airliners, loaded with passengers and jet fuel, into the twin towers of New York City's World Trade Center. They flew a third plane into the military nerve-center of the Pentagon, near Washington, D.C., killing 189 people. Heroic passengers forced a fourth hijacked aircraft to crash in rural Pennsylvania, killing all 144 aboard but depriving the terrorists of a fourth weapon of mass destruction.

As the two giant New York skyscrapers thunderously collapsed, some three thousand innocent victims perished, including hundreds of New York's police and fire department rescue workers. A stunned nation blossomed with flags, as grieving and outraged Americans struggled to express their sorrow and solidarity in the face of catastrophic terrorism.

President Bush responded with a sober but stirring address to Congress nine days later. His solemn demeanor and the gravity of the situation helped to dissipate the cloud of illegitimacy that had shadowed his presidency since the disputed election of 2000. While emphasizing his respect for the Islamic religion and Muslim peoples, Bush identified the principal enemy as Osama bin Laden, head of a shadowy terrorist network known as Al Qaeda. A wealthy extremist exiled from his native Saudi Arabia, bin Laden directed terrorist attacks from landlocked Afghanistan, ruled by an Islamic fundamentalist party, the Taliban. Bin Laden harbored venomous resentment against the United States for its support of Israel and its military presence on the sacred soil of the Arabian peninsula, and he also fed on worldwide resentment of America's enormous economic, military, and cultural power. Ironically, America's most conspicuous strengths had made it a conspicuous target.

When the Taliban refused to hand over bin Laden, Bush ordered a massive military campaign against Afghanistan. Within three months, American forces and Afghani rebels

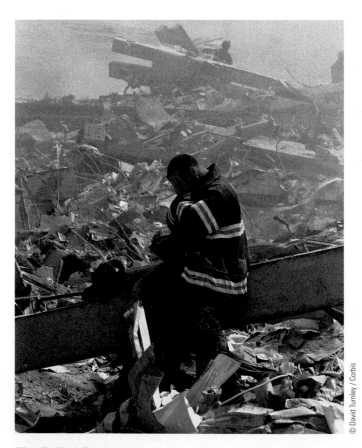

The Toll of Terror Grief overcame this exhausted fire fighter during the search for survivors in the wreckage of New York's World Trade Center

© David Turnley / Corbis

overthrew the Taliban but failed to find bin Laden, and Americans continued to live in fear of future attacks. Confronted with this unconventional, diffuse menace, antiterrorism experts called for new tactics of "asymmetrical warfare," employing not just traditional military muscle but also counter-insurgency tactics like innovative intelligence gathering and the training of local police forces.

The terrorists' blows diabolically coincided with the onset of a recession. The already-gathering economic downdraft worsened as edgy Americans shunned air travel and the tourist industry withered.

In the anxious atmosphere immediately after the September 11 attacks, Congress in 2001 rammed through the USA PATRIOT Act (officially, "Uniting and Strengthening America by Providing Appropriate Tools Required to Intercept and Obstruct Terrorism"). The Act permitted extensive telephone and e-mail surveillance and authorized the detention and deportation of immigrants suspected of terrorism. The Justice Department meanwhile rounded up hundreds of immigrants and held them without habeas corpus (formal charges in an open court). As hundreds of Taliban fighters captured in Afghanistan languished in legal limbo and demoralizing isolation in the **Guantanamo Detention Camp** on the American military base at Guantanamo, Cuba, public-opinion polls showed Americans sharply divided on whether the terrorist threat fully warranted such drastic encroachments on America's venerable tradition of protecting civil liberties.

Guantanamo Detention Camp *Controversial prison facility constructed at U. S. base in Guantanamo, Cuba, after the U.S.-led invasion of Afghanistan in 2001.*

Catastrophic terrorism brought a long chapter in American history to a dramatic climax. All but unique among modern peoples, Americans for nearly two centuries had been spared from foreign attack on their homeland. That unusual degree of virtually cost-free national security had undergirded the values of openness and individual freedom that defined the distinctive character of American society. Now American security and American liberty alike were dangerously imperiled.

Bush Takes the Offensive against Iraq

On only its second day in office, the Bush administration warned that it would not tolerate Iraq's continued defiance of United Nations weapons inspections, mandated after Iraq's defeat in the 1991 Persian Gulf War. Iraqi dictator Saddam Hussein had played hide-and-seek with the inspectors for years. After Saddam expelled all international inspectors in 1998, President Clinton declared that his removal ("regime change") was an official goal of U.S. policy, but no sustained military action against Iraq had followed.

In January 2002, just weeks after the September 11 attacks, President Bush claimed that Iraq, along with Iran and North Korea, constituted an "axis of evil" that gravely menaced American security. The Iraqi tyrant, defeated but not destroyed by Bush's father in 1991, became the principal object of the new president's wrath. Unlike the elder Bush, who had carefully assembled a broad international coalition to fight the Persian Gulf War, his son brashly determined to break with long-standing American traditions and wage a preemptive war against Iraq—and to go it alone if necessary.

The younger Bush thus stood revealed as a daring risk-taker willing to embrace bold, dramatic policies, foreign as well as fiscal. Itching for a fight, and egged on by hawkish Vice President Richard (Dick) Cheney and other "neoconservative" advisers, Bush accused the Iraqi regime of developing weapons of mass destruction (WMD) and supporting terrorist organizations such as Al Qaeda.

Most controversially, Bush also suggested that a liberated, democratic Iraq might provide a beacon of hope to the Islamic world and thereby begin to improve the political equation in the volatile Middle East. To skeptical observers,

In his 2002 state of the union address, President Bush declared:

"Iraq continues to flaunt its hostility toward America and to support terror. The Iraqi Regime has plotted to develop anthrax, and nerve gas, and nuclear weapons for over a decade. ... This is a regime that has agreed to international inspections, then kicked out the inspectors. This is a regime that has something to hide from the civilized world.
States like these, and their terrorist allies, constitute an axis of evil, arming to threaten the peace of the world. By seeking weapons of mass destruction, these regimes pose a grave and growing danger. They could provide these arms to terrorists, giving them the means to match their hatred. They could attack our allies or attempt to blackmail the United States. In any of these cases, the price of indifference would be catastrophic."

Supreme Court Justice Sandra Day O'Connor justified her decision in favor of affirmative action in the Grutter *case as follows:*

"By virtue of our Nation's struggle with racial inequality, [minority] students are both likely to have experiences of particular importance to the Law School's mission, and less likely to be admitted in meaningful numbers on criteria that ignore those experiences."

Justice Clarence Thomas dissented:

"Every time the government places citizens on racial registers and makes race relevant to the provision of burdens or benefits, it demeans us all. ... When blacks take positions in the highest places of government, industry, or academia, it is an open question today whether their skin color played a part in their advancement ... asking the question itself unfairly marks those blacks who would succeed without discrimination."

including America's European allies, his ambition to create a democracy in long-suffering Iraq, burdened with centuries of internecine conflict, seemed naively utopian. Secretary of State Colin Powell warned about the consequences of invading and occupying an unstable, religiously and culturally divided nation of 25 million people. "You break it, you own it," he told the president. Congress passed a resolution in October 2002 authorizing the president to employ armed force to defend against Iraqi threats to America's national security. But with United Nations inspectors unable to find weapons of mass destruction in Iraq, the U.N. Security Council declined to authorize the use of force against Saddam Hussein.

In this tense and confusing atmosphere, Bush, with Britain his only major ally, launched the long-anticipated invasion of Iraq on March 19, 2003. Saddam Hussein's vaunted military machine collapsed almost immediately. In less than a month Baghdad had fallen. From the deck of a U.S. aircraft carrier off the California coast, speaking beneath a banner declaring "Mission Accomplished," Bush triumphantly announced on May 1, 2003, that "major combat operations in Iraq have ended."

Owning Iraq

Bush's words quickly came back to haunt him and America's forces in Iraq. "Neoconservative" pundits in Washington had predicted that American soldiers would be greeted as liberators and that Saddam's ouster would lead to flowering democracy across the Middle East. In reality, post-Saddam Iraq quickly devolved into a seething cauldron of violence. The country's largest ethnic groups, Sunni and Shia Muslims, clashed violently, especially in the capital city of Baghdad. Both groups attacked American forces who, after their leaders disbanded the Iraqi army, were left to secure the country single-handedly. A locally grown insurgency quickly spread, and occupying Iraq became ever more perilous for American troops. Hatred for Americans only worsened with revelations in April 2004 that Iraqi prisoners in Baghdad's Abu Ghraib prison had been tortured and humiliated by their American captors. Amid this chaos, jihadist terrorists from around the region flooded into Iraq and established strong positions in Iraq, often fueling the intra-Iraqi conflicts to further their vision of radical Islam. Although Al Qaeda had no link to Iraq under Saddam, as Bush had falsely alleged, it certainly moved in after. These three battles—Shia/Sunni ethnic violence, counter-occupation insurgency, and jihadist terrorism—created a ceaseless cycle of bloodshed, in which American soldiers found themselves increasingly bogged down. By the end of 2006, more Americans had died in Iraq than in the attacks of September 11, 2001.

Reelecting George W. Bush

Americans had rarely been as divided as they were in the first years of the twenty-first century. Civil libertarians worried that the government was trampling personal freedoms in the name of fighting terrorism. Revelations in 2002 about flagrant corporate fraud at energy giant Enron, telecommunications titan WorldCom, and other prominent firms fed rampant popular disillusion with the business community. Cultural tensions brewed over the rights of gay and lesbian Americans when leaders in San Francisco and Massachusetts permitted same-sex couples to marry in 2004. Affirmative action continued to spark sharp debate, as the Supreme Court permitted some preferential treatment in admitting minority undergraduate and law students to the University of Michigan in 2003.

Amid this division, George W. Bush positioned himself to run for reelection. He proclaimed that his tax cuts had spurred economic growth by giving citizens more control. Targeting what he called "the soft bigotry of low expectations," he championed the No Child Left Behind Act of 2002, which mandated sanctions against schools that failed to meet federal performance standards. He played to cultural conservatives over stem cell research and called for a constitutional amendment to ban gay marriage. But most of all, he promoted himself as a stalwart leader in wartime, warning the country not to "change horses midstream."

After a bruising round of primary elections, the embattled Democrats chose lanky and long-jawed Massachusetts Senator John Kerry to represent their ticket. A more old-fashioned liberal than Clinton, Kerry pushed progressive visions of government and counted on his Vietnam war record to counter charges that he would be weak in the face of terrorism. But that plan backfired as Kerry fell under attack for his very public opposition to Vietnam once he returned from battle in the early 1970s. The Republicans also had success painting the senator as a "flip-flopper," changing his policy positions to fit opinion polls. In spite of increased public misgivings about the war in Iraq, Bush nailed down a decisive victory in November 2004. He received the first popular vote majority in more than a decade, 60,639,281 to 57,355,978, and won clearly, if by only one state (this time Ohio), in the electoral college, 286 to 252. This time his mandate was clear, constitutional, and uncontested.

Bush's Second Term

Reelection, George W. Bush announced, gave him "political capital," which he intended to spend on an aggressive domestic agenda. The appointment of two new conservative Supreme Court justices (John G. Roberts and Samuel A. Alito, Jr.) upon the retirement of Sandra Day O'Connor and the death of Chief Justice William Rehnquist seemed to bode well for his ambitions. But Bush overplayed his hand. Attacking the core of New Deal liberalism, Bush proposed a radical program to privatize much of Social Security, providing incentives for younger Americans to fund their own retirements through personal accounts. A massive outcry led by the American Association of Retired Persons and other liberal groups reminded Americans how much they loved Social Security, warts and all. Bush's proposal faded away within six months of his reelection. The same fate befell a proposed constitutional amendment to ban same-sex marriage, which had been a major issue in the 2004 campaign.

The president also took aim at the contentious issue of immigration reform, where he parted company with the conservative wing of his party. Bush opposed arresting and deporting the nearly 12 million undocumented people in the United States, as some nativists proposed. At the same time, he felt that simply normalizing their status would reward them for entering the country illegally. His compromise plan to establish a guest-worker program and a "path to citizenship" for the undocumented ended up pleasing no one. Congress rejected it in the summer of 2007, and the issue was dead for the rest of Bush's term.

Every second-term president since the 1960s had seen scandal mar his later years in office. Nixon had Watergate, Reagan had Iran-Contra, and Clinton had Lewinsky. The Bush White House was no exception, but this time the accusations were political, not personal. Bush's critics claimed that Bush's fierce loyalty to his staff prevented him from recognizing incompetence, and that he unlawfully expanded the power of the presidency under the guise of protecting America in the "War on Terror." In December 2005 journalists discovered that the government was conducting illegal wiretap surveillance programs on American citizens inside the United States, in violation of federal law. In 2007, scandal engulfed the Justice Department over the firings, for political reasons, of eight U.S. attorneys. Perhaps the most tragic and avoidable of Bush's missteps came in the botched response to the deadly **Hurricane Katrina**, which devastated New Orleans and much of the Gulf Coast in late August 2005, flooding 80 percent of the historic city and causing over 1300 deaths and $150 billion in damages. The response of the Federal Emergency Management Agency (FEMA) proved woefully inept, and Bush came in for still more criticism.

The continuing Iraq War was the biggest factor in fueling growing public disapproval of the Bush administration. Prewar claims about weapons of mass destruction and Iraq's connections to Al Qaeda and 9/11 had proved false, and a majority of Americans came to believe the war had been a mistake. Seizing on this disillusionment, Democrats narrowly regained control of both houses of Congress in the mid-term elections of 2006 for the first time since

Hurricane Katrina (2005) *The costliest and one of the deadliest hurricanes in the history of the United States, killing nearly 2000 Americans. The storm ravaged the Gulf Coast, particularly the city of New Orleans, in late August 2005.*

the Gingrich revolution of 1994. With his credibility badly damaged, Secretary of Defense Donald Rumsfeld resigned. In 2007 Bush launched a new surge of twenty thousand additional American troops that provided a modest measure of stability in Iraq. However, as the 2008 election cycle got under way, public opinion solidified against the war, and President Bush's approval ratings sank below 30 percent. Candidate Obama's promise to conclude the war in timely fashion powerfully aided his candidacy in the upcoming presidential election.

The Presidential Election of 2008

With neither the sitting president nor vice president running, the 2008 election was truly "open" for the first time in 80 years. The Democratic race soon tightened into a fiercely fought battle between the 46-year-old, first-term Illinois Senator Barack Obama and the pre-campaign favorite, former First Lady and New York Senator Hillary Rodham Clinton.

The ensuing nip-and-tuck contest, destined to catapult either a black man or a woman into the general election as a major party nominee split the Democratic party and drew millions of new voters into the primaries. The son of a black Kenyan father and a white mother from Kansas, Obama appealed to both the crusading spirit of the civil rights era and the newer ethos of tolerance that came naturally to the young in twenty-first century America. Capitalizing on an army of youthful volunteers, his record of early opposition to the Iraq War, and his astonishing eloquence, Obama defeated Clinton and rode into the general election on a wave of Democratic enthusiasm. He bolstered his national security credentials by selecting Delaware Senator Joseph Biden as his running mate.

In keeping with the country's anti-Bush mood, Republicans nominated veteran Arizona Senator John McCain, a Vietnam War hero and a self-styled "maverick" with a record of bipartisan reform. To rally the conservative and evangelical Christian wing of his party, McCain selected Alaska Governor Sarah Palin as his running mate. As McCain hoped, Palin galvanized the right-wing Republican base, but her inexperience and weak grasp of issues made her at least as much a liability as an asset to the Republican ticket.

Armed with an unprecedented war chest of nearly 700 million dollars, Obama seized the advantage in both the "air war" (television) and the "ground war" (his legions of volunteers). His strong performance in televised debates also lent the youthful Obama an aura of gravitas that some voters had doubted he had.

What appeared to bolster his chances most, however, was the worldwide economic collapse that began in the final six weeks of the campaign. The American housing price bubble had begun to burst in 2006, which in turn led to a huge wave of mortgage defaults, housing foreclosures, and decline in mortgage-based securities held by banks around the globe. By early October the credit markets froze, stock values plummeted, and Americans watched helplessly as their savings shrank. Economists of every stripe spoke of the gravest financial crisis since the Great Depression.

Barack Obama Riding the public's discontent with President Bush's Republican administration, Illinois Senator Barack Obama beat Arizona Senator John McCain in 2008 to become the first African American to reach the White House.

In contrast to the 1929 crash, it took days, not years, for a terrified Bush Administration to intervene on a gigantic scale. The Treasury Department and Federal Reserve System nationalized the country's two biggest mortgage companies, the Federal National Mortgage Association ("Fannie Mae") and the Federal Home Mortgage Corporation ("Freddie Mac"), and took over the world's biggest insurance company, AIG. Treasury Secretary Henry Paulson then persuaded Congress to authorize a whopping $700 billion to buy "toxic" mortgages and inject cash directly into the nation's biggest banks. Suddenly even small-government Republicans spoke of the need to regulate the financial sector. Obama seized the initiative by declaring that electing McCain would amount to a "third Bush term," and calling for big public investments in alternative energy and infrastructure repair—proposals that McCain said amounted to "socialism."

Huge voter turnouts delivered a historic victory to Barack Obama, who won 53 percent of the national popular vote. By overtaking his rival in such traditional Republican strongholds such as Virginia, Indiana, and Colorado, Obama prevailed in the Electoral College 364 to 175. Democrats gained seats in the House and Senate to enlarge the Congressional majority they had won in 2006. Obama's election opened a new chapter in the history of the country's race relations. It also presented the nation's first African American president the daunting challenge of governing a country struggling with wars in Iraq and Afghanistan and entering its roughest economic waters since the 1930s.

Obama in the White House

Inspired by Barack Obama's vision of "hope," a vast and exuberant crowd gathered in Washington, D.C., to celebrate the historic inauguration. In his inaugural address Obama struck a sober note by calling on Americans to "put away childish things" and enter "a new era of responsibility."

Obama's solemn tone was fitting, for he took office amidst a continuing economic collapse of epic proportions. The stock market and the financial system had been in freefall for months and remained so, as banks virtually stopped lending, business activity plunged, and hundreds of companies went belly up. Home construction nearly ceased and mortgage foreclosures soared. Most alarmingly, the economy was shedding a sickening 700,000 jobs a month. The unemployment rate rapidly climbed above 10 percent—the highest rate since the early 1980s.

Obama boldly seized the reins of power by immediately taking vigorous federal action to stop the bleeding and prevent an even deeper crisis. In his first hundred days he pushed through a series of major initiatives that included a new round of help for troubled banks, $275 billion to aid homeowners, and a massive new federal "stimulus" bill—the American Recovery and Reinvestment Act—that contained nearly a trillion dollars of new spending for jobs, infrastructure projects, education, and relief to state and local governments. The government also stepped in to bail out bankrupt automakers General Motors and Chrysler as well as distressed banks and insurance companies.

By the summer of 2009, the worst of the panic was over, but the economy had been badly wounded and continued to suffer. The unemployment rate settled in above 9 percent, while many discouraged workers eventually stopped looking for jobs. The "Great Recession" gnawed at the Republic's vital organs.

Though the economy preoccupied the nation, President Obama turned his attention to the long-sought goal of health care reform. After attempts to enlist Republican support bogged down in Congressional haggling, he was forced to rely on Democrats alone to pass a bill in March 2010 that guaranteed health insurance for nearly 32 million more Americans. It also enacted other reforms in the health insurance industry, including preventing denial of coverage based on pre-existing conditions, prohibiting the cancellation of seriously ill patients' insurance, and guaranteeing young adults up to age 26 coverage under their parents' policies. In July 2010 the Wall Street Reform and Consumer Protection Act overhauled the nation's financial regulatory system with new controls on banks and stock markets, and new curbs on the risky, high-flying practices that had contributed to the meltdown of 2008.

Obama's unflinching assertion of the need for forceful federal intervention in the economy, health care, and other matters revealed his commitment to the kind of activist presidency and expansive government role not seen since the days of Lyndon Johnson. Bill Clinton's claim that "the era of big government is over" faded as Obama liberally spent his own political capital, along with buckets of federal dollars, to achieve his goals and address the nation's needs.

Wars, Oil, and Political Backlash

Along with economic problems, Obama inherited America's twin wars in Iraq and Afghanistan. As a longtime opponent of the Iraq conflict, the new president sought to wind down that war while leaving behind a reasonably stable Iraq. Shortly after taking office, Obama announced that American combat operations in Iraq would end in summer 2010 and that all American combat troops would be withdrawn by 2011. Despite continuing violence and the persistent shakiness of the Iraqi government, the deadline for ending American-led operations was met on August 31, 2010. Still, about 50,000 American troops remained in the country to protect U.S. bases and support Iraqi security efforts.

Afghanistan was a thornier nettle to grasp. Obama had declared the Afghan war necessary to defeat Al Qaeda and prevent future terrorism. But Afghan *jihadi* (militant Islamic) fighters grew stronger against an Afghan government plagued by incompetence and corruption. More ominously, the Taliban and Al Qaeda found refuge across the border in unstable but nuclear-armed Pakistan, creating the danger of an expanded conflict there as well.

Pressed by some to bolster the American effort in Afghanistan, and by others to seek a way out of the increasingly costly conflict, Obama chose to do both. In December 2009 he declared that American troops would begin to withdraw in mid-2011—but that in order to achieve that goal an additional 30,000 U.S. soldiers would be sent immediately to combat the insurgency. Obama also put in place a new counter-insurgency strategy and a new U.S. commander, General David Petraeus, but casualties increased and outcries against the nearly decade-long conflict grew louder, especially among Democrats.

Obama soon faced an environmental calamity as well. On April 20, 2010, the Deepwater Horizon oil platform in the Gulf of Mexico exploded, killing 17 workers and spewing oil from its well nearly one *mile* below the ocean floor. Over the next four months the American public watched helplessly as nearly five million barrels of oil poured into the Gulf of Mexico, fouling beaches and killing wildlife from Louisiana to Florida. For four months the oil giant British Petroleum futilely attempted to stop the gusher of oil as frustration and anger mounted. By the time the well was finally capped in August 2010, it had become the worst oil disaster in U.S. history, exceeding the *Exxon Valdez* spill in 1989.

The government's inability to contain the Gulf oil spill added to a building political backlash against the initially gleaming Obama administration. The still-crippled economy struggled to make positive headway, but it was weighed down by the burden of debt and the reluctance of spooked consumers to spend. And as often in the past, economic fears contributed to outbursts of anti-immigrant sentiment. In April 2010 Arizona enacted a harsh law requiring state and local police to help enforce federal immigration laws. Although a federal judge put the statute on hold, Arizona's action was applauded in many other places, especially those with substantial Latino immigrant populations.

Meanwhile, a growing chorus of critics began assailing Obama's raft of "big government" and spending initiatives. Starting with vehement attacks on the proposed health care bill in the summer of 2009, there soon appeared a growing number of angry protesters who accused the Obama administration of promoting "socialism" and "unconstitutional" controls over individual lives. Calling themselves the "Tea Party" after the American Revolutionary Patriots, these noisy citizens combined a knack for street-theater demonstrations with nonstop internet and media fulminations against the president and his policies.

Congressional Republicans, who had been momentarily stunned into silence by Obama's overwhelming popularity, took heart from the Tea Party's passionate grass-roots mobilization and began fighting the administration tooth and nail. Obama was still able to win some hard-fought battles. His successful appointment of two new Supreme Court Justices, Sonia Sotomayor in 2009 and Elena Kagan in 2010, brought the number of female justices to an historic three. But other efforts, like a "cap-and-trade" bill to curb greenhouse gases and reduce global warming, fell victim to minority opposition.

As economic and political discontent simmered, Obama's public opinion approval ratings slumped. Having entertained extravagant hopes for dramatic change and bipartisan cooperation, many independents and even Democrats were discouraged by the stubborn persistence of the nation's problems and the administration's seeming loss of momentum. As the mid-term elections of 2010 approached, enthusiastic Republicans gathered steam and dreamed of regaining control of Congress. Riding the wild Tea Party bandwagon, however, proved a tricky balancing act. In several primary elections, right-wing Tea Party candidates defeated establishment conservative Republicans, putting several key races within reach of the Democrats.

Chapter Summary

The dynamic young "baby-boomer" Bill Clinton defeated President George H.W. Bush in 1992, and promoted an ambitious reform agenda within the context of his centrist "new Democrat" ideology. Clinton's efforts to reform health care and promote gun control met strong resistance, but his economic policies helped to spark a decade-long expansion. Presenting an aggressively conservative agenda, Republicans gained control of Congress in 1994 for the first time in fifty years. But overreaching by the Newt Gingrich–led Republicans enabled Clinton to revive and win a second term by defeating Kansas Senator Robert Dole in 1996.

In his second term, Clinton downplayed reform and successfully claimed the political middle ground. The booming economy created budget surpluses, and enhanced Clinton's efforts to develop even more free trade agreements in line with the successful North American Free Trade Agreement (NAFTA). Clinton recovered from early foreign policy stumbles in Africa and Latin America with a successful intervention in the former Yugoslavia. But efforts at Middle East peace stalled. Clinton's affair with Monica Lewinsky led to his highly partisan impeachment in 1998 and acquittal in 1999.

Texas Governor George Walker Bush defeated Clinton's vice president, Albert Gore, in a cliffhanging election that was finally settled by the Supreme Court. Bush promoted an aggressive and divisive conservative agenda of deep tax cuts at home and unilateral assertion of American interests abroad.

The terrorist attacks of September 11, 2001, were a watershed in American history, ending centuries of nearly cost-free national security. Bush invaded the Al Qaeda stronghold of Afghanistan, ousting the Taliban regime, and Congress passed the USA Patriot Act over civil libertarian objections. Bush

invaded Iraq in March 2003. U.S. forces quickly crushed Saddam Hussein's army, but became entrapped in low-intensity warfare against determined Iraqi insurgents.

The United States became culturally and politically polarized in the early years of the twenty-first century. George W. Bush ran successfully as a wartime president leading the fight against terrorism, defeating Democrat John Kerry in the election of 2004. But growing public discontent with the prolonged Iraq War and the Bush administration's inadequate response to the devastating Hurricane Katrina caused his political support to erode.

The campaign of 2008 featured a newcomer, Democratic Senator Barack Obama, the first African American presidential nominee, against veteran Republican Senator John McCain. A major financial and economic crash in the middle of the campaign prompted a strong response from the Bush administration, while enabling Obama to seize the political initiative and gain stature with the voters. Obama won a strong victory by drawing millions of new voters to the polls and breaking into traditional Republican strongholds.

Obama responded to the deep economic crisis with a massive "stimulus" spending bill and other federal initiatives. The worst of the economic collapse ended in mid-2009, but the "Great Recession" took a deep toll in lost jobs and homes. Obama succeeded in passing significant health care reform, but stirred the vigorous protests of conservative "Tea Party" protesters.

American combat operations in Iraq officially ended in summer 2010, but Obama sent additional forces into Afghanistan. Obama's public approval declined amidst the continued economic troubles and the fierce attacks of a re-energized Republican opposition to his policies.

KEY TERMS

paramilitary (695)
Whitewater (697)
vouchers (698)
Guantanamo Detention Camp (701)
Hurricane Katrina (703)

PEOPLE TO KNOW

William Jefferson ("Bill") Clinton
H. Ross Perot
Hillary Rodham Clinton
Newt Gingrich
Robert Dole
John McCain

Monica Lewinsky
George W. Bush
Richard Cheney
John Kerry
Sarah Palin
Barack Obama

Go to the History CourseMate website for primary source links, study tools, and review materials for this chapter.
www.cengagebrain.com

42

The American People Face a New Century

As our case is new, so we must think anew and act anew.
We must disenthrall ourselves, and then we shall save our country.

ABRAHAM LINCOLN, 1862

Well beyond its two-hundredth birthday as the twenty-first century began, the United States was both an old and a new nation. It boasted one of the longest uninterrupted traditions of democratic government of any country on earth. Indeed, it had pioneered the techniques of mass democracy and was, in that sense, the oldest modern polity. As one of the earliest countries to industrialize, America had also dwelled in the modern economic era longer than most nations.

But the Republic was in many ways still youthful as well. Innovation, entrepreneurship, and risk taking—all characteristics of youth—were honored national values. The twenty-first century began much like the twentieth, with American society continuing to be rejuvenated by fresh waves of immigrants, full of energy and ambition. The U.S. economy, despite problems, pulsated as a driving engine of world economic growth. American inventions—especially computer and communications technologies—were transforming the face of global society. Consumers from Lisbon to Tokyo seemed to worship the icons of American culture—downing soft drinks and donning blue jeans, watching Hollywood films, listening to rock or country music, even adopting indigenous American sports such as baseball and basketball. In the realm of consumerism, American products appeared to have Coca-Colonized the globe—for better or worse.

The history of American society also seemed to have increased global significance as the third millennium of the Christian era opened. Americans were a pluralistic people who had struggled for centuries to provide opportunity and to achieve tolerance and justice for many different religious, ethnic, and racial groups. Their historical experience could offer valuable lessons to the rapidly internationalizing planetary society that was emerging at the dawn of the twenty-first century.

Much history remained to be made as the country entered its third century of nationhood. The great social experiment of American democracy was far from complete. The ethical challenges posed by science and technology, environmental stewardship of a fragile planet, and overcoming inequality and prejudice all posed formidable challenges for the future. And the terrorist attacks of September 11, 2001, violently heralded a new era of fear and anxiety.

But men and women make history only within the framework bequeathed to them by earlier generations. Whether they like it or not—indeed, whether they know it or not—they march forward along time's path bearing the burdens of the past. Understanding when they have come to a truly new turn in the road, when they can lay part of their burden down, and when they cannot, or should not—all this constitutes the kind of wisdom that only historical study can engender.

FOCUS QUESTIONS

1. How did economic and technological changes alter the American workplace and workforce?

2. What ethical questions were raised by the revolutionary new knowledge in science and medicine?

3. What caused the growing economic inequality in the late twentieth and early twenty-first centuries, and what were the social and moral consequences of this trend for American society?

4. How has the feminist movement altered women's roles and transformed the character of American business, politics, education, and family life?

5. What major changes affected American family life in the half century since World War II, and what were the long-term economic and social consequences of the "aging of America"?

6. What lay behind the vast new wave of immigration from Latin America and Asia, and what challenges and opportunities did it pose for the future of American society?

7. How have American art, literature, and media reflected the dynamic character of American society in the late twentieth and early twenty-first centuries?

Economic Revolutions

When the twentieth century opened, United States Steel Corporation was the flagship business of America's industrial revolution. A generation later, General Motors' preeminence in automobile production signaled the historic shift to a mass consumer economy that began in the 1920s and flowered fully in the 1950s. Following World War II, the rise of International Business Machines (IBM) symbolized the transformation to the fast-paced "information age." By century's end, the phenomenal growth of Microsoft Corporation and the Internet heralded an explosive communications revolution. Americans now rocketed down the "information superhighway" toward the uncharted terrain of an electronic global village.

The communications revolution was full of both promise and peril. In the blink of an eye, ordinary citizens could gain access to information once available only to privileged elites. Businesspeople instantaneously girdled the planet with transactions of prodigious scope and serpentine complexity. By the late 1990s a "dot-com" explosion of new commercial ventures quickly expanded the market (and the stock-market stakes) for entrepreneurs leading the way in making the Internet a twenty-first-century electronic mall, library, and entertainment center rolled into one.

But the very speed and efficiency of the new communications tools threatened to wipe out entire occupational categories. Postal letter-carriers, travel agents, booksellers, bank tellers, stockbrokers, and others whose business it was to mediate between product and client might find themselves roadkill on the information superhighway. White-collar jobs in financial services and high-tech engineering could now be "outsourced" to countries such as Ireland or India.

Increasingly, scientific research was the motor that propelled the economy, and new scientific knowledge raised new moral dilemmas and provoked new political arguments. Pioneering genetic discoveries, for instance, had yielded new strains of high-yield, pest-resistant crops, but also, unfortunately, had unleashed genetic mutations that might threaten the fragile balance of the wondrous **biosphere** in which humankind was delicately suspended. By the dawn of the new century, a revolution in biological engineering pointed the way to radical new medical therapies—and to mouth-watering profits for bioengineering firms. Research into human stem cells held out the promise of cures for afflictions such as Parkinson's disease and Alzheimer's. But the Bush administration shared the concern of certain religious groups that harvesting stem cells involved the destruction of human life in embryonic form. Bush therefore limited government funding for stem cell research, as Americans continued to struggle with the ethical implications of their vast new technological powers.

biosphere *The earth's entire network of living plants and organisms, conceived as an interconnected whole.*

Other unprecedented ethical questions clamored for resolution. What principles should govern the allocation of human organs for lifesaving transplants? How, if at all, should society regulate the increasingly lengthy and often painful process of dying?

Affluence and Inequality

Americans were still an affluent people at the beginning of the twenty-first century. Median household income climbed above $52,000 by 2007, but dipped to $50,221 in 2010, thanks to the Great Recession. Yet even those Americans with incomes below the government's official poverty level (defined in 2009 as $22,050 for a family of four) enjoyed a standard of living higher than that of two-thirds of the rest of humankind.

Americans were no longer the world's wealthiest people, as they had been in the quarter-century after World War II. Citizens of several other countries enjoyed higher average per capita incomes, and many nations boasted more equitable distributions of wealth. In an unsettling reversal of long-term trends in American society, during the last two decades of the twentieth century the rich got much richer while the poor got an ever-shrinking share of the pie. The richest 20 percent of Americans in 2009 raked in half the nation's income, while the poorest 20 percent received a little over 3 percent. The gap between rich and poor began to widen in the 1980s and widened further thereafter. Between 1968 and 2009 the share of the nation's income that flowed to the top 20 percent of its households swelled from 40 percent to 50.3 percent. Even more striking, in the same period the top 5 percent of income receivers saw their share of the national income grow from about 15 percent to a remarkable 21.7 percent.

Widening inequality could be measured in other ways as well. Chief executives in the 1970s typically earned forty-one times as much as the average worker in their corporations; by 2006 they earned 245 times as much. In 2009, 50 million people had no medical insurance. At the same time, some 43.5 million people, 14.3 percent of all Americans (12.3 percent of whites, 25.8 percent of African Americans, 25.3 percent of Latinos, and 12.5 percent of Asians), remained mired in poverty—a depressing indictment of the inequities afflicting an affluent and allegedly egalitarian republic.

What caused the widening income gap? Some critics pointed to the tax and fiscal policies of the Reagan and Bush (father and son) presidencies, which favored the wealthy. But deeper-running historical currents probably played a more powerful role, as suggested by similar trends toward inequality in other industrialized societies. Among the most conspicuous causes were intensifying global competition; the shrinkage in high-paying manufacturing jobs for semiskilled and unskilled workers; the greater economic

Two Nations? While decaying neighborhoods and legions of the homeless blighted American cities in the early twenty-first century, affluent Americans lived the good life in booming suburbs and in the more suburbanized cities of the Sunbelt, such as this development of million-dollar homes around a country club in Las Vegas, Nevada.

rewards commanded by educated workers in high-tech industries; the decline of unions; the rising tide of relatively low-skill immigrants; and the increasing tendency of educated men and women to marry one another and both work, creating households with very high incomes. Educational opportunities also had a way of perpetuating inequality, starting with the underfunding of many schools in poor urban areas and the soaring cost of higher education. A 2004 study revealed that at the 146 most selective colleges, 74 percent of the students came from families with incomes in the top 25 percent, compared to 3 percent of the students from the bottom income quartile.

The Feminist Revolution

All Americans were caught up in the great economic changes of the late twentieth century, but no group was more profoundly affected than women. When the twentieth century opened, women made up about 20 percent of all workers. Over the next five decades they increased their presence in the labor force at a fairly steady rate, except for a temporary

A New World for Women By the beginning of the twenty-first century, revolutionary changes in the economy and in social values had opened new career possibilities to women, even while they still performed their traditional duties as mothers and homemakers. Commander Kathleen McGrath of the frigate *USS Jarrett* (bottom left) was the first woman to take a warship to sea in 2000, and Drew Gilpin Faust (bottom right) became the first woman to serve as president of Harvard University in 2007. Women athletes came into their own in the wake of the feminist revolution. Venus and Serena Williams (top right) enthralled the tennis world as individual champions and as a doubles team beginning in the late 1990s.

Reuters/Corbis

Ed Kashi/Corbis News/Corbis

Dana Rudick/Boston Globe/Landov

spurt during World War II. Then, beginning in the 1950s, women's entry into the workplace accelerated dramatically. By the 1990s nearly half of all workers were women, and the majority of working-age women held jobs outside the home. Most astonishing was the upsurge in employment of mothers. In 1950, 90 percent of mothers with children under the age of six did not work for pay. But half a century later, a majority of women with children as young as one year old were wage earners. Women brought home the bacon and cooked it, too. By 2004, American women participated in the workforce in higher numbers than in almost all industrialized countries except Russia and China.

Beginning in the 1960s, many all-male strongholds—including Yale, Princeton, and West Point—opened their doors to women. By the 1980s, women became the majority on college campuses. By the twenty-first century, women were piloting commercial airliners, orbiting outer space, governing states and cities, and writing Supreme Court decisions.

Yet despite those gains, many feminists remained frustrated. Women continued to receive lower wages —80 cents on the dollar in 2009—and they tended to concentrate in a few low-prestige, low-paying occupations (the "pink-collar ghetto"). Although they made up more than half the population, women in 2009 accounted for just 32 percent of lawyers and judges (up from 5 percent in 1970) and 32 percent of physicians (up from 10 percent in 1970). Overt sexual discrimination explained some of this occupational segregation, but most of it seemed attributable to the greater burdens of parenthood on women than on men. Women were far more likely than men to interrupt their careers to bear and raise children, and even to choose less demanding career paths to allow for fulfilling those traditional roles. Discrimination and a focus on children also helped account for the persistence of a "gender gap" in voting behavior. Women continued to vote in greater numbers than men for Democratic candidates, who were often perceived to be more willing to favor government support for health care, child care, education, and job equality.

As the revolution in women's status rolled on in the 2000s, men's lives changed as well. Men assumed traditional female responsibilities such as cooking, laundry, and child care. Recognizing the new realities of the modern American household, Congress passed a Family Leave Bill in 1993, mandating job protection for working fathers as well as mothers who needed to take time off work for family-related reasons.

Changing Families and Aging Citizens

The traditional **nuclear family**, once prized as the foundation of society and the nursery of the Republic, suffered heavy blows in postwar America. By the 1990s one out of every two marriages ended in divorce, although the divorce rate appeared to ebb a bit by the century's end. Seven times more children were affected by divorce than at the beginning of the twentieth century, and kids who commuted between separated parents were commonplace.

Traditional families were not only falling apart at an alarming rate but were also increasingly slow to form in the first place. The proportion of adults living alone tripled in the five decades after 1950, and by the 1990s about one-third of women age twenty-five to twenty-nine had never married. In the 1960s, 5 percent of all births were to unmarried women, but four decades later one out of four white babies, one out of three Hispanic babies, and two out of three African American babies were born to single mothers. Every fourth child in America was growing up in a household that lacked two parents. The collapse of the traditional family contributed heavily to the pauperization of many women and children, as single parents (usually mothers) struggled to keep their households economically afloat.

Child rearing, the family's foremost function, was being increasingly assigned to "parent-substitutes" at day-care centers or schools—or to television, the modern age's "electronic babysitter." Estimates were that the average child by age sixteen had watched up to fifteen thousand hours of TV—more time than was spent in the classroom. Parental anxieties multiplied with the advent of the Internet, an electronic **cornucopia** where youngsters could surf through poetry and problem sets as well as pornography.

But if the *traditional* family was increasingly rare, the family itself remained a bedrock of American society in the early twenty-first century, as viable families now assumed a

PRIMARY SOURCE
Women in the Workforce

PRIMARY SOURCE
U.S. Health Spending

nuclear family *A parent or parents and their immediate offspring.*

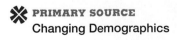

PRIMARY SOURCE
Changing Demographics

cornucopia *An overflowing abundance of good things, as in the bountiful outpouring of fruits and flowers in Greek mythology's "horn of plenty."*

variety of forms. Children in households led by a single parent, stepparent, or grandparent encountered a degree of acceptance that would have been unimaginable a generation earlier. Even the notion of gay marriage, which emerged as a major public controversy when the Massachusetts Supreme Court ruled it legal in 2003, signaled that the idea of marriage retained its luster.

Americans were living longer than ever before. A person born at the dawn of the twentieth century could expect to survive less than fifty years, whereas someone born in 2000 could expect a life span of seventy-seven years. Miraculous medical advances such as the development of antibiotics after 1940 and Dr. Jonas Salk's discovery in 1953 of a polio vaccine lengthened and strengthened lives.

Longer lives spelled more older people. One American in eight was over sixty-five years of age in 2009, and projections were that one of every five people would be in the "sunset years" by 2050. This aging of the population raised a host of political, social, and economic questions. Elderly people formed a potent electoral bloc that aggressively lobbied for government favors and achieved real gains for senior citizens. As late as the 1960s nearly a quarter of Americans over the age of sixty-five lived in poverty; three decades later only about one in ten did.

These triumphs for senior citizens also brought fiscal strains, especially on the Social Security system, established in 1935 to provide income for retired workers. Before Social Security began, most workers continued to toil after age sixty-five (if they were among the lucky few who lived that long). By century's end the majority of the elderly population relied primarily on Social Security checks for their living expenses. Contrary to popular mythology, Social Security payments were funded from the taxes of current workers, not from the retirees' own earlier payments. By the time the new century opened, the ratio of active workers to retirees had dropped so low that drastic adjustments were necessary.

At the beginning of the new century, as the huge wave of post–World War II baby boomers approached retirement age, it seemed that the "unfunded liability"—the difference between what the government promised to pay to the elderly and the taxes it expected to take in—might rise above $7 trillion, a sum that threatened to bankrupt the Republic unless sweeping reforms were adopted. Yet because of the electoral power of older Americans, Social Security and Medicare reform remained the "third rail" of American politics, which politicians touched only at their peril. Pressures mounted nonetheless to cut benefits, persuade older Americans to work longer, or take even more drastic action. In 2005, freshly reelected President George Bush made Social Security reform the centerpiece of his domestic agenda and proposed partially privatizing the system. Bush's plan would have given younger workers the option to invest some of their payroll taxes in individual retirement funds. But the electoral power of older Americans and the country's ultimate loyalty to a public social safety net brought the Bush plan to a stunningly quick defeat that spring. Plans to reshape the Social Security system lay dormant for the rest of the Bush years, even as some analysts claimed that payments to the nonworking elderly threatened to soak up fully half of the working population's income by about 2040.

The New Immigration

Newcomers continued to flow into modern America. They washed ashore in waves that numbered nearly 1 million persons per year from the 1980s into the early twenty-first century—the largest inflow of immigrants in America's experience. In striking contrast to the historic pattern of immigration, Europe contributed far fewer people than did the countries of Asia and Latin America.

What prompted this new migration to America? The truth is that the newest immigrants came for many of the same reasons as the old. They typically left countries where populations were growing rapidly and where agricultural and industrial revolutions were shaking people loose from old habits of life—conditions almost identical to those in nineteenth-century Europe. And they came to America, as previous immigrants had done, in search of jobs and economic opportunity. Some came with skills and even professional degrees. But most came with meager skills and scant education, and started work in low-paying manual jobs.

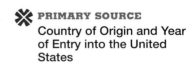

PRIMARY SOURCE
Country of Origin and Year of Entry into the United States

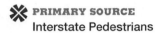

PRIMARY SOURCE
Interstate Pedestrians

undocumented *Lacking official certification of status as a legal immigrant or resident alien.*

amnesty *An official governmental act in which some general category of offenders is declared immune from punishment.*

PRIMARY SOURCE
Percent of the U.S.
Population Who Were...

The Southwest, from Texas to California, felt the immigrant impact especially sharply, as Mexican migrants—by far the largest contingent of modern immigrants—concentrated heavily in that region. By the turn of the century Latinos made up nearly one-third of the population in Texas, Arizona, and California and almost 40 percent in New Mexico—amounting to a demographic *reconquista* of the lands lost by Mexico in the war of 1846.

The size and geographic concentration of the Hispanic population in the Southwest had few precedents in the history of American immigration. Most previous groups had been so thinly scattered across the land that they had little choice but to learn English and make their way in the larger American society, however much they might have longed to preserve their native language and customs. But it seemed possible that Mexican Americans might succeed in creating a truly bicultural zone in the booming southwestern states.

Some old-stock Americans worried about the capacity of the modern United States to absorb these new immigrants. The Immigration Reform and Control Act of 1986 attempted to choke off illegal entry by penalizing employers of **undocumented** aliens and by granting **amnesty** to many of those already here. Anti-immigrant sentiment flared in California in the early 1990s when voters approved a ballot initiative that attempted to deny benefits, including education, to illegal immigrants, though it was later struck down by the courts.

Yet the fact was that foreign-born people accounted for only about 13 percent of the American population in 2007—a far smaller proportion than the historical high point of nearly 15 percent recorded in the census of 1910. Somewhat inconsistently, critics charged both that immigrants robbed citizens of jobs and that they dumped themselves on the welfare rolls at the taxpayers' expense. But studies showed that immigrants took jobs scorned by Americans and that they paid more dollars in federal taxes (withholding and Social Security taxes, as well as excise taxes) than they claimed for welfare payments. The story was different at the state level, where expenditures for immigrant education and health care often exceeded the net tax contribution of the immigrants themselves. Yet the infusion of young immigrants and their offspring was just what the country needed when faced with the challenges of an aging population. A more urgent worry was that unscrupulous employers might take cruel advantage of alien workers, who often had scant knowledge of their legal rights,

Debates over immigration were complicated by the problem of illegal immigrants. The intensity mounted in 2006, when xenophobic pundits and politicians began fanning the old flames of anxiety that millions of undocumented workers were usurping American tax dollars and privileges. That year the House of Representatives passed a punitive anti-immigrant bill that stirred widespread protests by immigrants and their supporters. Pro-immigrant groups argued that unlawful aliens had to be legalized so that they could receive the same protections as other workers. Amid this chaos, President George Bush proposed a bill to establish guest-worker programs for undocumented workers and create a path to citizenship, albeit after paying a fine. In the end, the compromise bill pleased no one and fell into the dustbin.

But the debate's legacy was large. The anti-immigrant venom spewed by many Republican politicians undercut hopes that the GOP might continue to attract Latino voters as it had in the 2004 presidential election. Latinos turned overwhelmingly to Barack Obama and the Democrats in 2008, especially after Obama pledged to pursue immigration reform. But the economic crisis and health care reform put immigration on the Obama administration's back burner. Anti-immigrant sentiment surged again in 2010, when Arizona passed a harsh new law requiring state police to question anyone they suspected of being an illegal immigrant and demand of them proof of citizenship or legal residency.

Ethnic Pride

Thanks both to continued immigration and to their own high birthrate, Latinos were becoming an increasingly important minority (see "Makers of America: The Latinos," pp. 716–717). The United States by 2008 was home to about 47 million of them. They included some 31 million Chicanos, or Mexican Americans, mostly in the Southwest, as well as 4 million Puerto Ricans, chiefly in the Northeast, and more than 1 million Cubans in Florida.

Pablo Martinez Monsivais/AP Images

The Oldest Americans Members of the Cheyenne River Sioux Tribe celebrate the opening of the Smithsonian Institution's National Museum of the American Indian in Washington, D.C., 2004.

Flexing their political muscles, Latinos elected mayors of Miami, Denver, San Antonio, and Los Angeles. After years of struggle, the United Farmworkers Organizing Committee (UFWOC), headed by soft-spoken and charismatic César Chávez, succeeded in improving working conditions for the mostly Mexican American "stoop laborers" who followed the cycle of planting and harvesting across the American West. Latinos, newly confident and organized, became the nation's largest ethnic minority when their numbers surpassed African Americans in 2003. Indeed, by the first decade of the new century, most newborns in California were Latino, a powerful harbinger of the state's demographic future.

Asian Americans also made giant strides. By the 1980s they were America's fastest-growing minority, and their numbers reached more than 15 million by 2008. Once feared and hated as the "yellow peril" and consigned to the most menial jobs, citizens of Asian ancestry were now counted among the most prosperous Americans. Indians, the original Americans, numbered some 2.4 million in the 2000 census. Half of them had left their reservations to live in cities. Meanwhile, unemployment and alcoholism had blighted reservation life. Many tribes took advantage of their special legal status as independent nations by opening gambling casinos on reservation lands, but the cycle of discrimination and poverty proved hard to break.

Cities and Suburbs

America's "alabaster cities" of song and story grew more sooty and less safe in the closing decades of the twentieth century. Crime was the great scourge of urban life. The rate of violent crimes committed in cities reached an all-time high in the drug-infested 1980s, then leveled off in the early 1990s. The number of violent crimes even began to decline substantially in many areas after 1995. Nevertheless, murders, robberies, and rapes remained shockingly common not only in cities but in suburbs and rural areas as well. America imprisoned a larger fraction of its citizens than almost any other country in the world, and some desperate citizens resorted to armed vigilante tactics to protect themselves.

The Latinos

Today Mexican food is handed through fast-food drive-up windows in all fifty states, Spanish-language broadcasts fill the airwaves, and the Latino community has its own telephone book, the *Spanish Yellow Pages.* Latinos send representatives to Congress and mayors to city hall, record hit songs, paint murals, and teach history. Latinos, among the fastest-growing segments of the U.S. population, include Puerto Ricans, frequent voyagers between their native island and northeastern cities; Cubans, many of them refugees from the communist dictatorship of Fidel Castro, concentrated in Miami and southern Florida; and Central Americans, fleeing the ravages of civil war in Nicaragua and El Salvador.

But the most populous group of Latinos derives from Mexico. The first significant numbers of Mexicans began heading for *El Norte* ("the North") around 1910, when the upheavals of the Mexican Revolution stirred and shuffled the Mexican population into more or less constant flux. Their northward passage was briefly interrupted during the Great Depression, when thousands of Mexican nationals were deported. But immigration resumed during World War II, and since then a steady flow of legal immigrants has passed through border checkpoints, joined by countless millions of their undocumented countrymen and countrywomen stealing across the frontier on moonless nights.

For the most part, these Mexicans came to work in the fields, following the ripening crops northward to Canada through the summer and autumn months. Others found work in the cities of the Southwest—El Paso, Los Angeles, Houston, and San Bernardino. Houses may have been shabby in the barrios, but these Mexican neighborhoods provided a sense of togetherness, a place to raise a family, and the chance to join a mutual aid society. Such societies, or *Mutualistas,* sponsored baseball leagues, helped the sick and disabled, and defended their members against discrimination.

Mexican immigrants lived so close to the border that their native country acted like a powerful magnet, drawing them back time and time again. Mexicans frequently returned to see relatives, and relatively few became U.S. citizens. In addition, the Mexican government sometimes intervened to discourage Mexicans from becoming citizens of their adopted country. In the 1910s and 1920s the Mexican consulate in Los Angeles launched a Mexicanization program among the immigrants, sponsoring parades to observe *Cinco de Mayo* ("Fifth of May"),

The migration from cities to the suburbs was so swift and massive that by the mid-1990s a majority of Americans were suburban dwellers. The nation's rather brief "urban age" lasted little more than seven decades after 1920, and with its passing many observers saw a new fragmentation and isolation of American life. Some affluent suburban neighborhoods walled themselves off behind elaborate security systems in "gated communities." By the first decade of the twenty-first century, the suburban rings around big cities such as New York, Chicago, and Houston were becoming more racially and ethnically diverse, though individual schools and towns were often homogeneous.

Suburbs grew fastest in the West and Southwest. Newcomers came not only from nearby cities but from other regions of the United States as well. A momentous shift of the American population was under way, as inhabitants from the Northeast and the Midwest moved southward and westward to job opportunities and the sun. The Great Plains faced the sharpest decline, hollowing out the traditional American heartland.

Some major cities exhibited signs of renewal, including New York, Chicago, San Francisco, and even the classic "city without a center," Los Angeles. Well-to-do residents reclaimed once-fashionable neighborhoods. But these latter-day homesteaders struggled to make their cities centers of residential integration. Cities stubbornly remained as divided by wealth and race as the suburban social landscape surrounding them.

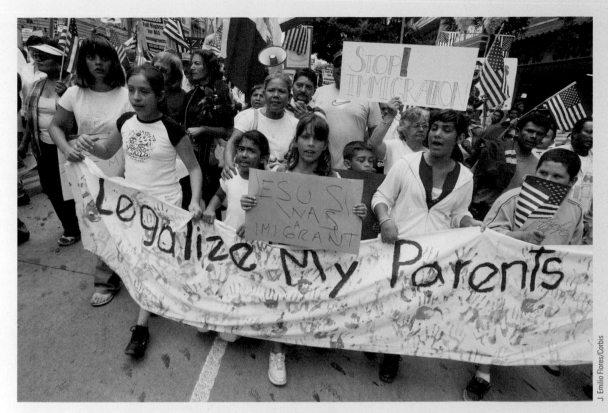

Demonstrating for Immigrant Rights, Los Angeles, 2007 Latinos march in downtown Los Angeles in support of legalizing undocumented parents who have children born in the United States. U.S. law gives the right of citizenship to anyone born on American soil ("jus soli"), but not necessarily to the parents of that child.

celebrating Mexico's defeat of a French army in 1862. Since World War II, the American-born generation has carried on the fight for political representation, economic opportunity, and cultural preservation.

Fresh arrivals from Mexico and from other Latin American nations daily swell the Hispanic communities across America. As the United States moves through the twenty-first century, it is taking on a pronounced Spanish accent.

Minority America

Racial and ethnic tensions exacerbated the problems of American cities. These stresses were especially evident in Los Angeles, which, like New York a century earlier, was a magnet for minorities, especially immigrants from Asia and Latin America. When in 1992 a mostly white jury exonerated white Los Angeles police officers who had been videotaped viciously beating a black suspect, the minority neighborhoods in South Central Los Angeles erupted in rage. Arson and looting laid waste to entire city blocks, and scores of people were killed. Many black rioters vented their anger against white police by attacking Asian shopkeepers, who in turn formed armed patrols to protect their property.

The Los Angeles riots vividly testified to black skepticism about the American system of justice. Just three years later, again in Los Angeles, the televised spectacle of former football star O. J. Simpson's murder trial fed white disillusionment with the state of race relations. After months of testimony that seemed to point to Simpson's guilt, the jury acquitted him, presumably because certain Los Angeles police officers involved in the case

In 1990 the African American intellectual Shelby Steele (b. 1946) declared in his provocative book, The Content of Our Character:

"What is needed now is a new spirit of pragmatism in racial matters where blacks are seen simply as American citizens who deserve complete fairness and in some cases developmental assistance, but in no case special entitlements based on color. We need deracinated social policies that attack poverty rather than black poverty and that instill those values that make for self-reliance."

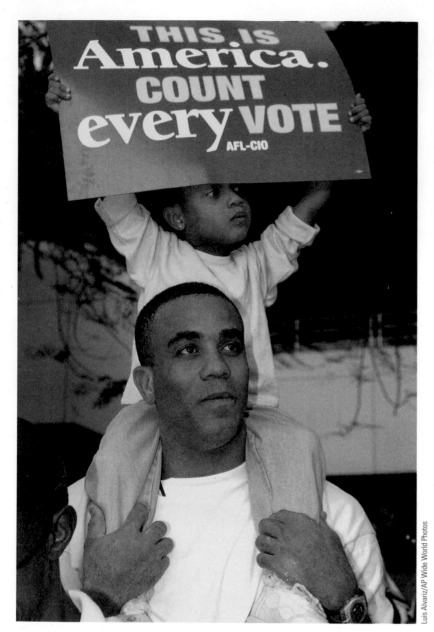

Luis Alvariz/AP Wide World Photos

Still Fighting to Vote An African American father and daughter participate in a rally in downtown Miami several weeks after the November 2000 election to demand a recount of dismissed presidential election ballots. Many Florida blacks complained that election officials had disproportionately disqualified their votes and unfairly turned them away from the polls, resurrecting the kind of obstacles that long had kept blacks from voting in the South.

civil trial *A trial before a judge or jury instigated by a private lawsuit in which one party seeks recovery of goods, financial compensation, or damages for loss or suffering from another private party or business. A* **criminal trial** *is instigated by an indictment for criminal law violations and is brought by a state prosecutor on behalf of the government ("the people"); it may result in fines, imprisonment, or execution.*

had been shown to harbor racist sentiments. In a later **civil trial**, another jury unanimously found Simpson liable for the "wrongful deaths" of his former wife and another victim. The reaction to the Simpson verdicts revealed the yawning chasm that separated white and black America, as most whites continued to believe Simpson guilty, while a majority of African Americans told pollsters that the original not-guilty verdict was justified. Similarly, complaints by African Americans that they had been unlawfully kept from the polls during the 2000 presidential election in Florida reflected many blacks' conviction that they were still facing systematic racial disenfranchisement.

American cities have always held an astonishing variety of ethnic and racial groups, but in the early twentieth-first century, minorities made up a majority of the population of many American cities, as whites fled to the suburbs. The most desperate black ghettos, housing a hapless "underclass" in the inner core of the old industrial cities, were especially problematic. Successful blacks who had benefited from the civil rights revolution of the 1950s and 1960s followed whites to the suburbs, leaving the poorest of the poor in the old ghettoes. Without a middle class to sustain community institutions such as schools and small businesses, the inner cities, plagued by unemployment and drug addiction, seemed bereft of leadership, cohesion, resources, and hope.

Some segments of the African American community did prosper in the wake of the civil rights gains of the 1950s and 1960s, although they still had a long hill to climb before reaching full equality. By 2009, 43 percent of all black families (compared to 68 percent of all white families) had incomes of at least $50,000, qualifying them (barely) as middle-class. Blacks continued to make headway in political life as well. The number of black elected officials had risen above the nine thousand mark, including some three dozen members of Congress and the mayors of several large cities. Voting tallies demonstrated that successful black politicians were moving beyond isolated racial constituencies by appealing to a wide variety of voters. In 1989 Virginians, only 15 percent of whom were black, chose L. Douglas Wilder as the first African American state governor. In 2001 President Bush appointed Colin Powell secretary of state. In Bush's second administration Condoleezza Rice became the first African American woman to hold the post. And in the 2008 election, Senator Barack Obama, whose father was born in Kenya, attained the once-unimaginable goal of election to the presidency.

By the early twenty-first century blacks also dramatically advanced into higher education, though the educational gap between blacks and whites remained. The political assault against affirmative action in California and elsewhere in the 1990s only compounded obstacles to advanced training for many young African Americans. But defenders of affirmative action chalked up a major victory in 2003 when the Supreme Court, in a key case involving the University of Michigan, affirmed that achieving racial diversity on college campuses was a legitimate means to secure a more equitable society. The court preserved affirmative action in university admissions as long as schools avoided using quotas, point systems, or other mechanistic ways of diversifying their student bodies—though the Court remained uneasy about letting such programs endure indefinitely. Justice Sandra Day O'Connor said: "We expect that 25 years from now, the use of racial preferences will no longer be necessary."

E Pluribus Plures

Controversial issues of color and culture also pervaded the realm of ideas at the turn of the twenty-first century. Echoing early-twentieth-century "cultural pluralists" such as Horace Kallen and Randolph Bourne, many intellectuals after 1970 embraced the creed of "multiculturalism." The new mantra stressed the need to preserve and promote, rather than squash, a variety of distinct ethnic and racial cultures in the United States.

In the middle of the twentieth century, thinkers had tended to emphasize race-blind tolerance and universal qualities of the human species that transcended distinctions of nationality, color, or creed. In the 1970s and 1980s, however, ethnic pride became the catchword, and multiculturalism replaced the aging symbol of the "melting pot" with the colorful complexity of the "salad bowl."

The nation's classrooms became battlegrounds for the debate over America's commitment to pluralism. Multiculturalists attacked the traditional curriculum as "Eurocentric" and advocated greater focus on diverse ethnic traditions. In response, critics charged that too much stress on ethnic difference would come at the expense of national cohesion and an appreciation of common American values.

The Life of the Mind

Despite the mind-sapping chatter of the "boob tube," Americans in the late twentieth century read more, listened to more music, and were better educated than ever before. Colleges awarded some 3 million degrees annually, and more than one person in five in the twenty-five-to-thirty-four-year-old age group boasted a college bachelor's degree in 2009. (Nearly one in three had an associate degree.) This expanding mass of educated people lifted the economy to more advanced levels while creating consumers of "high culture." Each year, Americans made millions of visits to museums and patronized thousands of opera companies and symphony orchestras—as well as countless popular music groups.

What Americans read said much about the state of American society in the new century. Among the most striking development in American letters was the rise of authors from ethnic groups now coming into their own. African American authors and artists were among those who increasingly made their mark. Playwright August Wilson retold the history of black Americans in the twentieth century, with special emphasis on the psychic costs of the northward migration (*Fences*, 1985; *Joe Turner's Come and Gone*, 1988; *Jitney*, 1978). Alice Walker gave fictional voice to the experiences of black women in her hugely popular *The Color Purple* (1982). Toni Morrison wove a bewitching portrait of maternal affection in *Beloved* (1987) and in 1993 became the first African American woman to win the Nobel Prize for literature. Kiowa author N. Scott Momaday won a Pulitzer Prize for his portrayal of Indian life in *House Made of Dawn* (1968).

Asian American authors also flourished, among them playwright David Hwang, novelist Amy Tan, and essayist Maxine Hong Kingston, whose *Woman Warrior* (1976) and *China Men*

In her touching novel The Joy Luck Club, *Amy Tan explored the complex dilemmas of growing up as a Chinese American:*

" 'A girl is like a young tree,' [my mother] said, 'You must stand tall and listen to your mother standing next to you. That is only way to grow strong and straight. But if you bend to listen to other people you will grow crooked and weak. ...' Over the years I learned to choose from the best opinions. Chinese people had Chinese opinions. American people had American opinions. And in almost every case, the American version was much better. It was only later that I discovered there was a serious flaw with the American version. There were too many choices, so it was easy to get confused and pick the wrong thing."

(1980) imaginatively reconstructed the lives of the earliest Chinese immigrants. Jhumpa Lahiri's *Interpreter of Maladies* (1999) explored the sometimes painful relationship between immigrant Indian parents and their American-born children.

Latino writers made their mark as well. Sandra Cisneros drew on her own life as a Mexican American child to evoke Latino life in working-class Chicago in *The House on Mango Street* (1984). Women writers and women's themes forged to the fictional forefront as the feminist movement advanced. Jane Smiley modeled her searing narrative of a midwestern farm family, *A Thousand Acres* (1991), on Shakespeare's *King Lear* and followed up with a hilarious spoof on university life in *Moo* (1995). E. Annie Proulx won widespread acclaim with her comical yet tender portrayal of a struggling family in *The Shipping News* (1993), as well as with her moving tale of homoerotic love between two cowboys in *Brokeback Mountain.* The rising interest in feminist and African American themes revived the popularity of the 1930s writer Zora Neale Hurston, especially her naturalist novel *Their Eyes Were Watching God*, first published in 1937.

New York became the art capital of the world after World War II, as well-heeled Americans supported a large number of painters and sculptors. The open and tradition-free American environment seemed especially congenial to the experimental mood of much modern art. Jackson Pollock pioneered abstract expressionism in the 1940s and 1950s, flinging paint on huge flats stretched on his studio floor. Realistic representation went out the window as artists such as Pollock and Willem de Kooning strove to create "action paintings" that made the viewer a creative participant in defining the painting's meaning. Pop artists in the 1960s, notably Andy Warhol, canonized on canvas everyday items of consumer culture, such as soup cans. Claes Oldenburg tried to stun viewers into a new visual awareness with unfamiliar versions of familiar objects, such as giant plastic sculptures of pillow-soft telephones.

On the stage, playwright David Mamet analyzed the barbarity of American capitalism in plays such as *Glengarry Glen Ross* and *American Buffalo,* in which he crafted a kind of poetry from the sludge of American slang. The AIDS epidemic inspired Tony Kushner's sensationally inventive *Angels in America,* a broad-ranging commentary, alternately hilarious and touching, about the condition of American life at the twentieth century's end. Film, the most characteristic American art form, continued to flourish, especially as a wave of younger filmmakers such as George Lucas, Steven Spielberg, Spike Lee, and the Coen brothers, as well as the innovative documentary artist, Ken Burns, made their influence felt.

Architecture also benefited from the building boom of the postwar era. Old master Frank Lloyd Wright produced strikingly original designs, as in the round-walled Guggenheim Museum in New York. Eero Saarinen, the son of a Finnish immigrant, contributed a number of imaginative structures, including two Yale University residential colleges that evoked the atmosphere of an Italian hill town. Chinese-born I. M. Pei designed numerous graceful buildings on several college campuses, as well as the John F. Kennedy Library in Boston. "Postmodernists" such as Robert Venturi and Michael Graves, inspired by the decorative details of earlier historical styles, rejected the spare functionalism that had dominated modern architecture for much of the century. The flight from stark modernism took fanciful forms in Frank Gehry's use of luminous, undulating sheets of metallic skin in his widely hailed Guggenheim Museum in Bilbao, Spain, and Walt Disney Concert Hall in Los Angeles.

The New Media

By the early twenty-first century, the Internet had dramatically transformed daily life for most Americans. First created by the government for Cold War intelligence sharing, the World Wide Web spread like wildfire through American homes, schools, and offices during the mid-1990s. The percentage of households with Internet access skyrocketed from 18 percent in 1997 to about 70 percent in 2009. In rapidly increasing numbers, America turned online to communicate, shop, and even work. The exploding "Information Age" drove the tremendous economic boom of the late 1990s during the "dot com" economy.

Even as the "dot com bubble" deflated after 2000, the Internet demonstrated its staying power. Online companies soon became giants in retail (Amazon.com), web searching and communication (Google), and even finance (e-trade). The Internet reshaped the traditional corporate world as well. By the end of the 1990s, almost every business, group, or organization—from used-car dealers to sports teams to college arts groups—had its own website.

Fulfilling the promises of its early boosters, the Internet seemed to have a democratizing effect, spreading power and information among more and more Americans. Young people in particular flocked to social networking sites such as MySpace and Facebook to make connections. YouTube allowed everyday users to post homemade videos for, literally, the whole world to see. And millions of people around the world with no more than a web connection and an opinion started a media revolution through their web logs, or "blogs." "Bloggers" lent their voice to issues from foreign policy to college life, offering their beliefs and opinions without fear and often without research.

As the "blogosphere" grew, it posed a major challenge to the media that, for hundreds of years, had shaped Americans' understanding of the news. Supporters argued that this "New Media" added fresh voices and new perspectives, but opponents questioned bloggers' expertise and accused them of spreading misinformation. And blogs were not the only threat the Internet posed to the "mainstream media." The "old media" daily newspaper and network television news found fewer readers and viewers. As with railroads and the telegraph in the nineteenth century and radio and television in the twentieth, computers and the Internet drove major readjustments in modern American economic, social, and cultural life.

The American Prospect

The American spirit pulsed with vitality in the twenty-first century, but grave problems continued to plague the Republic. Women still fell short of first-class economic citizenship, and American society groped for ways to adapt the traditional family to the new realities of women's work outside the home. A generation after the civil rights triumphs of the 1960s, full equality remained an elusive dream for countless Americans of color. Powerful foreign competitors challenged America's premier economic status. As job opportunities shrank in some of the nation's regions and expanded in others, as jobs shifted to cheaper labor markets abroad, and as giant corporations such as Enron collapsed through corporate scandal, many Americans began to fear their economy as a treacherous landscape even as it offered some of them astounding prosperity. The alarmingly unequal redistribution of wealth and income threatened to turn America into a society of haves and have-nots, mocking the ideals of democracy and breeding seething resentments along the economic frontier that divided rich from poor.

Environmental worries clouded the country's future. Coal-fired electrical generating plants helped form acid rain and probably contributed to the greenhouse effect, an ominous warming in the planet's temperature. The planet was being drained of oil, and disastrous accidents such as the grounding and subsequent oil spill of the giant tanker *Exxon Valdez* in 1989 in Alaska's pristine Prince William Sound demonstrated the ecological risks of oil exploration and transportation at sea. By the early twenty-first century, bolstered by the sharply escalating price of oil, the once-lonely cries for alternative fuel sources had escalated into mainstream public fascination with solar power and windmills, electric "hybrid" cars, and the pursuit of an affordable hydrogen fuel cell. Energy conservation remained another crucial but elusive strategy—much heralded at the politician's rostrum but too rarely embodied in public policy, as witnessed in the Bush administration's rejection of the Kyoto "global warming treaty" in 2001.

As the human family grows at an alarming rate on a shrinking globe, new challenges still face America and its historic values. The task of cleansing Spaceship Earth of its abundant pollutants—including nuclear weapons—was one urgent mission confronting the American people in the new century. Another was seeking ways to resolve the ethnic and cultural conflicts that erupted with renewed virulence around the globe in the wake of the Cold War's end. At the same time, new opportunities beckon in outer space and on inner-city streets, at the artist's easel and in the concert hall, at the inventor's bench and in the scientist's laboratory, and in the unending quest for social justice, individual fulfillment, and international peace.

The terrorist attack on America on September 11, 2001, posed yet another challenge to the United States. Shielded for over two centuries against assaults on its soil, it would now have to preserve its security in a world made smaller by global communication and transportation, without altering its fundamental democratic values and way of life.

In facing those challenges, the world's oldest republic had an extraordinary tradition of resilience and resourcefulness to draw on. Born as a revolutionary force in a world of conservatism, the United States stood in the twenty-first century as a conservative force in a world of revolution. It had held aloft the banner of liberal democracy in a world wracked by revolutions of the right and left, including fascism, Nazism, and communism. Yet through it all, much that was truly revolutionary also remained a part of America's liberal democratic heritage, as its people pioneered in revolutions against colonialism, racism, sexism, ignorance, and poverty.

The dream of "making the world safe for democracy," articulated nearly a century earlier by Woodrow Wilson at the end of the First World War, gained a new poignancy after September 11, when Americans expressed a yearning for greater equality, opportunity, and democracy in the Middle East—all in the hope of diminishing the root causes of international terrorism. The capacity to nurture progress, however, depended on the ability of Americans to improve their own country and to do so in the midst of threats to their own security. As Wilson wrote in 1892, long before he became president, "Democratic institutions are never done; they are like living tissue, always a-making. It is a strenuous thing, this living the life of a free people."

Chapter Summary

In the early years of the twenty-first century, the American culture and economy underwent further dynamic changes. Having passed from an age of heavy industry to one of information and mass culture, America now entered an era characterized by globalization and instant communication via the Internet and other media. Science and technology increasingly created the new forms of wealth, opening vast new human possibilities but also presenting serious ethical and environmental challenges. The benefits of the new wealth did not reach everyone, however, as the gaps between those with education and those without contributed to an increasingly severe inequality in Americans' wealth and income.

The decades-long movement into the workforce of women, including mothers of young children, opened ever-wider doors of opportunity and contributed to changes in men's roles as well as in family life. Women's continuing focus on issues of families and children made the issues of workplace discrimination and child care important features of the continuing struggle for equality. With fewer families being formed, the population began to age and the elderly became a potent lobbying force.

That the American population continued to grow was due primarily to a vast new wave of immigration, especially from Asia and Latin America. Though more racially and culturally diverse than earlier immigrants, the new arrivals were exactly like earlier groups in seeking economic opportunity and liberties unavailable in their homelands. Latinos, Asians, and Indians all asserted their own identities and pride. Mexican Americans were the largest of the diverse Latino groups, and their rapidly growing presence increasingly made the American Southwest a "bicultural zone." Some old-stock Americans feared that the new immigrants, particularly Latinos, were not assimilating as previous groups had. The issues of

"multiculturalism" came to the fore, and Americans debated whether too much emphasis on ethnic distinctiveness would undermine a sense of common culture and national identity.

The problems of poverty, increasingly concentrated in inner cities ringed by affluent suburbs, remained stubborn and frustrating to millions of Americans, including many minorities. The majority of Americans now lived in suburbs, mostly white and affluent, but with some minorities appearing in "inner-ring" communities. The African American community made great strides in education, politics, and other areas, but there was a growing gap between an upwardly mobile middle class and those left behind. America's cities were plagued by problems of drugs and crime, but in the 1990s and 2000s crime dropped and many cities began to show signs of renewal.

American culture remained incredibly dynamic and inventive, both in "high culture" and "pop culture." The new voices of westerners, women, African Americans, Asians, and others were increasingly influential and popular, contributing to the variety and energy of U.S. society. Beginning with the postwar "abstract expressionist" movement in New York City, American visual arts and architecture also led worldwide revolutions in taste and transformed the nature of urban life.

American democracy remains a dynamic force in a new global and technological age. Issues of economic inequality, environmental degradation, and ethnic conflict demand urgent attention and engagement by American citizens. Most critical of all, the nation must find a way to remain vigilant against terrorism without sacrificing the unique values and opportunities of democracy. Protecting the freedoms upon which the United States was built in an age rocked by instability locally and globally has become America's greatest challenge.

KEY TERMS

biosphere (709)

nuclear family (712)

cornucopia (712)

undocumented (714)

amnesty (714)

civil trial (718)

criminal trial (718)

Go to the History CourseMate
website for primary source links,
study tools, and review materials for this chapter.
www.cengagebrain.com

Declaration of Independence

In Congress, July 4, 1776

The Unanimous Declaration of the Thirteen United States of America

[Bracketed material in color has been inserted by the authors. For adoption background see pp. 99–100.]

When, in the course of human events, it becomes necessary for one people to dissolve the political bonds which have connected them with another, and to assume, among the powers of the earth, the separate and equal station to which the laws of nature and of nature's God entitle them, a decent respect to the opinions of mankind requires that they should declare the causes which impel them to the separation.

We hold these truths to be self-evident: That all men are created equal; that they are endowed by their Creator with certain unalienable rights; that among these are life, liberty, and the pursuit of happiness; that, to secure these rights, governments are instituted among men, deriving their just powers from the consent of the governed; that whenever any form of government becomes destructive of these ends, it is the right of the people to alter or to abolish it, and to institute new government, laying its foundation on such principles, and organizing its powers in such form, as to them shall seem most likely to effect their safety and happiness. Prudence, indeed, will dictate that governments long established should not be changed for light and transient causes; and accordingly all experience hath shown that mankind are more disposed to suffer, while evils are sufferable, than to right themselves by abolishing the forms to which they are accustomed. But when a long train of abuses and usurpations, pursuing invariably the same object, evinces a design to reduce them under absolute despotism, it is their right, it is their duty, to throw off such government, and to provide new guards for their future security. Such has been the patient sufferance of these colonies; and such is now the necessity which constrains them to alter their former systems of government. The history of the present King of Great Britain is a history of repeated injuries and usurpations, all having in direct object the establishment of an absolute tyranny over these states. To prove this, let facts be submitted to a candid world.

He has refused his assent to laws, the most wholesome and necessary for the public good. [See royal veto, p. 85.]

He has forbidden his governors to pass laws of immediate and pressing importance, unless suspended in their operation till his assent should be obtained; and, when so suspended, he has utterly neglected to attend to them.

He has refused to pass other laws for the accommodation of large districts of people [by establishing new countries], unless those people would relinquish the right of representation in the legislature, a right inestimable to them, and formidable to tyrants only.

He has called together legislative bodies at places unusual, uncomfortable, and distant from the depository of their public records, for the sole purpose of fatiguing them into compliance with his measures. [e.g., removal of Massachusetts Assembly to Salem, 1774.]

He has dissolved representative houses repeatedly, for opposing, with manly firmness, his invasions on the rights of the people. [e.g., Virginia Assembly, 1765.]

He has refused for a long time, after such dissolutions, to cause others to be elected; whereby the legislative powers, incapable of annihilation, have returned to the people at large for their exercise; the state remaining, in the mean time, exposed to all the dangers of invasions from without and convulsions within.

He has endeavored to prevent the population [populating] of these states; for that purpose obstructing the laws for naturalization of foreigners; refusing to pass others to encourage their migration hither, and raising the conditions of new appropriations of lands. [e.g., Proclamation of 1763, p. 81.]

He has obstructed the administration of justice, by refusing his assent to laws for establishing judiciary powers.

He has made judges dependent on his will alone, for the tenure of their offices, and the amount and payment of their salaries. [See Townshend Acts, p. 88.]

He has erected a multitude of new offices, and sent hither swarms of officers to harass our people and eat out their substance. [See enforcement of Navigation Laws, p. 90.]

He has kept among us, in times of peace, standing armies, without the consent of our legislatures. [See pp. 86, 91.]

He has affected to render the military independent of, and superior to, the civil power.

He has combined with others to subject us to a jurisdiction foreign to our constitution, and unacknowledged by our laws, giving his assent to their acts of pretended legislation:

> For quartering large bodies of armed troops among us [See Boston Massacre, p. 88];
>
> For protecting them, by a mock trial, from punishment for any murders which they should commit on the inhabitants of these states [See 1774 Acts, p. 91];
>
> For cutting off our trade with all parts of the world [See Boston Port Act, p. 91];
>
> For imposing taxes on us without our consent [See Stamp Act, pp. 86–87];
>
> For depriving us, in many cases, of the benefits of trial by jury;
>
> For transporting us beyond seas, to be tried for pretended offenses;
>
> For abolishing the free system of English laws in a neighboring province [Quebec], establishing therein an arbitrary government, and enlarging its boundaries, so as to render it at once an example and fit instrument for introducing the same absolute rule into these colonies [Quebec Act, p. 91];
>
> For taking away our charters, abolishing our most valuable laws, and altering fundamentally the forms of our governments [e.g., in Massachusetts, p. 91];
>
> For suspending our own legislatures, and declaring themselves invested with power to legislate for us in all cases whatsoever [See Stamp Act repeal, pp. 87–88.]

He has abdicated government here, by declaring us out of his protection and waging war against us. [Proclamation, p. 98.]

He has plundered our seas, ravaged our coasts, burned our towns, and destroyed the lives of our people. [e.g., the burning of Falmouth (Portland), p. 99.]

He is at this time transporting large armies of foreign mercenaries [Hessians, p. 98] to complete the works of death, desolation, and tyranny already begun with circumstances of cruelty and perfidy scarcely paralleled in the most barbarous ages, and totally unworthy the head of a civilized nation.

He has constrained our fellow-citizens, taken captive on the high seas [by impressment], to bear arms against their country, to become the executioners of their friends and brethren, or to fall themselves by their hands.

He has excited domestic insurrection among us [i.e., among slaves], and has endeavored to bring on the inhabitants of our frontiers the merciless Indian savages, whose known rule of warfare is an undistinguished destruction of all ages, sexes, and conditions.

In every stage of these oppressions we have petitioned for redress in the most humble terms; our repeated petitions have been answered only by repeated injury. [e.g., pp. 96–97.] A prince, whose character is thus marked by every act which may define a tyrant, is unfit to be the ruler of a free people.

Nor have we been wanting in our attentions to our British brethren. We have warned them, from time to time, of attempts by their legislature to extend an unwarrantable jurisdiction over us. We have reminded them of the circumstances of our emigration and settlement here. We have appealed to their native justice and magnanimity; and we have conjured them, by the ties of our common kindred, to disavow these usurpations, which would inevitably interrupt our connections and correspondence. They, too, have been deaf to the voice of justice and of consanguinity [blood relationship]. We must, therefore, acquiesce in the necessity which denounces [announces] our separation, and hold them, as we hold the rest of mankind, enemies in war, in peace friends.

We, therefore, the representatives of the United States of America, in General Congress assembled, appealing to the Supreme Judge of the world for the rectitude of our intentions, do, in the name and by the authority of the good people of these colonies, solemnly publish and declare, That these United Colonies are, and of right ought to be, FREE AND INDEPENDENT STATES; that they are absolved from all allegiance to the British crown, and that all political connection between them and the state of Great Britain is, and ought to be, totally dissolved; and that, as free and independent states, they have full power to levy war, conclude peace, contract alliances, establish commerce, and do all other acts and things which independent states may of right do. And for the support of this declaration, with a firm reliance on the protection of Divine Providence, we mutually pledge to each other our lives, our fortunes, and our sacred honor.

[Signed by]   JOHN HANCOCK [President]
                                                    [and fifty-five others]

Constitution of the United States of America

[Boldface headings and bracketed explanatory matter and marginal comments (both in color) have been inserted for the reader's convenience. Passages that are no longer operative are printed in italic type.]

PREAMBLE

We the people of the United States, in order to form a more perfect union, establish justice, insure domestic tranquility, provide for the common defense, promote the general welfare, and secure the blessings of liberty to ourselves and our posterity, do ordain and establish this CONSTITUTION for the United States of America.

Article I. Legislative Department

SECTION I. Congress

Legislative power vested in a two-house Congress. All legislative powers herein granted shall be vested in a Congress of the United States, which shall consist of a Senate and a House of Representatives.

SECTION II. House of Representatives

1. The people elect representatives biennially. The House of Representatives shall be composed of members chosen every second year by the people of the several States, and the electors [voters] in each State shall have the qualifications requisite for electors of the most numerous branch of the State Legislature.

2. Who may be representatives. No person shall be a Representative who shall not have attained the age of twenty-five years, and been seven years a citizen of the United States, and who shall not, when elected, be an inhabitant of that State in which he shall be chosen.

See 1787 compromise, p. 124.

See 1787 compromise, p. 125.

3. Representation in the House based on population; census. Representatives and direct taxes[1] shall be apportioned among the several States which may be included within this Union, according to their respective numbers, *which shall be determined by adding to the whole number of free persons, including those bound to service for a term of years* [apprentices and indentured servants], *and excluding Indians not taxed, three-fifths of all other persons* [slaves].[2] The actual enumeration [census] shall be made within three years after the first meeting of the Congress of the United States, and within every subsequent term of ten years, in such manner as they shall by law direct. The number of Representatives shall not exceed one for every thirty thousand, but each State shall have at least one Representative; *and until such enumeration shall be made, the State of New Hampshire shall be entitled to choose three, Massachusetts eight, Rhode Island and Providence Plantations one, Connecticut five, New York six, New Jersey four, Pennsylvania eight, Delaware one, Maryland six, Virginia ten, North Carolina five, South Carolina five, and Georgia three.*

---

[1] Modified in 1913 by the Sixteenth Amendment re income taxes (see p. 483).

[2] The word *slave* appears nowhere in the original, unamended Constitution. The three-fifths rule ceased to be in force when the Thirteenth Amendment was adopted in 1865 (see p. 51 and amendments below).

4. Vacancies in the House are filled by election. When vacancies happen in the representation from any State, the Executive authority [governor] therefore shall issue writs of election [call a special election] to fill such vacancies.

See Johnson trial, p. 349; Nixon trial preliminaries, pp. 636–637; and discussion of Clinton's impeachment, p. 698.

5. The House selects its Speaker; has sole power to vote impeachment charges (i.e., indictments). The House of Representatives shall choose their Speaker and other officers; and shall have the sole power of impeachment.

SECTION III. Senate

1. Senators represent the states. The Senate of the United States shall be composed of two Senators from each State, *chosen by the legislature thereof,*[1] for six Years; and each Senator shall have one vote.

2. One-third of senators chosen every two years; vacancies. *Immediately after they shall be assembled in consequence of the first election, they shall be divided as equally as may be into three classes. The seats of the Senators of the first class shall be vacated at the expiration of the second year, of the second class at the expiration of the fourth year, and of the third class at the expiration of the sixth year,* so that one-third may be chosen every second year; *and if vacancies happen by resignation or otherwise, during the recess of the legislature of any State, the Executive* [governor] *thereof may make temporary appointments until the next meeting of the legislature, which shall then fill such vacancies.*[2]

3. Who may be senators. No person shall be a Senator who shall not have attained to the age of thirty years, and been nine years a citizen of the United States, and who shall not, when elected, be an inhabitant of that State for which he shall be chosen.

4. The vice president presides over the Senate. The Vice President of the United States shall be President of the Senate, but shall have no vote, unless they be equally divided [tied].

5. The Senate chooses its other officers. The Senate shall choose their other officers, and also a President *pro tempore,* in the absence of the Vice President, or when he shall exercise the office of the President of the United States.

See Johnson trial, p. 349; and discussion of Clinton's impeachment, p. 698.

6. The Senate has sole power to try impeachments. The Senate shall have the sole power to try all impeachments. When sitting for that purpose, they shall be on oath or affirmation. When the President of the United States is tried, the Chief Justice shall preside[3]: and no person shall be convicted without the concurrence of two-thirds of the members present.

7. Penalties for impeachment conviction. Judgment in cases of impeachment shall not extend further than to removal from office, and disqualification to hold and enjoy any office of honor, trust or profit under the United States: but the party convicted shall nevertheless be liable and subject to indictment, trial, judgment and punishment, according to law.

SECTION IV. Election and Meetings of Congress

1. Regulation of elections. The times, places and manner of holding elections for Senators and Representatives shall be prescribed in each State by the legislature thereof; but the Congress may at any time by law make or alter such regulations, except as to the places of choosing Senators.

2. Congress must meet once a year. The Congress shall assemble at least once in every year, and such meeting *shall be on the first Monday in December, unless they shall by law appoint a different day.*[4]

---

[1]Repealed in favor of popular election in 1913 by the Seventeenth Amendment.
[2]Changed in 1913 by the Seventeenth Amendment.
[3]The vice president, as next in line, would be an interested party.
[4]Changed in 1933 to January 3 by the Twentieth Amendment (see p. 554 and below).

SECTION V.   **Organization and Rules of the Houses**

1. Each house may reject members; quorums. Each house shall be the judge of the elections, returns and qualifications of its own members, and a majority of each shall constitute a quorum to do business; but a smaller number may adjourn from day to day, and may be authorized to compel the attendance of absent members, in such manner, and under such penalties, as each house may provide.

See "Bully" Brooks case, p. 288

2. Each house makes its own rules. Each house may determine the rules of its proceedings, punish its members for disorderly behavior, and with the concurrence of two-thirds, expel a member.

3. Each house must keep and publish a record of its proceedings. Each house shall keep a journal of its proceedings, and from time to time publish the same, excepting such parts as may in their judgment require secrecy; and the yeas and nays of the members of either house on any question shall, at the desire of one-fifth of those present, be entered on the journal.

4. Both houses must agree on adjournment. Neither house, during the session of Congress, shall, without the consent of the other, adjourn for more than three days, nor to any other place than that in which the two houses shall be sitting.

SECTION VI.   **Privileges of and Prohibitions upon Congressmen**

1. Congressional salaries; immunities. The Senators and Representatives shall receive a compensation for their services, to be ascertained by law and paid out of the treasury of the United States. They shall in all cases except treason, felony and breach of the peace, be privileged from arrest during their attendance at the session of their respective houses, and in going to and returning from the same; and for any speech or debate in either house, they shall not be questioned in any other place [i.e., they shall be immune from libel suits].

2. A congressman may not hold any other federal civil office. No Senator or Representative shall, during the time for which he was elected, be appointed to any civil office under the authority of the United States, which shall have been created, or the emoluments whereof shall have been increased, during such time; and no person holding any office under the United States shall be a member of either house during his continuance in office.

SECTION VII.   **Method of Making Laws**

See 1787 compromise, p. 124.

1. Money bills must originate in the House. All bills for raising revenue shall originate in the House of Representatives; but the Senate may propose or concur with amendments as on other bills.

Nixon, more than any predecessors, "impounded" billions of dollars voted by Congress for specific purposes, because he disapproved of them. The courts generally failed to sustain him, and his impeachment foes regarded wholesale impoundment as a violation of his oath to "faithfully execute" the laws.

2. The president's veto power; Congress may override. Every bill which shall have passed the House of Representatives and the Senate, shall, before it become a law, be presented to the President of the United States; if he approve he shall sign it, but if not he shall return it with his objections to that house in which it shall have originated, who shall enter the objections at large on their journal, and proceed to reconsider it. If after such reconsideration two-thirds of that house shall agree to pass the bill, it shall be sent, together with the objections, to the other house, by which it shall likewise be reconsidered, and, if approved by two-thirds of that house, it shall become a law. But in all such cases the votes of both houses shall be determined by yeas and nays, and the names of the persons voting for and against the bill shall be entered on the journal of each house respectively. If any bill shall not be returned by the President within ten days (Sundays excepted) after it shall have been presented to him, the same shall be a law, in like manner as if he had signed it, unless the Congress by their adjournment prevent its return, in which case it shall not be a law [this is the so-called pocket veto].

3. All measures requiring the agreement of both houses go to president for approval. Every order, resolution, or vote to which the concurrence of the Senate and House of Representatives may be necessary (except on a question of adjournment) shall be presented to the President of the United States; and before the same shall take effect, shall be approved by him, or being disapproved by him, shall be repassed by two-thirds of the Senate and House of Representatives, according to the rules and limitations prescribed in the case of a bill.

SECTION VIII.   **Powers Granted to Congress**

Congress has certain enumerated powers:

1. It may lay and collect taxes. The Congress shall have power to lay and collect taxes, duties, imposts, and excises, to pay the debts and provide for the common defense and general welfare of the United States; but all duties, imposts and excises shall be uniform throughout the United States;

2. It may borrow money. To borrow money on the credit of the United States;

3. It may regulate foreign and interstate trade. To regulate commerce with foreign nations, and among the several States, and with the Indian tribes;

For 1798 naturalization see p. p. 144.

4. It may pass naturalization and bankruptcy laws. To establish an uniform rule of naturalization, and uniform laws on the subject of bankruptcies throughout the United States;

5. It may coin money. To coin money, regulate the value thereof, and of foreign coin, and fix the standard of weights and measures;

6. It may punish counterfeiters. To provide for the punishment of counterfeiting the securities and current coin of the United States;

7. It may establish a postal service. To establish post offices and post roads;

8. It may issue patents and copyrights. To promote the progress of science and useful arts by securing for limited times to authors and inventors the exclusive right to their respective writings and discoveries;

9. It may establish inferior courts. To constitute tribunals inferior to the Supreme Court;

See Judiciary Act of 1789, p. 135.

10. It may punish crimes committed on the high seas. To define and punish piracies and felonies committed on the high seas [i.e., outside the three-mile limit] and offenses against the law of nations [international law];

11. It may declare war; authorize privateers. To declare war,[1] grant letters of marque and reprisal,[2] and make rules concerning captures on land and water;

12. It may maintain an army. To raise and support armies, but no appropriation of money to that use shall be for a longer term than two years;[3]

13. It may maintain a navy. To provide and maintain a navy;

14. It may regulate the army and navy. To make rules for the government and regulation of the land and naval forces;

15. It may call out the state militia. To provide for calling forth the militia to execute the laws of the Union, suppress insurrections, and repel invasions;

See Whiskey Rebellion, p. 137.

16. It shares with the states control of militia. To provide for organizing, arming, and disciplining the militia, and for governing such part of them as may be employed in the service of the United States, reserving to the States respectively the appointment of the officers, and the authority of training the militia according to the discipline prescribed by Congress;

---

[1]Note that presidents, though they can provoke war (see the case of Polk, p. 263) or wage it after it is declared, cannot declare it.

[2]Papers issued to private citizens in wartime authorizing them to capture enemy ships.

[3]A reflection of fear of standing armies earlier expressed in the Declaration of Independence.

17. It makes laws for the District of Columbia and other federal areas. To exercise exclusive legislation in all cases whatsoever, over such district (not exceeding ten miles square) as may, by cession of particular States, and the acceptance of Congress, become the seat of government of the United States,[1] and to exercise like authority over all places purchased by the consent of the legislature of the State, in which the same shall be, for the erection of forts, magazines, arsenals, dock-yards, and other needful buildings;—and

Congress has certain implied powers:

This is the famous "elastic clause"; See p. 137.

18. It may make laws necessary for carrying out the enumerated powers. To make all laws which shall be necessary and proper for carrying into execution the foregoing powers, and all other powers vested by this Constitution in the government of the United States, or in any departure or officer thereof.

SECTION IX.   **Powers Denied to the Federal Government**

See 1787 slave compromise, p. 125.

1. Congressional control of slave trade postponed until 1808. *The migration or importation of such persons as any of the States now existing shall think proper to admit shall not be prohibited by the Congress prior to the year 1808; but a tax or duty may be imposed on such importation, not exceeding $10 for each person.*

See Lincoln's unlawful suspension, p. 308.

2. The writ of habeas corpus[2] may be suspended only in cases of rebellion or invasion. The privilege of the writ of habeas corpus shall not be suspended, unless when in cases of rebellion or invasion the public safety may require it.

3. Attainders[3] and ex post facto laws[4] forbidden. No bill of attainder or ex post facto law shall be passed.

4. Direct taxes must be apportioned according to population. No capitation [head or poll tax] or other direct, tax shall be laid, unless in proportion to the census or enumeration herein before directed to be taken.[5]

5. Export taxes forbidden. No tax or duty shall be laid on articles exported from any State.

6. Congress must not discriminate among states in regulating commerce. No preference shall be given by any regulation of commerce or revenue to the ports of one State over those of another; nor shall vessels bound to, or from, one State, be obliged to enter, clear, or pay duties in another.

See Lincoln's unlawful infraction, p. 308.

7. Public money may not be spent without congressional appropriation; accounting. No money shall be drawn from the treasury, but in consequence of appropriations made by law; and a regular statement and account of the receipts and expenditures of all public money shall be published from time to time.

8. Titles of nobility prohibited; foreign gifts. No title of nobility shall be granted by the United States; and no person holding office of profit or trust under them, shall, without the consent of Congress, accept of any present, emolument, office, or title, of any kind whatever, from any king, prince, or foreign state.

---

[1]The District of Columbia, ten miles square, was established in 1791 with a cession from Virginia (see pp. 135–136).

[2]A writ of habeas corpus is a document that enables a person under arrest to obtain an immediate examination in court to ascertain whether he or she is being legally held.

[3]A bill of attainder is a special legislative act condemning and punishing an individual without a judicial trial.

[4]An ex post facto law is one that fixes punishments for acts committed before the law was passed.

[5]Modified in 1913 by the Sixteenth Amendment (see p. 483 and amendments below).

SECTION X. **Powers Denied to the States**

Absolute prohibitions on the states:

On contracts see Fletcher *v.* Peck, *p. 173.*

1. The states are forbidden to do certain things. No State shall enter into any treaty, alliance, or confederation; grant letters of marque and reprisal [i.e., authorize privateers]; coin money; emit bills of credit [issue paper money]; make anything but gold and silver coin a [legal] tender in payment of debts; pass any bill of attainder,[1] ex post facto,[1] or law impairing the obligation of contracts, or grant any title of nobility.

Conditional prohibitions on the states:

Cf. Confederation chaos, pp. 120–121.

2. The states may not levy duties without the consent of Congress. No State shall, without the consent of Congress, lay any imposts or duties on imports or exports, except what may be absolutely necessary for executing its inspection laws: and the net produce of all duties and imposts, laid by any State on imports or exports, shall be for the use of the treasury of the United States; and all such laws shall be subject to the revision and control of the Congress.

3. Certain other federal powers are forbidden the states except with the consent of Congress. No State shall, without the consent of Congress, lay any duty of tonnage [i.e., duty on ship tonnage], keep [nonmilitia] troops or ships of war in time of peace, enter into any agreement or compact with another State, or with a foreign power, or engage in war, unless actually invaded, or in such imminent danger as will not admit of delay.

Article II. *Executive Department*

SECTION I. **President and Vice President**

1. The president is the chief executive; term of office. The executive power shall be vested in a President of the United States of America. He shall hold his office during the term of four years,[2] and, together with the Vice President, chosen for the same term, be elected as follows:

See 1787 compromise, p. 125.

See 1876 Oregon case, p. 361.

2. The president is chosen by electors. Each State shall appoint, in such manner as the legislature thereof may direct, a number of electors, equal to the whole number of Senators and Representatives to which the State may be entitled in the Congress; but no Senator or Representative, or person holding an office of trust or profit under the United States, shall be appointed an elector.

See Burr-Jefferson disputed election of 1800, p. 149.

A majority of the electoral votes needed to elect a president. *The electors shall meet in their respective States, and vote by ballot for two persons, of whom one at least shall not be an inhabitant of the same State with themselves. And they shall make a list of all the persons voted for, and of the number of votes for each; which list they shall sign and certify, and transmit sealed to the seat of government of the United States, directed to the President of the Senate. The President of the Senate shall, in the presence of the Senate and House of Representatives, open all the certificates, and the votes shall be counted. The person having the greatest number of votes shall be the President, if such number be a majority of the whole number of electors appointed; and if there be more than one who have such majority, and have an equal number of votes, then the House of Representatives shall immediately choose by ballot one of them for President; and if no person have a majority, then from the five highest on the list the said house shall in like manner choose the President. But in choosing the President the votes shall be taken by States, the representation from each State*

---

[1]For definitions see footnotes 3 and 4 on preceding page.

[2]No reference to reelection; for anti–third term Twenty-second Amendment, see below.

having one vote; a quorum for this purpose shall consist of a member or members from two-thirds of the States, and a majority of all the States shall be necessary to a choice. In every case, after the choice of the President, the person having the greatest number of votes of the electors shall be the Vice President. But if there should remain two or more who have equal votes, the Senate shall choose from them by ballot the Vice President.[1]

See Jefferson as vice president in 1796, p. 142.

3. Congress decides time of meeting of Electoral College. The Congress may determine the time of choosing the electors and the day on which they shall give their votes; which day shall be the same throughout the United States.

To provide for foreign-born people, like Alexander Hamilton, born in the British West Indies.

4. Who may be president. No person except a natural-born citizen, *or a citizen of the United States at the time of the adoption of this Constitution,* shall be eligible to the office of President; neither shall any person be eligible to that office who shall not have attained to the age of thirty-five years, and been fourteen years a resident within the United States [i.e., a legal resident].

Modified by Twentieth and Twenty-fifth Amendments below.

5. Replacements for president. In case of the removal of the President from office or of his death, resignation, or inability to discharge the powers and duties of said office, the same shall devolve on the Vice President, and the Congress may by law provide for the case of removal, death, resignation, or inability, both of the President and Vice President, declaring what officer shall then act as President, and such officer shall act accordingly, until the disability be removed, or a President shall be elected.

6. The president's salary. The President shall, at stated times, receive for his services a compensation, which shall neither be increased or diminished during the period for which he shall have been elected, and he shall not receive within that period any other emolument from the United States, or any of them.

7. The president's oath of office. Before he enter on the execution of his office, he shall take the following oath or affirmation:—"I do solemnly swear (or affirm) that I will faithfully execute the office of the President of the United States, and will to the best of my ability preserve, protect and defend the Constitution of the United States."

SECTION II.   Powers of the President

See cabinet evolution, p. 134.

1. The president has important military and civil powers. The President shall be commander in chief of the army and navy of the United States, and of the militia of the several States, when called into the actual service of the United States; he may require the opinion, in writing, of the principal officer in each of the executive departments, upon any subject relating to the duties of their respective offices, and he shall have power to grant reprieves and pardons for offenses against the United States, except in cases of impeachment.[2]

For president's removal power, see p. 349.

2. The president may negotiate treaties and nominate federal officials. He shall have power, by and with the advice and consent of the Senate, to make treaties, provided two-thirds of the Senators present concur; and he shall nominate, and by and with the advice and consent of the Senate, shall appoint ambassadors, other public ministers and consuls, judges of the Supreme Court, and all other officers of the United States, whose appointments are not herein otherwise provided for, and which shall be established by law: but the Congress may by law vest the appointment of such inferior officers, as they think proper, in the President alone, in the courts of law, or in the heads of departments.

3. The president may fill vacancies during Senate recess. The President shall have power to fill up all vacancies that may happen during the recess of the Senate, by granting commissions which shall expire at the end of their next session.

---

[1]Repealed in 1804 by the Twelfth Amendment (for text see below).

[2]To prevent the president's pardoning himself or his close associates, as was feared in the case of Richard Nixon. See p. 664.

SECTION III.

For president's personal appearances, see pp. 482–483.

Other Powers and Duties of the President

Messages; extra sessions; receiving ambassadors; execution of the laws. He shall from time to time give to the Congress information of the state of the Union, and recommend to their consideration such measures as he shall judge necessary and expedient; he may, on extraordinary occasions, convene both houses, or either of them, and in case of disagreement between them, with respect to the time of adjournment, he may adjourn them to such time as he shall think proper; he shall receive ambassadors and other public ministers; he shall take care that the laws be faithfully executed, and shall commission all the officers of the United States.

SECTION IV.

Impeachment

See discussion of Presidents Johnson, p. 349; Nixon, pp. 663–664; and Clinton, p. 698.

Civil officers may be removed by impeachment. The President, Vice President and all civil officers[1] of the United States shall be removed from office on impeachment for, and on conviction of, treason, bribery, and other high crimes and misdemeanors.

Judicial Department

Article III.

The Federal Courts

SECTION I.

See Judiciary Act of 1789, p. 135.

The judicial power belongs to the federal courts. The judicial power of the United States shall be vested in one Supreme Court, and in such inferior courts as the Congress may from time to time ordain and establish. The judges, both of the Supreme and inferior courts, shall hold their offices during good behavior, and shall, at stated times, receive for their services a compensation which shall not be diminished[2] during their continuance in office.

Jurisdiction of Federal Courts

SECTION II.

1. Kinds of cases that may be heard. The judicial power shall extend to all cases, in law and equity, arising under this Constitution, the laws of the United States, and treaties made, or which shall be made, under their authority;—to all cases affecting ambassadors, other public ministers and consuls;—to all cases of admiralty and maritime jurisdiction;—to controversies to which the United States shall be a party;—to controversies between two or more States;—*between a State and citizens of another State*[3];—between citizens of different States;—between citizens of the same State claiming lands under grants of different States, and between a State, or the citizens thereof, and foreign states, citizens or subjects.

2. Jurisdiction of the Supreme Court. In all cases affecting ambassadors, other public ministers and consuls, and those in which a State shall be a party, the Supreme Court shall have original jurisdiction.[4] In all the other cases before mentioned, the Supreme Court shall have appellate jurisdiction,[5] both as to law and fact, with such exceptions, and under such regulations, as the Congress shall make.

3. Trial for federal crime is by jury. The trial of all crimes, except in cases of impeachment, shall be by jury; and such trial shall be held in the State where the said crimes shall have been committed; but when not committed within any State, the trial shall be at such place or places as the Congress may by law have directed.

---

[1] i.e., all federal executive and judicial officers, but not members of Congress or military personnel.

[2] In 1978, in a case involving federal judges, the Supreme Court ruled that diminution of salaries by inflation was irrelevant.

[3] The Eleventh Amendment (see below) restricts this to suits by a state against citizens of another state.

[4] i.e., such cases must originate in the Supreme Court.

[5] i.e., it hears other cases only when they are appealed to it from a lower federal court or a state court.

SECTION III.   Treason

See Burr trial, p. 156.

1. Treason defined. Treason against the United States shall consist only in levying war against them, or in adhering to their enemies, giving them aid and comfort. No person shall be convicted of treason unless on the testimony of two witnesses to the same overt act, or on confession in open court.

2. Congress fixes punishment for treason. The Congress shall have power to declare the punishment of treason, but no attainder of treason shall work corruption of blood, or forfeiture except during the life of the person attained.[1]

Article IV.   *Relations of the States to One Another*

SECTION I.   Credit to Acts, Records, and Court Proceedings

Each state must respect the public acts of the others. Full faith and credit shall be given in each State to the public acts, records, and judicial proceedings of every other State.[2] And the Congress may by general laws prescribe the manner in which such acts, records, and proceedings shall be proved [attested], and the effect thereof.

SECTION II.   Duties of States to States

1. Citizenship in one state is valid in all. The citizens of each State shall be entitled to all privileges and immunities of citizens in the several States.

This stipulation is sometimes openly flouted. In 1978 Governor Jerry Brown of California, acting on humanitarian grounds, refused to surrender to South Dakota an American Indian, Dennis Banks, who was charged with murder in an armed uprising.

2. Fugitives from justice must be surrendered by the state to which they have fled. A person charged in any State with treason, felony, or other crime, who shall flee from justice, and be found in another State, shall on demand of the executive authority [governor] of the State from which he fled, be delivered up, to be removed to the State having jurisdiction of the crime.

Basis of fugitive-slave laws; see p. 275.

3. Slaves and apprentices must be returned. *No person held to service or labor in one State, under the laws thereof, escaping into another, shall, in consequence of any law or regulation therein, be discharged from such service or labor, but shall be delivered up on claim of the party to whom such service or labor may be due.*[3]

SECTION III.   New States and Territories

e.g., Maine (1820); see p. 171.

1. Congress may admit new states. New States may be admitted by the Congress into this Union; but no new State shall be formed or erected within the jurisdiction of any other State; nor any State be formed by the junction of two or more States, or parts of States, without the consent of the legislatures of the States concerned as well as of the Congress.[4]

2. Congress regulates federal territory and property. The Congress shall have power to dispose of and make all needful rules and regulations respecting the territory or other property belonging to the United States; and nothing in this Constitution shall be so construed as to prejudice any claims of the United States, or of any particular State.

SECTION IV.   Protection to the States

See Cleveland and the Pullman strike, pp. 431–432.

United States guarantees to states representative government and protection against invasion and rebellion. The United States shall guarantee to every State in this Union a

---

[1] i.e., punishment only for the offender; none for his or her heirs.

[2] e.g., a marriage in one is valid in all.

[3] Invalidated in 1865 by the Thirteenth Amendment (for text see below).

[4] Loyal West Virginia was formed by Lincoln in 1862 from seceded Virginia. This act was of dubious constitutionality and was justified in part by the wartime powers of the president. See p. 303.

republican form of government, and shall protect each of them against invasion; and on application of the legislature, or of the executive [governor] (when the legislature cannot be convened), against domestic violence.

Article V.   *The Process of Amendment*

The Constitution may be amended in four ways. The Congress, whenever two-thirds of both houses shall deem it necessary, shall propose amendments to this Constitution, or, on the application of the legislature of two-thirds of the several States, shall call a convention for proposing amendments, which, in either case, shall be valid to all intents and purposes, as part of this Constitution, when ratified by the legislatures of three-fourths of the several States, or by conventions in three-fourths thereof, as the one or the other mode of ratification may be proposed by the Congress; provided *that no amendments which may be made prior to the year one thousand eight hundred and eight shall in any manner affect the first and fourth clauses in the ninth section of the first article;*[1] and that no State, without its consent, shall be deprived of its equal suffrage in the Senate.

Article VI.   *General Provisions*

This pledge honored by Hamilton, pp. 135–136.

1. The debts of the Confederation are taken over. All debts contracted and engagements entered into, before the adoption of this Constitution, shall be as valid against the United States under this Constitution, as under the Confederation.

2. The Constitution, federal laws, and treaties are the supreme law of the land. This Constitution, and the laws of the United States which shall be made in pursuance thereof; and all treaties made, or which shall be made, under the authority of the United States, shall be the supreme law of the land; and the judges in every State shall be bound thereby, anything in the Constitution or laws of any State to the contrary notwithstanding.

3. Federal and state officers bound by oath to support the Constitution. The Senators and Representatives before mentioned, and the members of the several State legislatures, and all executive and judicial officers, both of the United States and of the several States, shall be bound by oath or affirmation to support this Constitution; but no religious test shall ever be required as a qualification to any office or public trust under the United States.

Article VII.   *Ratification of the Constitution*

See 1787 irregularity, pp. 126–129.

The Constitution effective when ratified by conventions in nine states. The ratification of the conventions of nine States shall be sufficient for the establishment of this Constitution between the States so ratifying the same.

Done in Convention by the unanimous consent of the States present, the seventeenth day of September in the year of our Lord one thousand seven hundred and eighty-seven and of the Independence of the United States of America the twelfth. In witness whereof we have hereunto subscribed our names.

[Signed by]

G° WASHINGTON

Presidt and Deputy from Virginia
[and thirty-eight others]

---

[1]This clause, regarding slave trade and direct taxes, became inoperative in 1808.

AMENDMENTS TO THE CONSTITUTION

Amendment I.   *Religious and Political Freedom*

For background of Bill of Rights, see pp. 133–134.

Congress must not interfere with freedom of religion, speech or press, assembly, and petition. Congress shall make no law respecting an establishment of religion,[1] or prohibiting the free exercise thereof; or abridging the freedom of speech, or of the press; or the right of the people peaceably to assemble, and to petition the government for a redress of grievances.

Amendment II.   *Right to Bear Arms*

The people may bear arms. A well-regulated militia being necessary to the security of a free State, the right of the people to keep and bear arms [i.e., for military purposes] shall not be infringed.[2]

Amendment III.   *Quartering of Troops*

See Declaration of Independence and British quartering above.

Soldiers may not be arbitrarily quartered on the people. No soldier shall, in time of peace, be quartered in any house without the consent of the owner, nor in time of war, but in a manner to be prescribed by law.

Amendment IV.   *Searches and Seizures*

A reflection of colonial grievances against the crown.

Unreasonable searches are forbidden. The right of the people to be secure in their persons, houses, papers, and effects, against unreasonable searches and seizures, shall not be violated, and no [search] warrants shall issue but upon probable cause, supported by oath or affirmation, and particularly describing the place to be searched, and the persons or things to be seized.

Amendment V.   *Right to Life, Liberty, and Property*

When witnesses refuse to answer questions in court, they routinely "take the Fifth Amendment."

The individual is guaranteed certain rights when on trial and the right to life, liberty, and property. No person shall be held to answer for a capital, or otherwise infamous crime, unless on a presentment [formal charge] or indictment of a grand jury, except in cases arising in the naval forces, or in the militia, when in actual service in time of war or public danger; nor shall any person be subject for the same offense to be twice put in jeopardy of life or limb; nor shall be compelled in any criminal case to be a witness against himself, nor be deprived of life, liberty, or property, without due process of law; nor shall private property be taken for public use [i.e., by eminent domain] without just compensation.

Amendment VI.   *Protection in Criminal Trials*

See Declaration of Independence above.

An accused person has important rights. In all criminal prosecutions, the accused shall enjoy the right to a speedy and public trial, by an impartial jury of the State and district

---

[1]In 1787 "an establishment of religion" referred to an "established church," or one supported by all taxpayers, whether members or not. But the courts have often acted under this article to keep religion, including prayers, out of the public schools.

[2]The courts, with "militia" in mind, have consistently held that the "right" to bear arms is a limited one.

wherein the crime shall have been committed, which district shall have been previously ascertained by law, and to be informed of the nature and cause of the accusation; to be confronted with the witnesses against him; to have compulsory process [subpoena] for obtaining witnesses in his favor, and to have the assistance of counsel for his defense.

Amendment VII. *Suits at Common Law*

The rules of common law are recognized. In suits at common law, where the value in controversy shall exceed twenty dollars, the right of trial by jury shall be preserved, and no fact tried by a jury shall be otherwise re-examined in any court of the United States, than according to the rules of the common law.

Amendment VIII. *Bail and Punishments*

Excessive fines and unusual punishments are forbidden. Excessive bail shall not be required, nor excessive fines imposed, nor cruel and unusual punishment inflicted.

Amendment IX. *Concerning Rights Not Enumerated*

The Ninth and Tenth Amendments were bulwarks of southern states' rights before the Civil War.

The people retain rights not here enumerated. The enumeration in the Constitution, of certain rights, shall not be construed to deny or disparage others retained by the people.

Amendment X. *Powers Reserved to the States and to the People*

A concession to states' rights, p. 133.

Powers not delegated to the federal government are reserved to the states and the people. The powers not delegated to the United States by the Constitution, nor prohibited by it to the States, are reserved to the States respectively, or to the people.

Amendment XI. *Suits Against a State*

The federal courts have no authority in suits by citizens against a state. The judicial power of the United States shall not be construed to extend to any suit in law or equity, commenced or prosecuted against one of the United States by citizens of another State, or by citizens or subjects of any foreign state. [Adopted 1798.]

Amendment XII. *Election of President and Vice President*

Forestalls repetition of 1800 electoral dispute, p. 150.

See 1876 disputed election. p. 333.

See 1824 election, pp. 181–182.

1. Changes in manner of electing president and vice president; procedure when no presidential candidate receives electoral majority. The electors shall meet in their respective States, and vote by ballot for President and Vice President, one of whom, at least, shall not be an inhabitant of the same state with themselves; they shall name in their ballots the person voted for as President, and in distinct ballots the person voted for as Vice President, and they shall make distinct lists of all persons voted for as President, and of all persons voted for as Vice President, and of the number of votes for each, which lists they shall sign and certify, and transmit sealed to the seat of government of the United States, directed to the President of the Senate;—the President of the Senate shall, in the presence of the Senate and House of Representatives, open all the certificates and the votes shall be counted;—the person having the greatest number of votes for President shall be the President, if such number be a majority of the whole number of electors appointed; and if no person have such majority, then from the persons having the highest numbers not exceeding three on the list of those voted for as President, the House of Representatives shall choose immediately, by ballot, the President. But in choosing the President, the votes shall be taken by States, the representation from each State having one vote; a quorum for this purpose shall consist of a member or members from two-thirds of the States, and a majority of all the States shall be necessary to a choice. And if the House of Representatives shall not choose a President whenever the right of choice shall devolve upon them, before *the fourth day of March*[1] next following, then the Vice President shall act as President, as in the case of the death or other constitutional disability of the President.

2. Procedure when no vice presidential candidate receives electoral majority. The person having the greatest number of votes as Vice President, shall be the Vice President, if such number be a majority of the whole number of electors appointed; and if no person have a majority, then from the two highest numbers on the list the Senate shall choose the Vice President; a quorum for the purpose shall consist of two-thirds of the whole number of Senators, and a majority of the whole number shall be necessary to a choice. But no person constitutionally ineligible to the office of President shall be eligible to that of Vice President of the United States. [Adopted 1804.]

Amendment XIII.   *Slavery Prohibited*

For background see pp. 321–322.

Slavery forbidden. 1. Neither slavery[2] nor involuntary servitude, except as a punishment for crime whereof the party shall have been duly convicted, shall exist within the United States, or any place subject to their jurisdiction.

2. Congress shall have power to enforce this article by appropriate legislation. [Adopted 1865.]

Amendment XIV.   *Civil Rights for Ex-slaves,[3] etc.*

For background see p. 343.

For corporations as "persons," see pp. 382-383.

Abolishes three-fifths rule for slaves, Art. I., Sec. II, para. 3.

1. Ex-slaves made citizens; U.S. citizenship primary. All persons born or naturalized in the United States, and subject to the jurisdiction thereof, are citizens of the United States and of the State wherein they reside. No State shall make or enforce any law which shall abridge the privileges or immunities of citizens of the United States; nor shall any State deprive any person of life, liberty, or property, without due process of law; nor deny to any person within its jurisdiction the equal protection of the laws.

2. When a state denies citizens the vote, its representation shall be reduced. Representatives shall be apportioned among the several States according to their respective numbers, counting the whole number of persons in each State, excluding Indians not taxed. But when the right to vote at any election for the choice of Electors for President and Vice President of the United States, Representatives in Congress, the executive and judicial officers of a State, or the members of the legislature thereof, is denied to any of the male inhabitants of such State, being twenty-one years of age and citizens of the United States, or in any way abridged, except for participation in rebellion, or other crime, the basis of representation therein shall be reduced in the proportion which the number of such make citizens shall bear to the whole number of male citizens twenty-one years of age in such State.[4]

Leading ex-Confederates denied office. See p. 343.

3. Certain persons who have been in rebellion are ineligible for federal and state office. No person shall be a Senator or Representative in Congress, or Elector of President and Vice President, or hold any office, civil or military, under the United States, or under any State, who, having previously taken an oath, as a member of Congress, or as an officer

---

[1]Changed to January 20 by the Twentieth Amendment (for text see below).

[2]The only explicit mention of slavery in the Constitution.

[3]Occasionally an offender is prosecuted under the Thirteenth Amendment for keeping an employee or other person under conditions approximating slavery.

[4]The provisions concerning "male" inhabitants were modified by the Nineteenth Amendment, which enfranchised women. The legal voting age was changed from twenty-one to eighteen by the Twenty-sixth Amendment.

of the United States, or as a member of any State legislature, or as an executive or judicial officer of any State, to support the Constitution of the United States, shall have engaged in insurrection or rebellion against the same, or given aid or comfort to the enemies thereof. But Congress may, by a vote of two-thirds of each house, remove such disability.

The ex-Confederates were thus forced to repudiate their debts and pay pensions to their own veterans, plus taxes for the pensions of Union veterans, their conquerors.

4. Debts incurred in aid of rebellion are void. The validity of the public debt of the United States, authorized by law, including debts incurred for payment of pensions and bounties for services in suppressing insurrection or rebellion, shall not be questioned. But neither the United States nor any State shall assume or pay any debt or obligation incurred in aid of insurrection or rebellion against the United States, or any claim for the loss or emancipation of any slave; but all such debts, obligations, and claims shall be held illegal and void.

5. Enforcement. The Congress shall have power to enforce, by appropriate legislation, the provisions of this article. [Adopted 1868.]

Amendment XV. *Suffrage for Blacks*

For background see p. 345..

Black males are made voters. 1. The right of the citizens of the United States to vote shall not be denied or abridged by the United States or by any State on account of race, color, or previous condition of servitude.

2. The Congress shall have power to enforce this article by appropriate legislation. [Adopted 1870.]

Amendment XVI. *Income Taxes*

For background see p. 483.

Congress has power to lay and collect income taxes. The Congress shall have power to lay and collect taxes on incomes, from whatever source derived, without apportionment among the several States, and without regard to any census or enumeration. [Adopted 1913.]

Amendment XVII. *Direct Election of Senators*

Senators shall be elected by popular vote. 1. The Senate of the United States shall be composed of two Senators from each State, elected by the people thereof, for six years; and each Senator shall have one vote. The electors in each State shall have the qualifications requisite for electors of [voters for] the most numerous branch of the State legislatures.

2. When vacancies happen in the representation of any State in the Senate, the executive authority of such State shall issue writs of election to fill such vacancies: Provided, that the Legislature of any State may empower the executive thereof to make temporary appointments until the people fill the vacancies by election as the Legislature may direct.

3. This amendment shall not be so construed as to affect the election or term of any Senator chosen before it becomes valid as part of the Constitution. [Adopted 1913.]

Amendment XVIII. *National Prohibition*

For background see pp. 513–515.

The sale or manufacture of intoxicating liquors is forbidden. 1. *After one year from the ratification of this article the manufacture, sale, or transportation of intoxicating liquors within, the importation thereof into, or the exportation thereof from the United States and all territory subject to the jurisdiction thereof, for beverage purposes, is hereby prohibited.*

2. *The Congress and the several States shall have concurrent power to enforce this article by appropriate legislation.*

3. *This article shall be inoperative unless it shall have been ratified as an amendment to the Constitution by the legislatures of the several States, as provided by the Constitution,* *within seven years from the date of the submission thereof to the States by the Congress.* [Adopted 1919; repealed 1933 by Twenty-first Amendment.]

Amendment XIX.   *Woman Suffrage*

For background see p. 497.

Women guaranteed the right to vote. 1. The right of citizens of the United States to vote shall not be denied or abridged by the United States or by any State on account of sex.

2. Congress shall have power to enforce this article by appropriate legislation. [Adopted 1920.]

Amendment XX.   *Presidential and Congressional Terms*

Shortens lame duck periods by modifying Art. I, Sec. IV, para. 2.

1. Presidential, vice presidential, and congressional terms of office begin in January. The terms of the President and Vice President shall end at noon on the 20th day of January, and the terms of Senators and Representatives at noon on the 3d day of January, of the years in which such terms would have ended if this article had not been ratified; and the terms of their successors shall then begin.

2. New meeting date for Congress. The Congress shall assemble at least once in every year, and such meeting shall begin at noon on the 3d day of January, unless they shall by law appoint a different day.

3. Emergency presidential and vice presidential succession. If, at the time fixed for the beginning of the term of the President, the President-elect shall have died, the Vice President-elect shall become President. If a President shall not have been chosen before the time fixed for the beginning of his term, or if the President-elect shall have failed to qualify, then the Vice President–elect shall act as President until a President shall have qualified; and the Congress may by law provide for the case wherein neither a President-elect nor a Vice President–elect shall have qualified, declaring who shall then act as President, or the manner in which one who is to act shall be selected, and such persons shall act accordingly until a President or Vice President shall have qualified.

4. The Congress may by law provide for the case of the death of any of the persons from whom the House of Representatives may choose a President whenever the right of choice shall have devolved upon them, and for the case of the death of any of the persons from whom the Senate may choose a Vice President whenever the right of choice shall have devolved upon them.

5. Sections 1 and 2 shall take effect on the 15th day of October following the ratification of this article.

6. This article shall be inoperative unless it shall have been ratified as an amendment to the Constitution by the Legislatures of three-fourths of the several States within seven years from the date of its submission. [Adopted 1993.]

Amendment XXI.

For background see p. 549.

Prohibition Repealed

1. Eighteenth Amendment repealed. The eighteenth article of amendment to the Constitution of the United States is hereby repealed.

2. Local laws honored. The transportation or importation into any State, Territory, or Possession of the United States for delivery or use therein of intoxicating liquors, in violation of the laws thereof, is hereby prohibited.

3. This article shall be inoperative unless it shall have been ratified as an amendment to the Constitution by conventions in the several States, as provided in the Constitution, within seven years from the date of the submission thereof to the States by the Congress. [Adopted 1933.]

Amendment XXII.

Sometimes referred to as the anti–Franklin Roosevelt amendment.

Anti–Third Term Amendment

1. Presidential term is limited. No person shall be elected to the office of President more than twice, and no person who has held the office of President, or acted as President, for more than two years of a term to which some other person was elected President shall be elected to the office of President more than once. But this article shall not apply to any person holding the office of President when this article was proposed by the Congress [i.e., Truman], and shall not prevent any person who may be holding the office of President, during the term within which this article becomes operative [i.e., Truman] from holding the office of President or acting as President during the remainder of such term.

2. This article shall be inoperative unless it shall have been ratified as an amendment to the Constitution by the legislatures of three-fourths of the several States within seven years from the date of its submission to the States by the Congress. [Adopted 1951.]

Amendment XXIII.

Designed to give the District of Columbia three electoral votes and to quiet the century-old cry of "No taxation without representation." Yet the District of Columbia still has only one nonvoting member of Congress.

District of Columbia Vote

1. Presidential electors for the District of Columbia. The District, constituting the seat of government of the United States, shall appoint in such manner as the Congress shall direct:

A number of electors of President and Vice President equal to the whole number of Senators and Representatives in Congress to which the District would be entitled if it were a State, but in no event more than the least populous State; they shall be in addition to those appointed by the States, but they shall be considered for the purposes of the election of President and Vice President, to be electors appointed by a State; and they shall meet in the District and perform such duties as provided by the twelfth article of amendment.

2. Enforcement. The Congress shall have the power to enforce this article by appropriate legislation. [Adopted 1961.]

Amendment XXIV.

Designed to end discrimination against poor people, including southern blacks who were often denied the vote through inability to pay poll taxes. See p. 646.

Poll Tax

1. Payment of poll tax or other taxes not to be prerequisite for voting in federal elections. The right of citizens of the United States to vote in any primary or other election for President or Vice President, for electors for President or Vice President, or for Senator or Representative in Congress, shall not be denied or abridged by the United States or any State by reason of failure to pay any poll tax or other tax.

2. Enforcement. The Congress shall have the power to enforce this article by appropriate legislation. [Adopted 1964.]

Amendment XXV.

Gerald Ford was the first "appointed president." See pp. 663–664.

Presidential Succession and Disability

1. Vice president to become president. In case of the removal of the President from office or of his death or resignation, the Vice President shall become President.[1]

2. Successor to vice president provided. Whenever there is a vacancy in the office of the Vice President, the President shall nominate a Vice President who shall take office upon confirmation by a majority vote of both Houses of Congress.

---

[1]The original Constitution (Art. II, Sec. I, para. 5) was vague on this point, stipulating that "the powers and duties" of the president, but not necessarily the title, should "devolve" on the vice president. President Tyler, the first "accidental president," assumed not only the powers and duties but the title as well.

3. Vice president to serve for disabled president. Whenever the President transmits to the President pro tempore of the Senate and the Speaker of the House of Representatives his written declaration that he is unable to discharge the powers and duties of his office, and until he transmits to them a written declaration to the contrary, such powers and duties shall be discharged by the Vice President as Acting President.

4. Procedure for disqualifying or requalifying president. Whenever the Vice President and a majority of either the principal officers of the executive departments or of such other body as Congress may by law provide, transmit to the President pro tempore of the Senate and the Speaker of the House of Representatives their written declaration that the President is unable to discharge the powers and duties of his office, the Vice President shall immediately assume the powers and duties of the office as Acting President.

Thereafter, when the President transmits to the President pro tempore of the Senate and the Speaker of the House of Representatives his written declaration that no inability exists, he shall resume the powers and duties of his office unless the Vice President and a majority of either the principal officers of the executive department[s] or of such other body as Congress may by law provide, transmit within four days to the President pro tempore of the Senate and the Speaker of the House of Representatives their written declaration that the President is unable to discharge the powers and duties of his office. Thereupon Congress shall decide the issue, assembling within forty-eight hours for that purpose if not in session. If the Congress, within twenty-one days after receipt of the latter written declaration, or, if Congress is not in session, within twenty-one days after Congress is required to assemble, determines by two-thirds vote of both Houses that the President is unable to discharge the powers and duties of his office, the Vice President shall continue to discharge the same as Acting President; otherwise, the President shall resume the powers and duties of his office. [Adopted 1967.]

Amendment XXVI.   Lowering Voting Age

A response to the current revolt of youth. See p. 659.

1. Ballot for eighteen-year-olds. The right of citizens of the United States, who are eighteen years of age or older, to vote shall not be denied or abridged by the United States or any state on account of age.

2. Enforcement. The Congress shall have the power to enforce this article by appropriate legislation. [Adopted 1971.]

Amendment XXVII.   Restricting Congressional Pay Raises

Reflects anti-incumbent sentiment of early 1990s. First proposed by James Madison in 1789; took 203 years to be ratified.

Congress not allowed to increase its current pay. No law varying the compensation for the services of the Senators and Representatives shall take effect, until an election of Representatives shall have intervened. [Adopted 1992.]

PACIFIC OCEAN

WASHINGTON
1889

OREGON COUNTRY
(By Agreement
with Britain, 1846)

OREGON
1859

IDAHO
1890

MONTANA
1889

NORTH DAKOTA
1889

SOUTH DAKOTA
1889

WYOMING
1890

NEVADA
1864

UTAH
1896

MEXICAN CESSION
(1848)

NEBRASKA
1867

LOUISIANA
PURCHASE
(From France, 1803)

COLORADO
1876

KANSAS
1861

CALIFORNIA
1850

ARIZONA
1912

NEW MEXICO
1912

OKLAHOMA
1907

GADSDEN PURCHASE
(From Mexico, 1853)

TEXAS
(Independent Republic,
Annexed 1845)

TEXAS
1845

PACIFIC OCEAN

HAWAI'I
1959

HAWAI'I
(Annexed 1898)

0 50 100 Km.
0 50 100 Mi.

RUSSIA

ALASKA
1959

CANADA

MEXICO

ALASKA PURCHASE
(From Russia, 1867)

0 200 400 Km.
0 250 400 Mi.

PACIFIC OCEAN

CANADA

Lake Superior

MINNESOTA
1858

WISCONSIN
1848

Lake Huron

Lake Michigan

MICHIGAN
1837

Lake Ontario

St. Lawrence R.

MAINE
1820

VT.
1791

N.H.

NEW YORK

MASS.

CONN.

R.I.

IOWA
1846

Lake Erie

PENNSYLVANIA

NEW
JERSEY
1790

ILLINOIS
1818

INDIANA
1816

OHIO
1803

MASON-DIXON LINE

DELAWARE

MARYLAND

MISSOURI
1821

KENTUCKY
1792

WEST
VIRGINIA
1863

VIRGINIA

ATLANTIC

OCEAN

MISSOURI
COMPROMISE
LINE
36°30'N

2000

THE ORIGINAL UNITED STATES
(By Treaty with Britain, 1783)

TENNESSEE
1796

NORTH
CAROLINA

ARKANSAS
1836

Mississippi R.

SOUTH
CAROLINA

MISSISSIPPI
1817

ALABAMA
1819

GEORGIA

Territorial Growth
of the
United States

LOUISIANA
1812

(Seized from Spain,
1810, 1813)

FLORIDA
(By Treaty with
Spain, 1819)

1820 Date of states admission to the Union

● Geographic center of population by decade

0	150	300 Km.
0	150	300 Mi.

Gulf of Mexico

FLORIDA
1845

BAHAMAS

PUERTO RICO
(Acquired from
Spain, 1898)

VIRGIN IS.
(Acquired from
Denmark, 1916–1917)

19°N

68°W

PUERTO RICO

VIRGIN
ISLANDS

18°N

0	25	50 Km.
0	25	50 Mi.

67°W

66°W

65°W

CUBA

HAITI

DOMINICAN
REPUBLIC

THIRTEEN COLONIES

THE ORIGINAL

GREENLAND
(DENMARK)

ICELAND

ALASKA
(U.S.)

CANADA

IRELAND

UNITED STATES

PORTUGAL

Azores
(Port.)

ATLANTIC OCEAN

Bermuda
(U.K.)

WESTERN
SAHARA
(MOROCCO)

MEXICO

BAHAMAS

DOMINICAN REP.

CUBA

Virgin Is.
(U.S.)

JAMAICA   HAITI

ST. KITTS AND NEVIS
ANTIGUA AND BARBUDA
DOMINICA

MAURITAN

BELIZE

Puerto Rico
(U.S.)

BARBADOS

CAPE
VERDE

SENEGAL

HONDURAS

ST. LUCIA

GUATEMALA

GRENADA

ST. VINCENT AND
THE GRENADINES

GAMBIA

GUINEA

EL SALVADOR

NICARAGUA

GUINEA-BISSAU

PACIFIC OCEAN

COSTA RICA

TRINIDAD AND TOBAGO

SIERRA
LEONE

PANAMA

VENEZUELA

GUYANA

FR. GUIANA
(FRANCE)

LIBERIA

COLOMBIA

SURINAM

SÃO TOMÉ

Midway Is.
(U.S.)

Hawaiian Is.
(U.S.)

Galapagos Is.
(Ecuador)

ECUADOR

Equator

PERU

BRAZIL

SAMOA

BOLIVIA

French Polynesia
(France)

PARAGUAY

TONGA

CHILE

Easter Is.
(Chile)

URUGUAY

ARGENTINA

0	1,000	2,000 Km.
0	1,000	2,000 Mi.

Falkland Is.
(U.K.)

160°W   140°W   120°W   100°W   80°W   60°W   40°W   20°W

80°N

60°N

40°N

20°N

0°

20°S

40°S

60°S

80°S

'C OCEAN

ORWAY   FINLAND
SWEDEN   ESTONIA
            LATVIA
            LITHUANIA
EN.   BELARUS
ERMANY POLAND
CZ.
AUS.   SLK.   UKRAINE
SLN. CR. HUNG.   MOLDOVA
ITALY   B. H. SE. ROMANIA
        MO.   BULGARIA
ALBANIA MAC.
        GREECE   GEORGIA
MALTA   CYPRUS   ARMENIA
TUNISIA   SYRIA
        LEBANON   IRAQ
        ISRAEL
                JORDAN
LIBYA   EGYPT   KUWAIT
                SAUDI
NIGER   ARABIA   UNITED
CHAD   ARAB EMIRATES
NIN   SUDAN   ERITREA   YEMEN
GERIA   DJIBOUTI
        CENTRAL
CAMEROON AFRICAN REP.   ETHIOPIA
        UGANDA KENYA
GABON   RWANDA
        DEM. REP.
NGO   OF CONGO
        BURUNDI   TANZANIA
                SEYCHELLES
ANGOLA   ZAMBIA   MALAWI
NAMIBIA ZIMBABWE
BOTSWANA   MADAGASCAR
                MAURITIUS
        MOZAMBIQUE
        SWAZILAND
SOUTH
AFRICA
LESOTHO

RUSSIA

KAZAKHSTAN   MONGOLIA

        UZBEKISTAN
                    KYRGYZSTAN
TURKMENISTAN   TAJIKISTAN
AZERBAIJAN
        IRAN   AFGHANISTAN   PEOPLE'S REPUBLIC OF CHINA
                        BHUTAN
            PAKISTAN   NEPAL
                BANGLADESH
                INDIA   MYANMAR
                        (BURMA)   LAOS
                    THAILAND   VIETNAM
                        CAMBODIA
            SRI LANKA   (KAMPUCHEA)
MALDIVES   BRUNEI
                        DARUSSALAM
                    MALAYSIA
        SINGAPORE

INDIAN OCEAN

N. KOREA
S. KOREA   JAPAN

PHILIPPINES

PACIFIC OCEAN

                Mariana   Wake I.
                Islands   (U.S.)
                (U.S.)
                                MARSHALL
                Guam   ISLANDS
                (U.S.)
        PALAU   FEDERATED STATES
                OF MICRONESIA
                                KIRIBATI

                                NAURU
INDONESIA
                PAPUA   SOLOMON IS.   TUVALU
TIMOR LESTE   NEW
                GUINEA
                        VANUATU
                                    FIJI

                                New Caledonia
                                (France)
        AUSTRALIA

                            NEW
                            ZEALAND

ABBREVIATIONS

AUS.   AUSTRIA
BEL.   BELGIUM
B. H.   BOSNIA AND HERZEGOVINA
CR.   CROATIA
CZ.   CZECH REPUBLIC
DEN.   DENMARK
HUNG.   HUNGARY
K.   KOSOVO
LUX.   LUXEMBOURG
MAC.   MACEDONIA
MO.   MONTENEGRO
NETH.   NETHERLANDS
SE.   SERBIA
SLK.   SLOVAKIA
SLN.   SLOVENIA
SWITZ. SWITZERLAND

20°E   40°E   60°E   80°E   100°E   120°E   140°E   160°E